TH

D0551787

BROADBAND NETWORK ARCHITECTURES

The Radia Perlman Series in Computer Networking and Security
Radia Perlman, Series Editor

BROADBAND NETWORK ARCHITECTURES

DESIGNING AND DEPLOYING TRIPLE-PLAY SERVICES

CHRIS HELLBERG, DYLAN GREENE, TRUMAN BOYES

PRENTICE
HALL

Upper Saddle River, NJ • Boston • Indianapolis • San Francisco
New York • Toronto • Montreal • London • Munich • Paris • Madrid
Capetown • Sydney • Tokyo • Singapore • Mexico City

Many of the designations used by manufacturers and sellers to distinguish their products are claimed as trademarks. Where those designations appear in this book, and the publisher was aware of a trademark claim, the designations have been printed with initial capital letters or in all capitals.

The author and publisher have taken care in the preparation of this book, but make no expressed or implied warranty of any kind and assume no responsibility for errors or omissions. No liability is assumed for incidental or consequential damages in connection with or arising out of the use of the information or programs contained herein.

The publisher offers excellent discounts on this book when ordered in quantity for bulk purchases or special sales, which may include electronic versions and/or custom covers and content particular to your business, training goals, marketing focus, and branding interests. For more information, please contact:

U.S. Corporate and Government Sales
(800) 382-3419
corpsales@pearsontechgroup.com

For sales outside the United States, please contact:

International Sales
international@pearsoned.com

This Book Is Safari Enabled

The Safari® Enabled icon on the cover of your favorite technology book means the book is available through Safari Bookshelf. When you buy this book, you get free access to the online edition for 45 days. Safari Bookshelf is an electronic reference library that lets you easily search thousands of technical books, find code samples, download chapters, and access technical information whenever and wherever you need it.

To gain 45-day Safari Enabled access to this book:

- Go to http://www.awprofessional.com/safarienabled
- Complete the brief registration form
- Enter the coupon code G9C5-LKZD-THSU-1JDH-4WYA

If you have difficulty registering on Safari Bookshelf or accessing the online edition, please e-mail customer-service@safaribooksonline.com.

Visit us on the Web: www.awprofessional.com

Library of Congress Cataloging-in-Publication Data:

Hellberg, Chris.
  Broadband network architecture : designing and deploying triple play services / Chris Hellberg, Dylan Greene, Truman Boyes. -- 1st ed.
    p. cm.
  ISBN 0-13-230057-5 (pbk. : alk. paper) 1. Broadband communication systems. 2. Computer network architectures. I. Greene, Dylan. II. Boyes, Truman. III. Title.
  TK5103.4.H47 2007
  621.382'15--dc22

                    2007005085

ISBN 0-13-230057-5
Text printed in the United States on recycled paper at R.R. Donnelley in Crawfordsville, Indiana.
First printing, May 2007

This book is dedicated to J.B.

CONTENTS

FOREWORD

The broadband industry has evolved significantly since it first came to the attention of the general public around the late 1990s, at the time of the dot-com euphoria. The initial focus was on best-effort Internet access at speeds significantly faster than dial-up modems or ISDN. This was enabled by the advent of new high-speed access technologies, including ADSL, cable modems, and WiFi. More recently, ADSL2+, SHDSL, VDSL2, WiMax, Fibre-to-the-Curb/Home, and HSDPA in 3G cellular networks have kept up the momentum of increasing the availability and speed of broadband access. The increased availability and affordability of broadband access have caused it to overtake dial access in many markets, with adoption rates faster than those seen for television, VCRs, and cell phones.

Once the initial Internet-centric broadband networks had been deployed, application developers and service providers turned their attention to other uses for these broadband access connections. The next phase of development saw the deployment of voice services that leveraged the IP transport and access speeds of broadband to offer cost-effective VoIP services, often with new features. These services could be offered independently of the access provider (such as Skype or Vonage) by relying on the sheer speed and capacity of broadband access to the Internet to facilitate adequate QoS. Alternatively, some broadband access providers evolved their architectures to provide fully engineered QoS between the customer's phone and the VoIP softswitch to guarantee QoS. This enabled them to ensure that the quality of the voice call would always be as good as analog primary-line voice (as measured by Mean Opinion Score [MOS]). The combination of data plus voice in such product offerings became known as "double play."

The broadband industry has entered a new era of "triple-play" service bundles, in which service providers offer data, voice, and video services in a single package. Typically, DSL network operators approach this by adding video services to their data and voice foundation products, whereas cable operators have added data, voice, and Video on Demand (VoD) to their foundation broadcast video products. Triple play then becomes an essential approach for broadband network operators to enable them to better compete with each other and reduce churn (the number of customers changing service providers). By offering a service bundle, some services have even been marketed as "free" in certain countries since their cost is offset by revenues from the other services in the bundle. Ironically, ADSL (which is the most widely deployed broadband access technology) was initially conceived in the late 1980s/early 1990s for video services such as Video on Demand (VoD). However, at that time the cost of video servers, video encoders, and set-top boxes made commercial deployment prohibitive. Hence, ADSL was "repurposed" for the emerging Internet access market.

This bundling of services over a single converged IP network to both reduce costs and increase functionality presents a number of challenges to network providers. Bundling will increasingly highlight the quality of network engineering as a competitive differentiator due to its profound impact on service performance, functionality, cost, and time-to-market for new products. In the era of single play, it was possible to simply rely on the increase in access speeds (such as moving from dialup to ADSL) to keep the customer happy. Most Internet access was used to surf the World Wide Web (WWW) or to send and receive e-mail. WWW content was predominantly static graphics and text with limited streaming. The only early streaming content was low-bandwidth radio stations. Hence, network providers could get away with simply using bandwidth to provide adequate QoS. They could also rely on TCP's packet retransmission feature in the architecture's TCP/IP protocol stack to cover up any IP packet loss due to inadequate engineering or intermittent congested network links. When the market moved to doubleplay, some network providers could still "get away with" sloppy network engineering just by using more capacity to transport the small, incremental bandwidth required for voice services so that most times call quality was just good enough. The lower pricing of the double-play service bundles meant that many customers would tolerate the occasional quality aberration. Of course, some network providers did properly engineer double-play services, but MOS quality of VoIP is not something that is easily used as a competitive performance metric in marketing to consumers. However, as the broadband industry has moved toward triple-play bundles, adding video to the service mix means that no shortcuts can be taken. Video has extremely onerous quality requirements, and any network engineering deficiencies are immediately apparent to the customer (in terms of subjectively annoying video artifacts or sound-track problems). Hence, this will really sort out "the men from the boys" in terms of network architecture and implementation.

As video compression evolves and deployment of HDTV over broadband networks increases, the sensitivity of the customer's Quality of Experience (QoE) to the network architecture and its implementation will increase. Inadequacies in network architectures that result in detrimental jitter, packet loss, and multicast channel change latency will be immediately apparent to the customer. Standardized approaches to multiservice broadband architectures do exist, such as DSL Forum TR-101, which provides a QoS and multicast blueprint. However, there is still a need to understand at a detailed design level how to integrate the various network components to implement a highly capable network. This book provides you with knowledge of the key design decisions and approaches so that you can architect a competitive broadband network for the 21st century.

The role of core networks in broadband architectures is predominantly to shift a lot of bits quickly and reliably. Hence, the design focus is on cost-effective, resilient "fat pipes." A degree of sophistication has been added as networks evolved to triple play—for example, point-to-multipoint MPLS LSPs for transporting multicast traffic. However, core networks generally stick to the architectural principles of big, quick, reliable, and simple. If the core of the network is the muscle, the edge of the network is the brains. The network "edge" is typically a regional Point of Presence (PoP) or metronode where traffic from end-user customers is aggregated. In contrast to the core of the network, the speed of traffic at the network edge nodes means it is technically viable to "touch the traffic" to invoke policies on a per-user basis. This can be used as the basis for many innovative products, such as bandwidth on demand, byte-metered services, and so on. It is also a key IP policy enforcement point to ensure that the triple play of data, voice, and video services can be transported to the customer with adequate QoS.

The architectural approach of applying policies to traffic on a per-flow, per-customer, and perhaps dynamically time-varying basis facilitates innovative network products. This seems set to continue as Deep Packet Inspection (DPI) technology is leveraged to provide application-aware networking. This leads to the concept of a programmable or self-configuring network. In the past, new network service deployment was often characterized by the "lift and shift" of boxes as new equipment and network links were deployed to support the new product offering. With modern broadband networks operating in highly competitive markets, delays in time to market are unacceptable. Hence, once the fundamental plumbing of broadband IP/Ethernet access and metro networks is deployed, new-product development ideally becomes a case of designing new policy profiles and adding these to the policy database. The panacea is customer self-provisioning via mass customization. For example, somebody running a florist business from home may want to turn on some additional voice lines on her broadband connection to take on student labor to handle the increase in calls before Mother's Day. Ideally they should be able to simply log on to a web portal, click an upgrade option, and have the additional voice lines automatically enabled. The network would simply invoke a new policy (at the edge and customer premises equipment), and the charges would automatically ripple through to the billing system, with no human intervention. The technology exists to make this feasible, but the key is the architecture of the broadband network and its associated policy management infrastructure.

Any network operator with deep-enough pockets can increase capacity and fiber link speeds in the core and metro. However, last-mile access will always be a potential bandwidth bottleneck, especially with the advent of HD-TV with IPTV. It can be complex to design broadband networks to most effectively exploit techniques such as hierarchical scheduling for QoS and leveraging multicast techniques. However, the resulting benefits in service capability, customers' quality of experience, reduced operational costs, more efficient use of capital invested in the network, and subsequent rapid product development justify it. Hence, an effective, efficient broadband network architecture and its associated engineering design and policy management are vital in today's competitive market and will become a key differentiator between network providers. This looks set to continue as network providers look beyond triple play toward quadruple play, in which cellular/mobile traffic is added to the service mix to provide fixed mobile convergence.

It is all very well to build an information superhighway. However, a highway results in carnage without the existence of rules and their enforcement. Hence, the design of the highway code, law-enforcement policies, and infringement penalty systems are critical to make the whole infrastructure work for multiple users. The same is true of broadband networks. This book helps you understand and engineer future-proof broadband network architectures capable of handling the complexities of bundled services and sophisticated traffic policies.

—Gavin Young
Chief Architect, Cable & Wireless Access
DSL Forum Technical Chair
January 2007

PREFACE

When ADSL hit the market in the late 90s, the residential broadband market started to really heat up. Dial-up Internet access, while being a well-understood and reliable service, could not keep pace with the demands of having homes connected at broadband speeds. Cable networks, with their hybrid fiber and coax networks, were also competing for similar customers as traditional Telcos. Thanks to cable operators, triple-play services had already gained a foothold in the customer conscience as a service bundle that can be provided by a single company. This eased the way for Telcos to also deliver their own triple-play service bundles over a single copper pair—the same copper pair that was used for many years as a simple telephone line.

A triple-play package is a bundle of an Internet, video, and VoIP service. Video services almost always have two components: a Video on Demand, and an IP Television (IPTV). IPTV takes traditional terrestrial and satellite channels and delivers them over an IP network to the customer premises. Multi-play services are an extension of this concept and divide Internet access into more sophisticated services with specialized Quality of Service handling.

Until the early to mid part of this decade, apart from some early-adopters, service providers were not given to broadening their residential data portfolio past Internet access. This mindset is rapidly changing, and the market is diverging into two segments. The first segment is the commodity ISPs, who provide a cheap and fast Internet service. The cost-barrier to entry is lower due to the lower service overhead; the competition here is fierce. The second segment is to whom this book is aimed—those providers in, or looking at, getting into the triple- and multi-play service market.

Several reasons drive the diversification. From a political perspective, many Telcos with wired access are finding their traditional revenues being eroded due to regulatory pressures. Triple- and multi-service bundles are an ideal way to maintain some service margin in an increasingly competitive market. For access seekers, regulatory intervention is a much cheaper way to expand network coverage compared to an expensive copper or fiber access network rollout. For both wholesalers and access seekers, there was a major drawback to video service deployment: ADSL does not have much bandwidth to play with. ADSL2+ pushes up the downstream limit to over 24Mbps, giving ample headroom for high-definition IPTV channels, while not making a severe impact on Internet performance.

This book is the perfect companion for anyone in the networking industry. If you are a journalist or analyst who wants more inside, in-depth information about next-generation broadband access networks, you will find it here. Or if you work at a vendor or service provider, the architectures and configurations enhance your technical understanding with practical applications of protocols and hardware.

ATM-based DSL networks are well understood and have been in the marketplace for many years. There are already one or two books on these broadband networks. However, this book fills the gap in the market for a leading-edge architecture guide of next-generation, Ethernet-based DSL networks and triple- and multi-play services. Because this book is more about architectures than focusing exclusively on technology, this book appeals to a wider audience than just technicians. Planners, financial controllers, managers, and network architects will also find useful information. The designs and techniques described in this book apply to many markets around the world.

The intent of this book is to inform the reader of best practices in the industry, and where there is still contention, the pros and cons of each alternative are laid out. For example, North American providers generally choose to go with a customer-specific VLAN architecture, whereas European providers prefer to use a service VLAN. Explanations of these terms and the advantages and disadvantages of each are two examples of the flexible approach that this book attempts to provide.

Many readers already in the industry will be familiar with the topics in each chapter, but the concepts in the latter parts of each chapter are not intended for beginners. For example, many of the MPLS concepts in Chapter 3, "Designing a Triple-Play Backbone," are not intended for those whose exposure to MPLS is for the first time. The description for each of the 12 chapters listed in the next section tells the reader the intended technical level, along with any recommended reading titles.

WHAT YOU WILL LEARN

After reading this book, the reader will have enough knowledge to work through the issues and challenges involved with designing and deploying a triple- and multi-play network. There may be times where there is not enough detail in a particular section. The intention has been to cover at least the basics, so the reader at least knows what issues are involved if they need to do more research. Most of the IETF RFC-based technologies have been referenced by URL for further investigation. Although Wikipedia might not be 100% accurate, for technical information it is a reliable and useful resource for unfamiliar topics. As of January 2007, PDFs of in-force ITU-T specifications are freely downloadable. These are quite specific in nature and are good when needing to delve deep into specific aspects of a DSL modulation, for example. Also included at the end of the book are two glossaries: a comprehensive glossary of terms, and a list of packet diagrams for many of the protocols described in this book.

MULTI-VENDOR ROUTING

We have tried throughout this book to give an independent rendering of broad-band network architectures. Because all of us currently are employed by Juniper Networks, the reader may see some emphasis given to Juniper's routing technologies and protocols as opposed to Cisco Systems. This is not intentional but merely a fact of life that we all live and breathe one routing set of equipment.

Where appropriate, we have posted listings throughout the book that show both Juniper and Cisco configurations whenever they differ large enough to draw attention to themselves.

Because the focus of this book is on architectures, the basic principles do not change depending on what vendor supplies your routing equipment. Often one vendor will be stronger in one area over another. For example, their system might be better at handling DHCP over PPP, or might have a limited VLAN capacity, so prefers the N:1 over the 1:1 approach. Therefore, vendors differ in their recommendations for broadband network architectures; this is normal. This book has tried to present neutral, but smart network choices; and where there is still contention in the marketplace, to present as much information as possible. So, armed with the right information, the reader can make the best choices for their network.

PLAYERS IN THE STANDARDS WORLD

IETF

The development of the Internet has been accomplished through the cooperation among various commercial entities, government agencies, and educational institutions spanning multiple countries, all working toward the common goal of improving communications. Although this development happens through a larger network of cooperation, a central administrative authority is required to produce protocol specifications, operational guidelines, address assignment, and other standards. The Internet Engineering Task Force (IETF) is the body that oversees the Internet standards process.

The Internet began as a U.S. Department of Defense (DoD) project as an experiment in the use of packet switching technology. This network, called ARPANET, started as only 4 nodes in 1969, spanned the continental United States by 1975, and had reached beyond the North American continent by the end of the 1970s. To coordinate this growth, in 1979 the Internet Control and Configuration Board (ICCB) was formed to oversee the design and implementation of protocols on the Internet. Renamed the IAB (Internet Activities Board) in 1983, then reorganized again in 1986 into the Internet Research Task Force (IRTF), the Internet Engineering Task Force (IETF) was also formed to concentrate on short to medium term Internet engineering issues.

The IETF produces standards and documents, which are not submitted to "traditional" standards bodies. The IETF develops "Internet-Draft" documents in open forums known as Working Groups (WG), which can be submitted initially by anyone and have a lifetime of six months. These documents can later be published as archival documents known as an "RFC" (Request For Comments), but cannot be changed after they are published. The IETF Working Group process is described in RFC2418. The IETF's mission includes (and is documented in RFC3935):

- Identifying and proposing solutions to operational and technical issues in the Internet
- Specifying development and usage of protocols and near-term architecture to solve technical problems for the Internet
- Providing a forum for information exchange within the greater Internet community, including vendors, users, researchers, agency contractors and network managers

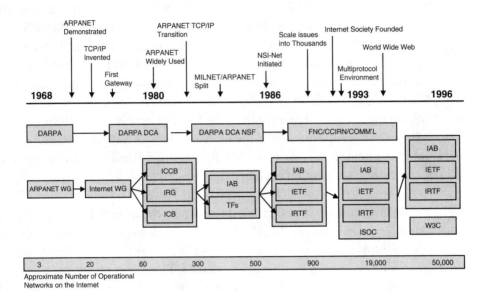

Figure I Evolution of the IETF

Over time, through various IETF working groups, the protocols and specifications that today's broadband networks consist of have been developed. The IETF standards include the fundamental protocols used today; from the Internet Protocol (IP), Transmission Control Protocol (TCP), User Datagram Protocol (UDP), routing protocols such as OSPF, RIP, ISIS & BGP, through access control protocols such as TACACS & Radius, Quality of Service, various Layer 2 control protocols, and other essential components in today's broadband networks. The following is a partial list of IETF working groups (WG) that have contributed to the protocols seen in today's Broadband networks, including ones described within this book:

- ANCP (Access Node Control Protocol)
- AAA (Authentication, Authorization and Accounting)
- ADSLMIB (ADSL MIB WG)
- AVT (Audio Video Transport)
- CCAMP (Common Control and Measurement Plane)
- DHC (Dynamic Host Configuration)

- DIME (Diameter Maintenance and Extension)
- DNA (Detecting Network Attachment)
- DNSEXT (DNS Extensions)
- DNSOP (DNS Operations)
- FECFRAME (Forward Error Correction Framework)
- IDR (Inter-Domain Routing)
- IPCDN (IP over Cable Data Networks)
- IPDVB (IP over Digital Video Broadcast)
- IPTEL (IP Telephony)
- IPv6 (IPv6 WG)
- L2TPEXT (Layer 2 Tunneling Protocol Extensions)
- L2VPN (Layer 2 Virtual Private Networks)
- L3VPN (Layer 3 Virtual Private Networks)
- MAGMA (Multicast & Anycast Group Membership)
- MIP4/MIP6 (Mobility for IP v4/6)
- MPLS (Multiprotocol Label Switching)
- PWE3 (Pseudowire Emulation Edge to Edge)
- RADEXT (Radius Extensions)
- SIGTRAN (Signaling Transport)
- SIP (Session Initial Protocol)

The IETF meets three times a year, in various locations around the world. Working Groups are divided into seven broad areas: Applications, General, Internet, Operations & Management, Real-time Applications and Infrastructure, Routing, and Security & Transport. The IETF consists of volunteers; there is no membership, and anyone can register for and attend any IETF meeting. See RFC4677 for a more detailed introduction to the IETF.

DSL FORUM

The genesis of DSL can be traced back to a number of key technical trials that were conducted around the late 1980s. Perhaps the most significant of those early efforts was conducted by Joseph Lechleider at Bellcore, who in 1989 was able to demonstrate the possibility of sending broadband signals and then followed this up with the astute observation that their application would be best served in an asymmetrical environment. Soon after this, John Cioffi pioneered discrete multi-tone(DMT), which enabled the separation of the signal into a number of frequency bands.

Telephony operators on both sides of the Atlantic, who at the time were grappling with the need for new services above and beyond traditional voice, were quick to take an interest. In a short space of time, a number of operators were deep into their own trials, many focusing on the possibility of using the new technology to deliver Video On Demand. While this particular application was a false start, it soon became clear that DSL would have a major role to play as enabling high-speed access to the Internet. When the Telecommunications Act was passed in the USA in 1996, the final piece fell into place and the technology had a truly viable future, both commercially and technically.

The momentum had been gathering pace for a while, and it was clear to key players in the DSL space that an official body was needed to bring the strands together. Following a meeting in New York, Debbie Sallee (Motorola) and David Greggains (Gorham & Partners) were instrumental in preparing people for what was to be the first official meeting of the ADSL Forum. That first meeting took place on October 7, 1994 at Church House in central London—54 people attended representing 43 organizations and 14 countries. The format and early goals were quickly established, and an interim steering group was appointed at the first meeting. A glance down the names appointed to that group shows many who would continue to play a major role in the Forum for many years to come:

Kim Maxwell, Independent Editions; Chairman David Greggains, Gorham & Partners; Secretary Dawn Diflumeri-Kelly, AT&T; Timothy Kreps, Amati; Mark Handzel, Orckit; Earl Langenberg, US West; Bill Rodey, Westell; Debbie Sallee, Motorola; Kamran Sistanizadeh, Bell Atlantic; Tom Starr, Ameritech; Alan Stewart, Network Interface Corp; Greg Whelan, Analog Devices; Gavin Young, BT; Federico Vagliani, Italtel.

The immediate goals of the DSL Forum can be seen as a microcosm of everything they have continued to achieve since inception in 1994. As the field trials continued to expand, so of course did the standards in use. The Forum was quick to recognize that in order for the technology to become "mass-deployable," it had to provide a base for the creation of a complete set of standards from the user to the network and everything above, below, and between. Second, and perhaps just as important, was a drive to promote the technology. In 1993/1994, many industry commentators and analysts were not convinced on the long-term future. And so began the Technical Committee and the Marketing Committee of the DSL Forum. Alongside these two key strands was a commitment by all original members to ensure that the Forum retained and promoted as much as possible an international focus.

Along the way a number of key milestones have shaped the importance of the Forum. In 1998, the ITU-T approved the ADSL Recommendation, and in 1999 the Forum officially changed its name from ADSL Forum to DSL Forum. Other key technical milestones are too numerous to mention; however, the approach has always been the same and is clear in its goals: Focus on the work most needed by the industry, converge on a single agreed-upon solution, and standardize this with Technical Reports that are voted on by a membership ballot.

The Forum currently has more than 200 members who meet four times a year at week-long meetings. These meetings continue to be invaluable as telecos, service providers, and equipment vendors thrash out best practices and architectures that enable rollout of new networks and services that are scalable, timely, and economical for all.

ITU

On May 17th, 1865, the International Telegraph Union was established—just over 20 years after Samuel Morse sent his first public message between Washington and Baltimore over a Telegraph line. The original 20 founders of the International Telegraph Convention initially set out to create a framework agreement that covered issues around international interconnection. In parallel, a common set of rules were developed to standardize the equipment used for international interconnectivity. This standardization was essential, because previous to this, international Telegraph communications required a laborious process to hand messages across international borders, as each nation typically had it's own systems and implementations.

After the telephone was patented in 1876, the ITU proceeded to develop international legislation for governing telephony. In 1906, with the introduction of the wireless telegraph and other early forms of radio communications, the International Radiotelegraph Convention was signed, which established the study of international regulations for radio telegraph communications. The 1920s saw the establishment of the International Radio Consultative Committee (CCIR), the International Telephone Consultative Committee (CCIF), and the International Telegraph Consultative Committee (CCIT). In 1932, the Union decided to combine the International Telegraph Convention and International Radiotelegraph Convention into a single entity—the International Telecommunications Union, which by this point covered both Wireless and Wireline communications.

Following World War II, the ITU formed an agreement with the United Nations (UN) to develop and modernize the organization, becoming a UN specialized agency. In parallel, the International Frequency Registration Board (IFRB) was established to coordinate the use of frequency spectrum. Then in 1956, the CCIT and CCIF merged into a single entity—the International Telephone and Telegraph Consultative Committee (CCITT). The 1950s and 1960s also saw the beginnings of space-based communications systems, with the launch of Sputnik-1 in 1957. The CCIR established a group responsible for the study of space-based radio communications in 1959. 1963 saw the allocation of frequencies to the various space services, and the beginnings of governance and regulation of radio frequency spectrum by satellites. In 1992, spectrum was identified for use in IMT-2000, the ITU developed global standard for digital mobile technology.

IMT-2000 was developed as a way to harmonize interoperability between the incompatible mobile telecommunication systems used around the world, by providing a technical foundation for new high-speed wireless broadband systems and devices capable of handling voice and data services. The 1990s also saw the ITU streamline into three distinct Sectors: the ITU-T for Telecommunication Standards, ITU-R for Radio communications, and the ITU-D for Telecommunication Development. A regular schedule of conferences was also established at this time.

With the strategic plan developed by the ITU in 1994 in Kyoto, a forum was established for the discussion of global telecommunications policy and strategies, known as the World Telecommunication Policy Forum (WTPF). The WTPF forum has hosted discussions on themes such as global mobile personal communications, telecommunications trade issues, and topics such as the Internet Protocol (IP).

CHAPTERS IN THIS BOOK

Chapter 1, "A History of Broadband Networks," describes the beginnings of broadband access networks, starting with the advent of the DSL family of technologies—CAP and DMT—and how this had an effect on deployment throughout the world. This tells the story of technology development from vendors and deployment milestones by service providers. There are also discussions of broadband access devices, access protocols, and the most common authentication and accounting protocol—RADIUS. The technical knowledge needed to understand this chapter is low.

Chapter 2, "Next-Generation Triple-Play Services," is an introduction to what triple- and multi-play services really mean. What does a video service actually entail? What are the components of a triple-play network, from a high-level perspective? How is VoIP integrated into the network? These questions are answered in this chapter. There is also a section on business connectivity, describing how services such as Layer 3 and Layer 2 VPNs are being deployed with DSL access. The technical knowledge in this section is medium due to heavy use of jargon and some of the more complex topics in each subsection.

Chapter 3, "Designing a Triple-Play Backbone," looks at how operators are implementing backbones that can carry triple-play services. The chapter begins with an overview of the most popular type of protocol on provider backbones—Multi-Protocol Label Switching (MPLS). The discussion quickly moves to describing a common service that providers have implemented—Layer 3 VPNs. MPLS networks are also used for their traffic engineering properties, and may not use any Layer 3 VPNs except for business services. Included are many examples of how IP multicast services can be integrated into these networks. The discussion starts from a common example of multicast and Protocol Independent

Multicast (PIM) and how traffic and protocols flow. There are many optimizations and enhancements possible with this model, such as using source-specific multicast and redundant rendezvous points, which are described here. An efficient way to transport multicast on an MPLS network using point-to-multipoint LSPs is explained here. Also included is a look to the future of next-generation backbone IPTV delivery using VPLS with point-to-multipoint trees.

The Broadband Network Gateway (BNG), often called a Broadband Remote Access Server (B-RAS), is an important point for service definition. The focus moves to integrating BNGs in to the network for triple-play services. This covers multicast protocols on the BNG, such as IGMP and additional features for PIM. Finally, implementing a highly available core network is a hallmark of any service provider, so there are protocols and strategies, such as BFD fast-reroute, that can be added to a network for added robustness.

The technical knowledge required for this chapter is medium to advanced because many of the principles described assume some prior experience with MPLS networks and multicast protocols.

Chapter 4, "Designing a Triple-Play Access Network," covers one of the most important aspects of a next-generation DSL network—the access network. There are two major components to this critical piece of infrastructure: the DSLAM, and the network between the DSLAM and the BNG, also called the aggregation network. DSLAM deployment architectures such as hub-and-spoke, daisy-chained are shown here. Designing the aggregation network is an important task. Examples described in Chapter 4 are using an MPLS network to transport customer traffic from DSLAMs to the BNG. Layer 2 tunneling technologies, such as VPLS, Martini or Kompella VPNs are also covered. Extensive deployment scenarios of these technologies is also shown as more traditional transport, such as CWDM, DWDM, or dark fiber.

The second part of Chapter 4 is the lively discussion as to the type of VLAN architecture to run between the DSLAM and the BNG: Should it be a 1:1, VLAN-per-customer model, or a service-per-VLAN model? The type of model chosen has important implications and should be designed correctly from the start. This chapter contains important information to enable the reader to make an informed decision for their VLAN architecture. Medium-level technical knowledge of MPLS protocols is also recommended for this chapter.

Chapter 5, "Choosing the Right Access Protocol," covers an equally lively debate in the industry—whether to use PPP or DHCP as the protocol between the BNG and the customer. Jargon and protocols, and deployment scenarios are explained here. As with any architectural choice in this book that does not have a clear answer, there are pros and cons to both approaches. Despite being quite narrow in focus, a low to medium level technical knowledge of PPP and DHCP is needed for this chapter.

Chapter 6, "Evolutions in Last-Mile Broadband Access," is a chapter for those who like to get deep into technical details on transport networks. This chapter takes a tour of the evolution of DSL networks, from the first ADSL deployments using Carrierless Amplitude/Phase Modulation to the standard Discrete Multi-Tone (DMT) in use today. Topics commonly associated with DSL lines—spectrum usage, cross-talk, special protocol features, and data rates—are explained in detail in this chapter. Line-level protocols covered include ADSL, ADSL2, ADSL2+, VDSL, VDSL2, and SHDSL. This chapter is appropriate for anyone with medium-level knowledge of transport protocols.

Chapter 7, "Wholesale Broadband Networks," covers what wholesale providers and access seekers need to know when working in a wholesale, unbundled environment. An unbundled environment is one where a local authority has mandated that an incumbent provide access to customers connected to the local loop. Types of unbundled services range from a simple Layer 3 IP wholesale service to a full unbundled copper service, which are two such examples that are covered. Some additional attributes and protocols associated with L2TP, such as tunnel fragmentation and proxy LCP, are also covered here. Low to medium level knowledge of L2TP and prior reading of Chapter 4 are sufficient for this chapter.

Chapter 8, "Deploying Quality of Service." Not a day goes by in discussions of next-generation DSL services without mentioning Quality of Service. This substantial topic is all about how to effectively deliver multiple services in a bandwidth-constrained environment. This covers the history of QoS in an IP environment, showing how IP precedence and Differentiated Services have had an important impact in helping to define a prioritization architecture. Uses of these mechanisms with QoS features, such as rate-limiting, shaping, RED and W-RED, and strict priority scheduling are a few of the features explained in this chapter. The concepts in this chapter do not require much prior knowledge and a low to medium level of understanding of access architectures in Chapter 4.

Chapter 9, "The Future of Wireless Broadband," presents a survey of the wireless technologies that complement today's traditionally wireline-based multi-service networks. With advances in 3G wireless technologies, such as growing data rates, advanced in service control, security and quality of service, it's becoming possible to deliver comparable services wirelessly as it is over wireline triple- and quad-play architectures. This chapter covers the history of wireless data, from the ETSI GSM and early CDMA days, through Wideband CDMA and UMTS, through today's evolving wireless broadband architectures, such as IMS, SIP, and non-SIP based fixed mobile convergence and wireless video. The chapter contains a survey of the different technologies, network architectures behind them, and evolving wireless broadband standards.

Chapter 10, "Managing IP Addressing," takes a look at one of the simpler tasks of a BNG—assigning an IP address. This chapter explains all the options available to a network operator, for both PPP- and DHCP-based networks. Whether this involves simple static address assigned via RADIUS or a more complex approach using dynamically signaled on-demand address pools (ODAP), many common approaches are described in this chapter. Keeping with the forward thinking trend of this book, there is also a section on the implications of IP address management in an IPv6 access network. The concepts in this chapter are of a low to medium technical complexity.

Chapter 11, "Dynamic User Session Control," is an overview of subscriber session management. It describes the important platforms that work behind the scenes to manage things like billing, provisioning, RADIUS, and the user database. This chapter also describes how advanced dynamic service provisioning can reduce the opex overhead of subscriber management, with such techniques as customer self-care web portals and automated service provisioning engines.

Chapter 12, "Security in Broadband Networks," presents some of the concerns carriers face when operating broadband subscriber networks. Subtopics include Denial of Service against infrastructure, and security of VoIP. The basic premise of the chapter is to present ideas around demarcation of levels of trust, and to discuss the problems that can occur when resources are exhausted or anomalous packets are received by systems. The reader should have a basic understanding of VoIP technologies when reading through the security concepts pertaining to VoIP. The majority of the chapter is of a low to medium technical nature.

Appendix A, "Glossary of Acronyms and Key Terms," is a comprehensive glossary of terms that are used throughout the book. Most technical terms and acronyms that are used throughout this book are expanded and explained in this section.

Appendix B, "Glossary of Packet Diagrams," contains packet headers and structures of common protocols that are used throughout the book. For example, if you find the concept of L2TP protocol difficult to conceptualize, there is an example showing how the protocols are layered on top of each other.

ACKNOWLEDGMENTS

In late 2004, I was asked the same question three times in as many months by three different customers: "Why can't you connect the switch into here and run PPPoE over this pseudowire?" After explaining the issue, I went home that night wondering why there wasn't a book that explains these sorts of topics. Similar books were either a few years old or focused more on individual technologies, rather than taking an architectural approach to designing next-generation broadband networks. So, with the help of two other authors, I decided to fill the gap in the market.

The idea of writing a book seems like a great idea at first. Setting off at such a leisurely pace in early 2006 was, with the benefit of 20/20 hindsight, a bit like entering the Tour de France with a tricycle—the best of intentions, but nothing to prepare you for the frightening pace ahead. Triple-play and multi-play services have been capturing technology headlines for several years, but over the last year of writing this book, the feverish rumble of interest from the industry has been growing louder day by day.

Keeping up with such a dynamic and demanding industry as telecommunications, while keeping one's day job, is an exciting role. Writing a book about it in one's spare time is a major undertaking, but at the same time, hugely rewarding. Service providers, enterprises, ISPs, vendors, and the Internet community are a continual source of innovation, whether it is simply a newer, slicker Internet service or a completely new one, such as seamless VoIP roaming between Wi-Fi and cellular access.

All three of the authors are roaming Professional Services consultants, and each works in a different part of the globe: one in Europe, the Middle East, and Africa; one in Asia-Pacific; and one in the Americas. Every few weeks, we'd confer on the book and its topics while each of us was working in a different country. It gives this book a uniquely global perspective, because it draws on best practices, architectures, and network trends rooted in the real world. Because the authors are distributed all over the world, this presents logistical challenges. Getting together for meetings is notoriously difficult. On conference calls, someone invariably draws the short time-zone straw and has to get up early or stay up late with a strong cup of coffee. Our editors, contributors, and reviewers are spread out over the globe, too. But with a good broadband connection, distances are no longer as great a problem. A quick, jitter-free VoIP call is cheap and painless when you need to bounce ideas off somebody. Sending large files to a reviewer is a snap with a zippy upstream connection. And when you need a break from work, dialing up last night's episode of *The Daily Show* is a few button-presses away.

This book would have been much shorter and less helpful without the networking experience of our many technical reviewers and readers. Particular thanks to Chee Teoh and Jonny Martin for their valuable support, suggestions, and extensive expertise. Thanks also to Tom Anschutz, Guy Davies, Cressida Downing, Thomas Haag, Robin Hartley, Robert Healey, Andrea Lasagna, Tom Lemaire, Per Lembre, Jerome Moisand, Michael Newbery, Ian Quinn, Brenden Rawle, Alessandro Salesi, Rafal Szarecki, Ronen Talmor, Sanjay Wadhwa, Bill Welch, John Whyte, and Gavin Young for their expertise and reviewing assistance. We'd also like to thank our employer, Juniper Networks, which helped allocate extra time, resources, and plenty of expertise to this project.

We would also like to thank the many people at Prentice Hall and Pearson Education who gave us guidance and added their book expertise: Raina Chrobak, Catherine Nolan, Songlin Qiu, Mark Taub, and Doug Ingersoll. We'd also like to thank Radia Perlman for her support. At Juniper Networks, we received much care and guidance from Aviva Garrett, with special thanks to Patrick Ames.

Finally, we owe much to our families and friends, who saw less of us during the year it took to write, edit, and review this book.

Chris Hellberg would like to thank his parents, Graham and Thelma Hellberg for their support, his managers Jos Bazelmans and Ramon Zanoni, Ash Pradhan for his guidance and inspiration, and the Juniper Networks Professional Services team.

Dylan Greene would like to thank his wife, Luciana, for all of her time spent listening to him talk about broadband architecture, which was promptly followed by her invaluable support editing chapters; his parents, Drs. David and Kathleen Greene, for supplying his first computer and the curiosity to learn more about it; his managers and mentors, Paul McNulty and Tayang Fu, for their insight and inspiration; and the following people for their review and support: Matt Kolon, Stefan Schneider, Nikhil Shah, Peter Macaulay, Pete Moyer, Steve Holman, Eugene Chang, Nate Alger, Eddie Parra, Avram Dorfman, Chris Montecalvo, LOA (Rob and Dawn in particular), FISC-T, and the entire Juniper Networks APAC, Americas & Professional Services team.

Truman Boyes would like to thank his best friend and partner, Jennifer Bayer; his managers and mentors, Tayang Fu, Paul McNulty, and Gary Richman; Dr. Phillip Stanley-Marbell for reviewing the book; and the following people for their support: Phil Russell, Ian Quinn, Vance McIndoe, Eugene Chang, Mao Cheng Chu, Yngwie Chou, Teong Quah, Avram Dorfman, Mitchell Stafford, Han Zhang, Francois Prowse, Campbell Simpson, Nathan Alger, Damian Holloway, Mike Hamilton-Jenkins, and the entire Juniper Networks Professional Services team.

About the Authors

Chris Hellberg has been working in the data communications industry for the past eight years for both telcos and vendors alike. He has design and operational experience with providers in Asia-Pacific and the EMEA region. He is currently a Professional Services Consultant for Juniper Networks in the EMEA region, specializing in B-RAS and core platforms. His role with Juniper is to assist customers with the design, test, build, and deployment phases of broadband access and backbone networks of all sizes. He lives in the United Kingdom, although he most often can be found transiting one of Europe's airports.

Dylan Greene is a consultant with the Juniper Networks Professional Services group. He has more than a decade of technical networking experience, having worked in a variety of environments from Tier 1 carriers, greenfield providers, financial enterprise networks, and mobile carriers to aerospace and defense projects. His primary expertise is in designing and deploying IP and MPLS networks, with a subfocus on network security. Prior to Juniper Networks, his work included academic computing, helping establish an early competitive regional ISP/DSL provider, a managed IDC/hosting provider, and working on large, multinational financial networks. He has been based in Asia-Pacific, Europe, and North America, and currently resides in Boston with his wife, Luciana.

Truman Boyes has designed and implemented large-scale carrier networks for the past ten years. He is a Professional Services Consultant for Juniper Networks in Asia-Pacific, where he is implementing next-generation networks that cater to larger subscriber growth and provide resiliency. He has designed networks all over the world that specialize in MPLS, Quality of Service, and advances in traffic engineering. He is active in numerous Internet and security-related technical forums. He lives with his partner in Wellington, New Zealand.

A History of Broadband Networks

With almost 190 million twisted-pair copper loops as an embedded base in the U.S. telco market and over 650 million *last-mile* copper loops worldwide, telecommunications companies (telcos) worldwide have sought to deliver converged broadband services to expand and thrive. Historically, the limited range of different services that could be offered over a single local-loop access has been one of the largest obstacles telcos faced when attempting to expand their service portfolios. As multiservice broadband network architectures continue to evolve, as described in this book, telcos can deliver a far richer range of voice, video, and data services than ever before.

Historically, the term *broadband* was used to distinguish multifrequency communications systems from baseband systems. Not long ago, telecommunications companies could offer only a limited range of highly reliable, lower-bandwidth services over their widely installed conventional copper twisted-pair telephone wire. Other options for delivering scalable, cost-effective high bandwidth services via existing wireless and physical media were also limited. Over time, as newer technologies developed, the term broadband has become synonymous with higher bandwidth services. This book discusses the architectures behind these services, beginning in this chapter with a brief history of broadband. Throughout this book, the term *broadband* in its contemporary sense is used. Digital Subscriber Line (DSL) is also used as the main technology for designing and delivering triple-play services. However, there are many other types of broadband technologies that can be used to support a triple-play service, from HFC cable, to wireless and fiber optic distribution using a PON system. Due to the authors' personal experience with DSL-based triple- and multi-play networks, DSL systems are the main technology of choice. An exception to this is Chapter 9, "The Future of Wireless Broadband," which describes the evolution of wireless broadband connectivity and services.

The mid-1990s was a critical time in the development of the telecommunications industry. Many innovations were turned into real-world deployable implementations during this period, including the rollout of Synchronous Optical Network (SONET) optical services, Asynchronous Transfer Mode (ATM), Frame Relay, and Integrated Services Digital Network (ISDN). These services all emerged during a particularly challenging time in the telecommunications market. Incumbent telephone companies were facing slowing and eventually peaking revenue growth from legacy services. This problem could be remedied only by developing new business lines and services to generate additional income. The legal landscape was changing as well, with significant emphasis and debate focused on deregulation and allowing competition in the historically tightly held carrier local-exchange marketplace.

At the same time incumbent telephone companies were dealing with these issues, cable operators (MultiSystem Operators [MSOs]) were facing a similar set of challenges. Faced with slowing revenues and growth, the cable operators, who already owned extensive high-bandwidth infrastructure, were prompted to seek new areas of growth for their businesses. This created an extremely competitive environment in the mid- to late-1990s between cable operators and telecommunications companies, each wanting access and revenue from the other's customers.

LEGACY ACCESS NETWORKS

The MSO-operated cable access networks have historically been based on a hybrid fiber/co-axial (HFC) design, whereas Local Exchange Carrier (LEC) telecom networks typically are based on twisted-pair copper access. This decades- and sometimes century-old copper network was initially oriented toward delivering low-bit-rate, highly reliable data and circuit-based voice services. Both HFC and copper access networks had sufficiently unique characteristics, thereby creating obstacles to each operator's intention to cross over and access the other's subscribers. However, significant motivations drove each type of operator's expansion; the struggle was sure to pay off handsomely for the winner in the form of increased Average Revenue Per User (ARPU). Cable operators sought to deliver data services to customers, and telecom companies sought to deliver video.

One of the technologies that this competition inspired was Asymmetric Digital Subscriber Line (ADSL). Telecom carriers saw a chance to deliver lucrative broadband video services using the unused spectrum in the existing global copper infrastructure. It was thought that high-data-rate services such as video on demand would drive customer demand, consequently funding the telecom industry's deployment of broadband technologies.

At the same time, around the period when these initial ideas were coming into focus in the telecommunications industry, the Internet was being adopted by the mass market at an exponential rate. This spurred the expanded adoption of a newly developing access technology, Digital Subscriber Line (DSL). The initial focus of ADSL during its inception was to support video streaming to the home, which allocated most of the radio spectrum in the downstream direction—hence its asymmetrical nature. After early Video on Demand (VoD) trials and the obvious booming market demand for Internet bandwidth, there was enough momentum to expand the industry's focus on DSL access technologies from video to multiservice broadband. Broadband was proving itself capable of offering additional high-bandwidth services such as Internet and Voice over Internet Protocol (VoIP).

COPPER

The most common telecommunications service is the Plain Old Telephone Service (POTS), available to millions of customer premises worldwide. Normally it is provided to the user via a 24-gauge twisted-pair copper wire from the telco's central office (CO or exchange). In copper wire-based transmission media, output power decreases exponentially as a function of distance, which creates loss. Initially these circuits were intended to carry only voice traffic, which often had to be *trunked* between telco exchanges to provide long-distance services. To conserve bandwidth on the trunks between exchanges and some residential areas, individual POTS subscribers typically were connected through *load coils* and *bandpass filters,* which amplified voice signals between 300Hz and 3,400Hz. But that attenuated, or reduced, higher-frequency signals. This enabled efficient frequency multiplexing on trunk connections between telco exchanges, because many of these 3,100Hz "calls" could be stacked on a single copper cable.

In a best-case installation scenario, the data capacity of a traditional POTS line is about 53kbps (due to these bandpass filters). The worst case peaks at 33.6kbps. This data rate is much lower than the potential capacity of a standard 24-gauge unshielded twisted-pair copper cable over a given distance according to standard sampling theories, when applied to the properties of the copper wire. Although telcos have been able to offer other data services over the same copper infrastructure using legacy modulation and encoding techniques, these services typically are quite distance-dependent and have severely limited bandwidth. To maximize the distance at which a signal can be accurately transmitted, copper wires typically are bundled in "twisted pairs," which reduces cross talk and interference. The higher the number of twists per a given distance, the greater the effect and thus the greater the distance a signal can be transmitted. Table 1.1 gives an overview of the different categories of unshielded twisted pair (UTP).

Table 1.1 Unshielded Twisted Pair Categories

Category	Bandwidth	Notes	EIA-568-A-Rated Attenuation dB Per 100M					
			1 MHz	4 MHz	16 MHz	26 MHz	100 MHz	300 MHz
CAT-1	Not rated for data	Pre-1980 POTS wiring.						
CAT-2	1MHz	Used in older Token Ring local-area networks (LANs). 4Mbps.						
CAT-3	16MHz	Three to four twists per foot. Known as "voice grade."	2.6	5.6	13.1			
CAT-4	20MHz	Often used for 10BASE-T.						
CAT-5	100MHz	Three to four twists per inch. 100Mbps-rated bandwidth.	2.0	4.1	8.2	10.4	22.0	
CAT-6	250MHz	10, 100, and 1000BASE-T.	2.2	4.2	8.3	10.7	21.7	

Technology Note: Sampling Theorem

Sampling is the name of the process of turning a signal into a numeric sequence. The Nyquist-Shannon sampling theorem, commonly known as simply "the sampling theorem," states that the "exact reconstruction of a continuous-time baseband signal from its samples is possible if the signal is bandlimited and the sampling frequency is greater than twice the signal bandwidth." The term "bandlimited" refers to the placing of a limit on the signal's upper frequency. Thus, a bandlimited signal is limited as far as how much detail it can accurately convey in a given amount of time. The theorem proves that evenly distributed samples create an accurate representation of the original signal if this bandwidth is less than half of the sampling rate performed on the signal. This basic theory can then be used in calculations to determine the ability of a given medium (such as 24-gauge unshielded twisted-pair copper wire) based on various characteristics. For example, with copper a signal's output power decreases exponentially with distance, creating loss. Other characteristics include noise levels created by factors such as cross talk, wideband noise, and other distortions. (The higher the frequency, the greater the attenuation. Thus, generally the harder it is to detect discrete signals or samples.)

The Internet's popularity grew in the 1990s. Telcos were faced with increasing competition from cable providers, which were rapidly building out HFC networks in the 1990s. The telcos needed to find a way to capitalize on their existing infrastructure to provide high-bandwidth data services to their subscribers.

Originally developed at Bellcore (now Telcordia), the ADSL specification began to receive serious attention from the telcos as a means to compete with the cable HFC networks. These networks were threatening to provide data services to legacy telco subscribers. The Bellcore ADSL service could offer high-rate data services and analog voice services over existing telco copper facilities. ADSL has some significant differences from HFC. ADSL provides dedicated resources and bandwidth to each subscriber from the DSLAM, whereas HFC, because it is a shared medium, shares an aggregate amount of bandwidth across multiple users on a given cable segment. However, in modern cable networks the bottleneck is not usually in the shared cable segment; rather, the bottleneck lies in the same place as in ADSL networks. This is in the aggregation network from the CMTS back (or Digital Subscriber Line Access Multiplexer [DSLAM] for an ADSL equivalent) to the IP edge.

One benefit ADSL has is that it integrates relatively easily with the existing POTS switched voice networks. DSL enables passive transmission of voice, narrowband data services, and DSL over a single copper twisted-pair cable. Using simple and inexpensive bandpass filters on both ends of the copper wire, analog voice service and high-speed data service are simultaneously provided to each customer premises without much expense to the telco or end subscriber. As shown in Figure 1.1, ADSL can run in parallel with a POTS voice service on the same copper cable by using higher frequencies. These are filtered using a bandpass filter before reaching the DSL modem to reduce the Radio Frequency (RF) interference to the modem.

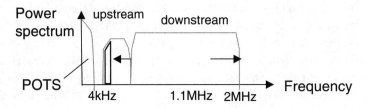

Figure 1.1 Spectrum distribution on a copper line with voice service.

DSL EVOLVES

Originally conceived by Bellcore in 1988, the ADSL specification saw initial adoption by two standards bodies: the American National Standards Institute (ANSI), and the ADSL Forum, an industry consortium created in 1994. These bodies proceeded to standardize the ADSL specification.

The early standards of DSL had two primary modulation schemes: Carrierless Amplitude Modulation (CAP) and Discrete Multitone (DMT). CAP, which was the most commonly deployed modulation technique, is a single-carrier modulation scheme that uses a wide passband (that is, it uses a large frequency range). Early on, CAP was an easily understood modulation scheme, because it is quite similar to the well-known Quadrature Amplitude Modulation (QAM) scheme. DMT, on the other hand, uses multiple discrete carriers, achieving higher-bandwidth rates by using many narrowband channels. Although these techniques have different modulation characteristics, both can provide the same service or interface to the higher-layer protocols. A higher-layer protocol is one further up the OSI stack. For more information on the OSI stack, read the Technology Note "OSI Seven-Layer Stack" in Chapter 11, "Dynamic User Session Control."

ADSL field trials began as early as 1993. They were piloted in the UK (BT) and Northeastern U.S. (Bell Atlantic) mostly using equipment that supported CAP modulation. Around the same time, ANSI T1E1.4 ratified DMT as a modulation technique, opening the door to higher data rates. It was felt that single-channel CAP modulation might not be able to deliver high-rate, multichannel video services as efficiently as DMT.

Then in 1994 a group of consultants for the International Copper Association (ICA) and representatives from Motorola met to discuss the need for a consortium of parties to develop and promote ADSL. Toward the end of the year, the ADSL Forum steering group was formed, with members representing a diverse group of telcos, equipment manufacturers, and other interested parties. The original steering group included representation from AT&T/Paradyne, US West, Westell, Motorola, Bell Atlantic, Ameritech, Analog Devices, BT, Italtel, Amati, Orckit, and others.

Although ANSI had specified DMT as the official modulation technique in ANSI T1.413, many of the Regional Bell Operating Company (RBOC) descendants of AT&T (primarily Paradyne/Globespan) were already midstream in their deployment of CAP-based equipment. Even though early implementations used the well-understood and common (and thus inexpensive) CAP, there were arguments that it would be difficult to scale the modulation scheme to greater bandwidths over time due to its single-carrier implementation. There was also concern that CAP was more vulnerable to interference. These were some of the reasons that led the ANSI T1E1.4 committee to adopt DMT.

The DMT standard initially called for 256 subchannels, each 4 kHz. 224 subcarriers are used in the downstream direction, and 25 in the upstream. There are some subcarriers that are not used, such as those used for POTS and the guardband between 3400 and 25kHz. Each sub-band is then individually modulated and combined using a QAM-like modulation with Trellis Coding. Digital phase modulation (a subset of QAM) is very similar to frequency modulation. However, instead of changing the frequency of the transmitted waveform, the phase and amplitude are changed to represent digital data.

Figure 1.2 shows the time line of these events.

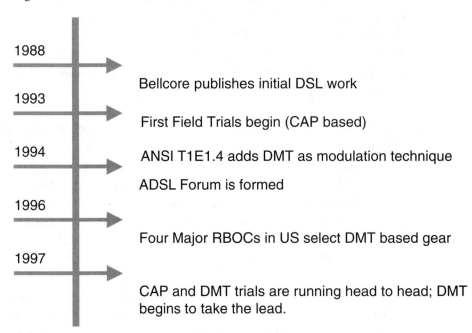

Figure 1.2 Evolution of early ADSL standards and supporting bodies.

Initial DMT support came from a camp of vendors including Alcatel, Amati, Westell, Orckit, and ECI Telecom. Alcatel brought early attention to DMT by winning contracts with four major RBOCs in the U.S. in late 1996 for DMT-based equipment. These windfall contracts later led the rest of the market toward standardizing on DMT, thus ending this important historical battle between modulation techniques.

The DSL Forum (DSL-F) has delivered many technical contributions that have been essential to the global, interoperable deployment of DSL. Technical work includes details of line encoding techniques, interoperability specifications, and end-to-end system architectures for delivering multiple services over a single DSL line. Some examples of these contributions are shown in Table 1.2.

Table 1.2 Some Important Contributions to DSL by the DSL Forum

Technical Area	Technical Reports
End-to-end network architecture	001, 003, 010, 011, 012, 042, 058, 059, 092, 101
CPE configuration	007, 019, 020, 032, 061, 064, 068, 069, 094
Interoperability specifications and testing	023, 026, 029, 031, 033, 045, 049, 055, 060, 067

THE TELECOMMUNICATIONS ACT OF 1996

The regulatory environment in which U.S. telcos operate dates back to the early 1900s. With the Mann-Elkins act of 1910, initial regulatory control was granted over means of interstate commerce. The Communications Act of 1934 overhauled this regulation, resulting in the creation of the Federal Communications Commission (FCC), a federal government body responsible for regulating interstate communications services. From 1934 onward, the regulatory environment set up by the FCC facilitated the creation, development, and support of the U.S. telecommunications industry.

The first major overhaul of the 1934 communications act happened with the Telecommunications Act of 1996. It was intended to deregulate the U.S. telecom industry and foster greater competition. One of the ways this would be accomplished was by requiring incumbent carriers to open access to their copper facilities to a new breed of Competitive Local Exchange Carriers (CLECs). Prior to the 1996 act, access to the "last-mile" copper facilities, over which the incumbent LECs had a near monopoly, was one of the largest hurdles that prevented competition in the U.S. telco marketplace.

Previously, the only way that competitive carriers could provide access was either to build their own last-mile access facilities—a prohibitively expensive prospect—or to use other techniques to ride on the incumbent's facilities without its knowledge.

One of the techniques that early Internet service providers (ISPs) used to provision DSL services involved what is known as a *dry copper loop* or *dry pair*. It consists of twisted-pair local loops that can be ordered from the telephone company. It runs between two points and is delivered without any electronics or circuitry. It may pass through the telco's central exchange, but it never touches any of the telco's electronic equipment. It's known by a variety of names:

- Burglar alarm wire
- Modified metallic circuit with no ringdown generators
- Voice-grade 36-circuit
- Local Area Data (LAD) circuit

The ISP simply attaches its own ATU-C and ATU-R (DSL termination equipment) to the two endpoints and starts delivering DSL service without any involvement from the telco other than the use of its copper. Most dry-pair services are priced at very low rates, typically from $7 to $20 per month, which gives ISPs a good deal of margin when delivering DSL services.

This architecture requires that the ISP's equipment be located close to the telephone exchange where the dry pair originates. Most DSL equipment has a fairly limited range and can only run over distances of less than 20,000 feet of total cable length. One of the coauthors of this book has experience deploying services in this manner. The ATU-C equipment was located in a facility directly across the street from a central office that served a metropolitan area. This facility formerly was used for alarm-monitoring purposes.

These types of early services were deployed by a number of up-and-coming CLECs and DSL ISP startups. Incumbent telcos were still establishing their own product offerings (and perhaps were waiting to see if earlier investments in ISDN might be able to pay for themselves before needing to be replaced). Telcos quickly identified these services as a loss of revenue, raised some technical concerns over their widespread deployment, and began to litigate the end of these tariffed services. This was one of the many hurdles the newly established CLECs had to face. Without practical, inexpensive, and easy access to the local exchange carrier's last-mile facilities, this spelled the beginning of the end for many of the smaller DSL ISPs and CLECs.

CHALLENGES TO DSL ACCESS NETWORKS

Many technical challenges arose from the quality of the local loop experienced by ISPs attempting to use dry-pair loops as well as the telcos' own early DSL deployments. Telcos, through service fees and cross-subsidization, spent a large amount of their operating budget each year maintaining their copper plant. In addition to maintenance, over the course of time additional capital expenditure is required in these facilities to increase the quality of these local loops to better support high-rate services such as DSL. Figure 1.3 illustrates the various parts of the local loop between the telco exchange and the end user.

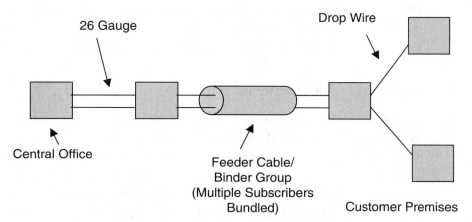

Figure 1.3 Telco local loop distribution between exchange and customer premises.

The best-case local loop is a continuous twisted pair with no changes in gauge throughout the run. It is properly insulated, consisting of no bridge taps and no loading coils, and it traverses the shortest possible path to the end-user premises. Unfortunately, in many denser and older facilities, this is often not the case. The quality of the loop and thus the service (speed and error rate) are directly impacted by any imperfections in the cable run. It is typical to find splices, bridge taps, corrosion, cross talk, and seemingly unnecessarily long runs that accommodate the original cable plan and rights of way that existed when the copper was first installed.

DSLAM EVOLUTION

As DSL line modulation techniques were under development, telco central office copper plants were opening due to copper loop unbundling happening in markets across the globe. Therefore, a scalable platform to terminate the telco end of new DSL local loops was required. Equipment vendors seized this opportunity and began developing a new breed of scalable DSL termination equipment, the Digital Subscriber Line Access Multiplexer (DSLAM). Initially, DSLAMs operated as a dense but relatively simple Layer 2 device. Early DSLAMs physically terminated copper loops and were responsible for handling line encoding. On the other side of the DSLAM, individual DSL subscriber connections could be aggregated into a higher-bandwidth *trunk* interface. Later

DSLAMs would evolve into multiservice platforms, coupled with ATM switching, Quality of Service (QoS) functionality, IP routing, different line encoding schemes, security, and otherwise, as described later in this book.

EARLY DSL TERMINATION

The DSLAM acts as a termination and aggregation device that sits on the edge of the physical copper network and logical service access network. The DSLAM has a number of copper pair interfaces on one side and one or more aggregated access interfaces on the other. As twisted-pair copper local loops enter the telco central exchange, they are "groomed" on a large copper cross-connect system called the Main Distribution Frame (MDF). Each individual subscriber's connection is then, through the MDF, terminated on a DSLAM port. Then it is returned, through a bandpass filter, to the MDF to be connected into a voice switch for standard POTS service.

On the trunk side of the DSLAM, with the early DSL Forum standardizing on ATM as the transport protocol, many early DSLAM devices included native support for ATM. More recently, Gigabit Ethernet-based trunk ports are now also supported on many DSLAMs. With many thousands of DSL connections terminated per central office, it's essential for telcos to carefully and efficiently allocate connections, bandwidth, and resources in the access network on the trunk side of the DSLAM. Because the prices of physical ports are generally not linear to the bandwidth serviced, telcos can gain large efficiencies by aggregating more subscribers onto a smaller number of higher-bandwidth trunk ports.

REMOTE LINE CARD SHELVES

Operators typically are faced with a fundamental trade-off in the economics of deploying new services to subscribers. Services typically are adopted over time, and in phases, based on a complex interrelationship between factors within the market, including pricing, macroeconomic effects, competition, and demand. Given a finite capital expenditures (CAPEX) budget that will buy a finite number of iterations of the new service, an operator has to decide how to optimally address the potential market. Because the adoption of this new service may be in phases, it often makes economic sense to be able to gradually deploy the service across a wider footprint rather than overbuilding capacity in a smaller footprint.

As a result, operators often want to deploy the minimum amount of technology required to support the demand of a given market segment and then scale up the resource as demand for the service increases.

Subtended DSLAMs, or Remote Line Card Shelves (RLCSs), allow operators to bring DSL capabilities into areas that may initially require only a small number of connections. As demand for bandwidth or subscriber connections increases, the appropriate resource can be increased, giving the operator a low break-even entry point into a new market segment, geographic area, building, or other facility, and bring about smoother economic growth that tracks the service's demand as closely as possible.

ATM DSLAMs

Many of today's DSL deployments are based on the DSL Forum's TR-025 model, shown in Figure 1.4, or the more recent TR-059 reference models. Both of these architectures aggregate the best-effort DSL access network (connectivity between the DSLAM and Broadband Remote Access Server [B-RAS] or Broadband Network Gateway [BNG]) using ATM). The DSLAM services act as the ATM aggregator toward the access network, through logical cross connections between ATM permanent virtual circuits (PVCs) on the access network side and individual DSL subscribers on the MDF side.

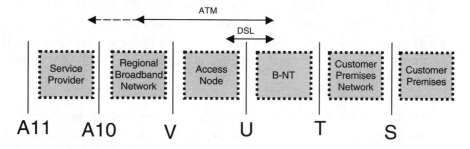

Figure 1.4 DSL Forum TR-025 architectural reference model.

In this model, the DSLAM cross-connects subscriber traffic between subscriber loop on the MDF with a logical port on the IP edge device, typically the B-RAS, which mainly handles Point-to-Point Protocol (PPP) subscriber session termination and tunneling. In the more advanced TR-059 reference architecture, shown in Figure 1.5, the B-RAS (or BNG) is located on the edge of the regional network.

It has additional functionality, including enhanced traffic management, advanced IP processing such as IP DiffServ-based QoS, subscriber management, Dynamic Host Configuration Protocol (DHCP), multiple virtual circuits (VCs) per subscriber, and RFC 2684 IP over bridged Ethernet, among other features.

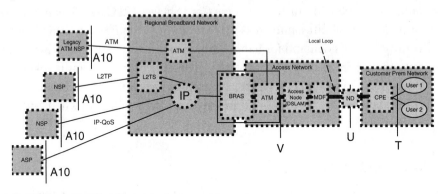

Figure 1.5 DSL Forum TR-059 architectural reference model.

ETHERNET DSLAMs

DSL networks are evolving toward higher per-user bandwidths and away from simple best-effort-only service toward the granular per-subscriber and per-service QoS required by many enhanced services such as video and voice. At the same time, the DSL standards and technology are shifting away from ATM as the access network medium. New, Ethernet-based DSLAMs are now emerging that support higher per-user and per-trunk port connection speeds, native multicast, packet-based QoS, high availability, Virtual Private Networks (VPNs), and other functionality, some of which was difficult to provide in an all-ATM based environment.

Ethernet-based DSLAMs generally are more *packet-aware* than other types of access nodes. They permit granular per-user and per-service markings and treatment of traffic, which typically are packet-based at the end nodes to begin with. DSL providers initially began by asking for PPP over Ethernet Intermediate Agent (PPPoE IA) and DHCP option 82 tags to be stamped on packets going into the BNG. This capability was later extended to pass other characteristics of the connection between the subscriber's CPE and the DSLAM to the BNG, such as line speed and interleaving. This type of functionality allows for more seamless integration between the access and IP networks.

SERVICE EVOLUTION

RESIDENTIAL ACCESS SERVERS

To deliver IP services across large numbers of narrowband or broadband connections, a new type of device was required to terminate all these user sessions. This new class of device required a broad combination of functionality, including routing, subscriber management, interface management, and quality of service. As a result, the standards groups worked to develop specifications to solve some of these problems. Many vendors also developed hardware and software products to fulfill the demands of these requirements. This section discusses the history and evolution of some of the key areas that have led to the functionality seen in today's BNG routers.

USER CREDENTIALS

Many of the basic functions found in today's BNGs have their roots in technologies and products that were developed over the years of narrowband and broadband access. Today's BNG is essentially an IP router with dense logical and physical interfaces, user authentication, protocols and interfaces to support billing and accounting, quality of service support, and other supporting functionality. Much of the user authentication, accounting, billing, and supporting functionality found in today's broadband gateway is derived from techniques used to support narrowband connections.

A key differentiator between older narrowband and today's broadband services is how services are provisioned. Narrowband services typically supported a single set of user authentication credentials. For example, a user might dial in for IP access to an organization such as a school, corporate network, or the Internet. Comparatively, broadband lends itself to supporting more services for an individual user because of its extra bandwidth. Over a single connection, a user might subscribe to multiple services, which are differentiated over the last mile by the customer premises equipment (CPE). For example, over the same connection a single user can run best-effort Internet, prioritized voice over IP, and even video services.

This type of expanded functionality has led to substantial developments in the supporting user authentication protocols and management systems compared with the days of narrowband dialup connections. Figure 1.6 shows some important milestones in the development of remote user authentication protocols.

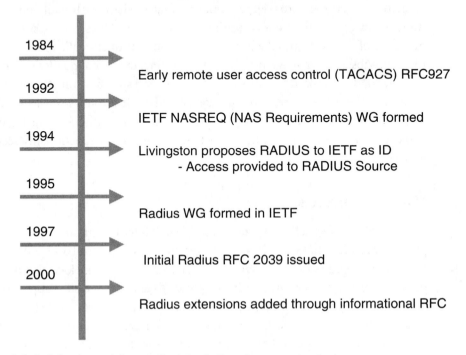

Figure 1.6 Evolution of some of the supporting authentication and management protocols.

One area of development in user access control traces its roots to as early as the mid-1980s, when early protocols were designed to provide access to remote terminals. The Terminal Access Controller Access–Control System (TACACS) protocol was initially submitted as an RFC by BBN in 1984 to enable remote user authentication of telnet sessions.

EARLY USER ACCESS IMPLEMENTATIONS

Alongside TACACS, other vendor-proprietary user authentication protocols were beginning to be developed. Early examples were created by companies such as Xylogics (Expedited Remote Procedure Call [ERPC]), Livingston's RADIUS, Telebit, Unisphere (now Juniper), Cosine, and others.

Xylogics' products included a range of dial access servers—the Annex series. These terminal servers typically supported asynchronous serial terminal access and could act as an aggregation and termination point for IP connections. The early Annex products supported protocols such as SLIP and PPP, giving remote users access to TCP/IP networks, including the Internet. Xylogics was eventually acquired by Bay Networks.

Another noteworthy early Network Access Server (NAS) was the Telebit Netblazer. Telebit was founded by one of the early creators of the concept of packet switching. Development of the Telebit product line originated from an offspring of the Cupertino, California-based company Packet Technologies. Packet Technologies eventually failed, splitting largely into Telebit and StrataCom (the builders of some of the first ATM switches).

Telebit's most widely known product is the Netblazer, thought of as one of the first on-demand dialup IP routers. The Netblazer was essentially a PC running custom software written by Telebit that integrated serial access devices (modems, ISDN), allowing users to remotely access IP networks using SLIP and PPP. This was a popular NAS used in many early ISPs and other dialup access networks. Telebit eventually sold part of its business to Cisco in 1996 and splintered off the rest of the business, closing its doors by the late 1990s.

An influential vendor that created one of the commonly used protocols seen in today's broadband devices was Livingston Systems. Its Portmaster line was another terminal access server that served multiple serial connections with SLIP and PPP access, giving remote serial connections access to IP networks. Livingston is credited with creating the RADIUS protocol, which eventually made its way into the IETF as a standard. Today RADIUS is used to support millions of Internet subscribers in networks across the world.

RADIUS received a lot of attention in the early 1990s during its first deployments in early Internet access networks such as MichNet. Early customization and deployment eventually led to demand to standardize remote user authentication protocols. Therefore, in 1992 the IETF responded by forming a working group dedicated to Network Access Server requirements—the NASREQ working group. This working group consisted of members of Merit/MichNet and had early involvement from vendors such as Livingston.

In 1994, Livingston proposed RADIUS as a standard to the NASREQ IETF working group. At the same time, Livingston offered access to the RADIUS source code, which then became the foundation for many other variations of RADIUS server implementations. RADIUS initially received a substantial amount of resistance from the IETF. Issues ranging from security to scope raised questions about its suitability as a standard protocol. However, after the IETF RADIUS Internet draft was released, nearly every NAS vendor in the market began supporting it. Its increasing popularity and user base eventually overwhelmed the resistance it initially received. Because multiple implementations and variations existed during the protocol's early phases, its deployed user base of vendors and users began demanding standardization on authentication, authorization, and accounting mechanisms. This pressure resulted in the formation of a dedicated RADIUS IETF working group. The initial group charter was to properly specify and "clean up" the protocol without adding new features or creating changes.

The result of this work is found in the initial RADIUS RFC, RFC 2039, which was issued in January 1997. It was followed by an informational RFC that specified RADIUS accounting as an extension to the RADIUS RFC. The original RFC was superseded by an updated version (RFC 2865) in 2000.

The combination of higher-speed line encodings, the evolution of broadband services, and increasing subscriber management needs spawned a market in the mid- to late 1990s to service the growing demand for broadband from service providers and telcos. Before that, vendors had placed substantial emphasis on improving core networks, which left room to grow around the high-speed network edge.

Providers were also seeking advanced features for offering valued-added services such as QoS, advanced subscriber management, VPNs, and so on. Many companies developed products to try to capture this market segment. Access server technology advanced due to improvements in the silicon and software used for dense, high-speed subscriber management and IP packet processing. The integration of previously separate systems, such as switches, routers, subscriber management, and quality of service, evolved and led to the introduction of a new type of dense, high-speed broadband aggregation device: the BNG.

Companies such as Cisco, Redstone, Unisphere, Redback, Laurel, Cosine, Springtide, and others built products during this period, resulting in many of the products commonly found in today's broadband networks. Ascend Communications led much of the pack in the high-speed dialup NAS market with its MAX TNT, which was one of the most successful dense dialup aggregation products in the market. The MAX TNT was deployed by the thousands in service providers such as AOL, Earthlink, and UUNET in the heyday of dialup Internet. Ascend eventually was acquired by Lucent.

Springtide, also acquired by Lucent, helped fill the gap between high-speed dialup and broadband aggregation. It approached the high-speed edge market by building a high-density, feature-rich edge router platform designed to support granular QoS, VPNs, and other features intended to allow providers to offer advanced services over broadband connections. The Springtide devices were deployed in the market, but eventually the line was discontinued by Lucent in the 2002–2003 timeframe.

Redstone, later Unisphere, eventually was acquired by Juniper from Siemens. It helped lead the way in large-scale, high-bandwidth, wire-speed broadband access devices with the ERX platform. With devices scaling into many gigabits per second, and with support for hundreds of thousands of simultaneous subscribers with rich functionality, the Juniper ERX platform is widely deployed. It is slated for use in many next-generation triple-play networks.

DSL FORUM BROADBAND ACCESS DEVICE REQUIREMENTS

With standardized user access protocols such as RADIUS and TACACS, advanced DSLAMs, and other supporting technologies available, the DSL Forum began specifying requirements for broadband access servers along with their architecture descriptions. In 1996, it created the DSL-F TR-001 system reference model. The initial TR-001 design, along with the TR-012 core network architecture, recommended PPP over an ATM transport layer over ADSL below the packet interface between the access node and user premises router.

In 1999, with early DSL deployments well under way, the DSLF documented an evolved architecture in TR-025. It provided more detailed requirements for the broadband access server as well as more detailed network architecture descriptions but maintained backward compatibility with the PPP over ATM-based

TR-012. TR-025 recommended four architectures to accomplish both backward compatibility and new services: Transparent ATM Core Network Architecture, L2TP Access Aggregation, PPP Terminated Aggregation (PTA), and Virtual Path Tunneling Architecture (VPTA). These four architectures are briefly described in the next section.

The TR-059 model, described in the next section and released in 2003, explicitly requires new functionality in the BNG, including the following:

- Supports PPP session aggregation into L2TP tunnels (LAC functionality)
- Terminates PPP sessions and assigns routing attributes based on subscriber profile (LNS functionality)
- RADIUS authentication
- IP over Bridged Ethernet (IETF RFC 2684)
- Dynamic address allocation using DHCP
- Multiple VCs per subscriber
- ATM VC termination and aggregation
- Policy-based downstream bandwidth allocation across ATM, PPP, Ethernet, and IP technologies
- Policy-based IP QoS marking
- Policy-based per-subscriber IP upstream policing
- DiffServ-based queuing and prioritization
- ATM, MPLS, and Ethernet traffic engineering support
- DiffServ-aware hierarchical scheduler
- Downstream per-subscriber rate shaping
- Upstream RED and WRED policing
- Optional multicast support
- Should support AAL-type agnostic VC/VP cross connection
- Supports the UBR, UBR+, CBR, VBR-nrt, and VBR ATM classes of service

The DSL Forum's TR-101 specification, released in 2006, details migration toward Ethernet-based DSL aggregation. Many new Ethernet-based features are required in TR-101, as described in depth throughout this book.

EVOLVING DSL ARCHITECTURE

As the features and speed of BNGs have evolved, so have the network architectures and service offerings. As contentious line modulation debates between CAP and DMT were resolved, many other issues had to be addressed to provide a viable end-to-end multiservice DSL architecture. The next significant area of debate that the DSL Forum undertook concerned which protocol should sit at Layer 2 of the OSI stack: ATM or native IP. Although this wasn't resolved for quite some time, many early DSL deployments began, based on the original ATM transport-based DSL Forum TR-001 reference model architecture. (Even today it still contains a large amount of the embedded DSL base.) This architecture is shown in Figure 1.7; Table 1.3 lists each abbreviation. Many of the basic elements and interfaces in TR-001 can be traced through the evolution of DSL architectures.

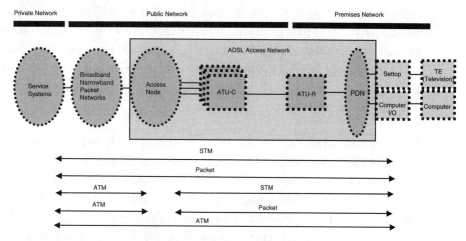

Figure 1.7 Early access architectures recommended by the DSL Forum in TR-001.

Table 1.3 TR-001 Reference Model Abbreviations

Abbreviation	Meaning
ADSL	Asymmetric Digital Subscriber Line
ATM	Asynchronous Transfer Mode
OS	Operating system
PDN	Premises Distribution Network
SM	Service module
STM	Synchronous Transfer Mode
TE	Terminal equipment

The Layer 2 debate focused on

- Quality of service
- The efficiency and overhead of transport of ATM versus native transport
- Processing complexity, which could impact the cost of devices
- Maturity and supportability
- Ease of service provisioning
- Compatibility with end-customer equipment

These subjects were debated at length, and in 1997 the ADSL Forum decided that services should be ATM-based. Although this was considered a success, with over 100 million ATM-based ADSLs worldwide, in 2004 the DSL Forum went in the opposite direction with the approval of the packet-based TR-059 and other IP-based TRs. It's hard to say if it would have been simply too much, too soon to have attempted native packet-based ADSL in 1997. Or perhaps with refinements to the technology in 1997 the outcome would have been different. It is now clear and relatively uncontested that the technology and market are there to drive a true fully IP-based system.

From the early ATM-based architecture described in TR-001 and shown in Figure 1.7 to the native packet-based architectures in more recent DSL Forum TRs (such as TR-059 and TR-101), the goal of providing multiple, simultaneous, high-quality services over a single copper loop has been maintained and has evolved over time. To understand the points of reference in the original TR-001 DSL Forum system architecture, Figure 1.8 shows the interfaces and devices. The terms are explained in Table 1.4.

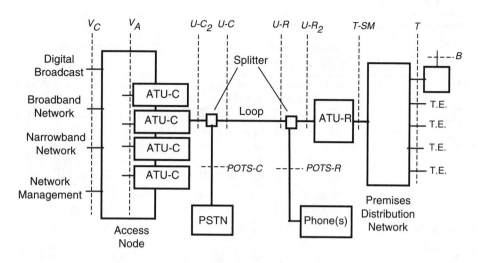

Figure 1.8 DSL system reference model according to the DSL Forum TR-001.

Table 1.4 Definitions for the TR-001 DSL System Reference Model, Shown in Figure 1.8

Interface or Device	Description
Access node	Local access concentration point for broadband and narrowband connections. The access node may be located at a central office or remote site. Also, a remote access node may subtend from a central access node.
ATU-C	ADSL Transmission Unit at the network end. The ATU-C may be integrated within an access node.
ATU-R	ADSL Transmission Unit at the customer premises end. The ATU-R may be integrated within an SM.
B	Auxiliary data input (such as a satellite feed) to a service module (such as a set-top box).
Broadcast	Broadband data input in simplex mode (typically broadcast video).
Broadband network	Switching system for data rates above 1.5/2.0Mbps.
Loop	Twisted-pair copper telephone line. Loops may differ in distance, diameter, age, and transmission characteristics, depending on the network.
Narrowband network	Switching system for data rates at or below 1.5/2.0Mbps.
PDN	Premises Distribution Network. System for connecting ATU-R to service modules. May be point-to-point or multipoint. May be passive wiring or an active network. Multipoint may be a bus or star.
POTS	Plain Old Telephone Service.
POTS-C	Interface between the PSTN and the POTS splitter at the network end.

continues

Table 1.4 continued

Interface or Device	Description
POTS-R	Interface between the phones and the POTS splitter at the premises end.
PSTN	Public Switched Telephone Network.
SM	Service module. Performs terminal adaptation functions. Examples are set-top boxes, PC interfaces, and LAN routers.
Splitter	Filter that separates high-frequency (ADSL) and low-frequency (POTS) signals at the network end and premises end. The splitter may be integrated into the ATU, physically separated from the ATU, or divided between high pass and low pass, with the low-pass function physically separated from the ATU. The provision of POTS splitters and POTS-related functions is optional.
T	Interface between the premises distribution network and service modules. May be the same as T-SM when the network is point-to-point passive wiring. Note that the T interface may disappear at the physical level when the ATU-R is integrated within a service module.
TE	Terminal Equipment. The device that processes data to and from the ATU-R and the customer devices. This could be a routing gateway and is often integrated with the ATU-R.
T-SM	Interface between the ATU-R and premises distribution network. May be the same as T when the network is point-to-point passive wiring. An ATU-R may have more than one type of T-SM interface implemented (such as a T1/E1 connection and an Ethernet connection). The T-SM interface may be integrated within a service module.
U-C	Interface between a loop and the POTS splitter on the network side. Defining both ends of the loop interface separately occurs because of the asymmetry of the signals on the line.
U-C2	Interface between the POTS splitter and the ATU-C. Note that ANSI T1.413 currently does not define such an interface and that separating the POTS splitter from the ATU-C presents some technical difficulties in standardizing this interface.
U-R	Interface between the loop and the POTS splitter on the premises side.
U-R2	Interface between the POTS splitter and the ATU-R. Note that ANSI T1.413 currently does not define such an interface and that separating the POTS splitter from the ATU-R presents some technical difficulties in standardizing the interface.
VA	Logical interface between the ATU-C and the access node. Because this interface often is within circuits on a common board, the ADSL Forum does not consider physical VA interfaces. The V interface may contain STM, ATM, or both transfer modes. In the primitive case of point-to-point connection between a switch port and an ATU-C (that is, a case without concentration or multiplexing), the VA and VC interfaces become identical (alternatively, the VA interface disappears).
VC	Interface between the access node and the network. May have multiple physical connections (as shown) and might also carry all signals across a single physical connection.

Newer DSL architectures had to support the changing regulations and competition landscape, such as open access for CLECs. Various techniques were debated, including native Layer 1/Layer 2 access to subscribers in cases where the regulatory body saw fit to unbundle the copper itself. Alternatively, just the DSL service can be unbundled and delivered to the retail ISP based on a Layer 3 interconnection. This entails one telco front-ending the physical access to the subscriber and then delivering subscriber data to the appropriate ISP. The delivery mechanism could be via native IP or L2TP. Chapter 7, "Wholesale Broadband Networks," describes the various wholesale modules.

The platform for developing future DSL architectures was established based on the foundation built by the TR-001 reference model and in the TR-018 core network architecture recommendations. TR-025, released by the DSL-F in 1999, described four architectures, allowing regional broadband carriers and service providers to interoperate in new ways while maintaining backward compatibility with existing TR-001 and TR-018 deployments. These architectures are Transparent ATM Core Network Architecture, L2TP Access Aggregation, PPP Terminated Aggregation (PTA), and Virtual Path Tunneling Architecture (VPTA):

- Transparent ATM Core Network Architecture, shown in Figure 1.9

  All protocols above the ATM layer traverse the regional ATM broadband network, and subscribers are terminated directly in the routing domain on the network service provider's equipment. There is no service interworking functionality. All functionality above the ATM level is the responsibility of the service provider.

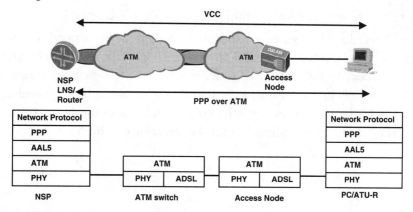

Figure 1.9 Transparent ATM core network architecture.

- L2TP Access Aggregation, shown in Figure 1.10

  This allows the subscriber PPP sessions to be tunneled through the regional broadband access network. Two functions are required: the L2TP Access Concentrator (LAC) on the regional broadband network side, and the L2TP Network Server (LNS) on the network service provider's side. This allows any IP network (not just ATM) technology to connect the regional broadband provider and the network service provider by tunneling the subscriber's PPP sessions over L2TP.

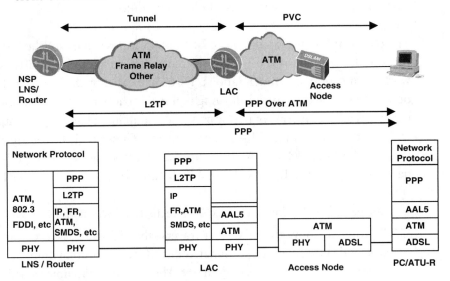

Figure 1.10 L2TP access aggregation.

- PPP Terminated Aggregation (PTA), shown in Figure 1.11

  This allows PPP sessions to be terminated on the broadband access server itself, within the broadband carrier's network. This allows the carrier to harness the PPP suite itself from within the ADSL access network instead of simply tunneling the PPP session to the network service provider. This architecture option was a driving factor in many of the advanced BNG architectures available today that are described in this book.

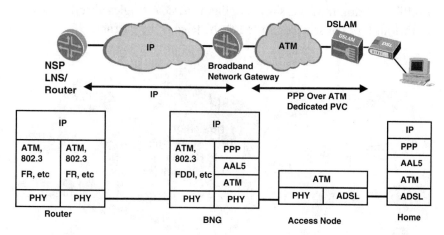

Figure 1.11 PPP Terminated Aggregation (PTA).

- Virtual Path Tunneling Architecture (VPTA), shown in Figure 1.12

    VP tunneling is similar to the first option, the Transparent ATM model. However, it provides an end-to-end SVC to carry the PPP session between the customer premises device and the access node.

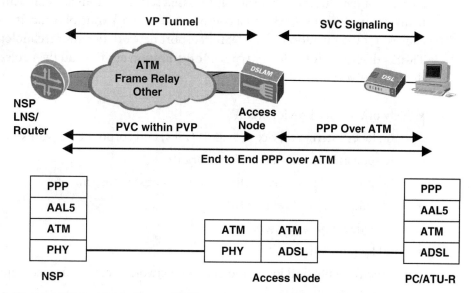

Figure 1.12 Virtual Path Tunneling Architecture (VPTA).

An ISP selection model is shown in Figure 1.13. A single subscriber gains access to various types of services hosted at the telco or its partners.

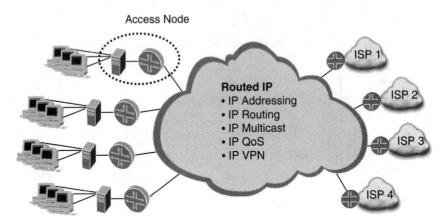

Figure 1.13 Routed wholesale DSL interconnects.

In 2003, the DSL-F released TR-059, which described architectural and service requirements for the support of IP QoS services on DSL networks. The model allowed for new functionality such as IP-based services, bandwidth on demand, many-to-many access, QoS, and a consolidated network control plane. It also allowed for the migration of the DSL transport network to newer technologies. TR-059 describes five different types of organization entities and their roles in the DSL network:

- Network Service Provider (NSP)
    - Includes Internet service providers (ISPs) and corporate networks.
    - Responsible for overall service assurance.
    - Responsible for authentication and IP address management.
- Application Service Provider (ASP)
    - Provides application services.
- Local loop provider
    - Provides a physical local loop between network access equipment and the subscriber's premises.
- Access Network Provider
    - Provides connectivity to the customer via the local loop.

- Regional Network Provider
  - Provides connectivity between the access network and NSP/ASPs.

TR-059 specifies a substantial amount of new QoS functionality, as well as subscriber and policy management capabilities. The architecture also creates the capability to support an access-media-agnostic IP-based regional access network, allowing for migration from ATM to other technologies, as shown in Figure 1.14.

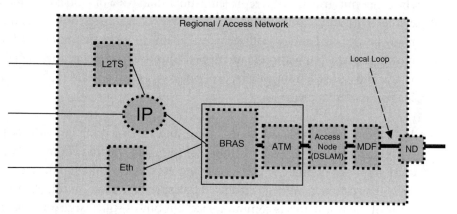

Figure 1.14 IP-enabled regional network.

Many of these early models provided simple Internet and VPN-based services. But emerging services required additional support for efficient multicast, MPLS integration, end-to-end quality of service, and so forth, as described throughout this book. Fully harnessing the capabilities of each new, evolving technology involves many people. Market researchers, media analysts, regulators, standards bodies, industry consortiums, and the end users themselves to some degree must all understand these new, evolving DSL technologies and architectures to put them to the best use. Carriers today are looking to move up the value chain by expanding into the content, application, and traffic management markets. They want to move away from the legacy of being commoditized *bit shifters*, participating only in the transport of data. This is one of the factors driving carriers toward triple-play services. At the same time, obstacles and hurdles must be overcome, both technical and nontechnical. Carriers require higher-layer application awareness in the network to move up the value chain. This currently is in conflict with common carrier status.

TODAY'S BROADBAND

With well over 100 million lines provisioned worldwide, DSL is truly a global and well-recognized technology. DSL deployment is even a political issue in many countries. Some governments track the overall number of DSL subscribers and subsidize large infrastructure deployments to attract businesses and development. This is much like bridges, electricity, and roads are subsidized to stimulate economic growth. DSL represents more than 63% of global broadband connectivity and is available in just about every developed country, as well as in many poorer economies. With service available to more than 75% (and rapidly growing) of the population in developed countries across Europe, the U.S., Japan, and Korea, among others, dropping prices and wide availability are helping fuel its deployment.

With applications such as Internet, voice, and video serving individuals, businesses, educational institutions, and governments, DSL has cut into a large cross section of society. Some of DSL's early success was attributed to the fee structure, in which customers were given a fixed line speed for a flat monthly fee. In some parts of the world, this is commonplace, but others still charge on a usage tariff, which is usually volume-based. It is still an open question how advanced services will be funded—if the demand itself is enough to support a flat fee, or if wider usage-based billing is needed.

To date, the vast majority of demand comes from simple best-effort high-speed Internet services, which are becoming increasingly commoditized as indicated by decreasing prices. Telcos are again looking at new ways to provide additional revenue-generating services over DSL. They are looking at where new customer bandwidth demands are coming from. Higher-speed Internet, VoD, broadcast/multicast media, and high-definition TV are all services that are well-aligned with consumer market trends.

This market is now expanding not from an embedded base of narrowband connectivity, but rather from subscribers who are accustomed to multimegabit-rate DSL. This market offers a path to higher revenue generation through the adoption of triple-play-type services. For these services (and revenue) to be realized, there is a much greater dependency on quality of service compared to today's service delivery. Line encoding schemes are increasing speeds through ADSL2+

and VDSL2 into the dozens of megabits-per-second (Mbps) rates that allow high-definition video and multimedia services. As a result, subscribers expect the same or greater quality and reliability they curently experience with their satellite, cable, or terrestrial service. Table 1.5 shows the data rates required by a handful of applications or tasks.

Table 1.5 Data Rates of Various Applications or Tasks Commonly Performed on DSL Lines

Service	Bandwidth
VoIP	16Kbps
H.263 full-screen videoconferencing	384Kbps
Basic web browsing	1Mbps
5 megapixel JPEG photo in 10 seconds	1.5Mbps
SDTV (MPEG4)	1.5Mbps
SDTV (MPEG2)	4Mbps
HDTV (MPEG4)	7 to 9Mbps
HDTV (MPEG2)	15Mbps
Uncompressed x-ray image in 2.5 seconds	25Mbps

With average DSL speeds in the single Mbps for upstream and low (3 to 5) Mbps for downstream, it is essential that line rates and quality evolve to compete with VSAT and cable-based content providers, which have much more downstream bandwidth available to them. ADSL2+ and VDSL2 are promising enhancements because they provide adequate bandwidth combined with appropriate QoS controls for triple-play services. A 20Mbps ADSL2+ connection could support HDTV, VoIP, and Internet simultaneously if traffic is correctly prioritized. The opportunity for telecom companies and service providers is enormous if they can meet these growing bandwidth demands using their existing copper infrastructure. Chapter 6, "Evolutions in Last-Mile Broadband Access," discusses in more detail recent DSLAM technology developments as well as other types of broadband access for comparison.

WHAT'S NEXT?

Higher data bit-rate DSL such as ADSL2+ and VDSL are being adopted, and other FTTx-type services such as Verizon's FIOS are gaining in the market. Therefore, it is a safe assumption that speeds to the end user are increasing and should continue to do so in the near/medium-term future. These new high bit-rate specifications are there to pave the way for a new suite of premium ser-vices, such as simultaneous data, video, and voice using advances in BNG tech-nology to offer dynamic services with granular QoS.

Regulations, as seen with the Telecommunications Act of 1996 in the U.S., can also play a role in deciding which services and technologies make it into wide deployment. For example, issues that are still being debated, such as "common carrier status," could punctuate the broadband landscape with unforeseen inter-connect costs. Common carrier status determines whether a provider is respon-sible for the content it delivers. The applicability of this status on individual operators recently became especially contentious when some telecommunica-tions providers were affecting traffic (reducing its priority or blocking it alto-gether) coming from off-net VoIP providers. Common carrier status may also have an impact on a carrier's ability to affect content on its own triple-play networks.

Enterprise adoption of high-bandwidth, low-cost wide-area network (WAN) services will enable new applications and interaction across the enterprise and externally with customers and partners. Lower-cost, high-bandwidth broadband connections allow telecommuters to work at home, saving transport costs for staff and office overhead for companies. Small and medium-sized enterprises can gain access to the types of services and applications that previously only larger organizations could afford, such as data replication across WANs.

The adoption of broadband services is also often looked at as an indication of economic growth in some countries. With greater access to the Internet and other broadband services, countries can bolster their educational systems, become more attractive to multinational corporations by providing the infra-structure they require and expect, and develop a strong pool of experience and skill around the technology itself, as well as the information available through the technology.

SUMMARY

After a long history, carrier networks and the services they can offer have evolved dramatically. They have gone from the simple low-bit-rate connections previously available in the legacy circuit-switched carrier's network to the flexible high-speed broadband services widely available today.

As carriers seek to move up the value chain by offering additional content and application services through triple-play networks, the supporting network architectures must continue to evolve in parallel. This evolution has been seen historically through the early DSL Forum architectures, from TR-001, TR-018 through TR-025, and forward to TR-059 and into TR-101.

Much of this evolution comes from constantly increasing capabilities on the same copper lines that have served subscribers for decades. Bandwidth is rapidly becoming widely available in more places and at a lower cost. Along with this development comes an increasing opportunity for service providers, carriers, and content providers, who can understand this evolving architecture, to deliver new types of services and reach new groups of potential subscribers.

NEXT-GENERATION TRIPLE-PLAY SERVICES

The IP networking world is buzzing with vendors releasing triple-play and multi-play ready products and platforms, service providers unleashing multimedia network extravaganzas on anticipating markets, and media pundits electrifying the buzz. In the beginning, triple-play referred to voice, video, and data services being delivered over an IP network. Multi-play extends this concept to refer to data services consisting of more than a single traffic type. These are premium data services. A gaming service, a high-speed download area, and a walled-garden network are examples of data services that can be treated differently to an Internet connection.

As explained in Chapter 1, "A History of Broadband Networks," data services meant Internet access. Of course, there was access to corporate networks using narrowband services (X.25, Frame Relay, ATM, and dial-up), but by far the most common use of a data service in terms of numbers of connections is Internet access. Over the last several years, service providers have been offering voice over IP (VoIP) services. Such service providers include both fixed and nonfixed operators. The former covers operators enhancing their service offerings with a voice network more feature-rich than POTS. The latter includes VoIP providers that rely on customers providing their own connectivity over the Internet to access the provider network. Vonage and Skype are two examples.

Not until video over IP services were popularized did the concept of triple play really take off. Video over IP services include television channels transmitted to households over an IP network (IPTV) and Video on Demand (VoD), which allows users to request on-demand movies and TV shows streamed over their IP network connection. But video content is not restricted to these general categories. For example, YouTube and Network Private Video Recorders (NPVRs) are two examples of how the market dynamic is changing to encompass more than simple VoD and IPTV.

This chapter discusses in more detail what triple-play services are about and what subservices can be offered as part of the three broad topics under the triple-play umbrella. Also covered are technical aspects of service delivery. For example, a general technical overview of a video server architecture is provided for reference.

NETWORK TOPOLOGY

This section gives a high-level overview of a generalized network topology and any protocols and devices of interest. The major components are: server head-end, external Internet peers, IP core, Broadband Network Gateway (BNG) edge, Ethernet aggregation network, DSLAMs, local loop, and the customer household. Many of these components are explained in more detail later in this book, but Figure 2.1 shows a simple overview of the server infrastructure in relation to the core.

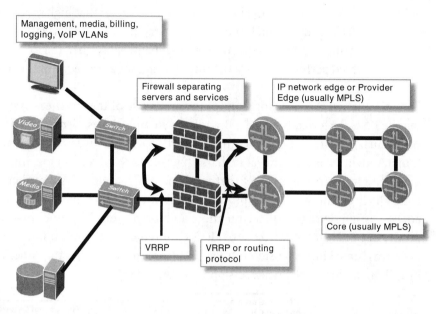

Figure 2.1 A high-level overview of servers, firewalls, IP edge, and core in a multiplay network.

One or two main data centers house the infrastructure servers, such as NMS, RADIUS, and log servers. Often colocated at these same data centers are servers for VoIP, IPTV, and VoD applications. These servers connect to switches using 100BASE-T and 1000BASE-T electrical connections, which are then fed into the core via optical GigabitEthernet or 10-GigabitEthernet links. To ensure that a failure of one IP router or switch does not affect connectivity between the core and server LANs, Virtual Router Redundancy Protocol (VRRP) provides a virtual IP and MAC address to the devices on the LAN. If one router fails, the other router assumes the role as the default gateway for the subnet.

If the network is running MPLS, edge routers are called Provider Edge (PE) routers, which are connected via point-to-point GigabitEthernet, 10-GigabitEthernet or SONET links to Provider (P) routers. Unicast and sometimes multicast IP packets are encapsulated into MPLS packets and are sent across the network of P routers toward a PE, at which point they are decapsulated back to IP packets. The core is a highly available, high-speed transport facility that switches MPLS packets to the destination label encoded in the packet header. To make the most of an

MPLS network, traffic engineering can be used to ensure that high-priority traffic is routed efficiently through the network using features such as fast reroute and link coloring. If packets are sent to a broadband subscriber, the PE should be the BNG, which performs service definition functions at the edge of the network.

Figure 2.2 shows the basic topology of the other side of the core network, including the BNG, historically called a Broadband Remote Access Server (BRAS). The BNG can be as simple as a router that forwards packets between the core and customer, providing little extra value than a high-density router. On the other hand, it can be a more complex router that implements dynamic per-subscriber IP policies, Quality of Service (QoS) profiles, rate limiters, packet manipulation, address assignment, session termination, and forwarding. The amount of complexity depends on the service provider's requirements. At a minimum, the BNG performs some kind of session termination from subscribers, using either DHCP or PPP in tandem with an address pool or RADIUS.

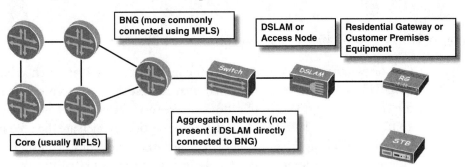

Figure 2.2 A view of the network from the core toward the subscriber.

The BNG connects to DSLAMs either using a switched aggregation network (also called a metro Ethernet network) or directly using dark fibre, CWDM, or DWDM. An aggregation network is useful when a switched layer between the DSLAM and the BNG provides cost-effective aggregation capacity. Such a scenario would arise if the bandwidth utilization per-DSL-port were not enough to justify connecting DSLAMs directly to the BNG. This benefit needs to be weighed against the expected traffic loads to and from DSLAMs. Also consider whether a switch can continue to offer enough statistical traffic multiplexing gains in the future.

DSLAMs terminate subscriber copper local loops and provide a DSL modulation service to the CPE. DSLAMs are also Layer 2-aware and take ATM AAL5 PDUs or Ethernet frames from the customer side and forward them to the BNG on the network side. If the DSLAM is Ethernet-capable, it forwards traffic toward the BNG as Ethernet frames with at least one level of VLAN tagging. Ethernet-capable DSLAMs are an important aspect of most of the designs in this book compared to the erstwhile DSLAMs, which use ATM as the interface toward the BNG. ATM-based DSLAMs also require the use of an ATM aggregation network, which is still common in many telcos. But the move is clearly toward Ethernet devices, which offer cost savings in the aggregation network and BNG due to the use of the cheaper Ethernet interfaces and the commoditized internal switching hardware.

The customer household is the network's demarcation point between service provider and customer. Services are delivered to the demarcation point, which may be a piece of equipment managed by the service provider. Or, in a simpler architecture, the customer may provide his or her own hardware. In both cases, they are called the Residential Gateway (RG), which is the Customer Premises Equipment (CPE). Most CPE are multi-play networks is complex pieces of equipment provided by the service provider that integrate a DSL modem and router. Sometimes only the DSL modem function is used; this means the CPE operates in bridging mode. In either case, it is useful for the service provider to manage the equipment for provisioning and remote diagnostics purposes, especially because the number of services a customer receives is more than just a basic Internet service. Connected to the CPE are one or more Set-Top Boxes (STBs), although most providers have only a single STB today. STBs take VoD and IPTV traffic coming from the network and send it to a TV connected via composite, SCART, HDMI, or RF outputs. STBs are controlled with a remote control, which is used to switch channels, browse videos, or, in some cases, send e-mail. Some STBs have a web browser built in to the STB User Interface (SUI). To let other devices connect to the broadband network, CPE have several Ethernet ports to connect PCs, gaming consoles, Macs, and other devices in the home. WiFi capability is commonly built into the CPE, which is useful for wireless phones with VoIP capability, PDAs, and any other nonwired device.

VIDEO OVER IP

As mentioned previously, video over IP is a broad term for a video service over an IP network. In this book, the focus of video over IP services is IPTV services delivered over multicast, and on-demand video services delivered using unicast. In general, the core and access networks can be built in a few different ways to support IPTV multicast. However, the multicast IPTV is a relatively straightforward service to categorize both at the network architecture level and at the service level. The service design is described in the following section. Microsoft has proposed a variation of the generalized multicast IPTV design, called MSTV. This is also discussed in the following section.

Unicast video services are more diverse. For networks with substantial network capacity, unicast video can in fact replace multicast IPTV services. This is called unicast IPTV. But to start with, the most identifiable service is basic VoD, similar to that found in hotels. Compared to hotel systems, not only is the range of content in multiplay VoD environments a lot wider than hotel systems, but the *concurrency rate* is a lot higher. Concurrency rate is the percentage of active video streams in the network versus the number of potential subscribers who can watch a video stream. These concepts and architecture are described in the section "Video on Demand."

Some additional video services, such as Network PVR (NPVR) and specialized content agreements, are value-added services that can enhance a provider's video value proposition. They are also discussed in "Video on Demand."

To show how media content flows from a satellite or cable source to the network, that section shows an example of a video head-end, which is where most content is encrypted before being sent to subscribers. Encrypted content is usually channels that are received from the content distributor already protected. They must be decrypted and then re-encrypted, but with the provider's certificate, before transmission to subscribers. This process is discussed in the section "Media Encoding, Security, and Encryption."

To tie together all these services and platforms, the middleware acts as the control point. It handles video service provisioning, interfaces with most of the video elements, creates billing records, and interacts with customer STBs. Clearly this is an important piece of the network, and is described in the section "Middleware."

IPTV

In most networks, IPTV services are generally characterized by efficient transport of television channels over a packet network using multicast. Multicast reduces utilization of network links between the video server and the customer by sending only a single copy of a media stream into the network. The network replicates the stream to individual subscribers closer to the edge, thus saving bandwidth in the core. The components involved before the core are the source video feed receiver and decoder, IP encoder, and encryption process. The media streams are then fed to the IP core. This process is described in the next section.

As mentioned previously, IPTV is not restricted to content via multicast. Networks with ample bandwidth to spare can get more control over the customer video stream if it is unicast. For example, it is easier to target advertising based on viewing habits to specific households if there is a uniquely addressable endpoint, that is, a unicast destination address. This is covered in the section "Unicast IPTV." Another example of a service that makes use of unicast streams is Pause Live TV. One implementation by Bitband makes use of cache servers deployed throughout the network. If the user pauses an IPTV stream, the STB switches from the multicast stream to a unicast stream.

Video Head-End

Figure 2.3 shows a simple video head-end reference architecture that is used for the discussion in this section.

The content in Figure 2.3 is supplied by satellite, but there are a variety of transport mechanisms. Terrestrial microwave links or even IP feeds from content aggregators are other possibilities. Digital streams are received off the satellite using the Digital Video Broadcast, Satellite (DVB-S) standard. These streams are received by the satellite, are frequency-stepped down, and are fed to a receiver that handles the demodulation of the DVB-S signal. They are then fed to a suitable output format for the decoder to work with. If the channel is encrypted, it is the decoder's job to decrypt the channel and forward it to the IP encoder. If the channel is not encrypted, it acts as a pass-through system and sends the stream directly to the encoder.

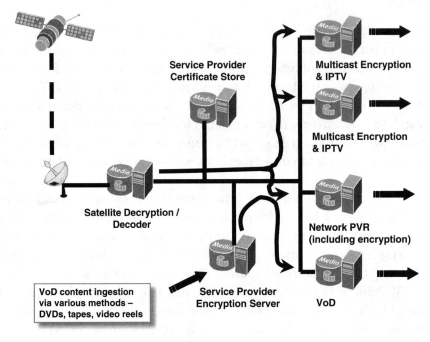

Figure 2.3 A simple head-end architecture fed by satellite.

The DVB-S and DVB-S2 systems transport the media streams in MPEG format, so the decoder's job is to take the unencrypted MPEG stream and feed it to the IP encoder. The IP encoder does the hard work of taking the MPEG stream, trans-rating or trans-coding it to a lower bit rate. Whether it is trans-rated or trans-coded depends on the amount of bit-rate reduction required. The MPEG video feed is encapsulated into IP packets. Any streams that were originally encrypted after being received from the satellite need to be re-encrypted before being made available to subscribers. Such streams are sent to an encryption engine, which encrypts the data using the provider's key or certificate. These streams can only be decrypted using an STB, which has received authorization from the certificate server. The certificate or key may have come via the middleware.

The encryption servers might be the last devices before the encrypted and unen-crypted multicast streams are sent to the IP core. The types of devices (if any) that are between the encrypters and the IP network usually depend on the high-availability architecture. Dedicated servers with a heartbeat mechanism between the two can provide a single multicast source to the network so that when one server fails, the other can resume the multicast forwarding duties. If the high availability (HA) mechanism is simple enough, the encrypters can also perform this feature.

This design uses a single IP source address for multicast group traffic. Each of the groups is distributed throughout the network using normal multicast forwarding replication, and the clients join the groups as needed.

Microsoft's MSTV

An alternative proposition by Microsoft is to extend the multicast distribution model with a hybrid unicast and multicast solution. One set of multicast *A-servers* (acquisition servers) sends the multicast groups into the network, similar to the architecture just described. In addition, a distributed layer of unicast *D-servers* (distribution servers) is located strategically throughout the network. The deployment architecture and location of the D-servers are intended to reduce the *channel zapping* latency for STBs.

From an architectural perspective, the primary use of D-servers is to compensate for the time interval between MPEG I-frames. An I-frame occurs every so often in the MPEG data flow and is a marker in the stream that can be used to build an instantaneous image on the screen. An MPEG decoder can only start decoding a stream starting with an I-frame. If an I-frame occurs more frequently in the stream, a receiver (such as an STB) can more quickly lock onto the stream and start the video output. But if the I-frame occurs too frequently in the stream, the video bit rate needs to increase, which is extra overhead. When an STB joins a new channel, a D server sends a unicast copy of the channel, beginning with an I-frame, at a much greater bandwidth (a burst in other words) than the multicast stream, to the STB. Simultaneously, the STB joins the multicast group in the network using IGMP. While the unicast stream is being used to display the channel to the television, the multicast group starts filling a video buffer. As soon as the buffer is sufficiently full, the unicast stream is terminated, and the STB switches to the multicast stream. Figure 2.4 shows a high-level architecture of the solution.

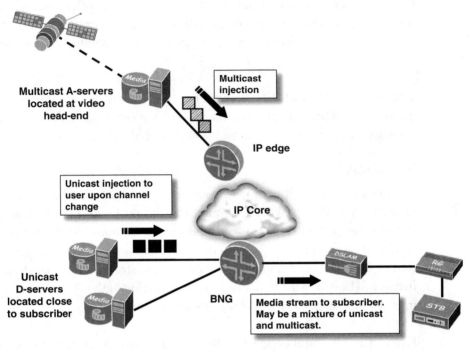

Figure 2.4 An MSTV architecture.

The solution requires servers to be distributed as close to subscribers as possible. This reduces the latency of the unicast stream between the STB and server. Also, the number of simultaneous connections that can be made between STBs and a server is limited by the server's video processing capacity and interface through-put. Even though the STBs are connected to a server for only several seconds, the network needs to cope with many simultaneous channel changes during peak viewing times. The efficacy of this solution depends on the individual network. As with any architecture, it is advised that you test its scaling properties well in a lab environment beforehand.

Unicast IPTV

MSTV is a hybrid unicast and multicast model. A pure unicast model drastically increases the requirements of network transmission, forwarding capacity, and server cluster performance. Each server needs to generate a unique stream for each client, and at 4Mbps for a Standard Definition TV (SD-TV) channel, the requirements quickly add up. Of course, this offers the highest flexibility for the service provider. A profile of each household's viewing habits can be built and targeted advertising created during the commercial breaks. Also, there are no issues with channel zapping latency due to I-frame interval and subsequent buffer fill. There are additional advantages for the service provider with a unicast stream. For instance, a service for rewinding, pausing, and fast-forwarding a program needs a unicast data stream. Multicast replication can be the standard delivery method until the user requests a pause, rewind, or fast-forward of the channel.

VIDEO ON DEMAND

Video on Demand as a concept is relatively well-known. Anyone who has been to a modern hotel has discovered VoD services available from the television in their room. There are two common models. The first is where popular movies run on a rotating schedule and, for a set period of time (24 hours, for example), you can watch the movie as many times as it comes up on the rotating schedule. This is not terribly flexible if you want to watch the movie right away. It is also difficult to implement video controls, such as pause and fast-forward, if the media stream does not have some kind of feedback loop to the server. This system is called Near Video on Demand (NVoD).The more preferred approach (at least from an end-user perspective) is a completely on-demand system in which the video stream is delivered to the user when requested. Usefully, a full on-demand approach is the way most systems are deployed nowadays; only a few older systems stream content on a loop system.

This section explains how VoD solutions can be deployed in a network service provider environment. At the press of a button, customers can watch the latest blockbuster movies or browse through hundreds of older cinematic releases from the comfort of their own home. One important aspect of a VoD over broadband service is, not surprisingly, a market differentiator over what traditional bricks-and-mortar movie shops offer. Breaking people's years-long habit of going to the local movie store and picking up a tangible, shiny disc needs more than just a strong marketing campaign. On-demand video over broadband has enormous potential over traditional media, but from the very beginning, clear advantages need to be pushed, such as previews of each movie or show, a large content archive, same-as or longer-than rental periods as DVDs and videos, and, most importantly, a compelling price. These less-technical, more-service-oriented issues are covered later in this chapter.

Basic Video on Demand

Except in the most grandiose of VoD rollout plans, a server architecture normally starts out small, with a centralized video head-end. One or more GigabitEthernet links (either bonded or discrete paths) link the VoD server switches with the IP edge. For maximum flexibility and to reduce IP address and load-balancing complexity (but at the expense of interface cost), 10-GigabitEthernet links can be deployed from the outset.

There are varying models of how the servers interact with the IP edge and STBs. One example, proposed by BitBand, is to have one or more *streaming gateways* in addition to the video content servers. When an STB requests a media file from the middleware platform (described later in this section), the STB is sent a control file that lists the video servers to which it can connect. Each VoD server that is listed in the control file is ranked by preference so that the client can choose the best server. The preference metric is an inverse indicator of load, so the more preferred server is the least-loaded one. For redundancy reasons, the streaming gateway doesn't send the details of just the best video server to the client. If a server fails midstream, the client can reconnect to a different server automatically without having to reconnect to the streaming gateway.

Various high-availability models exist. These can cover various failure scenarios—server failure, switch failure, router failure, or a combination thereof. Because explaining these scenarios in low-level detail could consume several chapters, Figure 2.5 shows a sample architecture with the components involved.

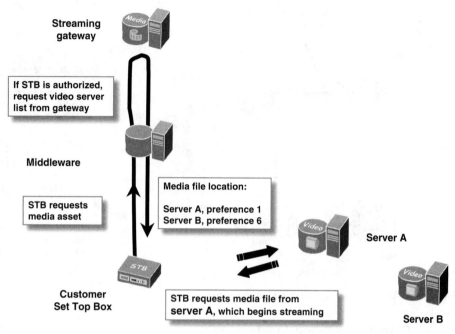

Figure 2.5 Video streaming setup.

Figure 2.6 shows a client re-requesting a media file to a different server after component failure. Less-impacting failures, such as a switch or router going down, cause a blip in the service until Layer 2 and Layer 3 protocols converge around the failure. Having a hot-standby server is difficult to achieve due to the amount of video session state that would have to be mirrored between the two servers.

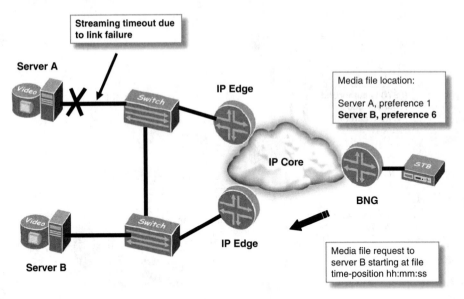

Figure 2.6]STB re-requests a file from the secondary server.

Distributed Video Clusters

To handle hundreds of concurrent video streams, the VoD server network needs to become more distributed. This has several benefits:

- It reduces latency between the server and the STB (although low latency is more important with an IPTV service).
- It creates Point of Presence (PoP) diversity to reduce the impact of a PoP going off the network.
- It improves bandwidth utilization in the core by moving VoD flows to the network edges.
- It reduces per-server bandwidth and CPU load.

When a new video PoP is built, it uses most of the components of the centralized video head-end, except on a smaller scale. Typically it has a central data center where all the TV shows and movies are stored. This data center also has certificate and encryption servers, middleware components, SUI content servers, and, of course, some video streaming servers. If the servers do not share a central content store, popular content can be preseeded to the individual servers based on anticipated demand ahead of a popular movie release. A second option is to simply let viewer demand dictate how content is seeded to the servers. A third option is a mix of the two; this option is the most common.

Tier 2 video PoPs are geared more toward pure video content delivery rather than housing middleware platforms and streaming gateways. Instead, these lower-bandwidth services are centralized at the Tier 1 data center. In much the same way that the content can be replicated to the Tier 1 streaming servers from the content store, the Tier 2 streaming servers (or the content store in the PoP) are seeded with the media files beforehand. The most optimal server from which an STB should request a media file can be determined dynamically using heuristics such as lowest server round-trip time (RTT) or a trace route method. Or the intelligence can be shifted to the network, where the STB's physical location can be derived using methods such as IP address coupled with a DHCP option 82 stamp or a PPPoE Intermediate Agent (IA) string. DHCP option 82 and PPPoE IA are identifiers that the DSLAM can add to indicate from which physical port a subscriber DHCP-based IPoE session or PPPoE session comes. Then, an IP address can be linked to one of the two identifiers, depending on the access protocol used. The STB can then be directed at a subset of video servers from which it can choose the one with the lowest preference. Of course, if a requested media file is not available at a Tier 2 PoP closest to the STB, the most effective option is to direct the STB to a central location where the media asset is available. This is only one example of how content and server distribution can be deployed.

> ➡ Caution: One of the important aspects to consider in the early phases of the design is how the high availability of a particular architecture should work from an end-to-end perspective. If this is treated as an afterthought or left until late in the design stage, it can mean a lot of unnecessary redesign work.

Maintaining Video Quality with Call Admission Control

The principle of Call Admission Control (CAC) in this sense is much the same as it was in the PSTN. A session (a video stream) is allowed or disallowed to proceed based on a CAC algorithm. It is essentially a binary result. If a CAC request is denied, it is not possible for a session to proceed, even in a degraded manner.

This is different from a QoS mechanism on routers and switches, which can prioritize traffic based on embedded markings in packet or frame headers. If traffic cannot be transmitted at a point in time, it is queued for later transmission. Such a prioritization mechanism relies on IP traffic streams being able to be statistically multiplexed down a single path. Normally this is possible because often non-VoIP and non-video IP streams are not of a consistent bit rate and can tolerate some variable delay in the packet delivery process.

Most video over IP streams are not so forgiving of poor network conditions. These conditions occur for a variety of reasons, such as link failures that cause suboptimal traffic routing, poor network capacity planning, or a DoS attack. The end result is too much data offered to network links with insufficient capacity to transfer all required packets.

As a general principle, the network needs to be built in such a way that video traffic is high priority and is forwarded without delay. If it isn't possible to reliably send a video or VoIP call from end to end (such as due to lack of network resources), the session should not proceed. This requires the CAC mechanism to work during session setup. In other words, first a request is made to see if the user has the right credentials (he has paid his bill and has passed the authentication check, for example). Then the network links are checked for resource availability. Only then is the stream delivered to the client. Relying on a mechanism that takes periodic snapshots or averages of network utilization is not a reliable method, because the traffic constitution could easily change between polling periods.

Implementing a CAC function with a VoD network can work by extending the video server's functionality to interact with an external server. The server can model the network topology and have an end-to-end (or part thereof), real-time view of VoD traffic flows. Because the video streaming server is the last point of contact for an STB before the video stream is sent, it makes the most sense to have this device interface with the CAC engine.

This is a general overview of CAC. For more in-depth information on VoD and multicast IPTV CAC, see Chapters 8 and 11.

MEDIA ENCODING, SECURITY, AND ENCRYPTION

A mandatory feature of all video over IP networks is content security. Digital Rights Management (DRM) is a hot topic for anyone going into the media distribution business. Music and videos purchased from sites such as iTunes Music Store and Amazon.com have licenses restricting how the file can be used. The license is enforced through the player, which is also needed to decrypt the file. The element of trust ends at the player, so one principle is that as long as the player's integrity is intact, the content can be sent safely to the client. Of course, crackers always keep up with the efforts of the content distributors and encryption engines in trying to break encryption schemes, so some systems that stream content to the desktop incorporate some extra host checking software to detect devices or software that is trying to circumvent DRM.

Using a dedicated STB instead of a software player makes it harder for crackers to bypass DRM mechanisms, because the host environment is now unfamiliar to the cracker. There are other benefits of streaming video to a dedicated STB, which are not directly related to DRM and security, such as a consistent operating environment controlled by the service provider. This makes it easier to troubleshoot and maintain compared to a user's PC.

Before we get into too many specifics, an explanation of a broader security perspective is needed. There are many types of encryption systems on the market that use Certificate Authentication (CA), which authenticates the identity of the client. DRM with content protection encrypts the content and controls when the media file can be played. Figure 2.7 shows one example of a provider architecture with a centralized video distribution system, certificate authentication, and content encryption.

After encoding, the middleware system analyzes the media files, or assets, to get their correct bit rate, title, runtime, and any other file details. The asset is then encrypted using the provider's certificate. The servers used to encrypt the asset can be the same as those used for IPTV encryption. After the asset is added to the content store and entered into the middleware system, it is available for delivery by the video streaming servers.

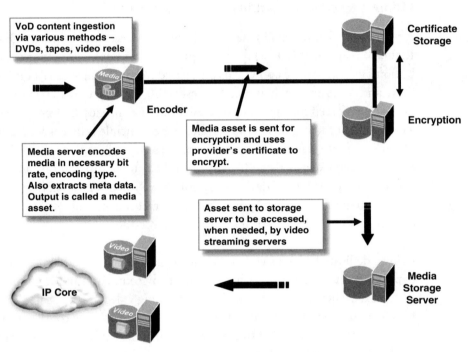

Figure 2.7 VoD asset encryption and delivery process.

Expanding on the example from earlier in this chapter that incorporates the Bit-Band video streaming servers, when an STB requests an asset, it contacts the middleware platform. The STB's identity is checked. It could be an IP address, an internal STB identifier, or a physical location gleaned earlier in the initialization process using DHCP option 82 or a PPPoE IA identifier. The identity is then used to check if the client has the right authorization for the VoD session. The authorization could be that the client's billing profile allows VoD streams, or that the requested movie fulfils a viewer age restriction, for example. One way of implementing parental control is for each person in the house to have his or her own PIN, which is entered when requesting a movie. Each PIN can be set up so that it can access all or only a subset of the content. TV shows and movies need to be rated as suitable for under-18s, for example. If the STB is allowed to receive the asset, it is sent a call entitlement, which includes information on how to decrypt the media file when it is streamed, how long the asset is valid (similar to a rental period), and other control information. In most cases, the media file is streamed over UDP—ideally, with RTSP sequencing information.

MIDDLEWARE

The middleware platform can be considered the heart of the IPTV and VoD system. It controls the SUI, which is the interface that the customers use to navigate through the menus on their STB. The SUI can be customized by the service provider and normally is delivered using standard protocols, such as HTTP and SSL. Many unencrypted elements in user interface pages can be cached in an HTTP proxy to allow the SUI subsystem to scale well. The Electronic Programming Guide (EPG) is a list of current and future shows on an IPTV system. This data can be sent either as a multicast stream that all STBs can join or as a file that is periodically retrieved from an HTTP proxy via unicast.

The middleware also interfaces with the DRM platform, which stores the site certificates and encrypts content for distribution either via an on-demand system or through multicast IPTV. The actual encrypted unicast video content is stored for distribution by the video streaming servers. The middleware typically stores only metadata related to the media assets.

When a user purchases a media asset, the middleware also issues billing records to the service provider billing engine. One name for these records is Entitlement Data Records (EDRs). An EDR can be generated once after the asset has been authorized for delivery, regardless of how many times the user watches the asset within his or her rental period.

VIDEO SERVICES

Technically speaking, a full video solution is quite complex. All this complexity can be in vain unless a clear service framework drives the network functionality. Many technically superior products unfortunately have been relegated to footnotes in the history books because of poor marketing and vision. Although there is no substitute for a well-thought-out marketing plan, this section lists some of the services possible with a video over IP network.

Network Private Video Recorder

A Network Private Video Recorder (NPVR) lets the user select a show, which is normally streamed as part of an IPTV service, to be recorded by the network. Then it is sent at a time of the user's choosing. This works in much the same way that people have been recording television stations on their TiVo or VCR for years. An NPVR service offers additional functionality not possible with a device in the home that does all the storing and recording. A recorder in the home can record only one or two channels at once, but if the service is more network-centric, there is no limit to the number of channels a user can record at the same time.

The technical implementation of the service need not be reflected in the service to the customer. For example, a provider can record just a single copy of each of the most popular channels, which can be enumerated to users as required. This saves storage space and lets someone later request a TV show or movie that she may have forgotten to record. Any shows that are not caught under this policy—a viewer wants to record a foreign movie, for instance—can be specially recorded as long as the request comes in ahead of the program.

Targeted Advertising

Being able to tailor advertising to the home is a huge potential for marketers. And they are bound to pay extra for this privilege. In much the same way that Internet search engines return advertising related to what the user typed in his search query, targeted advertising can deliver commercials based on a profile of the channels and what time they are viewed. To work alongside multicast IPTV services, additional groups could be dedicated to semi-targeted advertising. One multicast group could be for a demographic of 18-to-24-year-olds. When the commercial break starts, the STB could switch from the general channel group to a group used for that particular demographic.

Extensive Media Catalog

One of the competitive advantages that online stores have over bricks-and-mortar stores is that they do not need large shops to display their wares. Amazon.com, for example, can keep less-popular titles in distribution warehouses, and only when the media are ordered are they sent from the inventory. This is called long-tail marketing. Amazon.com's *Booksurge* concept takes this model one step further. If a book is out of print, no problem. An electronic copy of the book can be dispatched to a printing center, printed, bound, and sent to the customer as if it had been printed and sent directly from the publisher.

This is similar to the advantage that a service provider has with VoD over traditional bricks-and-mortar rental stores. Adding a few hundred movies to a program lineup involves adding an extra media storage array and is independent of how many users have *checked out* the movie. Physical space is not much of a concern.

An interesting value-add that IPTV services have over satellite TV providers is that the number of different channels that are offered does not increase network traffic load in a linear fashion—the usage is much better. The benefit comes from being able to have many niche channels added to the multicast group list. This increases the appeal of the television packages to a wider audience. And only when a customer wants to watch that channel is it added to the multicast tree. By contrast, a satellite provider consumes valuable bandwidth on its transponder for each channel it adds. The efficiency gains for a satellite provider occur when many households are connected to its service and only a few of the most popular channels are needed to fill its transponder capacity. For IPTV to have such a positive impact, the market dynamics need to be right. An ethnically diverse viewer base helps fuel the need for equally diverse content.

DATA SERVICES

Data services encompass anything that is neither video over IP nor VoIP—which is, in fact, a large basket of services. Where the triple-play concept has been expanded to cover multi-play is in data services. The data service began with Internet access and is the simplest and most understood service by service providers and customers alike. It is still the most common reason people get a broadband connection. However, Internet access is becoming commoditized through price; it is a war of attrition. Faster access through new technologies helps slow the commoditization process, but it is services and packages that differentiate one provider from the next. This section describes services that a provider can offer in addition to basic Internet access.

PREMIUM GAMING

Figure 2.8 shows a simple example of a multiplay environment. Individually, these services are not big technological advances but are branded as part of a service package. Using an end-to-end QoS and policy framework, a provider can differentiate itself from the competition. One of these services is premium gaming.

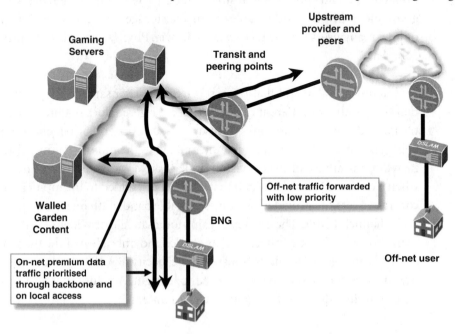

Figure 2.8 Prioritized gaming service.

To entice subscribers to a provider's network, locally hosted gaming servers are a popular draw card because of the enticement of lower ping times to the servers. Whether this is enough of an enticement for many subscribers depends on a variety of factors, not just the latency through the network to the servers. The branding image among the gaming community of a provider running hosted servers is a strong one. And so is network latency. If a gamer can shave a few tens of milliseconds off his ping by being with a provider, many enthusiasts make the move just for this reason. An even more attractive proposition for service providers and customers is to ensure that gaming traffic is treated with high priority when there is a real chance of network traffic congestion. Traffic congestion causes latency increases and, worse, jitter. The latency is surely a negative factor, but jitter has a worse impact on online games, which need fast, consistent feedback of players' movements to the servers. A well-engineered core should not be congested. The aggregation network and customer local loop are most susceptible to congestion. A customer doing heavy downloads at the time of online game-playing can disrupt her gaming session.

A solution is to mark all IP traffic going from gaming servers to on-net subscribers with a DiffServ marking that gives this traffic higher priority over less important best-effort traffic. Internet traffic can be marked with a DiffServ value of 0 and on-net gaming traffic as slightly higher than this—DiffServ AF11, for example.

Such a scheme could be applied to the network in a variety of ways. First, all packets coming from gaming servers and going to on-net subscribers can be marked with a nonzero DiffServ value. On the BNG, dynamic policies can be applied to subscribers who have purchased the gaming service, to modify their QoS policies, which would match the previously marked packets and transmit them ahead of Internet packets. Of course, this means that such data would be prioritized before reaching the BNG too, regardless of whether the destination is a paying premium customer. If this is viewed as a significant problem, a network-wide, BGP-based QoS signaling mechanism could be used. When a subscriber connects to the network, his /32 host route can be announced to the network with a special BGP community ID. When all BGP-speaking routers receive prefixes matching the special community, they can update policies in their forwarding tables, which gives traffic going to these destinations a slightly higher priority than best-effort. The scaling properties of this approach are poor. For all customers who subscribe to this service, there is a /32 route in the network, which consumes extra router control- and forwarding-plane memory. Despite there being services where subscribers can have a static address, which can trigger a /32 route in the provider network, these do not affect any QoS or filtering policy in router's forwarding databases.

A more scalable solution is to have dedicated address pools for subscribers who have a premium gaming service. These pools can be announced as aggregated networks from BNGs with BGP communities in a similar, but more scalable way than the per-subscriber /32 method previously mentioned.

WALLED-GARDEN SERVICES

Walled-garden services have been on the market for many years. CompuServ and AOL are two shining examples of walled-garden environments. Throughout the mid-1980s and early 1990s, CompuServ "was one of the largest information and networking services companies in existence."[1] Its model provided content that was available only if you connected via the CompuServ network. At the time, the World Wide Web (WWW) was not yet conceived, so this was an ideal way to access graphical content over the CompuServe network using CompuServ's Win-CIM client. But as the WWW gained popularity, providers who were hosting sites on CompuServ's network shifted their sites to the Internet to have access to a wider audience. Therefore, the network's popularity dropped sharply. AOL's walled-garden content was its primary focus until the popularity of the Internet started pushing AOL to another model.

Other examples of popular walled gardens still exist. Cellular handsets accessing the Internet often start inside a walled garden. Here, the service provider sends a portal to the customer. News aggregation, content subscription control pages, and e-mail portals are a few examples. If users want to access the Internet, the data volume tariff might be higher (or not free) to access off-net or non-walled-garden content, but the Internet is still possible. Sirius and XM satellite radio are walled gardens, because users need a special handset to receive the broadcasts, and some of the content is exclusive to these providers.

Some lessons can be learned from walled-garden content. Even if the access method is unique—that is, if users need a special device to access the content—a walled garden can still be popular. To access satellite radio, users need a special receiver. Nonetheless, users are prepared to buy hardware for the additional benefits of satellite radio—a large coverage area, a digital signal, no retuning to a different frequency when moving between areas, and content. For Internet access on cellular handsets, walled gardens serve a useful purpose to reduce the number of pages that are needed to navigate to commonly accessed pages.

It could be tempting to have a special area with premium content on a service provider's network for more traditional devices—PCs, Macs, gaming consoles. This has to be carefully thought through, because the danger is to restrict a user's

1 Wikipedia page on CompuServ: http://en.wikipedia.org/wiki/Compuserve

access to the wider Internet, as happened with CompuServ during the late '90s. Because the Internet is currently the network with the most people online, users want Internet access to chat with their friends and visit their home pages, blogs, and discussion forums. A simple model is to have a section of on-net content that is accessible with a special tariff and to have the Internet accessible by a more expensive tariff. If the provider offers flat rate (it does not bill according to volume), on-net content could be accessible with a faster speed than Internet content. One good example of having content available to off-net customers is gaming servers. If gaming servers are not available to off-net players, there might not be enough people continually active on the servers to make the service popular enough—a critical-mass problem.

One alternative is if a service provider is willing to pay the necessary license fees to a content provider so that it can rehost or rebrand the media and sell it as part of a package. One example of such a service discussed throughout this book is IPTV. But there needs to be a good reason that a user can't go to the site with his or her web browser and access the same content.

BUSINESS CONNECTIVITY

DSL lines are no longer just for residential access. Business customers are connecting to the Internet and their other offices using DSL access. Frame-Relay, ATM, and ISDN circuits cost a lot more to run than DSL-based ones, and DSL is proving to be a suitable alternative to these older modulations and encapsulations. Broadly speaking, three types of business services in the marketplace use DSL access: Layer 3 VPNs, Layer 2 VPNs, and enhanced Internet access.

Business Layer 3 VPNs

This business service is a provider-hosted Layer 3 VPN service and uses a DSL line as the access technology. The PVC or VLAN from the DSLAM is terminated on an edge router, providing connectivity to the business VPN cloud. Various encapsulations could be used on the local access. Also, the edge router could be different from that used for the residential BNG. The simplest approach is to reuse the residential broadband infrastructure and use the same PPPoE or DHCP-based IP over Ethernet (IPoE) addressing and encapsulation between the CPE and BNG. The BNG has Virtual Routing and Forwarding (VRF) configured for each Layer 3 VPN. Reusing PPPoE encapsulation makes it easier to dynamically provision a customer session to the correct VRF by using RADIUS to map a PPP username (such as username@realm) to a VRF. If the local loop addressing and encapsulation are DHCP and Ethernet, respectively, a more static approach is needed to map a customer VLAN (Ethernet backhaul) or PVC (ATM backhaul) to a VRF. For more information on various backhaul architectures, see Chapter 4, "Designing a Triple-Play Access Network." Figure 2.9 shows how the same access and aggregation network that is used for residential session transport can also be used for business VPN access. The remote user on the bottom logs in using PPPoE and the username sam@acewidgets.com and is placed in the business Layer 3 VPN. The Internet user, bob@isp.com, is placed in the global routing table.

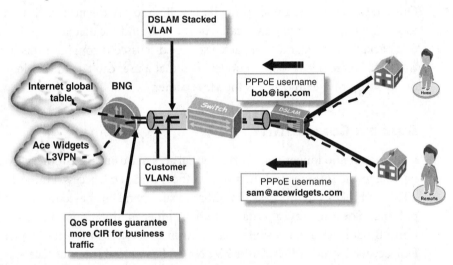

Figure 2.9 Business Layer 3 VPN access using residential broadband infrastructure.

Despite being a residential broadband infrastructure, many of the same QoS and SLA guarantees needed for business can still be achieved in the model shown in the figure. For instance, one of the most common requirements in a business Layer 3 VPN connection is to ensure a minimum bit rate from the IP edge to the CPE. This is known by various terms, such as Committed Information Rate (CIR), assured rate (Juniper JUNOSe terminology), bandwidth (Cisco IOS terminology), and transmit rate (Juniper JUNOS terminology). The circuit's peak rate may be much higher, but this is not guaranteed throughput if the same links that the circuit traverses are being heavily utilized by other customers. If the aggregation network between the DSLAM and BNG is oversubscribed, CIR rates can be managed on the BNG using QoS mechanisms. This makes the BNG *the* point of control to ensure that business connections receive their committed rates in the event of circuit or interface congestion. A cruder alternative to managing oversubscription in the aggregation network is to set the Ethernet priority in the Ethernet header and let switches and DSLAMs handle any congestion with simple scheduling. The disadvantage is that without some very complex traffic modeling, it is hard to ensure that an accurate assured rate is delivered to the end subscriber.

However, it is common for providers to opt for dedicated edge routers for business connections. One of the reasons is that bigger providers often have one group manage VPN services and another manage residential broadband. Using separate hardware helps streamline operations, design, and testing. Even when one group manages everything, there might be a purely architectural reason to have different routers. It might be for stability reasons, to reflect the importance of business connections by using dedicated hardware, or additional routing policy features available on a different platform. Because usually there are less business connections than residential, there are less changes occurring on a dedicated business router. These changes and *fingers in the network* are things that can also cause service outages. Figure 2.10 shows how a customer VLAN can be dedicated to a DSL port and is switched through a metro Ethernet network.

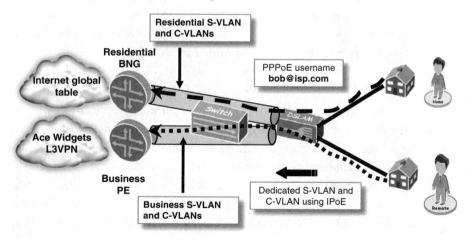

Figure 2.10 Business Layer 3 VPN access using dedicated circuits.

In the figure, a stacked VLAN (S-VLAN) tag identifies the DSLAM and a customer VLAN tag (C-VLAN) for the DSL port. There are several ways of switching the customer through the metro Ethernet network. The architecture shown in Figure 2.10 is the most recommended for several reasons. An outer S-VLAN tag for the DSLAM lets the architecture scale well in a large metro Ethernet network with many DSLAMs. A dedicated C-VLAN tag for the DSL port as opposed to a service-based VLAN for all business connections attached to a DSLAM ensures Layer 2 separation between customers. This provides a good level of security between DSL ports. It also suits more traditional routers that enforce QoS on a per-VLAN basis rather than per-subscriber. In the latter scenario, this would be the case with a service VLAN environment. More details about service VLANs, C-VLANs, and S-VLANs are covered in Chapter 4.

Business Layer 2 VPNs

In the access and aggregation networks, the architecture is much the same, except with Layer 2 VPNs, it is almost mandatory to have a dedicated C-VLAN. Ideally an S-VLAN between the DSLAM and the IP edge is used for scaling reasons. A Layer 2 VPN is a customer-managed VPN service. The service provider (SP) delivers a Layer 2 connection between two of the customers' CPE. A simple approach is for a CPE to have a DSL connection over which is a bridged Ethernet connection to the provider's PE. The SP runs an MPLS network and uses Layer 2 VPN circuits between two PE routers. At the other PE, a similar architecture is employed, with a VLAN to the other CPE. Bridged Ethernet (or pure Ethernet if using VDSL) is also used on the access link. All devices on the two LANs are on the same broadcast domain. This contrasts with the Layer 3 case, in which the two CPEs need to be running in routed mode.

Enhanced Internet Access

Internet access is a very important service for business customers, especially if their income is derived solely from an Internet presence. An Internet service can be delivered either using a stand-alone router at the provider, as described in the two preceding sections, or on the same BNG as residential broadband services. If a provider uses separate hardware to deliver services to business clients, business-grade Internet services are usually delivered on the same routers as those for Layer 3 and Layer 3 VPNs. What is business-grade Internet access? On a technical level, it can be supposed benefits from the hardware separation from residential access. Even if there is no physical service separation, a business connection usually has a higher CIR than a residential customer.

It is common for business customers to have provider-hosted Layer 3 VPNs and Internet access from a single provider. There are several ways of delivering these services to customers from a perspective of PE, VLAN, and CPE configuration. For instance, a single VLAN between the CPE and PE could be used to deliver all services, and the PE does the routing between the Layer 3 VPN and the Internet. Alternatively, one VLAN can be assigned per service, and the CPE handles the routing between the Layer 3 VPN and the Internet, and, if applicable, NAT between any private address and public Internet addresses. More details on these connectivity solutions are covered in Chapter 3, "Designing a Triple-Play Backbone."

VOICE SERVICES

Voice over IP (VoIP) is a hugely popular service and is being deployed by traditional wire line telcos, competing ISPs, and Internet-based VoIP providers such as Vonage and Skype. The competitive landscape is pushing traditional carriers toward migrating their traditional TDM-based switches to more cost-effective packet-based ones. Additional services can be delivered using online self-provisioning tools. A customer can log on to his or her portal, enable the second VoIP line into his or her home, and select a range of voice mail and unified messaging options. Many of the more powerful features of use to businesses can be ordered online, too. An extra ten outgoing lines from a business PBX can be enabled at the press of a button, for example.

This section explains some of the VoIP services that providers can offer to customers. Even though VoIP services can be offered over any IP connection, the target audience for this section is wire line providers delivering voice services. Purely Internet-based providers such as Vonage and Skype share some similar attributes, but their services are more Internet-based and are not covered here.

POTS ACCESS TO DSLAM

One of the simpler approaches to delivering a VoIP service is to deploy it in stages. Voice services that coexist with DSL connections have used a frequency splitter at the customer premises to separate the lower-frequency voice band from the DSL signals. A VoIP architecture does not need to be IP end-to-end. Instead, a voice switch at the central office (CO) or exchange can provide the interworking between the POTS and IP voice signaling. This avoids the extra complexity of having to deploy SIP-capable CPE. Many DSLAM vendors are integrating voice switch capability into their products, which enables the local loop at the CO to be terminated on the DSLAM for both voice and data services. This eliminates the need for external splitters and voice switch hardware if a single provider has exclusive use of the copper to the customer.

In terms of the service to the customer, the features are almost the same as POTS or ISDN, which have been used for many years. On the provider side, the voice switch in the CO takes any analog calls from the customer and sends them down a VoIP trunk to one of the soft switches. These soft switches perform call routing and billing. A sample end-to-end architecture is described in the next section. This is a good stepping-stone before a full-blown end-to-end VoIP architecture. Such an architecture might also be used in environments where a competitor wants to supply both a voice and DSL service to the customer, rather than allow the incumbent to have the voice-band service.

END-TO-END VoIP

This section explains the components involved in a simple VoIP architecture. Designing and implementing a VoIP network is complex business, so the intent of this section is to provide a casual introduction to how the signaling and media flow both within and beyond the network. Figure 2.11 shows a VoIP server network located on the left at one of the provider's PoPs. The server network consists of an SDH interconnect with a local voice provider. A VoIP VPN also is used as a private interconnect with another VoIP provider, either domestic or international.

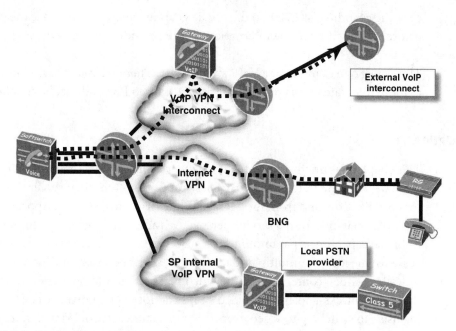

Figure 2.11 An end-to-end simple VoIP network architecture.

In Figure 2.11, a SIP CPE has a POTS phone connected. The SIP CPE presents a POTS interface to the phone and, at the same time, registers with the soft switch. After the CPE has registered itself with the soft switch, usually using a special username and password as an identifier, the soft switch then knows at which IP address a number can be reached.

As soon as the SIP user agent (UA)—the SIP CPE in this case—has registered with the voice switch, it can place calls with and receive calls from the network. In Figure 2.11, the CPE makes an international call via the external VoIP inter-connect. The UA signals its call intentions to the soft switch, which establishes a signaling session with the international provider's voice switch. If the call can proceed, the UA is directed to send its media session (the voice part of the call) to the soft switch or Session Border Controller (SBC) (described in more detail in Chapter 12, "Security in Broadband Networks"). This media session is repre-sented by the dashed line, which flows to the switch/SBC, and then via the VoIP gateway, shown at the top of the diagram. To add some complexity, for the pur-poses of illustration, the international provider requires that calls be received in a lower bit rate than the G.711 encoding that the provider uses internally. In this case, the encoding is G.729, so the media gateway needs to *trans-code* the call before sending it on to the international VoIP provider's voice switch.

This is just one example of a VoIP architecture. There are many variations, such as more integrated units performing media transcoding and media signaling.

SUMMARY

This chapter has briefly illustrated the network components that are described in more detail in the rest of the book. These range from the video server head-end to the MPLS core and from the aggregation network to the BNG. Approaching a multiplay network from a service perspective rather than being driven purely by technical capability is paramount for a successful deployment. This chapter discussed some ideas for multiplay data services, such as a premium gaming service or walled-garden content. From the video perspective, adding extra value that traditional bricks-and-mortar video shops cannot easily provide is key to enticing users to switching to video over IP. Some features are solved in a more routine manner, such as having a large range of content. Other services are more complex to implement, such as an NPVR service.

Finally, a VoIP service is almost as important as, if not more important than, an Internet service to deliver to customers. Some customers will want just a telephone connection without any data or video services, so, at a minimum, a stand-alone VoIP service needs to be available. This could be delivered using a method with only incremental complexity by using DSLAM-based VoIP trunks (implemented using H.248 trunking, for example) and using a low-pass frequency splitter at the customer premises. Or you might not bother with a splitter if only a PSTN service is provided. On a more complex level, providers can deliver VoIP services directly to the customer. For the more residential customers, the ideal option is to have one or more analog POTS ports on the CPE, to which they connect analog phones. The CPE then acts as a SIP UA on the phone's behalf. This is a VoIP service directly to the home. For more-complex business requirements, the SIP UAs are devices on the LAN and generate the necessary SIP or H.242 signaling and RTP data streams themselves.

QoS needs to be carefully managed for all these services. Chapter 8, "Deploying Quality of Service," covers quality-of-service implementations for effective triple-play networks.

Designing a Triple-Play Backbone

A triple-play network provides voice, video, and data services to customers. From the humble beginnings of simple Internet access, the next generation of broadband networks is delivering voice, rich video content, and speedier Internet services to households over IP networks. Having a reliable, high-capacity core with all the right protocols is an important prerequisite for delivering these services to customers. Most provider backbones have, in the past, been built with unicast services in mind—Internet and VoIP services being the most common ones. When a provider wants to offer IPTV services, this means an enhancement of the backbone is needed to support multicast data and protocols.

This chapter has four major sections. The first, "MPLS Backbone Networks," introduces Multiprotocol Label Switching (MPLS) backbone networks. MPLS is a technology used in provider backbone networks to allow multiple protocols to be carried over a converged routing infrastructure. This book's intention is to provide practical applications of the supporting architectures, protocols, and routing techniques. Therefore, MPLS-based backbones are introduced from the perspective of providing services to customers based on these technologies. This section gives answers to questions that providers face when delivering multiple services to customers over an MPLS network, such as whether to use policy forwarding, VRF route-target leaking for route distribution, multiple VLANs to separate services, or a mixture of these. This chapter also discusses Layer 2 and Layer 3 VPN services for providers that use VPNs to deliver services to customers.

For most providers, these services are targeted at business customers, but in some cases these architectures apply to residential services too. You need intermediate to advanced knowledge of routing and MPLS to understand the concepts and designs in this chapter.

The second major section, "Multicast Protocols in the Backbone," covers adding multicast protocols to the backbone, which enable IPTV distribution. You must consider several things when adding this capability to the backbone—whether MPLS will transport multicast and, if so, how. From a signaling perspective, it tells you which Protocol-Independent Multicast (PIM) mode to use. Finally, this section looks to the future of IPTV transport using Virtual Private LAN Service (VPLS). An excellent book on the subject is *Interdomain Multicast Routing* (Addison-Wesley Professional, 2002).

The third major section is "Running MPLS on the BNG." Because Broadband Network Gateways (BNGs, historically known as BRASs) are now highly capable multipurpose routers, they can participate in the MPLS backbone and become provider edge (PE) routers. Even in provider networks running MPLS, BNGs often are located outside the MPLS domain, creating a two-tiered routing and signaling structure. Integrating an MPLS-capable BNG to the rest of the backbone has benefits in terms of a more unified end-to-end network.

Finally, the section "Designing a Highly Available Core Network" has strategies for implementing protocols in the core to minimize the effect of router hardware or software failure. These strategies include features such as RSVP, make-before-break Label Switched Paths (LSPs), and Bidirectional Forwarding Detection (BFD) for rapid path failure detection.

MPLS Backbone Networks

The core network, commonly called the backbone, is the packet-forwarding workhorse of the service provider. It is a highly available platform with fast-forwarding rates between the routers. A backbone should be as simple an architecture as possible, because its primary task is reliable packet forwarding. The complexity lies in the network edge, because this is where the user services are created: policies, rate limiters, logical circuits, and address assignment all happen at the network edge. Keeping a clean separation between a complex edge and simple core is key for a reliable and scalable network.

Figure 3.1 shows an MPLS network of PEs providing Layer 2 and Layer 3 services to two customers across four separate sites. All these services share a common converged core. The services are created on the PE routers, and the routers in the middle (P routers) mainly do basic packet forwarding: they switch MPLS packets from one interface to the other. These P routers are not concerned with what data are carried within the packet payload.

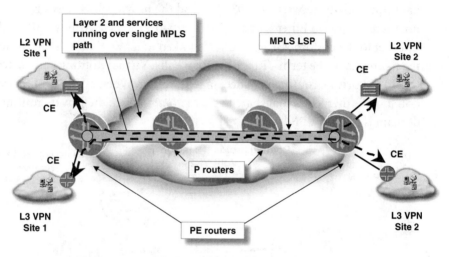

Figure 3.1 Topology of a sample Layer 3 VPN service deployed over MPLS.

One way of delivering an Internet service on a service provider network is to use a Layer 3 MPLS VPN (L3VPN). L3VPNs connect several IP networks within a private routing domain. The most common use of an L3VPN is to enable businesses to connect their sites. L3VPNs can also provide Internet access to Broadband Network Gateways (BNGs) located on the service provider network. Another use is to support internal services infrastructure within a provider's network. For example, a VoIP service can be delivered within a Layer 3 VPN to isolate the routing domain from other services. The downside is that any devices connected to the Internet VPN have no routing capability to get to the VoIP network, and vice versa. This section shows different ways these two services can be delivered to a business subscriber. The principles of using VPNs for service separation can then be applied to the architecture of a residential broadband ser-vice using BNGs. The first way to deliver these two services concurrently is to run two VLANs to the BNG—one for VoIP and the other for Internet access. In Fig-ure 3.2 a PE on the left is attached to a Customer Edge (CE) router on the right. CE is a term first defined in RFC 2547 and is a device that connects to a Provider Edge (PE) router. A CE usually exchanges routing information about the VPN with a PE. In cases where the CE does not exchange routing information using a dynamic routing protocol, such as RIP or BGP, static routes are used. There is a metro-Ethernet network between the two devices that provides Ethernet back-haul connectivity between the DSLAM and the provider's IP network. In the fig-ure there is a metro Ethernet network uses two VLANs to deliver VoIP and Internet to the customer. Each VLAN is linked to its VPN on the PE. Notice that the figure shows the term VRF rather than VPN. Virtual Routing and Forwarding (VRF) is a private routing instance on a PE router. When a VRF is in the routing domain of other VRFs that share the same *route-target*, the private routing domain is called a VPN.

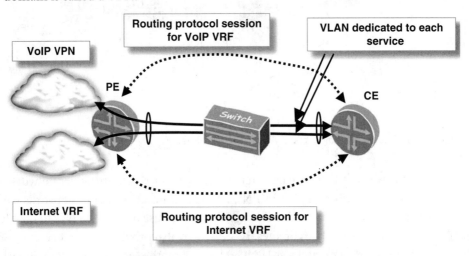

Figure 3.2 Linking a VoIP and the Internet to a BNG using multiple VLANs.

In summary, the scenario presented in the figure shows how a CE can forward traffic between two VPNs, given enough routing information. The mechanics of this approach also apply if the CE is substituted for a BNG that is not MPLS-aware.

POLICY FORWARDING

Instead of using a VLAN per service, a single VLAN between the PE and CE can transport the two services. A technique called policy forwarding is done on the PE to forward traffic to and from the customer into the correct VRF.

Technology Note: Policy Forwarding

IP packets typically are routed to a destination based on the header's destination address (DA). Even in an MPLS network, the destination address (or label) is still used to locate a packet's destination.

Policy forwarding changes this paradigm by enabling a router to use other information in the packet to make a forwarding decision. For example, a source address or a port number could indicate that a packet is part of a VoIP call and should be forwarded over a different path in the network.

Cisco IOS and Juniper JUNOSe software uses the term Policy-based Routing (PBR). Juniper JUNOS software uses the term Filter-based Forwarding (FBF). In general, depending on the router and corresponding software version, policy forwarding can have an adverse impact on the router's forwarding performance. Ideally policy forwarding is done in hardware to reduce the impact of enabling the feature.

The key to policy-based forwarding is to decide what should be matched in the packet and thus tie it to a service. With a VoIP, if a packet is addressed to a known media server IP address, this destination address can be used to tell the router where a packet should be sent. Figure 3.3 shows a packet leaving the CE with the destination address of a VoIP server. The PE uses a policy-forwarding configuration that is attached to the VLAN subinterface to match any packets with a destination address of 192.168.1.0/24 and shunts them to the VoIP VRF. This is needed because the Internet VRF, to which the circuit is attached, does not have a route for the VoIP network. The default route in the Internet VRF cannot be used because the servers are not located on the upstream provider's network (to which the default route points). In Figure 3.3, SA is Source Address and DA is Destination Address.

Listings 3.1 and 3.2 show Cisco IOS and Juniper JUNOS configuration based on Figure 3.3. The purpose is to show (in configuration terms) how to forward any incoming traffic with a destination address of 192.168.1.0/24 to the VoIP VRF.

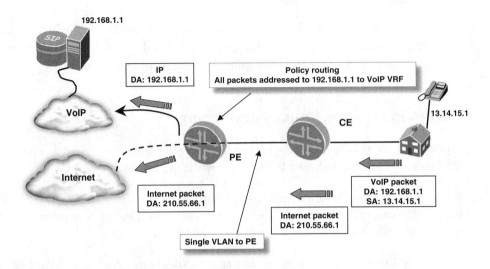

Figure 3.3 Sending VoIP traffic to a different VRF using policy forwarding.

Listing 3.1 Cisco IOS Policy Forwarding Configuration

```
ip vrf internet
 rd 65300:100
 route-target import 65300:100
 route-target export 65300:100

ip vrf voice
 rd 65300:101
 route-target import 65300:101
 route-target export 65300:101


interface gigabitethernet 1/0/0.100
 encapsulation dot1q 100
 ip vrf forwarding internet
 ip address 192.168.6.1 255.255.255.252
 ip policy-map to-voice-vrf input

ip policy-map to-voice-vrf permit 10
 match ip address voice-net
 set ip vrf voice

ip access-list extended voice-net ip any 192.168.1.0 0.0.0.255
```

Listing 3.2 Juniper JUNOS Policy Forwarding

```
interfaces {
  ge-1/0/0 {
    encapsulation vlan;
    unit 100 {
    vlan-id 100;
    family inet {
      address 192.168.6.1/30;
      filter {
       input to-voice-vrf;
      }
    }
   }
  }
}

firewall {
  family inet {
    filter to-voice-vrf  {
      term voip-nets {
        from {
          destination-address 192.168.1.0/24;
        }
        then {
          routing-instance voice;
        }
        }
        term default {
        then {
          accept;
        }
      }
    }
   }
}

policy-options {
  community com-internet target:65300:100;
  community com-voice target:65300:101;
}

routing-instances {
  internet {
   interface ge-1/0/0.100;
   instance-type vrf;
   route-distinguisher 65300:100;
   vrf-target {
     export com-internet;
     import com-internet;
   }
  }
  voice {
   instance-type vrf;
   route-distinguisher 65300:101;
   vrf-target {
     export com-voice;
```

Listing 3.2 continued

```
import com-voice;
   }
  }
}
```

Using the preceding configuration, VoIP data are forwarded to the correct VPN. Return traffic from the VoIP servers needs to be correctly routed back to the CE. Configuring PEs so that traffic is policy forwarded *to* the servers is easier than configuring return traffic back to the CE. The reason is because the servers reside in only a handful of IP networks. A lot more configuration is required on the PEs for return traffic because there are many different destination routes for subscribers. Policy routing is useful for some niche applications, but the configuration complexity and possible forwarding performance degradation on some routers mean that this is not a widely deployed type of configuration for large-scale applications.

A better alternative is for the PE to merge some of the Internet routes and some of the VoIP routes into a single VRF and then deliver both services down a single VLAN. Distributing routes between two or more VRFs is called route leaking. It involves configuring routing policy on the PE that selects which routes from the VPNs to import to the main VRF instance.

VRF ROUTE-TARGET LEAKING

The preceding section described policy forwarding, which uses relatively static configuration to determine packet-forwarding paths. Routing data from dynamic protocols such as BGP usually cannot be incorporated into the router's policy-based forwarding decision because the policy forwarding configuration often has to match fields in the packet other than the usual destination address. Route target leaking is a more flexible and dynamic way to allow traffic to flow between VPNs. In an MPLS Layer 3 VPN, routes that belong to the Internet VRF are tagged with a particular community and VoIP routes with another. To allow traffic to flow between the two VPNs, routing policy can be used to match dynamic routing information received from other PEs. If a BGP route passes the policy, it can be imported in to the master VRF. As soon as the routes are in the master VRF, they can be announced over a single routing protocol session to the CE. This also means only a single VLAN is needed to establish multiservice delivery over a single VLAN between the CE and PE. A similar process is done for traffic returning from the servers to the CEs. On the PE that connects to the VoIP servers, customer prefixes that use VoIP services are imported to the VoIP VPN.

The preceding paragraph has shown an example application of route-target leaking. However, a VoIP service that is provided to VPN customers usually uses a Session Border Control to interconnect between customer VPNs and a voice VPN. However there are still many applications where route leaking is useful in business VPN or multiservice residential broadband environment.

Figure 3.4 shows a business customer that is connected to the network with two services—Internet and VoIP. As described in the preceding section, a customer is attached to a VRF. This could be the customer's own VRF, an Internet VRF, or a VoIP VRF. In the diagram, the customer is connected to the Internet VRF because it is the routing instance with the most number of routes. The routing policy on London imports VoIP routes, so there is a suitable forwarding path to get to the servers on the 13.14.15.0/24 VoIP server network.

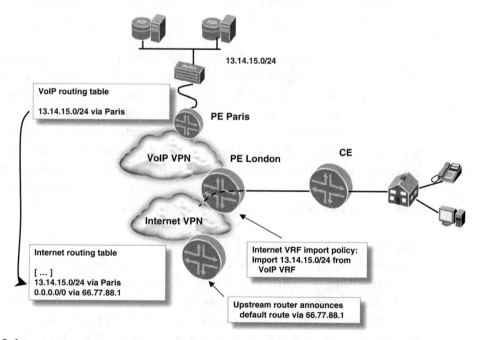

Figure 3.4 Leaking routes from the VoIP VPN to the Internet VPN.

This approach of using route target leaking is widely deployed in provider networks that use VPNs for service separation. It relies on BGP route target communities, which are a convenient way of attaching an identifier to a route, which can then be used in conjunction with routing policy throughout a network. Multiple route target communities can also be attached to a route for more fine-grained routing policy control.

Nevertheless, for providers that are new entrants to the market or that have little use for VPN technology except for business connections, the ideal approach is to put all public-facing devices in a common, global routing instance.

Hybrid VPN and Non-VPN Routing Models

The previous sections have focused on backbone networks that use VPNs for multiservice transport. This is common with incumbent telcos that are migrating customers off legacy ATM and Frame Relay VPNs to Layer 3 VPNs. Because these providers are comfortable with the concept of customer separation using VPNs, it is a common step to have service separation using VPNs.

However, such a pervasive use of VPNs is not required. In fact, in a residential broadband environment, it is actually more preferable to have a single routing domain for all common public services. This simplifies routing policy and packet forwarding because there does not need to be any complex route leaking or policy forwarding on PEs. In this model, the security implications in the network are effectively the same compared to the split-VPN approach, because the server and service layers enforce security rather than the PE network edges. VPN service separation does add some security advantage by being separated from other routing domains as long as VPNs are strictly isolated from each other by a firewall layer

A single multiservice global routing table is still compatible with an MPLS environment. An MPLS network can provide traffic engineering, fast reroute, and QoS capabilities using the signaling protocol—Resource Reservation Protocol with Traffic Engineering (RSVP-TE) extensions. Alternatively, the Label Distribution Protocol (LDP) signaling protocol can set up basic MPLS traffic routing paths. If a single multiservice, global routing table is used, Label Switched Paths (LSPs) are still signaled between PE routers. But instead of routes being advertised through-out the domain as labeled VPN routes, they are basic IPv4 or IPv6 routes. This means that they are all present in the main routing table instead of being inside individual VRF tables. However, the next-hop of the routes is resolved across the MPLS LSPs instead of the typical hop-by-hop IPv4/IPv6 routing.

NON-MPLS NETWORKS

Non-MPLS networks are a rarer occurrence. Service providers that do run a pure IPv4 core run a global routing table for all services, including the Internet. The properties of this network are similar to the scenario described previously of using MPLS for forwarding but not using a VPN. The difference is that it is not possible to have any MPLS-based QoS, end-to-end traffic engineering, band-width reservation, fast reroute, or VPN capabilities. These networks are common among smaller providers because the architecture is a tried and tested model that has been used for many years. The network size is usually smaller, so the over-head of MPLS with only a handful of routers may not be worth it (unless Layer 2 or Layer 3 VPN services are needed).

WHAT TYPE OF NETWORK IS BEST?

The designs presented in this chapter are weighted in favor of MPLS. MPLS solves many of the limitations of a hop-by-hop routing paradigm that has been in use since the Internet Protocol was the subject of a cutting-edge RFC.

If running MPLS is a fait accompli, the first question that needs to be answered is whether to use a global routing table for most services or to dedicate a VRF for each service. This is not so easy to answer. From a routing perspective, an Inter-net service is different from most other ones. For example, routes received from other peering routers can contain many BGP attributes that need to be inspected, sometimes modified, and then passed around the rest of the network. The net-work might not be a simple flat domain of BGP routers and could cross interpro-vider VPNs (see the following Technology Note), dedicated peering routers between Internet peers, or edge routers that are not running MPLS. If an Internet service is run in a VRF, to be effective, all PE routers should have as much routing-policy control over MPLS-labeled Internet routes as nonlabeled (non-VPN) ones. Such capabilities vary from vendor to vendor, but day-to-day they are sufficient to keep most operators happy. However, every so often a policy, routing, or IP application feature has limitations working in a VRF; this is common with many vendors. Often implementing such a feature in a VRF is a few releases behind the non-VRF case, but for other cases, the delay is significant or not planned. This comes down to careful planning and testing if the requirement is an Internet service within a VRF. One example of this overhead is a multicast service. Implementing multicast routing and forwarding in a Layer 3 VPN environment (using the Rosen draft) is a lot more complicated than a simple non-VPN architecture. Because the Rosen draft has several versions, the very latest support varies from vendor to vendor.

Technology Note: Interprovider VPNs

Interprovider VPNs (also known as Carrier-Supporting-Carrier VPNs) are a way for service providers to interconnect MPLS-based VPNs across provider domains. Because most providers cannot offer complete international or sometimes national connectivity, they can set up peering points. At these peering points, customer VPN routes are exchanged with other another service provider. This lets them expand their service coverage without the customers having to do it themselves.

Interprovider VPNs are also used within a single company to bridge separate administrative domains. These are common after mergers and acquisitions. These VPNs are sometimes used in a wholesale broadband access model, where the incumbent offers access to wholesaled subscribers through an interprovider VPN.

If VPNs are used for service separation, there needs to be a way of routing between them. Policy forwarding is one option, but it does not scale well when many services are applied to a customer interface, because the configuration is difficult to manage. It is a useful feature to solve tricky routing issues in isolated cases, but it is not an ideal candidate to use for rolling out multiservice access on a large scale. VRF route leaking is the most common solution for VPN providers to enable inter-VPN routing. The downside is that as the number of services grows, managing and configuring leaking for each service VPN becomes a significant overhead. Life can be made easier when a common set of services are managed from a single routing entity—either a "service VRF" or a non-VRF-based routing table.

That said, providers that deploy VPNs as the mainstay of their business often have no problem running Internet and other services in VRFs, because the overhead of configuring route leaking and complex BGP configuration is routine business. At the other end of the spectrum are ISPs, where the focus has been on providing Internet access and it's typical to put Internet and supplementary routes in the global routing table, which results in a simpler configuration.

MULTICAST PROTOCOLS IN THE BACKBONE

The last few sections gave a quick introduction to the designs of double-play core networks. The next set of services to cover is video, which includes both IPTV and unicast Video on Demand (VoD). As far as the core network is concerned, with the exception of QoS configuration, adding VoD is much simpler compared to multicast-based IPTV. This is because VoD has forwarding requirements similar to other high-priority traffic that may already be on the network. This section explains strategies for designing a multicast-capable core, covering both MPLS and non-MPLS networks. Associated supporting protocols and technologies such as point-to-multipoint LSPs, VPLS, and vanilla IPv4 are also explained. You must be familiar with the basic concepts of multicast. Some are explained in the section "Hybrid 1:1 and Multicast VLANs" in Chapter 4, "Designing a Triple-Play Access Network."

DEPLOYING NATIVE IP MULTICAST

Multicast has been around as long as unicast and is still undergoing continual changes to its routing protocols. Native multicast involves sending data around a network as pure IP packets rather than over some kind of tunnel (such as Generic Routing Encapsulation [GRE] or Layer 2 Tunneling Protocol [L2TP]) or over the top of an MPLS network. All routers involved with forwarding multicast data also participate in the multicast routing domain and have firsthand knowledge of and influence over how multicast flows over the network. PIM is the protocol in the core that distributes the routing information. Figure 3.5 shows the standard model of a PIM Any Source Multicast (PIM-ASM) network with a content injection point—New York, an RP, Chicago—and the interested receiver, the BNG. The content injection point first sends the group to the RP. The RP is also the router toward which all last-hop routers (the BNG in this case) send their PIM Join message. The BNG attached to Los Angeles sends a PIM Join to Chicago, requesting group 232.1.1.1.

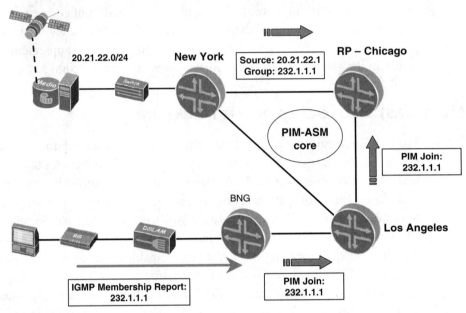

Figure 3.5 PIM any source multicast—stage 1.

Figure 3.6 shows the second stage of the RP delivering the group down the "tree" through Los Angeles to the BNG.

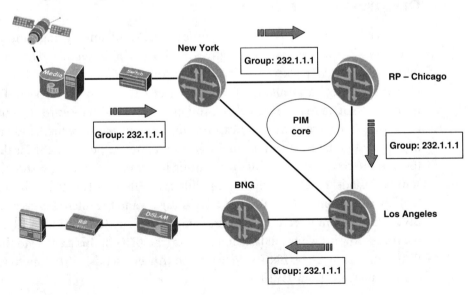

Figure 3.6 PIM any source multicast—stage 2.

PIM-ASM

PIM-ASM has been the most common way of deploying a multicast network. This means that any device interested in receiving a group can also transmit streams for the same group to the network. Such a model lends itself well to videoconferencing, where there could be several senders. This is not the case for IPTV, where only a single source (or at least only sources under the provider's control) needs to send the channels to the group. Multiple active sources for a single group would corrupt the video stream for all users. Filters can be put at the IP edges of a PIM-ASM network to keep any nefarious users from sending data to the network and disrupting the service.

In protocol terms, PIM-ASM means that a PIM receiver that wants to receive a multicast group (the BNG in Figure 3.6) needs to send a request to a router in the network called a rendezvous point (RP). The RP provides a liason service between the multicast senders and receivers. This liaising function is needed because a receiver does not know the group's source IP address until it has received the first packet of the stream. The RP sends IP packets for the group to the interested receiver. After the BNG receives them, it knows the stream's source address based on information in the IP header. The next step is to send a PIM Join directly toward the source. A direct path is then set up between the source and the receiver, which is called a Shortest Path Tree (SPT). Why send a Join to the source? If the RP were not on the shortest path between the source and receiver, and the Join were not sent to the source, traffic would continually flow through the network via the RP. This would be inefficient and would mean that the RP needs to handle much more data throughput. This could amount to hundreds of megabits per second, so limiting such roundabout traffic flow is a must.

This is tricky to digest in one go, so, in summary, these are the steps for a PIM-ASM network to deliver a multicast group:

1. The multicast source router that is connected to the source (called the designated router [DR]) registers its groups with the RP. The RP creates an SPT back to the DR. Multicast packets are forwarded down the SPT to the RP.

2. The last-hop router (adjacent to the interested receiver) sends a PIM Join for the group toward the RP. This creates an RPT back upstream to the RP.

3. RP delivers the group to the interested last-hop router down the RPT.

4. The interested receiver sends a Join for the group directly to the source address of the packet stream. This creates an SPT back to the DR from the last-hop router.

5. When the receiver receives the group from the source DR (along the SPT), it sends a Prune toward the RP so that it does not continually receive two copies of the same group. The RPT is pruned back to the point at which the last branch occurred. A branch is the point at which the SPT and RPT no longer share the same path.

If multiple anycast RPs are deployed for redundancy or network efficiency reasons, a second protocol is required to synchronize the RPs—Multicast Source Discovery Protocol (MSDP). MSDP runs between RPs to distribute information about the multicast groups in the network. Without it, not all RPs would have a full view of what multicast sources were in a network.

Technology Note: Multiple RPs

Multiple RPs are used for redundancy and load distribution in a PIM-ASM multicast network. Described in the section "PIM-ASM," RPs provide the mapping function between sources and receivers. Any source that needs to transmit to the network, first needs to register its groups with the RP. Also, the receivers need to register their intent to receive a group.

Adding one or more RPs for redundancy can be achieved in several ways—bootstrap router (an IETF PIM standard), Auto-RP (a Cisco-designed protocol using dense-mode PIM), or anycast RP. The most common, anycast, involves each RP having the same loopback IP address ID across all the redundant routers (this IP address is different from the unique Interior Gateway Protocol [IGP] router ID). The anycast IP address is announced to the rest of the network in the IGP so that when a PIM router receives several routes for the same IP address, it picks the path to the RP with the lowest IGP cost. Other routers might have a lower cost to reach a different RP because they are closer (in routing protocol terms) to the other RP. In the event of an RP failure, the route is withdrawn (hopefully) from the network, and all the routers choose the remaining RP as their preferred rendezvous point.

Something needs to synchronize the RPs because of the differences in multicast routing tables of each PIM router in the network. For example, one PIM router (or DR) might send registration messages to its closest RP to register its groups, but the interested receiver might have a lower-cost route to a different RP (remember that they all have the same IP address). Something needs to inform all RPs in the network about the location of the multicast senders so that they all have the same list of groups. This protocol is called MSDP[1], and its job is to synchronize all the RPs in the network. It runs over a TCP connection between the unique IP addresses of the RPs in the network. It periodically sends Source-Active messages to other peers when a new group is discovered to keep the group state fresh.

Figure 3.7 shows a network running multiple RPs with MSDP peering. The ingress DR (not shown) sends a register message to the RP address, which is 192.168.99.1. This is configured as loopback 1 on both routers. Because two RPs have this address in the network, the ingress DR sends the register to the one with the lowest IGP cost. The RP that receives the register sends the MSDP Source-Active message to the other RPs. If interested receivers send a message to any of the RPs, the RPs all have enough state to send a Join message toward the source and the consequent group toward the receiver. The "5"s in the image are the interface IGP metrics, which are added at each hop to the received route announcements.

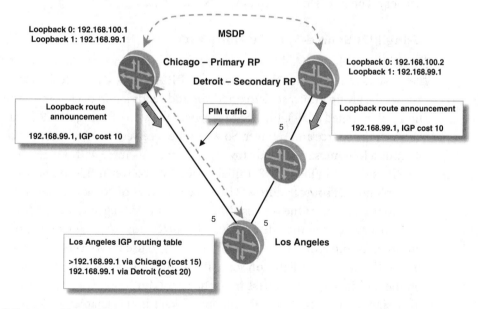

Figure 3.7 Anycast RP with MSDP peering.

[1] http://www.ietf.org/rfc/rfc3618.txt

Bootstrapping the ASM Domain with BSR

Buried further in the multicast tool chest, BSR (bootstrap router) is used to distribute the IP addresses of RPs around the network. Rather than statically configuring RP addresses on every PIM router, the BSR protocol can distribute this information automatically throughout the PIM domain when the domain is first initialized (or when the BSR goes down). First, each PIM router running the BSR protocol is configured with a priority value. It then becomes a candidate BSR (C-BSR). If it wants to become an RP for a group or a range of groups, this is also configured along with a priority; the router is now a candidate RP (C-RP). The router with the highest BSR priority becomes the BSR, which then arbitrates between the C-RPs to decide which RP is responsible for a given group or group range. In the event of a priority tie, the router with the highest IP address wins the point of contention.

If you're thinking that all this seems rather complicated, you would be right. PIM-SSM (Source-Specific Multicast) removes much of the complexity associated with PIM-ASM in one fell swoop. It eliminates RPs, MSDP, and BSR from the network; it is becoming the plumbing protocol of choice for IPTV service delivery. The next section explains how this works.

Using PIM Source-Specific Multicast

Recall that with PIM-ASM, when an interested receiver wants a multicast channel, it sends a request for the group to the RP. After the client receives the data, it knows the group's unicast source address and sends a Join back toward this injection point (called a DR). PIM-SSM removes the step of using an RP to map between the source and receiver. So when the receiver wants to receive a channel, it sends a Join message directly toward the group's source without going through an RP, as shown in Figure 3.8. Initially the PIM receiver needs to know the video stream's unicast source address. There are two ways of conveying this information to the network. One is to use Internet Group Management Protocol (IGMP) version 3, which can include the unicast source address along with the multicast group in its Join request. The second option is to use IGMP version 2 in conjunction with a feature available on some BNGs that fills in the unicast address based on the multicast group address from the client. Both these options are explained in "Using IGMP with PIM-SSM Mapping" later in this chapter. If the source of the media stream is down, there needs to be some way for the network to recover from this situation and choose a different source. This issue is covered in the section "Designing a Highly Available Core Network."

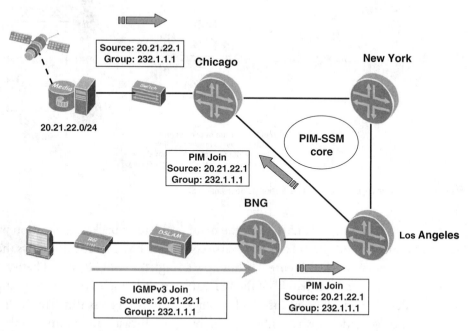

Figure 3.8 PIM Any Source Multicast.

USING P2MP LSPs FOR MULTICAST DATA DELIVERY

Until point-to-multipoint (P2MP) LSPs were conceived, LSPs could be only single paths between two PEs. A problem with overlaying multicast on top of these LSPs is that they have no knowledge of the underlying physical topology. Even if any of the LSPs share common links from the source, the multicast groups must still be duplicated across each of the LSPs. In such a scenario, it decreases the usefulness of multicast as a bandwidth-saving technology and increases the bandwidth used on the backbone linearly with the number of PEs, as shown in Figure 3.9. One solution is to run native multicast in the core, as mentioned previously. Many service providers like to be protocol puritans and run a core network with as little protocol clutter as possible (not necessarily a bad thing), so using PIM in the core to manage multicast routing is sometimes avoided.

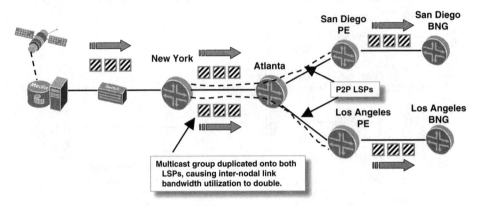

Figure 3.9 Traffic duplication of multicast using point-to-point LSPs.

Point-to-multipoint LSPs solve the main problem of packet duplication when point-to-point (P2P) LSPs transverse common links. Figure 3.10 shows the same physical network as Figure 3.9, but now a single P2MP LSP is used between the three routers. The "trunk" of the LSP carries only a single copy of the group until Atlanta, at which point the LSP branches out to two egress PEs. This MPLS forwarding model now resembles the native IP multicast one; common links transport only one copy of each group, regardless of the number of receivers. A signaling protocol such as RSVP or LDP is used to set up the P2MP LSP between the ingress router and all the egress PEs. Where the LSP branches into two or more paths, the router has enough information in the signaling protocol to build the LSP to the end PEs. At the branch point, the router sets up its forwarding plane to replicate MPLS packets from the upstream path across the multiple downstream paths, as it would for IP or IPv6. It is worth noting that despite being MPLS-based, this solution does not require the use of a Layer 3 VPN.

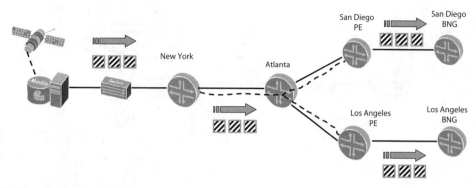

Figure 3.10 Point-to-multipoint LSP overview.

The Signaling Plane

Deployments of P2MP LSPs are normally based on RSVP-TE. The usual benefits of RSVP-TE, such as QoS, traffic engineering capabilities, and fast reroute, can be used with this signaling protocol. The two specifications that form the mainstay of the protocol are draft-ietf-mpls-p2mp-sig-requirement and draft-ietf-mpls-rsvp-te-p2mp. The first deals with generalized signaling protocol requirements and defines some terminology, and the latter describes the machinery used to signal P2MP LSPs. As soon as the path for the LSPs through the network has been computed (either using an offline tool or online using Constrained Shortest Path First [CSPF]), the ingress router sends RSVP PATH messages toward the egress (or leaf) routers. When the routers along the path receive the message and all bodes well for an established path (sufficient bandwidth and path constraints are being met), they send a confirmation message (RESV) back to the ingress point. Figure 3.11 shows how the RSVP PATH messages flow through the network to set up the first part of the LSPs.

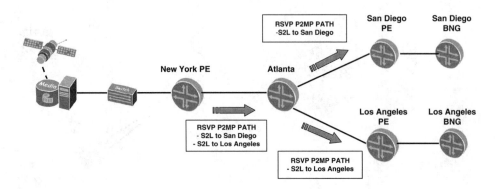

Figure 3.11 RSVP point-to-multipoint LSP setup—stage 1.

Figure 3.12 shows the paths being confirmed by the egress nodes sending RSVP RESV messages back to the ingress PE. Notice that each hop sends the label for the upstream router to use when sending it a P2MP LSP packet.

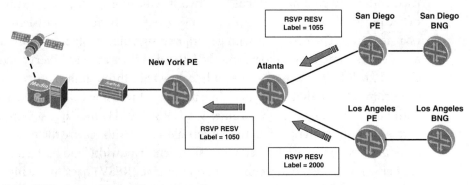

Figure 3.12 RSVP point-to-multipoint LSP setup—stage 2.

The Forwarding Plane

P2MP LSPs for multicast go well with the forwarding paradigm of the DR sending a single copy of a group to the network regardless of the number of receivers. They also offer a compelling alternative to running native multicast in the core. The network shown in Figure 3.13 has been replaced with a P2MP model like that shown in Figure 3.10. New York is the ingress point of the LSP and crosses a P router—Atlanta—before branching to the two PE routers, San Diego and Los

Angeles. When the IPTV channels are sent to the LSP at New York, only single copies of the multicast groups are sent. Atlanta is responsible for replicating the groups to the two LSP branches.

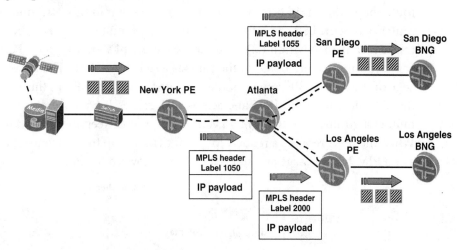

Figure 3.13 Point-to-multipoint packet forwarding.

If a service provider uses only LDP in the core and does not require traffic engineering, QoS capabilities, nor fast reroute, an Internet draft[2] has been written that details the requirements for using LDP- signaled P2MP LSPs. Another Internet draft[3] describes the protocol machinery for setting up the paths. The paradigm of setting up the LSPs differs from RSVP-TE. In the case of an RSVP-signaled LSP, if a leaf or egress router wants to join the LSP, the ingress router needs to signal the new addition to the tree by sending new PATH messages along the path. The routers can then set up all the forwarding state and graft on the new router. Instead with LDP, the leaf nodes (otherwise known as egress routers) send the request upstream, indicating that they want to join the LSP, at which stage the upstream nodes graft the leaf nodes onto the tree. A downside to both protocol drafts as well as deployments today is the lack of coupling the P2MP LSPs to the PIM protocol. This means that any routers that set up LSPs do so without any knowledge of the multicast topology. Instead, they build paths based on MPLS topology. This is where the IETF's work on writing a specification that enables efficient multicast forwarding over a VPLS network comes in (as covered later in this chapter).

[2] http://www.ietf.org/internet-drafts/draft-leroux-mpls-mp-ldp-reqs-03.txt

[3] http://www.ietf.org/internet-drafts/draft-minei-wijnands-mpls-ldp-p2mp-00.txt

Integration with PIM Source-Specific Multicast

As mentioned, the forwarding path of MPLS packets is at the mercy of LSPs routing in the network. Normally PIM dictates the multicast forwarding path at each router hop, which is in turn based on IGP metrics. But in this case, none of the routers along the LSP can influence the routing of multicast packets, because all traffic is contained within P2MP tunnels. Figure 3.14 shows a typical PoP that connects one or more BNGs to the core via a switch network. The routers at the edge of the core are PE routers and terminate the P2MP LSPs. In this instance, the BNG does not run MPLS and acts as a CE router. For it to be able to request multicast groups from the core, PIM needs to run between the CE and the PE. When the BNG receives a request for a multicast group from an end host, it creates a PIM Join message and sends it upstream toward the PE.

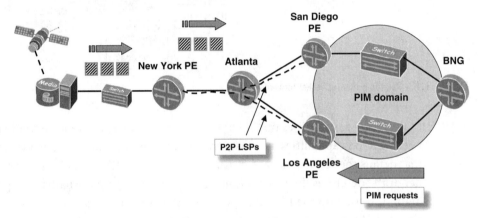

Figure 3.14 Integrating PIM-SSM with point-to-multipoint LSPs.

Before the BNG receives the group, the core needs to be set up to forward the IPTV channels to the P2MP LSP. Because no PIM is running in the core between the egress and ingress routers, the usual way is to statically route all groups to the P2MP LSP at the ingress point. Now that the channels are being sent to the egress router, it can deliver any of the requested groups to the BNG. To reduce protocol delay, the egress PE can also be set up in the same fashion as the core and can transmit all groups to the BNGs. If network bandwidth is skimpy and on-demand PIM is preferred, the "on-demand" portion runs as close as possible to the customer. Therefore, fewer routers are involved that need to set up the necessary forwarding state when a channel is requested. One point that needs to be mentioned is the protocol interaction with Reverse Path Forwarding (RPF).

RPF is used to prevent multicast forwarding loops in the network. If multicast RPF is enabled—and, in almost all cases, it is—when a router receives multicast data, it makes a note of the unicast source address and checks it against the routing table. It is looking for two things: the lowest-routing-cost route back to the source address, and the next-hop interface that the router uses if it has to reach the source. If the multicast data came in on the same interface as the RPF interface, all is well, and the router accepts the traffic. But if it came in on a different interface, the traffic is dropped. This is a safeguard against multicast traffic taking a poor path through the network.

To give this some context, the edge PE that the BNG connects to needs to have a route for the unicast source on the same interface where the P2MP LSP comes from. (Recall that the multicast traffic leaves the P2MP LSP at the PE.) It is possible that, during times of link failure in the network, the P2MP LSPs would be rerouted, and multicast would enter the PE at a different interface than where RPF routes for multicast traffic point to. Careful engineering of network metrics during LSP path planning should be done to ensure the alignment of RPF routes during LSP reroute. It is possible to disable RPF checks as a way to get around the problem, but if redundant multicast streams will probably enter a single PE, this solution becomes of dubious merit. In this case, both streams would be accepted, interleaved, and sent out the egress port, which is undesirable. RPF should be disabled only if a single media stream will enter a PE.

Technology Note: Other Uses for RPF

There are uses for RPF other than multicast loop protection. It is also used as a check against traffic being sent with spoofed source addresses. This is when a host such as a PC or server sends traffic with a source IP address set to one other than the one it has been assigned. By doing this, it masks the sender's identity, making it harder to track the source of malfeasant traffic.

A recommended protection mechanism involving RPF is described in BCP38,[4] which concerns enabling RPF checks at the edges of a network. This recommended-best-practices document recommends that edge routers verify the source address of packets entering the network against their routing table. If a match occurs, the packet is accepted; otherwise, it is discarded. The three ways of making a match are documented in a further BCP document:[5] strict RPF, feasible RPF, and loose RPF.

---

[4] http://www.ietf.org/rfc/rfc2827.txt
[5] BCP84

Strict RPF means that the interface where traffic arrives must match the interface that would be used to get back to the source address. Feasible RPF loosens the restriction that there can be only a single route back to the source. For example, if a router receives multiple BGP routes for a network, feasible RPF lets the router choose any of these routes for the RPF check. Such a case would arise if a customer were multihomed and traffic intentionally might not return via the lowest-cost path.

Loose RPF means that there just needs to be any possible route for the traffic, even if it is a default one. This means that traffic with forged source addresses could enter the network via a completely different path than what is expected or valid, defeating the purpose of the RPF check if a default route can match the source of traffic. BCP84/RFC2827 does document one or two use-cases for loose RPF.

Chapter 12, "Security in Broadband Networks," gives further examples of configuring RPF checks on BRAS routers.

DELIVERING MULTICAST USING VPLS IN THE CORE

Running multicast over Virtual Private LAN Service (VPLS) is getting lots of attention in the IETF lately—and for good reason. It is shaping up to be an ideal fit for a provider's internal IPTV transport mechanism and for delivering multicast VPN services to external customers as well. The biggest drawback of using VPLS for multicast forwarding is its lack of knowledge of the underlying physical MPLS topology (as described in the preceding section). This results in traffic being unnecessarily duplicated on common network links, as shown in Figure 3.9. Protocol enhancements are being written to allow VPLS to forward multicast traffic more efficiently and to integrate more closely with the underlying transport mechanism. For example, today VPLS uses many P2P LSPs for the transport mechanism. An alternative model is to use P2MP LSPs. Chapter 4 has further information on the basics of VPLS.

VPLS is not solely responsible for streamlining multicast replication in the network; it builds on other protocols, such as BGP, RSVP, and LDP, to create an efficient multicast topology. The discussion in this section is based on the concepts described in the "Multicast over VPLS" Internet draft.[6] The first optimization is where VPLS networks that need to carry multicast traffic use *multicast trees*, which are built using signaling protocols such as RSVP-TE, LDP, or PIM. The

---

[6] http://www.ietf.org/internet-drafts/draft-ietf-l2vpn-vpls-mcast-00.txt

second optimization is to allow ingress and egress PEs to auto-discover each other and to enable routers to create multicast trees between themselves. Both of these concepts are explained in the following sections.

Multicast Trees and VPLS

In a basic multicast setup with IPv4 and PIM-ASM, when routers want to join a group, they send messages toward the unicast source or the RP. Core routers deliver the multicast stream out of the interface via the one through which the original request was received. If another edge router wants to receive the same group, a core router can simply replicate the group out of the other interface that it received the new request on rather than the server's having to send a separate stream. Looking at this from a top-down perspective, it forms what is called a multicast tree and describes the path that a group takes in the network.

VPLS supported with P2MP LSPs does not suffer the problem of sending multiple copies of groups across common links that a normal VPLS network does. Because the underlying topology is based on a point-to-multipoint architecture, only one copy of a group is transmitted along a common part of the tree, regardless of the number of receivers. Only where the tree splits in two parts is the group duplicated out of the different interfaces. The P2MP LSP hierarchy with VPLS is the same as plain P2MP LSPs, so there needs to be an advantage from running all the extra signaling state in the backbone. The first advantage is that point-to-multipoint LSPs can be used for more than just the internal transportation of provider multicast. They can be reused when the service provider offers multicast VPN services to customers. These can coexist on the same LSP as provider multicast services. Because of the extra signaling protocols used in this mechanism, LSPs can be automatically provisioned.

Automated P2MP LSP Provisioning

One of the drawbacks of P2MP LSPs is the amount of static configuration needed on the PEs. In the case of LDP-based LSPs, each of the edge nodes needs to be configured with the details of the LSP tree to join. With RSVP-TE, the ingress router needs to be configured with the addresses of the egress PEs. The draft **draft-ietf-l2vpn-vpls-mcast** enables ingress and egress PE routers that are part of the same domain to discover each other and automatically build a point-to-multipoint topology as required. Figure 3.15 shows an ingress router—New York—attached to a multicast server. Several of the PEs are part of a single VPLS instance and announce their membership to the domain using BGP.

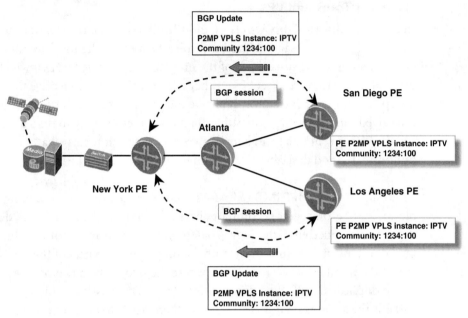

Figure 3.15 Multicast over VPLS—network setup stage 1.

At the same time, the ingress router announces the P2MP LSP name to the egress routers. So when an LSP arrives from New York, the egress routers (San Diego and Los Angeles) can properly map between a VPLS instance and the P2MP LSP. This step is shown in Figure 3.16.

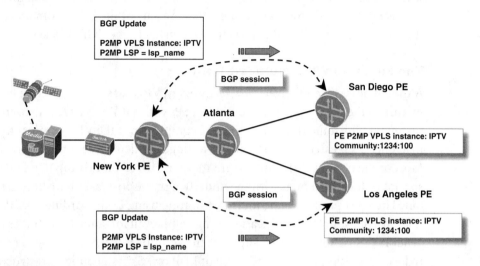

Figure 3.16 Multicast over VPLS—network setup stage 2.

So the ingress router knows to which egress routers to build the P2MP tree, it uses the IP addresses of BGP advertisements as the destination addresses of the P2MP tree. This is shown in Figure 3.17. The ingrass PE starts to signal the paths using RSVP-TE PATH messages.

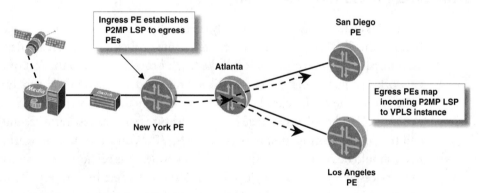

Figure 3.17 Multicast over VPLS—final stage.

LDP P2MP LSPs differ from RSVP-TE because the egress PEs add themselves to the tree rather than the ingress router's grafting them on, as in the RSVP case. The ingress PE is preconfigured with a Forwarding Equivalence Class (FEC), which can be thought of as an ID for the P2MP LSP. The FEC is sent to the egress PEs using BGP, and any egress routers that are part of the VPLS domain graft themselves onto the P2MP LSP ID that was given in the BGP message.

The Future of VPLS Multicast Delivery

Although it is still a relatively new technology, VPLS has had some time to mature in the marketplace. Basic P2MP LSPs without VPLS have also been on the market for some time. However, the complexity of the VPLS protocol machinery is greater, so development, testing, and deployment take more time. Most of the current VPLS implementations are based on existing P2P LSP ones, so a lot of the initial bugs with the underlying transport layer have been ironed out. The safe option of basic multicast routing using IP forwarding over P2MP LSPs or even simple IP multicast routing will prevail for some time. But as router vendors release software that supports the additional VPLS draft, the benefits of reduced provisioning time and reuse of LDP or RSVP signaling infrastructure will help make the switch to the more flexible network architecture. Just as once it was enough of a payoff to move to a more complex MPLS architecture that offered the benefits of services running on a "converged" platform, VPLS should help the switch from a P2P model.

RUNNING MPLS ON THE BNG

So far, this chapter has focused mainly on backbone and some edge architectures. Because the BNG is a multiservice router, some of the services that are deployed on it impact the way in which it is linked, at a protocol level, to the rest of the network. For instance, if Layer 3 VPNs are required on the BNG, it usually needs to be part of the MPLS cloud (unless Layer 2 Tunneling Protocol is used in the network). To take full advantage of MPLS features such as fast reroute, end-to-end traffic engineering, point-to-point LSPs, VPLS, and a unified network, the BNG should be connected to the MPLS backbone. This section discusses some of the services and protocols deployed on a BNG that affect its connectivity to the backbone, including Layer 3 VPN services and integrating multicast routing protocols with the BNG.

The BNG can connect to PEs via a switch aggregation network or directly using SONET, Gigabit Ethernet, or 10 Gigabit Ethernet. SONET is becoming less common in provider PoPs because Gigabit Ethernet is a cheaper alternative.

One issue with Gigabit Ethernet in the past has been the failure detection mechanism. When GE links are connected through a switch aggregation network, link failures cannot always be detected by loss of light and can take seconds to detect. To solve this problem, the industry is moving toward using Bidirectional Forwarding Detection (BFD). Basic BFD link detection mode is a lightweight protocol that sends simple keepalive packets to an IP address of a router sitting on the same broadcast domain. These keepalive packets can detect path failures similar to how ATM OAM cells are used for continuity-check virtual circuits (VCs) and are used by the router to bring down a subinterface if it times out receiving a response from the other end of the BFD session.

CONNECTING THE BNG TO THE WIDER WORLD

Connecting a BNG to the core using plain IP has been a common feature of broadband networks for some time. Because Internet access was the only service that was needed, sophisticated routing and forwarding methods were not used. Connectivity to the rest of the network and the Internet at large would be handled by configuring a static default route on the BNG pointing to the upstream router. Or, if some routing dynamism was needed, a routing protocol such as OSPF, IS-IS, and/or BGP would be used. Some service provider architectures lend themselves well to continue running their BNGs in a simple configuration when migrating to a triple-play architecture. For example, if the BNG routers do not provide any locally terminated VPN services and MPLS features are not of interest, the benefits of migrating the BNG to MPLS are minimal.

But if there is a service that requires terminating subscriber sessions in Layer 3 VPNs, the most common model is to terminate them on an L2TP LNS rather than locally-terminated VPNs. This entails the BNG extending subscriber PPP sessions over an IP network using L2TP and terminating them on a centralized router called a Layer 2 Tunneling Protocol Network Server (LNS). The advantage is that each BNG does not need local configuration of each VPN. It simply forwards each PPP session to one (or possibly one of several) centralized router that has the necessary Layer 3 VPN configuration for that subscriber. Because this functionality is agnostic to whatever packet mechanism is used underneath (MPLS, L2TP, GRE, IP, and so on), there is no affect on L2TP functionality if MPLS is deployed to the BNG. If IPoE services based on DHCP or static configuration are used, L2TP VPN services require a different approach. The first is to use L2TP Version 3, which is more flexible with the type of payload it may carry. The second option is to deploy local VPN configurations on the BNG.

Extending the MPLS domain to the BNG has the compelling benefit of creating a more unified network, making it possible to deploy end-to-end traffic engineering, QoS, and fast reroute capabilities. In this fashion, MPLS runs across the links between the BNG and core. All unicast traffic (such as Internet and VoIP) is transported using point-to-point LSPs from other routers in the network. The BNG runs internal BGP with the other PEs or route reflectors and participates in the backbone IGP. Aside from the usual benefits of MPLS, one of the advantages of designing the network this way is being able to deliver locally terminated Layer 3 VPN services to the BNG. The customer VRF is configured on the BNG so that a DSL modem can dial in and get access to its VPN, as shown in Figure 3.18. Each of the VRFs can use the same MPLS LSPs to forward VPN traffic to the other PEs in the network. The trick to differentiating traffic from one VPN to the other is to attach a different inner MPLS label to packets that are sent from a router. This inner label information is distributed using iBGP signaling. A unique label can be assigned to the whole VRF, a label per interface in the VRF, or even per prefix in the VRF. The method of assigning these labels varies from router vendor to router vendor, with some providing configuration knobs to tweak the algorithm of label assignment.

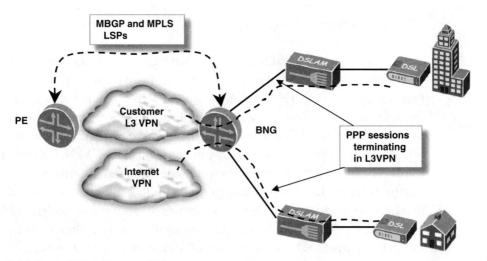

Figure 3.18 Running VPN services at the BNG.

VPN services are not the only services that benefit from MPLS-connected BNGs. High-priority traffic, such as Video on Demand and VoIP, can take advantage of specially reserved LSPs. These LSPs can take a shorter or more reliable path through the network than other LSPs that are used for best-effort traffic. These LSPs can be protected with fast reroute capability to minimize the impact of delays in IGP convergence and path resignaling. It is up to the provider whether lower-priority traffic can use the same LSPs as high-priority traffic. For more complex deployments, often low-priority traffic is forwarded on an LSP with a longer path and lower setup priorities. An LSP with a lower setup priority is one that, in the event of a link break in the network and if there is insufficient bandwidth to signal a new path at that priority, an LSP with a higher priority value can take its place. If an LSP is dedicated to a particular traffic priority, it is called an L-LSP (label-inferred LSP), compared to an E-LSP, which can carry multiple traffic priorities.

USING IGMP WITH PIM-SSM MAPPING

To request a multicast group from the core, PIM requests it from the upstream router. MPLS or IP forwarding is used as the underlying packet transport, and Internet Group Management Protocol (IGMP) is used by the subscriber to request groups from the BNG.

IGMP is a lightweight protocol that an end host, such as a set-top box, uses when requesting a multicast video channel. An IGMP packet, which is sent toward a PIM router, contains the multicast group address that the host wants to receive. The BNG also can act as an IGMP client of sorts. It is used when the router wants to statically join a group and have the core continually transmit it to the BNG. These are called static IGMP Joins.

Before we race ahead too fast, an explanation of the relationship between IGMP and PIM is needed. IGMP is used by a host (such as a set-top box) to request multicast groups from the network. With IGMP versions 1 and 2, when the set-top box requests a multicast channel, it sends an IGMP Membership Report packet upstream to the BNG that contains the group address it wants to receive. With IGMP version 3, this same packet is called a Join (Figure 3.19 shows an example). IGMP is also used to request that a particular group no longer be sent; the packet is called, unsurprisingly, an IGMP Leave. IGMP does not have much multicast topology information about the rest of the network, nor does it need such information, because it is a simple protocol for controlling multicast at the edges of the network. The hard routing part is left up to PIM. As soon as the BNG receives this IGMP request, it begins the process previously described of requesting the multicast group from the network, either directly from the source using PIM-SSM or from the RP using PIM-ASM. To illustrate the operation of PIM, Figure 3.19 shows the protocol operation with the BNG as a CE, rather than a PE. If the BNG is running VPLS (with the underlying transport being MPLS), there would be a different protocol setup in the core. This would involve a communications channel between the BNGs and the ingress PEs of the required multicast group membership. The architecture of this protocol interaction is still under discussion at the IETF.

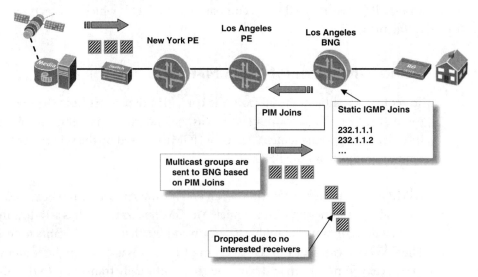

Figure 3.19 Dynamic PIM Joins. The network delivers the group to the BNG based on IGMP from the customer.

Static IGMP groups are used on the BNG for groups it *always* wants to receive from the core. These trigger PIM Joins that are sent to the core as soon as the PIM protocol is available for use on the router and the correct upstream PIM state (neighborships and RPF table) has been created. Figure 3.20 is similar to Figure 3.19, but the BNG is locally configured with two static groups—232.1.1.1 and 232.1.1.2—which triggers PIM Join messages to be sent upstream toward the core. The idea behind the static IGMP groups is to reduce the all-important zapping latency in the network by having the BNG always receive these multicast channels. Zapping is when someone changes TV channels. If these static Joins were not configured, some extra protocol latency occurs from having to wait until the BNG receives and processes the IGMP request from the STB, creates and sends the PIM request, waits to receive the channel, and then forwards it.

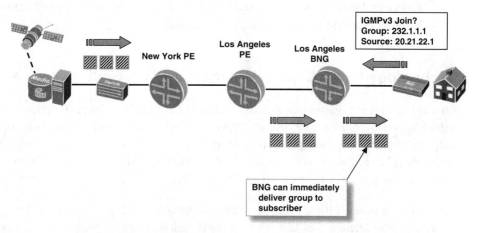

Figure 3.20 Static IGMP Joins—BNG preloading multicast channels.

IGMP has three versions; the two common ones are IGMP versions 2 and 3. Version 2 is more prevalent to date. Version 3 offers several compelling benefits over version 2. One is the capability for an STB to simultaneously request to leave one group and join another within a single packet. With IGMP version 2, this would require sending two separate packets, causing extra latency in the network due to having to process two packets. This is especially important to avoid when you need to rapidly change from one channel to the next. A second use of version 3 is for PIM-SSM. PIM-SSM requires the PIM receiver to know the group's source address beforehand. This address can be communicated in the IGMPv3 packet header.

The STB needs some help to determine the video source address to include in the IGMP Join that it sends to the BNG. At the time of writing, a divination protocol had not yet been written. One solution is for the boot configuration of the STB to have the address preseeded from the network. The STB's configuration architecture normally is dynamic enough that if any settings need to change (such as the address of the video server), a new configuration can be pushed to it from a central server.

If the STB cannot specify a source address in the Join packet, all is not lost. Even though IGMP version 3 has a field for the unicast source address, it does not have to be filled in. Version 3 can still be used while leaving the source address field inside the packet empty. Now we're back to the problem of discovering the source address. The solution is to let the PIM router fill in this information. This is called PIM-SSM mapping, and it is explained shortly.

Technology Note: Explicit Tracking and Immediate Leave

Every device on a router's subinterface (such as a multicast VLAN to a DSLAM) that sends and receives IGMP traffic is tracked by the router. If only one host is left on the interface, and it wants to leave the group, the router can immediately stop sending traffic out the interface when it gets the leave message. This was not possible with IGMP version 2, because the protocol did not allow the router to receive Join messages from all clients; one client on a LAN is designated the group speaker.

Cisco calls to the feature of tracking every join and leave of the LAN *explicit tracking*. Juniper ERX software has a slightly related feature called IGMP immediate leave, which means that as soon as it receives a Leave message on an interface, it stops transmitting out that interface. This should be used only on an interface where there is one IGMP client connected.

Cisco:

This feature can be enabled by configuring the following command under the interface:

```
ip igmp explicit-tracking
```

Juniper ERX:

This feature can be enabled by configuring the following command under either an AAA profile or the interface:

```
ip igmp immediate-leave
```

IGMP Proxy

One feature that has not been mentioned in this chapter is IGMP proxy, which is designed to handle scaling issues in the access and BNG edge. One that is familiar to many is the web proxy; it handles requests for websites on the Internet on behalf of the client sitting behind it. The IGMP proxy works in a similar way by dealing with multicast requests on behalf of the client (or clients) sitting behind it.

One of the more common uses is in a residential gateway (RG), which often functions as an IGMP proxy on behalf of the STB. When someone presses a channel button on the RG remote control, it causes the STB to send an IGMP request upstream to the RG, which intercepts the IGMP request and sends it to the network on its behalf. When the BNG sends the IPTV stream to the RG, it is forwarded to the STB. So why not let the STB send the request directly to the BNG? Similar to a web proxy, one of the reasons is to hide the addressing of the network sitting in the background. For example, the addressing between the STB and the RG might be a private network, so making the STB's identity visible on the network might not be desirable. Usually, however, the proxy is part of the operation of the RG to track which port the IGMP request came from.

The more important use of the IGMP proxy is described in Chapter 4. It involves the DSLAM handling requests on behalf of all the multicast clients sitting behind it so as to reduce the amount of traffic between the clients and the BNG. For example, if 300 clients are connected to a DSLAM, and they all ask to change the channel at a similar time by sending IGMP packets directly to the BNG (such as at the start of a commercial break), it could be inundated with requests. This is especially true when extrapolating this effect across many DSLAMs. The actual impact and the number of IGMP requests that could adversely affect a BNG's performance varies between vendors, of course. Using an IGMP proxy on the DSLAM can reduce the control traffic to the BNG by filtering out requests that the DSLAM has already sent and skipping directly to the step of delivering the multicast group to the client. For example, if the DSLAM is already sending an IPTV channel to one host and another host requests the same channel, the DSLAM can suppress the IGMP request to the DSLAM and add the new host to the list of receivers to which it should send the channel.

Usually an IGMP proxy goes hand in hand with IGMP snooping, which is a way for a router or switch to listen to traffic on a port. If it detects an IGMP Join, the switch withdraws the default (with IGMP snooping enabled) restriction, preventing the transmission of the group to that port. If this snooping function is not enabled, it causes the multicast to be sent out all ports (except the one it came through), because the destination address of the Ethernet frames is similar to broadcast frames, which need to be sent out all ports in the switching domain.

PIM-SSM Mapping

If IGMP packets from STBs do not have the source's required unicast address, the BNG can fill in this information based on local configuration. Because it is not possible to include a group source address in these packets, this situation could arise with IGMPv1 or IGMPv2. Another occasion when this could happen is with IGMPv3 and the packet has an empty group-source-address field. This may happen when an STB supports IGMPv3 but cannot supply the required source address.

This feature works by having the BNG contain a list of multicast groups and their corresponding unicast source addresses. When the router receives an IGMP Join—for, say, group 232.1.1.1—it takes the group from the packet and looks up its static mapping table (or sends a DNS request) for the unicast source address that corresponds to the group. Instead of sending a PIM-ASM request to the RP, it inserts the unicast address into the PIM request and can send a PIM-SSM directly toward the source.

Listings 3.3 and 3.4 show Juniper JUNOSe and Cisco IOS configurations to create a PIM-SSM mapping when receiving an IGMP packet that does not have a source address. The downstream interface toward the DSLAM is GigabitEthernet 0/0.100; it receives the IGMP requests from the downstream hosts. The upstream interface is GigabitEthernet 1/0; it sends PIM Join messages toward the source (10.1.1.1).

Listing 3.3   Juniper Networks: JUNOSe PIM-SSM Mapping Configuration

```
interface loopback0
 ip address 1.1.1.1 255.255.255.255

interface GigabitEthernet 0/0.100
 vlan id 100
 ip address 192.168.1.1 255.255.255.0
 ip igmp version 2

interface GigabitEthernet 1/0
 ip address 192.168.2.1 255.255.255.252
 ip pim sparse-mode
```

```
ip igmp ssm-map enable
ip igmp ssm-map static "multicast-groups" 10.1.1.1

access-list multicast-groups permit ip 232.1.1.0 0.0.0.255 any

router igmp
ip multicast-routing
ip pim ssm
```

Listing 3.4 Cisco Systems: IOS PIM-SSM Mapping Configuration

```
interface loopback0
 ip address 1.1.1.1 255.255.255.255

interface GigabitEthernet 0/0.100
 encapsulation dot1q 100
 ip address 192.168.1.1 255.255.255.0
 ip igmp version 2

interface GigabitEthernet 1/0
 ip address 192.168.2.1 255.255.255.252
 ip pim sparse-mode

ip igmp ssm-map enable
ip igmp ssm-map static 10 10.1.1.1

access-list 10 permit ip any 232.1.1.0 0.0.0.255

ip igmp ssm-map enable
ip igmp ssm-map static
no ip igmp ssm-map query dns


ip pim ssm default
```

Cisco IOS can support PIM-SSM mappings either by using a static table or by sending a DNS request to get the same information. Only a static mapping table is possible with Juniper Networks E-Series routers.

Table 3.1 summarizes the protocol terminology that has been used so far in this chapter.

Table 3.1 Summary of Multicast Protocols and Terminology

Protocol or Term	Meaning
BSR	Bootstrap router.
IGMP	Internet Group Management Protocol. A lightweight protocol that runs between PIM routers and hosts that want to receive multicast groups. IGMP can be used in IGMP proxy mode.
IGMP proxy	Allows a router to proxy an IGMP request on behalf of a host. This is found in CPE to hide STB addressing. More commonly found in DSLAMs to reduce the amount of IGMP traffic to the BNG.
IGMP snooping	A feature used on switches and DSLAMs to detect when a host on a port has requested an IGMP group. When the switch comes to replicate the group, it sends it out only the ports that it detected in the Join/Membership Report packet. This works the same in reverse for IGMP Leaves. Note that the switch still is a pure Layer 2 device and does not perform any IGMP routing.
PIM	Protocol-Independent Multicast. A multicast routing protocol that is used to start or stop routers sending multicast groups. The two types of PIM are PIM-ASM and PIM-SSM.
PIM-ASM	PIM Any Source Multicast. The most common way to signal multicast routing information. It uses a mapping agent called an RP, which receives information about active multicast sources in the network. Interested receivers request the group from the RP, which sends it out via the RPT. Interested receivers then switch to the SPT.
MSDP	Multicast Source Discovery Protocol. Runs in a PIM-ASM network between RPs. This TCP-based protocol synchronizes the RPs with information about all the multicast sources.
PIM-SSM	PIM Source-Specific Multicast. A way for a network to specify the unicast source address of a multicast group. This increases global multicast scalability and reduces state in the network due to the elimination of the RP. This is a better fit with an IPTV service compared to a PIM-ASM model. PIM-SSM obviates the need for a PIM-RP or MSDP.

DESIGNING A HIGHLY AVAILABLE CORE NETWORK

Compared to a best-effort Internet data service, a video service needs to be given high priority in the network, in terms of both service priority during times of congestion and overall service availability. This section starts with strategies for engineering the network to create a highly available multicast video service. Chapter 8, "Deploying Quality of Service," covers the design of a triple-play service bundle from a quality of service perspective to ensure reliable packet delivery throughout the network. The latter part of this section covers protocols and techniques to increase the backbone's availability and reliability.

USING MULTIPLE INJECTION POINTS WITH A SINGLE SOURCE ADDRESS

If a single media server is used, all the network redundancy in the world would not help if the single server needs to be rebooted or crashes. Luckily, a single media server deployment is an uncommon occurrence, so the next question is how to run these servers to reduce the downtime when one fails or needs to be bought down for maintenance reasons.

An STB can receive one multicast video channel from a single source at a time. If a server fails, either the network or the STB needs to switch to an alternate source. In current deployments, it is not common for STBs to be able to switch to an alternative source. One minor point is that such a scenario would require IGMP version 3, because this protocol can include the group's source address. Therefore, deployments today need the end-to-end architecture to be robust enough to withstand server failure, a component of the core transport network, and as much of the PoP hardware as possible. Of course, the closer the network is to the customer, the more expensive it becomes to offer full redundancy.

Multiple video injection points can be used by dedicating a server (or server cluster) to one or more edge routers. An active server transmits all the multicast groups to the routers, but only one of these routers actually forwards the traffic to the network, because the downstream routers choose only a single path to the source address when the PIM Join is sent upstream. The injection servers need to share the same source IP address, because the STBs (or BNGs with PIM-SSM mapping) usually have only a single address configured for a given multicast group. The trick is to configure each router interface that connects to a server/ server cluster to be configured with the same network address. This creates an anycast domain and functions similar to anycast RP. Each PIM receiver router chooses the lowest-cost route to send the PIM Join message. Each router interface has a common network configured for the anycast media servers and announces this to the IGP routing domain. Recall that RPF checks are performed throughout the network on multicast packets to ensure that traffic is coming from the shortest path back to the source. In this case, each router has multiple entries in its routing table back to the traffic source, so it chooses whichever route is the least-cost back to the source.

But a more important point and one that is more fundamental to the high-availability architecture is that only one server from a cluster should transmit a group at a time. If all servers were on a common LAN and more than one stream for a group is sent, the edge router would simply forward all packets for the group down the PIM tree, creating interleaved streams. Even though they may be for the same channel, only a single IP stream should be delivered to a client. Vendors delivering such a video solution have techniques to ensure synchronicity between the servers so that only one transmits at a time.

HIGHLY AVAILABLE ROUTING AND SIGNALING PROTOCOLS IN THE CORE

In addition to a highly available video head-end architecture, the underlying protocols, such as MPLS, BGP, and RSVP, also need certain reliability features to ensure that the applications that run on top of the network can assume that the backbone has a strong degree of resilience. This section discusses how various protocols and techniques can be used in the backbone to achieve this.

RSVP

By deploying RSVP-TE LSPs to carry multicast services across the backbone, end-to-end path protection, traffic engineering, and enhanced MPLS QoS can be provided. RSVP can be used to calculate and create a specific path between any two PE routers in the network. The path calculation can be performed offline or using the Constrained Shortest Path First (CSPF) algorithm. It can also be performed online and can take into consideration a variety of factors, known as constraints, to determine the path from the "head-end" to the "tail-end" of the LSP. Traffic enters the LSP at the "head-end" router and leaves the LSP at the "tail-end" router. Path constraints can include bandwidth guarantees, avoiding "double booking" of a common resource in the network (to make sure a primary and backup path do not traverse the same link or device, for instance).

After this path is created, two examples of how it can be protected are

* Make-before-break secondary path
* Fast reroute link-local protection

Make-Before-Break Secondary Path

By presignaling a "make-before-break" secondary LSP, which does not share any of the same links as the primary path, the head-end router is preseeded with a completely redundant path through the network. When a failure is detected anywhere in the LSP, the router directly upstream from the break uses RSVP to signal toward the head-end router that the LSP is no longer usable. As soon as the head-end router receives this message, it tears down the nonworking path and starts forwarding traffic that is destined for the tail end over the secondary path, which was calculated before the failure.

Nondeterministic Failover

RSVP processing, which happens within the control plane of the MPLS routers, can be triggered through a variety of events. Therefore, it is difficult to deterministically calculate the time required for traffic to be fully restored after a failure. The link failure has to be detected by the local router. Then RSVP can generate and send a notification message toward the head-end router, which also has to be processed. The delay time is at least the propagation delay between the point of the failure and the head-end, plus the time it takes the devices to process the message. In the meantime, the head-end router still forwards traffic down this path, all of which is dropped at the failed link. The greater the bandwidth of the links in the path, the more data that is dropped in front of the failed link.

Fast Reroute Local Protection

With fast reroute, traffic can be rerouted around a link failure more quickly. Each node in the end-to-end path (LSP) can calculate an alternative *fast reroute* path to the next downstream node to protect traffic during a failure. With fast reroute protection enabled on an LSP, each router in the path calculates an alternative way of getting to the next downstream router. This information can be seeded into the routers' forwarding plane to make the failover faster. As soon as a link failure is detected, a router can immediately switch traffic for that LSP via the alternative fast reroute path. This allows traffic that is currently in transit to continue to be forwarded along the new path, even while the routers' control plane is trundling along with the necessary signaling updates. These fast reroute paths can even be constraint-based. Although they can be expensive in terms of processing, features such as fate-sharing, bandwidth guarantees, and other factors can be used when creating the alternative paths. Using these constraints appropriately can allow for nearly seamless end-user experiences, even during a severe network event.

Failure Detection

A critical part of restoring a path, using either traditional RSVP signaling or fast reroute, is the initial detection of the link failure. Some transmission media provide signaling and hardware/driver-level notification when the medium becomes unusable (such as SONET/SDH). Other transmission media, such as Ethernet, have no such failure detection capability. Routers typically consist of a variety of integrated components, device drivers that handle specific interface media types, packet processing hardware, and control hardware. Router/vendor implementation and integration of these devices vary from one to the next, so media failure can be detected in a variety of ways. Conceptually, these failures are learned via either "interrupt"-driven events or a "polling" mechanism. Some transmission media are good at being interrupt event-driven. For example, when the protocol detects a SONET/SDH error, a message is sent up the control plane path to notify the rest of the router of the condition. Ethernet media, with no built-in failure detection capabilities, are sometimes left to be polled periodically. In this scenario, if a failure happens between polls, it is not detected until the next polling interval.

BFD

Bidirectional Forwarding Detection is a simple forwarding detection protocol that can detect failures from OSI Layer 4 and below. It does this by sending rapid UDP hello packets between two endpoints. These are typically adjacent IGP routing neighbors, but BFD can be extended for use in nearly any conceivable application. Today's implementations can provide failure response times in the 100 to 120ms range. This rate is improving over time and ultimately aims to provide 50ms failover times.

BFD and Ethernet

One of the most obvious uses of BFD is to provide failure detection for Ethernet media, which have no such inherent mechanism. Without BFD, an IGP adjacency running over an Ethernet link that experiences a failure would take anywhere from seconds to minutes to detect, depending on the timer values. OSPF, by default, would require a loss of three hellos sent at ten-second intervals before flagging a neighbor as down. This would trigger a new OSPF calculation to converge around the failed link, giving a failure time of over 30 seconds. Although these timers can be changed, there are architectural limits to how fast this mechanism can work. It is possible to increase the IGP hello rates enough to detect a failure in about 3 seconds with OSPF and 1 second with IS-IS, but this places a significant amount of strain on the control plane and typically is avoided. Most common configurations yield standard IGP detection times of 5 to 40 seconds. Using BFD over this same link with a sufficient per-second rate of BFD packets over the link can instead detect the failure in 100 to 120ms.

If BFD functionality (which is being constantly developed in its own IETF working group)[7] were to be enabled on the Ethernet, DSLAM, BRAS, and associated elements, rapid failover times could be achieved on these currently vulnerable points.

BFD for MPLS LSPs

BFD in its basic form is used primarily as a hop-by-hop failure detection mechanism. A typical core network also requires end-to-end protection. This can be done by extending a BFD session between LSP endpoints and sending rapid hello packets across the entire end-to-end path. Further details can be found in the IETF working group, because the specification was still being worked on at the time of writing.

This section uses several acronyms and terms; they are explained in Table 3.2.

Table 3.2 Summary of Core Protocols

Protocol or Feature	Meaning
BFD	Bidirectional Forwarding Detection. A lightweight protocol that sends UDP hello packets between two IP addresses. It is used to check a link's integrity. If a router misses keepalive packets from a remote host, it can consider the link down and can reroute traffic.
Fast reroute	A feature that involves presignaling an alternative path for an RSVP-TE LSP so that, if the primary "protected" path fails, traffic can be switched to the standby path with SONET-like speed.

continues

[7] http://www.ietf.org/html.charters/bfd-charter.html

Table 3.2 continued

Protocol or Feature	Meaning
IGP	Interior Gateway Protocol. The internal routing protocol in a network that distributes interface and loopback routes through the service provider domain. The two widespread protocols are IS-IS and OSPF. Both can inter-operate with RSVP using *traffic engineering extensions.*
LDP	Label Distribution Protocol. Used to signal LSPs in an MPLS network. Creating constraints in the LSP is possible using CR-LDP, but generally paths follow the IGP.
MPLS	Multiprotocol Label Switching. A way of encapsulating and sending any type of data through a network. It uses the concept of an MPLS label to tell routers where to send the packet.
RSVP-TE	Resource Reservation Protocol with Traffic Engineering extensions. Another signaling protocol for LSPs. Can ask the network to reserve bandwidth for the LSP, set constraints on how it is routed, and use link protection.

Integrating Core Protocols with Multicast

The preceding section dealt with the protocols that are used in the core to keep the transport layer in good shape—rapid link failure detection and fast reroute. This section covers the higher-layer protocols and functionality, such as PIM and RPs to provide high-availability multicast signaling. A pure IPv4 multicast core can use either PIM-SSM or PIM-ASM. PIM-ASM requires deploying RPs, so to make this function highly available to the rest of the network, anycast RP is deployed in conjunction with MSDP. Now if one RP in the network goes out of service (planned or unplanned), another RP can take over the role of mapping sources and receivers. Note that in the event of an RP failure, IPTV sessions that are already established between sources and receivers are unaffected. Only new IPTV sessions that need the use of the RP are affected until the network converges. PIM-SSM does not need the machinery of the RP, because the mapping function is done either by the BNG doing PIM-SSM group mapping or IGMPv3 from the STB. Although this might seem elegant at first glance, there is a disadvantage to not having an RP. With PIM-ASM, if a source stops transmitting, the RP eventually deletes this source address (also called [S,G]) from the list of valid sources for the group and switches to a different source for the same group. Normally such a reconvergence takes several seconds while the PIM state times out and works around the failure. This requires that only one media server transmit at one time; otherwise, interleaved streams would result. This allows the network to follow the multicast forwarding state (the RP Joins toward the source that is actually transmitting). With PIM-SSM using an anycast source redundancy mechanism, if one of the source streams fails but the route toward that stream is not withdrawn from the network, the tree cannot work around the failure. The hardest part of this approach is ensuring that only one server is transmitting at a time. If this problem can be solved on the video side, it may make sense just to go straight to PIM-SSM as the benefit to be gained with an RP is marginal.

As previously mentioned, PIM-SSM redundancy involves running an anycast domain and injecting the IPTV server's subnet into the IGP. Because the interested receivers are all programmed with a single source address when using PIM-SSM (with IGMPv3 or PIM-SSM mapping), if a server stops transmitting, an interested receiver cannot switch to a different stream for the same group. This is because perhaps only the stream has stopped, not any of the routers in between, so PIM Joins continue to be sent to an inactive server. A solution may be to use host BFD, which involves sending lightweight keepalives to the server to detect if it is still in the land of the "living." If the server is active, it causes the DR (the edge router connecting to the server) to insert a host route (/32) for the server into the IGP, acting as a beacon for PIM receivers to use. If the server goes down, the router withdraws the server's host route, causing the PIM receivers to send PIM traffic elsewhere, as shown in Figure 3.21.

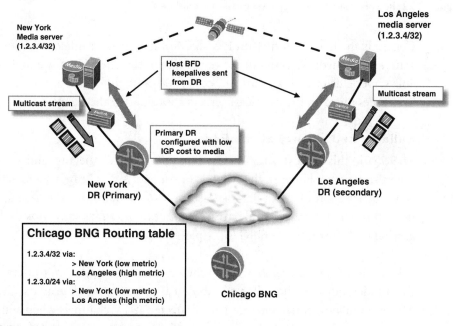

Figure 3.21 Host BFD with an active server.

Figure 3.22 shows the edge router withdrawing a route for the server based on BFD timeout.

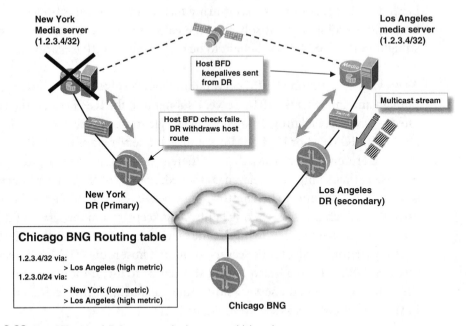

Figure 3.22 Host BFD with a failed server, causing host route withdrawal.

Generally the failure mode with PIM-SSM of having the route present for a source but a media stream not active is a rare occurrence. Usually a highly available server cluster with anycast source is good enough for current requirements. This relies more on the multicast servers coordinating the failover.

Building Redundancy at the Edge

The *edge* in this context is the BNGs, the routers they connect to, and any switching infrastructure between the two sets of routers. A BNG can be connected to a single upstream router, but in most cases, a BNG is multihomed to two upstream peers through diverse physical paths. This section provides some tips for integrating multicast into the BNG for triple-play services.

When multiple links stretch between the BNG and the upstream routers, ideally the multicast groups should be distributed as evenly as possible across the links. This is mainly to reduce the number of affected IPTV channels when a link fails. For instance, in the event of a link failure, PIM needs to re-request the groups that previously flowed across a failed link via an interface that is functioning. If the channels are spread evenly across the links, this reduces the number of channels that are affected during a failure.

If faster convergence time is required, the upstream routers can be configured with static IGMP Joins on their interfaces as well as static Joins on the BNG. Static IGMP Joins were discussed earlier in this chapter. They instruct a router to join a multicast group regardless of whether hosts are attached that are interested in receiving the group. Of course, when an interface on the BNG fails, it must resend some of the PIM Joins out a working interface and wait for the streams to be sent from the upstream direction. It is possible to have a scenario whereby the BNG is receiving the multicast groups on all interfaces, so when one fails, it can simply accept the data for the group from one of the other interfaces. How does it block the groups from all but one of the interfaces? This comes back to the RPF check, which allows only a single link to accept multicast data for a group. The downside of this solution is that it increases the bandwidth utilization on the links between the upstream routers and the BNG. A trade-off could be to create static Joins for the top handful of popular channels and leave the rest as dynamic. A benefit of using switched Gigabit Ethernet in the PoP between the upstream routers and the BNG is efficient multicast forwarding. If there is more than one BNG in a PoP, each of the broadband routers can be added to the switch domain. If they are all in the same broadcast domain, only one copy of the multicast groups needs to be sent from the upstream routers.

⬛➤ Caution: A word of caution needs to be mentioned with respect to this model concerning the PIM assert mechanism. If a broadcast domain with two core routers feeds multicast traffic to one or more edge devices (BNGs), the two core routers negotiate between themselves so that only one of them transmits onto the subnet. When one of the routers wins the assert election, the other "mutes" for a defined period (the assert timeout) and then starts transmitting again. They then reelect an assert winner, and the process continues. This means that briefly during every assert timeout, all BNGs receive two copies of the multicast streams. However, there is a much worse problem.

If a core router fails immediately after it has won an assert election, no traffic is sent by the other core router until the assert timeout is reached. The assert timers can be reduced, but that leads to more frequent duplication of packets onto the broadcast domain. Those packets must be correctly handled and, where appropriate, dropped by the BNGs. They also consume significant amounts of bandwidth (particularly in the case of IPTV channels, which average about 2 to 7Mbps each).

SUMMARY

This chapter has discussed how customers can prepare their network for double-play services that leverage their existing infrastructure, such as MPLS, Layer 2, and Layer 3 VPNs. Layer 3 VPNs can be reused to provide service isolation between different service domains. However, the architecture needs to be planned carefully so that customers can access both service domains at the same time (VoIP and Internet). Sometimes, the concept of separation using VPNs can be taken to an extreme, such that it becomes an inflexible architecture or the service boundaries become significantly blurred with route leaking. It can be easier to simply have a global routing table for all provider-hosted services, but of course this depends on the provider's network and how it anticipates building its network. Also it should be considered whether there is the expertise to maintain VPN policy. However, VPNs and the accompanying policy can be a perfectly legitimate model as long as the implications are well-known.

You also saw examples of how multicast can be transported in the core and what routing protocols can be used to set up the correct forwarding state. VPLS coupled with P2MP LSPs looks like a promising mechanism as the next step up from point-to-multipoint LSPs for multicast IPTV delivery. Vendors should start supporting this delivery method in the future as the IPTV market heats up.

Finally, a highly available multicast IPTV service is a highly desirable feature of triple-play networks, so various approaches were shown, mostly focusing on PIM-SSM anycast deployments and high availability techniques in the core. Anycast deployment has its drawbacks (such as lack of media stream failure detection in the network), but these generally are addressed by having an intelligent server cluster that can detect media stream failures.

DESIGNING A TRIPLE-PLAY ACCESS NETWORK

As the inexorable search for more and cheaper bandwidth continues apace, Ethernet Digital Subscriber Line Access Multiplexers (DSLAMs) and Access Nodes (ANs, a DSL Forum[1] term) are all the rage. They allow the platform to deliver next-generation multimedia applications over DSL technology. Thanks to faster uplinks and greater switching capacity, Ethernet DSLAMs can support speedier DSL lines as well as the triple-play services that are built on top of DSL. This chapter provides an overview of Ethernet DSLAMs and how they are deployed in service provider networks. It also explains the underlying technology and jargon and includes a section devoted to building a high-availability Broadband Network Gateway (BNG) solution.

This discussion assumes that you have some basic knowledge of DSL networks and are familiar with ATM and Ethernet technologies. The configuration examples provided in this chapter are taken from common vendor platforms and offer a basic example of how a technology can be deployed. You should use them as reference examples and not real configurations.

---

[1] http://www.dslforum.org

ETHERNET DSLAMS

Service providers are looking toward deploying enhanced multimedia services that demand greater bandwidth over digital subscriber lines. These services include gaming, video (both broadcast TV and video on demand), voice services, and greater Internet speeds. In the past, DSLAMs based on ATM technology provided DSL service to customers at the end of a copper loop. These DSLAMs were not well suited to connecting back to the core network at speeds much over OC3/STM1 levels, which posed a problem for providing higher-speed services to customers. Ethernet DSLAMs provide more upstream bandwidth at a lower cost than ATM hardware, which makes them an obvious fit to provide the incremental speed increase needed for the next generation of services.

To help you understand some terminology, BNG stands for Broadband Network Gateway. This is a general term for a router that provides broadband services to subscribers. This term was coined by the DSL Forum and is used throughout this book. Other terms commonly used are Broadband Remote Access Server (BRAS) and Broadband Service Router (BSR).

OVERVIEW OF AN ETHERNET DSLAM

The basic premise of the Ethernet DSLAM is the same as for ATM types. Subscribers enter the multiplexer from a local loop and terminate on an xDSL line card. Early versions of these line cards could connect only a few subscribers. Today, it is commonplace to see densities of 24 and 48 ports on a single line card in bigger Central Office (CO) located DSLAMs. The DSL Forum uses the terms Level 1, Level 2, and Level 3 to describe how many upstream layers of ANs a DSLAM is connected to. For example, a DSLAM that is directly connected to a BNG is a Level 1 AN. Other nodes that connect through the Level 1 DSLAM to the BNG are called Level 2 DSLAMs. Smaller DSLAMs, such as Level 2 DSLAMs[2], might have a capacity of only tens of subscribers, but this is because of their smaller sizes.

Each line card is typically connected to either a midplane or backplane, which is used as a common bus to exchange data between other cards in the chassis. As soon as a single chassis of line cards is full, further chassis can simply be added to the existing DSLAM as needed.

[2] TR 101, section 2.4

These interfaces are considered the downstream or access part of the network. The upstream is where the story gets interesting. Connected to this same chassis are one or more Ethernet line cards. These are usually Gigabit Ethernet or Fast Ethernet (vestiges of 10BASE-2 and vampire taps, surprisingly, are not found in current vendor brochures) and connect the DSLAM to the aggregation network. For redundancy, these uplink cards can be configured in a 1+1 standby mode. If the link is cut on one card or port (detected by loss of light), the other takes over the frame-forwarding duties.

An upgrade to an Ethernet DSLAM does not necessarily mean that the customer has to change any configuration on its side. Such a procedure can be relatively transparent if the DSL type (ADSL, ADSL2, ADSL2+) and protocol on the local loop are not changed during the upgrade.

SUBTENDED DSLAMs

An entire DSLAM does not need to be located within a single CO. Individual chassis (shelves) can also function as switches and enable multiple chassis to be chained together to increase network coverage. The two models of subtended DSLAMs are the daisy-chained model and the hub-and-spoke approach.

Daisy-Chained DSLAMs

Imagine the following scenario: a medium-sized town needs three DSLAM shelves to satiate DSL subscriber demand. One of the DSLAM shelves, which is considered the master shelf, is linked via long-haul (LH) fiber-optic transmission to the closest metropolitan BNG hub. To increase network coverage, a neighboring town needs its own DSLAM. Because the area is much smaller, it might not make sense to run a dedicated link from this DSLAM back to the metropolitan BNG hub. This is because dedicated transmission capacity from the small rural areas direct to the metropolitan hub is expensive, both in terms of transmission links and the cost of interfaces. Instead, the shelf is daisy-chained to the larger neighboring DSLAM, providing an incremental multiplexing function at the edge of the network before being trunked to the BNG.

The daisy-chaining approach increases the reach of coverage while keeping transmission and interface costs lower, but there are downsides to consider.

Imagine that as many as seven shelves are daisy-chained together. Managing the bandwidth for each shelf at each hop in the chain becomes an onerous task by having so many points to provision as well as inspect when fault finding. As management tools such as Ethernet OAM[3] mature, the operating expenses (OpEx) would theoretically decrease. Keeping the bandwidth the same between daisy-chained shelves (that is, all links are Gigabit Ethernet) can simplify things in the long run. Having too many daisy-chained shelves can increase the number of single points of failure, thus increasing Mean Time between Failures (MTBF) figures.

The daisy-chaining architecture is most suitable in rural areas where the distances between nodes are substantial. Figure 4.1 shows an example of daisy-chained DSLAM shelves.

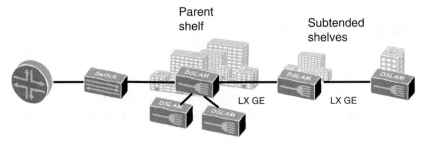

Figure 4.1 Daisy-chained DSLAMs.

Hub-and-Spoke DSLAMs

Hub-and-spoke subtending is the same concept as in other areas of data networking. Several *spoke* DSLAMs connect back to a master, or *hub*, which is then connected to the BNG via an aggregation network. In this topology, the transmission paths between the spoke and a hub shelf may often be duplicated in some cable stretches, which increases costs. However, in urban and metropolitan areas (where hub-and-spoke is normally used), the density of fiber-optic distribution networks is a lot higher than in rural areas. This means that duplication of transmission resources does not factor into the pricing equation as much as with rural builds.

Two benefits become apparent with this particular model. The number of network elements between subtended shelves and BNGs has been cut, reducing the

[3] IEEE 802.1ag

network's complexity. This is apparent in terms of both provisioning (subscriber circuits and aggregate paths) and troubleshooting. In a daisy-chained environment with limited inter-nodal bandwidth, it can be an ongoing challenge to provide adequate aggregate throughput for customers at each shelf. In the hub-and-spoke model, the VLAN architecture is reasonably flexible, because the hub has fewer sibling devices to manage. The VLAN models for a hub-and-spoke architecture are either stacked VLANs per shelf or a more flat VLAN structure across all the nodes. With a daisy-chained model, often a dedicated path needs to be provisioned to each shelf.

Figure 4.2 shows the hub-and-spoke approach, which the DSL Forum calls dual-facility subtending.

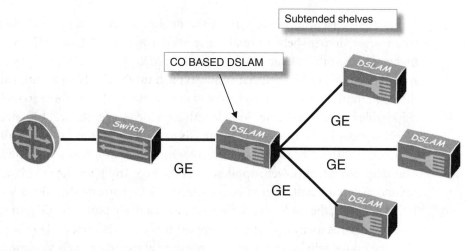

Figure 4.2 Hub-and-spoke DSLAM subtending.

OTHER TRANSPORT MODELS

The current rage is to build out fiber-optic transmission networks to new residential, commercial, and industrial zones and run a more localized copper distribution network. Smaller DSLAMs are installed in remote cabinets to service customers in that area.

In most cases, fiber was rolled out to remote locations before DSL networks gained popularity—or even existed. Unfortunately, the sword of Damocles was dangling above the rollout of the fiber runs. Because ADSL requires an analog line to carry data frequencies from 25kHz and 1.1MHz between the modem and DSLAM, having a piece of glass in the middle that can only natively transport digital signals prevented analog ADSL frequencies from sharing the same cable. Therefore, a way had to be found to provide ADSL to customers at the tail end of a fiber path. The solution was to install mini DSLAMs located closer to customers than traditional CO-based ones.

As a side note, in many parts of the world, analog and digital pair-gain devices were used to deploy multiple voice lines over a single copper pair where growth had outstripped available copper. Arguably, digital pair gain systems were the first instances of DSL technology, but they prevented the use of ADSL on the customer lines they served.

It may seem anachronistic to continue to deploy DSLAMs in remote cabinets when larger, denser shelves usually have lower costs per DSL port. However, higher-bandwidth DSL technologies, such as ADSL2, ADSL2+, and VDSL, require the node to be deployed closer to the household. Although improvements in framing overhead, codecs, and power usage all contribute to higher achievable bit rates, a shorter loop length is needed to get the real benefit of the newer standards. To have a smaller chassis footprint that can fit into roadside cabinets, features that are present in larger models are sometimes omitted. For example, redundant power supplies, secondary control plane line cards, and redundant uplink paths might be eliminated, thus reducing the node's overall reliability. Also, the nodes are designed to be relatively plug-and-play, so they may not have as many operational support tools as larger nodes. On the plus side, the nodes' reliability against environmental elements, such as snow, storms, and floods, is much better than traditional CO-based devices. Another benefit is due to the number of subscribers terminated on a Level 2 or 3 DSLAM being much lower. The impact of an outage is not as severe as that at Level 1 DSLAM, which could potentially affect hundreds of households and businesses.

DSLAM AGGREGATION

As mentioned earlier, one of the advantages of moving to an Ethernet architecture is to increase the bandwidth that can be provided to the DSLAM and consequently to customers. Ethernet versions are often cheaper than ATM versions because of the cheaper Ethernet switch fabric and cheaper commoditized Ethernet hardware. This has a flow-on effect to the aggregation network because the BNG as well because the pieces that make up the aggregation network are also Ethernet-based (as opposed to bridging Ethernet over an ATM platform). This results in lower interface costs and reduced data overheads. Designing the ideal aggregation network is not a simple task; it can involve complex cost-modeling techniques. This section acquaints you with the concepts and architectures associated with access networks, stretching from the DSLAM up to the BNG. Both incumbent service providers and new entrants to the market can use the information presented here during network design and deployment.

Linking the DSLAM with a bastion of bandwidth to the BNG is no straightforward task. Devising a cost-efficient way of shipping data between the DSLAM and BNG can be built on several layers of transport network. Traditional DWDM, CWDM, or dark fiber deployed with or without a SDH/SONET overlay are some options for the physical transport layer. If the price point of connecting DSLAMs directly to a BNG is not very good (the per-port cost on the BNG might be unpalatable), reusing an MPLS platform to aggregate a network of DSLAMs can provide some cost savings. Because of MPLS' capability to be protocol agnostic, it is well suited to transport different Layer 2 and Layer 3 technologies between Provider Edge (PE) routers. This lets BNGs be centralized and relay on a larger distribution of MPLS nodes to do the aggregation work. This chapter assumes that you are familiar with the basics of MPLS switching. To obtain a good understanding of MPLS, two highly recommended titles are *MPLS and VPN architectures*[4] and *MPLS-Enabled Applications*.[5]

PSEUDOWIRES

A pseudowire is a way of sending Layer 2 services such as Ethernet, Frame Relay, and ATM across a Packet-Switched Network (PSN). This section discusses MPLS-based PSNs. GRE and L2TP tunnels are also suitable PSNs for pseudowire transport; they are described in their respective IETF drafts. In the context of building a triple-play network, pseudowires are used in conjunction with an

---

[4] *MPLS and VPN Architectures*, Ivan Pepelnjak and Jim Guichard, Cisco Press
[5] *MPLS-Enabled Applications*, Ina Minei and Julian Lucek, John Wiley & Sons

MPLS network to transport Ethernet data from a DSLAM across an MPLS network to one or more BNGs. This section describes how a pseudowire circuit functions and then compares the two competing versions of pseudowires that have been deployed.

There are many monikers for a pseudowire service. Virtual Private Wire Service (VPWS) is a term defined in the IETF as the service of providing Layer 2 point-to-point connectivity.[6] Pseudowire Emulation Edge to Edge (PWE3) is an IETF term that refers to how Protocol Data Units (PDUs) are packaged or encapsulated before being transported over the network.[7] Terms from the vendor space are the Cisco AToM service (Any Transport over MPLS), which refers to both encapsulation and signaling for point-to-point circuits. A Circuit Cross Connect (CCC) is an early, proprietary point-to-point Layer 2 technology from Juniper Networks. Layer 2 VPNs (L2VPNs) and Layer 2 circuits are the two additional types of Layer 2 point-to-point services from Juniper Networks. In this chapter, unless otherwise mentioned, L2VPN always refers to a pseudowire service.

An advantage of MPLS networks is that they are protocol-agnostic. After a packet is encapsulated in an MPLS header, all the internal routers care about is switching packets based on a label, regardless of the underlying payload. This enables Layer 2 protocols, such as Ethernet, to be transparently transported over a routed domain. A long-standing joke in telecommunications circles is that there is no shortage of ways to build a new network to emulate legacy networks. An example is using a legacy Time-Division Multiplexing (TDM) network to build a shiny new MPLS network, only to emulate the original TDM network that was there in the first place.

The reason for introducing the context of pseudowires, MPLS, and broadband networks together is that sometimes the distribution of BNGs is not wide enough to connect every DSLAM in the network directly, or even via a metro-Ethernet network, to a BNG. The MPLS network can be used as Layer 2 backhaul instead of, or in conjunction with, an Ethernet aggregation network. One downside to this approach is due to all traffic being transported at Layer 2 across the

---

[6] IETF Layer 2 VPN Working group, http://www.ietf.org/html.charters/l2vpn-charter.html

[7] IETF Pseudo Wire Emulation Edge to Edge Working Group, http://www.ietf.org/html.charers/pwe3-charter.html

network to and from the BNG. This means devices at each end need to mark the Layer 2 frames before sending across the network so that correct QoS can be ensured. One of the benefits of being able to terminate traffic at the BNG as early as possible is that it allows traffic to be more effectively managed at Layer 3; the network adds more value rather than being a simple bit pipe.

Figure 4.3 shows a simple MPLS network consisting of two provider edge (PE) routers (Dunedin and Wellington) linked through a network of provider (P) routers. Router Dunedin is connected to the DSLAM via a switch. The DSLAM imposes a VLAN tag of 100 on all Ethernet frames that it sends to the DSLAM and then shunts them off to the PE router. This router has a subinterface on its Gigabit Ethernet port on which the frames are received. To send the frames across the MPLS network to the BNG, a pseudowire circuit needs to be created between Dunedin and Wellington. The same also happens in the reverse direction. When the BNG has to send traffic back to a subscriber connected to the DSLAM, router Wellington forwards these frames across the pseudowire to router Dunedin. In the diagram, the MAC address of "FF" is used as a short form for the all-ones broadcast MAC address.

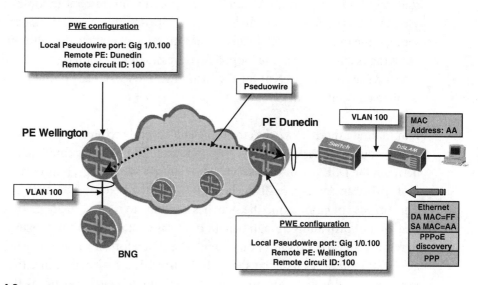

Figure 4.3 Overview of a pseudowire circuit.

Technology Note: PE and P Routers

A provider edge (PE) router is a router at the edge of an MPLS network that interfaces with the customer edge (CE) on the external side, and provider (P) routers on the core network side. Of course, CE routers do not have to be end customers. The term can be used for any device that connects to a PE, such as the service provider DSLAM shown in Figure 4.3. These terms are defined in RFC 2547.

Figure 4.3 shows a VLAN ID of 100 being transported across the network. This would be the case with a service VLAN approach (described in the section "VLAN Architectures: N:1 or Service VLANs"). An equally possible approach is if a 1:1 VLAN structure (described in the section "Provider VLAN Architectures: 1:1 and Multicast VLANs") is used, VLAN 100 (shown in the figure) could be a stacked VLAN of 100. For the sake of simplicity, any descriptions in this section can refer to either VLAN architecture unless otherwise noted.

It is important to note here that a PWE3 circuit exists between an interface on one router and another interface on a different router (or sometimes the same router, but this isn't strictly MPLS PWE3). A common misconception is that a pseudowire is built between the loopback addresses of two routers. Later, when some of the more technical details are explained, you will see that although the signaling occurs between the loopback addresses of two routers, entry and exit interfaces need to be present for the pseudowire to exist. Each of these interfaces is called an Attachment Circuit (AC).

Eliminating Ethernet switches from the end-to-end architecture is a popular activity during times of network consolidation. The switches could be those between the DSLAM and the service provider IP/MPLS edge, but more commonly they are large-capacity switches between the BNG and the IP/MPLS edge. The purpose of eliminating the switches could be to remove aggregation devices that are not providing enough benefit in terms of statistical multiplexing or just to remove an extra point of potential failure. Therefore, if there is an MPLS aggregation network like that shown in Figure 4.3, it may make sense to run pseudowires directly to the BNG and thus eliminate switches between the BNG and its directly connected PE. Unfortunately, at the time of writing, it is not a common feature in BNGs to be able to terminate both a Layer 2 VPN/pseudowire and PPPoE or DHCP subscribers within that VPN/pseudowire without the use of an external loopback cable. This feature is being talked about in some circles and will no doubt appear as a router feature in due course. But in most cases, integrating pseudowires with a BNG means some kind of VLAN trunking for decoupling the underlying data from the transport mechanism.

As mentioned, a PWE3 is a point-to-point circuit built between two ACs. The PE and P routers are not concerned with the payload carried in the MPLS packet (with the exception of the ultimate PE, which has to send it out in its native Ethernet format). Because these routers do not care about switching Ethernet based on MAC addresses, it is more scalable in the control plane compared to VPLS (described next). Using a pseudowire means that a large table of MAC addresses does not have to be maintained on each router. Also, a PE does not need to implement complex functions to run a PWE3 service because the PEs simply encapsulate Ethernet frames into a PDU and send them out a Layer 2 VPN tunnel. Figure 4.4 illustrates how routers interact with MAC addresses when forwarding frames across a pseudowire circuit.

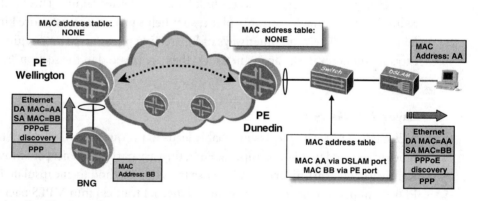

Figure 4.4 Pseudowire MAC addresses.

As with any network of point-to-point circuits, managing them can be a hassle. For example, if 100 DSLAMs are aggregated to a single BNG, 200 point-to-point endpoints need to be managed at the network edges, as well as 100 pseudowires between individual DSLAMs' PEs and the BNG's PE. Of course, a similar problem also existed with backhauling DSLAMs over an ATM network, because each DSLAM would be represented by just as many Permanent Virtual Paths (PVPs).

The difference is that an ATM network consists of homogeneous parts—all ATM switches that interface directly with the DSLAM and BSR. A VLAN can span heterogeneous switching domains—Ethernet switches and MPLS pseudowires—so there is at least one extra switching domain to provision in the process. Smart OSS systems can mitigate this problem, but it costs extra to test, deploy, and maintain such capability in the OSS systems.

One of the limitations of PWE3 circuits is redundancy. Because a circuit is associated with attachment circuit interfaces, if one of the ports fails on either end of the link, or a PE fails, the circuit breaks, and a reprovision is required to restore it to service. Nonetheless, vendors have created redundancy features for both types of pseudowires (Martini and Kompella VPNs). However, these are both redundancy features in the signaling plane. Of course, a router should also have good internal redundancy in case of control plane failure. This seems intuitive enough, so why mention it? Here is where the benefits of VPLS can help. A VPLS circuit can be set up in a point-to-multipoint fashion between the DSLAM PE and two other PE routers. These two routers can then connect to two separate BNGs, thus providing protection against access link failure or router failure. This kind of redundancy is in the forwarding plane, so it helps protect against more kinds of failure modes. There are other ways of buttressing point-to-point circuits with extra redundancy in the access network; they are covered in the section "Aggregation Network."

Layer 2 VPNs

A discussion of Layer 2 VPNs invariably leads to the question of which of the two types to use—Martini or Kompella. First, the easy part—the encapsulation. Both Kompella and Martini Layer 2 VPNs use the same method to encapsulate Layer 2 PDUs (in this context, think of them as Ethernet frames) into MPLS packets before transmission across the network. Various IETF drafts define the low-level requirements of encapsulating the frames in MPLS packets,[8] but the generalities are captured in draft-martini-l2circui-encaps-mpls. These drafts are all based on a common PWE3 requirements document—RFC 3916.[9]

---

[8] draft-ietf-pwe3-atm-encap for ATM encapsulation, draft-ietf-pwe3-ethernet-encap for Ethernet encapsulation

[9] http://www.ietf.org/rfc/rfc3916.txt

Before moving on to the differences between the two types of VPNs, you need to know some basic MPLS terms of reference before becoming one of the MPLS Layer 2 cognoscente. Figure 4.5 shows a base tunnel (also called an LSP) between Auckland and Dunedin. This LSP is the path that MPLS packets take when any data need to be transmitted between the two PEs. Stacked on top of this tunnel are all the services (including Layer 2 VPNs) that are run over MPLS. This stacking functionality is achieved by pushing multiple labels onto an MPLS packet. The outermost label in the stack defines the base tunnel, which is of interest only to the core routers (and sometimes the ultimate or last router in the path) that switch packets from one interface to the next. The routers along the path swap the outermost label as they push the packet along the path. For example, Hamilton swaps label 1011 with label 1060 as it forwards the packet along the path. The final PE router is usually interested in only the lowermost label (100 in the example), which tells it what service (or, in this case, pseudowire) the MPLS payload refers to.

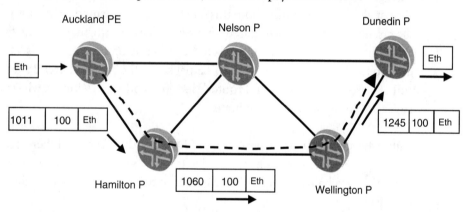

Figure 4.5 Basic MPLS routing.

With Layer 2 VPNs, in between the link-layer Ethernet header (not the underlying payload—Ethernet in the figure) and MPLS headers of the MPLS packet, an optional *control word* can be present to communicate control information to the other end of the circuit. It is used in the following cases:

- Sequencing of Layer 2 PDUs
- Padding the MPLS payload (if the underlying transport requires it)
- Control bits from the original Layer 2 need to be transmitted along with the packet

A control word can carry some QoS-like information from the original frame (for example, DE, BECN, FECN for Frame Relay or CLP for ATM). However, the PDU's QoS priority information is reflected in the MPLS EXP field as it's transmitted across the network. The EXP field is a 3-bit field in the MPLS header that is used in a similar way that ToS on an IP packet is used, or 802.1P on an Ethernet header. It reflects the priority of the underlying packet.

Martini

Martini Layer 2 VPNs are defined in draft-martini-l2circuit-trans-mpls. Label Distribution Protocol (LDP[10]) is used to signal the VPN service that is stacked on top of the base tunnel. The draft does not make any assumptions about what signaling should be used for the base LSP. The Martini draft specifies that the label exchange mechanism for the Layer 2 VPN (the innermost, or bottom label in the label stack) can be statically configured or dynamic, using LDP. However, LDP is almost always used to distribute this label binding information. At both ends of the circuit, the PEs are configured with two pieces of information. The first is the VC identifier (VC ID), which needs to be the same on each end. This VC ID is used to tie the inner label of the MPLS packet to the correct Layer 2 Martini circuit. The second is the far end router's loopback address, which is where the Layer 2 VPN/pseudowire terminates.

Figure 4.6 shows the peers performing LDP auto-discovery and then creating targeted sessions with each other. After the targeted sessions have been established, the routers exchange labels with each other to bring up the mesh of LSPs between the PEs.

---

[10] http://www.ietf.org/rfc/rfc3036.html

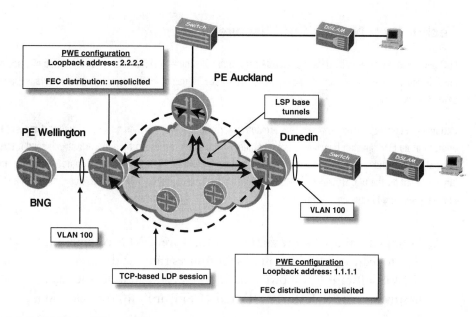

Figure 4.6 Establishing an LDP network.

After the LSP mesh has been built, a Martini circuit is established between two PEs. The configuration on each router specifies the local interface that the circuit goes from, its VC ID, and the destination router, as shown in Figure 4.7.

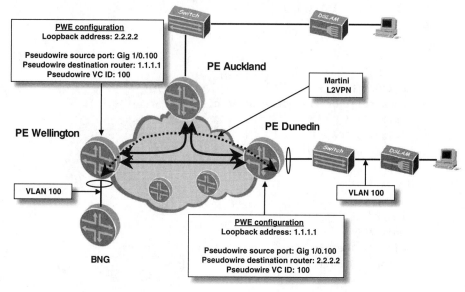

Figure 4.7 Establishing an LDP-based pseduowire.

Technology Note: LDP Discovery

LDP peers can automatically detect each other through a discovery mechanism. The two types of discovery mechanisms are basic discovery, which is used to detect LDP peers on directly connected interfaces, and extended discovery.

Extended discovery is used for peers that are not directly connected. As soon as an LDP router discovers the IP address of an LDP speaker based on announcements from other routers in the network, it can send a targeted unicast hello to the router with which it wants to make a session. In this way, peers do not have to be manually specified on the CLI. However, if MD5 authentication is required on TCP LDP sessions, peers should be manually specified in the configuration.

Listings 4.1 and 4.2 show sample Martini Layer 2 VPN configurations between the Dunedin and Wellington PEs for routers running the Juniper Networks JUNOS software. Not shown is basic router configuration, such as security filters, hostnames, and so forth, nor the IGP (OSPF or IS-IS) configuration.

Listing 4.1 Sample Juniper JUNOS Configuration—Dunedin PE

```
interfaces {
 lo0 {
  unit 0 {
   family inet {
     address 1.1.1.1/32;
   }
  }
 }

 ge-1/0/0 {
  encapsulation extended-vlan-ccc;
  unit 100 {
   vlan-id 100;
   encapsulation vlan-ccc;
  }
 }

 so-0/0/1 {
  unit 0 {
   family inet {
     address 66.1.1.1/31;
```

```
      }
      family mpls;
     }
    }
   }

   protocols {
    mpls {
     interface so-0/0/1.0;
    }

    ldp {
     interface so-0/0/1.0;
     interface lo0.0;
    }

    l2circuit {
      neighbor 2.2.2.2 {
        interface ge-1/0/0.100 {
          description "subinterface to Dunedin DSLAM";
          mtu 1500;
          virtual-circuit-id 100;
        }
       }
      }
     }
```

Listing 4.2 Sample Juniper JUNOS Configuration—Wellington PE

```
     interfaces {
      lo0 {
        unit 0 {
         family inet {
           address 2.2.2.2/32;
         }
        }
       }

      ge-1/0/0 {
       encapsulation extended-vlan-ccc;
       unit 100 {
        vlan-id 100;
        encapsulation vlan-ccc;
```

Listing 4.2   continued

```
      }
     }

    so-0/0/1 {
     unit 0 {
      family inet {
       address 60.1.1.1/31;
      }
      family mpls;
     }
    }
   }


    protocols {
     ldp {
      interface so-0/0/1.0;
      interface lo0.0;
     }

     mpls {
      interface so-0/0/1.0
     }

     l2circuit {
       neighbor 1.1.1.1 {
        interface ge-1/0/0.100 {
         description "subinterface to BNG - Dunedin DSLAM";
         mtu 1500;
         virtual-circuit-id 100;
        }
       }
      }
     }
```

Listings 4.3 and 4.4 show sample Martini Layer 2 VPN (AToM) configurations between the Dunedin and Wellington PEs, but for Cisco IOS. Again, the basic router and IGP configurations are not shown.

Listing 4.3 Sample Cisco IOS Configuration—Dunedin PE

```
mpls ldp discovery targeted-hello accept
mpls label protocol ldp
mpls ldp router-id loopback0 force

interface loopback 0
 ip address 1.1.1.1 255.255.255.255

interface GigabitEthernet 1/0/0.100
 encapsulation dot1q 100
 description "subinterface to Dunedin DSLAM"
 mpls l2transport route 2.2.2.2 100

interface pos 0/0/1
 ip address 66.1.1.1 255.255.255.254
 mpls label protocol ldp
 mpls ip
```

Listing 4.4 Sample Cisco IOS Configuration—Wellington PE

```
mpls ldp discovery targeted-hello accept
mpls label protocol ldp
mpls ldp router-id loopback0 force

interface loopback 0
 ip address 2.2.2.2 255.255.255.255

interface GigabitEthernet 1/0/0.100
 description "subinterface to BNG - Dunedin DSLAM"
 encapsulation dot1q 100
 mpls l2transport route 1.1.1.1 100

interface pos 0/0/1
 ip address 60.1.1.1 255.255.255.254
 mpls label protocol ldp
 mpls ip
```

Kompella

Kompella Layer 2 VPNs are defined in draft-kompella-l2vpn-l2vpn. Instead of using LDP to distribute the Layer 2 circuit information, Kompella Layer 2 VPNs use BGP. The draft does not specify any assumptions about how the base tunnel is signaled—it could be with LDP or RSVP. When an AC is provisioned on a PE, the details are sent to other PEs using Multiprotocol BGP (MBGP) Network Layer Reachability Information (NLRI). A similar process occurs at the far-end PE. As soon as both routers have sufficient protocol information, the circuit can be brought up.

Technology Note: NLRI

NLRI is the name of a field in a BGP message that contains routing information that is sent to other BGP routers. An NLRI field can be extended to carry more than just IPv4 routing information. For instance, Kompella VPN routing information is carried in a new set of NLRIs that are defined in the draft.

LDP uses a similar mechanism to support additional protocols, such as Layer 2 VPN routing information. LDP has been extended to add a new type of Forwarding Equivalence Class (FEC) field to distribute information about the Martini circuit.

Kompella includes a mechanism called autodiscovery. It allows PEs to send unsolicited Layer 2 routing information about their locally connected ACs to MBGP peers without having to specify the remote end of the circuit. For example, if a PE router had to create several point-to-point paths between an attached device and several other PEs, it would simply send out MBGP NLRIs to all its other MBGP peers to inform them of the ACs. When other PEs receive the corresponding BGP NLRIs for the other ends of their Layer 2 circuits, they then have enough information to be able to build the Layer 2 VPNs across the network.

If a PE router receives Layer 2 VPN routing information but doesn't have any CEs connected that are members of that VPN, it can discard the incoming BGP messages to save resources. An alternative approach commonly used nowadays is a technique called route refresh. If a router changes its routing policy or adds a VPN for which it needs to receive routes from other routers, it can request that other routers resend their routes.

Figure 4.8 shows base tunnels being established between Dunedin, Auckland, and Wellington using RSVP. These tunnels establish a bidirectional communication path that can be used to add MPLS services. MBGP sessions with Layer 2 VPN capability are established between the PEs so that all the peers can exchange information about their locally connected ACs.

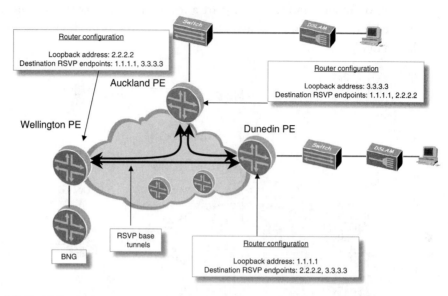

Figure 4.8 Establishing base tunnels in preparation for Kompella-draft Layer 2 VPNs.

A PE sends a route target, a site ID, and a block of labels for all ACs to other BGP peers. The site ID is an identifier that groups all the circuits for a given CE. These messages are exchanged as shown in Figure 4.9.

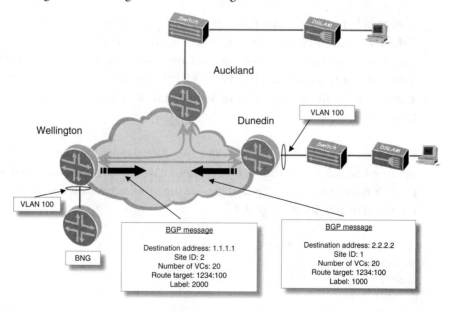

Figure 4.9 Exchanging Kompella-draft Layer 2 VPN BGP messages.

Routers Wellington and Dunedin share a common route target. They process the received routing information for the Layer 2 VPN and bring up the circuit as shown in Figure 4.10.

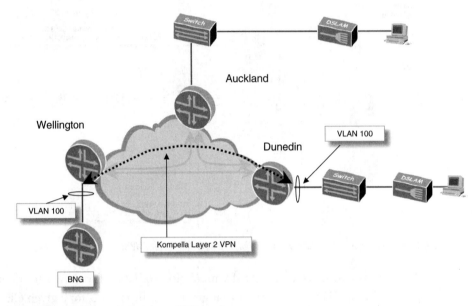

Figure 4.10 Establishing a Kompella-draft Layer 2 VPN circuit.

Kompella Layer 2 VPNs have several analogs to RFC 4864 (formerly RFC 2547bis) Layer 3 VPNs in terms of the signaling plane. First, all ACs (or, in this case, DSLAMs) that are part of a single Layer 2 domain use a route target to group links under a single VPN. Layer 3 VPNs also use the same concept of grouping by route target. The same signaling protocol—BGP—is also used in Layer 3 VPNs.

Listings 4.5 and 4.6 show a Kompella Layer 2 VPN circuit between two PEs. Because Cisco does not support this type of Layer 2 transport, only Juniper JUNOS is shown. The configurations use the same network topology that was used for Listings 4.1 through 4.4.

Listing 4.5 Sample Juniper JUNOS Configuration—Dunedin PE

```
interfaces {
  lo0 {
    unit 0 {
      family inet {
```

```
          address 1.1.1.1/32;
      }
    }
  }

ge-1/0/0 {
 encapsulation extended-vlan-ccc;
 unit 100 {
  vlan-id 100;
  encapsulation vlan-ccc;
 }
}
so-0/0/1 {
 unit 0 {
  family inet {
   address 66.1.1.1/31;
  }
  family mpls;
 }
}
}

protocols {
 bgp {
  group ibgp {
   peer-as 1234;
   type internal;
   family l2vpn;
   local-address 1.1.1.1;
   neighbor 2.2.2.2 {
   }
  }
 }

mpls {
   label-switched-path dunedin-wellington {
    to 2.2.2.2;
    primary dunedin-wellington;
   }

  path dunedin-wellington;
  interface so-0/0/1.0;
```

Listing 4.5 continued

```
    }

    rsvp {
       interface so-0/0/1.0;
     }
    }

    routing-instances {
     to-wellington {
      instance-type l2vpn;
      interface ge-1/0/0.100;
      route-distinguisher 1234:100;
      vrf-target 1234:100;
      protocols {
       l2vpn {
        site dunedin-dslam {
         site-id 1;
         interface ge-1/0/0.100 {
          remote-site-id 2;
          description "L2VPN to Wellington BNG";
         }
        }
       }
      }
     }
    }
```

Listing 4.6 Sample Juniper JUNOS Configuration—Wellington PE

```
    interfaces {
     lo0 {
       unit 0 {
        family inet {
          address 2.2.2.2/32;
        }
       }
      }

     ge-1/0/0 {
      encapsulation extended-vlan-ccc;
```

```
    unit 100 {
     vlan-id 100;
     encapsulation vlan-ccc;
    }
   }
   so-0/0/1 {
    unit 0 {
     family inet {
      address 66.1.1.1/31;
     }
     family mpls;
    }
  }
  protocols {
   bgp {
    group ibgp {
     peer-as 1234;
     type internal;
     family l2vpn;
     local-address 2.2.2.2;
     neighbor 1.1.1.1 {
     }
    }
   }

  mpls {
     label-switched-path dunedin-wellington {
      to 1.1.1.1;
      primary dunedin-wellington;
     }
    path dunedin-wellington;
    interface so-0/0/1.0;
   }

   rsvp {
    interface so-0/0/1.0 {
   }
  }

  routing-instances {
   bng-transport {
    instance-type l2vpn;
```

Listing 4.6 continued

```
    interface ge-0/0/1.100;
    route-distinguisher 1234:100;
    vrf-target 1234:100;
      protocols {
        l2vpn {
          site wellington-bng {
            site-id 2;
            interface ge-0/0/1.100 {
              remote-site-id 1;
              description "L2VPN to Dunedin DSLAM";
            }
          }
        }
      }
    }
}
```

Martini or Kompella?

Understanding the mechanics of how the two Layer 2 VPN methods work is useful, but scalability, manageability, and lessons from deployment are of most value in deciding which version to use. Luckily, choosing one over the other does not restrict the protocols that can be carried over the VPN. Both use the same method to encapsulate the Layer 2 payload before it is sent over the pseudowire circuit.

BASE TUNNEL SIGNALING   There is no difference between the two drafts in terms of base tunnel signaling. In terms of service signaling, a Kompella VPN requires BGP to signal circuit information. So if a service provider is running only LDP and does not require BGP (or does not use it on Layer 2 VPN PE routers), deploying Martini circuits means that there is only one protocol to manage. This is a likely scenario if PE routers are not running Layer 3 VPNs. However, if such capability is required in the future, BGP would need to be used as a signaling protocol anyway, so the point becomes moot.

LABEL SIGNALING   Because Martini circuits use LDP for VC label signaling, the protocol can establish targeted sessions to other administrative domains. BGP has the notion of AS boundaries, which requires a different approach. Kompella

VPNs require establishing interprovider VPNs when a Layer 2 circuit needs to cross provider boundaries. The flexibility of LDP in crossing administrative boundaries can be a boon for provisioning and operational groups. At the same time, it can cause hand-wringing for service providers because it limits control over network borders in terms of LDP messages. It is possible to configure LDP filters on some routers. However, the number of policy knobs that are available to tweak is significantly fewer than for BGP.

SCALING PROPERTIES IN THE CORE   Both solutions have similar scaling properties in the core because P routers do not contain any routing information for edge services such as Layer 2 VPNs. Routing information for Martini-draft circuits is carried over TCP-based LDP sessions between PEs, and Kompella VPNs use BGP, which is also over TCP. This means that P routers need to maintain state only for the base tunnels.

VPN SCALING PROPERTIES   Kompella has a nice scaling property for VPNs with large Layer 2 meshes because a CE and all its ACs are announced as a block of labels rather than as a discrete label for each circuit. This reduces the amount of message passing between routers and helps efficient label provisioning on routers somewhat. If a PE needs another set of labels after it has burned through the initial block for a CE, the PE issues another block of labels for future circuit additions.

RSVP VERSUS LDP   It is common for service providers that deploy Kompella VPNs to also deploy RSVP as the signaling protocol for base tunnels between PEs. However, this need not always be the case. Some large service providers choose to run LDP as the base tunnel protocol and run Kompella Layer 2 VPNs over LDP LSPs due to the added benefits of BGP and routing policy control.

FAST REROUTE   A generic issue with the use of LDP compared to RSVP is that there is no way to run fast reroute LSPs between the core and the edge. Nor is it possible to run traffic engineering from PE to PE. (More details on fast reroute can be found in RFC 4090.) To overcome this, a trend among providers is to run one-hop RSVP LSPs between routers and to deploy LDP on top of these tunnels. The LDP sessions can be used for both base tunnel label distribution and Layer 2

VPN label distribution. This gives the benefit of fast reroute while still letting LDP be used as the main signaling protocol.

VENDOR SUPPORT   An obvious point, but one to mention nonetheless, is vendor support. Some support both the Kompella and Martini drafts (Juniper Networks), and others support only Martini-draft VPNs (Cisco Systems).

Table 4.1 compares the Kompella and Martini pseudowire drafts.

Table 4.1 Comparison Between Kompella and Martini Layer 2 VPNs

	Kompella-draft	**Martini-draft**
Signaling	LDP or RSVP for base tunnel M-BGP for VPN tunnel	LDP or RSVP for base tunnel LDP for VPN tunnel
Layer 1 or Layer 2 payload encapsulation	Martini-encap-draft	Martini-encap-draft
Interprovider VPNs	M-BGP interprovider VPNs	Possible, but policy control is difficult
Core scaling	Good	Good
Edge scaling	MPLS label block per CE	MPLS label per AC per CE
Fast reroute and TE	Possible with RSVP signaling	Possible with RSVP signaling
Provisioning	Greater amount of router configuration Large P2P meshes are easier to provision	Simple router configuration Large P2P meshes are difficult to maintain

Other Uses for Pseduowires

Pseudowires can also be used to backhaul DSLAM connectivity to an access seeker (see Chapter 7, "Wholesale Broadband Networks," for an explanation of access seeker). Instead of transporting some or all pseudowires to the incumbent's BNG, some of these can be used to transport Layer 2 connections to the retailer. This is very useful for providers that do not use PPP as the access protocol (see Chapter 5 for explanations of the two common access protocols). PPP makes it easy to run L2TP between the incumbent and the access seeker for wholesale access to a subscriber's local loop. When doing a circuit hand-off from the incumbent to the access seeker, it is important to keep effective control on the routes or FECs between the two providers. This is where the benefit of BGP-based inter-AS Layer 2 Kompella VPNs really pays off.

TRADITIONAL TRANSPORT

Rather than using an MPLS Layer 2 aggregation network, service providers that have an existing transport network opt to use lower-layer transmission alternatives for DSLAM aggregation in concert with MPLS.

Dark fiber is a dedicated light path between the DSLAM or a local aggregating Ethernet switch and the CO. The light path can traverse several fiber cross-connects before reaching the final Fiber Distribution Frame (FDF) at the CO and can provide a simple way of connecting two optical endpoints. This option is more expensive from a fiber-utilization perspective compared to an SDH multiplexer, but it provides bandwidth speedsters with direct interfaces to DSLAMs and BNGs without needing to interface with more active DWDM hardware. Thus, if an increase in transport bandwidth is required on the endpoints (from 1GE to 10GE), only the optical interfaces at each end need to be upgraded, compared to a more expensive upgrade for an optical multiplexer. Such architectures are most common in short- or medium-reach distribution networks where the density of fiber is high and the maintenance cost lower. For example, wholesale metropolitan fiber networks can provide connectivity between the CO and DSLAM for a service provider without its own infrastructure. At the CO, dark fiber runs could be terminated either directly in the BNG or into an aggregating switch. In areas where the bandwidth distribution is low, a switched Ethernet network would work out better from a cost perspective. But as mentioned at the beginning of this chapter, you should carefully analyze the expected data throughput. This is especially prudent as per-subscriber bandwidth increases due to peer-to-peer traffic and video services, whether they be Standard Definition (SD-TV) or High-Definition (HD-TV). As the bandwidth increases, the aggregation benefits of a switch are not as pronounced.

Dense Wave Division Multiplexing (DWDM) in the context of backhaul carries user traffic (usually Ethernet) on one or more light paths. (They also are called lambdas, which derives from the scientific symbol for wavelength.) As with any multiplexing function, several devices can share a single cable, compared to a single dark fiber link, which carries a light path from a single device. A further benefit of DWDM is that the multiplexing is usually agnostic to different bandwidths sharing the same optical cable. A demultiplexer at the terminating end can split the Ethernet paths into either discrete Ethernet ports or different VLANs. This muxing and demuxing equipment is more costly than dedicated fiber paths and usually requires an expensive transmission plant. As a matter of semantics, a dark fiber can also carry CWDM or DWDM transmission. A more general definition of dark fiber just means that cable interface for the end systems is at the light layer, rather than some other equipment. The systems at each end could be SFPs that are plugged directly in to an AN, BNG, or switch. Or the system could employ multiplexing functionality as well. For the purposes of simplification, dark fiber refers to a system that has a non-multiplexing device attached, such as a DSLAM, AN, or a BNG.

An existing SDH or SONET network can be enhanced to support native Ethernet transport (rather than using ATM as the underlying protocol) by installing Ethernet interface cards in multiplexer nodes. DSLAMs are then directly connected to the nodes over short-haul copper or fiber cross-connects. This can be a cheaper way to provide Ethernet connectivity to a PoP without requiring a dedicated switch. Bear in mind, though, that existing SDH/SONET aggregators might have insufficient fabric switching capacity for the high throughputs needed for triple-play services even though the number of interfaces available might suggest otherwise. The saving grace is that in some urban and most rural areas where the local loop lengths are longer and thus DSL port synchronization rates are lower, greater coverage trumps the need for large aggregation bandwidths in the SDH nodes.

VPLS

Virtual Private LAN Service (VPLS) was created to emulate a LAN over a PSN. Like a pseudowire, VPLS can also run over GRE or L2TP tunnels. VPLS is an enhancement to straight pseudowire service, which is capable of only point-to-point service. Ethernet LAN networks are inherently multiaccess, so being able to properly emulate them requires a point-to-multipoint network. It is probably not immediately obvious why such a technology is gaining popularity among service providers. This section first gives an overview of how VPLS works and then describes the problems it can solve in a triple-play network.

Figure 4.11 illustrates the basics of VPLS. Wellington, the head office site shown in the figure, has two branch offices—Auckland and Dunedin—that need to communicate with each other without requiring a router at each site. In other words, the networks need a single broadcast domain so that each device on a LAN believes it is on one flat Layer 2 network. Each site is connected to the service provider routers over Ethernet (but the access types could theoretically be Frame Relay or ATM, too). If a full point-to-point Layer 2 mesh (using either Martini or Kompella drafts) were used, two VLANs from each CE would be needed so it can reach each of the other CEs. Of course, spanning tree would also be required to prevent any Layer 2 loops from forming. Taking this a step further, for large Layer 2 deployments, the overhead of managing all the point-to-point circuits, as well as poor redundancy models, can make VPLS a compelling choice for service providers to use instead of PWE3 circuits.

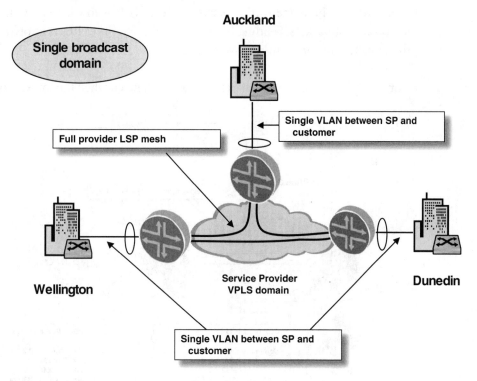

Figure 4.11 A basic VPLS network.

As with to point-to-point circuits, VPLS transport and aggregate a network of DSLAMs back to a BNG site. The physical architecture of a VPLS network looks very similar to the pseudowire service shown in Figure 4.3. The obvious difference on the surface is the service's point-to-multipoint behavior. First some inspection of the nuts and bolts of VPLS is needed to see how the two differ.

Genesis of a VPLS Network

When a VPLS domain is created, as with a pseudowire network, PE routers need to create a mesh of base LSPs among each other. This mesh can be created using either RSVP-TE or LDP signaling. MPLS services are then stacked on top. Next, the PEs perform some handshaking using either BGP or LDP messages (depending on the implemented draft) to indicate CE membership to the rest of the VPLS domain. These messages set up other PE nodes with enough information to track whence in the network a packet came, as well as to where they should send broadcast packets. Sending broadcast packets to other PEs is known as a process called *flooding* (this is covered later).

Figure 4.12 shows the VPLS messages that are exchanged when the routers come up.

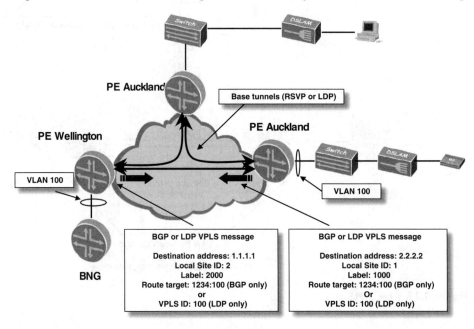

Figure 4.12 VPLS message exchange.

After Ethernet frames enter the PE via the DSLAM AC, the PE adds the source MAC address of the customer router (also called the residential gateway [RG]) and the source AC identifier to a bridging table. Like a standard Ethernet network, if router Dunedin does not know where to send an Ethernet frame, it broadcasts it to other routers in the same broadcast domain. And, implementing split horizon, it does not forward the frame out the AC from which it was received. Then Dunedin sends the frame to the other two PEs. In the scenario currently being described, Auckland is included in the VPLS instance, but the protocol exchange is not shown in the figure. This process of broadcasting frames to all other routers is called flooding. The BNG located at the Wellington site receives the frame and processes the data (in this case it is a PPPoE discovery packet), as shown in Figure 4.13.

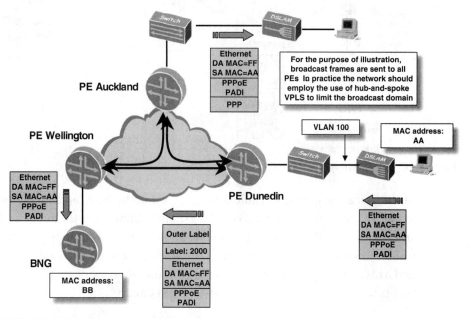

Figure 4.13 VPLS MAC flooding.

When the BNG sends data back to the subscriber (using a PPPoE Active Discovery Offer [PADO]), it sends the unicast Ethernet frame to the local router, which then sends it directly to PE Dunedin. PE Wellington knows where to send the frame based on the inner label that came from the broadcast frame from PE Dunedin. This information is implicitly understood by PE Wellington based on the inner label number that was used when the other PE sent the original broadcast frame around the network. In this case it was label 2000. The final step is shown in Figure 4.14.

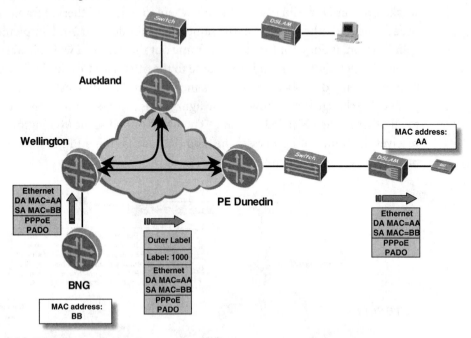

Figure 4.14 VPLS unicast reply.

At this stage, the only noticeable difference is that the MAC address is now used as part of the forwarding decision on PEs. This difference is the key to scalability and deployment discussions. Because VPLS is a point-to-multipoint service, troubleshooting requires more places to isolate the problem because of flooding and MAC learning. This problem is not so acute when there are only single endpoints to check in the case of a point-to-point circuit.

Also, each PE router needs to keep a table of every MAC address that it has received traffic for. If it is not the number of MAC addresses that might cause concern, it might be the rate of addresses that a router has to continually learn as a network goes about its normal business of flooding and learning. For example, when a DSLAM or PE restarts, a flood of MAC addresses suddenly enters the VPLS domain when the PPPoE or DHCP sessions come up. This could be hundreds of flows that need to be learned. A point-to-point pseudowire service does not have this aspect because there is only one place for the Ethernet frames to go—to the other end of the circuit. MAC-in-MAC encapsulation (explained later) is a positive step toward MAC address scaling issues in a VPLS domain, especially if a DSLAM does not perform some kind of MAC interworking itself.

Although it is more complex than a pseudowire service from a protocol and operational perspective, provisioning a large VPLS domain paradoxically turns out to be a lot simpler than provisioning a large mesh of point-to-point connections. Adding a new site to a VPLS domain is just a matter of configuring a new site on the PE node with the correct VPLS instance information, and the network takes care of the rest (almost!).

Why add all the complexity of using VPLS when more basic transmission options are available?

It may be cheaper for a service provider to purchase VPLS connectivity from another provider rather than to run its own transport network. Or a service provider may have an extensive MPLS network already, looking to expand it closer to DSLAMs, so it would be financially prudent to reuse common infrastructure and backhaul DSLAMs over the MPLS network.

Redundancy is also a big driver for running VPLS. If a DSLAM can send traffic to two PEs, and then to redundant BNGs, this can provide protection from a PE failure or perhaps an access path connecting to the BNG failing. Protecting the internal MPLS network against failure is normally part of creating a highly available core. It is different from a more isolated access or PE router failure. To be able to provide some kind of PE node redundancy, having awareness of MAC addresses among all the routers is required. More information on this topic can be found in a later section.

If traffic in a VPLS network is being forwarded from many sites to a central hub location (that is, no direct spoke-to-spoke connectivity), the PE's routers can be configured to reflect this traffic profile in their signaling information to limit unnecessary flooding. Having many DSLAMs connect to a central BNG (or even two BNGs for redundancy) is such a case. Here each spoke PE needs to import only the BNG MAC address from the hub rather than the whole domain's MAC addresses. This means that only the hub PE(s) needs to know the entire MAC address routing plan. Caution should be taken in the case where all DSLAMs must have knowledge of the entire MAC domain for security reasons. With any kind of network where there isn't an isolation of the broadcast domain between untrusted users, extreme caution should be taken to avoid attacks such as MAC spoofing. Usually a lot of work needs to go in to DSLAM and PE policy to ensure that users cannot cause MAC-level attacks against other users. Using a 1:1 VLAN architecture largely obviates this problem. See later in this chapter for an explanation of a 1:1 VLAN architecture.

VPLS Scaling

Much work is under way to improve the scaling properties of VPLS. Work is being done in three areas:

- PE full-mesh requirement
- Traffic routing efficiency
- MAC address scaling

As with the pseudowire service, there are two VPLS drafts: LDP-based and BGP-based. Several of the differences between the pseudowire drafts summarized in Table 4.1 also apply to the two VPLS drafts. This section looks at the drafts' scaling properties in terms of VPLS. It also looks at work going on in the IEEE, which is working on a standard (802.1ah) that, among other benefits, will also improve MAC scaling.

PE FULL-MESH REQUIREMENT   As the number of PEs grows, the number of LSPs required to fully mesh the network grows by the magic formula of $(n*(n-1))/2$ (which is more clearly written as $(n^2-n)/2$), where n is the number of nodes. This means greater signaling overhead and provisioning work to maintain the network. The LDP VPLS draft defines two methods to loosen the requirement of a full mesh of base LSPs between the PEs. It creates the concept of a Multi-Tenant Unit switch (MTU-s), which is a smaller edge device connected to a PE. It is still managed by the service provider but is not part of the core VPLS cloud. The MTU-s aggregates all CEs that are part of a VPLS instance before tunneling them to a PE (or PEs in the case of multihoming). The tunnel can be a stacked VLAN tunnel (Q-in-Q) or an MPLS point-to-point pseudowire. When the tunneled packets reach the PE, the stacked VLAN tag or pseudowire labels are stripped from the packet, and then normal VPLS forwarding in the core takes place. This approach is often called Hierarchical VPLS (H-VPLS).

A possible enhancement that is mentioned in the BGP VPLS draft is to use route reflection. The document also suggests that if a single layer of route reflection is insufficient, a hierarchy of route reflectors can be deployed. Yet a further scaling enhancement is to use one set of route reflectors for Layer 2 VPN services and another set for Layer 3 VPNs.

Technology Note: BGP Route Reflection

BGP route reflection is a way of lifting the requirement to have a full mesh of iBGP sessions between BGP-speaking routers. Rather than all routers in an iBGP domain having to peer with each of the other routers in the domain, one or more routers are designated a route reflector (RR). All routers have to peer with only the route reflectors, rather than with every router. The non-route-reflector routers are called route reflector clients.

The modus operandi of a route reflector cluster is for a router to send all updates to a route reflector, which reflects the updates to all the other route reflector clients. It won't replicate the routes to other routers in the domain that aren't route reflector clients (unless the routers are in a different AS). This means that the route reflectors themselves need to be fully meshed.

In a large network, even full meshes of route reflectors may not sufficiently scale. In this case, a route reflector could be a route reflector client of another RR cluster. This chaining effect is called an RR hierarchy.

These scaling enhancements are only in the BGP signaling plane. There is no suggestion of how to solve the issue of needing a full mesh of base LSPs between the PEs as the network expands. The techniques described in the LDP VPLS draft, such as the stacked VLAN tunnel or MPLS pseudowire, could be deployed in conjunction with a BGP-signaled VPLS domain even if LDP is not the preferred signaling mechanism.

TRAFFIC ROUTING EFFICIENCY The second scalability benefit of using an MTU-s is to aggregate all regional CEs so that traffic that remains local to the MTU-s can transit directly between CEs and does not need to be forwarded through the PE. If a common switch (MTU-s) or stacked VLAN tag were not used, each CE would need a dedicated path to the PE, which would then switch frames back out to the local sites, creating an unnecessary tromboning of traffic.

MAC ADDRESS SCALING   Of equal or possibly greater concern than the issue of full PE LSP mesh is the number of MAC addresses that need to be learned by all PE routers in a VPLS instance. As the number of MAC addresses increases, so does the flooding of broadcast traffic. Pseudowire links from MTU-s switches and stacked VLAN tunnels only help reduce the mesh of LSPs in the service provider network and make traffic routing more efficient. They do nothing to reduce the MAC learning in the core.

Two efforts are under way to address this. The first is an IETF group still in the early stages called Generalized Ethernet Label Switching (GELS). GELS is working toward switching MPLS packets based on a label encoded in the Ethernet header, rather than the one in the MPLS header. Although this is not one of the working group's primary goals, it would have the additional benefit of limiting the size of the MAC domain in the PEs. Switching MPLS packets based on a native Layer 2 header is similar to other GMPLS drafts, such as generalized MPLS over Frame Relay, ATM, and passive optical networks (PONs). Some of these capabilities are captured in a technology called Provider-Based Trees that the GELS working group has released. The drawback of this approach is that the core network links must be Ethernet. SONET links do not have the correct header to encode the label information. Another proposal is a subset of the 802.1ah IEEE specification and encapsulates an Ethernet frame within a second MAC header (called MAC-in-MAC). For this to address MAC scaling issues, a hierarchical Ethernet model is used. An edge switch (or MAC-in-MAC-capable PE) aggregates a set of CE connections within an S-VLAN. A second MAC header, which is generated specifically for MAC-in-MAC encapsulation, is added to the top of the original Ethernet frame and is forwarded to the core PE. This PE and the other PEs in the core VPLS domain see only a single MAC address for all Ethernet frames from a particular S-VLAN, which could be many customer sites. At the other edge of the VPLS domain, this extra MAC header is stripped to reveal the original addressing information that is flooded onto the rest of the network. Because this single MAC address is unique per regional S-VLAN (or, in IEEE parlance, an Ethernet UNI), it scales on the order of one MAC address per VPLS instance per PE. This contrasts with an unknown number of MAC addresses per VPLS instance per PE.

Quality of Service on a PWE3 and VPLS

To ensure that customer data are reliably forwarded on the aggregation network, the network needs to be dimensioned so that congestion does not occur. If congestion occurs, high- and low-priority data is indiscriminately dropped unless there is some of way of indicating packet priority to devices in the path. Quality of service (QoS) is implemented on a network to improve performance for important data during times of congestion.

Because pseudowires and VPLS are carried within an MPLS packet, there is a mechanism for marking packets with a priority value. Defined in RFC 3032, the 3-bit EXP field in MPLS packets can be used to indicate to MPLS routers how the packet should be treated. This is similar to DiffServ TE and 802.1P (discussed next), which are used to indicate the priority of IP packets and Ethernet frames, respectively. Also, if there is an Ethernet aggregation network, these EXP bits should be translated to 802.1P bits in case of congestion on the aggregation network.

Previously, it was noted that it is not common to terminate a pseudowire or VPLS instance on a BNG that simultaneously terminates subscriber sessions. As a result, VLAN trunking is needed between the BSR and MPLS network. To properly manage QoS, some interworking steps need to be applied between the two protocols. Figure 4.15 shows Ethernet frames leaving the BNG with 802.1P priority markings. 802.1P is an IEEE standard that defines the use of a 3-bit field within an 802.1Q header to indicate the frame's priority. As soon as these frames hit the MPLS PE, these 802.1P priorities need to be transcribed to MPLS EXP headers.

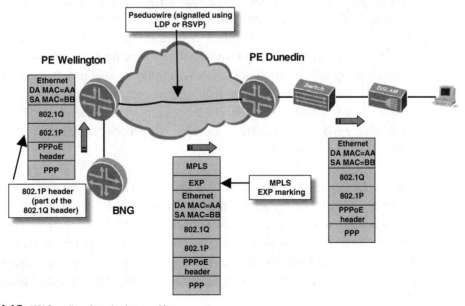

Figure 4.15 MPLS quality of service interworking.

Now all P and PE devices along the path know the priority of the Ethernet frame and can treat it according to service provider policy when there is congestion in the network. At the other end of the pseudowire, when the frame enters either the DSLAM or another Ethernet network, the 802.1P field is untouched by the MPLS domain and can be read by the switches along the path. Further information on QoS configuration and architectures can be found in Chapter 7.

VLAN Architecture: N:1 or Service VLANs

Just as important as the physical path of the aggregation network is the VLAN architecture. In the ATM world, it was a relatively easy task to allocate a PVC to a DSL port. Each customer PVC would be tunneled within a Permanent Virtual Path (PVP) to the BNG and would then terminate on an ATM subinterface. Nowadays, it is common to multiplex each customer session onto a single common VLAN to the BNG. PPPoE and IP over Ethernet (IPoE) are the protocols that can be used to encapsulate data between the BNG and the customer. The decision of which of the two protocols to use is discussed in Chapter 5.

The service VLAN is used when a service (such as video, voice, and/or data) is routed to a particular VLAN, rather than having multiple services share a VLAN. It is then possible to route one service to one BNG and route another service to a different BNG. It is worth noting that this differs from the terminology used by the IEEE. A service in an IEEE context is separated at the MAC layer rather than using the concept of a VLAN per service that is used here. This book uses the generally accepted definition of service VLAN that is used in broadband access networks rather than the IEEE context. Another point to note is that some services, such as VoIP, have two different types of forwarding behaviors. In a VoIP service, there is one connectionless UDP session used for the media and one TCP session used for the signaling.

Figure 4.16 shows a VoIP service VLAN that is routed from the first Ethernet switch to an MPLS PE router and then to the VoIP backend network. A separate VLAN is split out for multicast IPTV services. The third VLAN terminates on the Internet BNG, which terminates all customer sessions. Sometimes this same path is used for unicast Video on Demand (VoD) services. Other times it could be the IPTV BNG. Which of the two approaches is used depends on several factors:

whether the RG is in a routed or bridged mode, if the STB is required to use its own dedicated video VLAN. Ideally it should not be the STB requirements that dictate the network architecture, but rather the STB should be flexible enough to accommodate several types of access network builds.

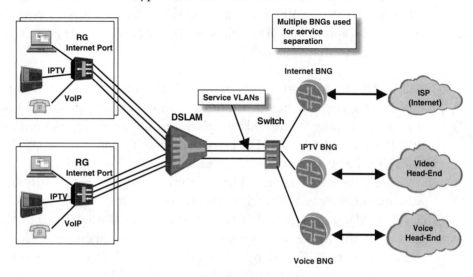

Figure 4.16 Service VLAN architecture.

Customer sessions could be split across multiple routers for functional separation of the services or to reduce the complexity of each BNG. For example, where there isn't a need for complex accounting and policy management, such as a multicast video service, this could then be delivered over a cheaper, less complex router or server. Another reason is to enable vendor diversity among the BNGs, although this is usually a secondary reason for splitting services into separate VLANs.

The more aggregation VLANs (and hence services) that a network has, the more complex the configuration and troubleshooting become. Therefore, it is best to keep the number of service VLANs used to a minimum where possible. An alternative is to use a single VLAN for all services and to terminate the sessions on a single BNG. This is a variant of a service VLAN approach and closely resembles a cable network in which all IP sessions share the same single broadcast domain.

Service Multiplexing

There are three ways of transporting services from the Customer Premises Equipment (CPE) and the IP edge. The first is a VC or VLAN per service, which is a straightforward way of splitting services into separate broadcast domains. The second is to use a VLAN for all services. The third is not as conventional and requires that equipment split services to different BNGs or edge routers based on the ether type value contained in the Ethernet header.

VC/VLAN PER SERVICE   However, when there is more than one VLAN per service in the aggregation network, the DSLAM must be able to link data from the CPE to a particular service and then place it on the correct aggregation VLAN. A PVC/VLAN can be dedicated to a service on the CPE and have the DSLAM bind each VLAN/PVC to the correct aggregation VLAN. This would mean that each PVC/VLAN interface on the RG needs its own IP address. Figure 4.16 shows a CPE that would have an IP address for each of the three PVC/VLANs. PCs on the LAN would normally get an IP address from a built-in DHCP server on the CPE, and any traffic that needs to be sent to the Internet would undergo NAT before being sent to the BNG. VoIP would have their own dedicated physical ports (such as FXO POTS ports) on the CPE. Video services would normally use an external STB to decode the video services and provide the correct video outputs to televisions. Each of these two services would still be linked to the respective PVC/VLAN.

Technology Note: NAT

Network Address Translation (NAT) is a way of translating IP addresses from one network to another. In a residential broadband environment, it is used to translate addresses from the private LAN in the home to the public Internet address given to the RG by the BNG.

For example, PCs attached to the RG might be given private addresses from the 192.168.1.0/24 network. The RG is given a public address—66.1.2.3, for instance. When the PCs want to access the Internet, their IP addresses are converted from a 192.168.1.x address to 66.1.2.3 as they pass through the RG.

Strictly speaking, this concept is called Network Address Port Translation (NAPT) or NAT overload. However, it is commonly called NAT. For more details, see RFC 1631.

As mentioned earlier in this chapter, caution must be taken to ensure that customers within a broadcast domain can't communicate with each other. Even though services are separated by VLANs, customers within each VLAN still share the same broadcast domain. In most cases, providers want to ensure that all traffic from a customer is forwarded through a Service Delivery Point (SDP), such as the BNG. Therefore, at many points in the network (aggregation network, DSLAM, and any VPLS PEs), frames must be securely forwarded to their correct destination. A broadcast domain that spans untrusted network ports is an ideal candidate for MAC-layer attacks unless care is taken to restrict where traffic can flow. A 1:1 VLAN architecture largely avoids these problems.

Of course, some protocols, such as multicast, lend themselves well to a single broadcast domain. Such a setup is described in the section "Provider VLAN Architectures: 1:1 and Multicast VLANs."

SINGLE VLAN PER DSLAM   One of the easiest ways of delivering a triple- or multi-play service is to allocate a single VLAN to a DSLAM and allow all customers to share that VLAN. The BNG could be multiple devices, which is called a multi-edge approach. Therefore, when a single BNG delivers all services to a subscriber, it is easy to enforce QoS because one device is aware of the bandwidth requirements of each service and the total subscriber session.

This approach also shares similar security drawbacks as mentioned above, with multiple subscribers sharing the same broadcast domain.

PROTOCOL PER SERVICE   Rather than run a PVC/VLAN per service, a single PVC/VLAN can be provisioned to the household and use different protocols for different services. Figure 4.17 shows that Internet and unicast video can be provided over a PPPoE session to a BNG, while VoIP is split into a separate VLAN based on the ether type field. The DSLAM then can demultiplex both protocols off a single PVC based on ether type. The IP address for the IPoE session can be provided over DHCP.

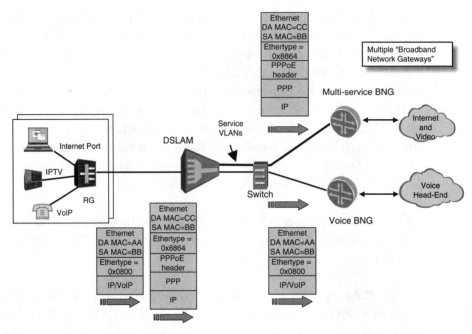

Figure 4.17 Protocol per service.

Protocol Interworking

It is the job of the DSLAM to multiplex each customer session onto a single VLAN. The local-loop protocol could be PPPoE over ATM, bridged IP over ATM, or Ethernet (with or without PPPoE) using Ethernet in the First Mile (EFM[11]), which is an option with VDSL.

All the protocols just mentioned rely on the aggregation network to broadcast data and create a bridging topology based on flooding and MAC learning. A DSLAM in its basic form functions in a similar way. Data coming from the CPE is identified based on a source MAC address and source DSL port, so the DSLAM knows where to send data for the subscriber when it receives packets/frames coming from the network to be sent to the CPE. Such a simple protocol mechanism for learning data-link addressing[12] means that you need to be careful when deploying this in an Ethernet DSLAM environment. For example, it is a trivial

---

[11] IEEE 802.1ah

[12] A data-link address is another term for a Layer 2 or MAC address. The term data link comes from the ISO network layer model.

matter to forge MAC addresses on clients and masquerade as another user or, even worse, a BNG MAC address.

Instead of running PPPoE from the CPE to the BNG, an alternative is to run PPPoA between the CPE and DSLAM and then PPPoE between the DSLAM and BNG. PPPoA is common for service providers that have an ATM aggregation network. A PPPoA session runs between the BNG and the CPE. However, when migrating to an Ethernet backhaul network, PPPoA cannot run between the BNG and the DSLAM. Therefore, a protocol interworking function on the DSLAM runs between the two protocols. The DSLAM now becomes a PPPoE client. It must create a new PPPoE session for each PPPoA session coming from the access network. Some vendors use a single source-MAC address for all new PPPoE sessions and then tag each one with an individual Host-Uniq or Session-ID tag to differentiate the sessions. Another approach is to use a unique MAC address for each session, although this solution is more wasteful from an address utilization perspective and also has negative flow-on effects on VPLS scalability in the core. Using a single MAC address for all sessions is a more scalable solution from a core network perspective; it works out to about one MAC address per DSLAM. Figure 4.18 shows an example.

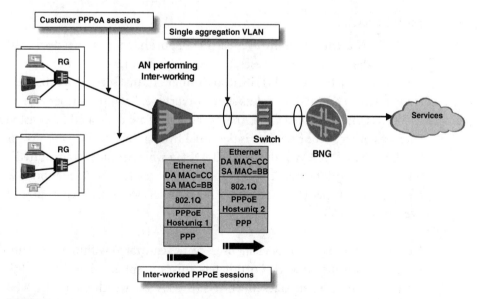

Figure 4.18 PPPoA protocol interworking.

Reasons for running protocol interworking could be to provide a phased migration allowing customers to continue to run PPPoA, while still being able to run PPPoE in the aggregation and BNG networks.

It should be noted that such solutions are completely proprietary and rely on the DSLAM vendor doing the *right thing*. For some providers with a large embedded base of PPPoA subscribers, there is no palatable alternative to doing such an IWF on the DSLAM.

PROVIDER VLAN ARCHITECTURES: 1:1 AND MULTICAST VLANs

Two alternatives to the service VLAN approach are the hybrid VLAN mode and the 1:1 VLAN mode. Why might the service VLAN be an inappropriate choice for some service providers? One of the limitations of a service VLAN is that there is no logical isolation between user sessions at the VLAN level. All PPPoE or IPoE users share the same logical segment and rely on the DSLAM and BNG to implement sufficient security filtering. Another limitation is related to QoS (as explained later). A hybrid VLAN or a 1:1 design can address both of these concerns. First, an explanation is needed of what is meant by the 1:1 VLAN.

1:1 VLANs

A 1:1 VLAN architecture involves each DSL port having its own dedicated Layer 2 path to the BNG. In most cases, there is a one-to-one correlation between a DSL port and a CPE or subscriber, so throughout this section, a subscriber generally refers to a DSL port unless stated otherwise. Each subscriber is separated by VLANs that are called C-VLANs because they are dedicated to a customer. Each customer's set of services is delivered from a BNG to the DSLAM down its C-VLAN. The DSLAM adds the C-VLAN tag when traffic is transmitted upstream toward the BNG. This is an analog of the typical ATM model, which dedicates a PVC per DSL port and delivers all services from a centralized BNG over the one PVC.

Of course, in the ATM model, all users were aggregated within a PVP tunnel for transport over the network. Fortunately, this concept also exists in the Ethernet world. It involves using stacked VLANs (S-VLANs), which is an extra VLAN on top of the original VLAN. This is also called Q-in-Q. If each customer VLAN from every DSLAM were transported as a single 802.1Q VLAN across the core, the network would not scale to the thousands of VLANs needed; stacked VLANs solve this problem. Figure 4.19 introduces the concept of the S-VLAN. The second 802.1Q tag is added to the Ethernet frame with the C-VLAN and trunks many customer VLANs across an S-VLAN tunnel. There are two ways to add the S-VLAN tag. The first, most common way is for the DSLAM to add the S-VLAN tag itself. Or, if there is an aggregation switch, it can add the S-VLAN tag based on the physical port to which the DSLAM is connected. The downside of having the switch add the tag is that if any Level 2 or Level 3 DSLAMs are connected to the first DSLAM, they cannot be individually identified with unique S-VLANs. This means that a single S-VLAN identifies all DSLAMs connected to that switch port. This option is shown in the figure.

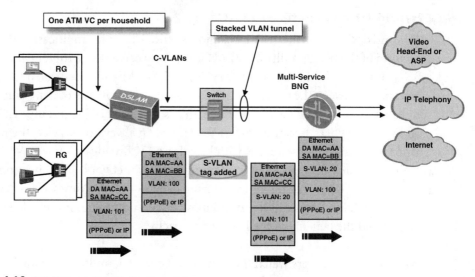

Figure 4.19 S-VLAN tags being added by the switch.

Without the stacked VLAN tag, provisioning would be an incredibly onerous task because of having to manage so many customer VLANs. Note that a stacked VLAN tag does not reduce the number of MAC addresses. Even though a tunnel is created from one side of the aggregation network to the other using an S-VLAN tag, all switches and VPLS routers still need to check the destination MAC address to work out where to send the Ethernet frame. This differs from the traditional concept of a tunnel, in which the routers doing the tunneling are unconcerned with the ultimate destination of the data contained in the encapsulated payload.

Address scaling properties in the aggregation network of the 1:1 model using stacked VLANs are similar to the service VLAN, because there are just as many MAC addresses to manage. In the 1:1 model, more resources are consumed at the BNG because of the number of customer VLANs that need to be managed. However, preconfiguration or bulk provisioning can ease this problem. The extra configuration at the DSLAM for 1:1 compared to a service VLAN approach merely involves having incremental C-VLAN identifiers rather than a single VLAN ID for all ports. Usually this is a negligible extra task. More information about bulk configuration can be found in Chapter 5 at the end of the PPPoA section.

Hybrid 1:1 and Multicast VLANs

A hybrid design takes the 1:1 VLAN and a service VLAN for multicast and creates a hybrid of the two. A multicast VLAN is one between an edge router (normally a BNG, although this is not mandatory) and a DSLAM and is dedicated to multicast traffic between the two. A full triple-play offering consists of data, video, and voice services. In basic terms, for video, this is multicast IPTV and unicast Video on Demand (VoD). Because unicast VoD is not an always-on service, the need for bandwidth is not as great as with broadcast TV. Broadcast TV (IPTV) uses multicast to deliver television broadcasts over an IP network. Thus, it is common to see such a service highly utilized during television prime times—much more so than VoD. First, some background information on multicast is needed to understand the benefits of the hybrid approach.

When multiple viewers watch the same IPTV channel, multicast forwarding can deliver the channel as a single stream along common parts of the network regardless of the number of viewers. Unicast video would require a stream from a central server for each interested viewer. As soon as the media streams no longer follow a common path, routers (or switches) replicate data to subscribers as needed.

For example, Figure 4.20 shows two customers, each requesting to view a channel at the same time on a 1:1 VLAN network. The multicast data are sent from the video server, across the core, and then to the BNG as a single stream. Because there is no longer a common logical path for the video channel to follow, the BNG needs to replicate the groups down each customer VLAN. You might say that the video channels share a common path between the BSR and the DSLAM—the S-VLAN. However, in terms of the C-VLANs, the streams are in discrete paths and can't leverage the benefits of a common channel. Replicating multicast streams to each C-VLAN at the BNG instead of directly onto a multicast VLAN would be undesirable from a traffic utilization perspective. It causes extra utilization on the BNG, on the aggregation network, and, to some degree, on the DSLAM. Delivering the video content as a single multicast stream to the DSLAM and letting it do replication is the better option. Of course, if the DSLAM cannot perform IGMP snooping, replication at the DSLAM is not realistically an option, and multicast video needs to be replicated over each C-VLAN.

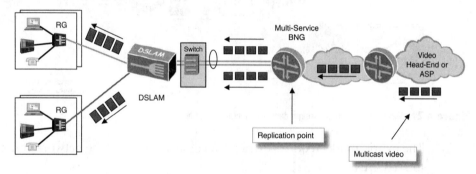

Figure 4.20 Nonoptimized multicast forwarding in a triple-play network.

Enter the hybrid VLAN. Figure 4.21 shows a single multicast VLAN stretching from the BNG, across the aggregation network, to the DSLAM. Now there is a common path to each DSLAM for multicast video content, so the only duplication of the media streams is on the last mile to the CPE. Bandwidth saved! Such capability isn't free. Extra intelligence needs to be built into the DSLAM so that it can track subscribers that have requested a particular channel for correct replication. When a CPE requests to view a channel, it sends a message to the BNG in the form of an IGMP request, asking it to begin sending the multicast data. As this message passes through the DSLAM, the DSLAM peeks inside the customer traffic and discovers that a CPE wants to join or leave a video channel. It then adds the DSL port to a table that tracks the ports it needs to replicate the channel to. Note that in this model, there is still only a single PVC/VLAN on the local loop between the DSLAM and the CPE. The way to separate multicast traffic from PPPoE is to use a different Ethernet ether type for PPPoE and IP over Ethernet (IPoE). This is inherent in the solution anyway because the multicast router sends IP over Ethernet frames with the correct ether type set in the Ethernet header. The same is true with PPPoE—they are set with a different ether type. When the DSLAM receives these frames, it simply forwards these frames on to the CPE. It is up to the CPE to perform the protocol demultiplexing function off the one PVC.

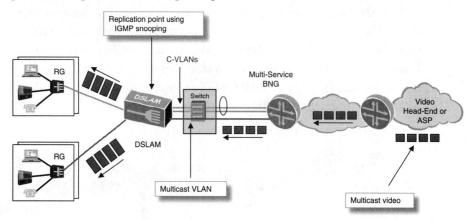

Figure 4.21 Multicast forwarding using a dedicated multicast VLAN.

The hybrid model requires extra protocol intelligence in the network compared to 1:1 VLANs:

- The DSLAM needs to inspect the IP payload of packets sent to the BNG to match IGMP control messages. IGMP snooping is not a new concept. However, when using PPPoE compared to bridged IP and DHCP, deeper inspection inside the packet is required. This does not appear to be a problem judging by the vendors who have implemented this feature so far.
- The DSLAM needs to act as an IGMP echo client to duplicate the IGMP request from the subscriber to the multicast VLAN. This causes the BNG to transmit the video down the correct VLAN. Notice that in Figure 4.21, the multicast data are delivered over the multicast VLAN, but the user session spans a dedicated C-VLAN between the CPE and the BNG. When the CPE sends the request to the network to deliver a multicast channel, the BNG receives the IGMP request and starts sending down the customer VLAN. Therefore, the DSLAM needs to duplicate the IGMP packet on the multicast VLAN to get the traffic flowing the right way.

- An alternative to the DSLAM acting as an echo client is for the CPE to perform the echo client function. The CPE sends two IGMP packets onto the PVC to the DSLAM. One is encapsulated in IPoE and the other is in the PPPoE session.

- When the multicast group is transmitted from the BNG, the DSLAM needs to correlate the incoming stream with the correct outgoing DSL ports.

Figure 4.21 shows a single BNG transmitting IPTV to the DSLAM as well as handling Internet and voice traffic. It is possible to split the function of transmitting multicast data to a separate router, as shown in Figure 4.22. Reasons for doing this might be to put multicast replication on a simpler and less expensive router or switch. It might also be to split functionality across different routers to reduce the device's complexity—not necessarily for price reasons, but to avoid overloading a router with multiple concurrent features. This is similar to Figure 4.17. However, the difference is that the Internet, voice, and VoD router can still identify a household based on a C-VLAN ID. In the service VLAN architecture, a customer can only be identified based on either a DHCP option 82 ID or a PPPoE Intermediate Agent (IA) ID.

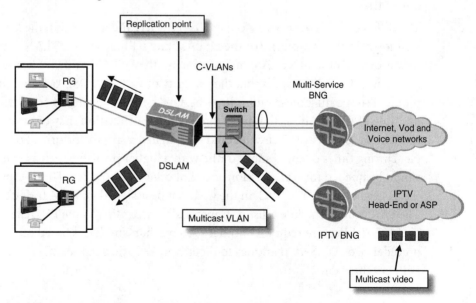

Figure 4.22 Multicast forwarding with a partially decentralized BNG model.

QoS

Each VLAN design has a different QoS implication. Some models move the required intelligence from the BNG to the DSLAM, and others do the reverse. Effective QoS needs a central point to manage user bandwidth during times of congestion. This could be on the BNG or at the DSLAM. The maturity of each of the devices' hardware and software has a large impact on which has the better QoS capability. In some cases, such as the hybrid or service VLAN model, the only option for central bandwidth management is usually the DSLAM, while in the 1:1 model this can be the BNG or DSLAM. More information about VLAN architectures and their implications are found in Chapter 8 "Deploying Quality of Service."

FEATURE COMPARISON

There is no one right answer to the question of which model to deploy. The ultimate design depends on many requirements and vendor capabilities. The following sections summarize the differences between the three.

Last Mile

The differences between a service per VLAN, a 1:1, and a hybrid in the last mile are mostly in the complexity of the DSLAM and CPE. A service VLAN usually means extra PVC and VLAN configuration on the DSLAM and CPE for service separation. The advantage is that the majority of CPE and DSLAMs have no problem supporting these multiple paths. One benefit of splitting services across multiple PVCs/VLANs is that upstream traffic prioritization may be easier to implement. Each Layer 2 circuit could be assigned a specific priority. For example, During times of congestion, traffic with a higher priority (such as voice) would be queued for transmission ahead of other traffic types. This is especially the case when a specific PVC on the CPE can be assigned an ATM traffic class. The SAR would schedule cells for transmission according to the PVC class. A single PVC architecture requires another QoS mechanism that is based on Layer 3 precedence or DiffServ markings to dictate packet priority. Most CPEs support DiffServ these days.

In the last mile, a 1:1 architecture is the simplest in terms of provisioning, because only a single PVC is configured on the DSLAM and CPE. Also, there is only one path to deal with when troubleshooting. A flow-on effect from having a single point in the network at which to manage QoS (the BNG) is that the DSLAM does not need extensive QoS capabilities to prioritize traffic, because this task has already been done at the BNG.

A hybrid model mainly affects the aggregation network, so its properties are similar to a 1:1 style. One difference is that if PPPoE is used as the control protocol between the household and BNG, the CPE needs extra intelligence built in to be able to handle IPTV streams being delivered over IP. This pushes up the gateway's cost. The last factor in a hybrid 1:1 and multicast VLAN combination approach concerns QoS. If traffic is adequately prioritized after it reaches the DSLAM, the DSLAM does not need significant QoS intelligence. If the network might transmit packets at a greater rate than the port speed, the DSLAM needs to be able to read Ethernet priority bit settings on the packets, and correctly prioritize and buffer traffic.

Aggregation Network

A service VLAN is the simplest design for the aggregation network because it needs only a single VLAN to be provisioned for each service, or even a single VLAN for all services. The use of a stacked VLAN tag is not common in either of these service VLAN models. The address scalability of the two models is roughly the same because the number of MAC addresses does not change.

- Because the DSLAM is functioning as a standard Ethernet bridge, it needs to implement sufficient security measures to prevent Ethernet frames from one DSL port from disrupting sessions on other ports. With a 1:1 VLAN architecture, Layer 2 separation inherently isolates traffic to a single broadcast domain and is good from a security standpoint. With a service VLAN, this approach is inherently insecure unless the DSLAM is correctly configured with the necessary security policy. Even then, this may not cover all cases if the attacker uses sophisticated-enough MAC address attacks. This can be ARP spoofing, MAC flooding, or simply customers running "hairpin" traffic streams. A hairpin model is mentioned in WT-101. It describes traffic from one DSL port going directly to another DSL port without transiting the BNG. A hairpin traffic model might actually be a service offered by a service provider, but this is not common in a residential broadband environment.

- QoS capabilities become a bit more limited in a service VLAN model. Identifying the DSL port that a PPPoE or IPoE session comes from is possible using a PPPoE intermediate agent or DHCP option 82, which can then be used to apply a QoS configuration to the session. Even so, hierarchical QoS becomes difficult if there is more than one DHCP or PPPoE session from a household. These sessions need to be tied to a single aggregate rate if DSL port shaping can happen.

- A 1:1 design means that a VLAN per subscriber is required. To effectively transport all customer VLANs from a DSLAM to a BNG, an S-VLAN tag is required. This adds an extra step to the provisioning process as well as extra complexity from VLAN stacking in the network. But practically this impacts only the BNG and DSLAM. For most DSLAMs, preconfiguration does away with this issue, because they usually have preconfigured VLAN and PVC port mappings in mind. If the BNG has bulk-configuration or auto-detection capability, it can automatically create interfaces based on the S-VLAN and C-VLAN of the incoming frame.

HIGH-AVAILABILITY BROADBAND ACCESS

The advanced IP-based triple-play services that carriers are now beginning to deploy come with assumptions about these services' availability and reliability. As time passes and advanced services proliferate, they become more commoditized and are expected to behave as utilities. Just as one expects power, water, heat, and other basic services to always be available, this same reliability and availability will be expected of voice, video, and other applications.

Many techniques exist for building resilient core networks where traffic is aggregated onto a smaller number of large links, which are typically then pervasively meshed. Physical and logical redundancy typically become sparser as you get further out toward the edge of the network, finally thinning the most when reaching the "last mile" single point of failure.

REQUIREMENTS

In this new world of utility-like reliability, substantial emphasis is placed on the carrier to minimize the effects of an outage. Ideally, the impact of an event (as measured by the number of subscribers affected) should be roughly linear to the distance where the failure occurred in relation to the subscriber. For example, a cut in a single copper pair into a subscriber's location should affect only that user; a problem with a DSLAM shelf affects only the users terminating on that shelf. Events should be as isolated as possible, and redundancy options should exist for each potential point of failure; this is known as localization.

MEASURING AVAILABILITY

Failures and the impact on the overall network-availability figure that an operator wants to achieve are impacted by a variety of factors, ranging from human to environmental. Overall network availability, as perceived by the end subscriber, is achieved through the careful and disciplined management of a large number of interdependent systems. Network availability goals are often stated in terms of an overall availability percentage, which is the amount of time over a one-year period that the network is usable. For example, 99.9% means that the network is down for about 500 minutes a year. 99.99% results in about 50 minutes a year of outage, and 99.999% availability means only 5 minutes a year of downtime.

Factors That Affect Availability

Network outages can be caused by any number of events. A backhoe might dig up the physical connectivity between points A and B. A miscommunicated change request from engineering could result in an incorrect configuration. Or simple human error can occur. Chances are that "Murphy's Law" will make everyone's worst contingency plan a reality at some point.

Although not every unique type of failure can be calculated and predicted, the overall pattern can be understood, and steps can be taken to minimize the effect of given types of events. Best practices exist that outline rigorous and thorough change management procedures and their review. Router operating systems can be built with a series of reliable mechanisms and exception handling routines that catch the unexpected. Also, protocols exist that can protect against any type of failure, operator-induced or otherwise. Figure 4.23 shows the areas to focus on when designing a highly available access network and BNG interface.

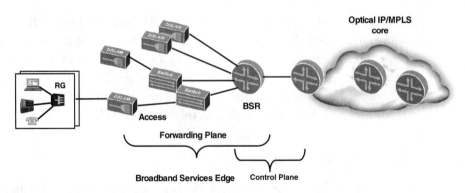

Figure 4.23 Focus areas for high-availability networks.

CPE/RG   The first point of failure, the subscriber-side equipment (CPE), is conventionally the least redundant. Typically there is little need to provide much redundancy at the subscriber location because the last mile is often only a single copper pair. In a residential service, CPE redundancy is not common. For a business service, multiple CPE can be used with a protocol such as VRRP running on the customer LAN to provide high availability of a routing gateway function.

LAST MILE   If adequate care is taken in the design of the physical copper plant, issues can be isolated and resolved quickly. However, unless a redundant physical path exists, the only way to restore service is with manual intervention.

After the subscriber's physical copper pair terminates on the provider's network, options for redundancy become available. DSLAMs can be divided into various redundant components and can be set to varying degrees of fault tolerance. In a residential service, the last mile is not protected. With a business service, a second line can be provided to the premises via redundant conduits. For a properly redundant last mile, there must be no shared infrastructure between the CPE and the Main Distribution Frame (MDF) or Fiber Distribution Frame (FDF). This includes conduits in to the exchange. Redundant last miles are very expensive to provide, but some customers are willing to pay the price for such access redundancy.

BACKHAUL NETWORK   The next point of failure that can exist in the infrastructure that connects the DSLAM back to the BNG is the backhaul network. Various designs and best practices exist to prevent this, but in many cases the BNG is not physically located near the DSLAMs it serves. In this case, some type of backhaul network is required. Backhaul networks can be built using anything from traditional flat switched Ethernet networks to advanced highly available MPLS-based networks using technologies such as PWE3 and VPLS. Several options exist for building a highly available aggregation network. If DSLAMs are directly connected to the BNG, there are fewer options for high-available solutions; but on the flipside, there are fewer things that could fail. A DSLAM could have two uplinks, in a 1:1 or primary/secondary configuration. If the primary connection were to fail, the DSLAM could enliven the secondary interface and terminate customer connections on the BNG to which the second interface is connected.

If there is an aggregation network, then connectivity can be set up in such a way as to allow CPE to see one or more BNGs during the PPPoE discovery phase. If a BNG were to fail, the CPE could re-establish its session with the other BNG. This would be the case with PPPoE. With DHCP and IPoE, VRRP could run between the two BNGs to provide a continually available upstream connection without the client needing to reconnect. There are some issues with QoS when connecting subscribers across multiple BNGs. These are covered in Chapter 8.

To allow a CPE to see multiple BNGs requires multipoint connectivity between the BNG and the DSLAM. An aggregation network could provide this multipoint connectivity with a VLAN (be it service VLAN or 1:1 C-VLAN) being terminated on one or more BNG Gigabit Ethernet Interfaces.

BNG ARCHITECTURE

The BNG has many moving parts because it is responsible for controlling the user's access to a variety of network services. These include authentication, accounting, IP routing, and maintaining interfaces and state for large numbers of concurrent users. The load on a BNG increases with the number of users a BNG device simultaneously terminates.

Modern BNG elements are built from a highly distributed architecture, with specialized processing and memory dedicated to discrete functions that have to be performed. Common architectures separate functionality across logical and physical boundaries. Some processing may be distributed across individual line cards, such as PPP state, and other processing can be performed centrally across the whole chassis, such as RADIUS user authentication. This leaves a trail of stateful information that must be coordinated and maintained in a variety of systems for each user within the BNG.

This stateful information can be viewed in two different ways: static information, which is known through the device's configuration, and dynamic information, which is learned as the device is operating. Static information can include things that are preconfigured, such as the number and types of interfaces, IP addresses of local interfaces, and static IP routes. Examples of dynamic information are dynamic IP routes learned through a routing protocol, PPP state required to keep sessions alive, DHCP addresses and interface bindings, user authentication state, and interface bindings.

The sheer volume of this stateful data and its constant dynamic nature are what drive the highly distributed architectures seen in today's large-scale BNGs. It is simply not practical to centrally process events such as constant user churn, authentication, interface state, and keepalives across thousands of interfaces, dynamic routing protocols, and all the other functions required. A highly centralized architecture also wouldn't lend itself well to fault tolerance. Every component in any network element has a calculable MTBF. It is true that having fewer components, each of which might have a high MTBF, could reduce the overall probability of a failure within the system, but it is also true that any such failure is likely to be catastrophic if there isn't a redundant component with available capacity to absorb the functionality of a failed component. Adding unnecessary complexity usually only hurts reliability. In the words of Albert Einstein, "Make it as simple as possible, but no simpler."

This redundancy that can be easily and scalably built into a distributed architecture provides the foundation for a highly available and reliable BNG. This is only one piece of the puzzle. A variety of techniques in software can be used to efficiently take advantage of this underlying foundation and get us closer to the seamless "connectopia" we seek, even under the worst of conditions. Next we will discuss some of the design and high availability (HA) tools that can be used to build a highly available BNG network.

HIGH-AVAILABILITY ETHERNET ACCESS ARCHITECTURE

As discussed earlier in this chapter, an Ethernet DSLAM does not need to be located in the same central office as the BNG. It is even possible for individual subtended shelves that are part of the same DSLAM to be in separate locations. This is typically done to distribute capacity across the network where it's needed. If planned properly, this can be very cost-effective.

It is important to ensure that connectivity is always available between the DSLAMs and BNGs. Redundant physical paths are required to achieve the highest level of availability between a BNG and DSLAM. Taking advantage of the physical redundancy usually requires a protocol to route around failed paths (unless the failure detection is a simple loss-of-light mechanism). This could be an MPLS network with redundancy in the core that is provided to upper-layer services such as VPLS and PWE3. For lower-level transport deployment, Resilient Packet Ring (RPR[13]) can be used to provide physical path redundancy, which is independent of the upper protocol layers.

Metro Ethernet

Interconnected Ethernet with redundant interfaces and a loop-avoidance protocol is commonly used. Ethernet switches operate at Layer 2 of the OSI stack. Their basic function is to forward Ethernet frames from the port on which they arrived via other interfaces, with the goal of getting the frame to its destination.

The Learning Bridge

When a frame arrives on a switch port for a destination that it previously did not know about, it first floods this frame out every port in the Layer 2 domain. As soon as it knows through which port(s) the destination MAC address is reachable, the switch builds a table that associates a MAC address with the correct destination port to avoid flooding subsequent frames through all ports.

[13] IEEE 802.17

This works in very simple topologies, but problems arise when redundant links and switches are added. Because simple Ethernet frames do not include any sort of loop detection or avoidance mechanisms (no TTL or path information is stored in the MAC header), flooded frames can be caught in a "bridge loop," where they are perpetually flooded back and forth over a potential backup path.

To address this, ports can be placed in a "blocking" mode, wherein these redundant paths are logically removed from the Layer 2 topology, thus breaking the loop that would otherwise be created. Configuring ports in blocking mode does not lend itself well to converging around dynamic topology changes. For this another mechanism is required—Spanning Tree Protocol (STP).

Spanning Tree Protocol

STP operates at Layer 2 of the OSI stack and is responsible for discovering a loop-free topology through a switched Ethernet domain. Because this topology discovery is performed dynamically, it can be repeated whenever a topology change is detected. It provides a degree of resiliency against topology changes. A variety of situations can cause the spanning tree domain to not function properly, resulting in outages that self-heal after a few minutes or outages that require manual intervention and troubleshooting to fix.

These issues include software bugs, mismatched port configurations (duplex, speed, or anything else that could possibly cause packet corruption), misconfigured spanning tree parameters, or even just the natural load of a rapidly and constantly changing large Layer 2 domain. Some of these issues become particularly acute in a large, shared Ethernet domain, such as what is found in the DSLAM and BNG backhaul network.

Ethernet Fault Detection

Some transmission media, such as SONET/SDH, have built-in fault-detection mechanisms that can be used to rapidly indicate a link failure and notify a network element so that it can react by finding a backup path. Ethernet has no built-in ability to detect transmission media faults beyond simple loss of carrier (optical or electrical). Faults can occur along an Ethernet path, with the end media being unaware of a problem down the line. With STP enabled, a periodic polling event needs to happen before any faulty links in the Ethernet domain are detected. This can take seconds or minutes to resolve.

PSEUDOWIRES

One of the drivers behind the rapidly growing adoption of MPLS by carriers is the potential cost savings and uses for Layer 2 transport over MPLS networks. This approach means that a common MPLS infrastructure can support multiple services to create a converged multiservice network. Today, Layer 2 MPLS transport can provide seamless point-to-point connectivity and even translational services that allow carriers to migrate Frame Relay, ATM, leased line, and Ethernet-based services to a common MPLS network.

MPLS-Based Function

Leveraging MPLS provides a single platform for service delivery without the costly overhead of managing multiple overlay networks while providing highly resilient, QoS-enabled transport. The MPLS control plane solves many of the reliability issues found in large switched Ethernet domains. It uses protocols such as Bidirectional Forwarding Detection (BFD) for fast failure detection, Constrained Shortest Path First (CSPF) for dynamic LSP topology calculation, and make-before-break fast reroute and its variations for SONET-like path restoration times. With the advent of DiffServ-TE, MPLS can also enable the topology to become aware of the different QoS levels serviced on the network.

Link Protection

Many Layer 2 transport implementations also support the concept of "protection interfaces," which can be used to provide APS/MSP-like redundancy between the PE and CE. In this case, two interfaces are provisioned between the PE and CE. One is used as the working interface, and the other is a protection interface. If the working interface fails, the protect interface is immediately available to start passing traffic into the Layer 2 VPN.

By leveraging the high-availability functionality inherent in MPLS, in addition to edge-interface redundancy in PWE and Layer 2 VPNs, a true highly available backhaul network can be deployed between BNGs and DSLAMs.

VPLS TOPOLOGY DISCOVERY

Using VPLS, it is possible to provide redundant, loop-free paths from a single CE to multiple PEs. This is similar to the "protect interface" functionality found in

Layer 2 VPNs and PWE3. Multihoming is mentioned in both the LDP and BGP drafts, but the BGP-based draft provides a more complete solution to the problem. Loop detection is provided as an inherent function of BGP (in this case, using different local preference to differentiate the two paths to a VPLS PE).

High-Availability Design Elements

A variety of high-availability (HA) options exist and are in use today for core IP networks of all types. For example, traditional IGP-based pure IP-core networks, as well as MPLS-enabled ones, can use a mechanism such as BFD to offer impressive failure detection times. In conjunction with BFD for simple failure detection, MPLS-TE can be concurrently deployed when complex traffic rerouting is required. Using MPLS, it's possible for multiple services, such as native IP transport, Layer 2 VPNs, Layer 3 VPNs, and VPLS, to share the network concurrently.

High-Availability BNG Element Architecture

A system's ability to survive unforeseen events is first mitigated by an effective design. A BNG consists of a large number of components. It is responsible for terminating many subscriber sessions, processing all the Layer 2 and Layer 3 signaling, AAA, and IP forwarding. Some of these functions are handled in hardware, and others in software. Thus, to provide true fault tolerance, both hardware and software redundancy must exist.

This redundancy is not free. It would be great to have two of everything, but not only is this extremely costly, but it also introduces additional complexity, which itself can cause more faults. A balance of component redundancy and clean, simple architecture is the ideal environment to provide a highly available BNG platform.

HARDWARE   A BNG typically consists of separate control plane hardware, data plane hardware, and support subsystems. Each of these individual hardware components can be protected by a hot-standby component:

- Power supply
- Environmental (fans)
- Control plane hardware

- Data plane hardware
- Interface media

Some efficiency can be gained when numerous identical yet discrete components are used simultaneously. Rather than the traditional 1:1 backup, in which a backup line card is dedicated to the active one, a more efficient option is to deploy a 1:N redundancy scheme. This type of redundancy allows a single component to act as a spare for N primary ones. Such an architecture, although it is more efficient from a resource perspective, has some limitations. This design protects against only a single failure in the system. Based on the overall MTBF of each component and the desired system availability, the level of redundancy can be calculated.

SOFTWARE   Having redundant hardware available to assume the responsibilities of a failed component is only one piece of the puzzle. The system also must be able to restore end-to-end state and services after a hardware failover. Within the control and data planes, a variety of data is stored and processed. The device's internal state could change at any moment. Users frequently connect and disconnect; interface keepalives are processed; authentication information is sent, requested, and stored; and forwarding table entries are calculated and used.

To provide seamless failover between redundant hardware, this state must be shared between the active and backup components. Some of this information can be considered "static" (such as device configuration), and other information is more "dynamic." Static information can be thought of as stored, preconfigured information that the device knows. Dynamic information, on the other hand, is discovered "on the fly" while the box is operating. Both types of information must be shared between active and backup components to facilitate seamless failover.

The static information, if shared (or mirrored) between the active and redundant components, gives the redundant component enough information to resume operation after it assumes the responsibilities of the erstwhile primary. Because the dynamic information changes rapidly, an accurate and complete snapshot of this information has to be available on the redundant component the instant a failure occurs for the redundant component to resume where the active left off.

Alternatively, some of this state can be built based on incoming control data from the network.

NSR   Nonstop Routing (NSR) is one of many marketing terms used to describe the combination of a variety of stateful failover techniques. The goal of NSR is seamless failover from a primary component to a standby without interrupting routing or forwarding. To achieve this, the device must be able to detect a failure quickly and then rapidly switch all external connectivity to a "warm" standby unit that has been preloaded with a fresh and accurate copy of the *current* state.

This means that routing protocol sessions, interface state, and other user state can be seamlessly moved between components in the BNG. This prevents any devices around it from knowing there was a glitch. Therefore, adjacent devices can maintain state during the failover, and end-to-end service quality is maintained.

GRACEFUL RESTART   Considered a precursor to NSR, Graceful Restart extensions are available in most of today's routing protocols. Graceful Restart is a capability signaled between two adjacent protocol neighbors. It indicates that a router should continue to be in the forwarding path, even if its control plane or routing protocol software is being restarted. The assumption is that during this restart, no changes can be made to the restarting device's forwarding table.

Without Graceful Restart, when an IGP (such as IS-IS or OSPF) detects that a neighbor has failed, the IGP typically tries to route around the restarting router. This causes at least two Shortest Path First (SPF) runs through the network—one when the failure is detected, and another after it has returned. Many modern routers implement a separation of forwarding and control planes. This could enable the router to continue forwarding packets even while the control plane and routing software are restarting. With Graceful Restart enabled, a restarting router's neighbors know to continue forwarding traffic to it provided that the routing topology around the device remained stable during the restart period. To help the restarted router restore its previous view of the network topology, the neighbors simply flood their protocol information back to the freshly restarted router. To prevent loops, if the routing table changes during the restart period, when the router comes back up, a full restart (including reroute) is automatically done.

ISSU The goal of many HA infrastructure features currently being implemented is to allow in-service software upgrades (ISSUs) without impacting the device's routing and forwarding capacity. With functionality such as Graceful Restart and NSR, devices with redundant hardware (either physical or logical) can load entirely new software releases that do not disrupt traffic flow. This capability is a major step toward a truly highly available network.

Figure 4.24 summarizes the functional blocks in the network that were discussed in this section. This includes process components, which also need to be built to ensure proper error handling in the network in case of misconfiguration.

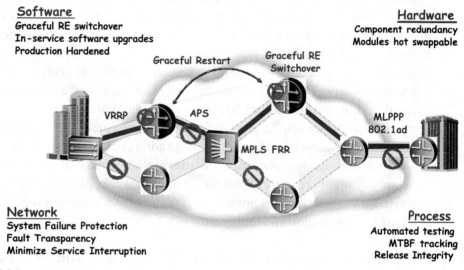

Figure 4.24 High-availability network and process components.

High availability is achieved through the cumulative effects of a number of components: software features, operational procedures, and an overall architecture that allows all these parts to work together. The network elements themselves play an important role in maintaining their own stability, but failures do happen. The network architecture has to consider the balance between the service guarantees sold to the end user, the factors and scenarios that could disrupt those guarantees, and the costs and details of how they can be mitigated.

SUMMARY

This chapter has outlined the many ways to build an access and aggregation network between the customer CPE and the BNG. Just like other aspects of building a triple-play network, there are various approaches to network design. On the local loop between the CPE and the DSLAM, a multi-PVC approach could be used. This is often the case where a service VLAN access architecture is used in the aggregation network. This distributes the network elements and relies on either static configuration for QoS or the DSLAM to perform service aggregation. Services are split across multiple routers for several reasons. One is because different groups in a company are responsible for different services. To delineate service responsibility, each group manages the router that delivers its service. Another reason is for vendor diversity, either for its own sake or because one vendor may have strengths in a particular area, such as a broadband service gateway, but not in other areas. In the first instance, to have vendor diversity on the cheap, one type of service can be delivered on vendor A's router, and a separate service could be delivered on vendor B's hardware. The alternative, more operationally expensive approach is to have multiple vendors in the network and all routers deliver the same services. The reason for the additional operational expenditure is usually software upgrades and knowledge capital. When routers need to be upgraded to support a new feature for one type of service, this affects not only all services on the same router, but also each router brand in the network. Thus, plenty of coordination and testing are needed.

Even though there is a central point at the DSLAM where traffic can be managed before being sent to the customer, there are not as many tools and features for dynamic service management compared to a dedicated BNG. Providers using a DSLAM in such a scenario are generally content with basic service prioritization among the VLANs/PVCs that carry services.

An alternative is the 1:1 centralized model, which delivers all services from a central broadband gateway. This enables QoS and service management to be done further in the network, before the aggregation network. Usually a stacked VLAN approach is used between the DSLAM and the BNG, which puts a subscriber in its own VLAN to the broadband IP edge. Using a central point to administer services is useful from a QoS perspective, and for easier implantation of Lawful

Intercept (LI). However, this functionality generally requires more expensive hardware to support all the features needed for a multiplay router.

Also discussed were methods of connecting DSLAMs to BNGs. These range from the cheap approach of using switches to aggregate traffic to the more expensive approach of connecting DSLAMs directly to the BNG using multiplexing equipment or dark fiber. In some cases, an MPLS network can be used to transport the Layer 2 traffic to and from the DSLAMs. This is used when there is already a network (or will be) that can support one or more Layer 2 transport types. These can include VPLS, pseudowire (Martini or Kompella transport). A further type of transport is MAC-in-MAC encapsulation, which improves the scaling properties of transporting Ethernet frames across the provider network. However, this is not yet in widespread use.

CHOOSING THE RIGHT ACCESS PROTOCOL

Access protocols can provide features such as automatic IP addressing, parameters for boot purposes, and enable a framework for authorization and authentication into service provider networks. Two examples, which are the focus of this chapter, are PPP over Ethernet (PPPoE) and Dynamic Host Configuration Protocol (DHCP). Strictly speaking, DHCP encompasses more functions than PPP. DHCP is a protocol to allocate IP addresses, Maximum Transmission Unit (MTU), communicate a TFTP server address, or any other parameters that are needed to prime a client when it boots up. It is also a protocol that runs on top of a multiaccess network such as Ethernet. The session part is generally called IP over Ethernet (IPoE).

PPP operates lower in the Open Systems Interconnection (OSI) model and runs directly on top of the physical layer. Other times it runs at a slightly higher protocol layer, such as ATM Adaptation Layer 5 (AAL5), but it was always intended as a point-to-point protocol. As such, it has slightly different goals and protocol approach than DHCP. It has such features as link-level status check—the Link Control Protocol (LCP) echo-request and echo-reply mechanism. It can determine whether a circuit is looped, and it supports encrypted authentication (CHAP). From an IP perspective, it supports assigning IP addresses, DNS, and WINS addresses to the device on the other end of the link. But extra features to configure a host, such as address lease timers, TFTP server addresses, and vendor-specific enhancements, have been left to other protocols.

Access protocols provide important functions to set up and enable the access network to deliver triple-play services. Most importantly, they play a significant role in assigning IP addresses to customer equipment. They also provide a mechanism to carry authentication credentials to the service provider. PPP can carry authentication protocols such as Password Authentication Protocol (PAP), Challenge Handshake Authentication Protocol (CHAP), and Extensible Authentication Protocol (EAP). DHCP can be used to authenticate the client's physical location, which is carried in a field called option 82. This option contains circuit identification information that tells DHCP servers and DHCP relays what was the originating circuit. In summary, both of these access protocols provide

- IP address and supporting data to client equipment
- Authentication mechanisms
- Connectivity for a client to the network

Even though the focus of each protocol is technically different, PPPoE and DHCP are used in a similar fashion to allocate IP addresses to subscribers. Both protocols can be used as part of a service provider's triple-play addressing architecture. PPPoE focuses more on address assignment and session state, leaving more sophisticated configuration up to other protocols. DHCP is a more fully featured protocol than PPPoE but lacks some of its stateful features. This chapter describes the basics of access protocols, describing PPPoE and DHCP in detail. The focus then moves to how they are implemented and the pros and cons of each.

PPP FOR BROADBAND NETWORKS

Over the past seven years, residential broadband services have mostly used ATM infrastructure. This is why Point-to-Point Protocol over ATM (PPPoA) was the dominant access protocol in service provider networks. As Ethernet supplants ATM, the protocols will accordingly become more Ethernet-centric. Remote Access Servers (RASs), which terminate dial-up connections, have primarily used PPP. It has been the protocol of choice because it has addressed the needs of service providers for providing authentication, protocol flexibility, and accounting.

PPP was originally defined by the IETF in RFC 1661. It provides a substantial amount of functionality:

- A way to encapsulate multiprotocol datagrams onto a single link
- A link control protocol
- Capabilities to configure and manage different network-layer protocols
- Handles authentication of the peer at the opposite end of the link
- Detects loops in physical media using magic number sequences

Technology Note: PPP Magic Numbers

Magic numbers are identifiers that are inserted into PPP control packets (called Link Control Protocol [LCP] packets) and are sent to the other end of the link in the form of an echo. The echo-request should be answered with an echo-reply containing the other end's magic number. The crux of the mechanism is for the received magic number to be different from the one that was sent. If the received magic number differs from the one that was sent, the link is not looped back to the local router.

PPP is connection-oriented. From a subscriber perspective, it indicates whether the connection to the service provider is up and IP connectivity has been established. The connection-oriented nature is a double-edged sword. On the positive side, the benefit is that both peers have an association with each other, and both have knowledge of the link state. When traffic is passed on the link, echo-request and echo-reply packets are not exchanged. The presence of data indicates that the link is working. During periods of inactivity, echo-request and echo-reply packets provide a link-checking mechanism to confirm that the other peer is still there.

But this results in a lot of state to maintain on the Broadband Network Gateway (BNG). With the large number of subscribers that BNGs terminate, this is fairly taxing on the routers. BNGs commonly terminate 32,000 customers on a single chassis. Newer equipment can, in theory, terminate more than 100,000 simultaneous subscribers on single router. The state mechanisms of PPP get even more complex if high-availability functionality is turned on within a BNG. The high-availability mechanisms mirror state between the active and standby control planes to provide stability to customer connections if a controller failure occurs. This point-to-point relationship between two PPP peers makes it difficult to introduce a hot standby routing gateway at the service provider. If a BNG fails at the service provider, all client sessions need to establish new sessions with a different gateway unless routers implement some proprietary redundancy mechanism.

PPPoA

PPP over ATM is still common in today's broadband networks, mainly because ATM was heavily used in carrier networks before the introduction of Ethernet DSLAMs. PPPoA provides some quality of service features, and traffic engineering capability. In this architecture, usually dedicated Permanent Virtual Circuits (PVCs) from customers can be multiplexed at the DSLAM onto a backhaul link toward the BNG. This is the same concept as Frame Relay, which also multiplexes multiple circuits onto a single link and uses the same acronym as ATM—PVC.

Since the days of dial-up, Internet providers have understood and deployed PPP-based services to their customers. As the progression to higher bit rate services gained momentum, it made sense to continue using PPP for Internet access services. Figure 5.1 shows a typical PPPoA topology.

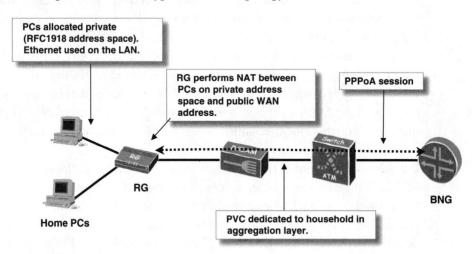

Figure 5.1 Diagram of a PPPoA session.

The PPPoA modem is usually a NAT-enabled router that provides basic routing functionality after it has established IP connectivity to the service provider. The

BNG is the PPP peer of the customer's modem. It authenticates the client when the user enters his or her credentials into the modem. The credentials are supplied either via PAP or CHAP to the BNG.

The PPPoA modem contains the ATM parameters to connect to the service provider. Each customer uses the same PVC details in the modem to enable a generic configuration to be saved on the modem. Typical ATM parameters used in the modem are VPI 8 and VCI 35. Virtual Path Identifier (VPI) and Virtual Circuit Identifier (VCI) values identify the virtual circuit on which to send traffic. See the Technology Note on PVPs near the beginning of Chapter 7, "Wholesale Broadband Networks," for more information on ATM Permanent Virtual Paths. The DSLAM terminates the DSL signal and sends the ATM cells to an upstream ATM switch. To unambiguously differentiate cells between DSL ports, the DSLAM modifies the generic circuit VPI and VCI values of 8 and 35 (or whatever they actually are) to locally unique values. Then the cells are forwarded to the ATM switch. When the BNG receives these cells, they have unique VPI and VCI values that it can associate with a particular DSL port.

To simplify the provisioning of connecting potentially thousands of PVCs on the BNG, automated circuit provisioning is a common feature of most vendors' broadband routers. It allows a service provider to input a few lines of configuration on the router to instruct it to dynamically create logical interfaces as needed rather than having to manually (or via automated provisioning from an external system) configure the interfaces.

In Juniper Networks' JUNOSe software, this is known as bulk configuration. It allows the operator to preprovision a range of VPI/VCI combinations in a few lines of configuration. The benefit is twofold. It keeps the configuration small, which means that there is less output to scroll through in the CLI. Also, by using this feature with dynamic interfaces, the ATM subinterface is not actually created until data are received on a given PVC. Because the ATM subinterface is not created if there is no traffic, this saves router resources at times when fewer customers are connected on the BNG. This capability is useful in oversubscription models where more "potential" PVCs are created than there are subscribers or capacity to connect them on the router. For example, if a provider is allocating blocks of PVCs per DSLAM and many PVCs in a block would never be used for customer connections, a provider can still preprovision all PVCs so that a PPP session can enter on any one of the circuits.

Cisco IOS allows for local-template-based ATM auto-provisioning with similar functionality. The ATM VC template is applied to a main interface with all PVCs on that interface auto-provisioned using values specified in the local template. These values may consist of, among other options, VPI/VCI combinations, OAM parameters, queue depth, and SAR shaping values.

Bulk configuration is not limited to ATM interfaces. Ethernet interfaces can also be preprovisioned so that when an Ethernet frame containing a PPPoE session enters the router, it can dynamically create the subinterface, reducing potential for error in the router configuration.

An Overview of PPPoE

Point-to-Point Protocol over Ethernet (PPPoE) is a client-server protocol that gives subscribers access to one or more BNGs. It differs from traditional PPP, which is strictly a peer-to-peer protocol by relaxing the point-to-point restriction. This enables it to function in a client-server model, with many clients connecting to PPPoE servers over a multiaccess Ethernet network, yet still run a point-to-point protocol on top. The two modes of running PPPoE to a household are bridged and routed.

PPPoE is divided into two phases: a discovery phase, which lets a client discover what services are available, and the PPP session stage, which is a subscriber's data channel. To differentiate between these two phases, a different Ethernet ether type is used on discovery and session frames. Ether type is a 2-byte header that is present on Ethernet II frames to indicate to the receiving end what type of protocol is present in the payload and thus how to decapsulate the frame. Additionally, a code field in the PPPoE header indicates if the frame is used as part of the discovery stage or session stage. The frame also contains a session ID field that uniquely identifies a PPPoE session. Having a different session ID allows multiple sessions to share the same MAC address. For example, a Residential Gateway (RG), which is also known as the CPE, might have two active PPPoE sessions, both of which might be sourced from the same MAC address but terminate on different BNGs for different services.

This section covers the two modes that PPPoE sessions can run in—bridged and routed. These have an impact mainly on the CPE architecture, but they also have scaling implications on the BNG. Bridged mode means that the CPE acts as an Ethernet bridge, forwarding PPPoE frames between the DSL WAN interface and the LAN. Routed mode has the PPPoE session terminated on the CPE, and the CPE routes packets between the LAN and WAN.

BNG Autodiscovery

When a client connects to a BNG using PPPoE, it initiates the discovery stage. Before the discovery phase happens, the client does not have any information about which devices are on the network or the services they offer. Therefore, the client sends a broadcast PPPoE discovery frame called a PPPoE Active Discovery Initiation (PADI). One or more BNGs reply to the initiation packet with a PPPoE Active Discovery Offer (PADO), containing an offer for service. The client selects one of the offers it has received from the BNGs and replies with a unicast session request packet to the selected BNG. This unicast session request is called the PPPoE Active Discovery Request (PADR). The PADR contains a tag containing the *service* the user is requesting. This is the same service name that the BNG sent in the PADO. The name of the service is arbitrary, but it can be used when a provider wants to offer multiple services on one or more BNGs that share a common Ethernet segment. For example, when a subscriber initiates the PPPoE dialer on his or her PC, a list of services could pop up, from which the user can choose one to connect. This causes a PADR to be sent to the BNG containing the name of the service. The final step in the discovery stage is for the BNG to send a PPPoE Active Discovery Session-confirmation (PADS).

PPPoE Resources

If the BNG does not have enough resources to support an incoming session request, it should not return a positive PADO. Instead, it should return a PADS with a specific tag (such as an *AC System Error*) indicating that the PPPoE server is running at or close to resource exhaustion and therefore is incapable of servicing the client. The PPPoE client can then display the embedded text string indicating that the service is unavailable due to resources and that the issue is not on the client's end of the connection.

It is quite common for a service provider to oversubscribe a BNG's client termination capacity. For example, the provider might use a single ATM PVC or VLAN for each household and terminate it on the BNG. Yet there could be several PPPoE sessions on this PVC if the CPE runs in bridged mode. The customer could consume three or more PPPoE sessions on the BNG, consuming extra resources. Most broadband routers can limit the number of PPPoE sessions per PVC to limit the overall impact of multiple PPPoE sessions.

PPPoE and MTU

The PPPoE RFC[1] limits the size of the negotiated PPP Maximum Receive Unit (MRU) between the PPPoE client and server to be no greater than 1,492 bytes so as not to exceed the IEEE Ethernet MTU of 1500 bytes. This is because the PPPoE and PPP overhead adds an extra 6 and 2 bytes, respectively. And because an IP packet can be up to 1,500 bytes on an Ethernet network, the MTU of the PPPoE session is thus limited to 1,492 bytes. If a PPPoE RG is running in routed mode, this causes packet fragmentation in the network, because PCs on the LAN send IP packets of 1,500 bytes, which the router must fragment due to the 1,492-byte MTU on the DSL link. Reassembling these packets requires extra resources on the receiving server, which must buffer all fragmented packets before it can reassemble them, creating potential for a denial of service (DoS) attack. It also introduces delay into the packet-forwarding process due to the reassembly. Servers have built-in strategies to avoid undue resource consumption due to packet reassembly, but it causes some impact nonetheless.

This issue is addressed in IETF draft draft-arberg-pppoe-mtu-gt1492-02, which describes how to improve the situation. A new PPPoE tag has been created that tells the AC what MRU the client is capable of receiving. It assumes that most Ethernet devices today bend the 1,500-byte limit and allow jumbo frames. Jumbo frames are those that are larger than the limit specified in the IEEE Ethernet specification. On older switches, such jumbo frames are dropped rather than being transmitted across the network.

Bridged Mode

Bridged mode means PPPoE sessions run between a PC in the home to the BNG. It is called bridged mode because the Residential Gateway (RG) is functioning as a bridge and forwards Ethernet frames between the home LAN and the DSL port. This topology is shown in Figure 5.2.

---

[1] http://www.ietf.org/rfc/rfc2516.txt

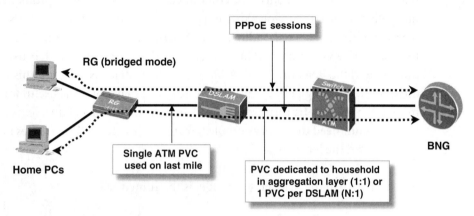

Figure 5.2 Topology of a PPPoE session with the CPE operating in bridged mode.

In the figure, an ATM switch is used in the aggregation domain between the DSLAM and BNG. Even though the protocol is PPP over Ethernet, an architecture using ATM as shown in Figure 5.2 is still possible. In fact, it is commonly deployed. It uses ATM AAL5 and bridged Ethernet over ATM to deliver PPPoE (in short, PPPoEoA) to the customer. There are several ways to deliver PPPoEoA using an Ethernet aggregation network. These are covered in Chapter 4, "Designing a Triple-Play Access Network." The two common ones are the 1:1 model, which dedicates a VLAN to each subscriber, and the N:1 service VLAN model, which uses a single VLAN for all subscribers on that DSLAM. In both cases, one or more PPPoE sessions are multiplexed onto a PVC with the Ethernet MAC addresses in the Ethernet header and the session ID in the PPPoE header acting as the demultiplexing keys. With an ATM aggregation architecture, the models are very similar. In the 1:1 architecture, a PVC is dedicated to each household, and one or more PPPoE sessions are run from devices on the LAN. Predictably with the N:1 architecture, a single PVC is used on the last mile but maps onto a shared PVC in the aggregation network. All users connected to a DSLAM share this single PVC. In the ATM aggregation environment, the most common approach is the 1:1 model.

In both the 1:1 and N:1 architectures, the demarcation point between customer and provider is still the CPE. However, because the CPE is in bridging mode, using in-band Layer 3 interface for troubleshooting is more difficult. This means

that when providers need to troubleshoot customer connectivity problems, prag-
matically they need to involve themselves further into the customer LAN. A simple ping to the customer IP address may not be sufficient. Of course, a dedicated
management PVC with an IP interface can be deployed between the customer
modem and the BNG or Network Management System (NMS), but this is in a
different forwarding path to customer traffic and may not be as useful for deter-
mining the nature of a forwarding problem. One of the strong upsides is that the
CPE does not need to be very complex. It simply bridges PPPoE frames between
the LAN and the local loop.

An alternative to the bridged RG model is the routed RG.

Routed Mode

The CPE can instead be placed in routed mode, which means that the PPPoE session is terminated on the Residential Gateway (RG). The RG forwards traffic,
using Layer 3 addressing information, between the Ethernet domain on the customer LAN and the PPPoE session on the WAN side. Usually this involves Network Address Translation (NAT) to allow devices on the LAN to share the same
public IP address on the WAN. This functionality is shown in Figure 5.3.

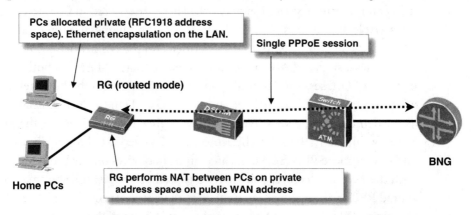

Figure 5.3 Layer 3 mode with a PPPoE session terminating on the CPE.

A common question that arises is which is the better of the two modes to
run—routed or bridged? Luckily this is a relatively simple choice for the service
provider, given the correct information. The attributes of routed mode are as
follows:

- It isolates the household LAN from the BNG, which is useful to limit what traffic reaches the provider. The CPE also acts as a Layer 3 demarcation point. This is handy as a central point of management when multiple services are delivered to a single household.

- It usually uses one PPP session per household. Although this simplifies routing, it is not possible to tailor services to a single subscriber, because all traffic undergoes NAT from the household. However, in most deployments to date, triple-play services are delivered to a household rather than a subscriber.

- CPE is more expensive compared to a bridged one due to extra protocol complexity.

The attributes of bridged mode are as follows:

- It allows multiple PPPoE sessions per household, creating more customized service.

- No complications with NAT application layer gateways (ALGs) on the RG.

- Limited CPE management and troubleshooting capability.

- It's not possible to implement Layer 3 packet filtering on CPE.

- No upstream packet fragmentation occurs, because the PPPoE session ends on an interface on the LAN device.

Bridged CPE may have made sense in a simple single-play environment, but in a complex triple-play environment, often the provider wants to provide and manage the CPE itself. This drastically cuts down on the involvement the provider needs in the LAN. A routed device at the customer premises provides a handy demarcation to manage any services that are delivered to the customer. Any devices on the LAN that send dubious broadcast traffic at questionable rates to the access network are blocked by the routed CPE because of broadcast domain isolation.

Most legacy DSLAMs or non-IP DSLAMS do not terminate PPPoE but provide transport or bridging of ATM frames from the customer DSL port to the ATM or Frame Relay backhaul. Some IP DSLAM vendors can terminate PPPoA from the subscriber and perform protocol translation from PPPoA to PPPoE. This is called PPPoA to PPPoE Interworking Function (IWF), but it is a proprietary scheme. The IWF can be used when migrating an aggregation network from ATM to Ethernet where there is an established base of PPPoA subscribers. The reason for the IWF is because PPPoA cannot run on an Ethernet network. However, switching over to PPPoE in a sudden transition could be considered too risky. Therefore, it may be preferable to continue running PPPoA on subscriber modems and migrate to PPPoE at a later stage. If the DSLAMs are configured correctly, many can support either protocol on the last mile. See the section "Protocol Interworking" in Chapter 4 for more details on PPPoA-to-PPPoE protocol interworking.

A major benefit of all PPP-related architectures is authentication and connectivity detection. Of course, PPPoE also benefits from having PPP as its cornerstone. Service providers can move from an ATM transport model to an Ethernet model and continue to maintain many aspects of their existing OSS and RADIUS systems because the protocol is very similar. If authentication is based on user credentials supplied in PPP through PAP/CHAP, existing backend systems that authenticate PPPoA customers can be reused with minimal modification.

DHCP FOR BROADBAND NETWORKS

DHCP is used in broadband networks as an alternative to PPP for IP address configuration and service provisioning. DHCP has been used for some time in local-area networks (LANs) as the preferred way to assign IP addresses, gateways, DNS servers, and various IP-centric options to clients. For example, DHCP can provide the IP address of a configuration server to a VoIP handset, which it can contact to download its configuration. A trademark of a flexible protocol is the ability for vendors to add their own capabilities to the protocol (while still falling within some guidelines that the specification dictates). With the passage of time, these vendor-specific attributes have been captured in IETF RFCs: RFC 1497[2] and, more recently, RFC 2132.[3] The origins of DHCP lie in the Bootstrap Protocol (BOOTP), written in the mid-1980s and extended through several RFC documents to communicate dynamic IP address and supplementary configuration information. The description in the specifications shows that the targeted types of devices for BOOTP and DHCP are small embedded devices, and this is still true today. For example, consumer Set-Top Boxes (STBs) and VoIP handsets are

[2] http://tools.ietf.org/html/1497
[3] http://tools.ietf.org/html/2132

both used in triple-play environments and are considered embedded devices. Service providers deploy DHCP for the simple purpose of giving PCs in the home an IP address to access the Internet but also in more complex scenarios of using DHCP to configure STBs and SIP handsets. This section covers both cases. This differs from PPP, which is really an address assignment mechanism and relies on other, higher-layer protocols for further configuration.

The usage of DHCP in broadband networks is gaining momentum because it is a good fit with the Ethernet connectivity that is being deployed in access networks. Providers also want a simple, scalable solution for IP address assignment. Here are some of the current and emerging features of DHCP deployments in broadband networks:

- Ethernet connectivity between the subscriber and the DHCP server
- The ability to uniquely identify a subscriber's local loop
- End device configuration
- Policy control on dynamic DHCP subscribers

DHCP deployments in broadband networks require Ethernet connectivity between the subscriber and DHCP server. This could be either bridged Ethernet over ATM, which is described in RFC 1483[4] (although the newer version is RFC 2684), or native Ethernet connectivity if using packet transport with Ethernet in the first mile. As just mentioned, most DSL networks have used ATM to transport data between the DSLAM and BNG, which means that DHCP is used as an Ethernet overlay protocol—Multiprotocol Encapsulation over ATM, described in RFC 1483. It explains how Layer 2 and Layer 3 protocols such as Ethernet and IP are encapsulated in Protocol Data Units (PDUs) for transport across an ATM network. This could be using either a bridged mode or a routed mode. As service providers migrate to Ethernet transport and slowly grandfather their legacy networks, the protocol operation is simplified by not having to deal with ATM protocol encapsulation and its associated overheads. Overheads here refer to the ATM CPCS padding, which is needed to bring the PDU up to the next 48-byte multiple, and to the 5-byte header present in every ATM cell. AAL5 refers to the type of encapsulation used in RFC 1483 and is designed to transport packets. Other types of adaptation layers are in use, such as AAL1 and AAL2, which are both used to transport constant bit rate (CBR) circuits across an ATM network.

[4] http://tools.ietf.org/html/1483 or http://tools.ietf.org/html/2684

Technology Note: Bridged IP

In the case of bridged IP over ATM, an IP interface is configured on top of the ATM PVC on the BNG and has an encapsulation type of bridged RFC 1483. The notion of "configuring interfaces on top of a PVC" comes from the concept of a protocol that has layers of protocols stacked on top of each other. See the Technology Note on the OSI seven-layer stack in Chapter 11, "Dynamic User Session Control." An ATM PVC is considered a data-link protocol that sits under a Layer 3 interface—a bridged IP interface, for example. In Cisco IOS nomenclature, this is called a bridged virtual interface (BVI), and on Juniper JUNOSe it is called a bridged IP interface. The interface on the BNG is explicitly configured to support an encapsulation type of bridged Ethernet over ATM (as specified in RFC 1483/2684). To enable Layer 3 functionality, the interface needs an IP address, which can be enabled by setting the interface to unnumbered and "nailing" it to a loopback interface. This Layer 3 configuration is used to enable routing functionality on the interface and enable more complex features, such as running DHCP relay (described next) and IP filtering.

Of course, this refers to the case in which ATM is still used in the aggregation domain. If native Ethernet transport is used between DSLAMs and BNGs, bridged Ethernet does not apply. With this type of transport, the encapsulation type is Ethernet, and the VLAN terminates on a subinterface on the BNG.

DHCP ADDRESS ALLOCATION MODELS

This section covers several common implementations of DHCP servers. DHCP servers can be characterized in two broad categories—one with all configuration and control residing on the BNG, and the other using a mixture of BNG and external DHCP server capability. The first, BNG-hosted DHCP, is the method by which the BNG acts as a DHCP server. All address pools, static addresses, and additional IP parameters are stored on the broadband gateway. A more centralized way of managing IP addressing is to have BNGs forward DHCP requests to a central server and let them allocate IP addresses to subscribers. There are three approaches to designing the network with centralized address assignment in mind. The first is DHCP relay, which means that the BNG forwards most DHCP packets to external servers with few changes to the original packet. The second is DHCP relay-proxy, which has the BNG take a more active role in the address management process by modifying some fields in the DHCP protocol exchange. In relay-proxy, the BNG has full state knowledge of which clients are active on the network and also provides a basic security layer between the real DHCP server and client.

The final DHCP implementation that is covered in this section is when the BNG acts as a BNG client. Here, the BNG can use an external DHCP server and request addresses on behalf of subscribers that connect to it.

BNG-Hosted DHCP

Almost all vendors' BNGs can act as a DHCP server, allocating addresses to clients which are either directly connected or those on remote networks. This is the simplest DHCP scenario because the configuration remains local to the router and there are no external systems to interact with. The configuration on the BNG entails enabling the DHCP server and creating one or more pools of addresses from which the server can allocate. When the router receives the first request from the client for an address, it is forwarded to the DHCP application so that an IP address can be offered to the client. This configuration is used when a simple address allocation mechanism is satisfactory and it's unimportant which address the client receives. Where there is simplicity, limited flexibility is sure to follow. A static address can be assigned to a particular client by configuring a MAC-to-IP address mapping on the BNG. But this approach is not terribly scalable for large numbers of clients. Also, DHCP feature development on a BNG often lags behind external server feature development, so if any new, customized DHCP functionality is needed, an external server is often the best way to go.

DHCP Relay

The DHCP relay agent functionality that exists in BNGs is an important tool for dynamic address assignment in broadband networks. It is used when an end client is connected to the BNG over a Layer 2 network or via a directly connected DSLAM and the client needs to be assigned various IP configuration parameters. When the client initiates the DHCP process, it sends a DHCP discover packet, which is broadcast using UDP to the IPv4 address 255.255.255.255. The discover is intended to solicit a reply from a DHCP server on the same broadcast network (hence the 255.255.255.255 destination address) and is similar to PPPoE PADI discovery. It is infeasible to deploy DHCP servers connected to every Layer 2 network, so DHCP relay is used on the BNG to listen for these DHCP broadcasts and forward them as unicasts to one or more centralized servers. The BNG then acts as a relay for some subsequent DHCP messages. But as soon as the client has been assigned an address, subsequent protocol exchanges, such as renewals, are unicast between the client and server.

Because the server is often several router hops away from the client, the BNG needs to insert an attribute to the unicast *discover* sent to the server. The attribute is called the giaddr, which is the IP address of the interface on which it received the request. One or more servers answer the DHCP request in the form of an offer with an IP address to use and send the reply to the BNG's address in the giaddr. This is then either broadcast or unicast to the local subnet. This first phase is shown in Figure 5.4.

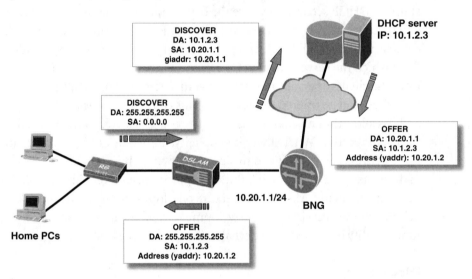

Figure 5.4 First phase of DHCP relay.

The second phase is the client requesting the offered address with a request packet, which is also sent to the 255.255.255.255 broadcast address. The BNG gets involved again to forward the request via unicast to the server that offered the IP address and again inserts the giaddr field into the request before sending. If the client is permitted to use the address, the server replies to the BNG with a DHCP ACK including the IP address, gateway, lease time, and any additional parameters that the CPE needs. As with the DHCP OFFER, the ACK is broadcast to the client on the subnet from where the request came. Because the replies are broadcast on the local subnet, a field inside the DHCP packet (the transaction ID) is used to differentiate the protocol exchanges between hosts on the same subnet. This phase is shown in Figure 5.5.

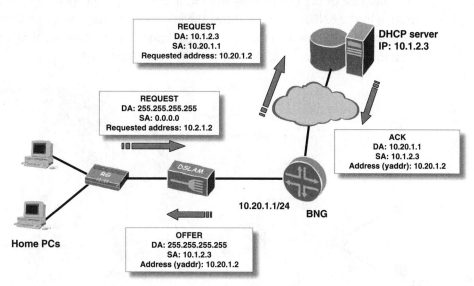

Figure 5.5 Second phase of DHCP relay.

One other piece of information that is usually inserted into DHCP discover and DHCP request packets before being sent to the DHCP server is DHCP option 82. It is defined in RFC 3046[5] and is officially called the DHCP Relay Agent Information Option. This option is used in addition to the client MAC address to identify the source of the request. In the service provider market, DHCP option 82 is the DSL port or local loop to which the subscriber is connected. This field is analogous to the A party or calling number that is tagged onto a residential telephone call to the phone network.

So why is a MAC address not enough to identify the client? And is the customer VLAN or PVC identifier also not enough information to be able to identity it? The answer to the first question is because the MAC address is easy to change on the client, and relying on an easily modifiable field is not good security practice if authentication of the physical location of the client is needed. Option 82 can be inserted into the DHCP packets either by the DSLAM or the BNG. It is transparent and external to the user, which means that it is harder to forge. The identifier's format is typically a DSLAM name, port designation, and logical circuit ID

[5] http://tools.ietf.org/html/3046

if it is inserted by the DSLAM, or an Ethernet/ATM-specific identifier if it is inserted by the BNG. Figure 5.6 shows the DSLAM inserting an option 82 field in to a discover packet, which the BNG forwards to the DHCP server. Notice that when the offer arrives back at the client, the field is removed.

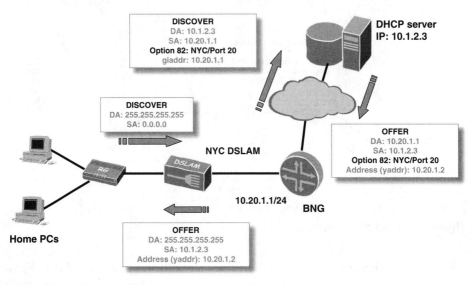

Figure 5.6 Option 82 insertion.

The answer to the second question about using the customer VLAN as an identifier relates to the design of the aggregation network and how the VLANs and PVCs are provisioned. For example, in a 1:1 VLAN architecture, each household has a dedicated VLAN between the DSLAM and the BNG and a stacked VLAN (S-VLAN) tag that identifies the DSLAM. Therefore, a local loop can be uniquely identified with an S-VLAN and C-VLAN pair. The complication arises if an N:1 VLAN architecture is used, which puts all traffic from one DSLAM onto a single broadcast network. Now there is no dedicated Layer 2 path between the BNG and the subscriber, so it is impossible to associate a C-VLAN and S-VLAN with a household. Therefore, the network needs the DHCP option to identify behind which DSL port a CPE makes the request.

Centralizing IP address allocation by using DHCP relay is more flexible and powerful than distributing DHCP servers located on each BNG. For example, most BNGs come with a limited DHCP server implementation that does not allow for configuring extra options that stand-alone servers have. These options could be vendor-specific attributes or a mapping between an IP address and a user's MAC address, which is stored in an external database. These tasks are best suited for an external server.

As soon as the client has completed its initial protocol negotiation with the server—after the server sends its ACK—the client communicates directly with the server to refresh its lease. A lease is the address assignment given to the client with a finite time that it is permitted to use the address and the associated parameters. To ensure continuity of service, the client *refreshes* or *renews* its DHCP lease before it expires (usually at 50% of the lease time) and asks the server for an additional lease. The renew message is sent unicast from the client directly to the server, which takes the BNG out of the loop. This is somewhat disadvantageous because the BNG no longer has any knowledge of clients silently going off the network or servers negating a lease extension (known as a NAK). This lack of state keeping is inflexible for some service providers that need to keep DHCP lease state on the BNG for services that need continual awareness of active clients. An enhancement to DHCP relay agent functionality is the DHCP relay-proxy, which makes the BNG a more active part of the protocol exchange.

Simple DHCP relay configurations are shown in Listings 5.1 and 5.2 for Juniper JUNOSe and Cisco IOS, respectively. Both configurations cause broadcast DHCP packets that hit the interface GigabitEthernet 1/0/0.100 to be relayed via unicast to the DHCP server, 10.2.3.4. In the listings, both function in relatively the same way. However, configuring the DHCP relay server address in JUNOSe activates the DHCP relay agent on all interfaces. Using IOS, DHCP relay is configured per interface.

Listing 5.1 Sample DHCP Relay Configuration—JUNOSe

```
interface loopback0
 ip address 10.20.1.1 255.255.254.0
!
interface GigabitEthernet 1/0/0.100
 ethernet description "Link to DSLAM port 100"
 vlan id 100
 ip unnumbered loopback0
!
interface GigabitEthernet 1/1/0.101
 ethernet description "Link to core"
```

```
vlan id 101
ip address 10.40.1.0 255.255.255.254
!


set dhcp relay 10.2.3.4
```

Listing 5.2 Sample DHCP Relay Configuration—IOS

```
interface loopback0
 ip address 10.20.1.1 255.255.254.0
 !
interface GigabitEthernet 1/0/0.100
 description "Link to DSLAM port 100"
 encapsulation dot1q 100
 ip unnumbered loopback0
 ip helper-address 10.2.3.4
 !
interface GigabitEthernet 1/1/0.101
 description "Link to core"
 encapsulation dot1q 101
 ip address 10.40.1.0 255.255.255.254
 !
```

DHCP Relay-Proxy

DHCP relay-proxy is an enhancement to DHCP relay. It still entails forwarding packets to an external DHCP server, but via a proxy agent on the BNG. As with DHCP relay, no modification is required on the client, and the client should not be able to discern much difference between DHCP relay-proxy and DHCP relay. When the client broadcasts a discover to the LAN, the BNG forwards the request to the DHCP server as before. When the offer is sent back from the server to the BNG, the BNG rewrites the server address field (option 54) within the DHCP packet to be an address of the BNG before broadcasting it to the client. As before, the client broadcasts a request for the server-offered address to the LAN, which the BNG intercepts and forwards to the server. The server confirms the lease by sending an acknowledgment back to the client via the BNG. The same as with the offer, the BNG replaces the server address in the server field (option 54) with the BNG itself.

Replacing the server address is one of the crucial differences between DHCP relay and DHCP relay-proxy. This means that the client exchanges all subsequent DHCP communications (releases and renews) with the BNG, which proxies them to the *real* server. This proxy function has several benefits. The first is a basic security layer that hides the real DHCP server addresses from the client.

Because option 54 has been rewritten to be the BNG address, the client sees only the BNG as the DHCP server. The second benefit is that because the BNG is implementing a proxy function, it can implement sanity checks on the packets before forwarding them to the real server. This limits the impact of malformed packets on the server. For example, an implementation could rate-limit requests from a client if it sends too many requests in a given time period. For optimal flexibility, this rate-limiter could be a configurable value. The third benefit is that the BNG is now fully aware of the state between the client and DHCP server. In theory, this last point would enable the BNG to replicate its DHCP state to another BNG and allow another router to take control without losing lease information. Of course, in any case, the DHCP server would also have this state, but getting this state to the BNG is the difficult part.

DHCP relay-proxy functionality is not covered under any RFC. However, the approximation of its functionality is based on the premise of the BNG running as a DHCP server with respect to the client. This allows for proxy-like functionality rather than the more transparent DHCP relay. Figure 5.7 shows how an implementation changes the destination address of a DHCP request packet state to the DHCP server's address during the renewing state.

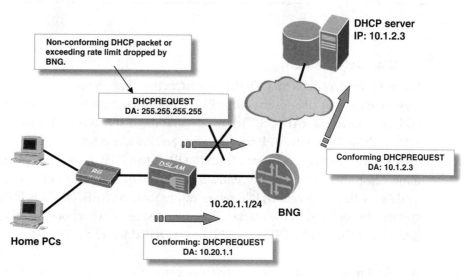

Figure 5.7 DHCP relay-proxy.

Table 5.1 summarizes the types of DHCP environments, their operation, and the pros and cons of each.

Table 5.1 Comparing the Three DHCP Options

	Operation	Pros	Cons
BNG-hosted DHCP	Address pools located on BNG. All addresses assigned locally.	Low management overhead.	Limited control over address allocation policy.
DHCP relay agent	DHCP packets relayed from BNG to central server. Addresses assigned from DHCP server.	Flexible address assignment.	Greater management overhead. Lack of BNG visibility with lease state.
DHCP relay proxy agent	DHCP packets relayed from BNG to central server. Addresses assigned from DHCP server. BNG masquerades as DHCP server.	Flexible address assignment. BNG has record of DHCP lease state.	More complex software functionality on BNG.

BNG as DHCP Client

Service providers deploying DHCP infrastructure have the option to use DHCP servers to provide IP addresses for PPP clients rather than assign from a local address pool or via RADIUS. This means that the BNG takes on the role of a DHCP client. When the PPP peer requests an IP address from the BNG, it triggers a DHCP message to be sent from the BNG to a DHCP server. This feature allows customers who want to centralize address allocation for PPP subscribers to do so with an external DHCP server rather than via RADIUS. This feature is not widely deployed in the market, because most providers choose to allocate IP addresses either via RADIUS for PPP or via DHCP server for DHCP.

As a final note on DHCP capability, work currently is under way in the DSL Forum to create a generalized keepalive mechanism, which is effectively targeted at non-PPP environments. A keepalive is inherent in PPP/PPPoE using the echo-request/echo-reply, but DHCP does not have an equivalent mechanism. The lease protocol exchange does not serve as an effective keepalive mechanism, because DHCP leases are typically measured in terms of hours or days, so the closest approximation of an active client is still within several hours.

CHOOSING BETWEEN PPP AND DHCP

DHCP and PPP have different origins, but both are in use today in broadband provider networks to distribute IP addressing information to PCs and RGs. PPP was developed as a successor to the Serial Line Interface Protocol (SLIP), which was used on point-to-point fixed-line and dial-up narrowband networks. Examples of narrowband networks are 2400bps serial lines, X.25 circuits, and dial-up lines. Due to limitations with SLIP, such as lack of link loop detection, single-protocol capability, and inflexible authentication methods, PPP was developed as its successor, and it's still in wide use today. In broadband networks, it was first used on point-to-point ATM PVCs, and then was extended for use on multipoint networks under the rubric of the PPPoE IETF RFC. On the other hand, although DHCP has its origins in BOOTP, it was designed for use on multipoint networks, such as Ethernet LANs, for address allocation. One of the advantages of DHCP is to ease the administrative burden of manually configuring static addresses to PCs and devices on a LAN. It does this by instructing a server to reserve addresses for certain clients and allocating them as necessary when requested.

ADVANTAGES OF PPPoE

The standard for PPPoE was written because providers wanted a way to use the PPP protocol on an Ethernet network. By its very definition, PPP has to run on a point-to-point link, so extra protocol encapsulation has been added to PPP to simulate a point-to-point link over which it can run. A broadband PPPoE access architecture means that a PPPoE session runs from each PC in the household or from a single PPPoE session from a dedicated CPE. These PPPoE sessions are Layer 2 paths that run across a multiaccess network to simulate a point-to-point link.

A commonly cited and important reason for using PPPoE is that it partially replicates the PPP and ATM environment where each subscriber has his or her own interface to which policies can be attached. This reduces the development time to adapt management systems to an Ethernet environment.

In almost all cases, service providers deploy PPP with some form of authentication. This could be the DSL port's circuit ID, inserted by the DSLAM into the PPPoA Intermediate Agent (IA) header. Alternatively this could be the more pedestrian combination of the username and password, or even a combination of the two. A variety of authentication modes exist, both encrypted and unencrypted. These range from Password Authentication Protocol (PAP) to Extensible Authentication Protocol (EAP). Only after the user is authenticated does he or she receive an IP address from the network.

If a party external to the service provider requires a particular customer's traffic to be duplicated to a legal intercept network, the username or port identifier can be located on the correct BNG and interface. The lawful intercept mechanism can then be activated on the user's interface.

If the user needs to be disconnected from the network, the PPP session can be terminated by one end sending a terminate request message to the other end. Alternatively, one end of the link can detect that the peer has disconnected through the lack of PPP echo-reply messages on the link.

A further benefit built in to the protocol is a keepalive mechanism, which means that one end of the link sends a PPP LCP echo-request to solicit a response from the other end of the link. This is called an echo-reply. These are lightweight packets (that is, they have little protocol complexity) that can be implemented on a router's forwarding hardware, thus saving valuable CPU cycles on the router's control plane for more demanding tasks. If one end of the protocol has silently disconnected, the other end of the link can eventually detect this through the loss of keepalives and remove the subscriber and PPP state from the network.

As discussed in Chapter 7, PPPoE is a natural fit with most wholesale networks due to the popularity of L2TP unbundling. L2TP version 2 is the most prevalent version of L2TP and is tightly coupled with PPP, making it difficult to run any other protocol on the access link. The exception is bit stream and copper unbundling, which do not use L2TP. L2TP version 3 solves this problem by being able to transport several types of Layer 2 protocols across a packet-switched domain, including Ethernet (which DHCP uses). Of course, thanks to PPP's authentication mechanism (that is, username and password), a PPPoE session can be dynamically terminated to an arbitrary L2TP LNS endpoint using the extra help of RADIUS.

Last, although they aren't built into the protocol's capabilities, time-based and volume-based usage have long been a feature of PPP networks. For example, a network access server (NAS) or broadband RAS (BRAS) that terminates PPP/PPPoE sessions usually sends the user's "time connected" and "bytes transferred" details to one or more RADIUS servers.

The benefits of PPPoE are as follows:

- It has built-in authentication mechanisms.
- The lawful intercept mechanism maps easily to techniques used in the dial-up world.
- It's easy to terminate a user session.
- It has a lightweight keepalive mechanism to determine peer status.
- It's straightforward to apply IP filters for service filtering or captive portal redirection based on existing RADIUS mechanisms.
- It's an ideal protocol fit for wholesale DSL providers.
- It has well-established practices for time- and usage-based accounting.
- It has many similarities to the tried-and-tested PPPoA access model.

DISADVANTAGES OF PPPoE

PPPoE also has several downsides. MTU complications causing IP fragmentation were explained earlier in the chapter. In the downstream, fragmentation usually causes a problem due to additional overhead of L2TP; but on the upstream direction, PPoE often causes fragmentation due to its 1492 byte MTU restriction.

Keeping the state of many thousands of subscribers on a router incurs greater CPU and memory usage on the BNG compared to a simple DHCP environment. A DHCP relay environment simply has to keep track of which IP address has been allocated out which interface. However, this state-keeping overhead increases for providers with a more complex DHCP environment. For example, applying IP policies and quality-of-service profiles on DHCP subscribers increases the state that must be kept on the BNG and becomes more pronounced when a DHCP keepalive mechanism eventually is devised and deployed.

Because PPPoE is a point-to-point protocol, the relationship between the BNG and other PPPoE endpoint is quite tightly coupled, because the ends need to keep the necessary protocol state. This makes it difficult to run a *hot standby* protocol that allows the session to fail over seamlessly to another endpoint if a gateway fails. For example, when running an IPoE architecture such as DHCP, the Virtual Router Redundancy Protocol (VRRP) can be used to provide one or more standby gateways for clients. If the primary gateway fails, the secondary one quickly takes the place of the primary gateway without any intervention from the client. The prevailing architecture in the market for redundant PPPoE gateways is to allow clients to choose between two or more PPPoE access concentrators in the *discovery* phase, but it still does not allow for seamless gateway failover. This type of architecture has two or more concentrators on the same broadcast network, each with its own service that a client can pick. Usually whichever of the two concentrators replies to the client's *discovery* first is the one on which the client chooses to terminate the service. When one fails, the client needs to establish a new session to the other gateway.

Most bridged CPE architectures do not lend themselves well to manageable triple-play environments, but PPPoE architectures in particular are even less flexible than their bridged DHCP counterparts. This is because PCs can't easily take advantage of other PCs sharing the same LAN in the same broadcast domain. Unless other routing solutions are employed, all traffic has to be routed via the BNG to get back to another device in the same household.

Because PPPoE was designed as a link management protocol to support limited implementations of upper-layer protocols, the protocol does not lend itself well to auto-configuring a CPE. This type of implementation is a lightweight protocol implementation, but it requires higher-layer protocols, such as TFTP/FTP or SNMP, to take care of more-complex CPE provisioning tasks. In summary, the limitations of PPPoE are as follows:

- MTU complications.
- Extra state-keeping is needed on the BNG.
- It isn't possible to implement hot-standby broadband gateways.
- If run in bridged CPE mode, slightly less LAN-based peer-to-peer routing occurs.
- It requires higher-layer protocols to fully provision CPE.

ADVANTAGES OF DHCP

DHCP was purpose-built for use in broadcast networks, such as Ethernet, so it is an ideal fit in Ethernet-based broadband access networks. It is suitable in both 1:1 and *N*:1 VLAN architectures. It has a large list of protocol extensions that lets providers configure DHCP clients to their specific requirements. Chapter 4 has more information on 1:1 and *N*:1 VLAN architectures. Using DHCP relay proxy agents on BNGs allows address allocation to occur from centralized servers and enables quick deployment of new DHCP protocol extensions.

A *session* in DHCP has a different meaning than in PPPoE. PPPoE establishes a connection between two endpoints or from the BNG to the client. Usually the two endpoints exchange keepalive messages to verify that the opposite end is reachable (although this isn't mandatory). DHCP does not have such a tight coupling between a client and server or its gateway router. The closest concept to a session in DHCP nomenclature is the *lease*. The lease, which was explained earlier in this chapter, is how long a client can use an IP address configuration. There is ongoing discussion in the DSL Forum as to how to represent a session in the access network. This applies to both PPPoE and the DHCP environment. A session is defined in this chapter, for the purposes of discussion, to be a lease between a DHCP client and a DHCP server, which could also be the BNG. Where necessary, a distinction between a true PPP session and a DHCP lease is made. In simple networks, DHCP deployments are more lightweight than their PPP counterparts, because less state is kept in the network, in both the CPE and the BNG.

Similar to the PPPoE environment, DHCP *sessions* can be established either between an RG and the external DHCP server or from PCs in the home LAN to the external DHCP server. The protocol can also run simultaneously on the household LAN between PCs and the RG and between the RG and the external DHCP server. In the latter case, the RG functions as a DHCP server and it runs in routed mode, with or without NAT enabled. NAT is disabled in a routed IPv6 scenario. The use of NAT in this context is to convert private IP addresses on the home LAN to a public address that is assigned to the RG. Figures 5.8 and 5.9 show examples of both modes.

In Figure 5.8, PCs on the LAN request IP addresses from the RG using DHCP. In a separate session, the RG requests an IP address from the DHCP server via a DHCP relay proxy agent on the BNG. This is called routed mode because the RG routes IP packets from the LAN side to the DSL side of the router. A public address is assigned to the WAN interface, and any addresses from the LAN undergo NAT.

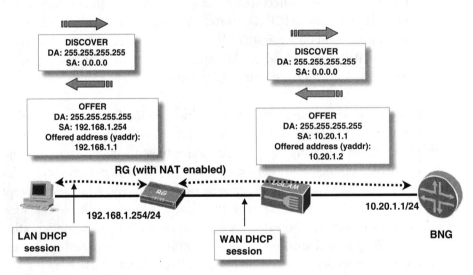

Figure 5.8 DHCP with a routed RG.

In Figure 5.9, PCs request IP addresses directly from the BNG using one of the DHCP modes explained earlier in the chapter. This is called bridged mode because the RG acts as a bridge, forwarding Ethernet frames between the DSL interface and the LAN interfaces. Each PC or device on the LAN receives a public IP address.

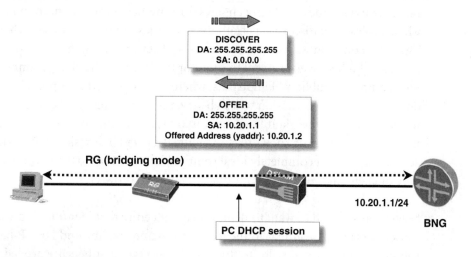

Figure 5.9 DHCP with a bridged RG.

In summary, the benefits of DHCP compared to PPPoE are as follows:

- It's designed with broadcast networks in mind—no MTU complications.
- It has redundant gateway capability with rapid failover—VRRP.
- It has many protocol extensions for automatic provisioning.
- Its simple implementation is ideal for lightweight clients and means little state overhead on BNG if using a simple service with few or no policies.

DISADVANTAGES OF DHCP

DHCP does not have any keepalive capability built into the protocol. An auxiliary protocol such as Bidirectional Forwarding Detection (BFD) is an option, and so is Ethernet continuity-check OAM. However, these protocols have not yet been widely deployed at scale within a routing node. This is because protocols such as these need to scale to tens of thousands of sessions and still need to progress from being implemented in the control plane to being implemented in the forwarding plane. Such a progression takes time, because protocol implementations need to stabilize before the careful programming of critical forwarding plane infrastructure.

However, state-keeping is not so important for services that do not need continuity checks between the BNG and client, such as a basic volume-based or flat-rate data usage product. Billing engines for time-based services need to know when a subscriber disconnects from the network so that they can stop charging. The most common way to address this lack of state-keeping in DHCP networks is to use a higher-layer protocol to monitor the status of the client's connectivity. For example, at public WiFi hotspots, where DHCP is used, a popup HTTP window with a persistent session to a web server is used to verify reachability from the client to the network. If the client disconnects or reboots, the session terminates so that the server knows to stop billing the client. For residential broadband access, this is not a completely ideal solution, because it needs to encompass any type of client and requires a continually open web browser.

Service providers that want to deploy an architecture that identifies individual subscribers by a key similar to the form "username@realm" find DHCP-based solutions extra work to tailor to their needs. Several identifiers are needed in a DHCP deployment to ascertain the identity of the client requesting a lease. A MAC address is the most basic way to identify the end device. The vendor ID is a useful piece of information encoded in the MAC address and can indicate what type of device the requestor is, such as a PC or an SIP phone made by a particular vendor. The second, more secure indicator of the requestor's physical location is DHCP option number 82, inserted by the DSLAM or BNG. This is added to all DHCP packets that originate from the household, so it can only identify the household, not the device or person requesting service. If a linkage between an assigned IP address and subscriber identity is needed, the most common option is to use a captive portal to allow login credentials to be entered via a web page. But usually an option 82 identifier is sufficient for most deployments.

With such a captive portal-based authentication model, any web page the user tries to visit causes the browser to automatically redirect the user to a provider's page, which prompts the user to enter his or her login credentials. These credentials could be a username and password, a credit card number, or some other key to identify the customer relationship with the provider. As soon as the user is authenticated into the network, a set of services can be applied to the subscriber session, one of which could be an "Internet" service. But a more elaborate service set could be applied to the subscriber session, such as both VoIP and Internet access with QoS control. Compared to a PPP environment, this external authentication layer requires extra intelligence on the BNG for handling automated service changes. Correspondingly, the web server infrastructure needs intelligence to handle the HTTP state machine of the user's session. This capability is covered more in Chapter 11. Running authentication through captive portals coupled with DHCP is common in the WiFi market, where users are mostly itinerant. Such authentication mechanisms are also found in specialized services, such as prepay access on a fixed DSL line. This captive portal can be used to identify either an entire household when the RG is running in routed mode (due to a single public address identifying the RG). Or it could identify a user if the modem is functioning in bridged mode. This brings DHCP into alignment with PPP to allow customized services on a per-user basis, but it requires a lot more work to achieve the same goal.

However, after a user has logged into the portal, operational support to link usernames with DHCP sessions is a multistep process because a system external to the BNG is required to associate the portal sessions, usernames, and IP addresses.

The traditional method to deploy DHCP in conjunction with a relay agent is to use an Ethernet subinterface with the access architecture in either the N:1 or 1:1 VLAN mode and to set this interface as IP unnumbered to a loopback. Any DHCP clients on the subnet receive an IP address in the same network as the unnumbered loopback address. Referring to Listing 5.1 and 5.2 (shown earlier) as an example, clients would receive an IP address in the network 10.20.1.0/23 by the DHCP server 10.2.3.4. Traffic destined for these would be routed out interface GigabitEthernet 1/0/0.100. With an N:1 architecture, if customized IP filtering or quality-of-service capability is desired for each end subscriber, it is not practical to use this configuration. This is because it would entail maintaining a master input and output access list and quality-of-service profile that would be attached to the GigabitEthernet interface and include customer-specific addressing information. There needs to be an attachment point for policies and quality-of-service profiles for each subscriber. Some BNG vendors support the functionality of applying such attributes to each DHCP client by creating a virtual interface for the session, but currently few vendors support this functionality.

In summary, here are the downsides of DHCP compared to PPPoE:

- Additional work is required to deploy per-user or per-household authentication and service customization.
- Not all vendors support dynamic interface creation for DHCP clients.
- Lack of session keepalives.
- Can only deploy in a wholesale L2TP environment with L2TPv3 or with MPLS pseudo wires.

ACCESS PROTOCOLS IN AN IPv6 ENVIRONMENT

Most of today's broadband networks implement only IPv4 routing. However, there are certainly compelling reasons to build broadband networks that cater to future growth and features. PPP can support many network protocols, but the most relevant protocol other than IPv4 is IPv6. Several BNG vendors already support the necessary enhancement to PPP to support IPv6—IPv6CP.

Most IPv6-enabled service providers have dual-stack support, which means that both IPv4 and IPv6 addresses are simultaneously provided to subscribers. The benefit of dual-stack is that subscribers can reach the IPv4- and IPv6-enabled networks at the same time without needing a sudden cutover. Chapter 10, "Managing IP Addressing," has more information on IPv6 protocol deployment.

SUMMARY

For providers who are newer entrants to the broadband market, DHCP can be an attractive proposition due to its simplicity, lower overhead, and rapid failover capability with VRRP. Currently no standards are written to handle the DHCP state replication between a primary and secondary BNG, but if the network is a simple DHCP relay architecture with no per-subscriber IP filtering or QoS profiles, little state *has* to be replicated, and the failover between the two routers could occur between two different vendor routers. For more complex setups with per-user policies, rate limiters, and QoS profiles, this state replication would need to be handled with proprietary methods, and multivendor options are not currently an option. Such inter-chassis state replication is currently a rare feature even for one vendor. Even though the feature set with DHCP is generally lower than PPP (lack of a keepalive mechanism and user identification), most providers can work around most issues that cause a feature disparity between the two protocols in simpler networks. Putting aside the issue of inter-chassis redundancy, adapting complex DHCP networks to support per-subscriber policies and QoS profiles is a newer and more involved approach than implementing the same functionality on PPPoE sessions.

Deciding between DHCP and a PPPoE local access is not easy, as this chapter shows. Each has its trade-offs. Many vendors tout one protocol over another. But if a service provider decides to deploy a multivendor network, the base set of features can vary significantly between platforms, and it is hard to deploy a network with a common capability. For providers with an established PPPoE (but running over ATM) or PPPoA network, PPP is the most pain-free route to take, because many of the protocol concepts and operational systems are already in place. Service providers already running PPPoE but on an ATM network may already have a high-availability system in place to allow a client to connect to a secondary gateway if the primary goes out of service. Most BNGs have redundant control planes, so any failure on the primary control plane can trigger the secondary control plane to come into service with the existing PPP state that was on the primary. This limits the downtime for clients, but this type of redundancy is limited to within a chassis. Provisioning PPP-based CPE in a service provider environment requires a bit of extra integration work because PPP does not come with a way to bootstrap the router with much other than an IP address and DNS server. Other protocols, such as TFTP, FTP, or SNMP, are needed to trigger a request for provisioning information. This is also a positive aspect because it keeps address and link-control protocols separate from device configuration. Having good separation between link control and device configuration makes troubleshooting easier, because the architecture is more modular than a one-protocol-fits-all model.

Evolutions in Last-Mile Broadband Access

Not surprisingly, copper phone networks that were originally designed for voice calls have proven to be a valuable way to shift other types of information to and from households. From the first residential modem, which used an audio coupler between a computer and telephone, to high-speed VDSL2 technology, the traditional copper local loop continues to be a viable option to deliver faster data rates, for both high-speed Internet access and richer multimedia services. This type of access supports incumbent operators with a vast copper distribution network as well as retail operators that want access to the copper network in a wholesale environment. The wholesale environment could be *naked DSL* access, which provides a copper interconnect between the retail provider and the incumbent for each household. The environment could also be bit stream access using L2TP or ATM/Ethernet interconnects. This chapter describes the range of DSL types in common use among carriers today, from the 8Mbps speeds of ADSL, to ADSL2+, to the 100Mbps speeds of VDSL2.

Although twisted copper pairs are the most ubiquitous way of providing data access, cable providers using hybrid fiber/coaxial (HFC) is the next most popular way of delivering residential broadband. These were briefly described in Chapter 1, "A History of Broadband Networks"; however, this chapter deals almost exclusively with ADSL.

One pervasive data delivery method is wireless, which can take many forms: WiFi, CDMA, GPRS, UMTS, and others. Because this is such a large topic, Chapter 9, "The Future of Wireless Broadband," is dedicated to wireless broadband access.

ADSL Access

Chapter 1 explains the history of ADSL, beginning with the early line Carrierless Amplitude Phase modulation (CAP) line coding deployed under the standardization auspices of the American National Standards Institute (ANSI). The progression was toward the Discrete Multitone (DMT) method deployed today under the International Telecommunication Union (ITU) G.992 and G.993 family of standards. This section discusses the most important ADSL standards to date, from the first—G.992.1—to the latest—ADSL2plus (also commonly called ADSL2+)—which is documented in G.992.5.

Generally speaking, ADSL is a way to transmit digital signals over one or more analog carriers, much in the same way that many other digital transmission standards work. The majority of ADSL-based services can coexist on the same physical cable as existing telephonic services, such as Plain Old Telephone Service (POTS) or ISDN. It achieves this using a technique called Frequency Division Multiplexing (FDM), which splits the two services into two frequency domains. POTS shares the lower part and ADSL, the upper part. In the ADSL domain, duplexing of the upstream and downstream parts occurs; the upstream is on the lower frequency range, and the downstream uses the upper frequency band.

ADSL stands for Asymmetric Digital Subscriber Line. Its name comes from the difference between upstream and downstream data rates. The downstream rate is always higher than the upstream speed. One reason for this is because one of the early motivations for ADSL was to transport streaming video to the home, which does not require a large amount of upstream bandwidth. A further application— residential Internet broadband—has historically utilized more traffic in the downstream direction. Also, the asymmetric nature of ADSL reduces Near-End Cross Talk (NEXT), which allows for greater density of services, longer loop lengths, and higher bit rates than would otherwise be achievable. This section covers all members of the ADSL family. It also describes SHDSL, which is a symmetric DSL service that better suits the needs of business connections that need more upstream bandwidth.

Technology Note: Crosstalk

In telecommunications, crosstalk is where one circuit, commonly a local loop, causes undesired interference to an adjacent circuit. This could be in the form of inductance or capacitance. A common example of crosstalk is where another party's voice call can be heard in the background of your telephone call. This is different from a party line, which intentionally wired several households together on a single circuit.

Crosstalk also causes issues for data transmission over copper pairs, including POTS ones. Humans can tolerate voice interference on POTS lines better than machines can. Because machines transmit digital data over copper pairs by using analog approximations of digital signals, any RF interference from other copper pairs can corrupt the information. There are two types of crosstalk discussed in the context of DSL systems: Near-End Crosstalk (NEXT) and Far-End Crosstalk (FEXT). NEXT occurs when the transmitting signal from one wire interferes with the signal in an adjacent wire. This is the opposite of FEXT, which occurs at the opposite, or far-end, end of the circuit. FEXT has less impact than NEXT because the signals are weaker at the other end.

One of the hallmarks of ADSL services is the effect that distance has on line speed. ADSL, for example, can reach speeds of up to 8Mbps on loop lengths of up to 6,000 feet (1.8km), but above that, the upper speed starts decaying. This happens because resistance, which attenuates signal, increases proportionally to both cable length and frequency. So as the cable length increases, so does the resistance, which also attenuates (reduces) the power of the higher frequencies more than the lower frequencies. Because the downstream portion of the line occupies the upper frequency band, this is the first to be affected, reducing the upper limit of the line speed.

Figure 6.1 shows how FDM lets the ADSL line share the same cable pair as POTS or an ISDN service. One semantic note: Frequency Division Duplexing (FDD) is where two frequency ranges coexist, such as an ADSL service, which duplexes the upstream and downstream frequency onto a single cable. Multiplexing is where more than two ranges share the same cable.

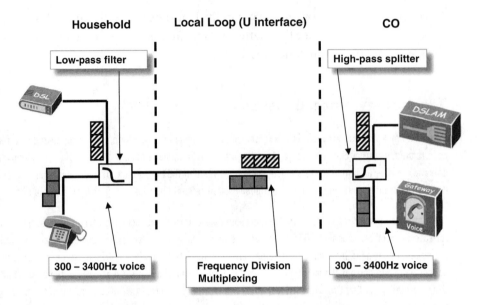

Figure 6.1 How ADSL coexists with telephone services sharing the same line.

Note that the low-pass filter is between the line and the POTS device. The DSL modem is connected directly to the line, not from behind the filter, as shown in the figure. The DSL modem has a high-pass filter that prevents POTS signalling from interfering with the DSL link and prevents the DSL modem from emanating frequencies in the voice or guard bands. This is part of the output Power Spectral Density (PSD) shaping, which is described later.

G.DMT

Several features of G.DMT are of interest to service providers. First, native STM or ATM data paths can be transmitted in the ADSL signal. Also, an Embedded Operations Channel (EOC) is used for statistics and diagnostics on the line. An interesting feature of the EOC is autonomous data transfer mode, which provides a 15kbps data channel that can transfer information such as the Customer Premises Equipment (CPE) vendor name, software or hardware revision number, serial number, and other informational parameters to the DSLAM. This is a useful way to track the location of CPE in the network based on the serial number transmitted in the EOC. Finally, a "dying gasp" is a message that can be sent from the CPE when a loss of power occurs at the CPE location. The CPE must have sufficient operating power long enough to be able to transmit this message. This gives information to the DSLAM. If there were a power fault instead of a line break, a dying gasp message would not be sent. The specification additionally allows ISDN and POTS frequencies to coexist with the ADSL signal.

Standards and Spectrum

The first ITU DMT-based standard to precede ANSI CAP was G.992.1, released in mid-1999. DMT-based ADSL allows simultaneous Plain Old Telephone Service (POTS) (including AC-based telephone ringing signals [25 to 50Hz]) and voice frequencies (300 to 3400Hz), and ADSL to share a single copper line. Some documents refer to the voice range as 0 to 4kHz, including the ITU Technical Recommendation itself. The use of the frequency range between 3400 and 4000Hz is to cover any additional spectrum that non-POTS services might need. For example, G.992.1 notes that the V.90 modulation standard might need frequencies between 3400Hz and 4000Hz as a guard band. In the standard, anything between the frequency ranges of approximately 25kHz to 1.1MHz is considered part of the ADSL spectrum, but the exact usage varies according to hardware manufacturer and local deployment requirements. Between 25kHz and 138kHz is allocated to the upstream direction, and 138kHz to 1.1MHz is in the downstream direction.

Data Encoding

The standard also explains how to encode data bits at the provider's ADSL modem, which is called an ADSL Transceiver Unit-CO (ATU-C), and at the remote CPE end, the ADSL Transceiver Unit-Remote (ATU-R). The encoding uses a constellation scheme. In the context of ADSL, this allows a chunk of bits (also called a symbol) to be represented by changes in frequency of the analog samples on the wire, as one example. Other ways to increase the line's information rate are to use phase shifts, amplitude shifts, or a combination of the two. To improve throughput, the use of Trellis Code Modulation (TCM) is strongly advised.

Technology Note: Shannon-Hartley Theorem

In reference to a scientific innovation, Isaac Newton once said, ". . . If I have seen a little further it is by standing on the shoulders of Giants." Many advancements in science have not been radical break-throughs, but additive enhancements. The Shannon-Hartley theorem is built on two important information theories: the Nyquist rate and Hartley's law.

Until the Shannon-Hartley theorem, a channel's capacity (a piece of copper) was modeled on Hartley's law, which was a way to calculate the rate at which information could be sent down a medium, given its band-width, suitability of transport for a given signal, and the reliability of re-creating the information at the other end. Of course, this acknowledged that noise is a limiting factor in a line's information capacity, but not how much of a factor it is. Shannon came up with a model that approximates the noise that is always present, in the form of white, or Gaussian, noise. Shannon incorporated this white noise into this theorem and achieved channel reliability through error-correction coding (see the section "Error Correction and Detection").

The theory is that a medium has a maximum capacity based on its signal and noise levels, the channel's bandwidth, and its frequency. The rate of information transfer has an upper bound, and no more informa-tion than this theoretical maximum can be transmitted.

Shannon's law is still relevant today and can be found in many spheres of telecommunications influence, including IETF mailing lists and mailing list discussions.

Technology Note: Trellis Coding

Trellis Coding (TC) is an efficient way of to use a data transmission medium. Most contemporary data trans-mission methods involve taking a series of bits and preparing them in some way before being transmitted.

A simple example of transmitting data over a copper wire could mean when a current is at a certain posi-tive voltage, it represents a 1 and the same voltage in the negative could be zero. A more complex scheme, such as QAM, uses sinusoidal waves to represent the bits. QAM makes use of two carrier waves that are combined, which allow both amplitude and phase changes to be carried as information to the receiver. The decoder can take these amplitude and phase changes and work out the encoded bit stream. Often these combinations are represented in a constellation diagram. Figure 6.2 shows an exam-ple of a 16-QAM diagram, which uses discrete points to represent the various combinations of bits that can be sent with particular phase and amplitude changes. Behind these diagrams are relatively complex mathematics, especially when dealing with more than two dimensions (as shown in the figure).

In simple terms, TC modulation is a way to improve a given modulation scheme by adding an extra constella-tion points (for reference, there are 16 points in the figure) to improve the signal to noise ratio of a channel.

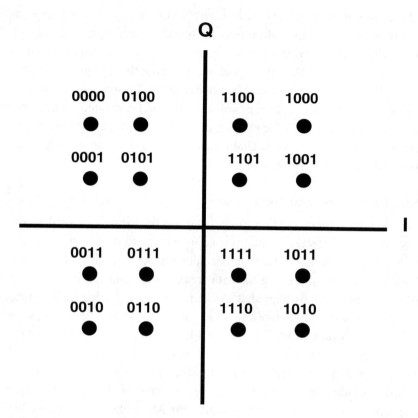

Figure 6.2 A 16-QAM constellation diagram.

Each point represents a series of bits and is based on a combination of signal phase and amplitude. When the receiving device demodulates the analog signal, it takes the signal's amplitude and phase and coverts them to a series of bits and vice versa on the encoding process.

This is one such example of a Trellis Coding scheme. There are many others, including QPSK, 64-QAM, and 128-QAM.

Data Modulation

As soon as the data bits are encoded, they are modulated onto the wire into multiple bins or subcarriers, each capable of transporting a stream of at least 32kbps of data. Each of these subcarriers is in its own frequency band, which is just over 4kHz in width. Up to 255 subcarriers are specified, although some are not used, giving a total downstream throughput of just over 8Mbps. One of these subcarriers is used for the pilot signal, reducing the throughput by 32kbps. The subcarriers can transport a variable number of bits (as long as the bins are a multiple of 32kbps); they usually are limited by the bit error rate. If it becomes too high (more than 1 in 10^7), the number of bits per symbol is reduced. Recall that a symbol is based on some constellation encoding, and the use of Trellis Code modulation with ADSL is advised.

Error Correction and Detection

To be tolerant of bit errors that might occur on the local loop, Reed-Solomon Forward Error Correction (FEC) is used to detect and correct such externalities. FEC works by sampling the original data, much like constellation coding used in TCM. Accompanying the original data are parity symbols, so if any part of the data stream becomes corrupted, it can be reconstructed using the additional parity data. This works much like any other parity-checking mechanism, such as a RAID-5 data storage array. If one drive is lost from the array, the data can be faithfully reconstructed using parity information that is spread across all drives. Of course, such data protection is not for free. An overhead, or tax, is incurred by sending redundant information, which reduces the real data rate. The amount of overhead varies according to implementation. More FEC data can be added to the original payload if the line is more prone to error. These FEC-encoded symbols are called code words, and they are fed into the next stage of the ADSL modem system, the modulator.

Reed-Solomon FEC codes are very good at correcting isolated errors but not very good at correcting a run of errors, such as those due to a transient burst of noise on the line. G.992.1 provides for interleaving, which helps spread out a code word in time such that channel burst errors are also spread through a block of data. This introduces extra latency to the ADSL line, because data must be queued in blocks, typically from 1 to 32ms, before both encoding. Interleaving is necessary to provide noise immunity for ADSL connections, particularly given the density of DSL lines now in service. Provision for a noninterleaved fast path is also provided, allowing providers to accept a trade-off between noise immunity and latency for latency-sensitive applications such as VoIP and gaming.

G.LITE

Defined in G.992.2, G.lite is a lightweight implementation of the ADSL specification from G.992.1, but it comes with some enhancements. G.lite has removed references to STM transport and defines only ATM data transport. An added feature is fast retrain, which allows an ADSL line to quickly recover from induced noise, such as a telephone on-hook/off-hook condition or other types of noise. It does have a significantly lower maximum downstream bandwidth—1.5Mbps. On the modulation level, the number of frequency subcarriers is limited to 127 in the downstream path and 31 in the upstream direction.

One of the advantages of G.lite is its lack of requirement for a central splitter at the customer premises, thereby eliminating a provider truck roll. At the time the standard was written, another advantage was a cheaper CPE. This was achieved in part by its reduced maximum frequency, which limited the amount of RF interference generated due to unbalanced customer premises wiring. In practice, most providers have skipped G.lite and run full-rate ADSL with individual filters per phone and a splitterless installation wherever possible.

ADSL2 AND ADSL2+

The next jump in the evolution of ADSL standards was ADSL2, defined in G.992.3. It allows for download speeds of just over 12Mbps for short loop lengths. This is achieved through improved line-encoding techniques, signal-processing algorithms, and various other low-level enhancements over the first-generation ADSL standard. On the electrical level, most of the characteristics are the same as ADSL. There is still a 4.3kHz subcarrier, and the operating range is also between 25kHz and 1.1MHz. ADSL2 still allows the DSL signal to coexist with either a POTS or ISDN system. The one exception is when the line is configured to be in an all-digital mode. This enables the ATU-R (CPE) equipment to use frequencies starting as low as 3kHz, which overlaps with the POTS frequency band. The benefit of being able to use these lower frequencies is that the maximum upstream rate is increased by 256kbps. If POTS is not required on the line, either because voice services are delivered via some other mechanism (VoIP) or because the channelized voice mode is used, 256kbps can be an ideal bandwidth increase, especially to try to deploy as close to symmetric services as possible (the same rate upstream as downstream). However, another technology is more suited to symmetric requirements—SHDSL, which is described later in this chapter.

ADSL2 FEATURES

After spending some time deployed in the field, the industry found several ways to improve asymmetric DSL services. These include a longer loop length and reducing the synchronization time (the time to train the two modems) to a few seconds. An equally desirable feature is the ability to dynamically adapt to changes in line conditions, called Dynamic Rate Adaptation (DRA).

The specification also explains how to support the simultaneous transmission of STM, ATM, and voice over ADSL. Voice over DSL enables concurrently transporting channelized voice services and cell-based ATM streams. Voice and data streams can be converged on a single platform if a provider wants to use the same equipment on the DSLAM to deliver both services rather than splitting them off to a separate POTS switch or soft switch.

Link bonding using the ATM Forum's inverse multiplexing (IMA) technique is also supported. IMA allows two or more copper links to be inversely multiplexed together to achieve higher data rates compared to just a single link. IMA enables cells to be distributed evenly across the links at the transmitting end, then reassembled at the other end in the correct order. Of course, two adjacent pairs both transmitting down the wire with a given power can cause interference with each other, so a conservative approach to spectral usage is employed on the lines. So as long as interference does not present a problem, it is possible to achieve a rate of the sum of the member links.

Longer Loop Length

ADSL2 extends the upper usable limit of the loop length to about 15,000 to 18,000 feet (4.5km to 5.5km), depending on the gauge of the local loop. This works by introducing variable framing overhead. ADSL requires a fixed framing overhead of 32kbps, whereas ADSL2 can have anywhere from 4kbps to 32kbps. This is useful in situations where the overhead-to-payload ratio is high, such as on 128kbps lines to squeeze a few extra kilobits per second from the line.

Faster Initialization and Dynamic Rate Adaptation

Users will be pleased with the faster initialization time for the line to train from a completely down state. Previously, the DSL signal light on an ADSL system would blink on the modem for about 10 seconds during the handshaking process. This process is significantly faster on an ADSL2 line and reduces the training time to about 3 seconds.

Equally beneficial to customers and providers is the ability to dynamically modify the synchronization rate in real time if the line has too many errors. This works by monitoring the bit errors in a subcarrier. If the rate becomes too high, it reduces the number of bits-per-symbol in use in that subcarrier. The bits-per-symbol rate continues to decrease to 0, effectively disabling that particular DMT subcarrier if the error rate does not decrease. As a result, it lowers the line rate without needing to drop the entire DSL line. If the noise was transient, some DSLAMs can train back up to a higher rate. This is a change from G.992.1, in which the whole line had to retrain when the bit error rate went above a certain threshold. To communicate these real-time changes to the rest of the network, Access Node Control Protocol (ANCP) in rate-adaptive mode (RAM) is an ideal protocol to handle the communication of the line changes from the DSLAM to the BNG. It works by using an out-of-band channel between the DSLAM and BNG. Whenever a line changes its synchronization rate, the new details are communicated back to the BNG. ANCP is described in more detail in the section "ANCP and the Access Network" in Chapter 8, "Deploying Quality of Service."

ADSL2+

The ITU then released the standard for ADSL2+; it significantly increases the downstream rate to about 24Mbps. It also increases the upper limit of the frequency range to 2.2MHz and increases the number of subcarriers to 512. All these extra subcarriers are allocated to the downstream transceivers. Because much of this specification builds on ADSL2 (G.992.3-4), the peak upstream rate is still roughly 1Mbps. An exception to this is Annex M, which increases the upstream peak rate to 3.5Mbps and increases the maximum upstream frequency from 138kHz to a potential 276kHz. Annex M is not too widespread due to the existing base of Annex A and B systems, which use 138kHz to 276kHz for the downstream path. NEXT is normally avoided in DSL by using a separate spectrum for transmitters and receivers; thus, there is potential for NEXT if the three types are mixed.

As described earlier, as both loop length and frequency increase, resistance also increases. This causes attenuation of the higher frequencies ahead of the others. As ADSL speeds increase, they become more dependent on a short loop length to keep the current loss low enough to support such high frequencies. For example, ADSL2+'s synchronization rate starts dropping from a peak of about 24Mbps at about 3,000 feet (900 meters). ADSL starts decaying at 6,000 feet (1.8km).

VDSL AND VDSL2

VDSL and VDSL2 dramatically increase transmission rates up to a potential 104Mbps. This is achieved similar to the step that ADSL2+ made from ADSL2—the frequency range on the copper is increased. The upper limit is now 12MHz. This section covers changes that VDSL will bring to the market and how service providers should think about designing their access network. For example, the change from ADSL2 to ADSL2+ meant that shorter loop lengths were needed to realize the benefit of higher line speeds—and even more so with VDSL and VDSL2. This also has implications for frequency spectrum planners, for both service providers and local regulators, because the increase in line frequency to 12MHz has the potential to cause much more interference than previous DSL standards.

One of the changes is that the ATU-C is now called the VDSL (or VDSL2) Transceiver Unit at the Optical Network Unit (VTU-O), and the ATU-R is now called the VDSL (or VDSL2) Transceiver Unit-Remote Site (VDSL-R).

VDSL PHYSICAL AND ELECTRICAL CHARACTERISTICS

As mentioned, the frequency band has been increased to 12MHz with the release of ITU VDSL recommendation G.993.1. To limit the degree of interference with ADSL systems, VDSL uses the frequency range in a different way than its predecessors. Recall that with ADSL2+ Annex M, the extra upstream bandwidth capacity was achieved by increasing the upstream frequency range to 276kHz (if needed). This meant that it overlapped with part of the downstream spectrum of non-Annex M systems, creating the possibility of unwanted interference between the two Annex systems. The problem is, an increase in upstream frequency is required to boost the speed. However, if the upstream starts encroaching in the range up to 276kHz, this would cause the same compatibility issue that ADSL2+ Annex M has. The approach of VDSL and VDSL2 is to shift up the lowest-frequency band to start at 138kHz and make it the first *downstream* carrier. This homogenizes the local loop so that adjacent cables in the binder are more spectrally compatible. The next band up is used for the first upstream part, followed by two more bands, which are downstream and upstream, respectively. Figure 6.3 shows this more clearly, including how it interoperates with VDSL.

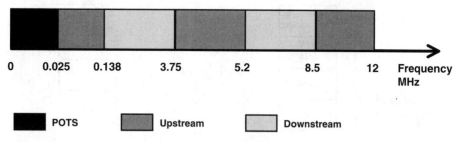

Figure 6.3 Frequency usage on a VDSL line that is shared with a POTS service.

To accommodate different regional requirements, these groups of frequencies can be split in three different ways using band plans. Even so, these band plans still follow the principle of four frequency bands, which are composed of two upstream and two downstream parts.

Ethernet Encapsulation

Expanding further on the advantage of using Ethernet in the first mile (EFM, described in 802.3AH), it reduces the overhead and complexity in both the CPE and the DSLAM. By eliminating a fixed 5-byte-per-cell overhead and CPCS padding, it optimizes bandwidth usage on the local access. At times, this overhead (also called cell tax) can be as much as 20%, depending on the packet size. Also, the complexity of the hardware at each end of the line is reduced, because an ATM SAR function is no longer needed if Ethernet encapsulation is required. However, in practice DSL chip vendors will continue to integrate both ATM and Ethernet capability in a single chip in both the CPE and DSLAMs for the foreseeable future. The active development and market shift are likely to precede a move to Ethernet encapsulation as VDSL becomes more popular.

Figure 6.4 shows an extreme (but possible) case of an ATM last-mile encapsulation producing more than 20% overhead.

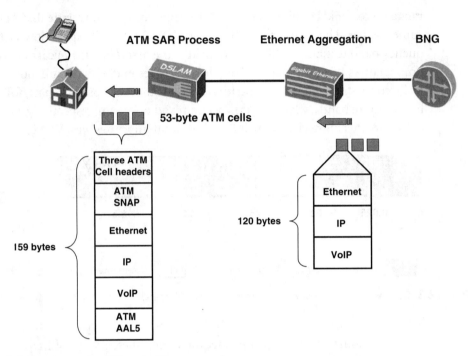

Figure 6.4 IP packet requiring 20% overhead for transportation.

QoS features are equal to, if not better than, ATM for Ethernet-encapsulated local loops. With an ATM-encapsulated local loop, devices at each end perform prioritization between PVCs based on each PVC's service class—CBR, UBR, VBR-nrt, and so on. However, no capability in the AAL5 protocol allows prioritization within a class. For example, with a single PVC access architecture, prioritization needs to be done some other way. A single virtual circuit or VLAN on a local loop using Ethernet and 802.1Q can contain up to eight different priority markings in the frame header, which allows priority multiplexing at the data link layer within a single virtual circuit. Of course, if multiple VLANs are used on the local access, each VLAN can also be assigned a weighting relative to the others, which provides the same inter-PVC prioritization as the ATM model.

VDSL2

In addition to increased frequency spectrum usage, the biggest benefit of VDSL2 is the ability to encapsulate native Ethernet on the local loop, rather than remain with traditional ATM encapsulation; of course, ATM (and STM, for that matter) can still be used.

Standards and Spectrum

G.993.2 pushes the upper frequency limit to 30MHz and increases the number of upstream bands to three and the downstream to potentially four. In the most optimal case, it is possible to reach speeds of up to 100Mbps upstream and downstream (200Mbps total), with loop lengths of up to 1,600 feet (500 meters). Of course, the rate drops dramatically as the distance from the DSLAM increases, as with G.993.1 VDSL. However, due to the mandatory use of Trellis Coding, an optional extra frequency usage in the first upstream band, and some other line optimizations, VDSL can continue to provide reliable operation on loop lengths up to 8,200 feet (2,500 meters). The first upstream band is similar to ADSL2+, Annex M, which extends the upper bounds of the upstream channel to 276kHz. Of course, the potential for interference still applies and needs to be considered by spectrum planners in each region.

Band Plans

With the greater frequency range and increased power usage in the downstream direction (up to 20dBm) used for VDSL2, it's important to consider compatibility with existing DSL-based installations and local regulations. For example, in the UK, the regulator permits a maximum frequency of only 7.05MHz on the local loop, so a special set of frequencies was created that satisfied local spectral requirements. Such requirements are captured as part of *band plans* or *profiles* in the ITU specification, which record various details, including frequency ranges and DMT subcarrier spacing (one of the profiles changes the subcarrier range from 4.3kHz to 8kHz). Eight profiles are defined. Some address regional spectral requirements, and others address compatibility between two local ADSL system installations.

The specification describes two modes of access node (AN) system configurations: cabinet-based and CO-based. The section "Copper Network Reticulation Considerations" describes the changes that need to occur in the local access network to support such high bit rates. One point that needs to be covered is that when VDSL2 systems are installed in a remote cabinet, if the system is configured to run in a certain band plan, existing ADSL loops may be adversely affected due to spectral incompatibility. Thus, several modes coexist better with ADSL. Therefore, it is important that this be incorporated into planning of the local loop.

COPPER NETWORK RETICULATION CONSIDERATIONS

When looking at graphs of theoretical VDSL access speeds versus loop length, it may seem that the high bandwidths needed to support Standard-Definition Television (SD-TV) and High-Definition Television (HD-TV) services can be extended along significant copper distances. In real deployments, the speed drops significantly after 4,000 feet (1,200 meters). Because POTS can reach distances of 18,000 feet (5.5km) or longer with bridge taps, carriers have exploited this distance capability. This means that most existing copper loops are a lot longer than the shorter lengths needed for high bit rate services. Therefore, VDSL deployments need to incorporate the deployment of fiber-fed DSLAMs in remote cabinets that lie close to customer premises. Delivering fiber to the DSLAM is called fiber to the node (FTTN). These nodes can be in either new or existing roadside cabinets. In some scenarios, however, the heat dissipation requirements, environmental noise-level bylaws, and space available in existing cabinets can restrict the deployment of some hardware types. This can mean relegating the VTU-O to a larger central office. The danger is that this reduces the coverage footprint of high bit-rate VDSL services. It also increases the copper loop length and the density of pairs in the cable binder, because the CO must service many more subscribers compared to a remote node. Thus, an increased amount of crosstalk occurs, and hence lower achievable speeds in the local-access network.

Multi-Unit Dwellings (MUDs) are ideal for this kind of distributed deployment. Such buildings could be apartment blocks, where an access provider installs DSLAM subracks in the basement for the rest of the building. Hotels can install such subracks to deliver high-speed access to guest rooms. They also can be useful in older buildings where it is infeasible to rewire rooms and conduits with CAT-5 or CAT-6 cabling for Ethernet services. Of course, the per-room installation cost then goes up, because modems need to be installed in each room.

In any case, the new VDSL services delivered over cabinet-fed DSL lines (rather than CO-fed) need to be spectrally compatible with existing DSL deployments. One example of when problems arise is when a short VDSL loop is deployed adjacent to a long ADSL loop; the power differences on each line are bound to cause interference in the form of NEXT. Power Spectral Density (PSD) shaping helps by reducing the power level of certain frequency subcarriers and potentially reallocating power elsewhere in the spectrum. Also, carriers can elect to set power levels lower than the upper limit of the PSD mask. This is useful in specific deployment scenarios where there is the potential for spectral interference at a given power level. Typically DSL modems of all types lower output power to the minimum required to maintain a given performance. As mentioned earlier in the chapter, having multiple band plans in the VDSL specification allows service providers to choose the best profile for their environment.

SHDSL

Single-pair High-Speed DSL (SHDSL) can be both a symmetric and asymmetric DSL technology and is ideally suited to business applications. All the DSL services, with the exception of VDSL2, are designed to be asymmetric. The applications originally envisioned for ADSL—Video on Demand (VoD) and Internet services—need more bandwidth in the downstream direction toward the customer. In the residential market, applications such as YouTube, Google video, Slingbox, and other subscriber-produced content are changing this model. Nevertheless, the traffic ratio is still tipped in favor of the downstream direction.

For providers that have deployed only ADSL services, the maximum upstream rate is about 800kbps. This is unsuitable for customers who want to deploy IP private branch exchanges (PBXs) with more than seven or eight lines or host a small to medium-sized data center or any other data services that need more than 1000kbps of upstream capacity. This bit rate is also the upper limit of ADSL. Just as 56kbps is the upper limit of analog modems running over the PSTN, both technologies rarely achieve their advertised maximums except in perfect lab conditions.

SHDSL addresses many of these limitations by providing a more business-suited service by allowing the line to operate with symmetric bit rates. Other features include support for a multiwire configuration, either to extend the service's reach or to increase the total bandwidth available on shorter loops. Signal repeaters can be used on the line to increase the signal distance if there are not extra cables for a multipair system that is being used for reach extension. Remote powering by the CO of the modem at the customer premises is supported. There are also several supported payload types—Transport Protocol-Specific Transmission Convergence (TPS-TC)—such as channelized and unchannelized T1 and E1 circuits, ATM, and packet mode. Finally, to improve resilience against line clocking slips, bit stuffing can be performed on the path.

However, to be a completely business-grade service, the SLA, in terms of Time-To-Restore (TTR) and service uptime, must be equivalent to other leased-line services, such as ATM and Frame Relay.

STANDARDS AND SPECTRUM

In North America, 1.544Mbps was the most common circuit of choice in the plesiochronous (PDH) transmission hierarchy. For a long time, it was delivered using Alternate Mark Inversion (AMI), which created a well-established base of equipment that required repeaters about every mile (1.5km). The successor, High-Speed Digital Subscriber Line (HDSL), was originally developed in the U.S. by Bellcore. It used 2B1Q line coding, which is much more spectrally efficient. Like AMI-provisioned lines, HDSL lines required two pairs to reach the full 1.544Mbps line speed. ANSI adopted it as an American standard. HDSL2 and SDSL soon followed. HDSL2 is more forgiving of poor line conditions and enables a T1-speed line to be provisioned over a single cable pair. To get rates slower than T1 speeds, the line can be channelized into multiple 64kbps time slots. It also makes line coding more efficient by adopting TC-PAM. In the North American market, SDSL has been deployed using proprietary 2B1Q line coding techniques to achieve variable bandwidth rates up to 1.544Mbps over a single pair. This technology is giving way to the international standard adopted by the ITU, SHDSL, defined in G.991.2. This is because equipment can be made with a single standard in mind (apart from annex differences), and economies of scale bring down the price of SHDSL chipsets.

A similar process of evolution occurred in Europe. E1 lines were first provisioned using the inefficient HDB3 line coding method. After HDSL was developed in the U.S., it was adapted to the European environment and was adopted as a standard by the European Telecommunications Standards Institute (ETSI). The main modification was to support the full 2048kbps on a dual-pair system compared with the 1544kbps system across the Atlantic. SDSL technology did not catch on in Europe, except by name. SHDSL, standardized by the ITU, was adopted by ETSI and renamed SDSL. Luckily, the two are compatible.

PHYSICAL AND ELECTRICAL CHARACTERISTICS

SHDSL, also known as G.SHDSL, is defined in ITU technical recommendation G.991.2. The specification went through two iterations. The first version defined support for a two-wire, single-pair service and an optional four-wire mode. The second version added an M-pair mode, which allows up to four pairs to be used concurrently. A cable pair is also called a span in G.SHDSL terminology. The use of M pairs increases the usable bandwidth in a linear fashion, according to the number of pairs (that is, n kbps * M). Depending on the Annex used, n could be anywhere between 192kbps and 5696kbps. The different data rates are described in the section "Transport Capacity." In the M-pair approach, the data are spread among each of the pairs just before modulation onto the wire. Each SHDSL frame is divided into four blocks, each of which is subdivided into 12 subblocks. Parts of each subblock are distributed among the spans and are reassembled at the other end. To compensate for differences in wire diameter, length, use of bridge taps, and any other impairments, each SHDSL Termination Unit (STU, similar to a VTU or ATU) implements a delay buffer of just over 50 microseconds to absorb propagation delay differences between the spans. This data interleaving is different from ADSL-based systems, which use ATM IMA to inversely multiplex multiple pairs to get increased data throughput. This involves spraying cells across the constituent links to evenly distribute data.

SHDSL also includes a transport-convergence-specific (TC-specific) sublayer for packet transfer, similar to how VDSL includes a TC specification for packet transfer. Because SHDSL is very liberal with its use of the radio frequency spectrum, it does not support sharing the same cable pair with either POTS or ISDN. The intention is that such services are handled by higher-layer protocols. However, SHDSL does support synchronous ISDN through the use of an ISDN-specific TC application sublayer. This is in comparison to VDSL and ADSL, which allow ISDN to share the same cable pair by using FDD.

SHDSL streams occupy the spectrum between 0 and 400kHz and place various limits on the maximum power usage at several ranges of the frequency spectrum and use PSD shaping. Of course, local spectrum usage dictates the ultimate frequency configuration.

One useful feature in the specification is the usage of signal regenerators. Up to eight signal regenerators can be used on a span, increasing the reach if the signal-to-noise ratio (SNR) becomes too great for non-regenerated line segments. To faithfully regenerate any such signal, such a piece of equipment needs to be active so that it can decode the SHDSL signal, reclock it, and provide an SHDSL repeater unit (SRU) to both sides of the regenerator. Such a regenerator can be remotely placed in diagnostic mode if required, by setting the necessary bit in the EOC channel. One important point is that SHDSL uses more optimized line coding techniques, so it uses fewer spectra than a T1/E1 line, which usually uses the spectrally inefficient AMI or High-Density Bipolar level 3 (HDB3) coding respectively. As a result, the loop length before needing a repeater is much longer with SHDSL. For example, a regenerator is not needed for loops shorter than 12,000 feet (3.6km), compared to every 5,000 feet (1.5km) on a typical AMI-encoded T1 line.

Modulation

The physical DSL level is called the Medium-Specific TC (PMS-TC) layer. Before an SHDSL data stream is encoded onto the wire, it is placed in a PMS-TC frame. Each frame contains 4 bits that can be used as stuffing bits to guard against frame alignment problems during a burst of noise on the line.

The ITU standard uses a 16-TC-PAM scheme, which makes efficient use of the spectrum by representing several bits in a single symbol. Other symmetric systems, such as HDSL, SDSL, and ISDN, use 2B1Q line coding. 2B1Q is less spectrally efficient because it can encode only two bit-patterns per symbol, compared to 16-TC-PAM, which encodes 4 bits per symbol.

The standard also allows remote equipment (STU-R or SRU) to be supplied with a 200V, 15W power source from the CO using the same cable pair as that used for data.

Transport Capacity

When SHDSL lines are operating in symmetric mode on a single pair, the maximum transport capacity can be anywhere between 192kbps and 5696kbps, depending on the mode and annex used. For example, Annex A is intended for use in North America and has a minimum rate of 192kbps and a maximum rate of 2304kbps, with steps of 64kbps in between. All implementations supporting this and the other annexes have limits placed on various radio frequencies through the use of PSD shaping. Annex B typically is used in European networks and specifies different frequency and power requirements than Annex A. Annex B also has bit rates up to 2304kbps. If the line is set in asymmetric mode, increments can be in 8kbps steps. Annex F extends the maximum data rate to 5996kbps.

Summary

This chapter has discussed last-mile access using DSL as the primary technology. Although several other types of access technologies exist, including wireless (covered in Chapter 9), this book has focused on DSL. Other techniques, such as Ethernet over Power, fiber to the home/curb/house, HFC, are also suitable candidates to use instead of, or in addition to, DSL. In the interest of space, this chapter has focused solely on DSL-related access. Table 6.1 summarizes the ITU standards mentioned in this chapter, their maximum bit rates, and the frequency ranges used by each.

Table 6.1 ITU DSL Recommendations and Their Speed Capabilities

Recommendation Number (Informal Name in Parentheses)	Recommendation Title	Approximate Maximum Speed Capabilities	Passband Frequencies
G.991.2 (G.SHDSL)	Single-pair High-speed Digital Subscriber Line (SHDSL) transceivers	2304kbps upstream 2304kbps downstream	0kHz to 400kHz upstream 0kHz to 400kHz downstream
G.992.1 (G.DMT)	Asymmetric Digital Subscriber Line (ADSL) transceivers	1Mbps upstream 8Mbps downstream	25kHz to 138kHz upstream 138kHz to 1104kHz downstream

continues

Table 6.1   continued

Recommendation Number (Informal Name in Parentheses)	Recommendation Title	Approximate Maximum Speed Capabilities	Passband Frequencies
G.992.2 (G.lite)	Splitterless Asymmetric Digital Subscriber Line (ADSL) transceivers	1Mbps upstream 1.5Mbps downstream	25 to 138kHz upstream **Annex A** 138 to 552kHz downstream or **Annex B** 25 to 552kHz downstream Note: Annex B uses overlapped upstream and downstream spectrum.
G.992.3	Asymmetric Digital Subscriber Line transceivers 2 (ADSL2)	1Mbps upstream 12Mbps downstream	**Annex A** ~26kHz to 138kHz upstream **Annex B** 120kHz to 276kHz upstream **Annex A** ~26kHz to 1104kHz downstream (overlapped upstream and downstream spectrum) or ~138kHz to 1104kHz downstream (nonoverlapped upstream and downstream spectrum) **Annex B** 120kHz to 1104kHz downstream (overlapped upstream and downstream spectrum) or 254kHz to 1104kHz downstream (nonoverlapped upstream and downstream spectrum)

Recommendation Number (Informal Name in Parentheses)	Recommendation Title	Approximate Maximum Speed Capabilities	Passband Frequencies
G.992.4	Splitterless Asymmetric Digital Subscriber Line transceivers 2 (ADSL2)	1Mbps upstream	~25kHz to 138kHz upstream **Annex A** 138kHz to 552kHz downstream (nonoverlapped upstream and downstream spectrum) or ~25kHz to 552kHz downstream (overlapped upstream and downstream spectrum)
G.992.5	Asymmetric Digital Subscriber Line transceivers Extended Bandwidth ADSL2 (ADSL2+)	1Mbps upstream 24Mbps downstream	**Annex A** ~26kHz to 138kHz upstream **Annex B** 120kHz to 276kHz upstream **Annex A** ~26kHz to 2208kHz downstream (overlapped upstream and downstream spectrum) or ~138kHz to 2208kHz downstream (nonoverlapped upstream and downstream spectrum) **Annex B** 120kHz to 2208kHz downstream (overlapped upstream and downstream spectrum) or 254kHz to 2208kHz downstream (nonoverlapped upstream and downstream spectrum)
G.993.1	Very high-speed Digital Subscriber Line (VDSL)	13Mbps upstream 22Mbps downstream	Various band plans from ~26kHz to 12MHz. Implementation depends on region.
G.993.2	Very high-speed Digital Subscriber Line 2 (VDSL2)	Up to 100Mbps upstream Up to 100Mbps downstream	Various band plans from ~26kHz to 30MHz

Table 6.2 summarizes the technologies and acronyms used in this chapter.

Table 6.2 Terms Used in This Chapter

Protocol or Term	Acronym	Definition
Access node	AN	A term adopted by the DSL Forum to generalize a device that implements an ATU-C function and optionally a switching function from other ANs.
ADSL Transceiver Unit, CO	ATU-C	The device at the CO or remote node terminating the ADSL signal from the ATU-R.
ADSL Transceiver Unit at the Remote End	ATU-R	The device at the customer that terminates the ADSL signal from the ATU-C.
Annex A, B, C, M		Examples of sections added to specifications to capture location-specific requirements. For example, Annex A in an ADSL context refers to an ADSL service delivered on the same cable as POTS.
Asymmetric Digital Subscriber Line	ADSL	A technology standardized by various bodies, including the ITU, which permits simultaneous high-speed data rates and POTS usage on an ordinary telephone line.
Bit swapping		A mandatory technique used in the low-level transmission layer of DSL transceivers. Changes data and power rates of individual subcarriers to compensate for induced noise but aims to keep the overall line rate the same.
Bridge tap		An open-circuit, unused twisted-pair section connected at some point along a subscriber line. A legacy from the days when copper pairs to households were often oversubscribed.
Carrierless Amplitude-Phase modulation	CAP	A single-carrier modulation technique used in the DSL market that uses adaptive equalization to compensate for attenuation and phase errors.
Digital Subscriber Line	DSL	A way to transmit data over one or more copper pairs. The two modulation standards are CAP and DMT. Current speeds are up to 100Mbps.
Digital Subscriber Line Access Multiplexer	DSLAM	A node that can be at either a telco's CO or a remote node in a roadside cabinet. It terminates many customer DSL lines by implementing multiple ATU-C or VTU-O functions.
Discrete Multitone	DMT	A technique used to subdivide the spectrum on a DSL line into many autonomous transceivers. Transceivers operate in parallel to deliver a fast data stream to higher layers.
Frequency Division Duplexing	FDD	When two frequency ranges are duplexed onto a single medium by a radio application. ADSL is an FDD system because the upstream and downstream portions are in separate frequency ranges and normally do not interfere with one another.

Protocol or Term	Acronym	Definition
Frequency Division Multiplexing	FDM	When more than two frequencies are used by a radio application on a single medium. VDSL uses FDM because it has several frequency ranges, for upstream, downstream, and POTS.
Layer 2 Control Protocol (now Access Node Control Protocol)	L2CP (now ANCP)	A way of controlling an AN remotely for operations and administration management. Also can be used by a BNG or other device to retrieve statistics from the AN.
Multi-Unit Dwelling	MUD	A building such as an apartment block where many dwellings share the same building.
Online reconfiguration	OLR	Allows subtle changes at the subcarrier level (for example, bit swapping) or more drastic changes such as changing the overall line rate. All OLR changes can be done without resynchronizing the line.
Packet Transfer Mode, Transmission Convergence	PTM-TC	The ability of a DSL line to support native packet transfer rather than through an intermediate protocol, such as ATM. Defined in G991.2 and the VDSL standards.
Plain Old Telephone Service	POTS	An analog telephone service operating in the voice band between 300 and 3400Hz. For most of its existence, it has been delivered using analog last-mile loops.
Power Spectral Density shaping	PSD	Controls the power used across different ranges of the DSL frequency spectrum.
Public Switched Telephone Network	PSTN	A general term for the telephone network supporting voice call switching. Voice calls include modulated data signals coming from analog modems using V.90 or V.24 modulation.
Reed-Solomon coding		A FEC scheme common in DSL systems. Check bytes are added to transmitted data to allow correction of data corrupted on the line. Reed-Solomon coding is a cyclic block-coding scheme first described in the early 1960s.
Seamless Rate Adaptation	SRA	A way to modify the overall DSL line rate without resynchronizing the modems at each end. A feature of the overall OLR capability.
Subcarrier		A fundamental building block of the DMT-based DSL system. Each ADSL subcarrier has a frequency range of ~4kHz and supports an ADSL transceiver.
VDSL Transceiver Unit-Central Office	VTU-O	A VDSL access node that provides VDSL service to a VTU-R.
VDSL Transceiver Unit-Remote End	VTU-R	A VDSL access node that terminates the transmit signal from the VTU-O and transmits a VTU-R signal to the transceiver at the other end. Often called CPE for simplicity.
Very high-speed DSL, Very high-speed DSL 2	VDSL	Standards defined in G.993.1 and G.993.2, respectively. Throughput rates are up to 22Mbps for the first standard and 100Mbps in one Annex of the second standard.

Cable access operators such as Time Warner have offered triple-play services for some time. Video and Internet services run over the coaxial cable between the head-end and the cable modem. Voice services may run using a reserved voice range in the coaxial, a separate twisted pair, or as packetized voice using a SIP or H.323 client connected to the modem. One of the big advantages of DSL over other broadband systems is the pre-existing access network. Copper loops run to any location where there is a POTS handset.

But working against DSL's ubiquity is fiber-to-the-premises rollouts. Even with VDSL2 potentially reaching rates of 100Mbps, fiber has the advantage of having a future-proof medium capacity. Upgrading its capacity is relatively easy by changing transponders at each end. Inherent in the solution are services being asymmetric in bandwidth. One advantage that it does not offer yet is low-cost installation; this is the major inhibiting factor of more aggressive fiber access rollouts. DSL has the advantage of being able to reuse infrastructure that has been over a century in the making—the local loop. By running ever higher bit rate services over the existing cooper infrastructure, cheaper DSL services shift the need for fiber deployments further into the future. In fact, the two can coexist to a large degree. Fiber-to-the-node is a common configuration when running VDSL services to remote cabinets or DSLAMs to the basements of MUDs. Fiber has the necessary capacity to support the large bandwidths needed for triple-play services, and DSL can provide sufficient bandwidth and sufficiently low cost in the last segment to the household—for now.

WHOLESALE BROADBAND NETWORKS

On the face of it, wholesaling broadband services allows other service providers to resell an incumbent telco's broadband services and enables access to the copper loops, allowing other providers to deploy their own services. The periodic Organisation for Economic Co-operation and Development (OECD[1]) Broadband Statistics report is a common benchmark to compare how participating OECD countries fare against one another in various metrics. One such metric is the number of connected broadband subscribers. Most countries in the OECD, including New Zealand, the United States, the United Kingdom, and the Netherlands, have government fiats for the incumbent to provide competitors some kind of access to its broadband network. This chapter provides valuable insight into how incumbent providers wholesale their broadband networks, and contains suggestions on how competitors can use wholesaled networks to their advantage in delivering their own services.

Following the invention of the telephone by Antonio Meucci and the subsequent patent by Alexander Graham Bell in the early 19th century, manual telephone exchanges were run using switchboards with human operators. A few years later, the process of connecting calls was automated with Strowger step switches, and later with crossbar technology. During this time, most telecommunications services were government-owned: *Reichspostamt* in Germany, the *General Post Office* (GPO) in the United Kingdom, and the *Postes et Télégraphes* in France. The

---

[1] http://www.oecd.org

governments owned the infrastructure needed to connect two telephone systems. As households were eventually directly connected to the telephone system, this important copper last mile between the household and the exchange was to become a serious point of contention in the communications sector. Today, most of the original government telecommunications companies are now privatized (or at least partially so). However, there has been one notable exception right from the period of the conception of the telephone, and this has been in the United States. The Bell Telephone Company, formed in 1877, was a private enterprise that eventually became the American Telephone and Telegraph Company (AT&T). It was eventually divested into several companies in 1982. In 1996 incumbent carriers (those owning the local loops) were forced to give other companies access to these loops. The prevailing wisdom was that opening the loop would bring competition among carriers and lower costs to customers.

This chapter deals with unbundling on a worldwide basis and discusses the various copper loop unbundling scenarios. When a telecommunication regulator mandates the wholesaling of the local loop, this can take several forms: full copper unbundling, Layer 2 bit stream access, L2TP, and Layer 3 wholesaling. In some instances, one or two of these wholesaled services are offered (or sometimes proffered) by the incumbent without needing directives from the regulator, but more often than not, all these services are mandated to be made available by the DSL provider.

LOCAL LOOP UNBUNDLING

This is the most basic form of unbundling. Depending on the wholesaling models included in an unbundling determination, the voice part, the broadband, or even both parts of the line can be opened up for competition. For ease of illustration, this section uses the terminology used in the United Kingdom to explain the different types of Local Loop Unbundling (LLU) services. Other terms for local loop unbundling are naked DSL and copper unbundling.

The three types of LLU services are full unbundling, also called Metallic Path Facility (MPF); shared line, also called Shared Metallic Path Facility (SMPF); and Subloop Unbundling (SLU). MPF involves the wholesaler offering the full use of the subscriber's copper pair to the retailer and lets the competitor deliver its own

DSL and voice services directly to the subscriber. Within the exchange, or Digital Local Exchange (DLE), the subscriber's local loop is routed via a cable tie to a meet-me room, where the wholesaler and retailer both connect. From there, the retailer picks up the subscriber loop with another cable tie and delivers it to termination equipment in the exchange. This equipment can be the retailer's own DSLAMs and PSTN termination equipment if they are physically colocated in the DLE. Or the hardware could be at a *distant location*, which means that a transport network could be between the wholesaler's exchange and the retailer's DSL and voice termination hardware. The transport network could be provided by the wholesaler or a third party. Without a backhaul transport service, the access seeker or retailer would need to deploy hardware in every region in which it wanted to provide service coverage. This requires significant capital expenditure for the DSLAM installation as well as operational expenditure for equipment colocation, hardware maintenance, and local loop diagnostics.

Despite describing the MPF service in the preceding paragraph in terms of DSL and voice termination, only a single service is delivered to the retailer over the copper pair. It is up to the retailer to split the two services into voice and DSL components with high- and low- pass splitters. By comparison, the wholesaler splits SMPF into voice and DSL components at the DLE. Voice can be handled by one party and the DSL service managed by another. If the voice and DSL parts are provided by different companies, the subscriber would receive two bills; with MPF, the subscriber would receive one bill from the retailer.

SLU lets a retailer have access to the copper loop at a point that is closer to the subscriber than the DLE. The interconnect point could be in a feeder cabinet or intermediate node. This is ideal if a service needs a shorter loop length than is available in the DLE.

LLU empowers the access seeker with almost complete control over the user experience, including DSL line speed capabilities, protocols (PPPoE, PPPoA, IP over Ethernet), service bundles, and quality of service (QoS). In some cases, the incumbent may offer some preinstallation diagnostic capability. Figure 7.1 shows how an access seeker may interconnect with an incumbent to provide an MPF service with LLU.

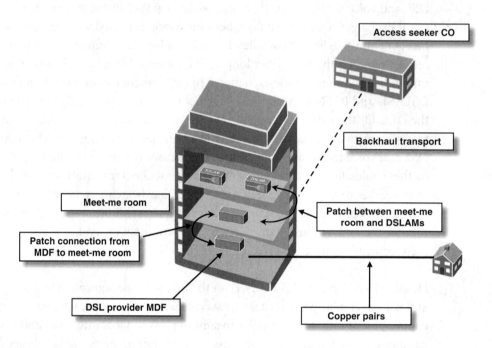

Figure 7.1 Copper loop unbundling.

This type of unbundling does not alter the routing of the copper in the ground. Local loops still enter the incumbent's exchange via cable conduits (also called binders) containing many cores (customer lines) and terminate on a Main Distribution Frame (MDF). The MDF is basically a large junction board containing metal jumpers to which each house's copper loop is attached. From this point, a cable *patch* is attached to the jumper to extend the household loop to another part of the exchange. In the case of an unbundled loop, the cooper pair runs to a *meet-me* room, which is a common area set aside in an exchange where access seekers connect the loops back to their own equipment.

When subscriber DSL connections are connected to the DSLAM, they are transported to a Broadband Network Gateway (BNG) over an aggregation network (or via dark fibre). Chapter 4, "Designing a Triple-Play Access Network," describes how the network between DSLAMs and BNGs can be built. If the access seeker does not have its own transport network, it makes sense to deploy

DSLAMs in locations where it is relatively inexpensive to purchase a dark fibre connection or pseudowire emulation service between the BNG PoP and DSLAM from a transport provider. If the LLU environment allows it, the wholesaler can sell transport back to a nominated retailer hub. Backhaul cost can be a significant factor if DSLAMs are deployed in remote locations, and the only transport option is expensive PDH or SDH/SONET technology. A cheaper option is metro Ethernet from the wholesaler. But this is usually still more costly in terms of recurring operational expenditure.

BIT STREAM ACCESS

Bit stream access involves the incumbent provider terminating the customer's DSL line and handing off the customer to the access seeker. The name implies interconnection at the physical level, but strictly speaking, a Layer 2 traffic stream is handed off to the access seeker. ATM PVCs and customer VLANs (C-VLANs) are transport mechanisms that are used to interconnect between wholesaler and retailer, but bit stream is a close-enough approximation.

ATM INTERCONNECTS

Figure 7.2 shows a typical model of a DSL network with an ATM backhaul. Each DSL port is mapped to a PVC that runs between the DSLAM and the BNG. Within the ATM network, the PVC is bundled within a PVP to make traffic management more efficient, because the network only needs to deal with traffic at the aggregate PVP level. The PVC is normally shaped to a specific rate at the BNG before it enters the ATM network. This enables the PVC to conform to the traffic contract that is set inside the ATM switch.

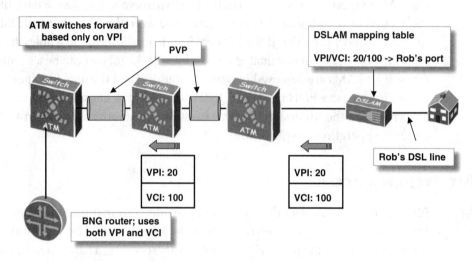

Figure 7.2 Overview of ATM PVCs and PVPs.

Technology Note: Permanent Virtual Paths (PVPs)

Transporting a PVC within a PVP is common practice among DSL service providers. Think of a PVC as a circuit that contains all traffic from a subscriber DSL port. Two pieces of information identify an ATM PVC—a Virtual Path Identifier (VPI) and Virtual Circuit Identifier (VCI). Many VCIs can be associated with a single VPT, which is the virtual path that bundles the PVCs. This makes it easier to deal with the routing of large numbers of PVCs throughout an ATM network.

In Figure 7.2, the PVP between the DSLAM and the BNG carries all PVCs within a bundle. When the DSLAM sends traffic to the ATM network, it marks the VPI and VCI numbers on each ATM cell to identify to which PVC the cell belongs. In the figure, when the ATM switches receive any cells with a VPI set to 20, they forward based purely on the VPI; the VCI is not used as part of the switching decision until the cell egresses the ATM cloud.

In contrast, a PVC is identified with both a VPI and VCI. A dedicated PVC between a customer port on the DSLAM and a BNG or other edge router is sometimes used when improved QoS support for the PVC in the ATM aggregation network is desired. To ensure that traffic within the PVC is treated with higher priority by the ATM switches than that in the PVP, the dedicated PVC is configured with its own traffic class and bandwidth guarantees in the ATM network. During PVC setup, the centralized ATM management system ensures that there are enough resources in the network to permit the PVC to be set up.

One type of wholesaled bit stream environment has an additional ATM path between the DSLAM and the access seeker's Network-to-Network Interconnect (NNI). Figure 7.3 shows the two ATM paths in use: one for the wholesaler's own use (VPI 20) and one for an access seeker, which has VPI 21. All wholesaled DSL ports from a DSLAM have their corresponding PVCs forwarded to the PVP that is destined for either an access seeker or the incumbent. At the NNI for the access seeker, each PVP corresponds to a DSLAM in the DSL service provider's network. Like a Russian doll, within each PVP are PVCs that correspond to each wholesaled port. During the provisioning process, the VPI and VCI that link a port to a PVC have been exchanged between the two providers. The figure shows the ATM path that a wholesaled customer takes through the network. The path goes through the DSLAM and follows the PVP through the incumbent's network to the access seeker. The NNI hands off VPI 21 to the access seeker, which routes the PVC to its own BNG.

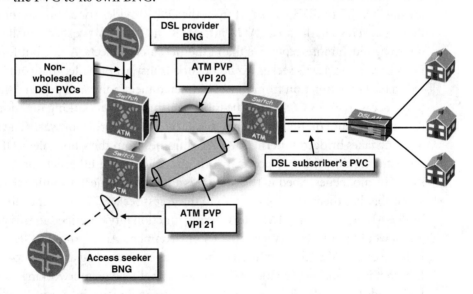

Figure 7.3 ATM topology with bit stream wholesale.

This bit stream model has a separate PVP from each DSLAM for each retail provider. Multiply this by the number of DSLAMs in the network, and that is a lot of paths to manage.

Normally the *maximum attainable downstream* and *upstream* bit rates are set by the incumbent at the DSLAM according to the upstream and downstream service speeds that the subscriber has purchased. No shaping is normally done on the PVC in the ATM network unless the wholesaler offers multiple PVCs per subscriber. This would usually be in the case of a PVC to be used for VoIP. To safeguard against the access seeker sending more traffic to the wholesaler's ATM network than has been agreed, the DSL provider can set a peak traffic rate on each PVP at the NNI. If this safeguard were not set, an access seeker could overwhelm the wholesaler's ATM backbone and links to DSLAMs with unexpected traffic loads.

The interconnect point is located at a wholesaler's DLE and consists of ATM links with bundles of PVCs within PVPs. These PVCs and PVPs are backhauled to an access seeker's central office (CO) and are terminated on a BNG, which means leasing SONET or SDH transport from the DSL provider (or a competitor if there is coverage in the area). ATM interfaces and transport costs normally work out to be much more expensive than Ethernet interconnects. A rare but fortuitous find for an access seeker would be for a transport provider that could provide a backhaul function from the ATM interconnect point and deliver Ethernet to the access seeker's CO. This is possible by using an interworking function commonly found on many switches as well as router vendor software. The interworking takes bridged Ethernet over ATM frames from the wholesaler's DLE, sends them across the transport network, and sends native Ethernet out the other side. The model described in this section is a 1:1 interconnect, meaning that each subscriber has their own logical path to the access seeker. The Ethernet-to-bridged-Ethernet-over-ATM interworking functionality described in this paragraph would not scale very well in a 1:1 environment. An *N*:1 model, described in the section "*N*:1 Ethernet Interconnect," scales when using an ATM-to-Ethernet interworking function. The reason is that bridge interworking between PVPs and stacked VLANS (S-VLANs) (using an analogous linkage of PVP and S-VLAN) is not easily configurable on a large scale on most routers or switches. Figure 7.5 (shown in a moment) shows an Ethernet backhaul architecture.

However, in an interworking model, the backhaul would be ATM, but before the access seeker interconnect, bridged-Ethernet-over-ATM is changed to pure Ethernet.

This is a complex protocol configuration. ATM interconnect models are well established in the industry, so this section is intended as supplementary information. Because the access seeker has a clear Layer 2 path to the customer, the perception is that bit stream interconnects perform better than Layer 3 or L2TP interconnects (see later in this chapter) from a QoS perspective. This is not always the case, because the incumbent is at liberty to implement any traffic management or oversubscription model within its own network. In times of high utilization within the provider's network, there could be PVP congestion if the guaranteed bandwidth allocated to the path is small. Interconnect agreements between the two providers often include provisions for guaranteed (also called committed) throughput on the PVP. This is normally calculated as a function of the number of DSL ports. Both parties should be aware of such rates when dimensioning their networks. This applies not only to ATM interconnects, but also to Ethernet interconnects, covered in the next section.

ETHERNET INTERCONNECTS

Due to its cheaper price and technical simplicity, Ethernet is becoming more pervasive to implement as the preferred interconnect technology between DSLAMs and the wider network. Until more Ethernet DSLAMs are deployed, most of the Ethernet interconnects will still handle traffic for ATM-based DSLAMs.

1:1 Ethernet Interconnect

Figure 7.4 shows an access seeker deploying an Ethernet switch rather than costlier ATM equipment at the interconnect point. An Ethernet DSLAM terminates the subscribers. The aggregation network or an MPLS network work as Layer 2 transports, carrying each subscriber within an S-VLAN. Because there are S-VLANs that carry all per-subscriber C-VLANs, the model is a 1:1 architecture. This is a close match to the architecture shown in Figure 7.3 with PVPs and PVCs.

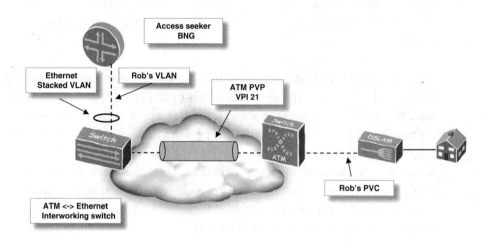

Figure 7.4 Ethernet wholesale interconnect topology.

Such interworking technology is a common feature in switches and routers that support both ATM and Ethernet interfaces. The protocol that is common between the two interfaces is the Ethernet MAC layer. It is commonly known as RFC 1483 or RFC 2684 bridging (RFC 2684 being a minor update to RFC 1483). Because Ethernet is the common protocol throughout the access seeker and DSL provider's networks, this restricts the protocol that can be used on the local loop to Ethernet. In most cases this is actually PPP over Ethernet, but because the wholesale model is bit stream access, the access seeker is at liberty to choose any protocol that sits on top of Ethernet—IP, PPPoE, IPv6, and so on. It is not possible to use PPP over ATM because it is not compatible with the underlying Ethernet transport layer unless the ATM performs protocol conversion between PPPoA and PPPoE. This is deployed in a few instances.

As far as provisioning goes, the linkage between the Ethernet VLAN and a customer DSL port is exchanged between the two providers' provisioning systems. The access seeker does not need to care about any VPI or VCI details, because these are part of the DSL provider's network. To make it easier to manage the potentially thousands of VLANs from the DSL network, the analog of the PVP is the S-VLAN. Each C-VLAN from a DSLAM is bundled within a stacked VLAN. To stay consistent with the ATM architecture, the stacked VLAN is bandwidth-limited to the agreed rate by the DSL provider. Bear in mind that an Ethernet handoff architecture does not obviate the need for judicious traffic management on the DSL provider's network.

N:1 Ethernet Interconnect

A service VLAN is a construct that has all PPPoE or IPoE (DHCP-based) sessions share the same Layer 2 broadcast domain. The workings of this model in a normal broadband access network are explained in the section "VLAN Architecture: Service VLANs" in Chapter 4. This section extends this model to the wholesale bit stream environment. In a normal service VLAN environment, one VLAN is dedicated to a service—the most common being the Internet service. In a wholesale model, it is almost always the Internet service that is delivered to the customer. In some markets, the incumbent delivers two paths to the retailer, one of which is used for VoIP services. The VoIP PVC is usually prioritized through the wholesaler's network. Each DSLAM has a VLAN for every access seeker. As a simple example, if there are five retail ISPs, the wholesaler offers its own Internet service, and 100 DSLAMs in the network, there would be 600 VLANs in the network.

Figure 7.5 shows a DSLAM, with two example connections. The network has two providers—the incumbent and one access seeker. VLAN 100 goes from the DSLAM to the BNG for the wholesaler's customers, and VLAN 200 goes from each DSLAM to the NNI for the access seeker. Subscriber Rob on the first DSLAM has a PPPoE session that spans his PVC on the local loop. The session is bridged onto VLAN 100 and then is terminated on the incumbent's BNG. The second subscriber on the same DSLAM—Veronica—has a connection to the access seeker—intertron.net. The PPPoE session spans the PVC on the local loop but is bridged onto VLAN 101 and is terminated onto Intertron.net.

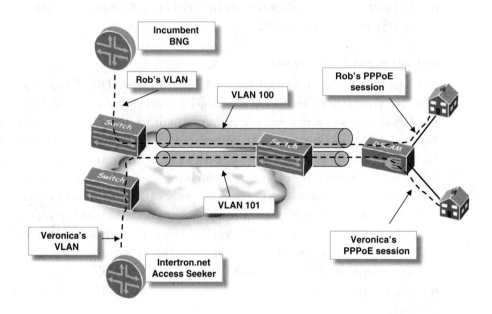

Figure 7.5 *N*:1 Ethernet interconnect architecture.

REDUNDANT BIT STREAM INTERCONNECTS

Because the bit stream model is based on Layer 2 interconnects, there are not as many ways as with Layer 3 or L2TP interconnects to implement highly available connectivity between a DSL provider and an access seeker. Because the model operates at Layer 2, the redundancy options are at Layer 2 and below.

Some routing protocols can use redundant links in a network, such as PNNI for an ATM network and per-VLAN spanning tree for Ethernet. Unfortunately, it is rare for a DSL provider to offer redundant bit stream access coupled with PNNI to handle the failover mechanism. This leaves physical redundancy techniques as the only real alternatives. A simple way to protect an ATM interconnect at the physical layer is to use a loss-of-light mechanism to detect if a link goes down. If the router or switch detects that it is not receiving a signal from the switch or router at the other end, it can switch to a backup link. In Figure 7.6, the primary interface is designated the *working* interface, and the standby interface is called the *protect* interface. In the event of a link breakage on the working path, the backup rapidly comes into service and takes over from the primary, as shown in Figure 7.7. In SONET or SDH protocols, K1 and K2 bytes in the line overhead (they can be thought of as bits of control information in the header) communicate the failover mechanism and actions (such as revertive behavior) between the two SONET/SDH endpoints. Rather than simply relying on a loss-of-light condition, a router or switch can make a link switch based on the configuration of these 2 bytes.

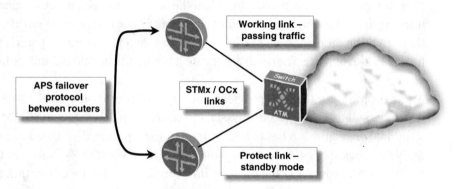

Figure 7.6 Automatic protection switching—normal operating mode.

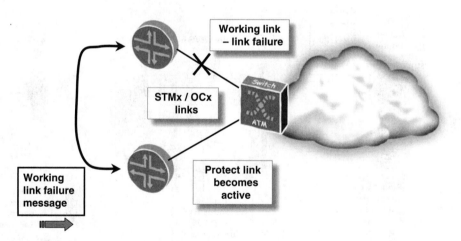

Figure 7.7 Automatic protection switching—link failure.

The protection mechanism can be configured as either revertive or nonrevertive, which describes the behavior of the router or switch when the primary link comes back up. Revertive causes traffic to automatically switch back to the original working link when it comes back up. If the primary link is flapping, returning it to service can cause unnecessary stress on the network's control plane. Therefore, most router/switch implementations include a configurable knob to revert to an interface after it has been stable for a period of time. Nonrevertive means that operator intervention is needed to switch the active path back to the original working link. The working and protect links can reside on the same switch, or they can be on different switches. Terminating them on different switches is better from a risk-avoidance perspective, because it allows for switch and link failure.

Another option for the DSL provider is to use Multi-Endpoint (MEP) PVPs, which designates two possible physical interfaces for a PVP from a DSLAM to terminate on. Figure 7.8 has two ATM interconnect points, designated as primary and backup. The ATM management system sets up the PVPs so that they leave the DSL provider at the primary interconnect. If a failure of any link or switch occurs between the DSLAM and the egress ATM port, the management system automatically reroutes the PVPs to terminate on the other ATM port.

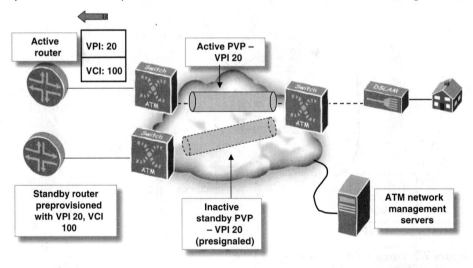

Figure 7.8 ATM multi-endpoint PVPs—normal operation.

Figure 7.9 shows how the path is rerouted when a failure occurs on the primary path.

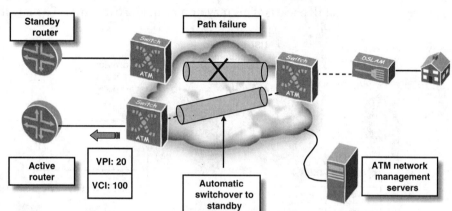

Figure 7.9 ATM multi-endpoint PVPs—path failure.

The downside is that no signaling protocol communication occurs between the access seeker and access provider switches after a switchover. As a result, the switches at the primary and secondary interconnect points need to be statically configured with the number and capacity dimension of each PVP that is carried. If the interconnect switches are routers rather than pure ATM switches, reserving PVCs on these routers is more costly in terms of resource usage compared to ATM switches; routers typically have a lower interface density than switches.

A further solution that is expected to gain more traction in the market place is pseudowire emulation interconnects. This involves using an MPLS network to deliver pseudowires of VLANs or PVCs to the interconnect point. The access seeker can run MPLS to the interconnect point to carry the pseudowires further in to their network or run straight ATM or Ethernet to their BNG.

LAYER 3 WHOLESALE

Layer 3 wholesale access is cheap and relatively easy to implement for access seekers. It involves creating a routed interconnect between the two providers and exchanging customer traffic at the IP protocol level. Figure 7.10 shows a router at the DSL provider's CO and a link to the router at the access seeker's network. The DSL provider terminates PPPoA, PPPoE, or IPoE sessions on its own BNGs for both its own customers if it is legally allowed under the unbundling regulations. It also terminates sessions for its own subscribers. Then traffic is routed to the access seeker as normal IP packets. This may or may not be over an MPLS network.

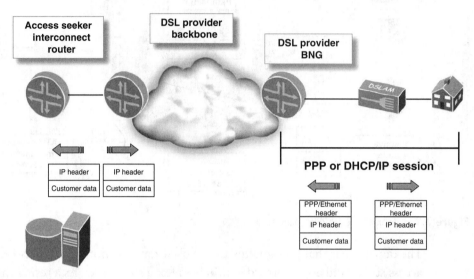

Figure 7.10 Layer 3 wholesaled interconnect.

A routing protocol runs between the two providers and instructs the access seeker's routers how to route traffic to the subscribers in the DSL provider's network. This is especially important if there are redundant interconnect points, which lets routing provide a better end-to-end redundancy mechanism than bit stream access models. This is thanks to a routing protocol (such as BGP), which gives a good indication that the path from a BNG to the access seeker's router is functioning. Ethernet or ATM bit stream interconnects normally do not have such availability information.

This model is ideal for some access seekers because all the hard work of subscriber termination, QoS, and service creation is handled by another party. But for these same reasons, many do not see this as an attractive proposition, because there is little room for service differentiation. QoS and packet policy control are impractical for an access seeker to implement in this type of architecture because the subscriber is several router hops and links away. Terminating subscribers on a BNG with bit stream access using PPPoA, PPPoE, or IPoE with DHCP provides a convenient attachment point to apply QoS or packet filtering policies. L2TP also provides a Layer 2 attachment point for QoS and policy attachment, as described next. The physical layer for Layer 3 interconnects is quite flexible. They could be ATM, Ethernet, SONET, Frame Relay, or essentially anything that supports IP.

L2TP WHOLESALE

Layer 2 Tunneling Protocol (L2TP) is one of the most popular ways to link access seekers to their customers that are connected to the wholesaler's DSLAMs. L2TP is a protocol defined in RFC 2661[2]. It extends a Layer 2 PPP session over a packet-switched network—an IP network in this case. PPP has been the de facto encapsulation standard for dialup access since Serial Line Interface Protocol (SLIP). PPP runs directly on top of physical links and requires a dedicated logical path between two endpoints (hence the term Point-to-Point Protocol). PPP works fine between dial-up user modems and Remote Access Servers (RASs), as well as between broadband modems and BNGs, but extra protocol machinery is needed to extend a PPP session across an IP network.

The right side of Figure 7.11 shows how users can connect to a narrowband RAS, which extends the user sessions to an off-site provider. L2TP is used by more than access seekers to provide residential broadband access. It can also be used in any instance in which an endpoint needs Layer 2 access to another endpoint over a packet-switched network.

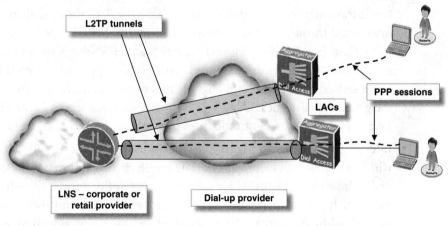

Figure 7.11 L2TP interconnect.

[2] http://www.ietf.org/rfc/rfc2661.txt

L2TP FOR NARROWBAND NETWORKS

One of the uses of tunneling PPP over L2TP is when a customer wants to handle her own IP addressing and policy control for dialup users but does not want the overhead of managing a network of dialup RASs. Instead, the dialup access provider forwards the PPP sessions over an IP network using L2TP. The PPP session terminates on a router called a Layer 2 Tunneling Protocol Network Server (LNS) at the customer premises. The router that originates the L2TP session is called a Layer 2 Tunneling Protocol Access Concentrator (LAC). L2TP dialup architectures are not part of mandatory unbundling but instead are a way to create centralized dialup services. Here are some examples of these services:

- Corporate roaming dial-in service: The corporate customer has an LNS at its premises. It handles IP addressing, Remote Authentication Dial-In User Service (RADIUS), and packet filters and runs a dedicated circuit to the dialup provider for L2TP traffic (and likely RADIUS). Alternatively, the corporate and dialup provider can route L2TP over the Internet with an IPsec tunnel providing the underlying transport security. RADIUS is a protocol used ubiquitously in networks to provide authentication, authorization, and accounting services to network devices. It is described further in the technology note later in this chapter.

- Provider-hosted VPN service: If the customer does not want to maintain any kind of remote-access hardware, the dialup provider can run the lion's share of this infrastructure—dialup RASs as LNSs. Figure 7.12 shows dial-in servers distributed throughout the network and a central LNS that terminates the L2TP tunnels (and PPP sessions). Rather than dedicating a router per customer, most providers use the more cost-effective approach of terminating L2TP sessions for several different customers on a single router and isolating the groups of customers using VRFs or virtualized routers. A Layer 3 interconnect circuit is used to get traffic from this LNS to the end customer.

- Internal provider session aggregation: This use of L2TP can optimize routing within a dialup provider network. The problem description is as follows: A dialup Internet access provider usually wants to offer a static IP address service, which enables customers to dial in from anywhere and always get the same IP address. Normally they would not get the same address for each session, because each dial-in RAS is configured with a unique pool of addresses to assign to customers when they connect. Without a static IP address service, when the customer dials up next time, they would most likely connect to a different RAS, which has a different pool of addresses it assigns to customers. And even if they connected to the same RAS, there are no guarantees that the assigned address would be the same one from the pool each time.

When a static address is given to the subscriber, it needs to be announced to the rest of the network through a routing protocol before the user can get anywhere. Providers are often concerned about the overhead of announcing potentially thousands of host routes into their network, as well as the continual protocol churn from the route advertisement and withdrawal. A solution is to terminate all subscribers that use static routes on a central LNS using L2TP. The static routes that are allocated to these subscribers are typically part of a pool of addresses the provider sets aside for such a purpose, so this pool can be announced as a single route from the LNS, obviating the need to announce thousands of routes into the network. But in most cases, as long as the majority of customers are part of dynamic blocks and static routes are used by the minority, a few thousand or even tens of thousands of host routes can work in medium to large-sized providers.

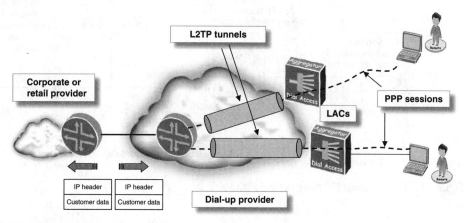

Figure 7.12 Dialup provider-hosted L2TP architecture.

L2TP FOR BROADBAND ACCESS NETWORKS

The most popular choice after copper loop unbundling is L2TP access to broadband subscribers. In this architecture, the incumbent owns the DSLAMs and

BNG routers and forwards the PPP session to the access seeker using L2TP. The preceding section gave you a basic understanding of how L2TP is used in the context of narrowband access. This section covers architecture solutions in the broadband world, including low-level details of L2TPv2 and L2TPv3 operation.

In broadband networks, L2TP is most commonly used to permit access to wholesalers' DSL ports for access seekers. This creates a dedicated Layer 2 path between the retailer and subscriber, giving the access seeker more control over the user session compared with the Layer 3 wholesale model. Layer 3 wholesale has several router hops between the subscriber and the access seeker, making it difficult to have the same level of subscriber control. The wholesaler still needs to restrict the speed of the connection according to the bandwidth rates the user has purchased. There are two options to achieve the rate-limiting: restricting the synchronization speed of the DSL port at the DSLAM, or limiting it at the wholesaler's BNG. When the wholesaler originates L2TP sessions, the wholesaler's BNG is a LAC. Figure 7.13 shows how a subscriber that is running PPPoE can be restricted to speeds of 2048Kbps downstream and 512Kbps upstream at the DSLAM. The wholesaled PPPoE session is extended to the ISP using L2TP.

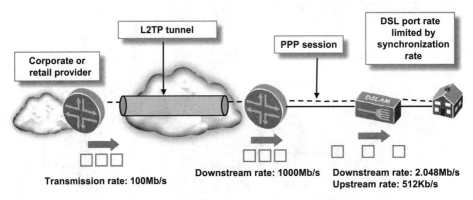

Figure 7.13 Rate-limiting L2TP throughput at the DSLAM.

Figure 7.14 shows the alternative approach of BNG doing the shaping. The subscriber connects to the DSLAM at the maximum downstream and upstream synchronization rates that the copper line can achieve given the loop conditions.

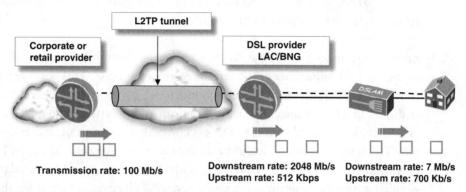

Figure 7.14 Rate-limiting L2TP throughput at the BNG.

In this example, the line speed for the customer *service* is still 2048kbps down and 512kbps up, regardless of what the copper rate is. But to limit the upstream and downstream traffic throughput, the wholesaler BNG now performs rate-limiting in both directions. In theory, the access seeker's LNS could perform the rate-limiting, but then the incumbent could not easily ensure that the access seeker's LNS is sending the correct traffic rate to the network.

Notice that even though the DSLAM's rate limit is much higher, the packets are still sent to the DSL modem at the purchased bandwidth rates because of earlier packet rate-limiting or shaping at the BNG.

Both designs have advantages. If the throughput is rate-limited at the whole-saler's BNG, the *serialization* delay of traffic sent from the subscriber is minimized. Serialization delay is the time it takes to transmit a given amount of data onto the *wire* and is based on the speed of the physical line. The biggest problem with serialization delay is when a large packet is being transmitted onto the wire and a smaller, delay-sensitive VoIP packet is waiting in a queue to be transmitted. As an extreme example, for a local loop rate-limited at the DSLAM to an upstream bandwidth of 128Kbps, a 1,000-byte packet would take ~62ms milli-seconds to transmit onto the wire. This would then cause jitter of at least 62ms before the VoIP packet could be transmitted. By moving the rate-limiting func-tion onto the BNG and allowing the modem to synchronize to the highest band-width possible, packets take less time to be sent on the wire. If the upstream were allowed to synchronize at 700Kbps, the time a VoIP packet would have to wait for a 1,000-byte packet is now around 10ms.

Another advantage has to do with QoS and provisioning. QoS is normally applied to each subscriber at the access seeker's own BNG. This permits prioritization between traffic classes when too much data are trying to be sent down the customer link line at once. The wholesaler can also prioritize wholesaled traffic as well as its own retail traffic, but this is currently the exception rather than the rule. When wholesalers are asked to support service differentiation in an L2TP environment, they need to be prepared with the right tools and knowledge. The simplest approach to setting up a multiservice L2TP environment is for the access seeker and wholesaler to have a common DiffServ code point scheme. This lets the access seeker mark traffic going to the subscriber. For instance, if a VoIP packet is sent from a session border controller (SBC) on the access seeker's network toward a subscriber connected via L2TP, the LNS can mark the outer IP packet header with the Expedited Forwarding group. When the IP packet arrives at the wholesaler's LAC, before the inner L2TP header is removed, the outer IP header is examined for the DiffServ marking. If a nonzero marking is found, the packet is placed in the correct traffic class within the router. As the subsequent PPP frame is scheduled for transmission on the customer-facing interface, the prioritization information is maintained, and the scheduler treats the frame with the correct Per-Hop Behavior (PHB). The next chapter contains a thorough explanation of these concepts and acronyms. Figure 7.15 shows this prioritization system with two classes of traffic supported by the wholesaler—VoIP and best-effort. The BNG or LAC on the right inspects the DiffServ Code Point on the outer IP header to determine what PHB it should apply to a packet.

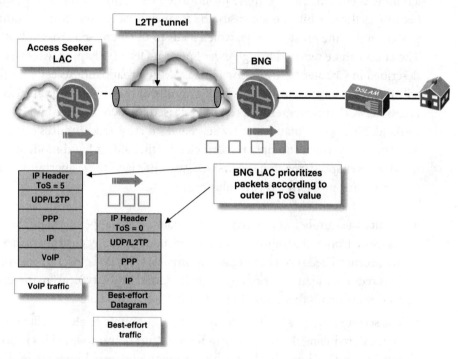

Figure 7.15 L2TP wholesale with multiclass services.

Applying QoS and upstream/downstream rate-limiting on a single device, the LAC, reduces the complexity and therefore the cost of the provisioning system. This is because it needs to configure only one device rather than the DSLAM and BNG. Provisioning need not apply solely to a one-off or a monthly change on the subscriber's line. Real-time service modifications, such as those described in Chapter 11, "Dynamic User Session Control," to increase or decrease the user's bandwidth are easier to manage when there is a single service definition point.

The downside of having loops synchronized at the maximum attainable bit rate is increased local loop cross talk. Cross talk occurs when the RF energy that a DSL line creates affects adjacent copper pairs in the binder, which is always the case when they are bundled in a multicore cable that is terminated at the DLE or a remote shelf. This effect is more pronounced when lines *train*[3] at high bit rates, because as the line bit rate increases, the frequency range and corresponding power on the line must increase, which leads to the increased cross talk effect. The effect can be reduced using Power Spectral Density shaping, which is described in Chapter 6, "Evolutions in Last-Mile Broadband Access," but there will always be some induced noise. An example of how line noise can affect an access network was written in a report[4] released in 2006 by Telecom New Zealand. Line noise (manifested by Self Far-End cross talk) induces errors in adjacent pairs, which can only be corrected by the DSLAM and modem retraining at a lower speed, making the line less susceptible to these aberrations. In summary, this problem has two solutions:

- Reduce the number of adjacent copper pairs. This happens when DSL providers move from a centralized model of terminating many customers in a CO to the decentralized model of deploying smaller DSLAMs closer to customers. This reduces the number of copper pairs found in the typical "many-core" binders, which is the main offender of induced cross talk.

- The second option is to limit the synchronization rate of all DSL lines at the DSLAM, reducing the frequency range and thus power usage. This is usually suitable for DSL lines that have a high-enough upstream bit rate to mitigate the effect of serialization delay. However, this is not feasible for DSL providers that are moving to ADSL2(+) and VDSL(2) models and that want to provide as much bandwidth as possible to subscribers. Ways to address this are found in Chapter 6, which describes the use of flexible band plans to reduce the impact of spectral interference. Analyzing the impact of DSL cross talk is time-consuming for a service provider, but this is an important problem to understand, because it can hinder the rollout of next-generation DSL services. Generally speaking, FTT*x* technologies are not impacted by this problem, because even with a fiber head-end and a localized copper distribution network, the number of adjacent pairs is not as great as with traditional copper POTS networks.

The only protocols that can use this L2TP model are PPP-based (PPP over ATM, PPP over Ethernet, or PPP over Ethernet over ATM). This is because the majority

---

[3] Train is a synonym for synchronized. It comes from the term used when the modem and DSLAM *train* against each other to discover maximum speeds, interleaving rates, and capabilities.

[4] http://www.telecom-media.co.nz/resources/adsl-performance-report-250706.pdf

of wholesale L2TP networks run L2TP version 2, which does not support transparent bridging of arbitrary protocols. Its successor, L2TP version 3, supports several Layer 2 protocols. Currently Ethernet, PPP, and IP are supported and are sure to encompass more encapsulation types in the future. For DHCP/IPoE networks to work in a tunnelled wholesale environment, L2TPv3 is needed due to its support for pseudowires, which can bridge Ethernet frames from one side of the tunnel to the other. Figure 7.16 shows a provider supporting L2TPv3 wholesaling, which allows for a dedicated Ethernet path between the customer modem and the LNS.

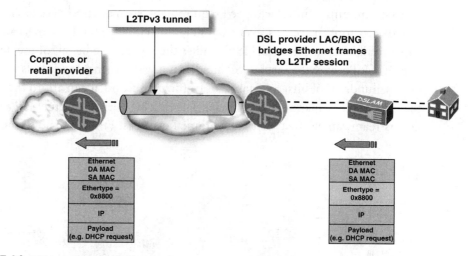

Figure 7.16 Bridging traffic with L2TP version 3.

Another model, which requires more provisioning overhead compared to L2TP, is to deliver these services over MPLS Ethernet pseudowires (PWE3s). PWE3 is described extensively in Chapter 4, so you should already be familiar with this technology. The reason for the extra provisioning overhead is that L2TP has commonly been deployed using dynamic RADIUS infrastructure, which allows provisioning from a central location. PWE3 does not have this luxury. Therefore, circuits need to be provisioned and configured on both endpoints of the network—on the incumbent's BNG and at the access seeker interconnect point.

L2TP TUNNEL SWITCHING

L2TP Tunnel Switching (LTS) is a way to aggregate L2TP sessions at one or more LNSs (called LTSs) and forward them to a second LNS. The LTS works like an LAC and initiates an L2TP tunnel to the next tunnel terminator, which is usually the last one in the chain. Figure 7.17 shows the principle of a *virtual ISP*. The virtual ISP simply receives L2TP sessions from the DSL provider and switches them to a smaller ISP. Why go through a virtual ISP when the smaller ISP could go straight to the DSL provider? The most common reason has to do with how the incumbent has set its access seeker interconnection policies. For example, there may be a minimum interface speed requirement, such as an STM-1 or Gigabit Ethernet, before an access seeker can interconnect. For small ISPs, this can be cost-prohibitive, so the virtual ISP handles the sessions on behalf of the down-stream ISP. Because the virtual ISP handles many subscribers and deals with tens of bits, hundreds of bits, or gigabits of traffic per second, it can afford the cost of the interconnect link to the wholesaler. The link between the virtual ISP and the downstream can be any type: radio, Frame Relay, Fast Ethernet, and so on.

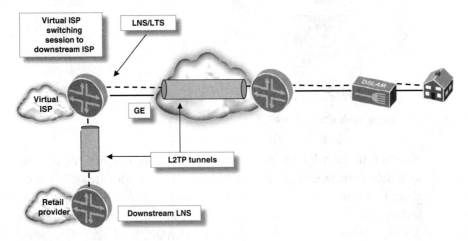

Figure 7.17 Virtual ISP using L2TP tunnel switching.

Another use for tunnel switching is within the DSL provider's network. The LTS aggregates L2TP sessions at a handful of tunnel server routers before handing them off to access seekers. This creates a smoke-screen effect, masking the consti-tution of the LAC configuration inside the DSL provider network. This means that ISPs do not have any direct communication with the LAC, which acts as a basic security layer. This is akin to how an SBC hides the VoIP server and end-point layer from the originating User Agent (UA).

This also means that any configuration modifications made to the wholesaler's LACs (IP addressing changes, router additions and removals) are transparent to the access seeker. The only L2TP relationship is between the ISP LNSs and the handful of LTSs. This cuts down on the provisioning overhead between access seekers and the DSL provider. Figure 7.18 shows a retail ISP terminating L2TP tunnels and session from a single LTS at the wholesaler.

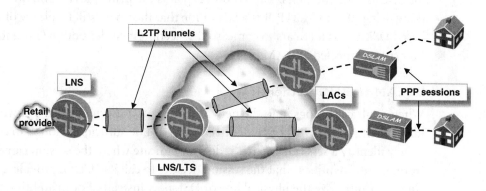

Figure 7.18 A DSL provider's internal L2TP session aggregation.

This model has some downsides—the first being cost. A virtual ISP has an essential cost of doing business. For a wholesaler, much extra hardware is needed to support a tunnel-switched network that is not necessarily mandatory to support an L2TP service. One type of deployment is for a wholesaler to dedicate one or more LTSs to an access seeker. If an access seeker has many L2TP sessions, the per-subscriber cost of the LTS router might be satisfactory, but for smaller-end ISPs with fewer sessions, the per-subscriber LTS cost for the wholesaler increases.

However, sharing LTS infrastructure is not foolproof. A common physical LTS means that if an end ISP fails to terminate an L2TP session, the originating LAC doesn't know whether the failure is at the final LNS or the LTS (it does not know that an LTS is in the middle). The danger is that the LAC could mark the LTS out of service for all other ISPs as well. Virtualizing the LTS to use different tunnel endpoint IP addresses for different ISPs avoids this situation.

SUBSCRIBER AUTHENTICATION

Chapters 4 and 5 describe ways in which a DSL provider can design the access network and the implications of different protocols on the architecture. If a DSL provider uses DHCP and IPoE as its addressing and encapsulation protocols, the options for a suitable wholesale solution are L2TPv3 or bit stream unbundling. L2TPv3 has been deployed in some providers, but L2TPv2 is by far the most common tunneling protocol in the market. It needs to be supported on the LNS and the LAC too. PPP and L2TP is still a very pervasive protocol combination in the wholesale market, primarily for two reasons: per-user authentication and historic implementations. This section explains the principles behind unbundling using PPP and L2TP. It is a fact of life that there will still be plenty of ATM-based DSL access for years to come, so this section includes both ATM- and Ethernet-connected DSLAMs.

DSLAM-to-BNG Authentication

When a subscriber logs in to the network, he sends a username and password to identify himself. This set of credentials might not be sufficient enough to completely identify a session, because it doesn't indicate where the session came from; it only identifies what the session decides to call itself. DSL providers often choose to authorize the physical line or DSL port instead of or in addition to the subscriber. Usually the credentials of the DSL line rather than the username/password dictate the speed characteristics of the DSL service. As soon as the subscriber identity is authorized, the provider can direct the PPP session to an access seeker based purely on line credentials, as shown in Figure 7.19, or based purely on the username and password.

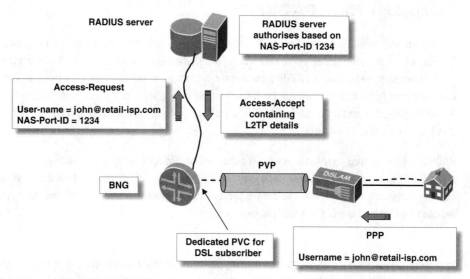

Figure 7.19 Line-based authorization.

What are the line credentials? In ATM-based networks, simply speaking, two bits of information usually identify a line: the VCI and VPI. The first one identifies the DSL port on the DSLAM; the second identifies the DSLAM itself. With these two values, a PPP session can be linked to a physical DSL port in the network. The identifiers are converted to a RADIUS attribute called a *NAS-Port-ID*, which is a numeric representation of the VPI, VCI, and some supplementary information (the ATM slot and port on the BNG, for example). The algorithm to calculate the NAS-Port-ID is vendor-dependent, but as a general rule, the BNG's slot, port, VPI, and VCIs are used to calculate the final value.

The NAS-Port-ID is sent to the RADIUS server, along with the username and password. With this information, the RADIUS server can authenticate the session based on the line credentials and can instruct the BNG to apply QoS and other rate-limiting attributes during the *Access-Accept* authorization phase.

Technology Note: RADIUS

Remote Authentication Dial-In User Service (RADIUS) is defined in RFC 2865[5]. It is a protocol that runs between a NAS and a RADIUS server to authenticate users who want to access a network. When a user requests access (based on sending a PPP username and password, for example), the NAS sends an *Access-Request* packet to the RADIUS server. If the RADIUS server is satisfied with the user credentials in the Access-Request, it sends an *Access-Accept* back to the NAS containing the services that the user can access. This last part is called authorization.

RADIUS does accounting, too. At the start of the user session, the NAS sends an *Accounting-Start* packet to the RADIUS server and correspondingly an *Accounting-Stop* at the end of the session. A third type of packet called an *Accounting-Alive* or *Interim Accounting* packet can be enabled to provide periodic accounting updates between the beginning and end of a user session.

➠ Note Interim accounting messages are especially useful if the BNG has a software or hardware problem and crashes in the middle of a user session. In this case, no accounting-stop record would be generated, because the BNG would have lost all state information for the sessions after it reboots. If users are billed based on volume usage, and thousands of accounting records are lost due to a BNG crash, this can represent significant revenue loss.

Time-based services are not as susceptible to this problem, because after the BNG reboots, it sends a message to the RADIUS server indicating that it has come back into service. The time between the *Accounting-Start* and the *Accounting-On* that the BNG sends after a reboot (with some adjustment for the time taken to reboot) is the session time.

LAC-to-LNS Authentication

When the access seeker receives the L2TP session on the LNS, it authenticates the subscriber session based on the username and password supplied by the client. The username and password can be authenticated either by using proxy Link Control Protocol (LCP) credentials from the LAC or by requesting that the client resend them. Proxy LCP is a concept that incorporates elements of both L2TP and PPP. PPP has a subprotocol called LCP that, among other things, exchanges a username and password between the two endpoints. Proxy LCP takes the username and password that the client sent to the LAC and passes them on to the LNS as part of the L2TP session setup.

[5] http://www.ietf.org/rfc/rfc2865.txt

Figure 7.20 shows an LAC creating an L2TP session to an access seeker's LNS. First the protocol exchanges some messages to set up the L2TP session. Then further messages are exchanged to set up each session within the tunnel. The first message is an ICRQ session-request packet. It is sent from the LAC to the LNS and contains session setup information. If the LNS is satisfied with the session setup details, it replies with an ICRP. This packet contains the LNS's own details. The final phase consists of the LAC replying with an ICCN packet, completing the session establishment. This packet contains the proxy LCP details, including the username and password that the client sent to the LAC during the earlier authentication phase.

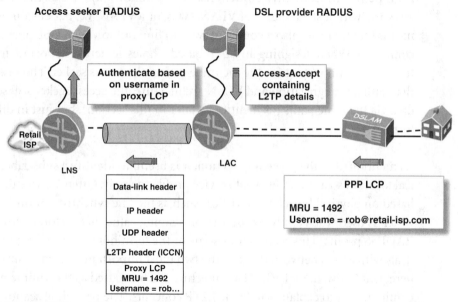

Figure 7.20 Proxy LCP in an L2TP environment.

There are a couple of reasons why proxy LCP is used. One is to keep the client from resending its authentication credentials during session setup. Because the LNS already has this information through proxy LCP, it can authenticate the client based on those credentials, saving setup time. This is especially important in scenarios with mobile handsets, which need short session setup times. A second reason is that some PPP clients do not function according to RFC and have protocol stacks that balk if the LNS asks them to resend their credentials. A stack is a concept based on the layering of protocols. For example, in a TCP/IP stack, TCP is stacked above IP, which is stacked above a data-link protocol such as Ethernet. An implementation of a set of protocols is called a protocol stack.

On the other hand, LNSs can choose to disregard proxied LCP information. This can be for any reason that the LNS chooses not to accept the attributes from the LAC. For example, there may be a Maximum Receive Unit (MRU) mismatch between the subscriber and the LNS. Or, as part of a provider policy, an access seeker may not trust the subscriber username and password that are sent from the LAC. MRU is a PPP LCP attribute that tells a PPP peer (a device at the end of a PPP link) the maximum size PPP frame it can receive.

DSL Port Identification

An Ethernet-DSLAM environment has two common ways to design the access network: with just a handful of VLANs/VCs, or a VLAN/VC per customer. This means that there are also a couple of ways to find out to which DSL port a user is connected. When designing an L2TP-based wholesale network, port identification is more important for the incumbent than the access seeker. The reason is that with any aggregation and VLAN architecture, the access seeker still sends data via the same paths (as mentioned later in this section), but just in different formats.

As mentioned in the preceding section, it is useful to identify a subscriber's physical location so as to know what service profile to apply. Often, service design is based on physical line characteristics (such as the line synchronization rate), which is used when applying the session shaping value that is stored in the line's RADIUS profile. This section uses some of the terminology from Chapter 4 that deals with access network designs; the two most important ones are summarized here. Until now, the 1:1 VLAN architecture has been used as the sample network configuration to explain wholesale L2TP concepts. The preceding section covered how the username and password can be used to authenticate the user at the end of a PPPoE session. In a 1:1 ATM architecture, the VPI and VCI (and potentially the ATM port and slot on the BNG) identify the source DSL port of a PPP session. This information can be encoded into an L2TP attribute called the Calling-Station-ID, which is sent from the LAC to the LNS. If required, the access seeker can use this information to identify the customer circuit. In the case of Ethernet-connected DSLAMs, the VPIs and VCIs are changed to S-VLANs and C-VLANs, respectively.

An alternative to the 1:1 is the service VLAN (also called the N:1 approach), in which N subscribers share a single VLAN. Described in Chapter 5, "Choosing the

Right Access Protocol," the PPPoE Intermediate Agent (IA) is a way to identify subscriber sessions when many clients share a single broadcast domain. This involves inserting a header into PPPoE discovery frames, which the BNG uses to identify a subscriber's port location. As in the 1:1 VLAN or 1:1 PVC architecture, the BNG (also functioning as the LAC) can send this circuit information to the access seeker in the L2TP session setup.

L2TP Fragmentation

A common issue for service providers when working with L2TP is fragmentation. An RFC[6] has been written to describe this problem and its solutions. When L2TP transports PPP across an IP network, it wraps the PPP frame in several bytes of control information in the form of a header before sending across the network.

When an IP packet is received at the LNS from upstream, it can be up to 1,500 bytes in size. After a liberal dosing of various headers, the packet can easily grow to over 1,550 bytes. For some types of media, transmitting a packet of such a size is not possible. For example, Figure 7.21 shows the LNS at the Horizon ISP connected to the DSL service provider using a Fast Ethernet link.

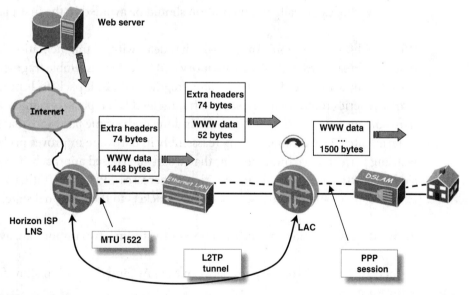

Figure 7.21 L2TP fragmentation and reassembly.

[6] http://tools.ietf.org/html/rfc4459

When the LNS receives the 1,500-byte IP packet from an Internet server, the following headers need to be added before being sent to the LAC over the Ethernet link:

- PPP header: 2 bytes
- PPPoE header: 6 bytes
- L2TP header: 12 bytes
- UDP header: 8 bytes
- IP header: 20 bytes
- Ethernet header with a single VLAN tag: 22 bytes
- Total: 70 bytes

Most newer switches obligingly transmit jumbo Ethernet frames, which are frames that are bigger than the Ethernet II specification. Such generosity extends only so far, and often, 70 bytes are just too many. The only way to get the data across to the other side is to perform *tunnel fragmentation*, which chops an L2TP packet into sizes small enough to pass through the links to get to the LAC. A configurable knob on routers is called a Maximum Transmission Unit (MTU), the maximum size of a packet that can be transmitted before requiring fragmentation. Nevertheless, ideally fragmentation should be avoided in the first place.

Why avoid fragmentation? Anyone who has dealt with IP fragmentation knows that it is a great burden on router memory and CPU to reassemble fragmented IP packets. The same goes for reassembling fragmented L2TP packets. Juniper Networks' E-series routers can reassemble fragmented L2TP packets using extra hardware on the LAC. On the LNS, this is done in the same hardware that is used to terminate L2TP sessions. Doing reassembly in hardware improves packet forwarding performance but is costlier than a software-based approach. The downside of a software implementation is that it increases CPU usage. Either way, extra resources are needed to re-form these packets to their original state.

To avoid fragmentation in each direction of the tunnel, two options are available:

- Increase the MTU of the path between the LAC and the LNS to allow for the overhead.
- Lower the MRU on the LNS, effectively limiting the maximum size of the packet that the subscriber can send.

If all the links support it, the first option is the most preferred, because it does not require any changes on the subscriber's PPP client software or have any impact on LAC resources. As far as the client is concerned, the LNS can support a 1,500-byte IP packet (or 1,492 in the case of PPPoE). This is supported on Frame Relay, ATM, and Gigabit Ethernet circuits, because they all should support MTUs larger than 1,518 bytes (IP + Ethernet header). However, setting MTU sizes larger than 1,518 bytes is not possible on all Fast Ethernet links. Even if the interface that is directly connected to the LAC or LNS is Gigabit Ethernet, the entire path between the wholesaler's LAC and the access seeker's LNS must support large packet sizes. Therefore, it is not a safe bet to increase the MTU unless you're absolutely sure of the end-to-end path. Path MTU Discovery (PMTUD) could be used to discover path information, but it only automates the process of obtaining the path MTU rather than knowing it explicitly through topology information.

The second option involves setting a configuration knob on the LNS to lower the MRU enough to allow for the L2TP overhead from the LAC. This limits the maximum packet size that the client can send to the LNS to avoid fragmentation from the LAC to the LNS. It requires some cooperation from client PPP implementations to accept the low MRU request from the LNS. Unfortunately, some operating systems are averse to negotiating their MRU to certain values and do not bring up their session (Microsoft Windows 2000 is such an example). This is a problem only if the PPPoE session is bridged through the CPE to the customer PC.

If the PPPoE session terminates on the CPE, during modem qualification, the provider can ensure that the PPP software supports this functionality. Alternatively, if the customer installs her own modem, it could be a mandatory feature of connecting to a provider network that the modem supports MRU renegotiation. Also, the LNS should be cautious about using the MRU from the client unless there is a good reason to do otherwise. The reason is the client CPE does not have enough path or interface MTU information to make a useful decision about the effective MRU for the session.

CPE in bridged or routed mode has pros and cons. These are described in a broader context in Chapter 4. From an L2TP fragmentation perspective, if the CPE is in bridging mode, the PPP session extends directly to the user's PC from the BNG. Therefore, when the PPP MRU is sent from the LNS to the PPP client, this is installed as the interface MTU on the PC. Therefore, the applications and the operating system on the PC work in concert and send packets out the PPP interface at the MRU size that is indicated by the LNS. As just noted, some operating systems may not accept certain MRU values from the LNS. Other systems may not accept renegotiating the MRU as the PPP state machine transfers from between customer PC and LAC to between customer PC and LNS.

Instead, if the PPP session terminates on the external router, the MRU is set on the router. When packets from the LAN reach the gateway, the router must fragment them before they are sent over the PPP link. Because most Ethernet devices on a LAN use an MTU of 1,500 bytes, this rules out the need for fragmentation on the LAN. This may not be a concern for service providers, because it shifts the reassembly burden to hosts on the Internet (or to an intermediate firewall that does the reassembly on the server's behalf). This could be avoided by setting the MTU to a value lower than 1,500 bytes, either through explicit configuration or through a technique such as DHCP option 26—Interface MTU. However, neither of these two Ethernet MTU-setting techniques is widely deployed.

HIGH-AVAILABILITY L2TP ACCESS

Chapter 3, "Designing a Triple-Play Backbone," discusses how to deploy a highly available core and video network. This includes building a highly available BNG access network. This section covers options available to the access seeker and incumbent when dealing with L2TP wholesale DSL broadband networks.

At the protocol level, L2TP creates tunnels between two IP addresses (normally loopback ones)—one on the LAC and one on the LNS. In RADIUS configuration terms, the LAC IP address is called the Tunnel-Client-Endpoint, and the LNS is called the Tunnel-Server-Endpoint. To forward L2TP traffic from the LAC to the LNS, a routing protocol runs between the routers of the wholesaler and access seeker to exchange loopback addresses. Recall that with the Layer 3 wholesale model, the network can use redundant links between the two providers. If path failures occur, the routing protocol reroutes traffic around the failed link. Multiple LNSs can be deployed in the access seeker's network in case one fails. They can be installed using several redundancy modes; here are the most common:

- Use the same loopback address on multiple LNSs in an anycast fashion. If one LNS fails, another LNS takes its place in the routing table.

- Configure the RADIUS server to return multiple tunnel endpoints to the LAC, and let the LAC choose between the LNS endpoints.

- Use a dedicated LNS load-balancer between the LAC and the LNSs.

ANYCAST LNS

Figure 7.22 shows an overview of anycast LNS. Each LNS announces the same loopback address to the network, but each with different routing protocol metrics. LNS London is the more preferred router, with a BGP local preference of 120; Paris is the secondary. When an L2TP tunnel-request enters the access seeker's network, it is sent to the LNS with the lowest protocol cost (a higher BGP local preference has a lower protocol cost). If LNS London goes down, the request would be routed to the LNS second-lowest cost—Paris.

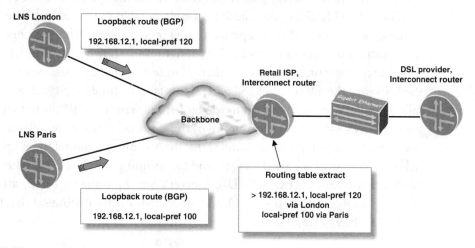

Figure 7.22 L2TP anycast.

Anycast has its limitations. Its failure mode requires that the LNS's loopback address be withdrawn from the network. This would require a major outage (planned or unplanned) of the LNS, that requires the route to disappear before the requests are rerouted to the secondary server. Additionally, when an LNS fails, all existing sessions are torn down and need to be reestablished with the standby LNS. An IETF draft—draft-ietf-l2tpext-failover-04—helps improve this situation. For example, if an LNS has a primary and backup control plane, this draft allows for some state to be rebuilt if the LNS switches control between primary and backup controllers. However, the industry is not yet in a position where full state can be maintained or rebuilt between two independent LNSs.

LAC-BASED LOAD BALANCING

The second, more palatable solution is for the DSL provider's LAC to have a list of LNS IP addresses it can choose from when creating an L2TP session. If the router vendor has the capability, the sessions can be load-balanced across the LNSs or used in a primary/secondary fashion. Local configuration on the LACs can be statically programmed with multiple LNS endpoints, but the more common and flexible method is to return this information using RADIUS.

The RADIUS *Access-Accept* packet that is sent from the RADIUS server to the LAC has several LNS loopback addresses embedded in it. For Juniper E-series routers, each of the LNSs are separated using tags. A tag is a RADIUS concept that groups attributes in a packet. The configuration shown in Listing 7.1 makes this clearer. It instructs the LAC to attempt to terminate L2TP sessions first on the LNS with the address 192.168.55.1. If this fails, it should try 192.168.66.1. A failure occurs when a tunnel acknowledgment message (SCCRP) is not received from the LNS within a certain amount of time. Tunnel tags are the suffixes on the end of each attribute, such as :1 and :2. All the attributes required to set up a tunnel with the first LNS have the tag :1, and the second group has tag :2. The actual configuration varies between RADIUS servers. Some put the tag on the attribute name (Tunnel-Server-Endpoint:1), and others require the attribute at the start of the value (:1:192.68.55.1).

Listing 7.1 Sample RADIUS Configuration—JUNOSe

```
retail-isp.com, Authentication-Type = Accept
            Tunnel-Server-Endpoint:1 = 192.68.55.1,
            Tunnel-Type:1 += L2TP,
            Tunnel-Medium-Type:1 += IP,
            Tunnel-Password:1 = "hardtoguess",
            Tunnel-Server-Endpoint:2 += 192.168.66.1,
            Tunnel-Type:2 += L2TP,
```

```
Tunnel-Medium-Type:2 += IP,
Tunnel-Password:1 = "hardtoguess"
```

The configuration shown in Listing 7.2 for Cisco IOS-based routers creates the same behavior as shown in Listing 7.1. A failure to connect to the primary LNS triggers an attempt to connect to the backup server. Notice that tunnel tags are not required in this case.

Listing 7.2 Sample RADIUS Configuration—IOS

```
retail-isp.com Password = "cisco" Service-Type = Outbound,
    cisco-avp="vpdn:ip-addresses=192.168.55.1/192.168.66.1"
    cisco-avp="vpdn:tunnel-id=lac-name",
    cisco-avp="vpdn:tunnel-type=l2tp",
    cisco-avp="vpdn:l2tp-tunnel-password=hardtoguess"
```

DEDICATED LNS LOAD-BALANCING HARDWARE

The third option is to use a dedicated piece of hardware to load-balance between the LNSs. A basic load balancer has a global IP address to which the LACs direct tunnels. The LNSs are placed behind this IP address and are assigned unique addresses. The better the load-balancer, the more effective the algorithm of distributing tunnels among the LNSs. The ultimate in load-balancing capability would be a device that can keep track of how many L2TP sessions and tunnels are active on a given LNS and direct sessions to the least-loaded server. The load balancer also keeps track of an LNS that silently fails so that it can reset that server's session counter. When the LNS is back in service, the balancer directs L2TP sessions throughout the server farm in such a way that the per-server load is normalized as quickly as possible. Sadly, these devices that make such intimate L2TP inspections of the protocol and effectively load-balance across many LNSs at scale are unavailable on the market today. An LTS with intelligent load balancing enhancements would be the most likely candidate to be on the market.

WHOLESALE ACCESS MODELS COMPARED

For access seekers, local loop unbundling provides the greatest control over their destiny. The entire service, from the physical layer on up, is under their control (perhaps with the exception of the initial copper provisioning in the incumbent's meet-me room). Such control comes at a price; the DSLAMs that the access seeker needs to install are not are cheap, nor are the backhaul costs from each exchange. Some governments require access seekers to deploy DSL in a minimum coverage area (for example, in all major cities). This drives up the initial investment that an access seeker must make to break into the market. This varies depending on the regulatory environment. There is also the whole other aspect of operational expenditure from maintaining the network.

Bit stream access gives the access seeker a Layer 2 path directly to the subscriber. The provider can choose any combination of protocol, addressing scheme, and service to deliver to the customer. Because the incumbent owns the DSLAM hardware, the wholesaler normally limits the DSL line speed in both the upstream and downstream direction according to what the user has purchased. This limits the scope of deploying automated provisioning systems to provide a service such as dynamic bandwidth adjustment. For example, the user could visit a web page and request a bandwidth increase for a short period of time, which automatically adjusts the download peak rate. Bit stream access is not as flexible as L2TP wholesaling when it comes to building redundancy into the interconnect points between the service provider and DSL provider. This is due to the lack of suitable routing protocols to handle multiple access links. On the positive side, it is less resource-intensive than L2TP because it does not require the extra protocol handshaking and state that L2TP needs. This extra state means that L2TP session scaling is a bottleneck in most LNSs. LNSs that perform L2TP termination in hardware are not so prone to performance impacts from many sessions, but the extra hardware drives up the expense. LNSs that do L2TP session termination in software are cheaper, but their session scaling is a lot lower, so extra devices are needed for increased scaling support. Because of the simplicity of bit stream interconnection, the routers are usually cheaper compared with L2TP interconnects.

Layer 3 wholesaled DSL networks are not as common, but they do exist in a few places. The network design is generally a simple one, with the DSL provider handling most of the hard work of connecting DSL subscribers to a network. The product differentiation between access seekers is normally relegated to applications rather than network-based services, such as speed control and Quality of Service (QoS). This simplicity may be just what the doctor ordered for some providers, but generally not the majority. The high-availability options for this type of network are the same as for L2TP. Layer 3 routing protocols such as OSPF,

BGP, and IS-IS can be used to take advantage of redundant links in the network. An L2TP network is more vulnerable to failure because it needs to make use of an extra device called an LNS.

L2TP is the most popular wholesaling choice for access seekers that choose not to deploy their own DSLAM kit. Because the protocol sits a few layers above the physical, more options are available to maintain a highly available L2TP termination network. The underlying Layer 3 routing protocols and the L2TP protocol itself can reroute around link or LNS failure. Because L2TP provides a Layer 2 path to the customer, QoS, packet filters, and accounting profiles can be easily attached to a user session. On the downside, the L2TP architecture suffers the same capacity limitations as bit stream and Layer 3 wholesaling because the DSL provider controls the upstream and downstream line rates. As mentioned previously, L2TP has extra protocol overhead, which increases the complexity and cost of the devices in the network that establish and maintain the tunnels. L2TP fragmentation can also be a problem unless it is planned for accordingly. Table 7.1 summarizes the options and their pros and cons.

Table 7.1 Summary of Wholesaling Options

Wholesale Type	Advantages	Disadvantages
Copper unbundling	Provides complete control over the user experience Allows quick deployment of new technologies (within local RF band plan stipulations)	Expensive to deploy Requires support infrastructure to deal with physical DSL layer issues
Bit stream access with ATM interconnect	Can reuse older ATM hardware on provider and access seeker networks Same protocol at end-user and retail provider. Can use ATM OAM for troubleshooting. Provides access seeker Layer 2 path directly to subscriber—protocol flexibility	Technology more expensive than Ethernet Failover mechanism less flexible than Layer 3 or L2TP access

continues

Table 7.1 continued

Wholesale Type	Advantages	Disadvantages
Bit stream access with Ethernet interconnect	Cheaper than ATM Easy upgrade path to higher-speed Ethernet interfaces. ATM interfaces greater than OC12/STM4 are not common. Provides access seeker Layer 2 path directly to subscriber. Almost as much protocol flexibility as ATM.	No SONET/SDH path status information for Ethernet-native failover mechanism Failover mechanism is less flexible than Layer 3 or L2TP access. If spanning tree for redundancy is used, design must be well thought out.
L2TP	Good failover capabilities Gives the access seeker Layer 2 access to the subscriber	Requires extra processing capacity on the router due to L2TP state keeping. Routers are generally more expensive. Not possible to run protocols other than PPP except with the newer L2TPv3 standard
Layer 3 interconnect	Simple solution—relatively easy to implement Low hardware overhead for access seeker DSL provider retains control over the user session	Access seeker has limited control over the subscriber session DSL provider retains control over the user session

SUMMARY

The flurry of wholesale DSL activity started while ATM was the flavor of the month for the transport network. It was also the protocol that ran on top of most of the installed DSL lines, which were all ADSL. Since then, there have been some tweaks in how the service is delivered to access seekers—offering Ethernet interconnects in addition to (or instead of) ATM interconnects, for example. The kinks in provisioning processes have largely been ironed out, and it takes days instead of weeks to install a wholesaled DSL line to an access seeker. Deploying automated provisioning interfaces between an incumbent and access seekers based on XML to exchange information on DSL port moves, adds, and changes is becoming popular. This streamlines what was once a task based on exchanging Excel spreadsheets or custom-built CSV files.

The most prominent argument against bit stream and L2TP unbundling of the local loop is that it disincentivizes incumbents from investing in next-generation networks. If their competitors can deliver services for their equipment that they have just poured millions into, this discourages investment in new infrastructure (or so goes the argument). Despite this, the market is still generally keeping pace with advances in DSL technology by deploying DSLAMs with ADSL2, ADSL2+, VDSL, and VDSL2 capability. ADSL has been the mainstay of the wholesale DSL line business for several years. But as providers upgrade their networks to deliver zippier line speeds over copper phone lines, the upgrade in technology is being offered to access seekers, too. This is likely not an altruistic act by DSL providers, but more of a pragmatic and/or regulatory one. To remain competitive and satiate customer demand, line speeds need to be continually upgraded. Maintaining a parallel legacy ADSL infrastructure purely for wholesale services would be costly. Taking wholesale products off the market would cause significant consternation from access seekers, which may result in extra regulator intervention.

Because providers are planning to deliver triple- and double-play services, technically any of the wholesaling products could be used when delivering these services. However, for effective service delivery, the architecture that gives the provider the most control over the network from end to end is copper loop unbundling. Avoiding jitter, delay, and congestion and providing enough bandwidth for triple-play services are of paramount importance. These tasks require intimate knowledge of their network's DSL network design, which incumbents are reluctant to divulge.

Basic assumptions can be made about network performance to deliver less-complex services, such as VoIP and Internet over a wholesaled network. For example, access seekers can indicate to the DSL provider the packets that should have priority over others during network congestion using IP precedence and DSCP markings. As long as prudent assumptions have been made about the minimum bandwidth guarantees the DSL provider will give, a VoIP and data service generally can coexist.

Deploying Quality of Service

8

Bandwidth is a scarce commodity for most broadband subscribers. As with anything that is in limited supply, there needs to be a way of effectively regulating and managing such a resource. Whereas 256kbps was considered insufficient capacity a few years ago, 10Mbps will take its place as the "slow band" access speed. In a few years, it will be 50Mbps. For some fortunate customers, bandwidth is in abundant supply. But for the majority, quality of service (QoS) differentiation is a feature often used in most broadband networks.

The terms class of service (CoS) and QoS are commonly used interchangeably, but in the past they defined subtly different things. QoS covers broader network performance aspects than CoS. CoS refers more to the autonomous treatment of traffic at a single router or switch hop using classes to aggregate and manage traffic with common behavior characteristics. It covers the differentiation of traffic into classes, managing jitter, preemption, latency, queuing, bandwidth, and scheduling. A subset of QoS capability roughly aligns with this and refers to differentiation and subsequent treatment of traffic from an end-to-end perspective (such as marking a packet with a global Differentiated Services [DiffServ] Code Point to influence end-to-end QoS behavior).

Broadening the scope, QoS can also cover higher-level characteristics that refer to one or more services, such as availability, packet reordering, timing accuracy, time-to-repair, time-to-provision, and accuracy of billing. A service description, which is supplied by the service provider, ideally defines the scope of the service and therefore what performance aspects are included as suitable QoS measurement metrics. There are often two service descriptions: an external service description written for customers, and a more-detailed internal service description for the service provider. External documents could include service availability criteria, penalties and credits for unavailable service time, per-class round-trip times in the provider core network, service charges, and other metrics. An internal document could be a brief ten-page business description or a hundred pages of detailed technical information, including oversubscription ratios, access network latency, and router configuration, among other information.

Obviously a whole book could be written on the subject. To keep with the technical theme of this book, this chapter covers the technical perspective of implementing QoS on an IP-based triple-play network. QoS is first described in a historical perspective, covering its use in the Public Switched Telephone Network (PSTN) and how this was important to help devise an IP prioritization scheme in the early '80s. To understand what QoS is trying to solve and with what tools, Differentiated Services and IP precedence classification are covered. These two pieces of information are used to identify and classify traffic. After classification and marking, the treatment of these packets is discussed—shaping, policing, and forwarding. There is also an explanation of related technologies and algorithms, including WRED, hierarchical policing, and queuing and scheduling. Because the aspects of QoS covered in this chapter overlap with the generally accepted definition of CoS, the two terms are used interchangeably throughout this chapter.

As with many other chapters in this book, configuration examples are given for several of the features described. And to keep with the theme of architectures, the last sections are devoted to the two edge architectures—centralized and distributed.

WHY IS QOS NEEDED?

QoS is not a new concept. Since the early days of the PSTN, there has been a way to prioritize telephone calls in a phone exchange. During an emergency, telephone exchanges can become overloaded, preventing important calls from getting through. In such an event, exchanges can be configured to ensure that emergency groups can place a call whenever they need to by guaranteeing capacity in the network for such calls. During the 1960s and 1970s, the United States Department of Defense (DoD) devised a more elaborate system of call prioritization as part of the Automatic Voice Network (Autovon). It used five priority levels:

- Flash override
- Flash
- Immediate
- Priority
- Routine

Normal calls would be tagged with routine priority. If a call required immediate service, a higher level could be selected on the telephone handset to drop an existing call that had a lower priority. This mechanism was called pre-emption. Even though the Autovon system was grandfathered in the early '80s and was replaced by the Defense Switched Network (DSN), the system's concepts were copied in the IP world, which also needs to be able to prioritize traffic.

LIMITED BANDWIDTH

The concepts in the IP world are similar. If more data are offered to the network than there is capacity available, there needs to be a way to tell the network which traffic has the highest priority. A classic example is the Olympic service, which has bronze, silver, and gold services. In a limited-bandwidth situation, packets from the bronze service are dropped first, so the receiving applications get less bandwidth. Silver services are the next to be dropped if the bandwidth is constrained even further. The effect of the packet drops on TCP-based applications is to reduce their transmission rate to avoid further drops.

JITTER

Packet jitter measures the variation in the time between the arrival of one packet and the next. Traditional digital telephone calls use a Time Division Multiplexing (TDM) system to send calls around telephone networks. These systems rely on precise timing to send voice signals between devices at the end of a link to ensure that a call can be reliably converted to and from a digital format to an analog one.

Because IP is an asynchronous protocol, Voice over IP (VoIP) calls do not have the luxury of a strict underlying TDM mechanism. Therefore, these types of calls are susceptible to jitter, in which packets arrive at differing temporal intervals. One of the important requirements of QoS is to first reduce the effect of jitter as much as possible to avoid impacting voice reproduction at the receiving end.

VoIP providers commonly monitor network paths to check that certain parameters do not go above thresholds in the service description. Many routers nowadays come with modules that can monitor the round-trip time and jitter between the router and another IP endpoint. A router sends probe packets to another IP endpoint. These usually are ICMP, but they can be UDP, TCP, or a higher-layer protocol, such as an HTTP. The router sends out several probes, and the average round-trip time, standard deviation, and jitter are calculated based on the return packets. If a reply to a probe exceeds a configurable threshold, an SNMP trap can be generated to tell the operator to investigate the source of the problem.

BUSINESS STRATEGY

Not all drivers for QoS are just technical solutions to a problem. A common market differentiator for a service provider is being able to offer a more comprehensive (and profitable) Service Level Agreement (SLA) to customers that can ensure that various traffic types are adequately prioritized. When the traffic is correctly prioritized on the link, the link capacity can be more effectively utilized by allowing best-effort (BE) traffic to burst to full rate when VoIP and video services are not active. In the opposite situation, BE traffic can be dropped or queued in deference to higher-priority services when they are active.

Also, some customers may not want the same oversubscription ratio as other customers on the same virtual link. For example, a VLAN or stacked VLAN (S-VLAN) between the DSLAM and BNG could contain connections to households or businesses that have different minimum rates (or committed information rates, explained later). QoS can make bandwidth guarantees for each customer within the same VLAN or S-VLAN. Other models can differentiate oversubscription ratios between VLANs and S-VLANs. These are discussed later in this chapter.

Many operators choose to run sufficiently sized links in their network to avoid having to deal with congestion problems for both themselves and external customers. Typically the QoS architectures described in this chapter are used in last-mile and aggregation parts of the network, where there is more susceptibility to congestion.

WHAT IS QoS NOT?

IP (and many other) networks take advantage of the fact that not all customers want to use the network at once. This means that core and backbone links are usually oversubscribed. Oversubscription is when a network is dimensioned to have lower aggregation and backbone capacity than the sum of the bandwidths of the edge links that feed into it. The oversubscription ratio is a quantifiable value by which the network has been oversubscribed. Exceptions to this rule are the Mother's Day and Christmas Day scenarios. These scenarios mean that at times, networks are used much more heavily than they usually are, and congestion is sure to arise. This is not restricted to data networking, and the solutions vary. To cope with the Christmas rush, Amazon has much more computing capacity than it needs for most of the year. Therefore, it has decided to offer a service called Elastic Compute Cloud, which lets other customers rent this spare capacity. In contrast, the telecom industry is aware of Mother's Day scenarios but often does not allocate extra capacity to cover the shortfall.

In most cases, traditional PSTN networks use fixed bandwidths for national calls (64kbps using G.711 encoding). Telephone networks have a long history of effective capability to route calls around congestion points using protocols such as Dynamic Nonhierarchical Routing (DHNR), Dynamic Adaptive Routing (DAR), and Real-Time Network Reporting (RTNR). In some cases, these have been adapted to support multiple traffic classes (RTNR). These protocols are much more flexible and responsive to changing conditions compared to static call routing, but there are still occasions when the network does not have enough capacity to handle the required call load.

IP networks are also susceptible to similar congestion scenarios, but they react in different ways than the PSTN. IP networks are not as flexible as PSTN networks at rerouting session-oriented connections around congestion because IP does not have the concept of a session. However, because of variable packet sizes and IP's asynchronous and connectionless nature, there are overall better statistical multiplexing gains compared to a more rigid PSTN. Nevertheless, there is still a limit to how much prioritization can benefit a network, because it cannot create bandwidth. For example, if network links are continually subject to overuse, QoS is not a suitable solution, because it is designed to handle transient traffic spikes. The solution is more effective traffic engineering and management of network growth.

HISTORY OF QoS

As previously mentioned, prioritization concepts from the PSTN have been copied in the IP domain. As written in *The Economist*,[1] "God, at least in the West, is often represented as a man with a flowing beard and sandals. Users of the Internet might be forgiven for feeling that nature imitates art, for if the Net does have a god, he is probably Jon Postel." Postel was the editor of the RFC document series (a collection of technical specifications of Internet standards). This includes RFC 791, which is a document describing the ubiquitous Internet Protocol. Envisioning the need for prioritization control in internetworks, the document describes several control fields in the IP packet header that indicate the datagram's priority:

- 111: Network Control
- 110: Internetwork Control
- 101: CRITIC/ECP
- 100: Flash Override
- 011: Flash
- 010: Immediate
- 001: Priority
- 000: Routine

These values, called IP precedence, closely map to the Autovon prioritization system. Routers inspect each packet's IP header for its IP precedence bit value to determine how to treat it as it progresses through the router's forwarding process. To deploy a homogeneous prioritization scheme, each router should treat packets that have the same IP precedence bit value with the same priority. Of course, each router on its own must enforce the prioritization between the traffic

---

[1] 8th February, 1997

types. Even though this system is more than 20 years old, the 3-bit IP precedence system is still in use today, on both the Internet and in private networks. This is being superseded by the Differentiated Services architecture. However some embedded devices, such as DSL routers, still deal with IP precedence because it is forward-compatible with the newer Differentiated Service (which is described shortly). For historical and backward-compatibility reasons, most router software continues to support IP Precedence too, although the preferred approach for the future is to work with the Differentiated Services architecture.

No real architecture documentation was written to instruct providers how to use the IP precedence bits. This caused implementations to differ from one organization to the next. The general rule was that the higher the precedence number, the higher the priority given to the packet. But it was and still is difficult to offer an end-to-end service guarantee across the Internet due to the lack of implementation uniformity. These 3 bits are part of a larger IP Type of Service (ToS) byte (8-bit field), which also defined an additional 3 bits to be set for other advisory characteristics of the packet—delay, throughput, and reliability. The remaining 2 bits were marked as unused.

Figure 8.1 shows how these values map to the IP header.

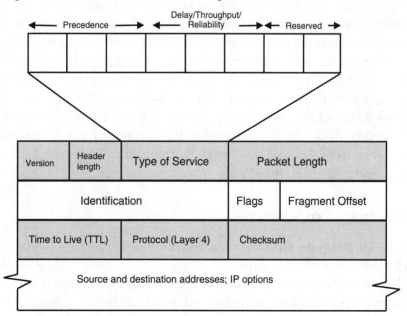

Figure 8.1 An IP header showing the various fields, including the 8 bits of the ToS byte.

INTEGRATED SERVICES

Enter Integrated Services (IntServ), which is a proposition to guarantee intermediate resources between two devices across the network or Internet. A signaling
protocol (Resource Reservation Protocol [RSVP]) was created to enable QoS-
aware endpoints to send requests through the network to reserve resources for the
duration of the application flow. These resources are specified in terms of the
bandwidth required and the nature of the flow. To ensure a consistent end-to-end
user experience, all routers along the path needed to maintain the signaling state
for each stream, which for core devices could amount to hundreds of thousands
or even millions of individual signaling streams. Unfortunately, this did not scale
well, and its original design did not gain much popularity in the market.

RSVP, one of the protocols used in IntServ, is commonly used in the industry
today but has been modified somewhat from its original purpose. Service providers use RSVP in traffic-engineered MPLS networks to establish Label
Switched Paths (LSPs) between provider edge (PE) and provider (P) routers. The
protocol's fundamentals—reserving bandwidth resources across the network—
have not changed. The past has come to haunt the present. Like the problem with
the original IntServ implementation, some larger providers dislike the scaling
properties of having many RSVP sessions between PE routers. These sessions
result in one or more LSPs between routers, which equates to a lot of state and
configuration overhead in the network. To mitigate the configuration burden at
the network edges when configuring the LSP mesh, the IETF has issued a draft
that enables routers to join mesh groups, which are a collection of MPLS routers
sharing a common label-switching domain. Some providers also choose to
deploy RSVP-based LSPs in the core but run Label Distribution Protocol (LDP)
at the edge, which cuts down on the RSVP mesh on the PEs. For more background on RVSP and LSP, see Chapter 3, "Designing a Triple-Play Backbone,"
and Chapter 4, "Designing a Triple-Play Access Network."

DIFFERENTIATED SERVICES

In a new networking architecture called Differentiated Services (DiffServ), the
IETF DiffServ working group devised a new use for the first 6 bits of the ToS-byte
field that provides a simple, scalable way to identify and manage traffic. This
framework provides QoS guarantees and introduces the concept of Per-Hop

Behavior (PHB). Traffic is first classified based on arbitrary characteristics, including source or destination IP address, source interface, or Layer 4 port information. After traffic is classified, it is marked with a DiffServ Code Point, which is a global indicator of what forwarding characteristics the traffic requires. The forwarding characteristics are prescribed in the various PHBs, which cover such properties as forwarding latency, jitter, loss, priority, and assured bandwidth.

Various combinations of the first 6 bits are described in RFC 2474.[2] The hexadecimal and integer equivalents of these binary values are also shown in this RFC. In contrast to the IP precedence values, each combination of bit values, called a Differentiated Services Code Point (DSCP), is part of a group, which describes how it should be treated by router hop in the network. For example, the EF (Expedited Forwarding) DiffServ group is described in RFC 2598.[3] It specifies that any IP packets matching this group should be handled with low loss, low latency, low jitter, and assured bandwidth. Figure 8.2 shows how the DiffServ field maps to the IP header.

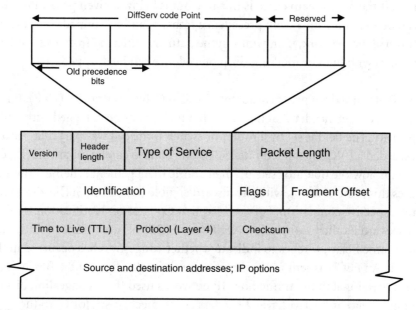

Figure 8.2 An IP header with the DiffServ field.

[2] http://www.ietf.org/rfc/rfc2474.txt
[3] http://www.ietf.org/rfc/rfc2598.txt

Notice that the first 3 bits of the DiffServ field overlap with the IP precedence field, because the DiffServ architecture was designed with backward compatibility in mind. For example, the EF DSCP has the binary value 101110. The CRITC/ECP IP Precedence priority, which has the value of 5, or binary 101, matches the first 3 bits of the DiffServ value. This priority is commonly used for VoIP traffic. With this in mind, a provider could migrate its backbone to a DiffServ architecture, while some of the periphery could continue to deal with IP Precedence and still maintain prioritization alignment.

Another DiffServ group is assured forwarding, described in RFC 2597.[4] It implements four classes within the group. Each of these subclasses can be used if granular packet handling within the group is required. A further attribute within the group is the drop precedence, which can be one of three values—low, medium, or high. The drop precedence is marked based on router configuration. For example, a data stream entering a DiffServ boundary (this can be thought of as the edge of the network) can be rate-limited to a given rate, called the sustained rate. If the data stream exceeds this rate but is below a given peak rate, packets can be marked with a drop precedence rather than be dropped. As these packets traverse the network, if any links in the path are suffering from over-utilization, packets with high or medium drop precedence can be dropped first.

ATM also has drop priority capability, called Cell Loss Priority (CLP). It is a 1-bit field in the cell header that indicates that the cell has been tagged with a high loss priority. The field is set by a router or switch if the cell was part of a packet that exceeded a PVC's sustained rate (SIR). The bit also can be set arbitrarily, depending on how the operator sets up their traffic management scheme. Frame Relay uses this same concept, with the discard eligible (DE) bit in its header to indicate retrospective congestion. Forward Explicit Congestion Notification (FECN) and Backward Explicit Congestion Notification (BECN) are notification frames sent by Frame Relay switches to indicate whether congestion has occurred in the network. An FECN is sent in the direction of the traffic flow, and a BECN is sent antidirectional to the traffic flow. IP networks used these congestion bits in Frame Relay and ATM Layer 2 headers as the mechanism for IP traffic engineering.

[4] http://www.ietf.org/rfc/rfc2597.txt

The IETF issued an RFC (RFC 2698[5]) that describes a two-rate, three-color marking scheme that can be used to implement a more complex rate-limiting scheme on a router. A sample implementation of this RFC could be to use each color to correspond to a drop precedence in the assured forwarding group. For a description of how rate-limiting works, see the section "Rate-Limiting." One of the immediate differences compared to a DiffServ architecture is that you have three ways to indicate the degree of congestion a packet has undergone. You mark the packet with green, yellow, or red.

Differentiated Services is the most popular implementation to provide service differentiation in today's service provider networks. It offers a lot more direction in terms of architecture and handling behavior compared to IP precedence. IP precedence is still in use among service providers for a couple of reasons: pre-existing implementations and sometimes IP precedence can offer all the functionality that is needed. Another reason is that it is common to find Customer Premises Equipment (CPE) that can only mark packets with IP precedence, rather than full-blown DSCP capability. One of DiffServ's advantages is the 6 bits of the DSCP field that overlap with the 3-bit IP Precedence field. It is possible for a packet to simultaneously have an IP precedence and DiffServ Code Point. This is useful for networks that use IP precedence in some subdomains and DiffServ in others, allowing packet classification to work seamlessly in both domains. See the sections "Classification" and "Trust Boundaries" for more details on this and other types of marking and classification architectures. Table 8.1 lists the Diff-Serv Code Points that are in common use among service providers and their equivalent IP precedence values.

Table 8.1 DiffServ Code Points and Their Equivalent IP Precedence

Per-Hop Behavior	Class	DiffServ Code Point	Drop Priority	Integer Value	IP Precedence
Best-effort					0
Assured forwarding					
	Class 1	AF11	Low	10	1
		AF12	Medium	12	1
		AF13	High	14	1

continues

[5] http://www.ietf.org/rfc/rfc2698.txt

Table 8.1 continued

Per-Hop Behavior	Class	DiffServ Code Point	Drop Priority	Integer Value	IP Precedence
	Class 2	AF21	Low	18	2
		AF22	Medium	20	2
		AF23	High	22	2
	Class 3	AF31	Low	26	3
		AF32	Medium	28	3
		AF33	High	30	3
		AF41	Low	34	4
		AF42	Medium	36	4
		AF43	High	38	4
Expedited forwarding		EF	Low	46	5

CALL ADMISSION CONTROL

Call Admission Control (CAC) has long been a feature of telephony and data networks to permit or deny a connection to be made between two endpoints. Connection requests are accepted or denied in essentially a binary fashion depending on available resources. Examples of these in data networks are SVC and PVC setup in ATM networks, MPLS with traffic engineering, and IntServ. In the PSTN, connection requests used to be put in a queue until resources become available, but it is rarer to find this type of "holding" admission control in PSTN networks these days. In earlier IP networks, CAC was not a pervasive technique for granting a user access to the network, because statistical multiplexing, QoS buffering, and prioritization were considered *good enough* tools at the time (and, for many applications, they still are). As more services such as video and voice are transported using IP, networks and their supporting server infrastructure are becoming more sophisticated and can make admission control decisions based on link utilization at various points in the network. Not exactly being relegated to the annals of history, IP network CAC capabilities are still evolving from day to day. Some examples of IP CAC capabilities in use can be found in Chapter 11, "Dynamic User Session Control." Another example is MPLS traffic engineering.

BUILDING BLOCKS OF QoS

Based on historical context and QoS capabilities in networks today, this section describes the various acronyms, technologies, and concepts used in triple-play networks. In addition to being used in multi-traffic-class networks (called multi-play networks for short), the underlying concepts and technologies are applicable in other environments where QoS is needed. Multi-play networks are considered to be those that support voice, video, and differentiated data services over IP. In other words, the data class has multiple services that are treated differently depending on the service characteristics. Traditional components of a QoS architecture are classification and marking, rate-limiting, queuing, and scheduling. Some of these components are used together with more complex QoS functionality, such as strict priority scheduling, hierarchical shaping, and hierarchical rate-limiting. This section describes the basic QoS concepts that can be applied in triple-play and multi-play architectures.

CLASSIFICATION

Classification is when a device identifies traffic by certain attributes and then assigns it a traffic class. Most of the attributes in the packet header can be used to identify the traffic class to which a packet should belong. For example, the source or destination address, fragment bits, Time to Live (TTL), and even Layer 4 information such as protocol type, TCP, or UDP port number can be used as matching criteria. Routers can also classify based on Layer 2 information in the frame. With Frame Relay and ATM, these were the DE and CLP bits, respectively. ATM has an additional prioritization mechanism that enables a PVC to be assigned to one of several classes, including variable bit rate real-time (VBR-RT); variable bit rate non-real-time (VBR-nrt), unspecified bit rate (UBR), and constant bit rate (CBR). When ATM transmission hardware sends data to these PVCs, prioritization occurs according to the type of PVC (CBR, UBR, and so on) rather than information in cell headers.

Matching IP header information such as source or destination address, protocol type, or port is commonly done at the edges of the network on CPE or provider edge routers. These devices have more feature capability (and, at times, capacity) to peer deep into packets compared to core devices. Also, traffic rates are lower at the perimeter. This works in favor of routers being able to perform detailed packet manipulation and inspection at wire speed, or close to it. A CPE is also called a Residential Gateway (RG). It can have many Application Layer Gateways (ALGs) that can identify multimedia streams and stamp the appropriate priority based on embedded protocol signatures. Providers can also use Session Border Controllers (SBCs), which are specialized protocol-aware (VoIP) devices to handle protocol classification and marking and, at times, CAC.

The previous classification method was called multifield classification, which means that several fields in the header (port, protocol type, address, and so on) can be matched in one pass. Classification can also be based on what is known as behavior aggregate (BA) classifiers, which are described in RFC 2836. This allows routers to identify traffic based on a single priority field and assign it to a traffic class. Packets with the same bit value are all deemed to share the same forwarding behavior characteristics throughout the network and are grouped in a single CoS handling type. The DiffServ field is not the only field that can be matched in a BA classifier; MPLS packets use the experimental field (EXP) header to reflect packet priority. Ethernet frames can use the 3 bits in the 802.1P VLAN tag header for prioritization purposes. In cases where two VLAN tags are in a stack formation, each VLAN tag in the stack can represent a different priority. Figures 8.3 and 8.4 show how priority bits are represented in MPLS, 802.1Q VLAN, and stacked 802.1AH headers.

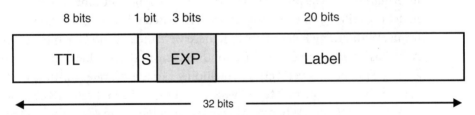

Figure 8.3 An MPLS header with EXP priority markings.

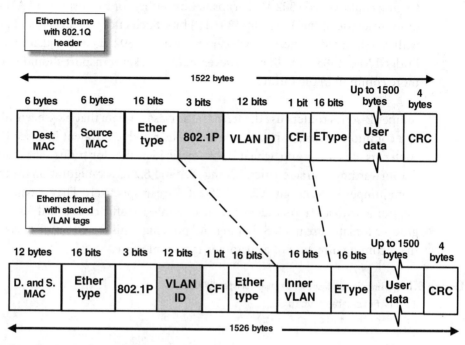

Figure 8.4 A single and double VLAN stack with priority markings.

Switches today are becoming more adept at performing deeper frame inspection than to just the Ethernet header, which means that IP-centric information can be checked for priority information, too. However, some switches do need extra hardware to perform inspection to a level deeper than an Ethernet header. As discussed in earlier chapters, stacked VLAN tags are a common choice for service providers to use to better scale their Ethernet infrastructure. In a stacked VLAN architecture using 802.1AH, each of the two VLAN tags can reflect priority information. With the inner VLAN tag reflecting the customer VLAN and the outer tag reflecting the DSLAM node, in theory each could have different priority values. The CPE could set the inner tag if the last mile uses 802.1Q encapsulation, and the outer tag could be set by service provider equipment, such as a DSLAM or an aggregation switch. VDSL and G.SHDSL DSL lines can support native packet transport, in contrast to ADSL-based services, which require ATM encapsulation to lie between the Ethernet and DSL layers. An example of native packet transport is an Ethernet service running directly on the DSL line. Ethernet tagging could include 802.1Q encapsulation, either for a transparent LAN service or to make use of the 3 priority (802.1P) bits. Such encapsulation is still possible with ADSL-based services, which can make use of 802.1Q encapsulation over a bridged RFC 1483 ATM line. However, native packet transport should make this more common in the future.

Juniper E-series routers use the term traffic class for data that have been allocated to a common internal forwarding group. The rough equivalent in Cisco IOS routers is the QoS group, which is a numeric identifier for traffic that shares similar forwarding characteristics. Listings 8.1 and 8.2 are configuration excerpts from Juniper JUNOSe and Cisco IOS software, respectively. They classify incoming traffic with an IP precedence value of 5 into a traffic class called **voip** or QoS group 7 for later use in QoS shaping and policing. This is a common task used on the incoming direction of a customer-facing interface.

Listing 8.1   Classification Configuration Example—Juniper JUNOSe

```
 1: traffic-class voip
 2:  fabric-strict-priority
 3:
 4: ip classifier-list cl-ip-prec-5 ip any any precedence 5
 5:
 6: ip policy-list pl-ip-sub-in
 7:  classifier-group cl-ip-prec-5 precedence 10
 8:   traffic-class voip
 9:  classifier-group * precedence 100
10:   forward
11: interface GigabitEthernet 1/0/0.100
12:  vlan id 100
13:  ip description "VLAN to subscriber"
14:  ip address 192.168.0.0 255.255.255.254
15:  ip policy input pl-ip-sub-in
```

The following list explains Listing 8.1:

- Lines 1 and 2: Create the traffic class that assigns traffic with common QoS properties in a group. Give it strict (very high) priority through the fabric.
- Line 4: The classifier that identifies the packet attributes to match—IP precedence 5.

- Line 6: Create the policy that instructs the router how to deal with packets matching classifiers.

- Line 7: The first match (classifier-group) is packets with IP precedence 5.

- Line 8: Assign packets matching this criterion to the **voip** traffic class. Because there is no **filter** keyword, packets are implicitly forwarded.

- Lines 9 and 10: Use the built-in catchall classifier to forward all other traffic without assigning it a traffic class.

- Line 15: Apply the policy to the interface for incoming traffic.

Listing 8.2 Classification Configuration Example—Cisco IOS

```
 1: class-map match-any class-prec-5
 2:  match ip precedence 5
 3:
 4: policy-map pm-set-qosgrp
 5:  class class-prec-5
 6:   set qos-group 7
 7:  class class-default
 8:
 9: interface GigabitEthernet 1/0/0.100
10: encapsulation dot1q 100
11: ip address 192.168.0.0 255.255.255.254
12: service-policy input pm-set-qosgrp
```

The following list explains the configuration lines in Listing 8.2:

- Lines 1 and 2: Create a class map that identifies the traffic to be matched in the policy map—IP Precedence 5.

- Line 4: Create the policy that instructs the router how to deal with packets matching the class maps.

- Line 5: The first match (class class-prec-5) is packets with IP precedence 5.

- Line 6: Assign packets matching this criterion to qos group 7 (roughly similar to a Juniper E-series traffic class).

- Line 7: All other packets match the class-default class. Statistics output shows the number of packets going out that interface.

- Line 12: Apply the policy to the interface for incoming traffic.

After traffic has been properly classified, actions such as rate-limiting, shaping, WRED discards, and QoS scheduling can occur, as described throughout this chapter.

MARKING

Marking is the process of marking classified traffic. After packets have been classified, a marking indicates the packet's priority to downstream switches and routers. Then downstream routers and switches need to match only a small field in the packet or frame rather than a more extensive set of fields. Marking can include the DiffServ Code Point in an IP packet, one of the 802.1P priority bits in an Ethernet frame, an EXP field in an MPLS packet, an ATM CLP bit, or a combination thereof. Packets and frames need to be marked only once for the markings to be able to re-read throughout the network. However, downstream devices can modify these markings based on local policy. For example, packets at a DSCP boundary arriving with DSCP AF21 can be remarked to DSCP AF31 to conform to a different marking scheme in another domain.

RATE-LIMITING

Rate-limiting (also known as traffic policing) is a mechanism to limit the throughput of a given type of traffic. A common use is on the ingress of a customer interface on a BNG to restrict the rate at which a customer can send data into the network. For example, high-priority VoIP traffic or even the total throughput that the customer can send can be "capped." Limiting a particular subclass of traffic rather than the total throughput is a useful marketing reason to differentiate between products with varying throughput rates so that products can be upsold. Rate-limiting could also occur for technical reasons, to protect the network from excessive high-priority traffic.

Rate-limiters are implemented using a token bucket algorithm. This uses the idea of a *bucket* of tokens or credits, which a router or switch works with to determine whether packets can be sent or dropped if they exceed a given rate.

In Figure 8.5, a rate-limit is configured, which is the speed at which tokens are added to the bucket. Each token usually corresponds to a byte of data that can be transferred, but this varies from vendor to vendor. Usually this is an internal implementation detail. At the same time the router forwards packets, it simulta-neously removes tokens from the bucket at the same rate that packets are for-warded. For example, if the router sends two 500-byte packets out an interface, it removes 1,000 tokens from the bucket. A second variable used in the token bucket calculation is the burst size, which is the depth or total number of tokens that the bucket can hold. When the rate-limiter is in action, the router withdraws tokens from the bucket for each packet it sends, and it also replenishes the bucket according to the configured rate-limit value. Sometimes, more packets try to exit the interface than there are tokens in a bucket (remember, the credits are replen-ished at a constant rate). This causes such packets to be discarded.

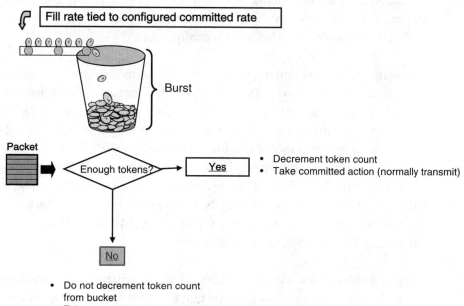

Figure 8.5 A single-token bucket rate-limiter.

Figure 8.5 shows a single-token bucket rate-limiter and the concepts involved in rate-limiting. Dual-token bucket rate-limiters are also a common mechanism in routers and switches. The concepts of a rate-limit and burst sizes from the single-token bucket also apply here. In dual-token bucket limiting, two buckets are used in the process rather than one. Packet colors are used in the rate-limiting process, which is part of the two-rate tricolor mechanism mentioned earlier in this chapter. The first token bucket is configured with a certain rate and burst size (peak rate and peak burst), and the second bucket is replenished at a lower rate and has a smaller depth. These are called the committed rate and committed burst, respectively. When a packet needs to be transmitted, the tokens are attempted to be withdrawn from the first bucket. If there are enough credits, the second bucket is checked. If there are still enough tokens, the packet is under the committed rate and can be marked green and sent. If there are enough tokens in the first bucket but not the second, the packet rate is between the committed and peak, which still allows it to be sent, but it is marked yellow to indicate that it exceeded the committed rate contract. This increases the packet's drop precedence. If there are not enough tokens in the first bucket, the packet is designated as exceeding the peak rate. If the packet is marked red, it is transmitted; otherwise, it is discarded. This behavior is configurable.

Note that packet color-marking is purely internal to the router. IP headers are not marked anywhere with a special color, but rather as packets traverse the fabric from the ingress port to the egress port. Each packet usually has an internal proprietary header that tells the router what color the packet is. Packet coloration can be used in later stages of the router's forwarding path, such as in Random Early Discard (RED) queuing to indicate a drop precedence. RED and Weighted Random Early Discard (WRED) are described in the section "Queuing." Additional actions can be taken on packets that exceed committed or burst rates, such as re-marking DSCP/IP precedence values, setting MPLS experimental (EXP) bit markings, Ethernet 802.1P headers, and so on.

Figure 8.6 shows how a dual-token bucket works with the different actions taken at each stage of the rate-limiter. Note that this kind of discussion centers around IP routers. This means that if there are not enough tokens to transmit an entire *packet*, it is discarded rather than transmitting a partial packet, which is what non-packet-aware switches do. Even though ATM switches aren't IP-aware, many are packet-aware through the Early Packet Discard (EPD) and Partial Packet Discard algorithm. The EPD and PPD algorithms enable ATM switches to discard all cells from a packet if only some of the cells exceed a rate limit. This avoids transmitting cells across a network that cannot be coalesced to form a full packet.

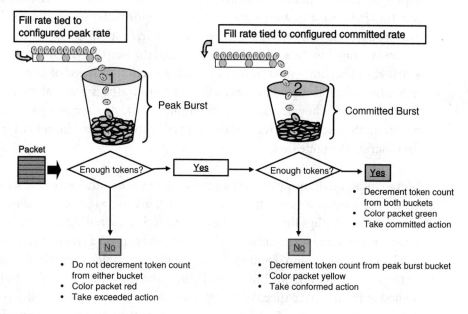

Figure 8.6 A dual-token bucket rate-limiter.

The third common type of traffic limiter is really a rate shaper, because data are placed on the wire for transmission at a continual, more constant rate than token-bucket-based policers. An issue with token bucket algorithms is packet clumping (groups of packets closely spaced together). When such datagrams are sent in a *bursty* fashion, rate-limiting cannot smooth them out. Shaping can smooth out bursty traffic better than rate-limiting or policing. Traffic shaping is usually implemented using a leaky bucket algorithm, which is often found in ATM switches. ATM networks are configured with very low tolerances for variations in incoming traffic rates, so packet (and eventually cell) clumping is undesirable. Therefore, algorithms in ATM scheduler hardware can pace traffic on the wire at very precise intervals to stay within traffic policer limits. The leaky bucket algorithm is also known as the Generic Cell Rate Algorithm (GCRA).

A newer type of rate-limiting found in some vendors' routers is hierarchical rate-limiting. This is a more powerful traffic rate management tool than a single- or dual-token bucket mechanism (although implementations use single- and dual-token bucket techniques at their foundations). It is designed for providers connecting subscribers to a multiservice edge, which makes it especially suited to triple-play environments. As a simple example, take the scenario of a double-play situation in which a customer uses both a best-effort Internet service and high-priority 256kbps VoIP service. Without hierarchical rate-limiting, the best-effort service is limited to the speed of the line, minus the VoIP service throughput. On a 2048kbps line, best-effort traffic can reach a maximum speed of 1792kbps rather than the full 2048kbps, even when no VoIP traffic is active at the time. This is because of how traditional rate-limiters work. As soon as a packet hits a rate limit, the packet is forwarded or dropped without regard for other types of data sharing the same link.

Hierarchical rate-limiting allows bandwidth that would otherwise be reserved for VoIP to be used by other traffic if no voice calls are in progress. This allows the use of the full 2Mbps line speed. The hierarchical rate-limiting nomenclature comes from having several classes of traffic feeding down a chain of rate-limiters in a hierarchical fashion. Figure 8.7 shows a more complex example. A high-priority video service is being limited to 2Mbps, and the other best-effort traffic is limited to the interface speed of 8Mbps, which could use the whole 8Mbps if there is no video. The 2Mbps limiter is to prevent the video data channel from starving resources from the best-effort class. Note that this hierarchical functionality can be used for both for incoming and outgoing traffic.

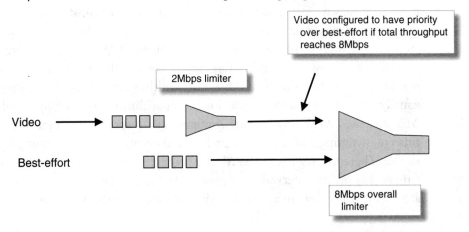

Figure 8.7 Hierarchical rate liming.

Listings 8.3 and 8.4 show the example from Figure 8.7 as a working configuration for both Juniper JUNOSe and Cisco IOS.

Listing 8.3 Hierarchical Rate-Limiting Configuration Example—Juniper JUNOSe

```
 1: traffic-class tc-video
 2:
 3: rate-limit-profile rl-interface hierarchical
 4:  committed-rate 8000000
 5:
 6: rate-limit-profile rl-ip-video hierarchical
 7:  committed-rate 2000000
 8:  committed-action transmit unconditional
 8:
 9: classifier-list cl-ip-tc-video traffic-class tc-video ip any any
10:
11: policy-list pl-ip-subscriber
12:  parent-group interface
13:   rate-limit-profile rl-interface
14:
15: classifier-group cl-ip-tc-video precedence 10 parent-group interface
16:  rate-limit-profile rl-ip-video
17:
18: classifier-group * precedence 100 parent-group interface
19:  forward
20:
21: interface GigabitEthernet 2/0/0.100
22:  vlan id 100
23:  ip description "Subinterface to subscriber"
24:  ip policy output pl-ip-subscriber
25:  ip address 10.1.1.1 255.255.255.0
```

The following list explains Listing 8.3:

- Line 1: Create a traffic class that video traffic is part of.

- Lines 3 and 4: Create the rate-limiter for the whole interface—8Mbps.

- Lines 6 through 8: Create a rate-limit profile that limits video traffic to 2Mbps. Set the committed-action to transmit 2Mbps even if best-effort is sending the full 8Mbps (using the **transmit unconditional** keyword).

- Line 9: Create a classifier that matches all data in the video traffic class. This means that video traffic needs to have already been assigned in this traffic class by another policy.

- Lines 11 through 13: Create a policy that will be applied to the subscriber interface. The parent-group is the master rate-limiter—8Mbps.

- Lines 15 and 16: Create a classifier group that identifies all video traffic and rate-limits it, but still subject it to the parent rate-limiter.

- Lines 18 and 19: Create the classifier group that forwards all other traffic but is still subjected to the parent rate-limiter.

- Line 24: Apply the policy to the interface for all outgoing traffic.

Listing 8.4 Hierarchical Rate-Limiting Configuration Example—Cisco IOS

```
 1: class-map match-all class-video
 2:   match precedence 4
 3:
 4: policy-map pm-vod
 5:   class class-video
 6:    police cir 2000000 bc 4500 be 4500
 7:
 8: policy-map pm-interface
 9:   class class-default
10:    police cir 8000000 bc 4500 be 4500
11:    service-policy pm-vod
12:
13: interface GigabitEthernet2/0/0.100
14:    encapsulation dot1q 100
15:    ip address 10.1.1.1 255.255.255.0
16:    service-policy output pm-interface
```

The following list explains Listing 8.4:

- Lines 1 and 2: Create a class map that identifies video traffic to be matched in the policy map—IP Precedence 4.

- Lines 4 through 6: Creates the child policy that polices video traffic to 2Mbps. Any traffic within this 2Mbps is fed back through the forwarding hardware to the parent policy—pm-interface.

- Lines 8 through 11: Create a top-level parent policy that limits the overall throughput of all traffic classes (including video) to 8Mbps.

- Lines 13 through 16: Create the interface and apply the service policy.

One note about the configuration in Listing 8.4 compared to the JUNOSe version. There is no equivalent for the **transmit unconditional** parameter in Cisco IOS, so when there is more than 8Mbps of traffic, there is no guarantee that video will get priority over best-effort traffic. A work-around would be to use a three-level policy and use prioritization at the middle-level policy with the **bandwidth** command.

Most operators who have dealt with routing configuration have configured a rate-limiter at one time or another. Usually rate-limiters use absolute rates such as 200kbps, 2Mbps, and so on. A more flexible approach is to configure a rate-limit as a percentage of the total bandwidth available. For example, a VLAN that is dedicated to a subscriber could have a total bandwidth of 1Mbps, configured on the subinterface. Three services each take a third of the link capacity—330kbps can be configured as a percentage—33% instead of 330kbps. If a different subscriber has a higher overall link speed of 2Mbps, the same rate-limit configuration can be applied, except with the higher, 2Mbps overall link speed. The router software calculates each service to be 666kKbps.

QUEUING

After traffic is classified, QoS processor modules use marking information to influence the traffic scheduler. When there is no contention for transmission capacity on the same outgoing interface, packet queuing does not occur. It is only when not all packets can be transmitted out the same logical channel at a given moment that traffic arbitration needs to occur. At this point, when the traffic with higher priority is forwarded, the lower-priority traffic can either be dropped or held in a queue for later transmission. One of the hallmarks of a QoS implementation is to be able to buffer packets in a queue if they need to be held until resources are available to send buffered traffic. It need not necessarily be a whole interface that is congested. A subinterface could be congested or a collection of subinterfaces sharing an S-VLAN could also be congested.

The term *queue* comes from each packet being stored one after the other in a First In/First Out (FIFO) fashion until the queue becomes full. As soon as this happens, packets are dropped rather than enqueued (placed on the queue). In a typical scenario, queues continuously vary their utilization rates depending on how traffic reacts to being buffered. For example, if a client receives TCP traffic such as HTTP or FTP that was delayed in transfer due to link-buffering some-where in the path, this is often a sign that congestion occurred. As a consequence, the server can decrease its congestion window size to avoid further congestion. This is triggered by an increased bandwidth-delay product, which is calculated based on the Round-Trip Time (RTT, also called Smoothed Round-Trip Time [SRTT]) and the transmission bandwidth. RTT is how long it takes for a packet to be sent to the other end of the network and for the corresponding acknowl-edgment to arrive back. Under normal conditions with no congestion, the aver-age RTT does not vary much. But when there is congestion somewhere in the network, packets are initially buffered in a router's memory, which leads to an average RTT increase. As long as the packet is buffered in router memory only long enough for the packet to be eventually processed by the receiver and a TCP acknowledgment to be received by the sender, the sender does not have to retransmit any packets.

In a worst-case scenario, router buffers would be exceeded. In other words, the queue utilization becomes too great, causing packets to be dropped from the end of the queue (known as tail drop). This action causes a more dramatic decrease in the server's sending rate, because it has to reinitiate the TCP fast recovery mechanism (with TCP NewReno)[6] or TCP congestion avoidance (with TCP Tahoe).

Technology Note: TCP Windowing and the Slow Start Mechanism

As part of the three-way TCP handshake process, the two endpoints exchange a parameter called a receive window size (RWIN). This is the number of bytes that can be sent to the other device before an acknowledg-ment (ACK) is needed to affirm that the data have been received. For example, between host A and host B, host A announces a 16K receive window to host B, and host B announces a 10K receive window to host A. In this case, host A can send 10,000 bytes of data to host B before it has to wait for host B to say it has received all the data. This *window* of data can be split across multiple IP packets.

A sliding window is a window size that changes over time. If the two hosts are connected across a satellite link, or what is known as a Long Fat Network (LFN), significant delay can occur between the two endpoints. Thus, it is advantageous to transmit a large window of data to the other end before expecting an ACK in return. Otherwise, the overall throughput would be limited because of a continual need to wait for ACKs. Sliding windows are also used to increase the transmission rate when there is available bandwidth, such as with the slow start mechanism.

[6] http://www.ietf.org/rfc/rfc2582.txt

Slow start is a solution to the following problem: If a host sends enough data to the other host to fill its TCP incoming window, it's possible that the other host is on a much slower-speed link. Therefore, many packets are dropped, and subsequently they need to be retransmitted. Slow start is more forgiving of differing link speeds. It works by transmitting a segment of data based on either a parameter from the other host or some default value. Based on each successful ACK, the transmitting side increases what's called its congestion window. When loss does happen, TCP implementations that are based on TCP Reno halve the congestion window and enter the fast recovery state. Older implementations based on TCP Tahoe drop the congestion window to one segment and restart the slow-start algorithm.

This state of dropping back to half the current window size or one segment is called congestion avoidance. It is detected when duplicate ACKs are received by the sending side. If the data never got to the receiving side, the receiving side keeps acknowledging the last valid segment it received. Ideally it would be better to avoid any drops and to take advantage of packet queuing to delay traffic until it can be sent rather than relying on retransmissions.

If one or more packets for a single data session are dropped, only a single session is affected. But if link congestion suddenly occurs on a wider scale (on a back-bone link, for example), packet drops can affect many data sessions. With TCP applications, all the transmitting servers simultaneously detect this loss and back off their transmission rates to avoid further congestion. So far, so good. The problem lies in the next step, when most of the devices gradually increase their transmission rates at the same rate (due to common TCP implementations across the operating systems) until packets for most of the sessions are discarded again. This cycle, called global synchronization, continues to repeat ad infinitum. Several algorithms have been proposed to break the cycle of all data for many sessions being dropped at once. One of these is Random Early Discard (RED), or a more complex variant—Weighted Random Early Discard (WRED).

RED is an active queue management algorithm that routers implement as part of their buffer-management mechanisms. A RED system has two important variables. The first is the average queue length, which states how full the queue of packets is over a given time (the time being on the order of microseconds, which essentially means instantaneous). The second is the discard ratio, which indicates how aggressively packets are discarded, or how probable it is that packets below a certain threshold will be discarded. To mitigate the problem of global synchronization, packets are randomly discarded from the queue according to the configured value rather than at the tail end of the queue. This more-subtle discard approach avoids impacting several flows at once.

Figure 8.8 shows a graph of different packet colors—red, green, and yellow—and their discard rates. These packet colors are the same ones from the two-rate tri-color marking described earlier. WRED enables enqueued packets to have a corresponding priority (green, yellow, or red), which is used to tell the router which packets are more likely to be dropped as the queue utilization increases. For example, a queue could contain high-priority traffic that passed through a rate-limiter above a committed rate and is colored yellow. Simultaneously, best-effort traffic could be colored red because of its lower priority in the rate-limiting configuration. When the WRED mechanism is operating, at 30% of the queue length, green packets might have a 10% drop rate, and yellow packets could have a 20% drop rate.

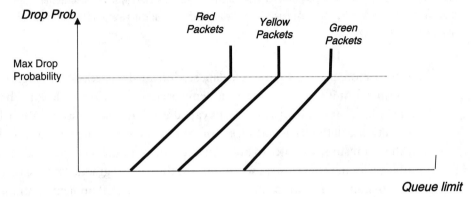

Figure 8.8 Weighted RED discarding.

Queuing theory other than a simple FIFO mechanism involves algorithms that are complex to understand and even more complex to test, administer, and implement. In practice, RED and WRED are deployed in some carrier networks with large numbers of micro flows to mitigate the effect of global synchronization. Unfortunately, RED configuration is a continual source of administration for a service provider, because there is no one formula from which to derive a configuration. One of the main reasons is because a lot of knowledge is needed about the types of traffic carried in a network to deploy an effective RED or WRED implementation. Using empirical evidence from the field is the most common way to tune queue configuration.

TCP traffic is by far the most prevalent transport protocol on the Internet, with UDP coming in second. UDP is a more lightweight protocol that does not implement any of the flow control or protocol handshaking mechanisms of TCP. Applications that use UDP are mostly VoIP, online gaming, video streaming, and videoconferencing applications. Generally speaking, without some kind of additional network performance monitoring capability built in, applications that use UDP do not respond to network congestion like TCP and decrease the transmission rate. Data flows from these applications are inelastic; so if there is insufficient bandwidth, they stop working unless higher layer protocols can feed back network performance information and take action, such as lowering the transmission rate

To complicate matters, these applications often have stringent timing requirements. Although some are reasonably tolerant of consistent delay—VoIP traffic being routed over a satellite link, for example—jitter noticeably affects these applications. As mentioned earlier, jitter is packets arriving at imprecise intervals, which makes it difficult for an application to reproduce a real-time media stream. Jitter buffers are used on end devices to reduce the impact of temporal irregularities. They work by storing the media stream for a sufficient amount of time to allow any delays and retransmissions to be cleared up before being output to the user. At the same time, such buffers should not be too big. Otherwise, the delay needed to fill them adversely affects the application. A prime source of jitter is network queuing. Too much can mean a packet has to wait an unsuitable amount of time before replaying the stream. ITU Recommendation G.114 considers a one-way delay of up to 150ms acceptable for voice applications.

As a general rule, traffic from applications that need quick turnaround times (such as gaming and VoIP traffic) should be buffered less than applications that are more forgiving of network latency. If both applications share the same queue (and, in the case of basic Internet traffic, they do), the need for a large buffer for interactive applications to avoid loss should be balanced against the need for interactive applications to have as little jitter as possible. As a consequence, buffer length is an often-changing datum point in a network.

Usually UDP applications are built to handle a few dropped packets, especially if the protocol employs some kind of Forward Error Correction (FEC). FEC allows a data stream to be faithfully re-created in the event of packet loss by pre- or post-pending additional information (or even preemptive acknowledgments) within the original stream to allow errors to be detected and corrected. An example of FEC is interleaving, which is used in many data transmission applications, including ADSL modems. Interleaving works by spreading the real data among several frames, which all contain enough supplementary information to be able to re-create the original data if some frames were corrupted. The additional redundancy against lost data comes at a price, which is increased latency on the local loop, because the real data cannot be fully transmitted until enough redundant or interleaved data is sent. Also there is reduced throughput from the extra data that need to be included as part of the FEC scheme.

One thing to keep in mind is that most flows on the Internet today are TCP-based. As mentioned earlier, UDP flows are usually inelastic, unless there is some higher layer feedback mechanism communicating network performance to the sending application. As a consequence, UDP flows usually do not respond to RED or WRED drops. So, the key is to identify UDP and TCP traffic as best as possible and separate them into different queues. The queues with UDP traffic can have WRED omitted. The queues that contain best-effort traffic can implement RED/WRED to avoid global synchronization.

SCHEDULING

Scheduling is one of the most important concepts in QoS. After traffic has been classified and distributed among several queues, it is up to a scheduling process in the router to ensure that all PHBs are maintained. Classification has no use unless the router can actually enforce data class arbitration. The term *scheduling* in a packet-based router is the principle of a scheduler allocating or scheduling a number of packets to be sent to a link. For example, if a provider configures a router that provides VoIP and best-effort Internet access to a subscriber, two queues hold buffered traffic—one for each class. A scheduler attaches to the physical interface and works at a very high speed, processing packets as they arrive to be sent out the interface. Normally VoIP packets are given strict priority (or Expedited Forwarding in DiffServ terms) scheduling, which causes them to be sent out the interface without delay. Only when there are no VoIP data to transmit does the best-effort class get an opportunity to be transmitted out the interface. Of course, this all happens at a very speedy rate. So as long as there is not too much strict priority traffic, best-effort traffic can be sent between strict packets. Strict priority traffic should be limited so as not to deny other traffic classes access to the outgoing link if there is too much strict traffic.

Because scheduling is such a substantial topic, with many mechanisms working in tandem, concepts are introduced step by step in this chapter, with each building on the previous feature. Round robin is discussed first. It is a simple algorithm to transmit data out a congested resource, such as a port or subinterface. Then this chapter discusses weighted round robin, which is an enhancement of basic round robin. As mentioned in the preceding paragraph, strict priority, LLQ, and Expedited Forwarding are terms that refer to traffic that is jitter- and delay-sensitive, such as voice. All three terms refer to the same thing. The first two are used by Juniper and Cisco, respectively, and the third is defined by the IETF as part of the DiffServ architecture. The term *strict priority* is used throughout this chapter, but it refers to the same thing as LLQ and Expedited Forwarding. Pulling these techniques together into a hierarchical QoS configuration is explained afterwards, from both a theoretical and practical perspective. The practical examples include sample hierarchical QoS configurations and their implementation in a DSLAM access network architecture. Finally, there is a short discussion of packet overheads and their relationships with rate-limiting and shaping algorithms.

Round-Robin Scheduling

It is important to schedule strict priority traffic so that it is sent with as little delay as possible. Usually a Weighted Round Robin (WRR) algorithm is used in QoS implementations. Rather than giving high-priority traffic strict treatment, WRR gives it a high weight in scheduling calculations. Before racing ahead too fast with acronyms and terminology, an explanation of WRR and scheduler weighting is needed. WRR is an enhanced version of round-robin scheduling, which is similar to how WRED is an enhancement of basic RED queuing.

If all packets are of equal size, a basic round-robin packet scheduler transmits an equal number of packets from each QoS object needing access to the outgoing interface. For example, a BNG might be connected to a DSLAM that has 100 single-play Internet subscribers, each with QoS enabled. Each subscriber has its downstream rate shaped to 15Mbps on the BNG. In reality, the shaping rate will likely be less than 15Mbps to account for overhead, but for the sake of simplicity, assume that the shaping rate is 15Mbps. But if all subscribers are trying to download at rates close to 15Mbps, there would be contention on the Gigabit Ethernet port because 1.5Gbps of traffic would have a hard time being sent out a 1Gbps port. This triggers QoS into action. To ensure that all subscribers get equal access to the port, the scheduler calculates a guaranteed rate that each subscriber shall receive, which ends up being less than 15Mbps. This calculation is the port rate divided by the number of subscribers:

```
1000Mbps / 100 users = 10Mbps per user
```

The best way to imagine how the scheduler works is to picture the subscribers being arranged in a loop, with the scheduler transmitting traffic for each subscriber for a short period of time and then moving on to the next one. As soon as it reaches the end of the subscribers, it is back at the start of the loop and continues with the first subscriber. The scheduler processes all subscriber queues, transmitting packets many times a second. The end result is that each subscriber receives a rough equal average of 10Mbps, which also means that no one can reach the peak rate of 15Mbps. There are two ways for the BNG to calculate the guaranteed rate. One is through implicit configuration, which is what the previous example showed using various megabit-per-second values based on a congested 1000Mbps port. Each subscriber received the same average rate. The second way is through explicit configuration, which leads to the next section describing WRR scheduling. In Juniper JUNOSe software, explicit configuration can be either an assured rate or a weight. In principle, an assured rate is the simplest to understand because it is configured in bits-per-second. The assured rate is the guaranteed rate at which the router will send traffic. The weight is more abstract and is a relative weight compared to other schedulers. Juniper JUNOS software calls it the transmit rate and can be expressed as a percentage of the interface speed or in kilo/mega/gigabits-per-second. Cisco IOS uses the term bandwidth distribution. For simplicity, it will be called the assured rate for the rest of this chapter.

At the other end of the spectrum, the shaping–rate limits the upper bound of the data rate. Continuing with the previous example, if on average most customers download at only 5Mbps, the total rate of traffic egressing the port is 500Mbps—half the port's capacity. However, one or two customers might be trying to download at a much higher rate with peer-to-peer applications; this can put a subscriber line at its maximum download capacity. In this case, the 15Mbps shaper kicks in to prevent excess traffic from being sent to the DSLAM and from being discarded due to exceeding the DSL port rate. An alternative to the shaper on the BNG is buffering such traffic at the DSLAM if the node has sufficient buffer capacity.

To summarize, two important concepts have been introduced so far:

- Shaping means limiting the peak rate of a subscriber's PPPoE, IP session, or other object (such as a VLAN or S-VLAN).
- Assured rate and transmit rate are synonymous terms for assigning a guaranteed minimum rate to an object (such as a VLAN, queue, or SVLAN). This could occur explicitly through configuration or implicitly based on the default configuration. Enough bandwidth must be available on the outgoing link to actually provide the assured rate.

Weighted Round Robin

Simple round robin is a good mechanism to apportion roughly equal amounts of bandwidth among a few or many subscribers. An equally common requirement is to give some subscribers more assured bandwidth than others. For example, providers often deploy a couple of basic Internet services, but with different assured rates, to give better performance when parts of the network are congested. This congestion may be deliberate to impair network performance for nonpremium services or during times of unexpected network duress.

Another use of a weighted round robin (WRR) scheduler is to provide a premium guarantee for business users and a nonpremium guarantee for residential customers. This is common for providers that use a switched aggregation network and use S-VLANs to isolate subscribers between DSLAMs. (See the section "1:1 VLANs" in Chapter 4 for an example of this architecture.) Subscribers within an S-VLAN are assigned different assured rates to guarantee minimum throughput when the path to the DSLAM is congested. The WRR scheduler uses the minimum rates or weights to calculate how much throughput subscribers in the S-VLAN receive.

Providers with a service VLAN can use a WRR scheduler, too. Rather than having an S-VLAN as an aggregation path between the DSLAM and BNG, the VLAN is the Layer 2 path. In this case, the subscriber sessions rather than VLANs are configured with the assured rate that reflects the oversubscription ratio that is sold to the customer.

Another use of a WRR scheduler is to apportion bandwidth between queues within a single subscriber session. For example, a customer might have a best-effort Internet and premium data service. The best-effort PHB is assigned a lower weight on the scheduler to make way for the premium downloads when too much data are contending for the same egress link. Hierarchical scheduling, which is a desirable feature in today's QoS implementations, is explained later in this chapter. It illustrates how the components previously described fit together in a hierarchical scheduler fashion for a robust QoS implementation.

Strict Priority and Low-Latency Scheduling

Strict priority traffic scheduling (also called low-latency queuing or DiffServ Expedited Forwarding) is a feature of almost all contemporary QoS implementations. It allows important traffic to be sent out a port with minimal queuing delay. Figure 8.9 shows an example of a strict priority implementation in which a customer has a VoIP service and a best-effort data service. The weighted round robin scheduler is halfway through a pass of scheduling traffic for all the subscribers on the port. Without a strict priority scheduler, VoIP traffic would have to wait until the RR or WRR scheduler has finished servicing all the other subscribers before sending VoIP packets. Instead, the scheduler excuses itself from the regular round-robin scheduling and begins processing VoIP traffic. As soon as these packets are no longer in the queue, the scheduler returns to where it was interrupted and continues with the round-robin scheduling. When a packet hits the VoIP queue again, it interrupts the round-robin process and recommences the strict scheduling cycle.

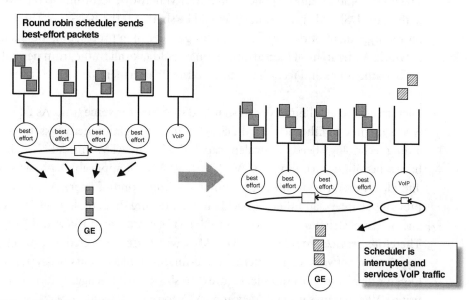

Figure 8.9 Strict priority scheduling.

One of the side effects of strict priority scheduling is that without a properly configured rate-limiter, the scheduler could always be busy servicing strict-priority traffic to the detriment of other traffic. Therefore, all strict traffic should have a rate-limiter configured—if not per-subscriber (ideally), then an overall limiter on the port.

Hierarchical QoS

QoS implementations in triple-play networks are at an advantage if they can manage traffic in a hierarchical fashion. The DSL Forum document TR-59[7] describes QoS architectures for DSL networks. One of its stipulations is a hierarchical scheduler on the BNG. One use for a hierarchical scheduler is if multiple queues are contending for access to the pipe to the subscriber. The hierarchical scheduler arbitrates between the queues before feeding the queues into an overall VLAN shaper (if a 1:1 architecture is used) or a subscriber shaper (if an N:1 architecture is used). Both of these VLAN configurations are explained in Chapter 4. Before the advent of Ethernet-based aggregation networks, ATM networks were the standard backhaul transport. Permanent Virtual Paths (PVPs) identified a DSLAM, and Permanent Virtual Circuits (PVCs) identified the individual households. PVPs were considered a pipe to transport circuits across the network in an aggregated fashion.

[7] http://www.dslforum.org/techwork/tr/TR-059.pdf

The PVP would usually be policed on the ATM network according to the size of the path to the DSLAM and optionally would be shaped at the BNG too. The BNG was more forgiving of bursty traffic by queuing rather than propagating bursts to the network. A hierarchical QoS arrangement would take all traffic from per-subscriber schedulers and feed the packets to the PVP shapers.

Hierarchical scheduling has been standard QoS fare for some time. As DSL networks migrate to Ethernet-based DSLAMs and aggregation networks, the superseding technology needs equivalent capability for the ATM world. BNGs should have scheduling capability on C-VLANs, S-VLANs (if applicable), physical trunks, and ideally on an aggregate application basis (more on this later). As discussed in previous chapters, an Ethernet backhaul architecture that employs a C-VLAN and S-VLAN structure is analogous to the ATM structure of PVCs and PVPs. Therefore, service providers with DSLAMs, which are connected to a switched aggregation network, can implement one-for-one replacements of several ATM QoS mechanisms. For example, Figure 8.10 shows an ATM aggregation network, using PVPs to represent DSLAMs and PVCs to represent subscribers. The second part of the figure shows the same 1:1 architecture, but in an Ethernet context.

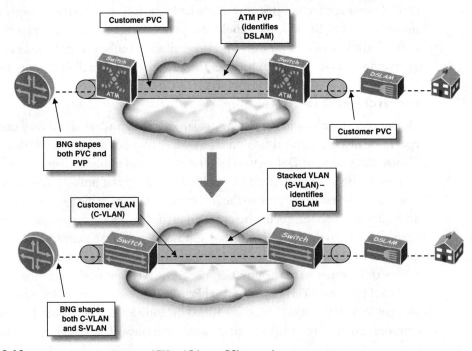

Figure 8.10 Architecture analogs between ATM and Ethernet DSL networks.

Figure 8.11 shows how these objects can be mapped into what is called a scheduler hierarchy diagram. It takes potential points of congestion (IP interfaces, C-VLANs, and S-VLANs) and orders them in a hierarchical fashion. The reason for representing potential points of congestion at a scheduler in the BNG is so that effective traffic prioritization can be managed on the BNG. This avoids congestion in the aggregation and access networks. Traffic flows into the queues at the top of the diagram and to the subscriber VLAN shaper. It then passes through an S-VLAN shaper before egressing the physical port. Figure 8.11 shows a hierarchy with a 1:1 VLAN architecture, which assigns a C-VLAN for each household and an S-VLAN for each path to a DSLAM.

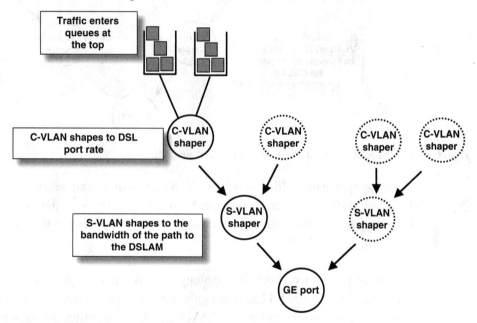

Figure 8.11 A QoS scheduler hierarchy based on a 1:1 Ethernet architecture.

If the access architecture is an *N*:1 or service VLAN topology, it means that all subscribers on a DSLAM share the same VLAN and are multiplexed by MAC address. The subscribers are separated by IP interfaces (JUNOSe terminology) or virtual access interfaces (Cisco IOS terminology). To manage aggregate traffic to a DSL port, a scheduler can be applied to the IP or virtual access interface. Figure 8.12 shows a scheduler hierarchy diagram for an *N*:1 service VLAN architecture.

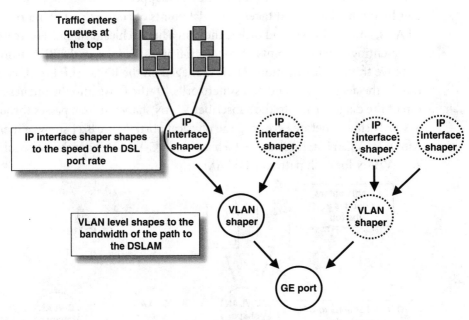

Figure 8.12 A QoS scheduler hierarchy based on an N:1 Ethernet architecture.

To manage aggregate traffic toward a DSLAM, a scheduler can be attached to the VLAN. All traffic from interfaces stacked above the VLAN flows down to the VLAN, which is the contention point that represents the trunk in the access network to the DSLAM.

From a QoS perspective, both the topology architecture in Figure 8.10 and the QoS hierarchy in Figure 8.12 have roughly the same capabilities of managing traffic on per-subscriber and per-DSLAM bases. One exception not shown is in the case of multiple PPPoE or DHCP sessions from each household. In this case, it is difficult to create an overall DSL port shaper that can effectively share bandwidth between all the sessions coming from a single household. Of course, it is possible to identify the sessions that share a single DSL port by using the PPPoE Intermediate Agent header or DHCP option 82 (both described in Chapter 5, "Choosing the Right Access Protocol"), but this does not bring them under a common shaper. It's rumored that improvements are coming soon to some BNG vendors that can group these sessions into a common rate-limiting domain. At the time of writing, this capability was not pervasive in the marketplace.

Most of the points of congestion in the access and aggregation network are represented by QoS objects in a BNG's scheduler configuration so that shaping can be applied earlier in the traffic path and consequently avoid traffic drops later in the network. C-VLANs are used in the hierarchy to represent the DSL port and thus enable per-subscriber traffic shaping. As per-subscriber bandwidth utilization increases, a common choice is to forgo an aggregation network and connect DSLAMs directly to the BNG using Dense Wave Division Multiplexing (DWDM), Coarse Wave Division Multiplexing (CWDM), or dark fibre. In this case it is not strictly necessary to use an S-VLAN and therefore not shape at the DSLAM level.

One exception is where subtended DSLAMs are used. The DSL Forum calls these level 2 access nodes. In this scenario, subtended nodes share the same GE link back to the BNG as the parent shelf. If there is a big disparity between the subscriber occupancy of the parent and subtended shelves, it is a good idea to group subscribers from each shelf within an S-VLAN and shape based on the outer 802.1Q tag. In the ATM world, this subtended architecture was commonly deployed to extend DSL coverage to remote areas. This meant that Level 2 and Level 3 shelves were fed with lower transmission capacity such as E1/T1 and E3/T3 links. At the same time, the parent shelves were connected with STM-1 or STM-4 interfaces. This disparity made it very important to manage aggregate traffic being sent to the lower-capacity node to avoid unnecessary discards after transitioning from higher-speed SDH/SONET to the lower PDH speeds. Based on observations so far, most providers are opting to go only as far as subtending to Level 2 because the bandwidths required for IPTV and unicast VoD make it unwise to multiplex too many DSLAMs onto a single link.

An emerging requirement from service providers is the ability to manage aggregate traffic rates, but with more capability than just at a logical path level. Take the example of a DSLAM directly connected to a BNG Gigabit Ethernet port over dark fibre. If there is ever a misdemeanor in provisioning or periods of non-normative best-effort traffic rates exiting the GE port, it can skew capacity planning estimations and consequently affect video and voice traffic. Oversubscription relies on each subscriber consuming an average, preplanned bandwidth rate for each class. Whether this is a kbps rate for data downloads or in terms of the number of concurrent video streams, the principle is roughly the same. If this average increases too much, it would start to encroach on port resources normally reserved for other services. This is where aggregate traffic management comes in. It allows a further level of prioritization after the C-VLAN and possibly S-VLAN schedulers in the BNG. Juniper JUNOSe calls this capability traffic-class-group prioritization. Traffic group prioritization enables better oversubscription in the access network. In a normal scheduler hierarchy, if an S-VLAN is congested due to large amounts of best-effort traffic, this would affect all types of subscriber traffic within that S-VLAN, including voice and video services. Prioritizing traffic before being sent in to the S-VLAN is more effective from a traffic management service perspective.

The following paragraphs show a common middle ground implementation for Juniper E-series and Cisco IOS to illustrate some of the QoS concepts that have been described. Figures 8.13 and 8.14 show JUNOSe and IOS scheduler diagrams, respectively. Figure 8.13 shows a hierarchy in which each subscriber has two traffic classes and is connected to the BNG using C-VLANs. The solid circles are part of a single chain of QoS hierarchy, representing objects that constitute a single subscriber. The dashed circles are other subscribers and S-VLAN shapers that share the same GE port.

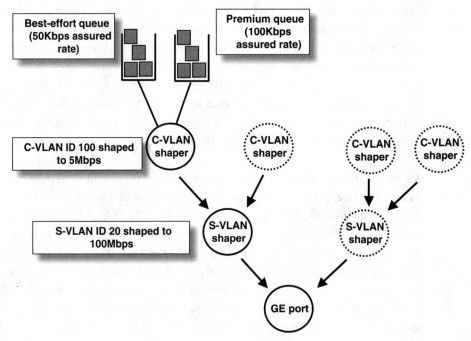

Figure 8.13 A JUNOSe scheduler hierarchy implementing C-VLAN shaping.

In both diagrams, traffic flows from top to bottom. The port is on the bottom, and the least aggregated traffic is at the top. As traffic progresses down through the hierarchy, it becomes part of more aggregated streams. Data flow into the queue based on traffic classification at the top level. WRED profiles can be applied to the queues. To classify traffic and then direct it to the correct traffic class, JUNOSe performs the classification action in an IP policy, which is then used by the QoS engine. To ensure that premium traffic gets more guaranteed bandwidth (100Kbps) than best-effort (50Kbps) during C-VLAN congestion, a scheduler profile is applied to each queue. They both contain assured rate parameters (100Kbps and 50Kbps) and could also contain a shaping rate, which would be the maximum rate that the queue can send. But in this case, shaping rates are not used on either of the queues, because the C-VLAN provides this shaping capability. Because each queue has a different assured rate, two different scheduler profiles are used in the configuration shown in Listing 8.5.

In technical terms, the next row down is the level 2 node level; it represents each of the C-VLANs. Another scheduler profile is attached at this C-VLAN point, which shapes the VLAN to the DSL port rate—5Mbps. The next level of hierarchy down is level 1, which is typically used to represent highly aggregated traffic. If DSLAMs are connected via a switch network, the paths to the nodes can be represented by S-VLANs, traffic class groups, or, as a simpler alternative, nothing at all. Figure 8.13 shows an S-VLAN shaper limiting the overall traffic to 100Mbps. S-VLAN shaping capability varies on Cisco platforms. Typically a separate device (such as a switch) shapes the aggregated traffic toward the DSLAM. Ideally, the switch should also have large buffers if it is to perform shaping on best-effort traffic that exceeds the contract rate. This is the main difference between the Cisco and Juniper examples.

Figure 8.14 shows a hierarchy similar to the Juniper example but without the S-VLAN aggregation layer. The top row is called the middle-level child policy. It splits traffic into the respective classes and then applies service policy actions such as policing, shaping, or assured bandwidth guarantees. At the bottom-level child policy (not shown in the example), only policing can be performed. Class-Based Weighted Fair Queuing (CBWFQ) actions such as shaping, assured bandwidth guarantees, and WRED need to be done in the middle-level child policy. The combined capability of the bottom-level child policy and the middle-level child policy is roughly equivalent to the queue level of Juniper E-series routers.

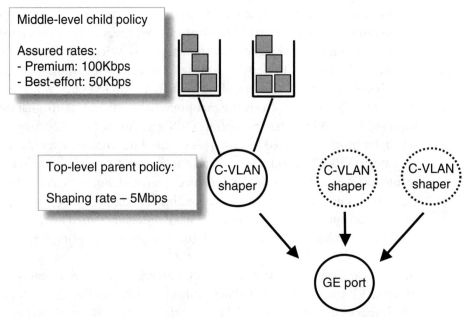

Figure 8.14 A Cisco IOS scheduler hierarchy loosely based on Figure 8.10, but without S-VLAN shapers.

The next stage of the hierarchy is to shape the customer subinterface. In a 1:1 VLAN architecture, this shaping point is a C-VLAN; in an *N*:1, this is the virtual interface on top of the CVLAN. In Figure 8.14, the final row is called the top-level parent policy. It is where the **shaping** command is applied to limit traffic to the customer DSL port rate. As mentioned, subsequent S-VLAN shaping is generally performed by external devices.

The configuration examples in Listings 8.5 and 8.6 show QoS configuration for both the Juniper E-series and Cisco IOS routers, following the examples in Figures 8.13 and 8.14, respectively. Both configurations incorporate weighted round-robin schedulers at the queue to arbitrate between the premium and best-effort classes. Each of the configurations is annotated to explain what each line does.

Listing 8.5 Juniper JUNOSe QoS Configuration for Queue and Subscriber Prioritization

```
1: traffic-class tc-premium
2: traffic-class best-effort
3:
```

```
 4: scheduler-profile 50k
 5:   assured-rate 50000
 6:
 7: scheduler-profile 100k
 8:   assured-rate 100000
 9:
10: scheduler-profile 100m
11:   shaping-rate 100000000
12:
13: scheduler-profile cvlan
14:   shaping-rate 5000000
15:
16: qos-profile subscriber-profile-basic
17:   vlan queue traffic-class best-effort scheduler-profile 50k
18:   vlan queue traffic-class tc-premium scheduler-profile 100k
19:   vlan node scheduler-profile cvlan
20:
21: qos-profile svlan-profile-100m
22:   svlan node scheduler-profile 100m
23:
24: interface gigabitEthernet 2/0/0
25:   svlan 20 qos-profile svlan-profile-100m
26:
27: interface GigabitEthernet 2/0/0.100
28:   svlan id 20 100
29:   qos-profile subscriber-profile-basic
```

The following list explains Listing 8.5:

- Lines 1 and 2: Create the two traffic classes—one tc-premium and one best-effort. The best-effort traffic class exists by default.

- Lines 4 and 5: The 50Kbps scheduler profile is used to provide a minimum guarantee of 50Kbps to the best-effort queue.

- Lines 7 and 8: The 100Kbps scheduler profile is used to provide a minimum guarantee of 100Kbps to the premium queue.

- Lines 10 and 11: This scheduler profile is used to shape the overall S-VLAN to 100Mbps.

- Lines 13 and 14: This scheduler profile shapes the C-VLAN to 5Mbps.

- Lines 16 through 19: Create the QoS profile that is applied to the subscriber interface. The QoS profile ties together the traffic classes and scheduler profiles.

- Lines 21 and 22: A separate QoS profile is defined for the S-VLAN shaper.

- Lines 24 and 25: The S-VLAN aggregation QoS profile needs to be applied on the physical interface.

- Lines 27 through 29: The subscriber QoS profile to shape to 5Mbps is applied to the C-VLAN subinterface.

Listing 8.6 Cisco IOS QoS Configuration for Queue and Subscriber Prioritization

```
 1: class-map match-any cm-prec-4
 2:   match ip precedence 4
 3:
 4: policy-map pm-vlan-shape-middle
 5:   class cm-prec-4
 6:     bandwidth 100
 7:   class class-default
 8:     bandwidth 50
 9:
10: policy-map pm-vlan-shape-top
11:   class class-default
12:     shape peak 5000000
13:     service-policy pm-vlan-shape-middle
14:
15: interface GigabitEthernet 2/0/0.100
16:   encapsulation dot1q 20 second-dot1q 100
17:   service-policy output pm-vlan-shape-top
```

The following list explains Listing 8.6:

- Lines 1 and 2: Create a class map that matches premium traffic—IP precedence 4.

- Lines 4 and 5: Create the middle-level child policy and the first class match for precedence-4 traffic, and give it a minimum guarantee of 100Kbps.

- Lines 7 and 8: Configure the next class to match all other traffic, and give it 50Kbps of guaranteed rate.

- Lines 10 through 13: The top-level policy shapes the VLAN. Only one class can be present in this policy—class-default. This shapes traffic to 5Mbps and also links the middle-level child service policy to it.
- Line 17: Assign the service policy to the interface.

Listings 8.7 and 8.8 show the CLI output to verify that the configuration has been applied to PPPoE sessions based on the configurations shown in Listings 8.5 and 8.6.

Listing 8.7 Verifying Juniper JUNOSe QoS Configuration for Queue and Subscriber Prioritization

```
BNG#show qos scheduler-hierarchy interface gig2/0/0.100

Scheduler hierarchy for the default traffic-class group
                                              shared      assured
                                         shaping shaping    rate
   interface resource                      rate    rate   or weight
--------------- ---------------------------- ------- ------- -----------
ethernet Eth2/0/0 ethernet port                              wgt 8
                svlan svlan node         100000000    ar 100000000
vlan Eth2/0/0.100    vlan node           5000000       wgt 8
vlan Eth2/0/0.100      vlan queue tc-premium           ar 100000
vlan Eth2/0/0.100      vlan queue best-effort          ar 50000
BNG#
```

Listing 8.8 Verifying Cisco IOS QoS Configuration for Queue and Subscriber Prioritization

```
BNG#show policy-map interface gig2/0/0.100
GigabitEthernet2/0/0.100

Service-policy output: pm-vlan-shape-top

Class-map: class-default (match-any)
315 packets, 18900 bytes
5 minute offered rate 0 bps, drop rate 0 bps
Match: any
Traffic Shaping
Target/Average Byte Sustain Excess Interval Increment
Rate Limit bits/int bits/int (ms) (bytes)
10000000/5000000 31250 125000 125000 25 31250

Adapt Queue Packets Bytes Packets Bytes Shaping
```

```
Active Depth Delayed Delayed Active
- 0 315 18900 0 0 no

Service-policy : pm-vlan-shape-middle

Class-map: cm-prec-4 (match-any)
0 packets, 0 bytes
5 minute offered rate 0 bps, drop rate 0 bps
Match: ip precedence 4
0 packets, 0 bytes
5 minute rate 0 bps
Queueing
Output Queue: Conversation 137
Bandwidth 100 (kbps) Max Threshold 64 (packets)
(pkts matched/bytes matched) 0/0
(depth/total drops/no-buffer drops) 0/0/0

Class-map: class-default (match-any)
315 packets, 18900 bytes
5 minute offered rate 0 bps, drop rate 0 bps
Match: any
Queueing
Output Queue: Conversation 138
Bandwidth 50 (kbps) Max Threshold 64 (packets)
(pkts matched/bytes matched) 0/0
(depth/total drops/no-buffer drops) 0/0/0
BNG#
```

Table 8.2 summarizes the terminology used so far in this chapter.

Table 8.2 Summary of Scheduling Protocols and Terminology

Protocol or Term	Definition
Assured rate	A term used by Juniper Networks that specifies a desired minimum rate of throughput that a QoS object receives in the event of congestion. Similar to a relative weight, except it is expressed as bandwidth rather than as an arbitrary numeric expression.
Bandwidth	A term used by Cisco Systems that specifies the desired minimum rate of throughput that a QoS object receives in the event of congestion.

Protocol or Term	Definition
Bottom-level child policy	A term used by Cisco Systems that is part of the three-level hierarchical policy. It is a child of the middle-level policy and can separate traffic according to class maps and can police each class.
Class-Based Weighted Fair Queuing (CBWFQ)	A term used by Cisco Systems. A mechanism to classify traffic based on packet or frame headers and apply QoS treatment using weighted fair queuing scheduling.
Class map	A term used by Cisco Systems to classify traffic. Has no effect until coupled with a policy map.
Low-Latency Queuing (LLQ)	A term used by Cisco Systems to denote traffic that must be sent without delay and with minimal jitter. Normally used for VoIP traffic.
Middle-level child policy	A term used by Cisco Systems for a service policy that is a child of the parent. Queue discard algorithms, queue lengths, shapers, and policers can be applied with this policy.
Parent-level policy	A term used by Cisco Systems for a service policy that is applied to an interface. It is a master shaper for traffic before it is sent out the interface. Child service policies can be attached to it.
Policy map	A term used by Cisco Systems. Matches packets based on class maps and assigns actions such as policing, shaping, queue management mechanisms, and packet re-markings. It has no effect until applied to an interface.
Priority command	A term used by Cisco Systems that is applied to a class within a policy map. It causes all traffic matching the class to be treated with LLQ.
QoS profile	A term used by Juniper Networks for the mechanism that unites QoS objects (queue profiles, scheduler profiles, traffic classes, and statistics profiles). It is assigned to the interface in the outbound direction to apply QoS treatment to traffic.
Round robin	A scheduling algorithm that withdraws packets from queues or nodes with equal priority. Queues and nodes are arranged in a loop.
Scheduler	A mechanism to allocate transmission resources among queues and nodes, VLANs, queues, PVCs.

continues

Table 8.2 (continued)

Protocol or Term	Definition
Scheduler profile	A term used by Juniper Networks to configure a scheduler's characteristics—assured rate and shaping rate. Has no effect until coupled with a QoS profile.
Shaping rate	Specifies the peak rate at which traffic can be sent from a QoS object. Any traffic exceeding the peak rate is queued if queue space is available. Smoothes traffic bursts.
Strict priority queuing	A term used by Juniper Networks to denote traffic that must be sent without delay and with minimal jitter. Normally used for VoIP traffic.
Traffic class	A grouping of traffic sharing common QoS characteristics.
Weight	A number of shares from a pool that determines the probability that a queue or node is scheduled. The pool's size is the sum of all the weight in the scheduler pool.
Weighted Random Early Discard (WRED)	A queue management algorithm that randomly discards packets in a queue. Is aware of packet coloration to modify discard aggression.
Weighted Round Robin	An advanced version of round-robin scheduling that allows a QoS object to have more or less affinity for scheduler resources compared to other objects in the same pool. Each QoS object has a relative weight to determine its affinity for scheduler resources compared to other objects.

Rate-Limiting and Shaping Overheads

Service providers regularly ask about one aspect of shaping. It has to do with shaping and rate-limiting overheads. Overhead in this context is any type of header or encapsulation added to an IP packet, such as a VLAN tag, Ethernet CRC field, or PPP header. Due to implementation differences across vendor platforms, a QoS shaping rate produces different transmission rates compared to a rate-limiter. For example, configuring a QoS shaper of 2Mbps on a customer VLAN might produce a shaping rate of 2Mbps on the wire—the wire meaning the traffic that is seen on the transmission link. But a rate-limiter of 2Mbps might result in a transmission rate in excess of 2000kbps. To further complicate matters, QoS shaping rates of 2Mbps may differ in transmission rates between vendors. Why the difference?

The answer to the first difference is reasonably conspicuous. As a general rule, it is the result of rate-limiting taking into account only the IP layer. Layer 2 headers such as Ethernet MAC addresses and VLAN tags are not included. For example, Juniper M and T series routers perform rate-limiting on the IP processor ASIC on the forwarding plane and normally deal only with plain IP packets. One exception is a rate-limiter that specifically works at Layer 2, such as with a Layer 2 VPN. Cisco IOS rate-limiting behavior is more nuanced; it depends on the platform and encapsulation type. With Ethernet encapsulation, policing includes PPPoE and the addressing header (MAC addresses and VLAN information) but no CRC. ATM policing includes little header information. Table 8.3 lists the current Cisco policing and shaping overheads. Table 8.4 lists those for the Juniper E-series routers.

Table 8.3 Cisco 10000 Policing and Shaping Overheads

	Policing	Shaping
Ethernet (no PPPoE)	IP packet but No Ethernet headers No VLAN header No CRC	IP packet and Ethernet headers All VLAN headers CRC
Ethernet (PPPoE)	IP packet but No PPPoE or PPP header No Ethernet header No Ethernet CRC No VLAN headers	IP packet and Ethernet headers All VLAN headers CRC
ATM (PPPoA)	IP packet and PPP header But No AAL5 padding No AAL5 trailer No cell header	IP packet and PPP header But No AAL5 trailer No AAL5 padding No cell header

Table 8.4 Juniper E-Series Policing and Shaping Overheads

	Policing	Shaping
Ethernet (no PPPoE)	IP packet but No Ethernet headers No VLAN header	IP packet and Ethernet headers All VLAN headers CRC
Ethernet (PPPoE)	IP packet but No PPPoE headers No Ethernet headers No VLAN header	IP packet and Ethernet headers PPPoE headers All VLAN headers CRC
ATM (PPPoA)	IP packet but No AAL5 padding No AAL5 trailer No cell header	LLC encapsulation: IP packet plus LLC header (3 bytes) NLPID (1 byte) PPP header But: No AAL5 trailer No padding No cell header VC MUX IP packet plus PPP header But No AAL5 trailer No padding No cell header

As described earlier in this chapter, QoS operations occur later in the forwarding process of router packet processing hardware. Due to internal implementation details, this can mean that some overheads are added to packets before they reach the QoS modules. Other times, internal padding bytes may be added to a packet to simulate overheads that are actually added after the QoS process, again due to vendor hardware implementation. In either case, this is intentional, because QoS shaping rates attain a transmission rate close to the line hardware type.

It can be difficult to design a rate-limiter for ATM that closely matches the interface speed, because specialized Segmentation and Reassembly (SAR) hardware is used to correctly encapsulate data on the link. This adds extra padding bytes to Protocol Data Units (PDUs), segmenting packets into cells and adding a cell header. A few years ago, accurate ATM-level shaping was not supported on non-SAR hardware, but this is changing. More vendors are beginning to support incorporation of ATM overheads into policing and shaping rates. To better approximate the rate at which an ATM interface will transmit on the wire with a given shaping rate, QoS cell mode simulates the overhead that would be incurred by the SAR just before transmission (padding bytes and cell headers). For example, a VoIP packet stream of 100kbps that is sent on an ATM-based ADSL local loop might be 120kbps after the extra ATM encapsulation is added. If the subscriber data stream is sent to the DSLAM from the BNG at too high a rate, data could be discarded at the DSL port. To avoid such a problem, providers have configured their BNG shapers with an approximation of the ATM overhead based on a best guess of the local loop's traffic profile and have subtracted the overhead from the ATM rate. In environments with Ethernet aggregation networks with ATM-based local loops, a QoS cell mode shaper lets the operator configure a subscriber's ATM shaping rate, even on an Ethernet interface. The BNG performs the calculation of the extra ATM overhead that an Ethernet frame would have and feeds this into the shaping algorithm in real time.

What is the significance of these seemingly unimportant facts? In an operational context, they do not have a large impact. It is in a service's planning, testing, and provisioning phases where it consumes resources. A common rumination is whether a service is marketed to the customer as an IP service or a Layer 2 service. If it is the latter and, for argument's sake, it is a 1Mbps DSL service to the customer, this might reach only 800kbps of IP. An IP rate-limiter has to be configured with a rate lower than 1Mbps. Due to differences in packet sizes, it might not provide the customer with true 1Mbps service. A better solution would be to use a QoS shaper to control the line speed more directly. This is the most common product sold to customers, because it takes the least amount of configurational "tweaking" to deploy. Some operators deliver an IP rate to customers. It is argued that this generates fewer support calls because customers can see the full advertised download speed on their PCs. This is most common on lower-speed lines, where it is easy to congest the local loop. As access lines become faster, users are less likely to notice the difference between a Layer 2 and Layer 3 rate.

The overheads described in Tables 8.3 and 8.4 often change from time to time, so it is useful to glean this overhead information in real time. This is shown is Listings 8.9 and 8.10 for Cisco IOS and Juniper JUNOSe, respectively. Each of the listings is based on the test of a 100-byte IP packet being sent through the router to an ADSL subscriber via a PPPoE session. The subscriber is identified with an S-VLAN and C-VLAN tag. The relevant configuration is shown first for each subscriber, with the corresponding CLI **show** output. The lines in bold show the bytes that are included in the rate-limiting calculation for the 100-byte packet, and the bytes in bold italic show the bytes that go toward the QoS shaping calculation.

Listing 8.9 Sample Output from Cisco IOS to Verify Rate-Limiting and Shaping Overheads

```
! The virtual template and vpdn-group configuration have been omitted
! from this listing

policy-map policy-output
 class class-default
  police cir 100000 bc 1000 pir 200000
  conform-action drop

interface GigabitEthernet6/0/0.100
 encapsulation dot1Q 20 second-dot1q 100
 service-policy output policy-output
 pppoe enable
end


rome#show policy-map interface fast6/0.100
 FastEthernet6/0.100

 Service-policy output: policy-output

 Class-map: class-default (match-any)
 1 packets, 130 bytes
 5 minute offered rate 0 bps, drop rate 0 bps
 Match: any
 police:
 cir 100000 bps, bc 1000 bytes
 pir 200000 bps, be 390 bytes
 conformed 1 packets, 130 bytes; actions:
```

```
drop
exceeded 0 packets, 0 bytes; actions:
drop
violated 0 packets, 0 bytes; actions:
drop
conformed 0 bps, exceed 0 bps, violate 0 bps
```

Listing 8.10 Sample Output from Juniper E-Series to Verify Rate-Limiting and Shaping Overheads

```
! Note: Profile configuration has been omitted from this listing
interface GigabitEthernet12/0/0.100
!
 svlan id 20 100
 pppoe
 pppoe auto-configure
 pppoe profile any ip
!


Milan#show ip interface GigabitEthernet12/0/0.100
GigabitEthernet12/0/0.100 line protocol VlanSub is up, ip is up
 Network Protocols: IP
 Unnumbered Interface on loopback0
 ( IP address 1.1.1.1 )
 Operational MTU = 1492 Administrative MTU = 0
 Operational speed = 100000000 Administrative speed = 0
 Discontinuity Time = 237125417
 Router advertisement = disabled
 Proxy Arp = disabled
 Network Address Translation is disabled
 TCP MSS Adjustment = disabled
 Administrative debounce-time = disabled
 Operational debounce-time = disabled
 Access routing = enabled: Using 192.168.1.3
 Multipath mode = hashed
 Auto Configure = disabled
 Auto Detect = disabled
 Inactivity Timer = disabled

 In Received Packets 0, Bytes 100
 Unicast Packets 0, Bytes 100
 Multicast Packets 0, Bytes 0
 In Policed Packets 0, Bytes 0
```

```
In Error Packets 0
In Invalid Source Address Packets 0
In Discarded Packets 0
Out Forwarded Packets 1, Bytes 100
Unicast Packets 1, Bytes 100
Multicast Routed Packets 0, Bytes 0
Out Scheduler Dropped Packets 0, Bytes 0
Out Policed Packets 0, Bytes 0
Out Discarded Packets 0

queue 0: traffic class best-effort, bound to ip
GigabitEthernet12/0/0.100.6
Queue length 0 bytes
Forwarded packets 1, bytes 134
Dropped committed packets 0, bytes 0
Dropped conformed packets 0, bytes 0
Dropped exceeded packets 0, bytes 0
```

ROUTER FORWARDING ARCHITECTURES

Today's higher-performance routers commonly implement a distributed, hardware-based forwarding architecture. One or more physical ports are connected to a line module or card. Each slot has dedicated packet processing hardware that performs many tasks, including packet decapsulation (removing Layer 2 header information if needed), classification, rate-limiting, and routing table lookup. When traffic needs to be sent to another line card in the router, it transits a fabric, which is a centralized high-performance packet switch that forwards packets between line modules.

Each line module also performs QoS tasks, such as buffering and scheduling. This is one of the last operations the router performs before placing a packet on the wire for transmission. The reason for putting QoS very late in the forwarding path is because most of the Layer 2 header and encapsulation data are included in the packet scheduling calculation. Usually scheduling is performed using dedicated hardware processors in the line card with the assistance of large packet memory, where data can be buffered in a queue rather than being discarded. As more cards are added to the system, because the line modules do most of the packet processing, the system can scale effectively with the bandwidth and capacity requirements. On the negative side, pushing packet processing to line cards drives up the system complexity because of the component synchronization needed for tasks including routing table distribution, fabric bandwidth arbitration, and statistics distribution.

A centralized forwarding architecture is still common in the industry, either due to an existing install base or in new routers that do not require high forwarding rates. CPE are often based on a centralized forwarding architecture, and most of the forwarding functions are implemented in software. This keeps the cost down. Also, because CPE architecture is simpler, complex edge forwarding functions can be implemented with a shorter development time compared to hardware-based designs. In a centralized architecture, packet processing, including QoS, is done in a single forwarding module, with fewer tasks given to the interfaces other than acting as a transmission interface and some limited encapsulation duties.

In larger centralized routers, as more line cards are added to the router, the central forwarding and switching module needs to do more packet processing and switching work. Centralized switching modules are usually rated to a high-enough capacity to easily switch packets between all interfaces on the router and maintain the required user sessions. However, at times system scaling could be affected if too many packet-processing duties in addition to basic packet switching need to be made in the forwarding path.

Figure 8.15 shows the flow of ingress and egress line modules performing packet processing duties with the fabric switch at the center, forming the linkage between the two cards. This is an example of a distributed forwarding architecture.

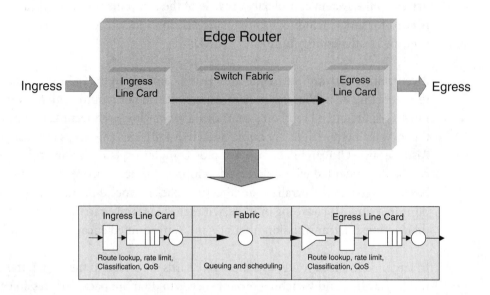

Figure 8.15 Distributed forwarding on modern router hardware.

Distributed Forwarding

In routers and switches, classification is important for both data entering the router (ingress classification) and traffic departing (egress classification). Ingress classification is important for devices that use a prioritized fabric backplane. In some architectures, this can cause discards or delays of high priority data transiting the fabric. This is called head-of-line blocking. In Figure 8.16, ingress classification is performed on the incoming interface before traffic is forwarded across a *fabric* or *backplane* to the egress interface. For example, if more than 1Gbps is being sent to the Gigabit Ethernet port on the right side of the diagram because both ports 1 and 2 are trying to send 1Gbps, traffic has to be buffered before it can be sent to the egress port. Without fabric prioritization and ingress classification, both high-priority and low-priority traffic would be indiscriminately buffered before eventually being sent to the egress port.

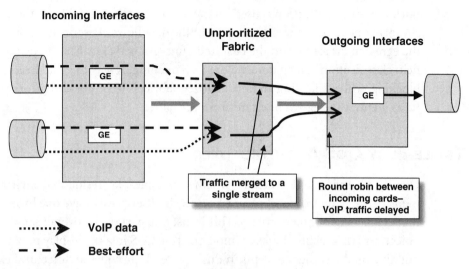

Figure 8.16 VoIP and best-effort data traversing an unprioritized fabric.

With effective fabric prioritization the router can put important traffic at the front of the queue to be sent to the egress port, as shown in Figure 8.17. The implementation of router and switch fabric is quite a specialized technique, so the two figures showing fabric priority differ in some respects—for example, where packets are actually buffered. However, they do show the general principle of fabric prioritization.

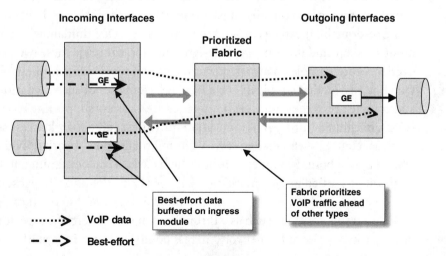

Figure 8.17 VoIP and best-effort data traversing a prioritized fabric.

Egress prioritization is also used when traffic is being queued to be sent out the port. Ingress classification is used on the incoming interface(s) from the core as a BA form due to the aggregated nature of the data flows. As soon as traffic reaches the egress interface toward the customer, fine-grained classification using multi-field classification can be done before CoS queuing. A way to avoid head of line blocking, while still using an unprioritized fabric, is to buffer and prioritize traffic as it enters the egress line card from the fabric.

TRIPLE-PLAY QOS ARCHITECTURES

Quality of service deployments—whether in triple-play residential environments, Layer 2 metro networks, or Layer 3 VPN services—have one broad goal: managing congestion effectively. This is just one part of the overall set of QoS objectives. This section looks at implementing QoS in a triple-play network, building on the earlier concepts in this chapter. It provides architectural examples of triple-play deployments in provider networks today. Many of the principles are also applicable to non-triple-play deployments: establishing trust boundaries, strict priority queuing for VoIP traffic, and round-robin scheduling between multiple traffic classes are examples.

TRUST BOUNDARIES

Trust boundaries are used at various points in a service provider network, but usually at the edges to establish a partition between the inside and outside areas of a QoS domain. It can be convenient to associate a QoS domain with an autonomous system, and if the network design is not too complex, these two generally overlap. More-complex network scenarios make it more difficult to establish QoS boundaries that simply match a BGP AS. Examples of such scenarios that add complexity to the QoS trust boundaries are Carriers supporting Carriers (CsC), integrated third-party application providers, and network access seekers (such as retail ISPs wholesaling services from broadband network providers). So what is a trust boundary? It establishes where packets can be admitted to the network with a particular QoS marking—DiffServ Code Points on IP packets, EXP tags on MPLS packets, 802.1P markings for VLAN tags, and so on. It can also include a traffic contract, such as a throughput of a certain traffic type, for example. If packets arrive at the network ingress points with spurious markings, usually the field is reset to 0.

The first scenario in this section is a service provider running a triple-play service, permitting 200kbps of VoIP traffic from each subscriber. This data is identified by the residential gateway (RG) at the customer premises, ideally marking these packets with a DiffServ Code Point corresponding to Expedited Forwarding. Sometimes the RG might only be able to make use of IP Precedence and sets the value to 5. A rate-limiter is applied on each customer's interface at the BNG. It limits the incoming rate of such traffic to 200kbps and re-marks any exceeding traffic with a Code Point that indicates a higher drop precedence. The trust boundary in this case is the BNG rather than the RG. Even though the BNG accepts the priority markings set by the RG, it does not trust them with blind faith. Rather, it uses them as a guide to what traffic is high priority. It uses the rate-limiter acting as a floodgate of sorts, so the trust boundary is the BNG. A similar principle can be applied to other subtypes of traffic (such as premium data). To reduce the amount of configuration complexity, rate-limiting so many classes on the BNG is not so common in residential networks. The most common approach to upstream traffic management is to use an inherent rate-limiter—the speed of the local loop—to restrict the total upstream rate. The next most popular approach is to use a line rate-limiter on the BNG. The DSLAM is configured to synchronize the customer modem as high as it can go given the line conditions. This last option reduces the configuration needed in the access network when the customer downstream or upstream rate needs to change, such as in an environment with highly dynamic service provisioning. As with any QoS design, it depends on individual provider preference. Some may decide it is unimportant how much high-priority traffic is sent to the network. The extra configuration overhead is the most commonly cited reason not to rate-limit. Those with more stringent bandwidth requirements tend to lean toward the per-class rate-limiters.

The trust boundary needs to stretch the entire perimeter of the provider network, so there is plenty more to manage than just the subscriber-facing interfaces. Two other important boundaries are Internet peering points and direct interconnect points with third-party providers. Internet peering points are places where much of the service provider's lifeblood flows, but it is not always metaphorically sanguine. In almost all cases, Internet traffic coming from upstream providers, whether multilateral or bilateral peers, is considered to be of a best-effort nature. Hence, any nonzero DiffServ markings are set to 0.

The second most important trust gateway also concerns data interconnects with third parties. Based on the L2TP and Layer 3 wholesale models described in Chapter 7, "Wholesale Broadband Networks," data-handoff points exist between the network access provider and the retail provider. Layer 2 interconnects do not have as strong a requirement to secure the trust border compared to L2TP and Layer 3-based interconnects because it is not typical to propagate Layer 2 QoS markings from one provider domain to the next. In almost all cases, this interconnect has the same policy as Internet exchanges, but this need not be so. Wholesale providers that want to offer differentiated services to retail providers and ultimately to the end customer can enable the interconnect for QoS handoff. This works for both L2TP and IP interconnects. One scenario is a retail provider delivering a double-play service to a customer that needs consistent end-to-end handling of VoIP traffic. For Layer 3 IP interconnects, the wholesale provider can dictate a set of DiffServ Code Points that retail providers must use for the various traffic classes, which are then honored down the network to the subscriber premises. L2TP traffic is more enigmatic to interpret because it is costly in terms of processing overhead to inspect customer IP traffic within the tunnel and to verify DiffServ Code Point markings. This is due to each customer IP packet being wrapped in an L2TP and UDP header before being sent as a bundled IP datagram from the LNS. MPLS has a similar problem to solve when routers need to know with what priority they should treat customer IP datagrams within the MPLS packet. The solution is to mark the outer MPLS label (or outer IP packet of the L2TP tunnel) with the same priority as the inner datagram if the intention is to honor the indicated priority from the retailer.

This architecture assumes a single PVC architecture all the way to the CPE. Alternatively, if a PVC-per-service model is in use, a PVC prioritization mechanism on the wholesaler DSLAM can differentiate between VoIP and best-effort data. This allows ATM cells for the high-priority VoIP PVC to be sent ahead of any large best-effort packets. Such a prioritization scheme is useful for low bit-rate services that could be affected by serialization delay. The PVC provisioning scheme used by the wholesaler is communicated to the retailer so that it knows which circuit to use for which service.

It is possible that the retailer could send all traffic to the network with a high priority, which may need a rate-limiter to protect the incumbent's network. It can be argued that here the risk to the network access provider is lower because an interconnect agreement commonly guarantees a minimum bandwidth rate across the network. This means that priority markings do not necessarily affect core network dimensioning. Instead, they are used more to prioritize traffic on the customer interface on the BNG. The argument for not implementing per-class limiting is that it would require continual tweaking as the number of sub-scribers increases. This could be mitigated with percentage-based rate-limiting, but this is not foolproof and still entails some ongoing operational effort.

VoIP QoS is not necessarily the only enhanced wholesale service. Retail providers could deliver video services, a walled-garden area, or application hosting, which still require sophisticated QoS treatment. This leads to the next section: third-party application providers. This is another entry point into the provider net-work that needs to be included in the QoS trust border. In most cases, these pro-viders specialize in a specific service area (such as only VoIP or only video) so that marking all ingress traffic with a single priority value is a sufficient stance to take. One thing to be aware of: If a service has different traffic types that need to be treated with different forwarding behavior. For example, VoIP has a media stream and a control stream, each with different PHBs. Therefore, marking all traffic for a service with the same priority marking might not be completely foolproof.

Service-provider-owned servers are a subtly different matter. Packets entering the network from a server are still marked with the DiffServ Code Point that pertains to the service within the packet. These Code Points can be set by the server itself, by the switch that the server connects to, or on the first Layer 3 hop from the server. Most applications on these servers can be configured to send data streams with a certain marking. However, if any Code Point scheme needs to be changed in the network, many servers would need to be reconfigured. Most high-end switches can set 802.1P markings on a per-port basis, and some can do DiffServ modification, too. Even though routers are especially suited to IP-based forward-ing, they can use 802.1P information in the Ethernet header to set the DiffServ or MPLS EXP field for routers further down the forwarding path. Setting per-packet priority on the switches based on the source physical port makes more sense when several servers that deliver different services are colocated on the same VLAN. Doing this on a router without awareness of the source physical port that the server is connected to means that the only way to distinguish between the services is using the source IP address or TCP/UDP port—not a terribly scalable solution.

Figure 8.18 illustrates the trust boundaries that have been discussed in this section.

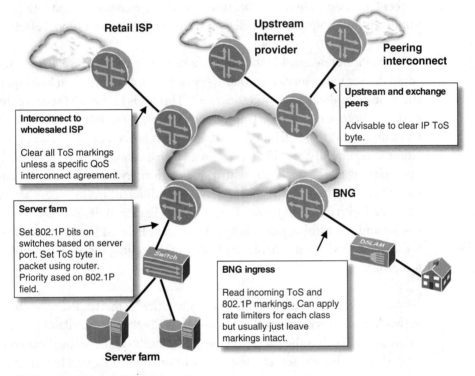

Figure 8.18 Trust boundaries in a triple-play network.

Common Carrier Status

There is ongoing debate at both an operational and political level as to a provider's *common carrier* status. One of the arguments against re-marking packet Code Points to 0 is that it breaks the principle of end-to-end transmission—that is, a packet should be unmodified from sender to receiver. It also means that a carrier's own VoIP streams can be marked with a high priority and that off-net VoIP providers such as Skype and Vonage are dropped in times of congestion. Counterarguments to the first argument are that packet headers are continually being modified at each router hop by the TTL decrement operation anyway; also, TCP MSS adjust operations are commonly done by BNGs and L2TP Network Servers (LNSs), which alter TCP headers to work around MTU issues in tunneled networks. The second point is more contentious. There is no single answer as to the best way to handle packets marked with nonzero priority markings, because it comes down to local provider policy. Nevertheless, many providers do choose to mark such packets to 0 to secure their border to keep matters simple. The argument goes that if packets are not re-marked to 0, it is hard to fully dimension the network if uncontrolled externalities exist (such as incoming packets with a high IP precedence or DiffServ Code Point).

CENTRALIZED BNG

Figure 4.19 in Chapter 4 shows a triple-play access network architecture using a centralized BNG design. Any 1:1 VLAN architecture essentially uses a centralized BNG architecture, meaning that a single edge router delivers most, if not all, services to a subscriber. Despite being a centralized architecture, it is accepted that a 1:1 model does incorporate a distributed element for multicast. This means that an external router delivers IPTV services over a common VLAN in the aggregation network.

The layout and design are explained extensively in Chapter 4, so this section discusses their qualities from a QoS perspective. The IP edge at which a customer connects to the network needs to know the customer's DSL port speed. It should also be able to implement some queuing for downstream traffic, which exceeds the port rate, so as to avoid packet drops at the DSLAM. In the majority of centralized deployments, the BNG is the device doing the per-subscriber packet management, because it has large buffering capability and usually more sophisticated QoS features than a DSLAM.

The centralized model supports DSLAMs that are directly connected to the BNG or ones that use a switched backhaul network, as shown Figure 4.19. In the case of a switched backhaul network, it is common to shape aggregate traffic to the DSLAM when oversubscribing the aggregation network. Some BNGs can do simultaneous S-VLAN and C-VLAN shaping, and others require the use of an external switch to shape the outer tag.

From a purely QoS perspective, one of the biggest advantages of a centralized architecture over other models is a single point of control for all subscriber traffic and, if applicable, the switch aggregation network. This limits how many devices need to be reconfigured for a line speed change or to enable a new DSL port. Note that if the copper distribution network from the DSLAM to households is densely packed, it may be an unavoidable fact that, due to excessive line noise from adjacent cable pairs in the binder, line speeds may need to be limited at the DSLAM. This results in the extra reprovisioning step of having to modify the DSLAM and the BNG for service speed changes.

Running a Distributed Multicast Edge

Using a common VLAN for multicast is an important feature of a triple-play network to save substantial bandwidth in the aggregation domain, and in the fabric switches of both DSLAMs and edge routers. This is described in Chapter 4 in the section "Provider VLAN Architecture: 1:1 and Multicast VLANs." Whether the multicast VLAN connects to a different edge router than a BNG or to the BNG itself is not of great importance. What is important is that when someone turns on his or her set-top box (STB) and starts watching an IPTV channel, this should not cause drops at the DSLAM due to IPTV and best effort contending for limited egress bandwidth. Prioritization can help only to a certain degree if the per-port buffer is not very large. The solution is usually to restrict the less-important traffic at the unicast edge router before it reaches the DSLAM.

This leverages the IGMP client architectures described in the DSL Forum document TR-101. The two types of IGMP clients are RG-based and access-node-based, and both ultimately achieve the same thing. The RG-based approach is used if the replication functionality is not available in the BNG. In this case, the RG replicates IGMP Joins and Leaves to an IPoE session that shares the same VLAN as the PPPoE session. The IPoE *session* is a slightly nebulous term that exists to conceptualize multicast traffic sharing the same logical PVC or VLAN, because PPPoE data are still considered a discrete channel. It doesn't represent a Layer 2 or Layer 3 relationship between two routers in the traditional sense. When the DSLAM or access node (AN) receives these IGMP packets, they are sent on the multicast VLAN for further processing by the multicast edge router. The other IGMP packet continues within the PPPoE session to the unicast BNG, which then could decrement the shaping rate of best-effort traffic by the same bandwidth as the video stream. If the customer stops watching the TV channel, the STB sends the necessary IGMP packets down both IPoE and PPPoE sessions. This causes the BNG to update its QoS shaper for best-effort data and increases it to its original rate.

AN-based IGMP client replication has been written into TR-101 to let the DSLAM snoop into the DHCP or PPPoE session for any IGMP packets and echo them on the multicast VLAN. The end result is the same as with RG as an echo client: the BNG and the multicast router both receive the IGMP traffic. Sometimes the DSLAM can perform a proxy function on the multicast VLAN to limit the amount of IGMP data sent to the router. For example, if two people want to watch the same channel, the multicast router does not need to receive both requests on its multicast VLAN; one is sufficient, so the DSLAM suppresses the second function. This proxy function is described in the section "IGMP Proxy" in Chapter 3, "Designing a Triple-Play Backbone."

Earlier in this section, a scenario was described in which the multicast VLAN needed to be the same router as the unicast one. This is for a feature called reverse OIF mapping. It involves somewhat of a role reversal of the packet flow from the one described earlier. The RG sends IGMP traffic to the BNG without modification or proxying by the DSLAM. Based on the packet's source IP address, the BNG can determine which subscriber it relates to and can therefore adjust the unicast shaping rate accordingly. This architecture is somewhat less flexible than the previous one because it means that the same router that delivers unicast must also be used to transmit multicast. The scaling properties of the second scenario are slightly worse in theory because many IGMP packets are concentrated on a single interface rather than distributed across the router, which could affect the scaling of some vendor software implementations.

Figure 8.19 shows the steps involved with a forward OIF map. The RG sends an IGMP request up both the PPPoE and IPoE session.

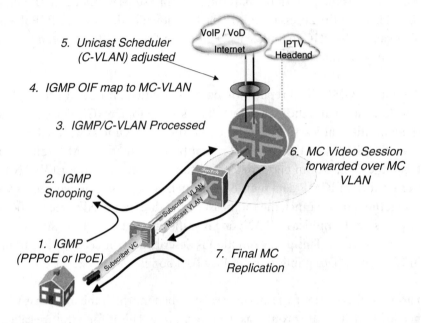

Figure 8.19 The processes involved in OIF bandwidth adjustment.

OIF mapping, shown in step 4, is a way to integrate a multicast VLAN with a BNG, which uses a separate VLAN to multicast for subscriber data. Each subscriber could have its own VLAN, or a common VLAN could be reserved for a unicast data service. In either case, if IGMP traffic is signaled in the subscriber session but multicast data needs to be sent in a separate VLAN, OIF mapping can reroute the requested group out the common multicast interface. Usually a BNG also makes an automatic best-effort shaper adjustment to account for the multicast group that the CPE receives. If multicast transmission is handled by a different router than the BNG, OIF mapping can still apply. Rather than the BNG sending the multicast group out a common interface and making the per-subscriber QoS adjustment, it can make the OIF mapping to a null interface, which signifies that an external router is handling multicast transmission. The QoS adjustment is still made on the BNG, but the external router deals with IGMP traffic on each VLAN and sends the groups as needed.

If DSLAMs are directly connected to the BNG, it does not make sense to have an external router for multicast connected to the DSLAM. One link (or links if redundant connectivity is used) can carry both unicast and multicast traffic.

Centralized BNG with Service VLANs

The preceding section explained QoS from the perspective of a C-VLAN and S-VLAN architecture. If DSLAMs are connected directly to the BNG, a C-VLAN per subscriber simply can be used. This section covers strategies for deploying an effective QoS architecture in a service VLAN environment while still maintaining a centralized subscriber management ethos. One thing obviously absent from a service VLAN is a logical Layer 2 identifier such as a C-VLAN per subscriber, which previously made it easy to tie a DSL port shaper to a logical interface. In a service VLAN environment, as soon as someone logs in to the network, shapers are tied to the session. Without some extra protocol help, it still is not possible to know what port a subscriber is connected to. With this extra identification, more sophisticated QoS features can be applied to the session. As described in the section "VLAN Architecture: Service VLAN" in Chapter 4, option 82 for DHCP and PPPoE intermediate agent (referred to as PPPoE+ by Huawei) are the protocol enhancements to tell the BNG which DSL port the subscriber is connected to. For a PPPoE environment, during the subscriber authentication phase the RADIUS server can return the subscriber QoS profile in the Access-Accept packet for a PPPoE session. In a DHCP environment, a more sophisticated BNG can dynamically apply QoS profiles to subscriber sessions when they receive a lease from the DHCP server.

In a service VLAN environment, instead of a C-VLAN shaper representing the Layer 2 path to the customer, the QoS profile is attached to the subscriber's Layer 3 interface. Cisco IOS calls this the virtual access interface, and Juniper JUNOSe uses the term IP interface. The VLAN is the identifier for all traffic that is associated with a particular DSLAM and should be shaped in the BNG before it is sent to the aggregation network. Figure 8.20 shows the interaction between a PPPoE intermediate agent and a QoS configuration for each subscriber. DHCP could equally be used with option 82 in this architecture.

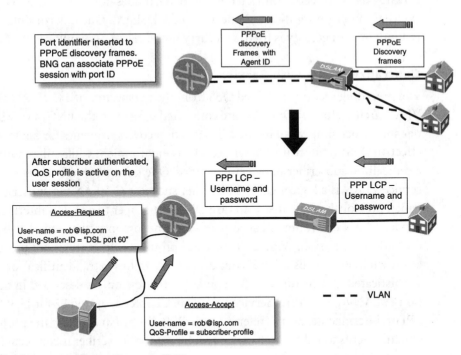

Figure 8.20 A centralized BNG with a service VLAN.

DISTRIBUTED BNGs

The traditional distributed model of running each service VLAN to a separate router competes for popularity with the 1:1 approach in Ethernet-centric triple-play networks. This section covers the service VLAN architecture, but using a more centralized approach.

The premises behind distributing services to different routers are discussed in Chapter 4, so the focus here is how it affects a quality of service implementation. When splitting services to different routers, the single aggregation point for a DSL subscriber's services is the DSLAM. By its very nature, a distributed network can only realistically make effective QoS enforcement as close to the customer as possible compared to the centralized model, where everything is done on the BNG. A similar example of such an architecture is shown in Figure 4.16 of Chapter 4, where Internet traffic is sent to a traditional BNG. VoD and multicast IPTV data come from one or more separate routers. Finally, VoIP data are on a separate VLAN that runs to a Session Border Controller (SBC) for specialized metering and firewall functions designed specifically for VoIP traffic. Each of these routers marks packets with DiffServ markings according to the type of packet, such as DiffServ 46 for VoIP. 802.1P fields are also populated to indicate the preferred treatment to downstream switches and DSLAMs.

In high-bandwidth Ethernet networks, some providers are not very interested in dynamic service edges. Hence, simple switch-based edges are sufficient from a QoS perspective until the link utilization starts encroaching on important services. A simple prioritization mechanism between various services with a medium-sized buffer on the access device works satisfactorily for transient bursts, too. But perhaps the customers frequently cause congestion on their access link (such as a DSL line with one or more streaming HDTV video channels, simultaneous VoIP calls, and data downloads). In that case, a more sophisticated approach including deeper buffers, WRED, and hierarchical QoS offers a more feature-rich alternative.

ANCP AND THE ACCESS NETWORK

Much of the discussion in this chapter has focused on making sure the edge network elements are aware of the access speed link to the customer. In most cases, providers like the flexibility of having a way to dynamically update the BNG and user database when some attribute in the access network changes, such as the synchronization speed of a DSL line. In the centralized model the BNG needs this information to shape traffic before it reaches the DSLAM for a DSL service or the optical line termination (OLT) for a broadband Passive Optical Network (PON). Why have a dynamic method in the first place? Why not have the access line configured statically? The main reason is because of the effects of line noise inducing errors in adjacent lines carrying DSL signals. A DSL line can adapt itself by lowering its synchronization speed when the number of errors in a subcarrier becomes too great. A lower synchronization speed is less susceptible to induced errors. For an access technology that is not subject to electromagnetic interference, such as PON links, the protocol described in this section—Access Node Control Protocol (ANCP)—is not as important.

At the time of writing, ANCP was defined in draft-ietf-ancp-protocol[8] and was at version 0 of the draft. By the time this book is on the shelves, this should be updated to either an RFC or a new draft. This protocol is built on General Switch Management Protocol (GSMP) version 3, which is a way to control and report switch configuration, which can include DSL switches, too. In an ANCP context, the DSLAM establishes an out-of-band (OOB) TCP communications channel with the BNG and sends attributes about a subscriber line, such as various upstream and downstream rates, interleave delay, port type, and OAM status. If any of these values change, the new attributes are sent to the BNG, even if the DSL port does not reset from a retrain.

Because the communications channel is OOB, when the DSLAM sends a message about a specific port to the BNG, there needs to be configuration on the router so that it can associate port details from ANCP messages with the physical port to which the subscriber is attached. The DSLAM is configured to send the subscriber details with its chassis ID and the subscriber's slot and port. Usually there is some degree of flexibility in how the identification string is structured. In broadband environments where each customer subinterface is statically configured on the BNG, the ANCP port identification string can be entered as part of the router configuration. In environments where subinterfaces are created dynamically on the router based on the incoming Ethernet VLAN or ATM VPI/VCI numbers, an embedded DHCP option 82 or PPPoE intermediate agent string can provide the necessary linkage between ANCP and the port details.

One of the benefits of this capability is that a BNG can dynamically update its QoS configuration based on port status messages from DSLAMs. So if a line dropped from 16Mbps to 10Mbps, the BNG can update its shaping configuration to match the new port speed without reauthenticating the subscriber. Depending on the implementation, the BNG might need to send a RADIUS request for the new QoS shaping parameters or make the QoS adjustment locally itself. In either case, the end result is the same. To make sense of how these pieces fit together, Figures 8.21 and 8.22 show the first step of a CPE synchronizing with the DSLAM and, as part of the PPPoE protocol exchange, an intermediate agent (IA) identifier being embedded in discovery packets. Simultaneously, the

---

[8] http://www.ietf.org/internet-drafts/draft-ietf-ancp-protocol-00.txt

DSLAM sends the port details to the BNG containing the same string as the IA. This mode is called QoS Rate-Adaptive Mode (RAM).

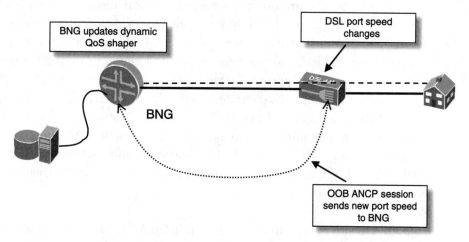

Figure 8.21 The first step in the ANCP process—informing the BNG of the initial DSL port speed.

Figure 8.22 shows the second step of the router making a dynamic QoS adjustment to the subscriber's shaper based on a new port speed message it received.

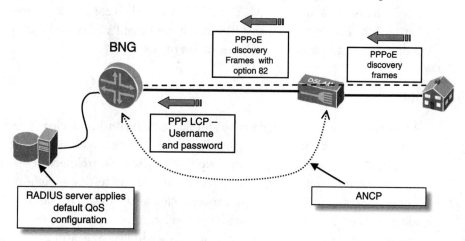

Figure 8.22 The second step in the ANCP process—dynamically updating the subscriber's port speed in the BNG.

Because ANCP is still a new protocol, it is not yet widely supported in DSLAMs. To communicate port speed information to the BNG from the DSLAM without ANCP, the DSLAM can add the port speed to PPPoE discovery frames or DHCP packets. This works in a similar way to embedding the subscriber port designator with PPPoE IA or DHCP option 82. Support for this mechanism is more widespread than ANCP due to common support of PPPoE IA or DHCP option 82. The downside of this approach is that port speed and status (such as interleaving and encapsulation) can be communicated only at the start of a PPPoE session or DHCP lease (in the case of a centralized DHCP infrastructure). Any line speed changes can be communicated to the BNG only when the PPPoE session restarts. Or, in the case of DHCP, any embedded line speed information needs to get from the DHCP server, which receives lease renew packets, to the BNG, which can make use of the line information.

ANCP can also be used to control switches. On ATM-based DSLAMs, BNGs sometimes used ANCP to set up the correct multicast forwarding state on the DSLAM. For example, if ATM DSLAMs were multicast-aware on the upstream network-facing side, a PVC usually would be dedicated to each group. When a subscriber joins a group, the BNG can perform a CAC function and then send an ANCP message to the DSLAM. The DSLAM would create a cross-connect between the upstream multicast PVC and a multicast PVC on the local loop. This is one such example of an implementation of ANCP.

SUMMARY

As shown in this chapter, QoS is no simple topic. It consumes a lot of resources during a network's design and operational phases. The topics in this chapter—classification, scheduling, queuing, rate-limiting, sample architectures—put you in good stead to apply these concepts in designing and testing a triple-play network. The configuration examples also go a long way toward explaining the sometimes dark art known as quality of service. A lot depends on the type of access architecture, whether it is N:1 or 1:1, distributed or centralized. In terms of QoS, there are some implications when choosing between N:1 and 1:1, but the differences are more prominent when comparing distributed centralized architectures. A distributed network has QoS enforcement points at the edge of the network—typically the DSLAM or switch. It is less likely to have such sophisticated and dynamic shaping and scheduling features as a BNG, so there could be some loss of functionality for future services that a provider wants to deploy.

Vendors are continually devising new and innovative QoS-related features designed for multiplay networks. Vendors also want to help operators deploy more dynamic services that require less configuration on their routers, to increase revenue and act as market differentiators. Most of these are to better support DSL Forum document TR-59—QoS adjustment due to IGMP requests and hierarchical shaping. This document is a popular reference for any provider that is serious about its triple-play QoS environment.

THE FUTURE OF WIRELESS BROADBAND

From the first single-cell mobile telephone services in the 1940s through today's second-generation, third-generation, and beyond mobile telephone services, wireless voice service has been and still is one of the most convenient and widely used means of modern communication. Wireless mobile networks are deployed in more than 120 countries around the globe by more than 200 operators. By 2006, there were nearly 2.5 billion mobile telephone subscribers worldwide. This number is expected to surpass 3.7 billion by 2010, when it's predicted that more than 40% of handsets will be 3G-capable. This trend is supported by the 65 million Wideband Code Division Multiple Access (WCDMA) subscribers served globally as of May 2006, indicating a rapid pace of growth that started with the first 3G WCDMA deployment at NTT DoCoMo in late 2002. Wireless service provider revenue is anticipated to surpass wireline revenue in 2007.[1]

The rapid adoption of wireless service worldwide over the past two decades (see Figure 9.1) has grown nearly in parallel with the adoption and expansion of the Internet (see Figure 9.2). As the Internet has grown and brought the Internet Protocol (IP) further into the mainstream in both enterprise and residential marketplaces, large numbers of users have grown dependent on its ubiquitous presence. The combination of the Internet's success and wireless mobile communications has presented an enormous opportunity to offer integrated "fixed/

[1] Source: marketresearch.com, Wireless Intelligence

wireless" services. This integration gives users access to the same types of services, seamlessly, over both fixed or wireline media, as well as wireless networks.

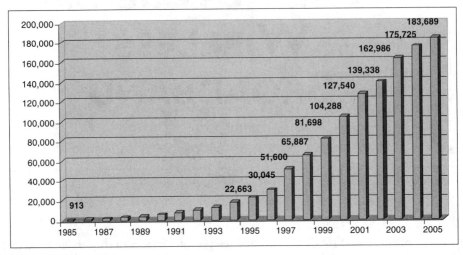

Figure 9.1 U.S. cell site growth trend.

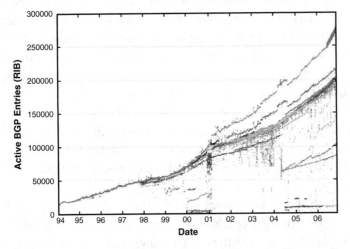

Figure 9.2 Border Gateway Protocol (BGP) table growth trend. (Source: http://bgp.potaroo.net/)

The wireless network has already taken advantage of new wideband codecs with up to 8kHz of fidelity, affording better sound quality to mobile phones than possible on legacy wireline phones with 3.1kHz of fidelity. In the past, wireless phone users were accustomed to lower voice quality in exchange for mobility. With new and advancing codecs, this has changed. Users are now getting used to equal or better wireless voice quality than they can find on wireline phones. As codecs and other features develop over time, wireless subscribers are upgrading their handsets more often, which allows for the easy introduction of new services.

ROAD MAP TO WIRELESS BROADBAND

Mechanisms for mobile wireless broadband were defined many years ago, but they have only recently gained mainstream interest and adoption by mobile wireless operators. Wideband wireless applications have evolved substantially over recent years due to advances in radio frequency (RF) interfaces and backhaul networks, driven by a growing market demand for media-independent ubiquitous services. End users demand the same applications and expect the same level of quality for both fixed/wireline and wireless networks.

IMT-2000

Much of this evolution has happened under the umbrella of the IMT-2000 (International Mobile Telecommunications 2000) specification, approved by the International Telecommunication Union (ITU) in Helsinki in 1999 as part of the ITU-R M.1457 recommendation. IMT-2000 includes five radio interfaces, which are the basis for standards-based third-generation (3G) wireless communications. The five radio interfaces are as follows (more information is provided later in this chapter):

- **IMT-DS (Direct Sequence):** Includes W-CDMA and Ultra-FDD, used in UMTS. Used in 3GPP standards.

- **IMT-TD (Time Division):** Includes TD-CDMA and TD-SCDMA (standardized by 3GPP in UMTS as Ultra-TDD HCR, Ultra-TDD LCR).

- **IMT-MC (Multi-Carrier):** Known as CDMA2000, next generation of 2G CDMA (IS-95). Used in 3GPP2 standards.

- **IMT-SC (Single Carrier):** Known as Universal Wireless Communications (UWC) and implemented as part of Enhanced Data rates for Global System for Mobile Communications (GSM) Evolution (EDGE).

- **IMT-FT (Frequency Time):** Known as Digital Enhanced Cordless Telecommunications (DECT).

These are all separate systems, requiring either separate mobile stations (MSs) (handsets or dual-mode radios) using different technologies. There are also other wireless broadband radio interfaces and technologies that are not part of IMT-2000, which include specifications such as 802.11 (WLAN), 802.16 (WiMax), Ultra Wide Band (UWB), ZigBee for wireless personal-area networks (WPANs) as defined in 802.15.4, and various satellite interfaces, among others. A common characteristic seen across many of the better wireless standards road maps is "harmonization." Good standards are often extensible, including provisions that allow for integration with different technologies in the future. Examples of this harmonization can be seen throughout this chapter. Some examples are the IP Multimedia Subsystem (IMS) architecture, which creates a standardized service platform that can be used by terminals equipped with disparate access technologies, Fixed Mobile Convergence (FMC) solutions, and others that can be found in the following sections.

Although the ITU provided 3G radio specifications through IMT-2000 (also called IMT-3G), further work is required to provide architectural standardization, thereby permitting vendors and operators to implement globally standard 3G networks. This standardization work has happened in two major bodies: 3GPP (Third-Generation Partnership Project), which produces specifications based on an evolved GSM system, now known as UMTS; and 3GPP2, which produces specifications based on IS-95, now known as CDMA2000. Figure 9.3 shows the evolution of these standards. It's also noteworthy that these standards will evolve toward the marriage of 3GPP LTE and CDMA2000 EVDO Rev C in the future, where both standards will strive to use the same channel bandwidths and achieve similar data rates.

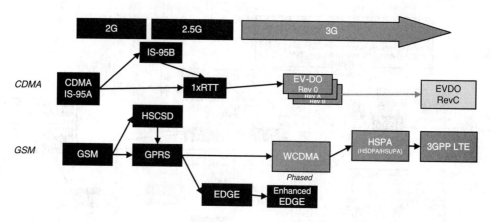

Figure 9.3 CDMA and GSM paths from 2G to 3G.

GSM EVOLUTION/3GPP

The 3GPP collaborative agreement was formed in December 1998 to facilitate cooperation between the previously disparate standards groups: ETSI (European Telecommunications Standards Institute), ANSI (U.S.), ARIB/TTC (Japan), CCSA, ATIS, and TTA (Korea). The 3GPP standards were based on the original ETSI GSM specification, dominant in Asia Pacific and Europe. GSM accounts for nearly 65% of global mobile phone subscribers. GSM-based data services took their roots as Circuit-Switched Data (CSD) in the early GSM specifications dating back to 1991 and 1992, where a single Gaussian Minimum Shift Keying (GMSK) modulated GSM timeslot was entirely consumed for data transmission. This provided users with a 9.6kbps data service. Higher-speed service could be delivered via High-Speed Circuit-Switched Data (HSCSD), which simply tied together four GSM timeslots, allowing users about 50kbps and consuming four radio timeslots per connection MS. This is depicted in the GSM evolution shown in Figure 9.4.

Connection-oriented CSD services generally are not the most efficient way to use a scarce resource (such as the RF constrained radio interface) to transmit IP packet-based data. They occupy an entire GSM radio timeslot, even when no

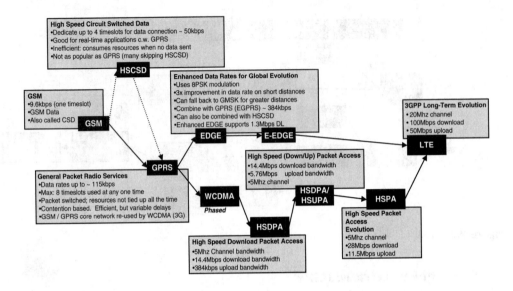

Figure 9.4 ETSI GSM path to WCDMA.

data or small amounts of data are being transferred. Many IP applications are "bursty" in nature and can gain large efficiencies through statistical multiplexing, which can be accomplished through packet switching. With packet-switched communications, the network delivers a data packet only when the need arises. Thus, for packet-switched radio interfaces, one radio channel can be shared between several mobile devices simultaneously, allowing much more efficient use of the radio interface and frequency spectrum.

General Packet Radio Service (GPRS) gives GSM users direct IP network access while achieving significantly higher spectral efficiency than previously available circuit-switched data services. GPRS affords individual users data rates over 100kbps and does so using a statistically multiplexed packet-switched radio interface that consumes a maximum of eight timeslots shared by multiple end users. Although efficient higher bandwidth per end user can be provided via GPRS, contention and congestion on the radio interface cause higher and sometimes variable delays. This means that although GPRS is useful for many "burst-tolerant" applications (e-mail, file transfers, web browsing), "interactive" types of IP applications (VoIP, streaming video, Push to Talk) can be less forgiving on a GPRS connection.

The next step in the GSM-based evolution was EDGE. EDGE modified the radio link modulation scheme from GMSK to a phased-shift keying modulation scheme, 8 Quadrature Phased Shift Keying (8QPSK). This high-order PSK modulation allows multiple bits to be encoded per symbol transmitted while also minimizing bit error rates. This gave a throughput increase of at least 3 times that of GSM GMSK while still using the same radio bandwidth. EDGE in combination with GPRS, known as E-GPRS, can deliver single user data rates over 300kbps. It's also possible to combine 8QPSK with HSCSD to provide dedicated high-speed circuit-switched connections over the same air interface.

The 3GPP standards are specified in releases, which are used to describe both the baseline network architecture and its evolution. The 3GPP architecture provides a transition platform (established in the form of 3GPP Release 98, which describes a pre-3G baseline GSM architecture that the preceding releases build on) or evolution path for GSM-based wireless networks. This architecture and evolution include the wireless "air interfaces" as well as the terrestrial access network and support systems, providing a path for operators and vendors to evolve their networks toward Universal Mobile Telecommunications System (UMTS) in phases. One of the benefits of this approach is that it is accomplished through incremental changes, tracked in 3GPP "releases" that minimize the disruptiveness and costs associated with the evolution:

- **Release 98:** Establishes a pre-3G GSM network baseline.
- **Release 99:** Specifies first UMTS 3G networks and incorporates CDMA air interface.
- **Release 4:** Adds features including an all-IP UMTS Terrestrial Radio Access Network (UTRAN) streaming packet (PS)-based MMS service. Splits CS into separate bearer and control.
- **Release 5:** Adds IMS (see the section "IMS") and HSDPA, end-to-end QoS, and SIP-based services.

- **Release 6:** Integrates WLAN, adds HSUPA and MBMS, and adds enhanced IMS features such as Push-to-Talk and GAN.
- **Release 7:** Efforts to provide better QoS (lower latency, jitter). Adds Voice Call Continuity (VCC), additional Fixed/Mobile Convergence (FMC) features, and HSPA+.
- **Release 8:** Currently under development.

UMTS utilizes a wideband CDMA (W-CDMA) or time-division CDMA (TD-CDMA) radio access interface to provide high-bandwidth (up to 11Mbps) services to mobile stations in phases, as described in the phased 3GPP releases. At the time of writing, carriers are already deploying the next phase of 3GPP radio interfaces: HSDPA. HSDPA allows for download user data rates of up to 14.4Mbps using a 5MHz-wide channel. More detailed information about HSDPA can be found in the section "HSDPA/HSUPA" near the end of this chapter.

CDMA EVOLUTION/3GPP2

The 3GPP2 collaboration dates back to 1998 during early IMT-2000 discussions. It was formed to define third-generation (3G) specifications and standards for non-GSM-based mobile telecommunications systems that were based on CDMA. The 3GPP2 effort consists of five Standards Development Organizations (SDOs) that collaboratively develop 3G CDMA specifications. The five SDOs that make up the 3GPP2 effort are ARIB (Association of Radio Industries and Businessmen, Japan), CCSA (China Communications Standards Association), TIA (Telecommunications Industry Association, North America), TTA (Telecommunications Technology Association, Korea), and TTC (Telecommunications Technology Committee, Japan).

3GPP2 specifications are produced by the project's four Technical Specification Groups (TSGs), which consist of representatives from each of the project's member companies. These groups are TSG-A (Access Network Interfaces), TSG-C (CDMA2000), TSG-S (Services and Systems Aspects), and TSG-X (Core Networks). Each of the TSGs reports to a centralized 3GPP2 steering committee that guides the overall development effort.

Early CDMA IS-95A data service was provided through IS-95A, based on the original interim standard (IS) developed by Qualcomm. This is also known by the Qualcomm brand name "cdmaOne" and is often referred to as the primary 2G CDMA technology.

Code Division Multiplexing (CDM) is a multiplexing scheme based on the mathematical properties of orthogonality. By dividing channels with "code" markers, rather than by time or frequency (such as in TDMA or FDMA), CDMA can achieve high spectral efficiency. The original IS-95A, based on the IS-95 standard developed in 1995 for the North American PCS 1900MHz band, could support voice and data traffic channels up to 14400 bits per second. A follow-on phase, IS-95B, gave a user access to multiple code channels simultaneously, thereby increasing the traffic channel throughput to between 64kbps and 115kbps. However, this was not widely deployed, because most operators opted for 1xRTT instead.

1x Radio Transmission Technology (1xRTT, or 1x for short) was the first generation of the CDMA2000 air interface to reach wide deployment. It occupies a single pair of 1.25MHz radio channels. The first 1xRTT revision offered more traffic channels than IS-95, which resulted in more voice and data capacity. 1xRTT Revision 0 was typically deployed for 144kbps per user, although it could support higher rates. 1xRTT can also coexist with IS-95, allowing for easy deployment and migration because it uses the same core network as IS-95 and the air interfaces do not interfere. With the next release of 1xRTT, Revision A, more than 300kbps could be delivered across a single 1.25MHz channel. These channels could also be combined, allowing mobile operators to offer 3xRTT services (three 1.25MHz radio channels).

The next step in the evolution of CDMA2000 to be deployed is known as Evolution Data Optimized CDMA, or 1xEV-DO. EV-DO is an evolution of CDMA2000 1xRIT, with high data rate (HDR) capabilities added and a TDMA component added below the code division layer. The EV-DO air interface is documented in IS-856. Revision 0 EV-DO supports data rates of up to 2.5Mbps toward the user and about 154kbps up. Revision 0 EV-DO is generally classified as a 3G technology. Revision A, which was being deployed in North America in 2006, can support up to 3.1Mbps downlink and 1.8Mbps in the opposite direction over the same 1.25MHz channels. In the future, EVDO Revisions B and C will expand the radio channel bandwidth to 5MHz and increase user data rates to 14.7Mbps down/4.7Mbps up and 100Mbps down/50Mbps up, respectively. These channel bandwidth and user data rates are comparable to 3GPP's Long-Term Evolution (LTE). Figure 9.5 shows the CDMA evolution.

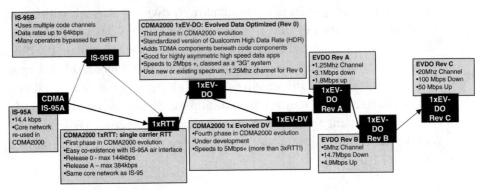

Figure 9.5 CDMA evolution to CDMA2000.

WIRELESS ACCESS NETWORK BASICS

Both 3GPP- and 3GPP2-based systems are built on a collection of components, organized into a core network. This section is intended to familiarize you with some of the general principles common to different types of wireless networks (3GPP- and 3GPP2-based). Figure 9.6 illustrates the basic components of a wireless core network:

- The Radio Access Network (RAN) services the radio interface to end users (called mobile stations [MS]).

- Terrestrial Access Network, known as the UMTS Terrestrial Radio Access Network (UTRAN) for UMTS and GSM EDGE Radio Access Network (GERAN) for EDGE. This is also referred to as the "core" network. This functionally is divided into two logical segments. One is the circuits, switching and routing elements. The other is the various supporting systems, databases, and network elements:

- Packet Core (PS) for packet-based services

- Circuit Core (CS) for circuit-based services

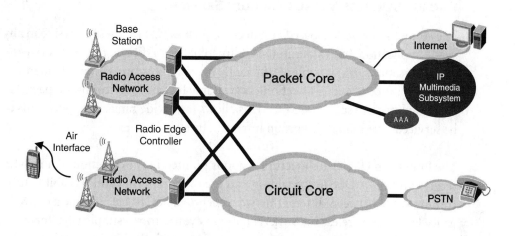

Figure 9.6 Common mobile network functional components.

An MS connects over the air to a local Base Station Controller (BSC), which then sends traffic into the terrestrial core toward its final destination. This can be done via circuit switching to the PSTN, other mobile users, or a packet network such as the Internet.

Although the end result functionality is roughly analogous, different terminology is used to describe the elements and functions of the various components of the mobile core network depending on the type of network (UMTS or CDMA2000). These are described in Table 9.1.

Table 9.1 3GPP Versus 3GPP2 Terminology

Terminology	3GPP (WCDMA/UMTS)	3GPP2 (CDMA2k/1x)
Base station	Node-B	BTS
Base station controller	RNC	BSC
Circuit edge device	MSC/MGW	MSC
Packet edge device	SGSN, GGSN	PDSN

PACKET SERVICES VERSUS CIRCUIT SERVICES

The strength of a packet-based architecture such as UMTS does not reside in any single application, but rather in the ability to deliver a diverse range of services and applications. It's possible to efficiently deliver both connection-oriented (constant bit rate) and connectionless (variable bit rate) services over a packet-based architecture such as UMTS. This allows for a wide range of applications to be serviced over a single common infrastructure.

The long-term UMTS architecture vision is pointed in the direction of an all-IP service evolution. Due to the widespread use of the Internet and IP's ability to communicate between different network technologies, IP has become a convergence layer that wireless networks can use to evolve from a simple voice/data access platform to a larger structure for services. With IP's ability to provide circuit-like services (through signaling and quality of service) in parallel with a whole new range of applications, IP is in a position to lead mobile communications into new directions and dimensions.

There are many inherent advantages to using packet switching in the wireless network, from enhanced mobility, the efficiency of statistical multiplexing for dealing with bursty traffic, security aspects, and simplified interoperability to convergence with other IP applications and services. This is causing a phased shift from legacy circuit services in wireless networks toward packet. The IP protocol is allowing service providers and operators to develop new and innovative services while enhancing their existing infrastructure. One of the main drivers of IP services is the range of new multimedia applications in addition to basic IP telephony.

A packet-based core network is also a platform on which advanced signaling systems and protocols can run, such as IMS (described later in this chapter) and Session Initiation Protocol (SIP). SIP is an IETF application layer control signaling protocol used to create, manipulate, and terminate sessions between one or more participants. These sessions can be between two or more participants; can be audio, video, or other data service-based; and can be either real-time or non-real-time in nature. SIP allows a great amount of flexibility in how sessions are controlled. For example, both calling and called peers can specify exactly where calls should be connected. SIP also allows session redirection and user location tracking, and it is standards-based and easy to implement by IP developers. SIP also has flexible support for session establishment and termination, which happens in five phases: user location, user capabilities, user availability, call setup, and call handling. More of SIP's capabilities are explored throughout the remainder of this chapter.

GPRS SYSTEM

Because 3GPP standards are based on an evolved GPRS network, Figure 9.7 depicts the basic entities and interfaces that make up a GPRS system. Table 9.2 describes each component and its function.

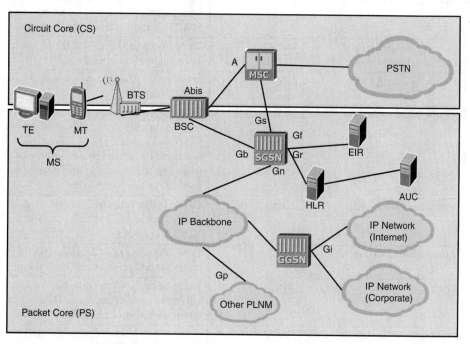

Figure 9.7 Baseline GPRS network topology.

Table 9.2 GPRS Network Elements and Functionality

System Name	Acronym or Abbreviation	Function
Terminal Equipment	TE	End-user terminal (computer, PDA, laptop) that transmits and receives packets.
Mobile Terminal	MT	The MT communicates with a TE that it serves, and over the air to the BTS. The MT is associated with a GSM subscriber.
Mobile Station	MS	The combined functionality of a TE and MT.
Base Station System	BSS	Consists of a Base Station Controller (BSC) and a Base Transceiver System (BTS).
Base Transceiver System	BTS	Provides all radio-related functions.
Base Station Controller	BSC	Separates MS-originated circuit-switched calls from packet data before forwarding CS calls to the MSC/VLR and PS data to the SGSN.
Gateway Mobile Services Switching Center	GMSC	Routes incoming CS calls to the MSC where the MS is currently registered.
Mobile Switching Center	MSC	Performs telephony circuit-switching functions for GSM CS calls.
Visitor Location Register	VLR	Database that contains information about all MSs that are currently in the MSC location area or SGSN routing area. The SGSN contains the VLR functionality for packet-switched communications. The VLR can be an integrated component in the MSC as well for CS calls.
Home Location Register	HLR	Database that contains information about every subscriber that has service from the given GSM/GPRS operator.
Authentication Center	AUC	GSM entity that provides authentication and ciphering functionality for GSM mobile stations.
Equipment Identity Register	EIR	Database that contains information about mobile equipment, which can be used to block calls from stolen, defective, or unauthorized MSs.
Serving GPRS Support Node	SGSN	A primary component in the GSM/GPRS network. The SGSN forwards IP packets addressed to/from an MS within the SGSN service area between the BSC and GGSN. Also handles GPRS ciphering, authentication, session management, mobility management, MS logical link management, and billing output.

System Name	Acronym or Abbreviation	Function
Gateway GPRS Support Node	GGSN	A primary component in the GSM/GPRS network. The GGSN tracks GPRS sessions, associates subscribers (MS) with the appropriate SGSN, generates billing data, and forwards IP packets between MS and external networks.
Air interface	Um	GSM Radio interface
GSM interface	A, Abis	Legacy GSM interface
GPRS interface	G(x)	GPRS packet interfaces

3GPP STRUCTURE

The 3GPP collaborative agreement was formed in December 1998 to facilitate cooperation between previously disparate standards groups: ETSI (European Telecommunications Standards Institute), ANSI (U.S.), ARIB/TTC (Japan), CCSA, ATIS, and TTA (Korea). The 3GPP is an organization of working groups that develops 3G standards and specifications.

The 3GPP organization is overseen by the Project Coordination Group (PCG), under which various Technical Specification Groups (TSGs) report. The PCG provides oversight and steering, manages timelines, coordinates partnerships, and performs other project management functions. Each TSG is responsible for developing, approving, and maintaining technical specifications within its reference. TSGs can also organize into working groups and liaise with other working groups as needed.

Figure 9.8 shows the organization of 3GPP TSGs as of September 2005.

The technical specifications produced by the TSGs follow a very specific naming convention. It is used to denote the series, maturity, relevance to 3G, GSM, or combined systems and type of document (service description, architectural, or protocol specification). The 3GPP naming scheme is shown in Figure 9.9.

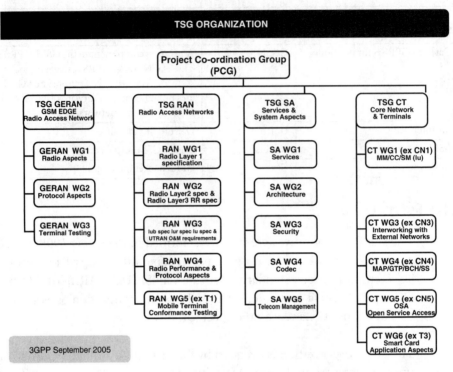

Figure 9.8 3GPP Technical Specification Group hierarchy as of September 2005.

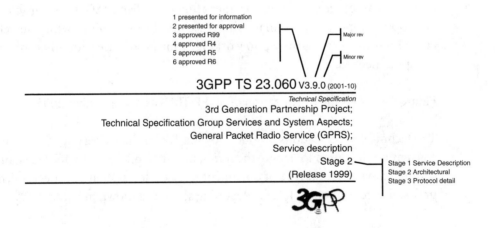

Figure 9.9 3GPP Technical Specification naming and numbering scheme.

3GPP ARCHITECTURE

The 3GPP architecture provides a platform for a number of advanced converged services to wireless users. This is accomplished by adding components to each 3GPP release during its evolution. As these features evolve and seamlessly interoperate on the network and device levels, the applications and services that run on them will do so as well. This means that the implementation of new platforms, devices, and applications are developing with the underlying assumption of a converged service environment, where voice services seamlessly coexist with data services such as Internet, multimedia, presence, and messaging.

3GPP Release 99 (R99) divided the wireless core into two networks: packet- and circuit-based, as shown in Figure 9.10. This created a service platform that retained compatibility with GSM (via the CS domain) and added access to high-speed data services and managed QoS. The "legacy" CS domain provides circuit-oriented services based on Mobile Switching Centers (MSCs) (later Media Gateways [MGWs]). The PS domain provides IP connectivity through the Serving GPRS Support Nodes (SGSNs) and Gateway GPRS Support Nodes (GGSNs). These two devices act as the gateways between wireless data networks and other IP networks such as the Internet or other private networks.

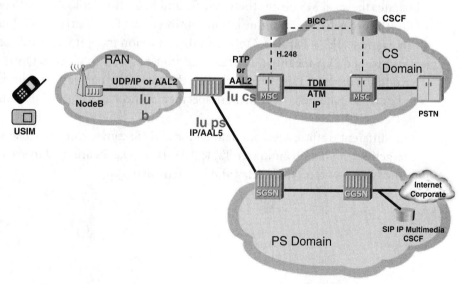

Figure 9.10 3GPP Release 99 topology.

The medium-term 3GPP vision, starting with R4 and R5, adds the capability for the IMS platform as an extension of the PS domain. This transition adds native IP support to the 3GPP interfaces (away from legacy TDM- or ATM-based). This allows the UTRAN core to be built on an MPLS network, as many carriers are beginning to do. This transition to an "all-IP" core makes IP a convergence layer that has evolved from a simple data transit layer to a larger service-enablement platform, opening a range of new wireless applications and services. This allows providers to offer a full range of IP-based multimedia applications in addition to basic telephony.

3GPP QoS

The overall 3GPP QoS concept and architecture is specified in TS 23.107. The goal of the QoS architecture is to provide end-user-perceived end-to-end QoS throughout the 3GPP system. This is accomplished through an evolution of standards that map common QoS behaviors to the various 3GPP components and interfaces. TS 23.107 specifies a set of four UMTS traffic classes that must be maintained over each bearer interface to provide end-to-end QoS. The bearers are illustrated in Figure 9.11, which depicts the UMTS QoS architecture. This includes the local MS bearer (between TE and MT), the Radio Access Network (RAN), core network, and translations for interfaces facing external endpoints (for example, IETF TSPEC). Only with this common mapping and architecture is end-to-end QoS meaningful. Many additional aspects of wireless QoS are beyond the scope of this book, including the particular per-hop, per-domain, and inter-domain behaviors that are specified in the 3GPP QoS TS documents.

Four different traffic classes are defined for UMTS: conversational, streaming, interactive, and background (see Table 9.3). These classes are used to separate traffic types based on their delay and loss sensitivity.

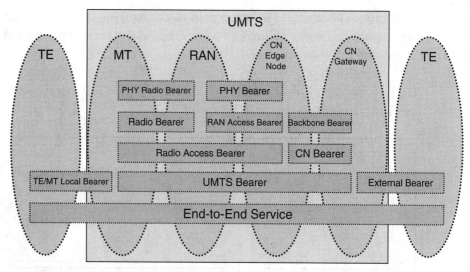

Figure 9.11 UMTS QoS architecture.

Table 9.3 UMTS Traffic Classes

Traffic Class	Conversational Class (Conversational RT)	Streaming Class (Streaming RT)	Interactive Class (Interactive Best Effort)	Background Class (Background Best Effort)
Characteristics	Preserves time relation (delay variation) and overall delay Conversational pattern (low variation and low delay)	Preserves time relation (delay variation)	Request-response traffic Preserves payload integrity	Destination is not expecting the data within a certain time Preserves payload integrity
Example	Voice	Streaming video	Web browsing	Background e-mail transfers

IMS

With the newly created packet services (PS) domain created after 3GPP R99, 3GPP networks were given a new capability to offer packet-based services in addition to legacy circuit-based services. For operators to deliver new data services, as well as equivalent legacy call services over the packet services domain, IP-based call control is required. This is where the IP Multimedia Subsystem

(IMS) fits in. It's intended to be a central component in supporting IP-based wireless services to give operators a common platform for controlling and billing for these new IP-based services.

The IMS framework abstracts the wireless network into three layers: service, control, and transport, as shown in Figure 9.12.

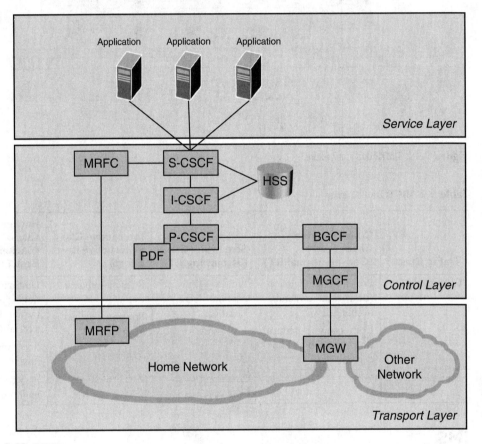

Figure 9.12 IMS layers.

The transport layer in IMS is responsible for the end user's basic access functions, such as security and media-independent interoperability, as well as basic access and transport. The transport layer is connected via elements such as Media Gateways (MGWs) to the control layer.

The control layer is where policy decision, routing, and subscriber management functions live. This layer controls the applications that reside in the service layer, meaning that IMS service applications need not be aware of details within the transport layer.

In the service layer, applications can be hosted and abstracted from the control and transport layers, thus making IMS applications extensible to any control and transport media supported by IMS.

This is accomplished through a set of IETF standardized interfaces. IMS was first defined in 1999 as part of the 3G.IP industry forum. It has since been introduced into the 3GPP standards group. It was first specified as part of 3GPP Release 5, where SIP-based packet services are provided. 3GPP2's CDMA2000 Multimedia Domain (MMD) platform is also based on 3GPP's IMS, with support for CDMA2000 defined.

IMS adds seamless interoperability between legacy and newer IP-based mobile services. This means, for example, that 3GPP handsets can communicate via an integrated SIP stack, allowing operators to provide native VoIP services through the PS network, with support for end-to-end QoS, roaming, security, and service continuity both intra- and inter-domain. IMS also enabled an application framework and platform that supports new converged services, allowing mobile device developers to create new applications based on the converged environment. In R6, IMS added support for WLAN interworking. Additionally, with the incorporation of TISPAN in R7, IMS becomes a platform that allows fixed/mobile convergence. IMS fundamentally strives to support the following:

- Agnostic access media: Support for fixed/mobile/wireless access media, including GPRS, UMTS, CDMA2000, WLAN, WiMax, DSL, and cable, as well as legacy circuit-switched-based services such as POTS and GSM.
- Architecture-agnostic: IMS functionality available regardless of underlying access media or architecture.
- Terminal/user mobility: Support for seamless roaming, handoffs, and so on.
- Extensive/rich IP services: VoIP, Push to Talk over Cellular (POC), messaging services, presence services, content sharing, and other native IP-based services.

One of the foundations of this new IMS-based fixed/mobile converged future rests on the abstraction of the functions of each architectural component. The multiservice all-IP core creates the basic platform on which integrated signaling and control can be developed and different access media can be accessed through media gateways. This in turn provides a path away from legacy "single-service" networks and toward an integrated multiservice platform, as shown in Figure 9.13.

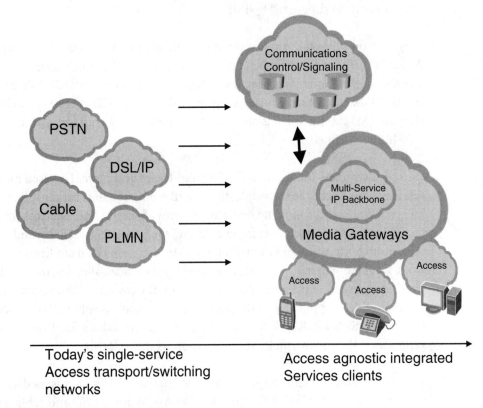

Figure 9.13 Evolution of a multiservice mobile core.

IMS ARCHITECTURE

IMS is a collection of functions interconnected via standardized interfaces. IMS functions are not necessarily implemented in dedicated devices or nodes, because functions can be grouped at the implementer's discretion. Although current networks still require legacy circuit-switched call support, initiatives such as

IMS will help operators provide all user services through the mobile packet core. Eventually, this will result in a fully packet-based core.

IMS Core Network

The IMS core network consists of a collection of entities and interfaces that connect them, as shown in Figure 9.14. The key IMS entities and their primary functions are listed in Table 9.4.

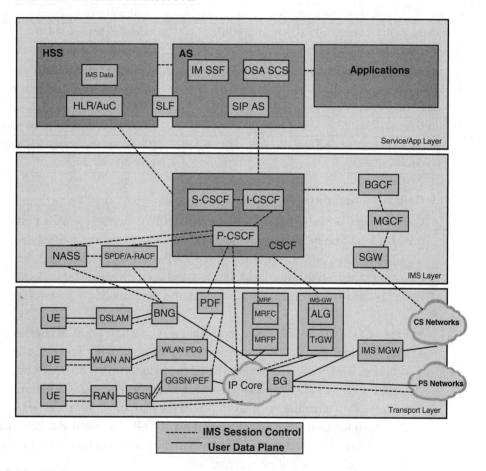

Figure 9.14 IMS core network.

Table 9.4 IMS Entities

Entity	Acronym or Abbreviation	Primary Function
Call Session Control Function	CSCF	Call control
Media Gateway Control Function	MGCF	Controls call state for connections
IP-Multimedia Media Gateway Function	IM-MGW	Terminates bearer CHs and media streams
Multimedia Resource Function Controller	MRFC	Controls media streams
Multimedia Resource Function Processor	MRFP	Controls bearers on Mb
Subscription Location Function	SLF	Queried for subscription data
Breakout Gateway Control Function	BGCF	Selects network for PSTN breakout
Application Server	AS	SIP, OSA, CAMEL server, and so on
Signaling Gateway Function	SGW	Performs signaling conversion
Security Gateway	SEG	Protects domains/enforces security
Global Text Telephony Specific Entities	GTTS-E	Routing calls through text modems
Home Subscriber Server	HSS	Master user database

Call/Session Control

Call/Session Control is handled by a series of SIP proxy/server roles that comprise the Call Session Control Function (CSCF) and that are divided into three major functions. Collectively, they process SIP signaling packets and can do so across administrative boundaries (such as between provider networks). The three functional blocks are described next and are shown in Figure 9.15:

- Proxy CSCF (P-CSCF): A SIP proxy that acts as a first point of contact for the IMS terminal. The P-CSCF is analogous to the session border controller (SBC) function. The P-CSCF is discovered by the IMS terminal through either DHCP or GPRS PDP context during registration. The P-CSCF communicates with the IMS terminal via IPsec and is in the path of all SIP messages, giving it the capability to inspect all SIP messaging. The P-CSCF can also behave as the Policy Decision Function (PDF) to authorize policy control. It is also responsible for generating billing records.

- Interrogating CSCF (I-CSCF): A SIP proxy that serves on the border between administrative domains. Used as an entry point for SIP messages into a domain.

- Serving CSCF (S-CSCF): A central SIP signaling device located in the IMS terminal's home network that both acts as SIP server and performs session control. The S-CSCF handles SIP registrations, sits along the path of all SIP signaling, decides which application servers SIP messages will be forwarded to, provides routing services, and enforces operator policy.

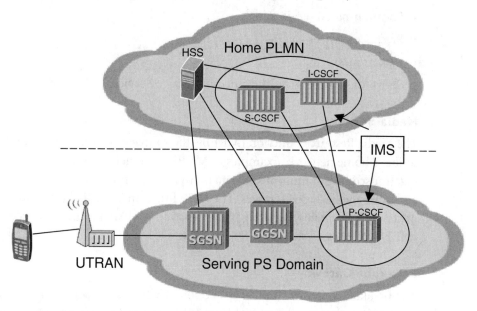

Figure 9.15 3GPP call/session control functions.

Application Servers

IMS application servers (ASs) host and execute IMS services. The S-CSCF function interfaces with each AS via SIP, creating the platform for dynamically signaled external IMS applications. Examples of application server hosted IMS services are

- Push to Talk
- Caller ID

- Call waiting
- Call forwarding
- Call holding
- Call transfer
- Lawful interception
- Conference calling
- Voice mail
- Location-based services
- Presence services
- Instant messaging
- Short Message Service/Multimedia Message Service (SMS/MMS)

Media Servers

The Media Resource Function (MRF) is the source of media content in the subscriber's home network. Examples of MRF media include multimedia conferencing, transcoding of multimedia data between different codecs, announcements, and other media-based services. The MRF function is divided into two components, with a separate signaling plane function (the MRFC) and media plane (MRFP) devices.

Breakout Gateway

The Breakout Gateway Control Function (BGCF) is a SIP server that is used for call routing when a call is placed from IMS to an end user in an external circuit switched network, such as the PSTN or PLMN.

A-IMS (Advances to IMS)

In addition to the standard 3GPP adopted IMS architecture, various industry efforts are under way to expand IMS by adding capabilities. A series of mobile operators and vendors, including Verizon Wireless, Cisco Systems, Lucent, Motorola, Nortel, and Qualcomm, are creating the A-IMS architecture, with the goal of efficient deployment of both Session Initiation Protocol (SIP) and non-SIP services.

The A-IMS effort does not currently claim to supersede the 3GPP accepted IMS architecture. Instead, it adds features such as a whole-network "Security Manager," extensions to enable the uniform treatment of SIP and non-SIP applications, dual IP address anchoring, tri-layer peering, and an approach for multitiered service interaction management. One of the goals of A-IMS is to support existing and future non-IMS applications in an IMS-aware environment. This could give users seamless access to network services, regardless of the application or network access technology.

FIXED/MOBILE CONVERGENCE (FMC)

Alongside the evolution of the 3G network, a clear trend is emerging around converged fixed-line and mobile telephony, known as Fixed/Mobile Convergence (FMC). With the alignment of the mobile, broadband, and PSTN access and signaling layers, it is possible to provide services with a single handset device that can switch between different network types in an "ad hoc" fashion. The goal is to provide end users with ubiquitous, seamlessly integrated service, regardless of how they are connected.

Mobile handset manufacturers and network operators are already beginning to address this opportunity, as seen in multimode/radio handsets and services starting to make their way to the market. Multiradio handsets that incorporate wireless and mobile radios, as well as faster processors for supporting advanced codecs, signaling protocols, and other advances, are becoming more and more common. Handsets are currently available, and further developments are occurring at a rapid pace by manufacturers such as Motorola, Nokia, and Siemens. It is in both the operator's interest, as well as the end user's, to provide service continuity and seamless handovers between access networks.

Operators are already beginning to deploy FMC products using a variety of emerging standards and proprietary solutions. Services are available from carriers such as BT (U.K.), SingTel (Singapore), T-Com (Germany), Orange (France, U.K., Netherlands, Spain, Poland); virtual operators such as Hello (Norway); and tier 2 operators such as Neuf Cegetel (France). The details of these services vary, ranging from free and reduced-rate international calling while the subscriber is connected via his or her home WLAN connection, to flexible cellular billing plans, roaming, and other capabilities.

FMC services are appealing to both wireline and wireless operators, as well as end subscribers. For the wireline operator, FMC presents an opportunity to hold on to broadband residential and enterprise subscribers, who ultimately need a wireline connection to support the local access WLAN. Wireless operators view this as an opportunity to pull users away from wireline-based voice services. End users enjoy the convenience of having a single handset and flexible billing options afforded by this type of service.

WLAN INTEGRATION

In Release 6, 3GPP specifies 802.11 (WLAN) access interface interoperability in TS 23.934. This includes the interface giving WLAN connected user terminals access to IMS services. It also allows IMS to control user access (Authentication, Authorization, and Accounting [AAA]), charging, roaming support, and other interoperability.

3GPP WLAN integration includes end-to-end subscriber authentication, which relies on USIM/SIM-based authentication mechanisms. This gives an established 3GPP subscriber access to WLAN services based on their existing subscriber relationship with a given carrier. This simplifies billing, allows for roaming, and provides a platform on which the subscriber's services (such as IMS-based services) can "follow" the subscriber regardless of whether he or she is connected via the UMTS mobile network or WLAN. The 3GPP authentication process can then be used to perform access control to a local WLAN network/local Internet connection via the WLAN.

The architecture also specifies the billing mechanism using the Charging Gateway/Charging Collection Function (CGw/CCF) and Online Charging System (OCS) entities. The AAA is supported in the backend by existing HSS/HLR/AuC subscriber records, and roaming is accomplished through a proxy AAA function between operators. The overall architecture is depicted in Figure 9.16.

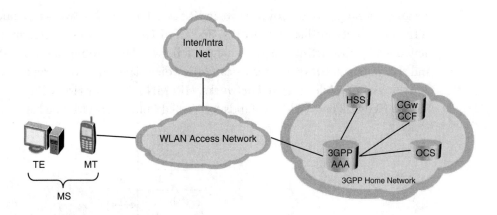

Figure 9.16 3GPP Release 6 WLAN integration topology.

DUAL-MODE HANDSET (DMH)

Imagine using a dual-radio UMTS and 802.11-capable handset to place a SIP-based VoIP or video call to another user, who is perhaps somewhere on the PSTN or another external network. When the user and handset are only within range of the 3G radio network (BTS), the UMTS SIP session is serviced over WCDMA, through the 3GPP network. Mobility on the 3GPP network normally happens between cells and is seamless to the end user. FMC seamless integration and dual-mode functionality becomes useful at the point where the user comes within range of an 802.11 WLAN access point. A handoff of the SIP session between the UMTS network and the WLAN network would be optimal for the mobile network operator, who wants to conserve WCDMA spectrum, as well as the end user, who wants to pay as little as possible for the call. This requires a substantial amount of signaling between various media gateways, routers, session border controllers, soft switches, and other elements to accomplish this handoff. This is one of the goals of fixed mobile convergence.

GENERIC ACCESS NETWORK (GAN/UMA)

The Generic Access Network (GAN) concept, formerly known as Unlicensed Mobile Access (UMA), was adopted by 3GPP for use in R6 and R7 in April 2005. It is defined in the 3GPP TS 43.318. GAN, shown in Figure 9.17, is a system that permits roaming and handover between IP-based local-area networks (including WLAN or Bluetooth-based networks) and GSM/GPRS or UMTS-based mobile networks. By abstracting the access network between the Mobile Station (MS) and the mobile network, operators can offer voice, data, and IMS services to users on both mobile and fixed networks. HPLMN stands for Home Public Land Mobile Network and VPLMN stands for Visited Public Land Mobile Network.

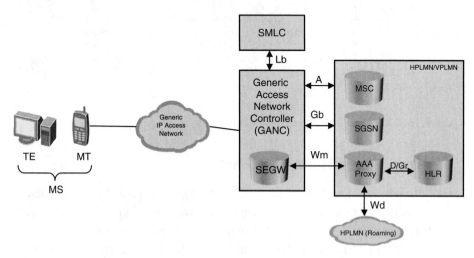

Figure 9.17 GAN architecture.

The GAN environment requires a new element, the Generic Access Network Controller (GANC), as well as new functionality in the MS. The architecture works by abstracting the connection between the MS and GANC, allowing almost any IP access network to sit between the two. Security is handled through an IPsec ESP layer established between the Security Gateway (SEGW) located within the GANC. At this point, the architecture coexists with a standard GSM/GPRS Radio Access Network (GERAN) via standard interfaces. The GANC then communicates via a standard A interface with the MSC for the CS domain and the Gb interface to the SGSN for the PS domain. To the mobile core, the GANC appears similar to a BSC, so handoff events also appear similar to a standard BSC-BSC handoff. GAN can be thought of as a means to abstract or backhaul GSM/UMTS transport over an IP network, with integrated support for security, roaming, handoffs, and billing.

SIP-Based FMC

Although GAN/UMA is available and solves the dual-mode handset handover problem at the access network layer, there is significant momentum around a parallel alternative approach: an application layer FMC architecture, based on SIP and IMS. An IMS-based solution is independent of the access network type and is therefore extensible to any access media. As illustrated earlier, in the "IMS Architecture" section, the IMS framework divides service and control functions into three layers.

The transport layer is responsible for the end user's basic access functions: security, media-independent interoperability, and basic access and transport. Connected through elements such as Media Gateways (MGWs), the transport layer is tied into the control layer. The control layer is where policy decision, routing, and subscriber management functions live. This layer controls the applications that reside in the service layer, which through this tiered model are abstracted as to what the transport layer sees. This is unlike the GAN/UMA approach, which is closely tied to the access network. With IMS, dual-mode access and other FMC services are controlled from the service/application layer. For example, an application such as VCC, which resides in the service layer, can stitch together end-to-end connections across disparate networks within the transport layer by signaling calls through a VCC anchor point.

This approach offers a substantial amount of control over FMC services. For example, beyond simple dual-mode access handovers, applications such as VCC can also move active sessions between separate devices (such as a handover between a mobile phone and a desk/home phone) and can enable sessions to be routed via the least-expensive media based on flexible policy. SIP-based call control may also have scaling advantages over other (GAN/UMA) approaches, because the VCC server only needs to handle control traffic because all media traffic is handled by the MGWs. Work is currently under way in various standards bodies, including the IETF, to define standards-based approaches to FMC (such as draft-yafan-fmc-arch-XX.txt).

VOICE CALL CONTINUITY (VCC)

Available in 3GPP Release 7, Voice Call Continuity (VCC) is specified in TS 23.206. VCC is an IMS application that provides the capability to transfer calls between the CS domain and the IMS. VCC provides for voice call origination, termination, and domain transfers from CS to IMS as well as from IMS to CS. VCC is implemented in the subscriber's home network, where calls to and from VCC User Equipment (VCC UE) are "anchored." This anchoring is used to provide voice continuity during domain transition events.

To perform domain transfers, the VCC application is aware of a number of aspects of a given user's session. The VCC UE's circuit-switched domain status (attached/detached), the VCC UE's IMS domain status (registered, deregistered), operator policy, the VCC UE's media capabilities, and the IMS media components, among other items, are collected from various 3GPP/IMS entities and are tracked for use in domain handoff decisions. Figure 9.18 illustrates a domain handoff.

VCC requires a set of additional functions and interfaces in addition to the standard 3GPPR7 entities and interfaces. These include the Domain Transfer Function (DTF), Domain Selection Function (DSF), CS Adaptation Function (CSAF), a Customized Applications for Mobile Enhanced Logic (CAMEL) service that can interact with the CSAF, and a VCC-capable user terminal, known as the Voice Call Continuity User Equipment (VCC UE).

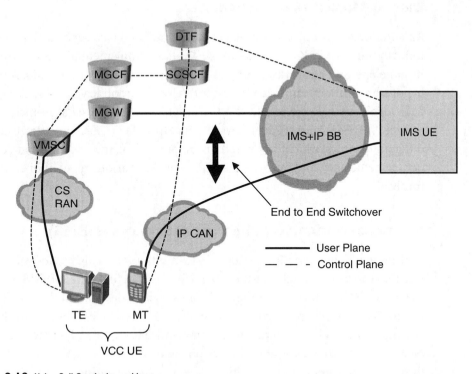

Figure 9.18 Voice Call Continuity architecture.

WIRELESS VIDEO INTEGRATION

With over 30 million subscribers worldwide currently served by 3G services, mobile broadband is today an active, tangible, billable service. However, despite its current and projected growth, there are challenges to be faced in evolving the technology. CDMA-based technologies in general are spectrally inefficient. Although QoS models are in development, true end-to-end quality of service has yet to be fully realized. When coupled with the higher latencies inherently produced in the multitiered 3G network architectures, delivering reliable, consistent, low-latency services is difficult. Despite these hurdles, wireless broadband services are increasingly in demand from various types of operators, fed by growing subscriber demand.

DIGITAL MOBILE VIDEO BROADCAST

An additional service that complements the voice and data services that operators can provide via 3G today is Mobile TV. Early implementations already exist in some operator networks; examples can be seen in Korea and Britain. A number of standards and approaches exist for delivering mobile video, including Digital Video Broadcast-Handheld (DVB-H), Multicast Broadcast Multimedia Services (MBMS), and Media Forward Link Only (FLO). Each architecture has different qualities, which vary based on factors such as spectral efficiency, core network efficiency, and business plan efficiency for various types of operators involved.

MULTICAST BROADCAST MULTIMEDIA SERVICES (MBMS)

MBMS, shown in Figure 9.19, is a point-to-multipoint media broadcasting service that can be delivered over the UMTS network architecture. MBMS became part of 3GPP in Release 6, through TS 23.246, which describes the overall architecture. The MBMS architecture supports two bearer modes—broadcast mode and multicast mode—each designed to maximize both the radio network and core network resources as efficiently as possible. The MBMS service is realized through some additional capabilities added to existing entities in the 3GPP PS domain. MBMS adds functionality to the GGSN, SGSN, UTRAN, GERAN, and UE. In addition, a new element, the BM-SC (Broadcast Multicast Service Center), is also added.

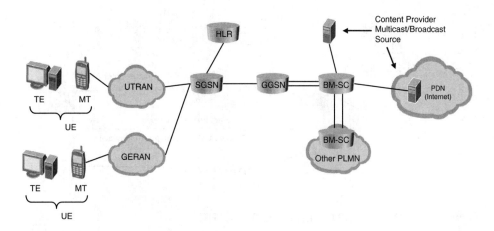

Figure 9.19 Multicast Broadcast Multimedia Services (MBMS).

DIGITAL VIDEO BROADCASTING-HANDHELD (DVB-H)

Digital Video Broadcasting-Handheld (DVB-H) is an ETSI standard for the uni-directional broadcasting of datagrams to handheld devices. It can broadcast IP datagrams, as well as other formats. DVB-H is specified in ETSI standard EN 302 304. DVB-H was designed with the specific requirements of portable and mobile (handheld) terminals in mind, such as mobility (Doppler shift compensation), low power consumption, and weight. To optimally service these types of portable devices, specific features are needed in the serving transmission system. DVB-H is also intended to be a global standard that can be used in various frequency bands, independent of other services. DVB-H supports 5MHz-wide channels, enabling its use within a wide range of licensed spectra, from a mobile wireless operator to a DVB-T broadcaster.

DVB-H, shown in Figure 9.20, is the result of a set of commercial requirements that grew out of the terrestrial DVB-T digital TV service to allow DVB operators to expand DVB broadcasts to mobile terminals. Among other things, this resulted in increased competition with conventional wireless operators. Also part of the DVB-H standard is the functionality to transport IP datagrams through the Internet Protocol Data Cast (IPDC) service. This layer adds a forward error correction layer to the top of DVB-H, which allows for more reliable transmission of IP datagrams. It is also possible to integrate DVB-T with GPRS or UMTS to allow for the reception of return traffic from properly equipped user terminals.

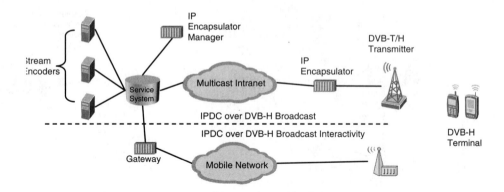

Figure 9.20 DVB-H allows DVB-T to integrate with GPRS or UMTS.

DVB-H can also be combined with a broadcaster's DVB-T network. This allows for simultaneous broadcasts to fixed terrestrial terminals and mobile terminals, sharing the same transmission network. This requires only a few changes to the standard DVB-T transmitters to support the DVB-H signaling and cell information. The actual media can be multiplexed before reaching the transmission network, allowing the two to coexist side by side (see Figure 9.21).

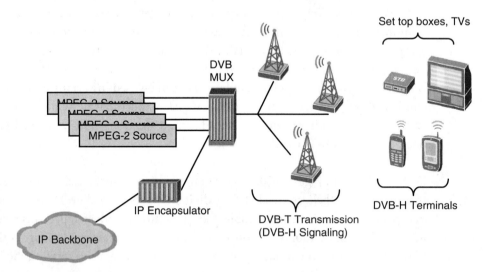

Figure 9.21 DVB multiplexing.

MEDIA FORWARD LINK ONLY (FLO)

Forward Link Only (FLO) is a system developed by Qualcomm to deliver media services to mobile terminals. It places specific emphasis on spectral efficiency, mobility, and mobile terminal power consumption. At the time of writing, in early 2007, carriers in North America (Verizon, AT&T/Cingular) and the UK (BSkyB) have begun testing and deploying MediaFLO. The major functional components of this specification are shown in Figure 9.22.

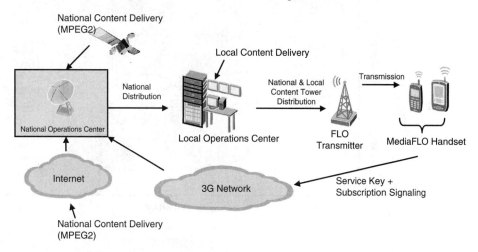

Figure 9.22 Qualcomm's media Forward Link Only (FLO) architecture.

WIRELESS BROADBAND EVOLUTION

Each generation of mobile air interface, from the original analog interfaces through today's 3G interfaces, has evolved with the goal of providing increased services while minimizing the per-bit costs the operator sees. This evolution is typically expressed in the form of higher end terminal bandwidth, decreased latency, increased spectral efficiency, and mobility.

The overall UMTS road map from GPRS takes the RAN from the legacy GSM/GPRS interfaces through WCDMA, offering end users speeds in the hundreds of kilobits to low megabits per second. This barely accomplishes performance comparable to residential DSL, and typically with much higher latencies. The next generations of wireless broadband will require bandwidth in the multimegabit to

100-megabit range, with lower and more controllable delay characteristics. The protocols that will achieve this are already in development and deployment. Figure 9.23 compares the 3G air interface road map with DSL and mobile broadcast bandwidths.

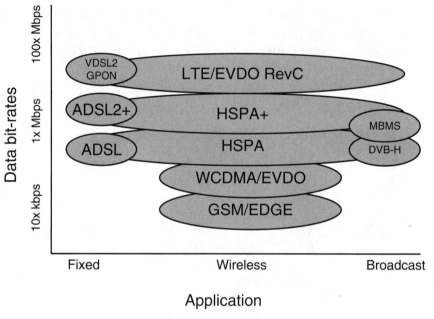

Figure 9.23 Fixed, mobile, and broadcast media bit-rate alignment.

The next generation of WCDMA-based air interfaces being deployed by many 3GPP-based operators is High-Speed Packet Access (HSPA). HSPA is a term used to describe enhancements made to the UMTS radio interfaces in 3GPP releases 5 and 6. HSPA is a generic term that refers to both the downlink and uplink interfaces, which are known separately as High-Speed Downlink Packet Access (HSDPA) and High-Speed Uplink Packet Access (HSUPA).

Initial HSPA implementations are focused on HSDPA, which allows downlink transmission speeds at rates up to 14Mbps. It can be implemented within the standard 5MHz carrier used in UMTS networks, allowing HSDPA to coexist with first-generation UMTS networks, available since 3GPP Release 99. Because the HSPA standards deal with only the air interface, no changes are needed in the core network infrastructure, other than any increased capacity required to handle the new HSPA traffic. Early HSDPA deployments have shown round-trip latency in the 60ms range, which should increase VoIP and other real-time application performance.

HSDPA/HSUPA

HSDPA works by establishing a shared high-speed downlink channel, known as the High-Speed Downlink Shared Channel (HS-DSCH), which is shared between multiple users. Using fast scheduling techniques, the HS-DSCH is divided into up to 15 parallel channels, with a very short "duty cycle," or Transmission Time Interval (TTI), of 2ms each. These channels can be simultaneously used by a single terminal for an entire TTI or split between multiple users as needed. Due to the fast scheduling techniques and short 2ms cycle, the system can quickly allocate bandwidth where it's needed. This scheduling technique is comparable to that used in WLAN networks.

HSDPA also supports a fast Automatic Retransmission reQuest (ARQ) mechanism, allowing corrupted datagrams to be retransmitted inside a 10ms window. This helps facilitate higher TCP throughput by creating a more reliable transport layer. Using these techniques in conjunction with new enhanced modulation and code schemes, HSDPA can offer theoretical speeds up to 14.4Mbps. It may be possible to increase this throughput in the future through further technology enhancements such as the adoption of multiple antenna systems such as Multiple Input Multiple Output (MIMO), as found in Release 6.

In 3GPP Release 6, the HSUPA uplink air interface, also called Enhanced Dedicated Channel (E-DCH), is redefined. HSUPA can support speeds ranging from about 1Mbps to 14.4Mbps. HSUPA uses a dedicated channel, unlike the shared channel found in HSDPA. HSUPA achieves its higher bandwidth through fast radio (Node B) scheduling, ARQ, and new signaling and data channels. HSDPA and HSUPA are sure to improve as the technology is more widely deployed.

Looking at Release 7, 3GPP is architecting a system to provide higher bandwidth and lower delay air interfaces. One goal is to be able to handle the same or greater voice capacity on the PS interfaces as R99 CS can handle. Some of the Release 7 goals include enhancing VoIP quality, reducing delay to the 20 to 40ms range, increasing peak bandwidth rates to the 40 to 50Mbps range, and other enhancements to enable more mobile broadband services. This is commonly referred to as HSPA+.

BEYOND CDMA

With the widespread subscriber adoption of higher bandwidth services, packet-based mobile voice, rich media, gaming, video, and other advanced services, operators are setting long-term capacity targets that far exceed today's air interface capabilities. To reach these long-term capacity goals, spectrum allocation will have to evolve from today's standards, which include CDMA's 1.25MHz channels and WCDMA's 5MHz channels. Future standards are aiming at wider band channels up to 20MHz to provide higher transmission rates to end users.

Global spectrum allocation plays a major role in how and which technologies are developed by operators, vendors, and standards groups. Operators will require large amounts of spectrum in the right bands to cost-effectively deliver higher-speed mobile services. It's important to note a major trade-off that exists in all radio networks: higher frequencies allow for more capacity but have shorter ranges for a given power output. This translates directly into costs for the operator, because higher-frequency services typically require more cell sites, backhaul network, and equipment to deploy. Most wide-area mobile radio networks are designed for use in the 800MHz to 2600MHz range, which is generally considered to offer the optimal trade-off between speed and coverage.

As a result of this demand for higher bandwidth, optimized coverage, and optimal spectral efficiency, most radio interface standards are moving away from CDMA-based carriers to Orthogonal Frequency Division Multiplexing (OFDM)-based schemes. OFDM is generally perceived to be more spectrally efficient than CDMA, is less susceptible to interference, and offers very efficient granular bandwidth to terminals and advanced scheduling algorithms. This gives OFDM-based modulation schemes more control over quality of service, as well as higher bandwidth. OFDM modulation schemes have already been adopted in mobile broadcasting systems such as Qualcomm's FLO and DVB-H.

Although a number of OFDM-based modulation schemes exist, both 3GPP and 3GPP2 are evolving their radio interface road maps away from CDMA and toward OFDM. This can be seen in 3GPP's 3G Long-Term Evolution (LTE) UTRAN work, which is the planned successor to WCDMA and HSPA, targeted for 3GPP Release 8. On the 3GPP2 side, 20MHz channel OFDM is being evaluated for CDMA2000 EVDO Revision C. The two systems' services become married at this point; 3GPP LTE and EVDO RevC offer equivalent data rates and a converging service delivery platform. OFDM is already a very mature and widely deployed technology, partially thanks to its use in the 802.11 WLAN protocol. Figure 9.24 shows the overall evolution of radio multiplexing schemes.

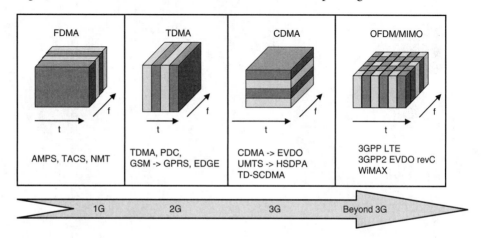

Figure 9.24 Radio interface multiplexing evolution.

SUMMARY

After a long history, the cellular network's legacy of circuit-based services is beginning to converge on packet-based technologies. They can offer not only the same legacy voice services but also a wealth of new IP-based data services. Although users are becoming accustomed to many of these new services through wireline residential and enterprise networks, the lines are blurring between wireless and wireline. Significant opportunity exists where the line blurs, because users should be able to expect the same levels of connectivity regardless of the means by which they are connected, such as we're currently witnessing with the rise of FMC solutions.

As these mobile broadband technologies evolve, those who subscribe to a video service, voice service, and Internet service at home via a triple-play DSL connection can expect to see these services "follow" them onto the mobile network. This evolution will create many opportunities for both existing subscriber services and new services that will become possible only through the converged wireline/wireless broadband architecture.

Managing
IP Addressing

Broadband networks bring many customers and connections into a central router, which presents its own set of challenges vis-à-vis IP addressing. This chapter discusses the methods that service providers can use to better manage customer IP address assignment and routing techniques employed within these broadband networks.

Connecting many customers to a broadband network means that there are also many routes and IP addresses to manage. In traditional dial-up and broadband networks, each customer is assigned a single IPv4 and possibly an IPv6 IP address. This address is assigned to a residential gateway that either provides a NAT function (routed mode) or is directly assigned to a computer on the customer LAN (bridged mode). Which mode is used depends largely on how the service provider chooses to deploy its broadband service. IPv4 usually entails all devices in the household to sharing a single address and making use of NAT functionality on the residential gateway. An IPv6 environment usually means each device on the LAN has a unique, globally routable address.

Each BNG typically simultaneously serves thousands of customers and acts as a service and routing aggregation point. At the network level, services are defined using a mixture of rate-limiters, QoS profiles, and routing policy in the provider network. Services can be implemented using dynamic features such as captive portals and Session Border Controllers (SBCs). Chapter 11, "Dynamic User

Session Control," describes how to implement dynamic user session control. This chapter is concerned with the less sublime and more mundane aspect of network design—address assignment and its supporting infrastructure. Both PPP-based and Dynamic Host Configuration Protocol (DHCP)-based designs are covered; there also is a section on deploying IPv6 broadband access networks. In the first sections, unless otherwise noted, all protocols and scenarios apply to IPv4. The latter part of the chapter discusses IPv6-specific and IPv4-to-IPv6 migration strategies.

SETTING UP THE CONNECTION TO THE BNG

In a PPP environment, a CPE establishes a PPP session with the BNG using one of the transport mechanisms: PPP over Ethernet (PPPoE), PPP over ATM (PPPoA), or PPP over Ethernet over ATM (PPPoEoA). PPPoE and PPPoEoA are of most interest throughout this book, because these are the protocols that run on next-generation Ethernet-based DSL networks. Some providers choose to run a PPPoA to PPPoE interworking function on the DSLAM, but ultimately the protocol that reaches the BNG is always PPPoE. The initial phase of LCP consists of authenticating the user based on the username and password. After the CPE and BNG have completed LCP negotiation, as part of IPCP, the BNG assigns an IP address to the customer router. A Point-to-Point Protocol (PPP) session is now at the open (or established) state between the two routers. The PPP session does not have to use a /30 or even a /31 IP network, as commonly found on more static point-to-point links. The addresses on the BNG and customer equipment can be in completely different ranges, such as 10.1.1.1 on one end of the link and 192.168.1.1 on the other. In most cases, the BNG uses the same address on its end for all subscriber connections, regardless of what address it assigns to the other end. The most common scenario that precipitates this configuration is a feature called unnumbered interfaces. This allows every subscriber interface on the BNG to share a single IP address. This IP address is commonly a loopback interface—a virtual interface on the router can be used for other functions, including routing protocols, management access, RADIUS traffic, and unnumbered interfaces. Technically speaking, the address on the BNG end of the link is not applied to the link itself. Instead, the BNG end is unnumbered and references a loopback address for any IP processing that needs to be done on the link.

How does the BNG know which address to assign the customer? There are several ways to allocate an address to a PPP session. The address could be out of a local or remote address pool, a static assignment via RADIUS, or using a DHCP server. The most straightforward approach of assigning addresses from local address pools is covered next.

LOCAL ADDRESS POOLS

Since the early days of dial-up access, local address pools have been used to simplify the task of assigning an address to a dial-in subscriber. In the broadband world, the mechanism is the same. It works by configuring the NAS or BNG with a group or groups of addresses called pools. Each group of addresses in a pool is called a range, and each range can be in a completely different network. For example, a pool could have one range from 192.168.1.1 to 192.168.1.254 and a second range from 192.168.7.1 to 192.168.8.254 (note that the two networks 192.168.7/24 and 192.168.8/24 are adjacent, but not aggregatable). When a subscriber logs in, the BNG allocates an address from the pool to the subscriber connection. Figure 10.1 shows a new connection at the BNG that attaches through an unnumbered interface. The sessions are assigned a free address from an address pool.

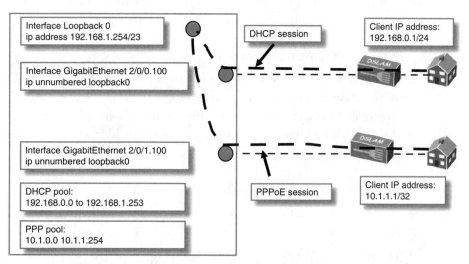

Figure 10.1 The BNG assigning addresses to subscribers from address pools and using an unnumbered interface.

In Figure 10.1, the loopback0 interface has an IP address configured that is part of a /23 network. The reason for the /23 network is that the DHCP sessions are also associated with the same loopback address. If DHCP sessions use a particular loopback interface, the address needs to be in the same network as the client that is on the Ethernet broadcast domain. This lets ARP and IP routing function properly. On the other hand, the client on the end of the PPP link can be assigned an address in a different subnet than that on the BNG due to PPP's point-to-point nature.

Not all vendors assign addresses from the pool in the same way. On Cisco IOS routers, the router always chooses the lowest free IP address in the pool. Juniper JUNOSe routers use a running pointer to allocate the next-highest free IP address in the current range. For example, assume that a BNG has an address pool with a single range from 192.168.1.1 to 192.168.1.254. Two subscribers log in and are assigned addresses 192.168.1.1 and 192.168.1.2. The running pointer on the JUNOSe router allocates the address 192.168.1.3 to the next subscriber that logs in, regardless of whether the first two addresses may no longer be in use. The theory has to do with relative address autonomy. The intention is to avoid having a newly logged-in subscriber receive residual data for a subscriber who just logged out and who had the same address. As the running pointer reaches the end of the range, it starts back at the beginning and uses addresses that have been returned to the pool. The next two sections delve into the lower-level details of Cisco IOS and Juniper JUNOSe address pool assignment.

Juniper JUNOSe Configuration

Juniper E-series routers support only locally configured address pools. Each pool has a name and one or more IP address ranges. A range needs a beginning and ending IP address and can span multiple networks (networks, were once considered pre-CIDR addresses). The router can assign an address from an address pool in three ways:

- Returning the pool name via RADIUS
- Not returning a static route via RADIUS, resulting in the router's using a local address pool
- Using a domain map to specify the address pool to use

The first is the most common approach and is accomplished by configuring a pool locally on the router and referencing it in a RADIUS *Access-Accept* packet. To illustrate how the router can assign addresses, the following is a list of requirements for the configuration:

- An address pool with two ranges. One address range must encompass the networks 192.168.0.0/24 and 192.168.1.0/24.

- A second address range that encompasses the network 192.168.99.0/24

- A second pool with a single range from which addresses out of the network 10.1.1.0/24 are assigned

The configuration is shown in Listing 10.1.

Listing 10.1 Juniper JUNOSe Pool Configuration

```
ip pool pool1 192.168.0.1 192.168.1.254
ip pool pool1 192.168.99.1 192.168.99.254
ip pool pool2 10.1.1.1 10.1.1.254
```

If the intention is to assign an address to the subscriber from the first pool, the RADIUS Vendor-Specific Attribute (VSA) *ERX-Address-Pool-Name* = "pool1" needs to be included in the user's RADIUS profile so that it is sent back in the Access-Accept packet. It is not possible to know ahead of time which range will be chosen, because it depends on the pool utilization on the router when the subscriber connects. The second range is used only if the router gets to the end of the first range in its running pointer and no free addresses are left in the range. The BNG then starts assigning addresses from the second range—192.168.99.1 to 192.168.99.254.

If there is no address pool name or static address in the RADIUS reply, as long as the default command **ip address-pool local** is not changed, the BNG starts assigning addresses from the first configured pool, pool1. If addresses from all ranges of pool1 are exhausted, the BNG starts assigning addresses from pool2. This works fine if connections are those of a single retail service provider on the BNG. But for instances in which a BNG has multiple wholesaled customers (in the case of Layer 3 wholesaling) or multiple VPN-type services on the same virtual router, it is very important to explicitly specify a pool name in the RADIUS profile. Not doing so would mean that the router could assign an address to the customer from any pool. Assigning the wrong address to the subscriber due to omitting the pool name is a bad situation.

The last way to assign an address from a pool is to use explicit configuration in a domain map. The domain map is a way to configure several aspects of the subscriber authentication process for a given domain, including the pool to use upon successful authentication. If the BNG uses a domain map and authenticates the subscriber using RADIUS, but the server does not return a pool name, the command **address-pool-name** in the domain map instructs the router to begin assigning addresses from this pool.

If a pool name is specified with a domain map or through RADIUS, and if all addresses have been used in all ranges within a pool, the router does not try to use another pool. The subscriber is rejected.

Cisco IOS Configuration

The configuration on Cisco IOS is very similar to Juniper JUNOSe. In fact, the configuration shown in Listing 10.1 is the same, so it is not repeated here. Cisco IOS also has a way to configure address pools remotely using RADIUS; they are discussed in the section "Remote Address Pools."

There are two ways for a Cisco IOS BNG to assign an address from a local address pool:

- By returning the name of an address pool in a RADIUS Access-Accept
- By specifying a pool in a virtual template (either implicitly or explicitly)

The RADIUS configuration to assign the pool named pool1 to a subscriber connection is similar to the ERX. A VSA of Cisco-Avpair = "ip:addr-pool=pool1" needs to be returned to the BNG in the Access-Accept packet. The BNG then assigns an address to the subscriber from the pool named pool1.

The second method is to specify the names of the pools in the virtual template using the command **peer default ip address pool [pool1, ...]**. If the router services customers using this command, even without a specific pool name, the configuration works well. But if the router has address pools locally configured for other providers, there is a limit to the number of virtual template interfaces that can be created. This has adverse scaling implications. The reason is that each unique reference to an address pool for a realm under a Cisco Virtual Private Dialup Network (VPDN) group needs a different virtual template reference.

A behavior difference between Cisco IOS and Juniper JUNOSe occurs when a local pool is referenced in a JUNOSe domain map or an IOS virtual template. With JUNOSe, if the RADIUS server returns an address pool when **address-pool-name** is configured under a domain map, the router uses the RADIUS-supplied pool name. With IOS, if the RADIUS server returns an address pool when the command **peer default ip address pool** is configured under the virtual template, this overrides the RADIUS attribute and uses the locally configured value instead.

VRF Address Pools

Virtual Routing and Forwarding (VRF) is an MPLS construct that provides an isolated routing domain for a customer. This routing domain can span multiple routers, called PEs, to which other customer sites connect. If the VRF extends across multiple routers, it is called a VPN. VRF Lite is a Cisco term for a VRF that provides an isolated routing domain but does not use MPLS to route traffic to other sites in the private network. Either VRF or VRF Lite can terminate broadband subscribers into their own isolated routing domain. This VRF can be on either a BNG or a remote L2TP Network Server (LNS). Assigning subscribers to a VRF is most commonly done on an LNS because configuration is more centralized. Address allocation in a VRF is very similar to normal address allocation that is used outside a VRF. For example, framed IP addresses, framed routes, and local and remote address pools can all be used to allocate addresses to subscribers in a VRF. Of course, extra RADIUS attributes are needed to direct the subscriber to the appropriate VRF, too.

REMOTE ADDRESS POOLS

Cisco IOS supports a feature called On-Demand Address Pool (ODAP), which is for centralized management of address pools and is well suited to large broadband networks. The concept of ODAP is essentially a growing or shrinking IP pool based on thresholds of address utilization on the specific router. This feature becomes especially important when a provider does not have enough public IP address space to accommodate a full subscriber count on all BNGs. Naturally this relies on more itinerant subscriber behavior compared to a fixed subscriber to BNG binding. This gives much higher utilization of address space, which makes ODAP an attractive proposition. Usually when subscribers are at a fixed location, their CPEs are online all the time. This feature allows the service provider to share address pools around the network, depending on usage rather than provisioning address pools large enough to handle peak load on each individual BNG. The following example explains how this works in a service provider network environment.

An ISP with three BNGs has allocated a /19 subnet (just under 8,200 hosts per BNG) to each gateway. Each BNG can technically handle tens of thousands of customers. However, with an IP pool being a /19 network, only 8,190 hosts can be connected at any one time. The ISP has three /19s for all broadband customers, and it expects to have between 6,000 and 8,000 customers connected to each BNG. Without requesting additional address space from an IP registry, the provider can configure the BNG to share unused IP address space among the other routers. This allows one BNG to have up to 9,000 subscribers at peak time yet a different BNG to have only 6,000. This results in better address usage throughout the network.

Automatic Pool Configuration

Cisco IOS also has a feature that enables the BNG to download address pools and the associated static routes when it starts up. If new pools need to be downloaded to the router, the process is to provision the new pool in the RADIUS server and reference it in a user profile. When a subscriber authenticates and the new pool name is sent to the BNG in the Access-Accept, the BNG sends a special request to the RADIUS server to try to retrieve the new pool and static route.

PPP Address Assignment Using a DHCP Server

Because a DHCP server already has a good mechanism for assigning addresses, some providers prefer to reuse it to assign all addresses to clients, be they DHCP or PPP. The usual reason is that significant DHCP infrastructure is already in place for existing services and a provider wants to expand its network to support a PPP-based infrastructure. Referring to Figure 10.2, when a subscriber logs into the network via PPP, he or she requires an address from the BNG. The BNG itself acts as a DHCP client and sends a request to the DHCP server on behalf of the PPP customer. The BNG and server complete the full DHCP protocol exchange with the BNG. Afterwards, the BNG continues PPP negotiation with the CPE and assigns it the address that was received from the server.

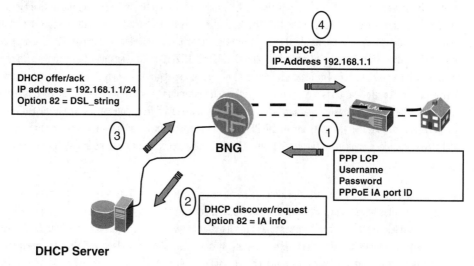

DHCP Server

Figure 10.2 BNG as a DHCP client.

This feature helps providers that want to use a unified addressing infrastructure. Nevertheless, there are features that would be present in a typical PPP and RADIUS combination that are not currently available when using a DHCP server. For example, it is not possible to use RADIUS Change of Authorization (CoA) to support dynamic services, nor is it possible to export comprehensive RADIUS accounting data. Some BNG vendor implementations that heavily revolve around DHCP may support applying IP policies to PPP sessions using a separate protocol mechanism, but this is the exception rather than the rule.

Technology Note: Address Compatibility

Even though addresses can reside in completely different ranges on each end of the PPP link, some poorly designed PPP stacks have been found in provider networks that do not function correctly in some situations. These problems generally are restricted to cheaper CPE. One example of a problem is when the provider's IP address is in a completely different *range* than the address that the client was assigned. The example to illustrate this issue follows the one shown in Figure 10.1. The figure shows a provider address of 192.168.1.254 and a CPE address of 10.1.1.1. A malfunctioning CPE fails to bring up the link because the device expects the BNG to be in the range 192.168.0.0 to 192.168.255.254. This harks back to the early days of the Internet, where classful addresses were used—that is, pre-CIDR. For example, an address such as 10.*x.x.x* was considered to be a Class A address with a mask of 255.0.0.0, and 132.181.0.0 was considered to be a Class B address with a mask of /16. The ideal solution is to not permit such misbehaving CPEs to be deployed in the network. But if a provider does not want to impose such restrictions, reconfiguration of the BNG is required. The reconfiguration is to ensure that any addresses that are assigned from pools or statically via RADIUS have roughly similar ranges on the BNG end of the PPP link. If many disparate ranges are in use, it can be a substantial piece of work to implement the work-around. Luckily these types of CPE are no longer too common in the market.

A second problem arises with certain addresses being assigned to clients. This time it is not the client, but network servers that have issues with the client address. Older operating system software, which follows classful address rules, treats some IP addresses as broadcast or network traffic and drops packets that originate from clients that use such addresses. Unfortunately, this problem is more widespread than the previous one, and the server software is outside the provider's domain of influence.

An example is where a provider uses a /23 network range for a pool and allocates an address to a subscriber with an all-1s or all-0s host address from the erstwhile Class C space. A problematic address would be 212.1.0.255. Providers fix the problem by splitting the /23 (or lower) network into separate /24 ranges that avoid the all-0s or all-1s addresses. This means that at least two addresses cannot be used for subscriber sessions in that range, resulting in increased pool management and provisioning complexity.

ASSIGNING ADDRESSES TO DHCP CLIENTS

DHCP address assignment requires a special server to allocate addresses to clients. When a DHCP subscriber connects to the network, the first packet that is sent is a discover packet. The BNG can do several things with the request. One is to relay it to an external DHCP server, which has a database of IP address pools that map to clients' MAC addresses. Instead of trying the client's MAC address, a more flexible approach is to use a special option in the DHCP packet called option 82. This option, added to DHCP packets by the DSLAM or BNG, is a field that identifies a subscriber's physical DSL port. If the client MAC address or option 82 field does not match an entry in the external server's database, an IP address can be assigned to the client from one of the pools in its database. A DHCP request (called a discovery packet) could come from any point in the network. If the external server does not match the client's identity, the server needs to know from which pool it should assign an address. The reason for this is to correctly match the BNG network associated with the customer VLAN or PVC. To do this, the server uses a field called the *giaddr*, which is the interface address to which the subscriber is connected. If the interface is unnumbered, the giaddr is the loopback address that the physical interface references. The server searches for a network that the giaddr is in and assigns an address from that range.

If the DHCP server finds an entry in its database for either the option 82 field or the client's MAC address, it returns this address to the client in a DHCP offer packet. Again, the address that is assigned to the client needs to be in the same subnet as the interface on the BNG so that the client has a valid gateway to route traffic through.

The model so far has focused on CPEs that have a Layer 2 path directly to the BNG and therefore use the broadband gateway as the DHCP server—or DHCP relay in this case. The end clients could be either Residential Gateways (RGs) (routed mode) or devices on household LANs (bridged mode). Both models are deployed in provider networks. In the former case, the RG is in routed mode and would typically NAT between the LAN and the upstream side to the BNG. In almost all cases, the RG usually assigns addresses from a private (RFC 1918) network to the clients. The exception is if a routable subnet is assigned to devices behind the LAN and there is no NAT, but this is not the typical case for residential networks. The latter of the two cases is called bridging and is where the BNG allocates addresses to devices directly on the LAN. When the RG is in bridging mode, one or more PVCs on the DSL side of the RG are configured in bridging mode. The RG transparently bridges Ethernet frames between the LAN and the PVCs. To ensure that frames are forwarded to the correct PVC, the RG maintains a bridging table to map between the MAC address and destination port. Instead of all clients on the LAN being able to forward traffic to any of the PVCs, the RG can statically map between a given Ethernet port on the LAN and a PVC.

A benefit of having an RG in routed mode is that it separates the LAN's broadcast domain from the rest of the network. The Layer 3 border on the RG limits the impact of NetBIOS broadcasts, misbehaving LAN devices (malicious or otherwise), or any other broadcast traffic. It also means that there is a central point of management (the RG), which is useful if the operator wants to look at per-application Layer 3 statistics on the RG. If all traffic is bridged, there is no chance to apply any IP packet filters on the RG or to look at IP-level statistics. Additionally, for bridged mode, there is no Layer 3 endpoint on the customer premises to ping for troubleshooting purposes.

On Juniper Networks' E-series, the system creates access-internal routes for routes assigned by an external DHCP server, just like PPP, so they can be redistributed to another protocol. Usually the redistribution of access-internal (subscriber) and even static routes is not necessary. Only the static aggregate route is normally announced to peers. The reason is that most DHCP deployments have address pools fixed by location. Any static addresses that clients have are part of a special section of the pool that is reserved for static addresses.

To enable DHCP relay on Juniper JUNOSe, the command in global configuration mode is

```
set dhcp relay [ server address ]
```

The equivalent command on Cisco IOS is configured on each interface facing the client VLAN or PVC:

```
ip helper-address [ server address ]
```

The limitation with a pure DHCP relay implementation is that the BNG does not have visibility of all protocol exchanges between the client and server. For example, any address renewals between the client and server are sent unicast between the two end hosts. A feature called DHCP relay-proxy allows the BNG to masquerade as a DHCP server yet still forward all protocol packets to the real server.

This is a useful feature to use when DHCP state is needed on the BNG. Alternatively, if a BNG can perform some kind of transparent snooping of the unicast DHCP traffic, this would keep the BNG updated with the client state, too.

Local DHCP Server

Most BNGs today have built-in DHCP servers that can assign addresses to both DHCP and PPP clients. These servers have sufficient capability to carry out most of the duties required of a DHCP server, including allocating static addresses for some subscribers. Of course, a dedicated DHCP server has a lot more flexibility when dealing with clients that require vendor-specific options in their interactions with user databases. This is quite common for triple-play networks that are heavy users of DHCP and that need specific customization and reporting capability on DHCP usage. Nevertheless, some providers assign addresses to CPE using DHCP but rely on upper layers such as TFTP or HTTP to program the rest of the CPE. They are not concerned with the address that a client receives from a pool.

Static DHCP Addresses

The principle of assigning static DHCP addresses is straightforward. A server has several addresses in a range set aside for static addresses. Which one the server assigns depends on the client identifier. This could be the MAC address, option 82, or perhaps a key embedded in the DHCP packet that the client sends to the server. The server must assign an address to the client that is in the same network as the BNG's interface address; otherwise, routing does not work properly. So if a user with a static DHCP address roams among different places in the network—between different WiFi hotspots, for example—some extra protocol features need to work in concert. Having the same address wherever the user roams means that the network address on the BNG must be the same everywhere. At the same time, the gateway would need to be different so that the server gets the correct giaddr for the interface location that the client is connecting to. Alternatively, some other mechanism could identify the location, such as an option 82 field. Referring to Figures 10.3 and 10.4, after the user is assigned the static address, the BNG needs to announce a /32 host route to the other BNGs so that there is a path to send traffic for that client. The next problem is, if all clients are on the same subnet, how can a client with a static address get to a different client in the same subnet located on the other side of the network through several routed hops? Proxy ARP. When Randy wants to send traffic to Horatio, Randy's PC sends an ARP request to the network for the Layer 2 address of Horatio's PC. Because Horatio's gateway is on the other side of the network, the BNG to which Randy is connected replies to the ARP request and uses its own MAC address as the destination address. Randy's PC should send traffic to reach Horatio back via the BNG. When the BNG receives these packets, it uses the /32 route for Horatio that was announced by New York and forwards the packets through the core and out to that BNG. The /32 is chosen over the local interface route because it is more specific. The same happens for packets traveling in the reverse direction. Figure 10.3 shows the ARP process when Randy wants to find out the destination Layer 2 address.

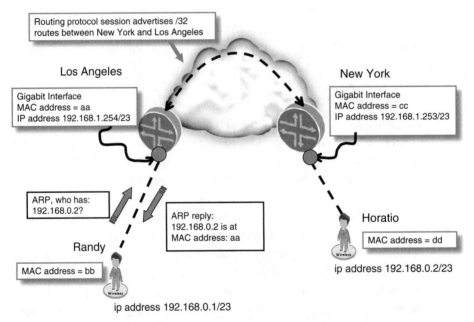

Figure 10.3 Resolving MAC addresses with proxy ARP.

Figure 10.4 shows the packet forwarding process after the correct destination address has been resolved.

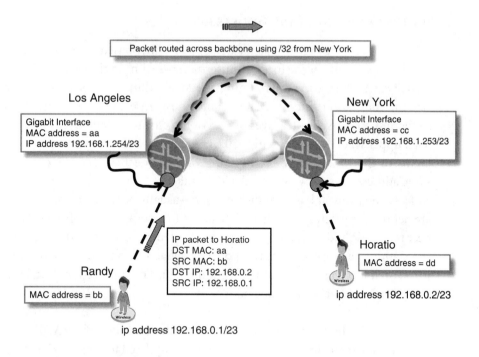

Figure 10.4 Routing traffic based on proxy ARP.

One of the issues with this architecture is dealing with PCs that leave the network without properly releasing their address. Suppose a subscriber pops up at another part of the network and wants the same address that is active on another router when the original DHCP lease was not properly released. There needs to be a way to synchronize the network and to allow the new session to come up and have full routing capability. This happens if users are roaming between WiFi hotspots yet still keeping their session active—macro mobility. One way to solve this limitation is to use a special gateway that performs a NAT function between the static client address and a global address. This approach requires extra hardware, although this is performed in the access point itself by some vendors. Another solution is to tune down the DHCP lease time so that if the client hasn't renewed the lease, the static address assignment times out and the host route is removed from the network. This can substantially load the DHCP server, so it is not an ideal solution.

ASSIGNING STATIC PPP ADDRESSES

A static address is assigned to a particular subscriber based on an identifier—usually a username in the form of "username@realm" in the case of PPP. In DHCP cases where users are roaming, the MAC address can be used to authenticate the end station's identity. This is notoriously insecure on a public network, so there should be an extra layer of security to ensure the end user's integrity. Such upper security layers include 802.1x with EAP, SSL-encrypted captive portal logins, or CHAP-authenticated PPPoE sessions, in decreasing order of security. A static address is useful when the device at the other end needs the same IP address every time it logs into the network—usually because one or more servers are behind the gateway that provide services to external users who need to connect to a static address. Another commonly cited reason is that the user needs a static address as part of a security policy to get access to his or her corporate network, or at least his or her authentication server. The first section describes PPP using RADIUS to allocate static addresses.

When a PPP subscriber is provisioned with a static address, the RADIUS database that stores the profile for the username is updated to include a field for the *Framed-IP-Address*. This is the RADIUS attribute returned in the access accept packet that instructs the BNG to assign the user the address in the RADIUS packet. This mechanism is relatively straightforward, so it does not need much further explanation. One implementation point worth mentioning for Juniper JUNOSe is that if both an address pool and a Framed-IP-Address are returned in the Access-Accept, the static address is used. Cisco IOS has the opposite behavior and uses the address pool instead.

Framed Routes

Framed routes are used to allow customers to route additional networks through their broadband connection. The discussion so far has assumed either that a single address is assigned to subscriber CPE or that it has been assigned directly to a PC on the LAN. NAT would be employed if the former case were used. Framed routes have relevance only when a session terminates on the RG and NAT consequently is disabled; it is uncommon for a PC to act as a router. The BNG assigns a /32 address to the CPE during the IP address negotiation phase of PPP, which is called IP Control Protocol (IPCP). The BNG receives the framed route from the

RADIUS server in the access accept packet and adds the route to its routing table with a next hop of the CPE's /32 WAN address. The CPE has the network configured on its LAN interface. Other hosts on the LAN are assigned addresses from this subnet and can route out the CPE without undergoing NAT.

Framed routes can be used by service providers as easy revenue-generators. A premium can be levied on top of the monthly subscription fee for assigning a routable pool of addresses to the customer. This is a much more effective solution for many hosts compared to setting up pinholes with NAT (such is the case with just a Framed-IP-Address). Usually the address pool is small—a /29, for example. To show how the RADIUS attribute is formed, take the example of a customer being assigned a /32 of 192.168.1.20 on the WAN interface of her DSL modem. To route the network 10.1.1.0/24 out the DSL modem, the following RADIUS attribute is returned in the Access-Accept packet, along with the Framed-IP-Address:

```
Framed-IP-Address = 192.168.1.20,
Framed-Route = "10.1.1.0/24 192.168.1.20"
```

Of course, the addresses shown in the code snippet are private addresses, but would be public ones on a production network. When a Framed-Route is installed in a Cisco IOS router, it appears in the routing table as a static route, which can then be redistributed by BGP. Juniper JUNOSe has a separate protocol for framed routes, called access routes. The next section describes how these routes can be advertised to the rest of the domain using redistribution.

ROUTING SUBSCRIBER ADDRESSES

So that all routers know where to send traffic back to subscribers, they need a route back to the PPP session. Route aggregation theory says that the farther you progress from the source of the route, the more aggregated the route should become. This means that routers outside a provider's autonomous system do not need to know the status of each host route. For example, other service provider routing peers would be more interested in the aggregate route of all subscribers in a 192.168.0.0/23 block, compared to an individual subscriber session with the address 192.168.1.1. Within the originating provider's network, similar principles apply, but they are not as strictly applied compared to a more public domain such as the Internet. A BNG that has a pool of addresses in the network of 192.168.0.0/23 does not need to advertise each subscriber route within that range to the rest of the autonomous system (AS). Instead, it can announce the generalized route to the rest of the network. This is sufficient for the rest of the AS and indeed the Internet to reach any subscriber within that network range.

The most straightforward approach to creating an aggregated route on a BNG is to configure a static route for the network and point it to a discard interface. On Juniper JUNOSe and Cisco IOS the command is to create a static route and use a next hop of a special interface called "null 0":

```
Bangkok_01(config)# ip route 192.168.0.0 255.255.254.0 null 0
```

Routers always prefer a more specific route match when looking up a destination to forward a packet to. So if a router has an aggregate—192.168.0.0/23—and a specific route in that aggregate—192.168.1.1—it always chooses the more specific route of 192.168.1.1. This is always the case in a BNG environment where each subscriber has his or her own host (or network route) but other routers have a less-specific route. If a router checks its forwarding table (like a routing table, but in the forwarding plane) and there is no specific match for the destination address, it discards the packet. The "null 0" interface is a special interface that is always up and discards packets routed through it. Why the static route? It creates the aggregate in the first place.

Aggregate routes are important for efficient routing tables and reducing routing churn on core service provider networks.

Efficient Routing Tables

Take the example of two BNGs in separate cities, each connected with 10,000 subscribers. The subscribers want to exchange VoIP with each other and therefore require routes between the BNGs. In a simplistic approach, each of the host routes (/32 routes for each subscriber) could be announced to the other router, but that would mean that 20,000 routes are installed on each BNG. It is more efficient in terms of router resources to create an aggregate route that encompasses the host routes on each router and then advertise this aggregate to the other router.

If the BNG in one city needs to forward traffic to a subscriber on the other broadband gateway, it needs only a single route that summarizes all customer addresses on the other router. The receiving BNG performs a best-match lookup for the destination address that matches a subscriber attached to a locally connected interface.

Reduce Routing Churn

If BNGs announce all subscriber routes in to the network as host routes, it can create a significant load on the network. These subscriber routes are announced by a BNG when the subscriber connects and then are withdrawn when the customer disconnects. Running this type of dynamic routing on a large scale for host routes would severely affect router resources due to continual SPF calculations. However, having several thousand or even tens of thousands of host routes in the network for static addresses is not a huge overhead in the scheme of things. But in terms of dynamic pools (when subscribers are allocated addresses from a pool of addresses), this is extra routing information that is not needed. One trick to save some router resources when triple-play traffic transits an MPLS VPN network is to use route target filtering. Not all routers in the network need a full Internet routing table for broadband traffic, so if these routes are in their own VPN, PE routers can be configured to filter routes for VPNs that they do not have any configuration for. Both Cisco IOS and Juniper JUNOS enable route target filtering by default.

Network Configuration

To control the routes that are advertised into the network, routing policy is needed. This is useful to announce host routes for subscribers with static addresses and to block all others. The difficult part is that all routes originate from the same protocol, whether static or not. One method of route distribution is to redistribute all subscriber host routes into a backbone routing protocol (usually BGP), but using a policy filter. All redistributed routes are then vetted by the policy before making it into the routing protocol. The policy permits addresses that are not part of the advertised aggregate route to be redistributed into the destination protocol and block all others that are part of the aggregate. Figure 10.5 shows the control flow for subscriber routes being redistributed to another protocol.

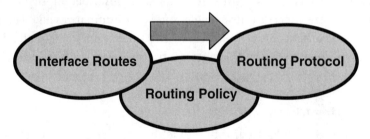

Figure 10.5 Control flow for redistributing subscriber routes.

Listing 10.2 shows how to configure a pool and its associated aggregate route in JUNOSe and IOS.

Listing 10.2 Pool Configuration

```
1: ip local pool pool1
2: ip local pool pool1 4.4.4.1 4.4.5.254
3:
4: ip route 4.4.4.0 255.255.254.0 null0
```

The address pool named pool1 supplies IP addresses for 510 hosts. The static route for the subnet with a next-hop of the null0 interface allows the aggregate route to be redistributed into other routing protocols. The second part of the configuration is JUNOSe-specific and performs the actual redistribution and filtering, as shown in Listing 10.3. The difference between JUNOSe and IOS configuration in the second part is marginal. Instead of redistributing access-internal routes, connected routes are redistributed.

Listing 10.3 Juniper JUNOSe Route Redistribution Configuration

```
1: ip prefix-list "isp-pools" seq 5 deny 4.4.4.0/23 ge 32
2: ip prefix-list "isp-pools" seq 10 permit 0.0.0.0/0 le 32
3:
4: route-map isp-pools permit 10
5:  match ip address prefix-list isp-pools
6:
7: router bgp 65001
8:  redistribute static
9:  redistribute access-internal route-map isp-pools
```

The following list explains Listing 10.3:

- Lines 1 and 2: The prefix lists provide a set of addresses that should be permitted. This paraphrases to the following:
  - Do not accept /32 (host routes) within the 4.4.4.0/23 prefix.
  - Accept all other routes.
- Lines 4 and 5: A route map, which is effectively the routing policy and matches on IP addresses that are permitted in the prefix list named isp-pools and accepts them.
- Lines 7 through 9: The BGP routing process has static and access-internal routes redistributed into the BGP process. The access-internal routes receive some special treatment. This treatment is that the route map named isp-pools is applied during the redistribution process of access-internal routes. Without the **route-map** statement, all access-internal routes in this routing instance would be redistributed into BGP.

The resulting configuration allows /32 host routes that are assigned statically via RADIUS to be announced while simultaneously suppressing the host routes that are assigned from address pools. In the listing, the address pool is 4.4.4.0/23. To redistribute routes assigned using the Framed-Route RADIUS attribute, JUNOSe needs a special redistribution command called **redistribute access** under the BGP/IS-IS/OSPF protocol. Such routes on Cisco IOS are static routes, so the **redistribute static** command is sufficient.

As described earlier, the principle of routing aggregation is important for the BNG to announce routes to the provider's network and to the greater Internet. So when these prefixes are announced to Internet peers, individual contiguous prefixes should be announced as a single route. The previous two listings show aggregate routes for pools on the BNG and static routes assigned via RADIUS being sent to other peers. So how do these routes get aggregated before being sent to Internet peers? When customers are assigned static addresses, they are usually assigned from a block of addresses set aside for such a purpose. This block may or may not be contiguous with the larger address pools, but in either case, these static routes are ideally announced to Internet peers as a single block. The peering router has a locally configured static route to null0 (or an equivalent) that encompasses the static address block and an encompassing route for the address pools. Figure 10.6 shows how the routes are announced and at which points the aggregation occurs. Where aggregation is not possible and static routes on peering routers is not feasible due to the amount of configuration, the individual sub-aggregates from the BNG may be used instead, but this is not considered good netiquette.

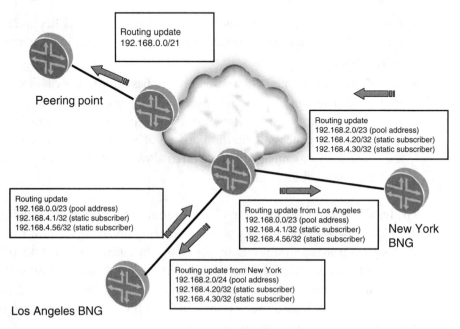

Figure 10.6 Internet peering routers and BNGs aggregating subscriber routes.

Providers may have a router aggregation layer between the BNG and the core network that can take host routes and slightly larger address blocks and announce a covering route to the core. However, with the high bandwidths involved in triple-play services (such as video), it becomes more economical to connect BNGs directly to the core and forgo the aggregation layer.

Route Aggregation Using L2TP

It might be an undesirable burden for the provider to have so many host routes, even just for subscribers with static addresses. This could be exacerbated with the churn of the addresses being announced and withdrawn. Some providers terminate all subscribers with static addresses on an L2TP Network Server (LNS) and then announce the covering aggregate route for all static addresses rather than the individual host routes from the LNS. Such aggregation is also useful for Layer 3 wholesale environments in which the incumbent provides PPP termination on its BNGs for small retailers. Each retailer has a pool of addresses that the incumbent has to divide between all its gateway routers. The smaller the retailer, the more inefficient the distribution of addresses becomes. Some BNGs may be more heavily loaded than others, so it is an ongoing process to shuffle addresses to where they are most efficiently utilized. Of course, if the router supports ODAPs, it should be used as it is designed to solve just this problem.

CUSTOMER LAN ADDRESSING

IP addressing on the customer LAN is significantly easier than addressing in the network. Thanks to the routing environment being relatively static and smaller in size, a provider can ask itself a few straightforward questions before deciding on a home-addressing architecture. There are only a few options to pick from: routed or bridged mode, NAT or no NAT, and, to a small extent, DHCP or PPPoE. This section is dedicated to IPv4 architectures in the home.

PPPoE OR DHCP

Whether PPPoE or DHCP is the access protocol does not have a major bearing on how the LAN addressing is structured. The biggest factor of the LAN addressing design is whether the CPE is in bridging mode or routed mode. Bridging mode means that the CPE forwards all Layer 2 frames from the customer LAN to the BNG and vice versa. Routed mode stops these frames and forwards only routable IP datagrams to and from the BNG. This mode also means that the DHCP or PPPoE access protocol terminates on the CPE rather than on a LAN device. Bridging mode has only one way of running, but routed mode has two ways—one with NAT and one without.

In terms of LAN addressing, if the CPE is functioning in routed mode, choosing one access protocol over another does not have such a big effect on the final design. The variables that have a bigger impact are management systems, IP addressing and identity management, existing historical access network deployments, CPE vendor support and capability, BNG vendor support and capability, and, at times, philosophical discussions.

PPP is probably the most common access protocol in the broadband market today, followed by DHCP, mainly due to its historical use in dial-up and older DSL networks. Although both can be made to work in a triple-play network, achieving the same functionality in a DHCP environment takes extra effort compared to PPP. As a small example, the DSL Forum is currently discussing what could be used as a keepalive mechanism for DHCP sessions. This would be analogous to the PPP LCP echo mechanism, which has been part of the protocol since its inception. Nevertheless, many providers in the market have deployed DHCP, and some new providers will also follow suit. An extensive discussion of DHCP versus PPPoE appears in Chapter 5, "Choosing the Right Access Protocol."

ROUTING OR BRIDGING

Most CPEs today are capable of using a routed or bridged mode to support a triple-play solution. The routed mode on the CPE may or may not include NAT (but usually does). If NAT is used, it is not possible to route any subnets to devices on the LAN side, because addresses are masqueraded by the NAT function before being sent to the BNG. NAT also impacts user applications that need to run more than a simple TCP or UDP connection to a device on the Internet. The CPE needs to be configured to properly pass traffic through NAT for applications that need to receive connections from outside the LAN (such as a file transfer using an instant messenger program). Universal Plug and Play (UPnP) helps by allowing an application to automatically connect to the CPE and make the necessary port reconfiguration. This is common in many new applications, and many CPEs support this now. Of course, devices that don't support UPnP have been around for several years, since the early days of broadband, so customers have become accustomed to working with these drawbacks. For newcomers, it takes some research to get used to. It is advisable for a provider to either deliver a CPE that supports UPnP or at least certify only those modems that do support it if they are provided via third-party channels.

Routed Mode

In routed mode, LAN devices are assigned addresses out of private address space using a DHCP server on the CPE. Sometimes, a video Set-Top Box (STB) needs to be assigned an address in its own subnet for some security or integration requirement. This could be achieved by binding the RG Ethernet port that connects to the STB to a second PVC on the local access network. This PVC would be routed to a central DHCP server for special address assignment. An alternative to a centralized DHCP model is to have the CPE reserve a dedicated address for the STB based on the vendor ID portion of the MAC address. Supporting an STB static address requires extra configuration on each CPE and would depend on its location. If the security requirement is to authenticate the customer location, the PPPoE IA header or DHCP option 82 could be used instead.

In the uncommon case that NAT is not used in routed mode, a unique, globally routable subnet needs to be assigned to the LAN. This could be applied using static preconfiguration on each of the devices attached to the CPE, or the CPE can run a local DHCP server to allocate the public addresses. In any case, the CPE needs to be preconfigured with this addressing information somehow. If a provider is using its own CPE in the household, presumably some automated mechanism exists to push a configuration to the CPE to deal with provisioning of its DHCP server.

Bridged Mode

If the CPE is in bridged mode, it does not play much of a role in the architecture; it functions simply as a frame forwarder between the LAN and the uplink interface. As such, the CPE can simply be a modem, which is a significant cost saving. In terms of addressing, changing it to bridging mode means the following:

- Each device on the LAN has its own fully routable IP address.
- If PPPoE is the access protocol, there are problems with peer-to-peer traffic on the LAN. The reason is that PCs no longer have a routing relationship with one another. Traffic between LAN devices needs to go via the BNG. On the other hand, there are no complications with port forwarding on the gateway.
- If DHCP is used, devices on the household LAN can communicate directly with each other due to the multipoint nature of Ethernet, as opposed to the point-to-point nature of PPPoE. This can be achieved with either a 1:1 or N:1 VLAN architecture in the access network. In the latter case, the DSLAM needs to be carefully configured to ensure that DSL ports cannot bridge between one another. Also, careful consideration needs to be paid to ARP to ensure that no

MAC address hijacking is possible. A 1:1 VLAN architecture on the upstream network can be used with DHCP, which improves security concerns of subscribers forwarding traffic between DSL ports.

- Unless the service provider implements some kind of firewall for subscribers, devices are directly exposed to the Internet. Routed mode with NAT provides a rudimentary level of security by filtering incoming connections from the Internet (at least in the default configuration).

- If a bridged architecture is employed that uses service VLANs, this has QoS implications. It means that the subscriber QoS cannot be managed on a centralized BNG. Instead, the DSLAM must perform prioritization and queuing among the subscriber PVCs unless a bandwidth carve-out model is used.

- Sometimes, an STB needs to be dedicated on its own STB PVC. This could be due to either provider preference to run a service VLAN architecture, or an STB vendor requirement that a common VLAN is used for addressing and authentication purposes. Again, the design of this architecture needs to ensure that traffic cannot be routed between DSL ports and that MAC addresses cannot be hijacked.

Routing or bridging is the factor that affects the design the most, with routing appearing to take a slight edge in popularity over bridged mode. The most commonly cited reason is for management capability and service demarcation. This simplifies the addressing structure, because there is almost always only one IP address per subscriber in the network to deal with.

TRIPLE PLAY WITH IPv6

For those working in the broadband access industry, IPv6 has been a topic of gentle interest for several years. The subject pops up every so often around the water cooler. It starts with the buzzword of IPv6 and then moves back to the problem of support and what happens when the address space runs out. Some ISPs or Internet access providers can deliver a connection to the IPv6 backbone (previously called the 6bone) and provide an IPv6 routing table. Sites on the IPv4 Internet are also available now on the IPv6 backbone, Windows XP has had IPv6 support for several years, and Windows Vista has IPv6 support enabled by default. If there has not been a concerted spam attempt using IPv6 transport already, there is sure to be in the near future, as spam writers leapfrog the capabilities of anti-spam groups. Viruses are sure to eventually proliferate through unsecured application ports and firewalls, just as with IPv4. But on the bright side, service providers can support triple-play applications on IPv6, too.

The Asia Pacific region is by far the most enthusiastic deployer of IPv6 in the residential broadband market. To support IPv6, routers and switches need to be upgraded to support the new addressing structure and the supporting protocol infrastructure. This chapter outlines some of the high-level changes in Layers 2 and 3 to the IP forwarding and addressing paradigm. It then discusses how broadband routers and address allocation are being addressed by service providers.

PROTOCOL CHANGES

The first obvious change to IPv6 addresses is that they have increased in size from 32 bits to 128 bits. This is not the only change. During the conceptualizing process of IPv6, the protocol writers also tinkered (and continue to tinker) with various other parts of the IPv6 concept. The IPv6 header has been simplified, and more than half the fields from the IPv4 header have been eliminated. In addition to the primary fields in the header—source and destination addresses—other fields are discussed in the next section.

Additionally, there are changes in the supporting protocols, address class space, and address allocation. For instance, Address Resolution Protocol (ARP) has been replaced with ICMP-based neighbor discovery, and there is an equivalent to IPv4 router discovery under IPv6. Similar to the IPv4 address space, some types of addresses have been restricted to only certain uses and are defined in RFC 4291.[1] For example, some addresses can be used only locally on a link, and others can be used for only multicast data. There are also impacts as to how the 128-bit address space should be allocated in address blocks, which are delegated to organizations and households. This is covered in the section "Deployment Scenarios."

---

1 http://www.ietf.org/rfc/rfc4291.txt

IPv6 Header

Changes to the IPv6 header include the following:

- A larger field size to support the larger IPv6 addresses
- The removal of the CRC field (allowing upper and lower layers to detect corrupted packets)
- The TTL changed to a hop count (where it was originally intended to be a time-based counter)
- The introduction of the flow label.

Figure 10.7 shows how the IPv6 header is structured.

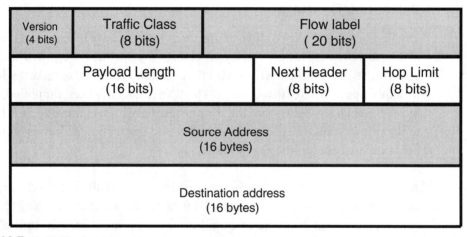

Figure 10.7 The IPv6 header structure.

ROUTER HARDWARE AND SOFTWARE SUPPORT

Router hardware and software need to be upgraded to support similar functionality on IPv6 that was present in IPv4. These include routing protocols, firewall filters (also called access lists), broadband access features, and system management functions (DNS, NTP, SNMP). Many of these features have been in router software for several years, especially protocols that are mandatory to support an IPv6 routing infrastructure. These include IPv6 route lookup, packet forwarding, Interior Gateway Protocol support (IS-IS or OSPF version 3), MBGP support, IPv6 access lists, and firewall filters. Many new routers on the marketplace have distributed packet-processing functionality implemented in FPGAs, ASICs, general processors, or a combination of these. The implementation of these features in hardware is more complex than in a software-driven forwarding environment. Therefore, new IPv6 features (of which the equivalent exist in IPv6) may take longer to develop in a hardware-based router purely because the demand for features in IPv4 is currently greater than in IPv6. This section discusses the various components that are affected in an IPv6 forwarding environment and what is required to support them. Of course, the market is very dynamic. New vendors are entering the market, and existing vendors are developing new software and platforms that all need to go through similar development cycles that other vendors and software trains have undergone. Therefore, IPv6 is expected to ride on the coattails of IPv4 development for some time to come.

IPv6 Forwarding Support

Basic IPv6 support is considered to be when a router can look up a destination address in a forwarding table and send the packet toward the correct destination. This also includes the capability to apply filters to discard or take actions based on Layer 3 or Layer 4 information in the packet. Several routers implement address lookup tables and firewall filters in Content Addressable Memory (CAM), which can perform fast lookups of packet addresses and firewall filters regardless of the number of entries (or relatively negligible delay). Of course, the number of CAM entries is limited in some older platforms. So as the size of the Internet table increases, this places extra demands on the CAM model to flexibly support IPv4 and IPv6 addressing and filtering capabilities. Also, the same memory limitations that plague CAM devices also affect other implementations that use Static Random Access Memory (SRAM) and Double Dynamic Random Access Memory (DDRAM). IPv6 VPN support is a little more complex than IPv4 VPNs, so in the past this took extra time to develop. The development time was mostly in the control plane, due to the extra BGP support and VRF enhancements. On the forwarding plane, the change was simpler and required using an MPLS next hop, rather than an IPv6 next hop.

Routing Protocol Support

The three dynamic routing protocols that are used in larger IPv6 network deployments are IS-IS, OSPF version 3, and BGP. The first two are Interior Gateway Protocols (IGPs), and the latter is used both within the provider and between providers. Usually providers choose one of the IGPs for their backbone. Sometimes providers run *protocol islands* that use the other IGP and redistribute information into the backbone. But an ideal world would have one IGP across the whole network. Additional protocols that have IPv6 support are RIPng and IPv6 static routes. The most common use of RIPng (the successor to RIP and RIPv2) and IPv6 static routes is as a lightweight way to provide routing information for remote sites connected to a provider's IP edge. However, this model is more prevalent in the business and enterprise model than in residential broadband access.

In terms of IGPs, both of the two popular IGPs support distributing IPv6 routing information. IS-IS was designed as an extensible routing protocol by the OSI, so adding IPv6 support for router vendors was a matter of adding the necessary IPv6 Type-Length-Value (TLV) fields to the protocol. Migrating from OSPF version 2—the version that distributed IPv4 routing information—required a completely new protocol rewrite, which increased the time required for development and testing. There are many arguments both for and against both protocols, but the biggest one in favor of IS-IS was its easy enhancement to support IPv6. The reason was that the extra development time and complexity of OSPFv3 meant more chance for bugs to creep into the software.

There are two modes for BGP to support IPv6 routing information. The first is to run IPv4 Multiprotocol BGP (MBGP) and distribute IPv6 Network Layer Reachability Information (NLRI) as just another field in an MBGP update. This approach is used for many other protocols that need to be transported over an IPv4 BGP session—Layer 2 and 3 VPN information, multicast routes, labeled unicast routes, and others. This is a suitable approach if there is no IPv6 connectivity between two sites or if a provider wants to use IPv4-based transport for BGP for the sake of simplicity. Two MBGP NLRIs have been defined to support basic IPv6 prefixes (not VPN or labeled unicast routes). One announces a prefix's reachability (MP_REACH_NLRI), and the other withdraws it (MP_UNREACH_NLRI). The second mode is to run BGP over a native IPv6 session.

SUPPORTING PROTOCOLS

As discussed earlier in this chapter, additional protocols are used to support an IPv6 infrastructure. To handle address assignment, a host can obtain a global

IPv6 address in two ways. The first is through stateless autoconfiguration, as described in RFC 4311.[2] This involves a host that wants to be allocated an address sending an ICMPv6 Router Solicitation (RS) packet using multicast. Routers on the subnet send a Router Advertisement (RA) packet back to the client with one or more subnets that are used on the link. The routers also send the gateway addresses that the client can use to route out of the subnet. A mechanism called Router Discovery (RD) makes use of Router Advertisement and Router Solicitation. It is a lightweight mechanism to indicate the routers and subnets that the client should use. It does not allocate a full 128-bit address to the client. The last part of the assignment is configured using a derivation of the Extended Unique Identifier-64 (EUI-64). It involves taking the first three octets of the host's MAC address (the company_id) and adding the hexadecimal numbers, FFEE, and the instance ID. This 64-bit identifier is applied as the host portion of the IPv6 address.

Router Discovery (RD) does not replace DHCP because the protocol is used simply for prefix and router advertisement to hosts on the LAN. The second address assignment method is called stateful autoconfiguration. The usual implementation of this function is DHCP version 6, which can assign similar information as the RS/RA mechanism but also DNS and NTP server addresses. ARP has been replaced with an ICMPv6 mechanism. It is part of the same family of protocols as RD but is called Neighbor Discovery. The function is similar to ARP, because it involves a host sending out a Neighbor Solicitation (NS) request (but with a multicast destination address) for a link-layer address of an IPv6 address. The host responds with a Neighbor Advertisement (NA) and its link-layer address.

This section has discussed the various support protocols for IPv6 that are of interest mainly on the LAN. On the links between the CPE and the BNG, the protocols more of interest to service providers are DHCPv6 Prefix Delegation (DHCP-PD) and PPP IPv6 Control Protocol (IPv6CP). The first is used to allocate an IPv6 prefix to a CPE, which can then start assigning addresses to devices on the LAN using stateful or stateless configuration. The prefixes in the DHCP-PD are the /64 or /48 subnet allocated to the LAN and other options such as DNS server addresses. IPv6CP is an additional control protocol that is part of PPP. It

2 http://www.ietf.org/rfc/rfc4311.txt

works in a similar fashion to IPCP and is used to allocate an address to the CPE. Also similar to IPCP, the protocol does not assign any addresses for use behind the CPE. This needs to be done via another mechanism, such as DHCPv6, which is described in the next section. These supporting protocols are on the household CPE. The IPv6 forwarding and routing protocol sections are all features that need to be supported on core and edge devices. Additional protocol support for Multicast Listener Discovery (MLD) version 1 or 2 is needed on DSLAMs, aggregating switches, and CPE to support IPv6 multicast. MLDv1[3] is the IPv6 version of IGMP but is implemented using ICMP. MLDv2[4] is a backward-compatible enhancement of MLDv1 but with SSM support. It can be thought of as the IPv6 version of IGMPv3. As with IGMP, MLD support is required to snoop inside IPv6 packets for multicast reports, joins, and leaves and set up the correct bridging state. One recommendation is that, when vendors implement MLDv1 or MLDv2 support in their switches and DSLAMs, the destination address rather than the destination Ethernet MAC be used in the snooping table. This is because the number of IP addresses that can map to one Ethernet MAC address increases from 2^5 in IPv4 to 2^{80} in IPv6. An extra protocol that is used in both IPv4 and IPv6 networks is the Multicast Router Discovery (MRD) protocol, which is a protocol to discover multicast routers on a segment. So even though it is not specific to IPv6 (although it does have IPv6-only semantics), it should start gaining momentum in provider networks soon.

DEPLOYMENT SCENARIOS

A lot of IPv6 broadband access deployment experience comes from Asia. There is even an Internet draft on the subject (draft-shirasaki-dualstack-service) describing IPv6 deployment experience from one provider. This section describes various approaches to running IPv6 in the access network and in the household. It assumes that the IP edge and core have been upgraded to support the protocols required for delivering a triple-play service.

PPPoE Model

A provider makes a conscious decision to run either PPPoE or DHCP on the aggregation network between the CPE and BNG. The reasons for choosing one

3 http://www.ietf.org/rfc/rfc2710.txt
4 http://www.ietf.org/rfc/rfc3810.txt

way or the other in an IPv6 environment are the same as for IPv4 and are discussed in Chapter 5.

Usually a BNG is deployed with simultaneous support for IPv4 and IPv6 protocols to allow for easy migration. Such a configuration requires a BNG with *dual-stack* support. Figure 10.8 shows how the protocols interact.

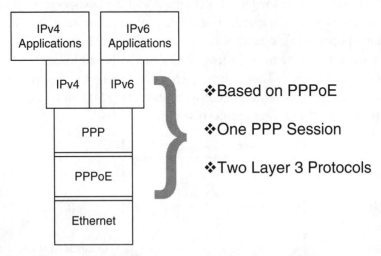

Figure 10.8 The dual-stack BNG model.

In some deployments, the CPE runs in Layer 3 mode, meaning that the PPPoE session terminates on the CPE. The CPE performs PPPoE discovery and session phases and then moves to PPP Link Control Protocol (LCP) and then Network Control Protocol (NCP). In the case just shown, two NCPs are negotiated—IPCP and IP6CP. In this model, the CPE can route either IPv6 or IPv4 traffic over the PPP session to the BNG. This is useful for accessing services on the Internet that have only IPv4 capability. Those with IPv6 addresses can be routed over the CPE using the IPv6 session. Such splitting of traffic is done by hosts on the LAN, which use their operating system's address resolution mechanism to check whether a DNS name has an IPv6 address, IPv4, or both. Based on local configuration, and if IPv6 has been correctly configured, they would send an IPv6 packet to the CPE to be sent to the wider Internet.

Before advancing too fast, one major part has not been covered yet. The IPv6 address assigned to the CPE over the PPP session is only a link-local address between the CPE and BNG. The CPE has no knowledge yet of the provider's DNS servers or the subnet on the LAN. To discover this information, the CPE sends a DHCPv6 solicit message to the BNG over the PPPoE session. In the advertise reply from the BNG, several options are included in the packet, but the most important ones are the DHCP-PD option and the DNS servers using Opt-DNS. These are options 26 and 23, respectively (although option 26 is actually a suboption of option 25). When the CPE receives the LAN's prefix (either /48 or /64), it assigns this as the network from which to allocate addresses to PCs and other clients on the LAN. These clients then make a request to discover their addresses using either stateful (DHCPv6) or stateless (RD) autoconfiguration. Figure 10.9 shows the different protocols used.

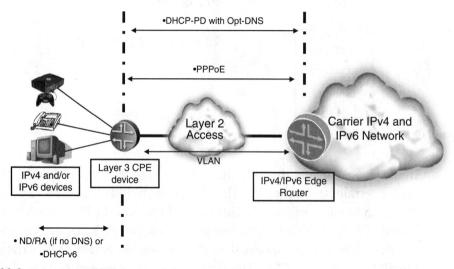

Figure 10.9 IPv6 access using PPPoE.

On the BNG side, most of the AAA mechanisms are the same. When the PPPoE arrives at the BNG, the router sends a request to the RADIUS server and authorizes the session based on the PPPoE IA header, the username/password, or a combination of both. The method used to allocate the prefix to a DHCP server can take several forms. One is when RADIUS returns the access accept, the reply can contain the customer prefix (/48 or /64). If a DHCP server is used locally on the BNG, the BNG can associate this prefix with the subsequent DHCP request from the CPE. The common piece of information is the DSL port, which is recorded from the PPPoE phase based on the PPPoE IA header or DHCP in the option 82 field. A second option is to use an external DHCP server solely to allocate the prefix and ancillary information to the CPE. In this case the BNG would relay the DHCP packets to an external server. A third option is a more static approach but still uses DHCP on the BNG. A prefix can be tied to a circuit based on static configuration. When a request comes in to the BNG from that circuit, the prefix is allocated. A slightly more dynamic method would be to associate the address from the DHCP configuration with some kind of dynamic route.

DHCP Model

A purely DHCP approach is popular for several reasons. A pure DHCP environment is more lightweight than PPPoE, can use a redundant router with VRRP, and supports many configuration options natively in the protocol. On the other hand, it still suffers the same drawbacks as the IPv4 version of DHCP. As mentioned in the preceding section, these differences are discussed in Chapter 5.

Even though the PPPoE model supports a CPE in either Layer 2 or Layer 3 mode, a pure DHCP approach is more conducive to running either bridged or routed. If the CPE is in Layer 3 mode, instead of having an underlying PPPoE connection to the BNG, the address for the WAN link is allocated using DHCPv6 natively over the Ethernet VLAN. This includes the DHCP-PD and the Opt-DNS fields to allow the CPE to allocate addresses to the LAN. One notable difference with this model, and also with the PPPoE model, is that the CPE does not perform any NAT. With 2^{64} or 2^{80} addresses, there is hardly a case for it. Figure 10.10 illustrates the relationships between the various protocols.

A Layer 2 model sets the CPE as a pure Layer 2 device and allows the PCs and other devices on the LAN to receive an address directly from the BNG using either DHCPv6 or the router discovery mechanism. If the household devices use router discovery to discover their addresses, a stand-alone client can receive this information from an external server. Figure 10.11 shows this configuration.

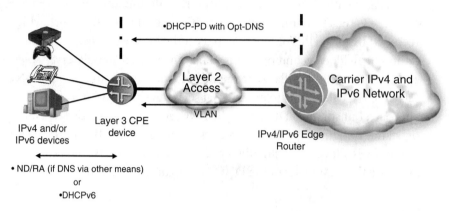

Figure 10.10   IPv6 access using DHCP with the CPE in routed mode.

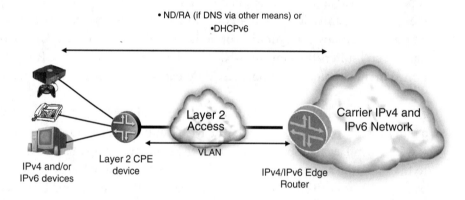

Figure 10.11   IPv6 access using DHCP with the CPE in bridged mode.

The household's /48 or /64 prefix is programmed directly on the BNG and is allocated with either router discovery or DHCPv6. As with IPv4-based DHCP, having a routed CPE between the devices on the LAN and BNG acts as a simple buffer mechanism between the two domains, filtering out Layer 2 broadcast and multicast traffic from the household.

IPv6 L2TP

If updating the backbone would be a substantial amount of work, IPv6 can be deployed sooner by running L2TPv2 or L2TPv3 over the IPv4 network, and IPv6 on the PPPoE session terminated at the LNS. This allows the underlying network between the LAC and LNS to be upgraded at a later stage. It is also ideal for retail providers that want to run an IPv6 service when the incumbent DSL provider cannot support IPv6 yet. Figure 10.12 shows how this would work.

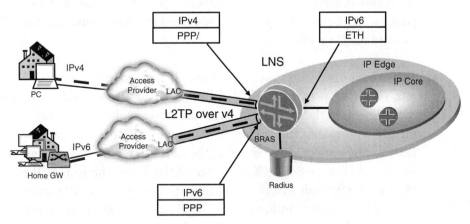

Figure 10.12 Using L2TP to support the IPv6 over IPv4 infrastructure.

SUMMARY

Assigning addresses to subscribers is standard fare for service providers. Without an address, there is little chance of a customer receiving services. This chapter has explained how address pools can be used to allocate addresses to customers with PPP or a local DHCP server in the BNG as a simple distributed allocation mechanism. Of course, this does not provide a great deal of flexibility if the provider wants more control over address allocation. Instead, address assignment can be centralized using the RADIUS Framed-IP-Address attribute for PPP or static reservations from a pool when using DHCP.

An important technique to master is address aggregation in the network, both from the BNG to the internal network and to the rest of the Internet. On the BNG, address pools are summarized into a static route that is continually announced to the network. This works by pointing the route's next hop to a special discard interface called null0. It is inevitable that customers will want static addresses, so in most cases, providers announce these /32 static routes into their core (ideally BGP to reduce the number of SPF calculations and make use of indirect next-hops). Even though there could be thousands or tens of thousands of these routes, this has not caused a problem for many providers. For providers that prefer to keep the routing topology as aggregated as possible, they can terminate these subscribers on a dedicated L2TP LNS. The reasons could be either to avoid announcing so many host routes into their backbones or to make address pool use more efficient. Aggregated addresses are then announced from the LNS to avoid the /32 route distribution.

Finally, customer addressing is more straightforward in terms of capability trade-offs. The access protocol (DHCP or PPP) is largely determined based on other requirements in the network. To present a single address and consistent client to the BNG, providers often opt to terminate the access protocol session on the BNG to ease remote management of the CPE and reduce the amount of interaction needed with remote PCs and other LAN devices. This is more the case in triple play, which needs a device that can do video, voice, and data integration. In the past it was more common to see PPPoE and DHCP sessions extended through to the LAN by using a bridged CPE configuration.

DYNAMIC USER SESSION CONTROL

Network access providers are continually fighting the battle against becoming commoditized bandwidth providers. In the case of regulated local loops, what was once the domain of the incumbent provider for telephony and Internet access is being encroached by access seekers who are keen on providing cheaper and faster digital data delivery. Internet-based VoIP providers such as Skype and Vonage are also eroding the mainstay of most telcos' bread and butter—PSTN calling minutes.

More than just providing streaming television over broadband access, providers are looking at enhancing their portfolio with dynamic service provisioning as a differentiation metric in the market. As services converge onto a single MPLS platform, this type of provisioning is becoming within the grasp of service providers.

This book has dealt with the network side of triple-play architectures—access, core, and wholesale. Chapter 8 "Deploying Quality of Service," discusses how services and business logic can be enforced in the network using quality of service and IP policy configuration to ensure a satisfactory quality of experience. Using the metaphor of network layers, which the OSI model has made de rigueur in quotidian networking discussions, these topics have dealt with what is considered to be Layers 1 through 4—the physical, data link, network, and transport layers. This chapter deals with the other three layers (session, presentation, and application), as well as the informally known eighth layer—the subscriber. As the joke goes, if the network has a problem, the first layer to check is the user—Layer 8. As mentioned in the following Technology Note, many textbooks present the OSI layer and map several applications, protocols, and functions (such as image formats, HTTP, and multimedia transport codecs) to the session, presentation, and application layers. Generally in the networking industry, anything over Layer 4 is not differentiated by layer, but rather by function. This nomenclature is also applied throughout this chapter.

Technology Note: OSI Seven-Layer Stack

The Open Systems Interconnection Reference Model (OSI Model) is widely used as a reference model in the computing and networking industry to separate the functional layers of a network stack. Each of the seven layers performs a particular function, such as data encapsulation or applying an IP address to a packet before being sent over the network. The model works such that a layer can use only the functionality of the layer directly below it, with a lower layer exposing its functionality to only the layer directly above.

The first four layers are usually of most interest to networking folks—physical, data link, network, and transport. The physical layer deals with electrical and encoding functions. The data link layer deals with data transfer and addressing between network devices on a local network, such as an Ethernet LAN. The network layer handles addressing packets to the correct destination across a network, such as the Internet. The transport layer allows the separation (also called multiplexing) of multiple applications on a single host to share a single network address. Devices such as HTTP load balancers profess to function at Layer 7—the application layer—as they perform application inspection.

Practically speaking, the Department of Defense (DoD) model maps more usefully to the communications protocol of the Internet today—TCP/IP, which uses layers similar to the first four OSI layers. It then uses a fifth layer to represent the application. This model is not as common due to the recommendation of the ISO body to use the OSI layer as a networking standard. And it also makes popular reading in network textbooks as a reference model to make a one-size-fits-all model.

This chapter discusses dynamic service provisioning of Small and Medium Enterprise (SME) customers, which is being integrated into broadband networks. Depending on the amount of dynamism and integration with the broadband gateway routers, service provisioning can be deployed on stand-alone vendor servers, coupled with existing service provider RADIUS infrastructure, or a mixture of both. This chapter covers three scenarios. Peering into the looking glass, this chapter also discusses the future of how service providers can exchange provisioning and service information between each other using public interfaces and APIs. Finally, this chapter looks at implicit service control using SBCs to provide security between VoIP domains. You don't need a strong technical background to understand the early concepts in this chapter.

RESIDENTIAL AND SME DYNAMIC SERVICE PROVISIONING

Having a user click a web page and request a new DSL line or a speed increase on his or her existing circuit has been commonplace in the service provider world for a few years. In the former case, a work order would usually be created from a provisioning system to dispatch a technician to an exchange to connect the right cables in the central office (CO) to enliven the copper line. In the latter case and in an ideal world, a provisioning engine would make a real-time adjustment on some network elements that adjusts the user bandwidth and perhaps make a pro rata charge adjustment on the user's bill. Alas, in practice this streamlined process is the exception rather than the rule. Some providers have implemented such impressive systems, but others are still working with manual backends, or semi-automated ones that require coordination between several systems and extensive message and error handling. This means that things can go wrong in lots of places.

On the other hand, unless a provider is setting up shop from scratch, integrating a dedicated dynamic service provisioning system into an existing network is no easy task, especially because it involves many *southbound* network interfaces to element management systems and other interfaces to billing engines, user databases, and user self-provisioning systems. This section explains what is available to service providers in this market space and the differing levels of network integration. For example, a couple of products on the market act as centralized *service gateways* that run everything from captive web portals to south-bound linkages with routers to apply service policies to user interfaces. Other types are interfaces to routers that act as a conduit between a provisioning system and the network. AxiOSS is one product that is a hybrid of the two. It can provision individual user services and maintain its own service and inventory database. At provisioning time, it can log on to network devices and make the necessary changes to activate a user service.

Most larger vendors that make routers and specialized broadband router equipment have their own service provisioning platform. For several reasons, it can take a lot of work to implement platform-independent provisioning systems that can interface with many vendors' devices. First, there is usually a tight coupling between provisioning platforms and the routers, resulting in a proprietary (or close to it) southbound interface between the network elements and the SPE (described in the section "Service Provisioning Engine"). Even with an open interface, the third party needs to invest significant capital to build a system that is compatible with several vendor architectures and that can scale to millions of subscribers. This is especially important in the residential market, where the network sees much state change compared to the business and enterprise market, where configuration is fairly static. But as providers are requiring multivendor support among broadband platforms, switches, and DSLAMs, a vendor maintaining a closed provisioning interface is becoming a hard stance to maintain due to the increasing popularity of centralized network provisioning tools.

BASIC SERVICE MANAGEMENT ELEMENTS

Before progressing to the various models that have been deployed in service provider markets, a look at the elements involved in service provisioning is useful. The service provisioning area has many moving parts, and various degrees of integration with a provider network are possible using third-party products.

Billing Platform

Love it or hate it, this is the most cherished platform of a service provider and is a complicated system that is well protected from other system interfaces. As the name implies, a billing engine handles billing of services, including rebates. In larger networks, these interface with mediation engines that convert between network-centric service details, such as Internet volume information in megabytes, and convert them into a service charge. Generally these platforms are not built in-house, but have been installed by third parties. The internal operation of a billing platform is not discussed here except where it involves triggers after activating and deactivating services from the provisioning engine, usually via the mediation platform. Usually the user provisioning web interface is not concerned with having access to the billing platform, even via a mediation engine. Users often want to query their account and billing statement online, so there is usually an external interface to the billing system via this vector.

Rating Engine

A related piece of equipment is the rating engine, which converts between network-centric details and bill-centric data. A good example of what a rating engine can do is to take RADIUS records from the RADIUS servers and convert the volume usages into a monetary format before being fed to the billing engine. For users on a flat-rate volume plan, the usage would be zero-rated in monetary terms before being sent to the billing engine.

Mediation Engine

As mentioned previously, the mediation engine acts as an intermediate step between the network and the billing engine. This is used for security to ensure that data coming from the network passes muster for sanity checks.

User Database

Many traditional wireline service providers have a billing relationship with a subscriber but only tie these services to a household. This typically means that the user database consists of lists of copper circuit identifiers, with database linkages to customer IDs. As users become more mobile, services need to follow their roaming patterns. For example, a user could roam from a fixed ADSL line, to a mobile handset, to a roaming dial-up connection via a provider such as iPASS, and the only constant identity may be a username and password. As providers upgrade their billing engines and revise their user databases, the linkage between phone line and customer must become more flexible to deliver next-generation services.

There is no hard and fast rule about database format. A common capability for many database servers is having a proprietary internal data format but providing several interfaces to access the data, such as LDAP or SQL. During organic growth of a service provider, where new services that require a database are added, multiple databases can be located throughout the network. One may have a database of MAC addresses for SIP User Agents (UAs), and another could have broadband access profiles. It is hard to divine the future of database requirements for an existing provider, but one trait that is important to strive to maintain is real-time synchronicity between the databases. This could be provided through directory aggregation point such as Novell's meta-directory. Some pieces of information are useful to have in the database, apart from the obvious ones: billing address and person. Supplementary information, such as a list of network port identifiers that take formats such as RADIUS NAS-Port-IDs or Calling-Station-IDs, are useful to have as part of a user database. These can be used when identifying the physical location of a login request. This is often used to restrict the services that a location can request (regardless of the username) in addition to applying QoS profiles (or service policies) pertinent to a line.

User provisioning and provider-side provisioning platforms need access to the user database to trigger subscription activations, deactivations, and modifications. Nightly bulk transfers of these service requests were common in the past, but users today expect to have more rapid service changes. Real-time service activation is regarded as a must-have feature, too.

RADIUS Platform

Remote Authentication Dial-In User Service (RADIUS) is a protocol that runs between network elements and an authentication server. It is used to authenticate and authorize users into the network. Originally written to give users access to dial-in networks, it has been extended for use in broadband networks. Additionally, some of its basic protocol operation has been modified to allow authentication servers to push attributes to a BNG for real-time provisioning and service activation. RADIUS platforms have interfaces to the user database for authentication and accounting purposes. For more technical information on this protocol, see the RADIUS Technology Note in Chapter 7, "Wholesale Broadband Networks."

The RADIUS platform also has an important role to play in user and network accounting. BNGs send accounting records to RADIUS servers, which record information such as session time, username, and traffic volume.

Web Portal

The web portal has captured the hearts of service providers as the de facto interface to allow customers to activate, deactivate, and modify services and to view profile and billing information. The two types of portals are the customer care web portal and the captive portal. The first is a web page where users can log into and change their service subscriptions, such as electing to increase their DSL line speed or subscribe to premium content. These are converted into a message that a backend network server, such as the SPE, can action. A real-time message format could be SOAP/XML, HTTP, or a Java API.

The captive portal is one that is triggered automatically when the user attempts to browse to a web page. For example, if a household is already connected to a DSL line but no services are applied to it, when a user tries to visit a web page, his or her session can be redirected to a captive web portal. The user can then create a billing relationship with the provider and subscribe to various services such as an "Internet service." If the user chooses not to subscribe, a free "walled-garden" service could be provided to the customer rather than no service at all. An example of such a captive portal is a wireless Internet access point, where, as soon as a subscriber attempts to visit a website, he or she is presented with a login page. In some cases, there are agreements between the location provider, such as a hotel or airport, and the wireless provider where the wireless provider lets the user browse to hotel-affiliated or airport-related sites (such as arrival schedules) free of charge.

Service Provisioning Engine

The Service Provisioning Engine (SPE) lies at the heart of a dynamic provisioning system. The web portals integrate tightly with it to trigger updates to the user database and initiate real-time changes on the routers, sometimes directly or via a Southbound Network Interface (SNI) server. Also, the provisioning engine may need to trigger additional auxiliary events, such as sending postage marketing information to the customer, and, if applicable, trigger the billing engine to reread the user profile. This capability is commonly available from router vendors, with varying degrees of functionality. An important feature to look for when choosing a provisioning engine is the number of external interfaces that can link to other systems. XML/SOAP and Java APIs are two of the most popular interfaces that should be included at a minimum. Although suitable products are available on the market today, which function as a provisioning engine, service providers may choose to design and create this function themselves to avoid vendor lock-in.

Southbound Network Interface

The SNI takes requests from the provisioning engine and communicates with the network elements to initiate changes on subscriber sessions. This function may be performed by a vendor's own equipment due to the specialized nature of the protocol that each router platform implements. Also, third parties such as AXIOM have products dedicated to providing a provisioning interface to many vendors' equipment. The interface to the router, DSLAM, or switch could be via a COPS channel, SNMP commands, unsolicited RADIUS packets or even via the CLI. On some occasions this function could also be performed using in-house development methods if the specification of the interface to the router is available to third parties. One implementation is to use a RADIUS interface with CoA (Change of Authorization) packets sent from a server to the BNG or NAS, allowing an existing session's parameters to be modified. Using RADIUS protocols can leverage preexisting in-house development, but it introduces additional burden on the service provider to extend the software development of its existing platforms.

A CLI interface usually is the option of last resort if there is nothing else. The reason is that in a highly dynamic BNG environment, services are constantly changing for many hundreds or thousands of subscribers. A CLI interface is designed for a machine-to-human interface rather than a machine-to-machine interface—it is not always optimized for fast service provisioning tasks. In more static environments, where a router configuration may not change much, a CLI interface could work out okay if this is the only interface made available to the SNI.

Subscriber-Facing Network Elements

SNEs are considered the devices in the network that the subscriber has contact with to facilitate their connection. The DSLAM (or access node in DSL Forum parlance) terminates the subscriber's DSL line, and the BNGs are used for Layer 3 termination and wholesale unbundling. Other network elements that may not always be present in every network but that are still considered subscriber-facing network elements are Layer 2 Tunneling Protocol Network Servers (LNSs) and aggregation switches. Some of these elements need to interface with the SNI server, especially the BNG. For the residential and SME market architectures, the BNG is the Policy Enforcement Point (PEP). One school of thought is to have all intelligence on a central BNG where the subscriber terminates so that it has complete knowledge of the subscriber services for effective quality of service (QoS) enforcement. A second architecture put forth is to distribute the functions of policy and QoS enforcement throughout various elements in the network. For reasons of brevity, only the centralized architecture model is discussed here.

SERVICE PROVISIONING FLOW

Whether a provider builds most of the SPE itself or the bulk of it is implemented using "off-the-shelf" tools, both use roughly the same components previously mentioned. This section shows what happens in the background when a user clicks a button in his subscription profile to boost his broadband line speed from 4Mbps to 8Mbps. Each vendor solution naturally has variations on the functional flow shown next, but for the most part, the concepts at a high level are the same.

First, the user logs in to his web portal, which sends a request to the SPE to get a list of the currently subscribed services. The SPE queries the database and sends the reply back to the web server. The user selects a boost on his line speed from 4Mbps to 8Mbps, which triggers a request to be sent to the SPE to kick the rest of the network into action. Figure 11.1 shows the processes that interact to trigger the service change.

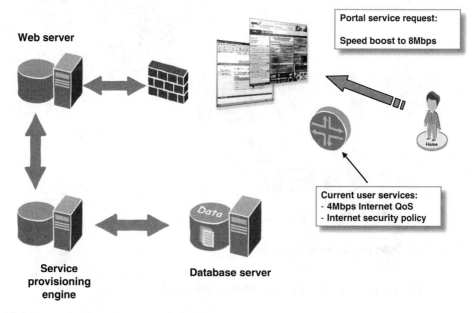

Web server

Portal service request:

Speed boost to 8Mbps

Current user services:
- 4Mbps Internet QoS
- Internet security policy

Service
provisioning
engine

Database server

Figure 11.1 User service change through a web portal.

Following Figure 11.2, when the SPE receives the request, it records the change in the user database and makes a note in the audit database. Any external messages such as e-mails and updates to the billing engine are triggered at this stage. The SPE needs to know whether the user is active in the network in case real-time changes need to be made to the subscriber session. It can get this information either from network elements that have synchronized their state over the SNI or based on standard RADIUS updates coming via traditional accounting interfaces. If the subscriber is active, the SPE sends a request to the BNG via the SNI to change the transmit rate limiter from 4Mbps to 8Mbps. If this is successful, an acknowledgment is sent back to the SPE to confirm the policy change.

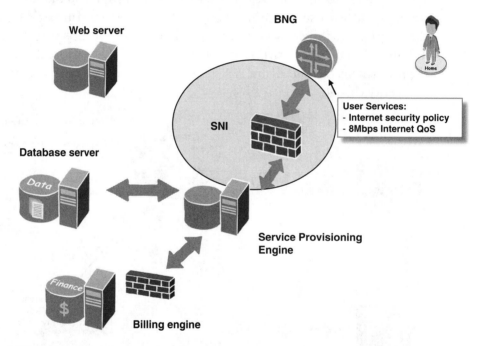

Figure 11.2 Network changes for service change.

BASIC DYNAMIC SERVICE PROVISIONING

Basic dynamic service provisioning involves users being able to provision services themselves, usually through some kind of web portal but with the service provider choosing to handle most of the service provisioning intelligence itself by implementing its own provisioning engine, RADIUS infrastructure, and web portals. To make changes to subscriber sessions in real time, providers are demanding more flexible provisioning interfaces from vendors. Automatic modifications via the traditional CLI interface do not scale up to handle any respectable number of subscribers. SNMP is an unsuitable tool for complex provisioning tasks. Finally, service providers are not always comfortable with using proprietary protocols across SNIs. One aspect that falls more under advanced dynamic service provisioning is real-time Call Admission Control (CAC) capability. For example, deciding whether to allow a VoIP call or video stream to proceed based on available bandwidth in the network is a CAC function that cannot rely on simple QoS prioritization. CAC is covered in more detail later.

RADIUS is more widespread as the protocol of choice to distribute simple- to medium-complexity policy information around the network. RADIUS can assign IP and QoS policies, which correspond to subscribed services, to network devices. IP policies can be assigned by either standard RADIUS attribute 242 filters or by using Vendor-Specific Attributes (VSAs). In technology development curves, vendors often release new functionality using proprietary VSAs until standards bodies catch up and provide for standardized methods. For example, VSAs allow a vendor to release its own proprietary features without having to go through the IETF and IANA, two Internet standards bodies. Standard Attribute-Value Pairs (AVPs) are those ratified in the IETF and recorded with IANA. Despite many features being common across vendor platforms (such as packet filters and rate limiters), most choose to use their own VSAs rather than go through the IETF process and get them defined in RFCs. This amounts to differences in only the low-level attribute definition[md]the interfaces and processes remain the same across vendor platforms. One notable exception is IETF RFC 4769, released in late 2006 and written by the DSL Forum.

This document describes RADIUS VSAs that are used to communicate characteristics of the DSL line from the BNG to the RADIUS server. The intention of that RFC is to provide a common set of attributes that vendors can implement to describe the DSL line status.

Figures 11.3 through 11.6 show the scenario of a subscriber connecting to the network with PPP. In Figure 11.3, the subscriber authenticates against the network with a PPP username and password, which the BNG uses to create a RADIUS packet. This is sent to the RADIUS server. The subscriber is then assigned a set of IP and QoS policies via RADIUS, which correspond to the set of subscribed services.

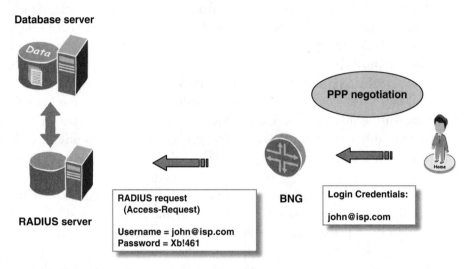

Database server

RADIUS server

RADIUS request
(Access-Request)

Username = john@isp.com
Password = Xb!461

BNG

PPP negotiation

Login Credentials:

john@isp.com

Figure 11.3 Initial PPP negotiation.

Figure 11.4 shows the RADIUS server replying to the BNG with a positive acknowledgment—an access accept. The reply contains an IP policy called "walled-garden" and a QoS profile that limits the subscriber throughput rate to 2Mbps. Because the authorization was successful, a message is sent to the subscriber, which brings the session fully up.

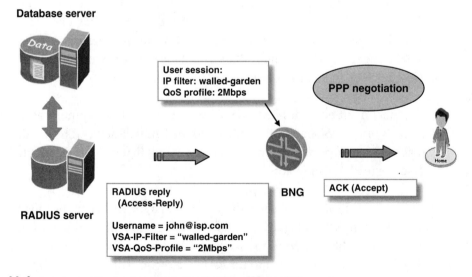

Database server

User session:
IP filter: walled-garden
QoS profile: 2Mbps

PPP negotiation

RADIUS server

RADIUS reply
(Access-Reply)

Username = john@isp.com
VSA-IP-Filter = "walled-garden"
VSA-QoS-Profile = "2Mbps"

BNG

ACK (Accept)

Figure 11.4 Assigning an address and services to the subscriber—PPP negotiation.

Figure 11.5 shows how a DHCP subscriber can be authenticated to the network. Recall that basic DHCP does not have authentication built in. DHCP option 82 is the ideal method to authenticate the location of the CPE. After receiving the DHCP discover, which includes the port identifier, the BNG relays the packet to the DHCP server.

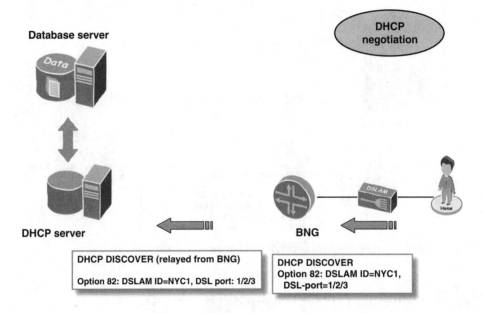

Figure 11.5 Initial DHCP negotiation.

Figure 11.6 shows a successful reply from the DHCP server, but this time the scenario is more complex. It is one example of how a BNG can apply services (via QoS and IP profiles or policies) to a DHCP session. After the subscriber DHCP lease is confirmed, a request can be made of the RADIUS server to send any policies or profiles for that DHCP option 82 string.

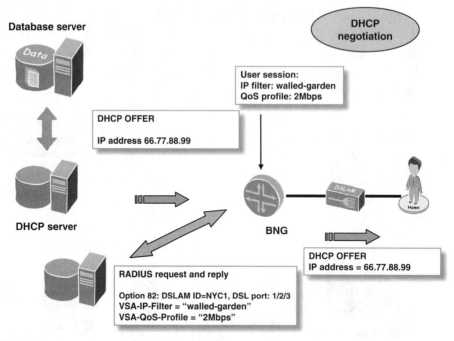

Figure 11.6   Assigning an address and services to the subscriber—DHCP negotiation.

Technology Note: Attribute 242 Filters

Each RADIUS attribute has a type ID to indicate what the attribute is to authentication servers and network access clients. Attribute 242 is a standard Attribute-Value Pair (AVP) that enables an operator to create IP filters (also known as ACLs) in a RADIUS packet. On most BNGs, filters need to be pre-defined if VSAs are used (as discussed next), but with attribute 242, the actual composition of the filter can be returned via RADIUS.

Technology Note: Vendor-Specific Attributes

In contrast with standard attributes such as attribute 242, Vendor-Specific Attributes (VSAs) allow a vendor to add its own attributes to the RADIUS protocol. Currently the RADIUS protocol has all standard attributes documented in IETF RFCs and recorded with IANA (http://www.iana.org), which maintains and allocates protocol and IP address numbers. The protocol has reserved attribute number 26 to allow any vendor to create its own subattributes within that AVP.

Doing this allows vendors to extend the protocol without having to go through the IETF to have each attribute ratified.

This functionality has been standard fare for many years. Any changes that needed to be made to a subscriber's service (such as a line speed change) required the user to log off and then back on again to trigger the new policies to be activated by the BNG. Even in the distributed BNG model, where the speed enforcement point is in the DSLAM, it required a resynchronization of the line to adjust the line speed. Ever since the introduction of ADSL2, DSL lines can modify their line speeds using online reconfiguration, which does not require a line retrain to activate.

Newer functionality appearing on the market allows the operator to send a special RADIUS packet to the BNG containing the new services to be activated and deactivated on a subscriber session. These changes are made in real time without requiring the user to log off and on. Each vendor has its special variations on this theme, but generally speaking, they function in a similar manner. One implementation used by Juniper, Cisco, Redback, and other vendors uses a standard Change of Authorization (CoA)[1] attribute that is sent unsolicited to the BNG. It modifies the services that a subscriber has subscribed to. One other method that Redback uses is to send an SNMP trigger packet to the BNG, which causes a RADIUS request to be sent to the server to receive the new subscriber profile from the RADIUS server. Again, this does not require reauthentication. One variation is a feature called Directory-Enabled Service Selection (DESS), used by the Cisco Service Selection Gateway (SSG). It has the BNG communicate directly with a Lightweight Directory Access Protocol (LDAP) server to discover a subscriber's profile. The SSG can also have a similar modus operandi as with Redback and Juniper and use RADIUS for profile information. An example of the functionality flow using RADIUS CoA is shown in Figure 11.7.

---

[1] http://www.ietf.org/rfc/rfc3576.txt

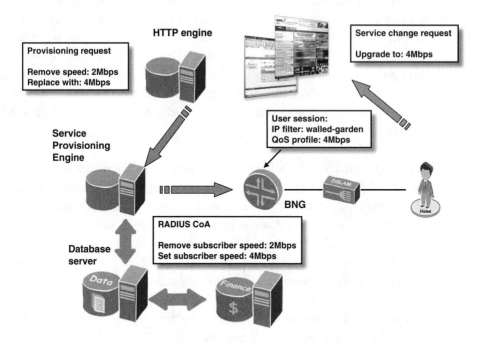

Figure 11.7 Real-time service change with the RADIUS CoA.

Figure 11.8 shows an example of the functional flow for a service change from 2Mbps to 4Mbps using an LDAP interface directly between the BNG and database server.

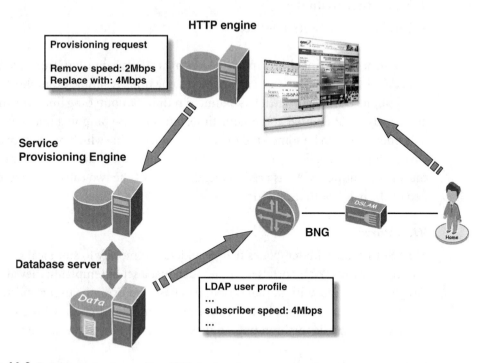

HTTP engine

Provisioning request

Remove speed: 2Mbps
Replace with: 4Mbps

Service
Provisioning Engine

Database server

BNG

LDAP user profile
...
subscriber speed: 4Mbps
...

Figure 11.8 Real-time service change with an LDAP directory change.

Both of these methods use protocols over the SNI that are in widespread use: LDAP and RADIUS. This type of architecture can be a prudent reuse of existing directory and RADIUS architecture if a simple dynamic service provisioning engine is needed.

ADVANCED DYNAMIC SERVICE PROVISIONING

An advanced dynamic service provisioning model uses the same interfaces between the SNI and SPEs. In this case, however, these instances are located deeper inside the provider network. A more sophisticated SPE that is designed from the ground up may integrate several core features into a single package (but distributed across several):

- User database (described earlier in this chapter)
- Web portal

- Middleware controller
- Southbound network interface

An element that is not always integrated into an advanced provisioning platform is a CAC engine. CAC has been around for some time. A simple example of it is a TDM phone exchange, which has a limited number of outgoing lines. If two outgoing calls are attempted at the same time, but only one outgoing line is available, there needs to be some kind of arbitration to decide which one gets priority (for example, one call may be to an emergency service), because the other call must be disallowed. CAC is used to dictate which of the two calls can proceed in lieu of the bandwidth limitation.

Web Portal

Most SPEs come with templates that providers can modify to suit local marketing requirements. Web portals are more than just a set of templates; they also are designed to interact with the subscriber database and drive the user provisioning process. Providers usually like to customize this interface to fit in with the style and feel of their existing branding, so these templates need to be extensible.

Middleware Controller

The middleware controller is at the heart of the SPE and is the most sophisticated of all the components. It receives requests from the web server for subscriber provisioning changes and converts them into requests for a server to activate over the SNI to activate on router elements if they need to be done in real time. It also triggers billing events and deals with any accounting data from the network.

The middleware controller needs good scripting capabilities built in. Common scripting includes Perl, Python, and JBoss. There should be a good range of APIs to allow service providers and third parties to build their own plug-ins. For instance, a plug-in might need to connect to an external credit card processing application and retrieve a user's credit history before that person is allowed to continue with a service purchase. Or if music downloads are made available through the SPE, it might need to connect to a third-party to pass on the details of the music downloads.

Technology Note: Middleware Plug-Ins

Much of the middleware's usefulness comes from modules called plug-ins, which are mini applications written to perform a specialized task related to a service or services. For example, a provider might use an Intrusion Detection System (IDS) that requires the SPE to interact with the IDS using a simple protocol such as HTTP. Based on the server's message, the SPE could decide to implement a special filter to block the intrusion attempt and trigger an e-mail to be sent to the customer. Plug-ins have hooks into the SPE state machine that dictate the module's functional flow, such as when to trigger external events and how to behave in error conditions.

Southbound Network Interface

Juniper's SDX is an example of an advanced dynamic provisioning engine that uses (among other protocols) a Common Open Policy Service (COPS)[2] interface to allow real-time subscriber attribute changes. COPS is a protocol specification written by the IETF that uses the concept of a Policy Enforcement Point (PEP), which in this case is the BNG and policy decision point (PDP), which is the database of user policies on a server. The PEP makes requests of the PDP based on a local event (say, a subscriber connecting). The PDP replies with an action to take, such as applying a rate limiter or a new QoS profile. COPS was built from the ground up as a service provisioning protocol, so it has features such as a reliable transport mechanism between the PEP and PDP (TCP), keeping regular state checks between the two (keepalives).

For comparison, RADIUS is a simpler, cruder example of a protocol that is used for southbound network provisioning. Although this protocol can be used for service provisioning by service providers and vendors, it is not a perfect fit for the task. First, UDP is the underlying protocol of RADIUS. In fact, the successor to RADIUS, DIAMETER, uses TCP or STCP as its underlying reliable transport mechanism rather than UDP. Second, COPS-PR was designed with the ability for the PDP to send policy changes to the PEP for real-time service changes. RADIUS has been modified to support similar functionality with the CoA, which lets the RADIUS server send unsolicited packets to the BNG for service changes. But this changes the protocol from its original design of a NAS-to-server protocol to one that works in both directions.

[2] http://www.rfc-editor.org/rfc/rfc2748.txt

RADIUS has been around long enough to support similar functionality. It has a huge deployment base, so it will be around for some time yet. But there are advantages to using a protocol that was built from the ground up with service provisioning in mind.

A similar argument goes for SNMP. This protocol can be suitable for making small provisioning changes or peeking at the router status, but it has limitations as a bulk configuration tool.

Call Admission Control

In a multiplay environment, Call Admission Control (CAC) means limiting the number of concurrent video streams of VoIP calls according to either available bandwidth in the network or due to policy control. Comprehensive bandwith CAC means tracking every link in the network that will transport the stream and ensuring that enough bandwidth is available for a session to proceed. It's unlikely that providers will implement full end-to-end bandwith CAC any time soon because of the amount of management overhead to monitor every router link when the network is functioning. This says nothing about a network failure. It can prove useful in areas that have real potential for congestion, such as in the aggregation network between the BNG and DSLAMs, and on local loops. Why not simply rely on QoS prioritization at the BNG? For best-effort Internet traffic, this is adequate, but for high-quality video and VoIP services that can tolerate very little loss under an "all or nothing" model, there needs to be a mechanism to completely disallow a call or stream to proceed if not enough bandwidth is available. For example, if a DSL line is synchronized at 10Mbps and can transmit only one HD-TV (High Definition Television) channel at 7Mbps, there is no point in allowing a second stream to be sent. Not only will the second stream not work due to insufficient bandwidth, but the first stream will be detrimentally affected, and any best-effort traffic will be starved of bandwidth. The same model applies for VoIP—the service is an all-or-nothing proposition. For example, if one VoIP call is active on a subscriber link and a second call is made, but without CAC, both calls would fail if there is not enough bandwidth for both. For fixed bit rate sessions, such as VoIP, statistical multiplexing of traffic does not work as well as more flexible traffic types.

Why not use this CAC model for other types of traffic? In the context of triple-play networks, VoIP and video streams are hosted by the service provider. The provider has knowledge of network capacity (or at least the important links), from the DSL line all the way to the application servers. Therefore, a CAC engine can decide at each point in the network whether there is enough capacity to permit a new call or video stream to proceed. Any other type of multimedia service, such as client-side videoconferencing and VoIP, is considered an off-net hosted service. Thus, it is not part of this model, because the provider is unaware of the characteristics of the media's signaling and payload streams. Without this information, it is not possible to fully accept or reject a client's request for media access. Therefore, the model needs to fall back to traditional priority-based QoS on the BNG (Chapter 8 has a more in-depth view of QoS). Such third-party services and applications are usually given a lower QoS priority than provider-hosted applications.

CAC deployment in residential triple-play networks is picking up at a moderate pace. Today some providers are making CAC calculations based on real-time local loop and simple aggregation network traffic flow information. Any potential for congestion at more complex aggregation layers, such as those with switches, is commonly handled in two ways. Either enough overhead is budgeted during capacity planning and plenty of bandwidth is assigned to video and VoIP services, or the middleware is programmed with enough network topology information to make a useful CAC decision. The decision to allow or disallow an extra stream is important for preserving overall service quality, because allowing a stream for which there is no capacity affects not only that stream, but all services currently running through the congested part of the network. As CAC systems become more prevalent and intelligent, they can incorporate knowledge of more parts of the network. For instance, suppose the local loop has enough bandwidth to send a Video on Demand channel to a house, but there isn't enough bandwidth on a core MPLS LSP to a PoP. The request from the STB could be rejected with an appropriate error code to the middleware, which is translated to something user friendly, then sent to the STB. A user message is displayed on the television indicating some kind of network problem. This congestion is obviously a situation to be avoided at all costs, but it illustrates an extreme example of how the feature could work. Ideally, instead of trying to close the proverbial stable door after the horse has bolted, a "high water" bandwidth utilization mark could trigger warnings to be sent to network terminals to warn of impending congestion.

Part of an effective CAC model on the local loop requires a minimum bandwidth at which the DSL port must synchronize. If the line cannot achieve any greater than this minimum rate, there are two options for service delivery. One option is that the line could be set to not train up, and therefore no service is provided. This is an undesirable option because it does not give the customer the option of choosing a data-only service. A more preferable option is that a line could be considered not suitable for triple-play service delivery, providing only Internet and VoIP. One other issue of complexity to consider is if the line *can* train at a high enough speed, a Set-Top Box (STB) can request video content that is usually a combination of multicast and unicast. Based on the minimum synchronization rate, only a certain combination of High Definition (HD) and Standard Definition (SD) multicast channel combinations can be requested by one or more STBs at the households. The STB is one place where the combinations of channels can be restricted. As an additional measure of protection, most BNGs implement per-subscriber multicast CAC functionality. For unicast Video on Demand services, the session combinations may be limited at the video server using either a built-in CAC mechanism, or CAC requests can be forwarded to an external server.

Per-subscriber multicast CAC is a feature that makes use of the signaling protocol that is used to join and leave multicast channels—Internet Group Management Protocol (IGMP). A BNG knows which channels (also called multicast groups) a household has requested based on IGMP packets sent from STBs. But first, some discussion about IGMP. Referring to the hybrid VLAN model discussed in Chapter 4, "Designing a Triple-Play Access Network," IGMP packets may come from subscribers via the multicast VLAN (MC-VLAN), the customer VLAN (C-VLAN), or even, at times, via both links. If the BNG receives IGMP packets on the C-VLAN, there needs to be a way to send the channel to the DSLAM via the multicast VLAN rather than down the customer VLAN. This is achieved using a multicast feature called forward Outbound Interface (OIF) mapping, which tells the BNG the correct multicast interface to use when IGMP requests arrive on the C-VLAN. If this mapping feature were not used, multicast traffic would be copied out each customer VLAN, defeating the purpose of DSLAM replication. In Figure 11.9, an IGMP request is sent from the home to the network. When the DSLAM receives this request, it snoops inside the packet and sets up the multicast bridging table. The BNG receives the packet and rather than send the group out the C-VLAN, the OIF causes the multicast data to be sent out the multicast VLAN.

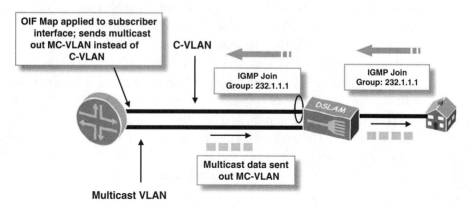

Figure 11.9 OIF mapping.

A variation on this theme is reverse OIF mapping (see Figure 11.10). This means that instead of the BNG receiving IGMP requests on the C-VLAN, it gets them on the multicast VLAN. Because the multicast VLAN is a single broadcast domain, the BNG needs to inspect the packet's source address and map it against an IP address that it has in a reverse OIF mapping table. Ideally, to save development time, this would be an existing subscriber IP address table on the BNG. As soon as the IP has been tied to a subscriber C-VLAN, the BNG knows which household requested the group.

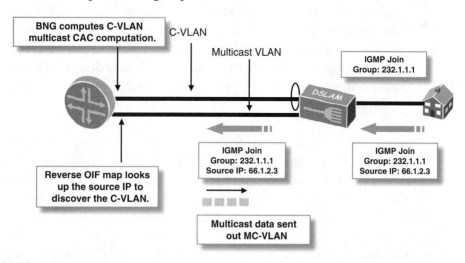

Figure 11.10 Reverse OIF mapping.

The difference between forward and reverse OIF mapping depends on the multi-cast access architecture, which relies heavily on DSLAM multicast capabilities. Putting all multicast traffic (both IGMP and video channels) on the MC-VLAN is the most common method because it is the most intuitive. Requests come in to the BNG on the MC-VLAN, and traffic leaves using the same router interface. However, to be able to implement more advanced features such as per-subscriber multicast CAC and QoS shaping adjustments on the C-VLAN (see Chapter 8 for information on BNG QoS multicast configurations), the BNG needs to know which groups each household requests. Forward OIF mapping is more intuitive because it does not involve any IP address mapping on the BNG. It relies on having a 1:1 relationship between a household and a C-VLAN.

How does this tie in with subscriber CAC? Recall that only a handful of SD-TV and HD-TV channel combinations can be sent to a household. Because each of these channels can have different video bitrates, the BNG needs to know the bandwidth of each channel. It also needs to know the total multicast bandwidth that can be sent to the household. One piece of functionality to acquire this knowledge is called a multicast bandwidth map, and it comes in two flavors: static and dynamic. With static bandwidth maps, a list of multicast groups and their corresponding bandwidths is entered via the CLI on the BNG. Dynamic bandwidth mapping means that the streams' throughputs are sampled in real time. The next step is to communicate to the BNG the maximum multicast throughput that a subscriber can receive. This can be done via either CLI or, more flexibly, RADIUS. Now that the BNG knows how much bandwidth each group takes up and what the multicast limit is on each C-VLAN, it can put these two elements together to create basic CAC functionality on a broadband edge router and deny a video stream request to a household if it requests too much bandwidth at once.

One scenario presents a significant problem with this architecture. The previous discussions relied on the BNG doing CAC on client requests. Recall that DSLAMs perform IGMP snooping on multicast group join-requests that are sent to the BNG. Unless a CAC mechanism is implemented on the DSLAM, it is possible that the DSLAM snoops an IGMP request on the customer session and starts sending it to the household even if the BNG may block the channel due to CAC. This creates a condition whereby the BNG is out of synchronization with what the DSLAM is transmitting.

One solution is to deliver multicast traffic to each subscriber over his or her unicast data session. Because the BNG can implement CAC on each circuit before multicast is delivered to the subscriber, an alternative is to implement complex CAC algorithms on the DSLAM that are aware of each channel's bandwidth and how this relates to a subscriber's link speed. This functionality would need to have good hooks into dynamic provisioning systems to update users' CAC profiles remotely. Such DSLAM functionality still has a way to go before it is widespread.

A third option is the Access Node Control Protocol (ANCP), which makes use of a Layer 2 Control (L2C) mechanism to control the DSLAM's forwarding state. When the subscriber requests a multicast group, the DSLAM does not send the group to the household unless the BNG sends a message to the DSLAM to allow the stream to proceed. When DSLAMs were aggregated on an ATM network and on the upstream path, one PVC was dedicated to a channel, this approach had some interest in the industry. For the Ethernet-connected DSLAM model, the jury is still out as to how L2C may interact with the DSLAMs to build the forwarding state.

A fourth option or group of options is to move the CAC functionality to the STB and allow it to communicate with a server in the network. There are several options as to what this server could be and what protocols would be used. The server could be the BNG, which communicates with a backend, or a dedicated CAC server. Potential protocols include RSVP and HTTP. The resources could be granted during a message exchange on a per-channel basis or a per-session basis. Possibly a more static option is for the STB to receive a configuration file from the network, letting it know what it can and cannot access. However, the STB's responsiveness based on real-time overall network utilization is limited, even if the network can push changes to the STB's configuration in close to real time.

In summary, there are no obvious answers, yet, to a scalable IPTV CAC solution for each type of VLAN/aggregation network architecture. Perhaps the most straightforward one that still allows dynamic session control is a dedicated C-VLAN to the customer that also carries IPTV traffic to the subscriber. If network PVR services take off in a big way, this will move much of the video content to a unicast model anyway, making the case stronger for this model. It does mean that the cost and per-subscriber bandwidth usage go up by a significant amount, because much of the network no longer has any multicast optimization.

SUMMARY

Setting up a dynamic service provisioning engine can seem like a daunting task for service providers, and the purported benefits can seem like they are peddled by snake-oil salesmen. This was in the past. Today the market has matured; it has a handful of vendors that offer more reputable products. These products come with ample modularity for service providers to select multiple levels of SPE integration, depending on the amount of customization required. Third-party products range from simple servers that take requests from in-house provisioning systems initiating real-time subscriber service changes on network elements, to full-blown provisioning engines. Having a good set of interfaces on the provisioning engine to allow building of third-party plug-ins is an important feature to include on your checklist. Also important is a good set of software toolkits to build external interfaces to databases, billing engines, and web portals. Running a multivendor broadband router network is common in the provider market, so a system that can interface with more than one brand of network element to make provisioning changes is a useful (and sometimes mandatory) feature. It's not surprising that router vendors have not rushed to develop modules on their systems for interacting with other vendors. But at least the basic software toolkits are there to develop the necessary applications.

SECURITY IN BROADBAND NETWORKS

The Internet is still a friendly place with friendly people. They are your neighbors, and they have home networks just like you do. However, there are lines of delineation between zones of trust, and just as there are doors on houses and businesses, there are gateways between points on broadband networks. This chapter describes the security concerns that face service providers and presents some solutions.

Broadband Network Gateways (BNGs) are IP aggregation points for thousands of customers. It is important to note that the BNG is the IP termination point where routing occurs and where the IP service starts. The other elements, such as residential gateways, access nodes, and Ethernet aggregation networks, provide transport.

Service provider networks have two primary goals when providing security. First is protecting the service provider domain. This means that the service provider needs to protect its network from external parties, including customers and external networks. Second, it is usually high on the list to protect customers from external networks. After all, the service provider's goal is to provide a reliable and useful service. If conditions create dissatisfactory service, the customers will likely find another provider.

Some security concepts overlap between protecting the service provider and protecting the customer. The next section and "Residential Gateway Security Features" delve into these topics.

DENIAL OF SERVICE

The last ten years have seen significant denial of service (DoS) attacks across the Internet. They have created havoc for providers and have caused network outages, billing issues, unavailable websites that provide both commercial and noncommercial content, and frustration for millions of users. These attacks come in many flavors and sizes and typically have a single goal: to make a particular host, network, or service unavailable.

Reasons for DoS attacks vary. The DoS attacker subculture has focused on building namesakes or repertoire for the size (in terms of time lost) or significance of service they have affected. UNIX systems in the 1980s saw attacks by single users inflict damage to shared systems. Some attacks focused on creating the maximum number of processes that a system could handle. The mid-1990s saw DoS attacks that focused on e-mail and FTP services, with the goal of filling server storage and effectively preventing valid e-mail and files from being transferred to the server. These attacks usually were not destructive to the network, but rather focused on particular systems. Thus, they commonly were rectified by systems administrators.

Attacks over the next few years became more network-focused. In 1997, with a release of source code and attack method, millions of Windows 95 computers on the Internet became susceptible to an attack called WinNuke, which crashed the computer. These attacks were possible over the Internet simply by sending a small string of data to a listening port on the computer. The target of these attacks appeared largely focused on individual hosts or subnets. Because the traffic volume was light, network providers were not very concerned about revenue loss due to attacks.

This all changed with flooding attacks, which consumed vast amounts of network backbone traffic. One of the most recognized attacks is the "smurf" attack, named after the application bearing the same name. This technique used the functionality of many routers at the time that allowed packets that were sent to remote IP broadcast addresses to be delivered to Layer 2 broadcasts. This functionality, combined with IP spoofing (changing or spoofing the source address of traffic) attacks, led to a situation in which a single IP ping that was delivered to an IP network could generate amplified ICMP responses from hundreds of hosts. If the initial transmission to the targeted network was sourced with a spoofed IP address, then hundreds of responses would be sent to the victim network that owned the spoofed IP address. The real attacker was essentially a third party that created the network storm. Tracing these types of attacks was difficult, because it involved networks sending massive amounts of traffic to other networks, even though one network did not originate the request. Even worse, it was possible to source a network address that amplified traffic and to use this IP source address to send to other amplifiers. The real attacker simply observed the behavior (usually by pinging servers on the targeted networks and monitoring round-trip latency) as the two targeted networks began flooding each other until either their or their upstream carrier's networks reached capacity.

Smurf attacks are no longer common for a number of reasons. Best-practice documents from network vendors and discussions within network operator forums helped quell the issues by making network changes that disabled the use of IP directed broadcasts, which is how a smurf attack starts. Additionally, one of the most important network changes that has been introduced on the edge of many providers is the concept of Reverse Path Forwarding (RPF), which makes it easy for service providers to prevent IP spoofing.

Reverse Path Forwarding

The concept of RPF checking is simple. Routers that implement RPF checks accept IP packets when they have a route to the source of the packet on the same interface on which they receive the packet. For instance, if the router has a route table entry for the prefix 192.168.10/24, which is reachable via interface GigabitEthernet2/0.100, and this interface has RPF checking enabled, the router will accept only packets from hosts within the 192.168.10/24 address range on this particular interface. This function in the router checks the reverse path for a received packet and accepts it if the router would normally send a packet to that address via the same interface.

RPF checking on BNGs is essential. On most hardware-based routers, the RPF check does not cause any noticeable forwarding delay, although it allows packets to be checked for spoofing. If this functionality is enabled on all subscriber interfaces, it may not stop attacks, but at least it will ensure that packets which originate from the subscribers are using their valid addresses, as shown in Figure 12.1. This makes tracking attacks much easier.

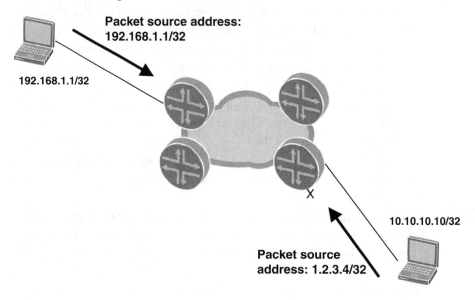

Figure 12.1 RPF in action.

RESIDENTIAL GATEWAY SECURITY FEATURES

The home router, now commonly called a Residential Gateway (RG), carries a greater number of features than before, which protect the subscriber from Internet attacks. The device needs to be able to protect itself from common TCP anomalies and attacks such as LAND, Ping of Death, TCP syn floods, TCP reset attacks, and invalid Internet Protocol packets. These types of attacks are common on the Internet; they target the IP stack that is implemented on devices. Devices that are vulnerable to these types of attacks usually reset or crash if they receive these attacks.

Providers would have a difficult time troubleshooting the connection's transient behavior if the customer's gateway was being attacked. It is important for service providers to reduce the number of help desk calls that are associated with lack of connectivity. Therefore, it is advisable that service providers select or recommend devices that provide an adequate level of security for the home premises. When security is ensured or tightened, it becomes easier to position more reliable services, because the service is not as vulnerable to degradation.

RG features vary depending on vendor and model. Here are some of the basic security features that should be available on residential gateways:

- Configurable firewall with the ability to log the packets that match specific rules
- Ability to block or not respond to ping on the WAN interface
- Session Initiation Protocol (SIP) Application Layer Gateway to open ports for voice traffic
- Ability to create VLANs on Ethernet ports to allow for segmentation between different home networks
- Classification of traffic based on five-tuple (source, destination, protocol, source ports, destination ports) and possibly TCP flags. This is useful for QoS configuration on the residential gateway, because it allows traffic flows to be classified, and then scheduling mechanisms can create the proper prioritization for the traffic.
- Network Address Translation / Port Address Translation (NAT/PAT)
- Port forwarding to allow external hosts to reach internal hosts on specific ports
- Demilitarized zone (DMZ) configuration for specific hosts

With a combination of provider-based security mechanisms and security features that are implemented in residential gateway products, the subscriber network can focus on using and enjoying services and not worrying about each packet that is directed its way.

BROADBAND NETWORK SECURITY AND VoIP

Traditional telephone systems give the residential customer a telephone service without providing a gateway to the service's signaling mechanisms. Phone systems allow limited commands from subscribers, usually limited to the on-hook/off-hook and DTMF inputs and in some cases, R2 signaling. Since the 1970s, the phone system has moved away from in-band signaling, and rightly so.

In some respects, voice over IP (VoIP) systems allow customers to interface with calls' signaling mechanics. VoIP still has the split concept of the voice stream and the signaling flows, yet implementations of VoIP have essentially placed the signaling interface back with subscribers. This is why security of VoIP for broadband networks is critical.

Let's compare some concepts between standard phone networks and VoIP networks. Standard phone networks typically have no user-supplied credentials to the phone system. There are exceptions, such as party lines, and call-gate calling features, where PIN codes are entered to enable specific calling patterns, such as to permit a long-distance call. However, most commonly, upon picking up a telephone handset, the call is already authenticated, because the actual line authenticates the customer. The fact that the POTS line is actually located at the subscriber's residence is enough authentication that the call is being placed by the appropriate party. VoIP services are different. They are not bound to the subscriber's physical location. Because IP packets can originate from anywhere on an inter-network, additional models for trust are needed.

These are the VoIP security issues that face service providers:

- Reliable authentication of subscriber details
- Prevention of fraud
- Mitigation against potential DoS attacks on the VoIP service
- Lawful interception capabilities within the service provider network

Subscriber registrations for VoIP services using SIP are performed in clear text in most implementations. Within a single service provider domain, this is not that much of a concern, because the provider can control the access and has a relationship with the residential voice subscriber.

THE SECURITY OF VoIP AND CREDENTIALS

Enforcing reliable authentication of subscriber details goes hand in hand with prevention of fraud. With valid authentication details, an IP host can place calls that may incur charges to a subscriber and the service provider. If the subscriber SIP credentials are compromised, it becomes possible for an attacker to place calls that are billed to another party. For this reason, it is highly recommended that service providers generate the passwords that are used for SIP devices. User-generated passwords would pose a risk and liability to the service provider should a brute-force method be applied to the SIP registrar in an attempt to find valid credentials.

Using managed residential gateways with VoIP support, or when more advanced users (possibly with softphones or WiFi VoIP phones) receive credentials for the network, these credentials should be generated by the service provider to ensure there is some randomness in the choice of credentials.

SESSION BORDER CONTROLLERS AS APPLICATION LAYER PROXIES

A soft switch is the name for an IP-capable telephony switch and protecting them is essential because of the importance placed on the switching infrastructure. Carriers that are interested in providing VoIP to PSTN handoff, or even PSTN replacement technologies need to ensure that the connections to their actual switches are handled in a secure fashion. Session Border Controllers (SBCs) help protect this switching infrastructure by creating an additional security layer between clients and the switching domain. SBCs provide back-to-back user agent support, which acts as an application layer proxy.

SBCs can provide additional control in VoIP networks. Features include the following:

- Network address translation
- Deep packet inspection on SIP / H.323 VoIP signaling packets
- Quality of Service (QoS) markings and prioritization based on call details
- DoS prevention and detection
- Lawful interception capabilities

Carrier-grade VoIP solutions are also best served with Intrusion Detection Systems (IDSs) that can inspect VoIP signaling packets (SIP/H.225) and analyze protocol anomalies that may cause issues with voice gateways and soft switches. These SIP and H.225 packets could be malformed, and consequently would exploit the protocol stack on the voice gateways. Such anomalies may be packets that have the following characteristics:

- SIP header refers to nonstandard procedures or non-RFC-compliant methods
- SIP packet fields are too large
- SIP max-forwards are a nonrecommended value
- SIP unknown headers

IDS systems that reside on the path to the SBC or voice gateway should perform this protocol inspection and alert on issues, as illustrated in Figure 12.2. Because crackers generally try to explore the system behavior before launching a direct attack, it is wise to investigate issues before you actually have a system fault or compromise.

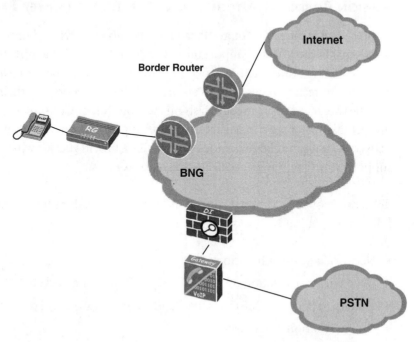

Figure 12.2 IDS protecting a voice gateway.

As shown in Figure 12.2, the deep inspection firewall inspects all flows that are directed to and from the VoIP gateway. For SIP phones and SIP clients that are built into residential gateways (RGs), the VoIP flows traverse the BNG, cross the service provider core, and then pass through the deep inspection firewall. The firewall ensures that properly formatted packets and valid content are being directed to the gateway.

Some SIP trunks can be reached over the Internet. For this reason it is important to inspect SIP flows to and from the Internet. The deep inspection firewall can reach the border routers or additional provider edge routers to reach other networks.

TRANSPORT SECURITY ISSUES WITH VoIP NETWORKS

As soon as subscribers get used to the benefits of advanced calling features and cheaper calling rates that are associated with VoIP, they will want to take these services with them when they are on the road, at the coffee shop, or at the airport. The problem is that many if not most of these mentioned networks carry a degree of risk that cannot be fully quantified. The public network that a computer or device connects to may have any number of vulnerabilities or potential hackers.

Many public access points do not use WEP or WPA security because of the difficulty in getting users to connect. With an open access point and no encryption, it is possible to eavesdrop or sniff the wireless packets from a WiFi-enabled SIP phone or even a softphone that runs on a laptop. Inside the wireless channel, the Ethernet frames may contain SIP registration messages and credentials for the user that could easily be reconfigured on another WiFi handset or in another client. The attacker can then place calls that will be billed against the original roaming user.

Immediate solutions to the issue are to establish VPNs (either IPSec or SSL) back to a service provider before passing credentials in clear text. This approach is an expensive solution in terms of the computing power and software required in the handset. Furthermore, devices might not have the VPN software built in.

The target architecture to deal with this issue is provided in Secure SIP or SIP over Transport Layer Security (TLS). RFC 3261 specifies this security framework in the TLS subsection. Business-grade IP phones that are being produced today contain this functionality. The hard part is finding providers that support TLS VoIP services.

Additional risks that need to be considered when taking IP phones onto untrusted networks are the devices' software vulnerabilities. For example, there have been reports of WiFi IP phones that in their default out-of-the-box configuration allow SNMP *get* and *set* commands. This lets the device be reconfigured by anyone on the Internet. Another WiFi handset model has a default telnet daemon that allows access based on default usernames and passwords. Once inside the phone, an attacker can modify system variables and operating system registers. With some in-house testing, providers could weed out most of the risky models of phones and recommend the approved models to their consumer base if the phones are not provided as part of the service subscription.

WHOLESALE VoIP SECURITY ON BROADBAND NETWORKS

One of the goals of Next-Generation Networks (NGNs) that carriers are deploying is not only to enable new service creation, but to reduce costs. The cost reduction is achieved by delivering multiple services on a single network instead of maintaining many disparate networks, each with its own expensive circuits and equipment. Many carriers currently sell toll-quality voice through standard residential phones. With the launch of VoIP services it would be important not to devalue all the existing PSTN business through arbitrage, but it is wise to complement the service by offering less expensive calling rates on services that cost the provider less. VoIP would cost the provider less because the infrastructure required to carry and terminate the call is cheaper.

Telecommunication companies that have a large local presence in a specific region may want to explore the option of taking in additional revenue streams by selling voice termination to international or other local providers. A wholesale environment has a loose relationship between the wholesale provider and the customer purchasing voice termination or call routing.

The purchasing customer may be in another country, and she might want to buy local dialing rates in the provider's country. With VoIP all of this is possible, although it does mean that the provider needs to expose part of its network to the Internet. Session border controllers should be placed at the network edge in the DMZ, as shown in Figure 12.3. This allows VoIP trunks over SIP (SIP peers) to be established between autonomous systems. Figure 12.3 shows a service provider with connectivity to the Internet via its border router, and connectivity to other private networks. For resiliency and scaling purposes, the provider may use dedicated session border controllers between private networks.

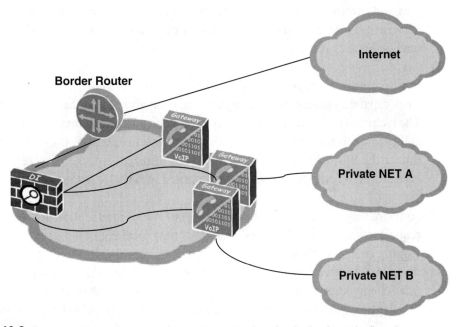

Figure 12.3 Session border controllers connecting to various networks and to the deep inspection firewall.

In the figure, the telecommunications provider may serve as an interim network between Private NET A and Private NET B. Calls between these networks may be routed directly within the SP network, and special functions may be applied for these call destinations.

A provider that wants to wholesale the termination of voice minutes on its VoIP infrastructure may consider attracting international companies by making the service available over the Internet via SIP.

LAWFUL INTERCEPTION IN BROADBAND NETWORKS

Government and law agencies have begun applying pressure to carriers to ensure that the carriers will provide mechanisms for agencies to trigger the monitoring of specific traffic flows and to send this data directly to the agencies. It is a complex and controversial subject for numerous reasons, but most importantly because it creates a security paradigm between a carrier and a somewhat trusted outside force.

From a business perspective, the agency is an untrusted entity. But from a network capability perspective, the agency has been given a significant level of trust. The technical implications are real. Most specifically, lawful interception is the ability to intercept entire IP streams, usually both to and from the customer, and mirror the IP streams to law agencies that scrutinize the packets for illegal or relevant content (once the flows are recomposed into useful data).

Software feature sets on routers in the area of lawful interception are dictated by requests from carriers that need to comply with local regulations regarding wiretapping and surveillance laws. For example, within some localities it is required that general network operators will not be able to detect that a particular interface is being intercepted. This means that there is a level of abstraction on lawful interception functionality and the details that troubleshooting operators can see.

TRIGGERS ON BNG INTERFACES

The BNG can trigger lawful interception capabilities by Command-Line Interface (CLI) commands or with RADIUS Change of Authorization (CoA) messages. CoA messages can allow a RADIUS server to modify subscriber attributes, such as enabling the mirroring of traffic to or from the subscriber session to an analyzer port (outbound mirrored port). This functionality is intended for lawful intercept capabilities, but it also works well for network troubleshooting when trying to diagnose protocol issues with clients.

CONFIDENTIALITY

Mirroring the data is not enough in some networks. Because the intercepted traffic could actually be an attack on a top-secret government computer, the data needs to be confidentially transferred over the service provider core. In some implementations this can be handled with an IPSec or SSL VPN tunnel between the interception point and the mediation point (the agency). This capability is important to some law agencies to prevent prying eyes (within the service provider) on the attack by sniffing backbone traffic.

DENIAL OF SERVICE ON AUTHENTICATION SYSTEMS

Each time a broadband subscriber connects to a service provider, resources to authenticate the user are consumed. Regardless of whether the user is connected via DHCP, PPPoA, PPPoE, or IPoE, internal system processes are spent processing the user's authentication attempt. Service providers need to protect their network from misconfigured clients and malicious users who may expose resource limitations in back-end authentication systems.

For example, consider a common setup for PPPoA/PPPoE subscribers in which PAP/CHAP credentials are configured in an ADSL modem. The modem may be configured to reconnect upon link failure, so the modem constantly retries to authenticate a subscriber. When the modem attempts to authenticate a subscriber, the BNG takes the supplied username/password credentials, queues them in RADIUS requests, and issues requests of a RADIUS authentication server.

Commonly, there are fixed numbers of outstanding RADIUS messages that can be processed or queued on both the BNG and RADIUS authentication servers. At the same time that this single modem is attempting to reconnect, hundreds of other RADIUS authentication requests might be occurring. The danger to the service provider is that with rapid succession of attempts on a single subscriber connection, it may be possible to prevent valid authentication attempts from other subscribers due to insufficient resources in the network. Usually the end client cannot be trusted to do the right thing, therefore the BNG should implement good control protocol rate-limit mechanisms to protect itself from attacks, whether intentional or not.

SOLUTIONS FOR ENHANCING SECURITY ON AUTHENTICATION SYSTEMS

The following sections contain some ideas and concepts that can improve authentication systems on carrier networks. By no means is this a complete list. Some of the ideas may be difficult to integrate into existing provisioning and OSS systems. The goal is to recognize the important role that authentication systems play within carrier networks and to reduce the risk to service degradation.

AUTHENTICATE AND ACCEPT ALL REQUESTS

One approach is to provide a RADIUS authentication accept along with other RADIUS Vendor-Specific Attributes (VSAs) that allow the subscriber to connect and receive an IP address inside a routing context with no connectivity to real services. Basically, for a user who supplies invalid credentials, the system accepts the user and places him in an area that does not provide external services, such as the Internet. This could be combined with a web redirecting portal that tells the user that he has entered invalid credentials, tells him how to troubleshoot the issue, and supplies him with a procedure for rectifying the situation.

This strategy reduces the strain on the back-end systems and the BNG, because most PPP clients are satisfied that they have connected when they receive an IP address. It is important to mention that this technique is of value only if the client is a valid PPP client and not a malicious attack. Specially designed client applications have been created by attackers that generate authentication attempts at line-rate speeds. This has caused some BNGs to begin dropping authentication requests from valid authentication clients.

Authenticating to the network with PPP credentials (username and password) may not be necessary if the provider grants access based on a subscriber line versus access based on the user-defined attributes. This form of authentication is identical to how a telephone is used today.

PASSWORD-FREE NETWORKS

When the concept of using a password to get access to the network does not exist, a few things become apparent. First, a security element (theft of accounts to do password compromise) is removed. Second, delivering the service is easier. Application services such as VoIP and other subscriber-centric services may still require a password or some form of authentication. But by removing the network-level password, a provider may benefit financially by reducing Operational Expenses (OpEx) from fewer support-related calls concerning password issues. However, the main benefit of this approach is to begin trusting infrastructure more and subscriber-supplied passwords less. A PPP environment still has ways to accomplish the same concept. Having a standard username and password, preferably ones that are the defaults on the residential gateway, can allow the service provider to easily enliven the service.

LOAD BALANCING OF AUTHENTICATION SYSTEMS

Placing network load balancers in front of the AAA systems allows peak loads to be distributed across multiple AAA servers, as shown in Figure 12.4. Load balancers typically have their own method of high availability or resiliency. Application health checks allow the load balancers to monitor if a particular AAA server is responding. These make use of AAA packets that are sent from the load-balancers and solicit a reply if all is in order These checks are a good measure to use so that the load balancing functionality does not forward packets to systems that are not responding.

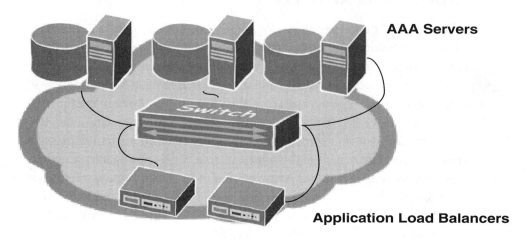

Figure 12.4 Application load balancers.

SECURING VIDEO DISTRIBUTION SYSTEMS

When securing video distribution systems, it is best to split the topic into two separate areas of discussion. The first is security concerns when joining broadcast channels, and the second is security concerns with video on demand (VoD) systems. Additionally, you can restrict which channels may be joined at a network layer. We talk about it in this section.

MULTICAST JOIN STATE AND SPEED WITH BROADCAST CHANNELS

Internet Group Membership Protocol (IGMP) is used by clients to join multicast channels or groups. An issue that has been discussed in great detail within networking forums is the speed at which channels may be changed on IP backbones that serve multicast streams. The goal is to provide not only fast channel changes, but also efficient network utilization.

IGMP join time needs to be fast, but because these packets are control packets, they need to be inspected by the BNG to ensure that a flood of IGMP packets does not bombard the BNG. Suspicious flow detection, which is discussed later in this chapter, detects IGMP thresholds on a per-customer basis and enforces sane joins-per-second.

Some providers use static joins to popular groups on a multicast VLAN that faces the aggregation network and then the access node. The statically defined groups would be defined on the BNG and may reference the normal suite of broadcast television channels. The intended behavior is to provide faster join times, because the group would already be available on the aggregated network and quite possibly would already be available on the access node. For more unique programming content, such as The Whale Channel, the IGMP messages would be transparently snooped on the access node and would flow all the way up to the BNG. The BNG would then join the specific group that contains The Whale Channel, and the forwarding of traffic would flow down to the customer.

MULTICAST GROUP ACCESS LISTS WITH BROADCAST CHANNELS

The BNG may have policies that enforce which channels a user may receive. On Juniper Networks JUNOSe and Cisco Systems IOS, these policies are enforced on a per-interface basis by consulting an access list that accepts or rejects specific groups that are referenced in an IGMP message. Service providers typically create a handful of profiles for video packages they want to offer, such as the following:

- Gold package (all multicast groups)
- Movie package (premium movie groups)
- Sports package (major international and local sports channels)

Corresponding access lists that reference the groups are applied to individual customer interfaces.

Many video systems now rely on securing content by using Public Key Infrastructure (PKI), encrypting all the video content, and decrypting the content at the set-top box—although a good safeguard is still to have some IGMP access-lists on the network edge, perhaps for unencrypted groups that are part of a package for which the user needs to subscribe.

VIDEO ON DEMAND SECURITY

VoD services allow users to choose video content and have it delivered on-demand to their video clients. The technology behind the scenes uses centralized or distributed servers that provide a series of time/resource slots in which clients connect. The servers stream the content and the clients buffer a few seconds of the stream in case of packet or frame drop in the network. Because the video stream is dedicated to a single client, it makes sense that this traffic would be delivered unicast to the client.

Firewalls and Intrusion Detection and Prevention (IDP/IDS) systems with application layer support for securing video servers are important to protecting the video area within the network framework. This includes features such as preventing SYN or UDP attacks to the infrastructure, corrupt protocols, or simply too many requests from a single client. Most carrier-grade firewalls can cope with large traffic flows and high bit rates and can prevent SYN and RST attacks against infrastructure.

Due to the nature of video, it takes only a short duration of degradation on the carrier network's VoD servers to create a serious problem. Losing only a single frame in MPEG streams can cause a noticeable issue for the subscriber. For this reason, some VoD solutions use dedicated servers that buffer large portions of the streamed video content and allow the client or set-top boxes to re-request portions of the data. All of this happens at the application level. It's important to protect these VoD servers from even accidental resource exhaustion caused by subscriber-initiated requests.

PROTECTING THE CONTROL PLANE IN THE ROUTING INFRASTRUCTURE

Modern BNGs provide rate limiting on a per-protocol basis from the forwarding plane to the control plane. The router's rate-limiting capability allows the BNG to protect itself from erroneous or malicious clients that send a high rate of packets that require the control plane to inspect or respond.

In a typical broadband access environment, a BNG runs subscriber management protocols such as PPPoE and DHCP and routing protocols such as BGP toward the core. The BNG is a termination point for thousands of customers. Therefore, if a flood of control packets arrives at the router, prioritization of protocols toward the control plane should occur. The primary goal of this behavior is to prevent failure of critical control plane functionality, such as the loss of BGP sessions if ICMP traffic is directed to the BNG.

BNGs must be able to distinguish between the different types of protocols that arrive at the network interface cards and provide a throttling mechanism on a choke point between the forwarding plane and the control plane. One way to think of this behavior is that the router identifies traffic by protocol, such as ICMP, BGP, PPP/LCP, or OSPF. The router then assigns specific internal rate limiters by protocol. This is a double-edged sword. If a single user were to fill a central PPP packet queue, other PPP customers would be affected. Therefore it makes more sense to detect anomalies and provide mechanisms to quell suspicious flows of protocol traffic from specific customer interfaces.

SUSPICIOUS FLOW DETECTION

Suspicious Flow Detection (SFD) functionality in BNGs is a major plus, because it allows the router to analyze traffic, detect suspicious traffic flows, and then disable interface stacks for a period of time. This requires the maintenance of state information, which can be quite expensive. However, if implemented correctly, the system can achieve a good level of protection required to mitigate the effect of protocol attacks.

One example implementation of SFD is supported in Juniper's JUNOSe operating system. The low-level protocols are analyzed at the BNG and it tracks the rate on an individual subscriber basis for a multitude of protocols, including ARP, DHCP requests, PPPoE PADI messages, ATM 1483 OAM and LMI, IP, ICMP, and MPLS. In the event that a specific flow is marked as suspicious, all packets pertaining to the flow are dropped on the line card until the flow expires or when the flow is no longer marked as suspicious.

Some examples of control protocol flooding that should be prevented in BNGs are IP TTL floods, extremely rapid DHCP requests, IP options, router alert, and PPP LCP echo/request. The consequence of not detecting and eliminating this traffic from the network edge is a poorly performing network and edge element. Thousands of users may be affected if these control packets are not properly eliminated at the edge. However, some requests can be effectively controlled only at an interface to the server layer by a firewall because of the complex protocol inspection that needs to be done. Filtering network-level and some application-level protocol flows scales better at the network edges. But if the protocol machinery is relatively complex or there is a need to continually maintain IP address lists, this may scale better at a centralized point.

NetFlow/J-Flow/C-Flow Statistical Collection

Collecting traffic flow statistics (not to be confused with suspicious flows) on BNGs provides a method to understand the traffic at a more granular level. Flows are collected based on sampling of traffic that is forwarded. A flow typically consists of information from the IP header and transport-layer header, such as IP source address, IP destination address, protocol, source port, destination port, and sometimes, router interface. A flow record or multiple flow records are sent to configured collection hosts for each flow that is sampled. Flows are given an identifier in the flow record to allow correlation on offline systems to determine if multiple flow records refer to a single flow.

The raw data of flow records can then be compiled into useful offline tools that produce detailed graphs and stochastic modeling of network traffic with a bit of intelligence. The benefit of using NetFlow instead of, or in combination with, standard interface graphing is that you can create graphs that show top packet forwarders, protocols that occur most frequently, detection of Distributed Denial of Service (DDoS) networks and attacks, and forensic details to trace attacks that have already occurred.

As soon as the information is collected from routers in the network, the flows can be stored in databases and archives on servers. Here, relevant information can be gathered by parsing the information into readable graphs and statistics. If attacks or spam originate from the service provider network and logs are supplied from a reporting IS, an operator can search for traffic flows that correspond to the reporting party. Then the operator can determine if and when the traffic actually did source from the alleged perpetrator.

The other added benefit concerning security is the ability to watch, trend, and possibly respond to new network anomalies. These might include a new worm or virus that is infecting machines on the Internet and, in turn, infecting additional hosts. If the overall traffic volume remains steady, it would be difficult to realize that the worm is running rampant through the network. One way to tell would be if the flow statistics showed a new port (possibly used by the worm to spread) that is increasing in usage at a tremendous rate.

PACKET FILTERS

Applying strict packet filters to BNGs to protect against control protocol attacks is not as vital if SFD is enabled. The listening ports for various protocols typically are bound to specific interfaces and routing instances. For example, if BGP is enabled on core-facing interfaces in the default routing instance, customers who are terminated into another routing instance can not open a TCP session with the BGP daemon on the router.

Packet filters to protect users from worms and trojans may be necessary to protect the user's service and the Internet's stability. Global routing was destabilized by the SQL Slammer worm as it began scanning multicast address ranges. This generated a large number of source addresses (SAs) on networks running Multicast Source Discovery Protocol (MSDP).

Other worms such as Code Red simply created such an incredible scanning and infection rate that the bandwidth congestion on links created BGP time-outs. The BGP time-outs turned into flapping behavior, which led to BGP dampening, which caused widespread network unreachability.

For these reasons it is at the operator's discretion to apply packet filters that help protect the routing infrastructure and, in some cases, protect the clients directly, even if this means giving the subscriber a filtered IP connection.

BLACKHOLE/SINKHOLE ROUTING

When DDoS attacks enter from either the provider's customers or other networks, it is necessary to get a handle on the traffic—and quickly! Backbone network operators may already be familiar with blackhole or sinkhole routing. The concept involves preconfigured policies on the network that are enacted when traffic is singled out and referenced in the policy. Blackhole routing usually allows a provider to drop traffic for a specific prefix or route the traffic to a discard/null interface. BGP policy can influence or trigger blackhole routing by tagging the appropriate BGP community that is matched in BGP policy around the network.

Sinkhole routing is useful for the same purpose and is essentially the same concept, except that the traffic is routed to an analyzer. This is very similar to lawful
interception. However, with a sinkhole, the traffic usually comes from another
network or multiple networks, and the idea is to capture a better understanding
of it, or simply to discard it. These may be DDoS attacks that are being received
from multiple autonomous systems (ASs) that are peers of the provider. Figures
12.5, 12.6, and 12.7 show a sequence of these variations in action.

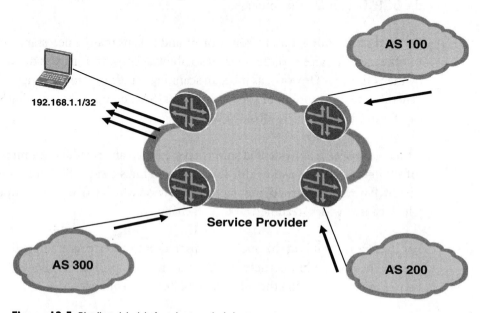

Figure 12.5 Distributed denial of service to a single host.

Figure 12.6 shows how the DoS traffic can be blocked at the ingress of the network. One way to achieve this is to match the destination address of the flow or
flows and advertise these routes to the other routers in the AS via IBGP with a
special community value. This community value instructs routers to discard traffic matching that destination.

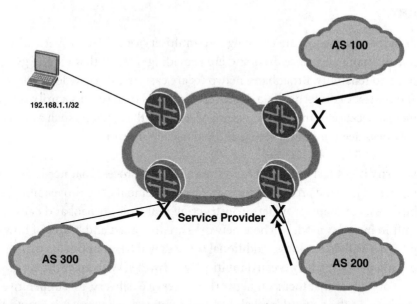

Figure 12.6 Sinkhole of traffic to an attacked host by discarding the DoS flow's source address at the border routers.

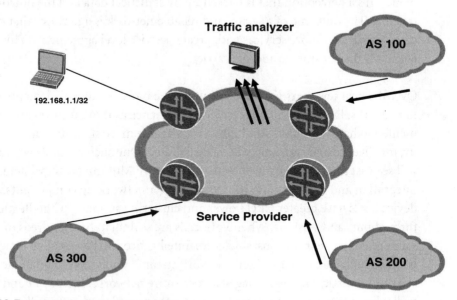

Figure 12.7 Sinkhole of traffic to an attacked host.

SUMMARY

Broadband networks are evolving into multiservice networks. Networks are supporting more and more users and are providing services that require greater control and reliability. Broadband networks are carrying voice, video, more data, and best-effort Internet data. Each service has its own set of security requirements. Because of the critical nature of some of the services, such as voice, the networks need to ensure secure and reliable architectures.

Security is not just access lists and firewalls. It's a process that needs to be ingrained into the protocols, the systems, the elements, the provisioning, and the business. For many providers, constructing multi-play broadband networks is a shift in business models. These networks are the bread and butter of how the provider will do business. Additional services will be components that can be provided on the newly created multi-play networks. With an entire series of business objectives that focus on network and service delivery, it is imperative to think about the network's reliability. If the network is secure, it is bound to enhance the service's reliability. Higher reliability is a concept, much like performance. It's a perception that is backed up by statistical data and the outcome is tangible. The outcome of a secure and reliable network is a network that can carry and deliver more services with greater service level agreements. This is beneficial for the consumers and the carrier.

Over the next few years we will continue to see more intelligent elements added to networks. Firewalls will increase in performance as more features are implemented in hardware ASICs and FPGAs. To handle more state and more complexity, intelligence and signaling will be distributed. One such example where we will see vast improvements will be the focus on IP Multimedia Subsystem (IMS) integration and concepts into routers and other networking components. Single-device SBCs have greater CPU power and clustering support to handle higher throughputs and sessions. When VoIP calls are scaling to the hundreds of thousands of concurrent sessions, single-box intelligence will have scaling issues. This is why intelligence of VoIP signaling, VoIP streams, and video channel membership and statistics will be managed across entire networks. Intelligent and controllable routers, which are already getting standards-based APIs, will simply become control points. The opening and closing of ports and access for signaled sessions will be controlled on the intelligent network as a whole.

The concept of broadband networks with multi-play services has sparked the creation of many additional protocols. These protocols will be scrutinized by security professionals and systems hackers. Protocols and hacking techniques will become more complex. The architects, designers, engineers, businesspeople, and users are at an important point in time. Broadband networks that deliver all services will become more widely deployed, and the reliance on them will increase. This will push security technologies to delve into more complex attacks and inspection, thereby creating a better service for consumers and a better network for providers.

Glossary of Acronyms and Key Terms

1:1 VLAN structure—In general terms, 1:1 is an architecture that matches one resource to one user or requestor. In a broadband access context, it is a VLAN architecture that assigns one VLAN per DSL port, or household.

2B1Q—2 binary, 1 quaternary. A physical-layer line-coding scheme that was used in early HDSL lines. The signal has four voltage levels, each of which represents 2 bits. One of its benefits over the early AMI scheme is its improved electromagnetic spectrum efficiency.

5-tuple—A compact way of expressing a combination of source IP address, destination IP address, transport protocol type (TCP or UDP), source transport port, and destination protocol port. A 5-tuple commonly identifies a traffic flow because throughout the life of a TCP or UDP-based session, the ports remain the same.

802.1AD—An IEEE specification that defines several aspects of Ethernet provider bridges. The most important aspect is the notion of the service provider VLAN tag, or S-VLAN, as it is called in this book.

802.1AH—An IEEE specification that defines aspects of Ethernet provider backbone bridges. The two important topics in this specification that are discussed in this book are MAC-in-MAC encapsulation and Ethernet in the First Mile (EFM).

802.1P—An IEEE specification for Ethernet that is used in specifications IEEE 802.1Q and IEEE 802.1D. It uses 3 bits on an 802.1Q header. These 3 bits allow for eight classes that can indicate the frame's priority to switches and routers.

802.1Q—Also called VLAN trunking. Allows devices to share the same physical path but be separated into different logical paths. This lets users be restricted to a given Layer 2 broadcast domain. A VLAN tag allows for up to 4,095 different VLANs.

AAA—Authentication, authorization, and accounting. Refers to the processes triggered when a user tries to access the network (authentication) and what the user can access (authorization). Also provides accounting back to the network for the user's session (accounting).

AAL5—ATM Adaptation Layer 5. The fifth layer is an efficient way (compared to other ATM adaptation layers) to transmit packets over an ATM network. Other ATM adaptation layers, such as 1 and 2, are used for voice transmission, for example.

AC—Attachment circuit. A term associated with pseudowires (also called Virtual Private Wire Service [VPWS]) to identify the circuit on the access side of the network. The attachment circuit is linked to a pseudowire for transmission across the network.

ACK—Acknowledgment. Used in many aspects of data communication to denote the message from a receiver acknowledging the data that were transmitted by the sender. The most common example is TCP, which uses ACKs to acknowledge received TCP segments.

ACL—Access control list. In networking, a list of terms that control what parts of the network a packet can access. For example, an ACL may reject traffic originating from a customer that has a destination address of the service provider's management network.

ADSL—Asymmetric Digital Subscriber Line. A technology standardized by various bodies, including the ITU that permits simultaneous high-speed data rates and POTS usage on an ordinary telephone line.

aggregate route—Used to improve a routing table's efficiency. Aggregate routes usually have one or more constituent routes, which are also called more-specific routes. A single aggregate route, which covers all the constituent routes, is usually announced to other routers in the network instead of announcing many constituents.

ALG—Application Layer Gateway. A program running in a device, such as a residential CPE or even a BNG, that can inspect packets and understand the protocol conversation contained inside. Most ALGs take action based on data inside the packets, which could include dynamically modifying firewall or NAT rules or rewriting some of the packet contents.

AMI—Alternate Mark Inversion. A line coding method, also called bipolar encoding, that was used in early T1 systems. It involves sending alternating positive and negative voltages for a binary 1. To avoid clock loss, successive sets of eight binary 0s are replaced with seven 0s, and the eighth is changed to a 1.

AN—Access Node. A term coined by the DSL Forum to refer to a device that aggregates subscriber connections—usually DSL, although the DSL Forum has allowed for Ethernet-based connections, too. In common usage, it is known as a DSLAM.

ANCP—Access Node Control Protocol. An extension of General Switch Management Protocol (GSMP). Can be used to control access switches and retrieve port statistics from remote switches and DSLAMs or ANs. One of the newest uses of this protocol is for an access node to push the synchronization rate of a DSL line up to the BNG.

ANSI—American National Standards Institute. Coordinates standards development in the U.S. A couple of notable standards are ANSI C and T1.413 Issue 2—ADSL.

anycast—A way for different routing systems to advertise the same prefix into a single routing domain. This allows clients to use the server or router that is closest in terms of routing protocol cost. Used commonly with PIM-SSM and root DNS servers. (See http://www.isc.org/index.pl?/ops/f-root/.)

API—Application Programming Interface. Lets an application exchange data and perform actions against another application using function calls. An API is a more direct way of accessing an application's capabilities compared to a higher-level interface, such as a web interface.

APS—Automatic Protection Switching. A system that provides link protection by having a standby link available to rapidly switch to in the event of a link or operator intervention. Most APS systems are SONET-based and aim to provide sub-50ms failover to a secondary link in the event of a link failure. Although APS systems can be based on other technologies, such as Ethernet, they function slightly differently.

AS—Autonomous System. Originally defined under the auspices of the BGP specification, an AS is a collection of networks under the control of a single entity. A more recent definition in RFC 1930 delves into more details on what constitutes an AS, which can span more entities of control. Each AS has an Autonomous System Number (ASN).

A-server—Acquisition server. The A-server, part of the Microsoft TV solution, ingests video content at the video head-end. The A-server also broadcasts multicast IPTV channels to the network.

ASIC—Application-Specific Integrated Circuit. An integrated circuit that is purpose-built for a specific task, compared to a more general-purpose IC, such as an FPGA. ASICs are used for many different applications, including high-performance forwarding and packet manipulation inside routers and BNGs.

asset—See *media asset.*

assured rate—A term used by Juniper Networks' JUNOSe software. Specifies a desired minimum rate of throughput that a QoS object receives in the event of congestion. Similar to a relative weight, except that it is expressed as bandwidth rather than as an arbitrary numeric expression.

ATM—Asynchronous Transfer Mode. A data transfer protocol that uses 53-byte cells, of which 5 are header and 48 are data. ATM uses local circuits called PVCs, which are connection-oriented links between two endpoints in the network. Used extensively in broadband networks as both an aggregation layer between the DSLAMs and BRASs and as an access protocol between the ATU-C and ATU-R.

ATU-C—ADSL Transceiver Unit–CO. The device at the CO or remote node that terminates the ADSL signal from the ATU-R.

ATU-R—ADSL Transceiver Unit–Remote End. The device at the customer that terminates the ADSL signal from the ATU-C.

Auto-RP—A proprietary but widespread method to distribute information in a multicast network to map RPs to multicast groups. It makes use of two dense-mode multicast groups, 224.0.1.39 and 224.0.1.40, to discover and communicate the group-to-RP mapping information throughout the network. It is seen as an advantage to static PIM configuration. In networks without an RP, such as PIM-SSM domains, auto-RP is not needed.

bandpass filter—A radio frequency filter that allows frequencies within only a specific range to pass.

bandwidth—In radio communications, refers to a channel's frequency capacity in hertz. In data communications, it may also refer to a channel's frequency capacity. But in more common usage, it refers to a link's effective data capacity, expressed in bits per second (bps) or a multiple thereof, such as kilobits per second (kbps).

BFD—Bidirectional Forwarding Detection. A recent specification compiled by the IETF that uses a lightweight mechanism to check a path's continuity. A UDP packet is sent from one host to another. To confirm the path is up, the sending end expects to receive a reply in a short period of time. This works in a similar manner to the PPP keepalive mechanism, but it is more functional because it can work over multiple network hops.

BGP—Border Gateway Protocol. Originally defined in RFC 1771 and updated in RFC 4271, it replaced Exterior Gateway Protocol (EGP). It is used to communicate routing information both within an autonomous system and external to a routing system. The largest deployment is on the Internet.

BGP community—A numeric attribute that can be part of a BGP route. A BGP community is used as a way of adding extra information to a route, which has significance to operators. As a DoS mitigation technique, if a provider receives a route with a prearranged community from a customer, it can blackhole traffic to that route to avoid overwhelming the customer with DoS traffic.

BNG—Broadband Network Gateway. Coined by the DSL Forum, the updated term for a device traditionally known as the BRAS. A BNG is a device with enough capacity to support a large number of subscribers (on the order of tens of thousands) and sometimes more than 100,000. BNGs also have features for advanced, per-subscriber accounting and policy support with extensive access protocol support, such as PPP and DHCP.

BRAS—Broadband Remote Access Server. A term that has been in use for many years to identify the IP device that terminates customer sessions. B-RASs also terminate large numbers of customers, but as the number of customers using broadband access grows, these routers need to become even more powerful. A notable evolution of the BRAS is from the move toward using Ethernet, Gigabit Ethernet, and 10-Gigabit Ethernet interfaces to groom customer sessions from the access network.

bridged mode—Used in this book to denote the forwarding mode of a CPE or RG. Bridged mode means that the CPE/RG forwards Ethernet frames between the WAN and LAN ports based on destination MAC address. RGs can forward frames to the WAN even when there are multiple VLANs or PVCs. RGs maintain a bridging table similar to that in a normal switch to understand which frame goes to which destination.

broadcast domain—A logical network segment that allows devices to communicate with one another without going through a router. For this to work, all devices need to be on the same subnet and VLAN (if applicable). Typical examples of broadcast domains are when all users in an office share the same LAN or in a household if users are sitting behind a routed gateway.

BSR—Bootstrap router. Used to distribute the IP addresses of RPs around the network. Rather than statically configuring RP addresses on every PIM router, the BSR protocol can distribute this information automatically throughout the PIM domain when it is first initialized.

cable binder—In the broadband residential market, a sheath or cable conduit that groups phone and data cable pairs from homes to an exchange.

CAC—Call Admission Control. In a multi-play context, a way to control network access for real-time media traffic, such as VoIP and video over IP. When a user requests to make a call or stream a video, an intermediate system decides whether to let the connection proceed based on available network resources.

CAM—Content-Addressable Memory. A type of memory that is used when needing to quickly search a large list of entries and return a result in a single pass. This type of memory is very effective at high-seed searches and is used in many switches and routers, which must maintain large routing tables and access lists.

CAP—Carrierless Amplitude-Phase modulation. A single-carrier modulation technique used in the DSL market that uses adaptive equalization to compensate for attenuation and phase errors.

CBWFQ—Class-Based Weighted Fair Queuing. A term used by Cisco Systems. A mechanism to classify traffic based on packet or frame headers and to apply QoS treatment using weighted fair queuing scheduling.

CE—Customer edge. A term first used in RFC 2547. Identifies the device at the customer premises that connects to the network. A CE connects to a provider edge (PE) at the provider premises.

CHAP—Challenge Handshake Authentication Protocol. Used in the authentication phase of PPP sessions, CHAP is a way to encrypt a password before it is sent to the peer at the other end of the link. CHAP can be used to authenticate one or both ends of a link by an authenticator issuing a challenge request to the peer.

CIDR—Classless Interdomain Routing. A specification initially drafted under RFC 1519. Moves IP routing away from the class-based system of class A, class B, and class C spaces to a more flexible structure. The broad principle is that the structure lets an IP route have any mask and not be dependant on the prefix itself to dictate its subnet mask.

CIR—Committed Information Rate. A value used to indicate that, in the event of congestion somewhere in the provider's network, the CIR is the guaranteed throughput that the client receives. This compares to Peak Information Rate (PIR), which defines the maximum rate the client can receive in the event of no congestion in the provider's network.

CLP—Cell Loss Priority. A 1-bit field in the header of an ATM cell that identifies a cell's probability for discard if there is congestion in the network. Cells with a CLP of 1 are more eligible for discard during congestion.

CO—Central Office. A building housing provider equipment, often known as an exchange.

CoA—Change of Authorization. A message that is sent from a RADIUS server to an access server or BNG (with the exception of a NAK or ACK from the BNG, which is sent to the RADIUS server). CoA packets are used in several applications, such as initiating lawful intercept (LI) sessions, disconnecting users, or more complex operations such as modifying user services.

codec—Coder/Decoder. A piece of hardware or software that encodes information, such as voice or video content, in a digital format suitable for storage or transmission. A decoder performs the same task, but in reverse, taking data that are stored or received and converting it into the original information.

COPS—Common Open Policy Service. A protocol for exchanging simple messages between a Policy Decision Point (PDP) and a Policy Enforcement Point (PEP). A PDP is the policy server, which controls the distribution of policies and policy requests. A PEP enforces the policies on the network that have been sent from the PDP.

CoS—Class of service. Refers to the autonomous treatment of traffic at a single router or switch hop using classes to group and manage traffic that have common forwarding requirements. It covers the differentiation of traffic into classes, managing jitter, preemption, latency, queuing, bandwidth, and scheduling.

CPE—Customer Premises Equipment. A device at the customer premises that could be either a Layer 2 or Layer 3 device that connects to the provider equipment. In a residential environment, a CPE is often called a residential gateway (RG).

CRC—Cyclic Redundancy Checksum. A mathematical algorithm performed over a block of data to detect any corruption of data in transit. In data communications, a CRC is usually added to the end of Layer 2 frames. In Layer 3 and Layer 4 protocols, IP and UDP/TCP have checksums in their respective protocol headers.

CsC—Carrier supporting Carrier. A way for one service provider to use a third-party MPLS provider to link its MPLS networks. For example, a provider with MPLS networks on the East and West Coasts of the United States could connect its two network islands using a third-party MPLS provider.

CSPF—Constrained Shortest Path First. An algorithm that is an extension of SPF. SPF is an algorithm that calculates the least-cost path to get to a destination, whereas CSPF can take into consideration extra constraints when calculating the least-cost path to a destination. CSPF is commonly used in traffic-engineered MPLS networks.

customer VLAN—A term used in 1:1 VLAN structures in which each customer is assigned a dedicated VLAN. This VLAN is an 802.1Q tag, which may coexist with a second 802.1Q tag. A second VLAN tag would be called an S-VLAN.

C-VLAN—See *customer VLAN.*

CWDM—See *wave division multiplexing.*

DA—Destination address. A packet's destination IP or IPv6 address.

DDRAM—See *RAM.*

DHCP—Dynamic Host Configuration Protocol. A host configuration mechanism to allocate IP addresses and MTU and communicate a TFTP server address or any other parameters that are needed to prime a client when it boots up. DHCP is a protocol that runs on the top of a multiaccess network such as Ethernet.

DHCP option 82—DHCP includes the ability to add options to the protocol packets. One such option is option 82, called the relay information option (defined in RFC 3046). The option can be filled in by intermediate switches, DSLAMs, or even the BNG to identify the subscriber's source port.

DiffServ—Differentiated Services. An architecture that uses 6 bits in the ToS byte. These 6 bits indicate to routers the type of forwarding behavior with which they should treat the packet. Each behavior is categorized into a per-hop behavior (PHB).

discovery—See *PPPoE discovery phase.*

DLE—Digital Local Exchange. A term used in the UK for a CO or exchange.

DMT—Discrete Multitone. A modulation scheme that uses individual sub-carriers or bins that each occupy a separate frequency band. If radio frequency interference affects data in one bin, it does not necessarily impact other sub-carriers. The DSL family of specifications uses DMT modulation.

DMZ—Demilitarized Zone. A network area, usually created by a firewall, that is reserved for a server farm. Different DMZs can be used for different types of servers. The important principle is that these servers are in a domain separate from LAN and Internet data, which can have policies applied to carefully control ingress and egress traffic.

DNS—Domain Name System. A system that associates system names (called Fully Qualified Domain Names [FQDNs]) with IP addresses and vice versa. Such a system resides on a server and listens for requests on UDP and TCP port 53.

DR—Designated router. Used in several contexts in telecommunications. When discussing an IGP, such as OSPF or IS-IS, the DR is a router on a multiaccess segment, such as Ethernet, which originates route advertisements on behalf of other routers on the segment. In a multicast context, a DR can be a router that splits a multicast tree from an SPF to an RPF tree, a PIM router that sends IGMP group-query messages to a LAN segment, or a router that is attached to the multicast source that sends PIM register messages to the RP.

DRM—Digital Rights Management. A general term that covers several different ways that publishers can control viewers' or listeners' access to digital technologies. Some schemes limit the number of times the content can be heard or viewed, and others are based on time.

D-server—Distribution server. The D-server is part of the Microsoft TV architecture and is the primary component of the Instant Channel Change (ICC) solution. When a user changes the channel, the D-server sends a unicast burst of the new channel (at a greater bit rate than the actual video channel) to the STB. Beginning the unicast burst with an MPEG I-frame and bursting higher than the video rate allows the STB to quickly fill its buffer and reduce channel zapping latency.

DSL—Digital Subscriber Line. The family of standards that encompass high-speed data transfer over POTS lines. Current DSL standards include G.SHDSL, ADSL, ADSL2, ADSL2+, VDSL, and VDSL2.

DSLAM—Digital Subscriber Line Access Multiplexer. A device that aggregates DSL subscriber connections. A DSLAM is usually a chassis with a number of line cards, each of which terminates one or more DSL lines. These are called south-facing cards. There are also one or more north-facing cards that connect the DSLAM to the aggregation network.

DSL Forum—An organization that helps develop standards and recommendations for DSL network deployments. Recommendations include QoS architectures, management, testing standards, interoperability, and migration to Ethernet architectures. The DSL Forum meets four times a year.

DTMF—Dual-Tone Multifrequency. A system to enable in-band signaling over the telephone line to the voice switch or other device at the other end of the connection. The most common use is when dialing a phone number to make a telephone call. DTMF uses a frequency matrix, so when a number or symbol is pressed, the handset sends two frequencies down the line.

DWDM—See *Wave Division Multiplexing*.

EAP—Extensible Authentication Protocol. An authentication framework for use over point-to-point links or multiaccess networks. Rather than being an authentication mechanism, it provides functions and methods to negotiate the authentication mechanism. EAP is commonly used with an 802.1X-capable access server.

EOC—Embedded Operations Channel. A 15kbps data channel in a DSL line that is used for line statistics and diagnostics. Some datum points that can be transferred include CPE vendor and software or hardware version number.

Ethernet—A multiaccess data transmission protocol. On LAN segments, it allows devices to share a common Layer 2 broadcast domain and uses Carrier Sense Multiple-Access with Collision Detection. Ethernet is also used between routers on point-to-point links. It is becoming increasingly popular in the service provider industry because of its cheaper price point.

EXP bits—Experimental bits. The 3 bits used in an MPLS header to indicate packet priority, giving up to eight traffic classes.

fast reroute—Initially developed by Juniper Networks for use on MPLS networks, it was later modified and standardized under RFC 4090. Fast reroute uses redundant paths in MPLS networks to create backup, or presignaled LSPs to protect primary paths. If a primary path fails, a router can quickly switch traffic to a standby path.

FDD—Frequency Division Duplexing. When two frequency ranges are duplexed onto a single medium by a radio application. ADSL is an FDD system because the upstream and downstream portions are in separate frequency ranges and normally do not interfere with one another.

FDM—Frequency Division Multiplexing. When more than two frequencies are used by a radio application on a single medium. VDSL uses FDM because it has several frequency ranges, for upstream, downstream, and POTS.

FEC—Forwarding Equivalency Class. A relationship between an MPLS label and a routing path. For example, in an MPLS network, a PE can set up an RSVP-TE MPLS path to another PE. To reach the PE at the end of the path, the router uses the FEC, which is the other PE and MPLS label that it must use.

flow—See *traffic flow.*

forwarding database—Also known as Forwarding Information Base (FIB). Used in routers to denote the final information table that a router uses for packet forwarding decisions. After a router has processed routing updates and populated its routing table, it calculates the forwarding table and applies this to the forwarding hardware or software.

FPGA—Flexible Programmable Gate Array. A versatile processor that can be programmed using a language, such as C. Often used on BNGs that need complex edge functionality due to diverse packet modification and processing tasks.

Frame Relay—A data communications protocol that supports transport of variable-length frames across a network. Multiple Layer 2 paths, called PVCs, can be multiplexed on a single physical channel, using a Data Link Connection Identifier (DLCI) at the top of the frame to differentiate the paths.

FTP—File Transfer Protocol. A protocol developed in the early 1980s that is purpose-built for transferring files between hosts over a TCP/IP connection. One of the protocol's trademarks is its control and data channel behavior. In active mode, when a client requests a file over its control channel, the server creates a new data channel to the client, which needs special support in the form of an ALG in any intermediate firewalls or NAT agents.

FTTx—Fiber to the x, where x means a location to where fiber-optic connectivity is provided. Examples include the curb, the premises, and the home. Using fiber-optic connectivity instead of DSL can provide large amounts of bandwidth to customers, depending on the necessary attachments on each end of the fiber.

G.711, G.729—VoIP codec schemes standardized by the ITU. G.711 is a full 64kbps uncompressed PCM stream that is used when trunking digital voice calls around national voice networks. G.729 is a voice codec scheme that reduces the bandwidth required by compressing the voice channel to anywhere between 8 and 12kbps.

gauge—See *wire gauge*.

Giaddr—Gateway IP address. A field in DHCP packets that is filled in by a device that relays DHCP requests to another DHCP server. Such a router is called a DHCP relay agent.

HDTV—High Definition Television. A broadcasting system that has much better resolution than traditional analog formats, such as NTSC and PAL, and also SDTV.

HFC—Hybrid Fiber Coaxial. A system that uses both fiber and coaxial cable reticulation to connect customers to a service provider network. The most common example is in cable networks, which use fiber aggregation to the cable head-end and coaxial cable reticulation along roadsides to connect the household.

host route—A route that identifies a single IP address. Also known as a /32 route. These types of routes have several applications, including that described in Chapter 7, in which a subscriber receives a static IP address with which he or she can roam throughout the network. Another example is for blackholing, where a specific host route is targeted in a DoS attack and also affects other routes. The /32 route can be black holed at an upstream provider to mitigate the impact of the DoS attack on other traffic.

HTTP—Hypertext Transfer Protocol. A protocol originally used to transfer HTML pages over the Internet. Web browsers implement HTTP to download and upload web pages and other data. HTTP can transfer many other types of data besides HTML pages, including images, music files, and multimedia presentations.

IA—See *PPPoE intermediate agent*.

ICCN—Incoming Call Connected. An L2TP message sent by an LAC to an LNS to indicate that an L2TP session setup was successful.

ICMP—Internet Control Message Protocol. An ancillary protocol used on the Internet to signal informational or error conditions. For example, ICMP is used to send PING messages from one host to another to determine if the other host is up. Another type of ICMP message is sent to a client when a port on a server cannot be reached due to administrative restrictions.

ICRP—Incoming Call Reply. A message sent from the LNS to the LAC during session setup. It is sent in response to an ICRQ.

ICRQ—Incoming Call Request. A message sent from the LAC to the LNS during session setup. It is the first message that is sent to the LNS for the call setup request.

IETF—Internet Engineering Task Force. A group set up to oversee the development of Internet-related standards.

I-frame—An I-frame is an image that is part of an MPEG stream. It is a compressed image of a video frame and is sent every so often in the stream. The principle is that an I-frame contains a full copy of an image and does not need knowledge of any previous frames in the stream to reconstruct the image. Most other MPEG frames rely on data from previous images to construct the current frame and to achieve high compression rates.

IGMP—Internet Group Multicast Protocol. A lightweight protocol that runs between PIM routers and end hosts that want to receive multicast groups. IGMP also can be used in proxy mode.

IGP—Interior Gateway Protocol. A routing protocol that runs within an autonomous system. Examples include OSPF and IS-IS. There is no hard-and-fast rule about what routes these routing protocols should contain, but at a minimum, they distribute routing information about the routers' links and loopback addresses.

IPCP—IP Control Protocol. A sub-protocol of point-to-point protocol (PPP). PPP has several phases and protocols to use when it sets up the connection. One is Network Control Protocol (NCP), which consists of one or more sub-protocols. Any protocol that is transported across a PPP link needs an associated NCP. To transfer IP packets, the necessary sub-protocol of NCP—IPCP—is first negotiated during NCP negotiation.

IPoE—IP over Ethernet. Whenever IP packets are transported over Ethernet, this is called IPoE. The underlying physical layer could be an Ethernet network, such as 10BASET, 100BASET, or GigabitEthernet. It could be an ATM network that is transporting Ethernet frames using an encapsulation protocol such as RFC 1483, but to avoid confusion, this should be called bridged or routed Ethernet over ATM.

IPTV—IP Television. Sending broadcast television over an IP network—currently, mostly using multicast IP forwarding. However, unicast can also be used if there is enough bandwidth in the network to support it.

ISDN—Integrated Services Digital Network. A data communications protocol standardized by the ITU that provides a digital line from the exchange to the customer premises. This compares with POTS, which is an analog line from the exchange to the customer premises. A simple ISDN system is 2B+D, which is two 64kbps B-channels and one 16kbps D-channel.

IS-IS—Intermediate System to Intermediate System. A routing protocol developed by the OSI that distributes routing information within an autonomous system. The underlying transport for IS-IS datagrams (called protocol data units [PDUs]) is CLNS rather than IP. However, PDUs can contain routing information for IPv4 and other protocols.

ITU—International Telecommunication Union. An organization under the jurisdiction of the United Nations (UN). Coordinates standards related to data communications.

IWF—Interworking Function. A general term for a system that interworks data communications between two separate systems. One example is a PPPoA to PPPoE IWF, which converts data between the two protocols. Another is a radio-to-packet IWF, which interworks a packet radio data session on the access side and a frame-based data session on the network side.

jitter—A measure of the variation of the time between the arrival of one packet and the next. Large jitter causes problems in VoIP networks and is best avoided for optimal performance.

Join—See *PIM Join*.

Kompella L2VPN—One of the two MPLS pseudowire (also called Layer 2 VPN) specifications (the other is Martini L2VPN). Kompella L2VPNs use BGP to distribute the service-level (or pseudowire) label binding information.

L2TP—Layer 2 Tunneling Protocol. This protocol has three versions; version 2 is the most popular. L2TP version 2 uses PPP to create a Layer 2 path between two networks over a packet-switched network. This could be used to provide wholesale Layer 2 connectivity between a DSL subscriber and the access seeker. L2TP version 3 allows more protocols than just PPP on the channel. Ethernet is one notable example.

L2VPN—See *Layer 2 VPN*.

L3VPN—See *Layer 3 VPN*.

LAC—L2TP Access Concentrator. A device that aggregates connections from an access network and forwards incoming connections (called calls) over an L2TP tunnel to an LNS. Each forwarded connection is called an L2TP session.

latency—The time delay between two hosts on a network or internetwork, usually measured in milliseconds. For example, the latency between a host in Australia and a host in New Zealand is about 22 milliseconds.

Layer 2 VPN—A private Layer 2 connection. Usually refers to a point-to-point connection between two endpoints, although it could refer to a multipoint connection, such as a VPLS. To avoid ambiguity, usually a pseudowire service is called a Virtual Private Wire Service (VPWS) and a multipoint connection is called a Virtual Private LAN Service (VPLS). In Juniper Networks' JUNOS software, a Layer 2 VPN refers to a Kompella-based VPWS.

Layer 3 VPN—A private Layer 3 routing domain. Usually refers to a provider-hosted Layer 3 VPN service, such as that described in RFC 2547bis (updated by RFC 4364). Previously a Layer 3 VPN consisted of the service provider delivering multiple ATM or Frame Relay PVCs to the customer, which managed the Layer 3 VPN service on its own routers.

LCP—Link Control Protocol. A sub-protocol of point-to-point protocol (PPP). Like NCP, LCP is a direct sub-protocol of PPP and implements several important features of PPP: MRU negotiation, authentication, keepalive management, and loop detection.

LDAP—Lightweight Directory Access Protocol. A specification to allow easy reading and writing of a database. LDAP uses distinguished names (DNs) to identify records in a database and a set of simple methods to add, modify, or delete existing records by using a key/value pair structure.

LDP—Label Distribution Protocol. A standards-based protocol that is based on Tag Distribution Protocol (TDP). LDP uses UDP-based autodiscovery before establishing a TCP session over which label-to-FEC bindings are exchanged between routers. LDP peers can also be manually configured to establish a TCP session. One case is used when exchanging Martini VPWS labels between two PEs.

LI—Lawful Intercept. A feature used on BNGs, NASs, and voice switches to allow government agencies to intercept user data traffic or voice calls.

LLQ—Low-Latency Queuing. Used by Cisco Systems to denote traffic that must be sent without delay and with minimal jitter. Normally used for VoIP traffic.

LLU—Local Loop Unbundling. Gives access seekers access to the copper local loop, usually based on government regulation. LLU has several variants—SPF, MPF, and bit stream access, to name a few.

LMI—Local Management Interface. Used in Frame Relay to exchange information about the link to the network and the status of PVCs. LMI signaling occupies its own PVC.

LNS—L2TP Network Server. A device that terminates L2TP sessions and tunnels from LACs.

local loop—The copper circuit that runs between the exchange and the household. The copper could be composed of several discrete segments of copper wire connected as one electrical circuit.

LSA—Link State Advertisement. A packet that is sent from an OSPF router to other OSPF routers to describe reachability information about a link or route.

LSP—Label-Switched Path or Link-State PDU. A Label-Switched Path is the path through an MPLS network that traffic takes. The signaling could be either RSVP-TE or LDP. Link-State PDU is an IS-IS term for a packet that distributes reachability information about a route or link. It is similar to an OSPF LSA.

LTS—Layer 2 Tunnel Protocol Tunnel Switch. A device that acts as both an LAC and an LNS. It receives L2TP sessions or calls from an LAC and switches them to another LNS without decapsulating the enclosed payload.

MAC (address)—Media Access Control. A layer defined by the IEEE that refers to a sublayer of the Ethernet protocol. The MAC layer sits between the Physical (PHY) layer and the Link Layer Control (LLC) and controls access to the media. A MAC address is a Layer 2 address of a device attached to an Ethernet network. A MAC address is also called a hardware address.

Martini L2VPN—One of the two MPLS pseudowire (also called Layer 2 VPN) specifications (the other is Kompella L2VPN). Martini L2VPNs use LDP to distribute the service-level (or pseudowire) label binding information.

MBGP—Multiprotocol BGP. A capability of BGP to carry reachability information for protocols other than to IPv4. This includes Layer 2 and Layer 3 VPN reachability information. Each protocol is identified with an address family identifier (AFI) and sub-address identifier (SAFI).

media asset—In the video content management area, an asset is a digital copy of multimedia content. This could be a TV show, a movie, recorded radio, or any other content for streaming to clients. Assets are managed using sophisticated content management systems with large storage arrays.

meet-me room—A room in an exchange that is used to house local loop cross connections between the incumbent and an access seeker.

middleware—A complex platform that is at the heart of an IPTV and VoD deployment. Middleware handles many tasks, including dealing with entitlement requests for STBs that ask to view VoD content, issuing Entitlement Data Records (EDRs) for billing purposes, delivering the SUI to the STB, and delivering any Electronic Programming Guide (EPG) information.

MPEG—Motion Picture Experts Group. An organization overseeing the development of standards related to the storage and transmission of digital video and audio.

MPF—Metal Path Facility. A term used by British Telecom (BT) to denote a fully unbundled copper loop. An unbundled local loop has two parts—a POTS part and a non-POTS part. With MPF, both services are unbundled and delivered to the access seeker.

MPLS—Multiprotocol label switching. A technology used in provider backbone networks to allow multiple protocols to be carried over a converged routing infrastructure. MPLS uses one or more extra packet headers, which are added to the underlying payload. Header information includes a label number, a (Time-To-Live) TTL, Bottom of Stack (BoS), and EXP.

MRU—Maximum Receive Unit. An attribute that is negotiated during PPP setup. It is sent by a PPP peer that wants to indicate the maximum frame size it can receive.

MSDP—Multicast Source Discovery Protocol. A protocol that runs between multicast rendezvous points (RPs) to communicate the status of multicast groups. An MSDP session is often used between RPs that use an anycast PIM router ID. It is also used between service providers to exchange multicast routing information.

MSO—Multiple System Operator. A provider that operates many cable television systems.

MSS—Maximum Segment Size. During the three-way TCP handshake, the peers exchange this attribute, which indicates the maximum TCP segment that it can receive. In most cases, this is 1480 bytes, which is the maximum Ethernet payload size of 1500 bytes minus the typical IP header of 20 bytes.

MTU—Maximum Transmission Unit. An attribute of an interface that indicates the maximum-sized packet or frame that can be sent out the interface. If the packet that is being sent out the interface is too large, it is usually fragmented, which separates the packet into multiple parts, each equal to or smaller than the MTU. In some cases, if the device in question originates the packets, the operating system can automatically pack the data into small-enough chunks to avoid fragmentation.

multicast—A packet-forwarding method that makes efficient use of network resources when many users or receivers want to receive the same content. IPTV is an example of content that can take advantage of multicast packet delivery. It works by forwarding only a single copy of the media or data stream through the network, regardless of the number of receivers. Only when there is no common path between the viewers (such as a local loop) is the media replicated onto each of the links.

N:1 VLAN structure—In general terms, an N:1 VLAN matches one resource to many users or requestors. In a broadband access context, this is a VLAN architecture that assigns one VLAN to N subscribers or households.

NAK—Not acknowledged.

narrowband—In radio communications, a channel that has a small range of frequencies. In data communications, the principle is similar but has some subtle differences. An NAS is considered a narrowband access technology because it uses only the POTS frequency range (300Hz to 3400Hz). Broadband access, such as ADSL, uses a much larger spectrum range. Sometimes, if a line is limited to a speed such as 128kbps, it is narrowband rather than called broadband. This is regardless of whether the line is limited at the BNG or at the DSLAM.

NAS—Network Access Server. A term for a narrowband dialup access server.

NAT—Network Address Translation. A method to modify IP addresses from their original numbers. NAPT is an extension that also allows modification of the TCP or UDP port information within the packet. NAPT has various uses, but the most common one is for devices in the household to share a single IP address on the Internet.

NEXT—Near-End Crosstalk. Transmission interference from one RF system into another, usually due to both sharing the same frequencies. Hundreds of ADSL transmitters (ATU-C) at COs cause NEXT. However, because the power level is very high at the CO, it does not cause much of an impact.

NMS—Network Management System.

NNI—Network-to-Network Interface. An interface that exists between two provider interfaces. An example is a backbone internodal link between two provider ATM switches. The converse is the user-to-network interface (UNI).

NPVR—Network Private Video Recorder. A technique for the network to record TV or radio programs on the user's behalf.

NTP—Network Time Protocol. A system to automatically and accurately synchronize network devices to a common clock.

OAM—Operations and Administration Management.

ODAP—On-Demand Address Pool. A variably sized address pool that can be dynamically assigned to a router based on subscriber demand.

OECD—Organisation of Economically Developed Countries.

OIF—Outgoing InterFace. Commonly used in multicast networks. Denotes an egress interface of a multicast stream. More than one OIF is called Outgoing Interface List (OIFL).

Option 82—See *DHCP option 82.*

OSI seven-layer model—Open Systems Interconnection. A networking model created by the International Organization for Standardization (ISO) to arrange functionality in terms of a stack. Electrical and physical standards and operation are at the bottom of the stack. Other levels, such as network and transport, are in higher layers of the stack.

OSPF—Open Shortest Path First. A link-state routing protocol used to distribute routing information in an autonomous system. It uses IP for transport and is one of the two common IGPs, along with IS-IS.

OSS—Operational Support System.

P2MP LSP—See *point-to-multipoint LSP.*

PAM—Pulse-Amplitude Modulation. A technique to modulate symbols onto sinusoidal wave patterns for transmission over an RF channel. The pulse-amplitude type of modulation involves changes to the wave's phase and amplitude. These types of modulation patterns can be represented as constellation diagrams.

PAP—Password Authentication Protocol. A basic authentication protocol that is part of PPP. It involves sending a password in clear text between PPP peers to authenticate the peer.

PATH—See *RSVP path.*

PBR—Policy-Based Routing. Allows routers to make forwarding decisions based on packet data other than the usual destination address (DA). This can include source port, destination port, source interface, and so on.

PDH—Plesiochronous Digital Hierarchy. A family of digital transmission standards that transports data over radio and cable-based systems. PDH systems include T1, E1, T3, and E3 systems.

PDP—Policy Decision Point. Part of the COPS specification. The server that stores the policies for distribution to the PEPs.

PDU—Protocol Data Unit. A general term for a block of data that is carried as part of a protocol. Examples of PDUs are link-state PDU (LSP), which is a type of IS-IS advertisement, and an AAL5 PDU, which is an encapsulated datagram or frame, including the AAL5 trailer.

PEP—Policy Enforcement Point. Receives policies from the PDP, enforces them, and reports the status of the enforcement back to the PDP.

PE router—Provider Edge router. A term coined in RFC 2547 to identify a router at the edge of the service provider that performs both MPLS switching and interfacing with the CE.

PHB—Per-hop Behavior. A term used in Differentiated Services (DiffServ) that describes how a router should treat an incoming packet with a particular DiffServ Code Point (DSCP). Characteristics of packet treatment include jitter restrictions, loss tolerance, and latency bounds.

PIM—Protocol-Independent Multicast. A protocol that runs on the top of IPv4 or IPv6 to control multicast distribution in a network. PIM has several protocol characteristics, including Joins and Prunes, which are sent between routers to indicate the routers that need to receive or not receive multicast groups.

PIM-ASM—PIM Any-Source Multicast. The first type of multicast. Allows any source to transmit data to the network for a given multicast group. As a consequence, all other receivers that have joined the group receive this data. For some applications (mainly collaborative ones, such as video-conferencing), this is a desirable feature. For other applications, such as IPTV, this is an undesirable feature. Requires the use of a Rendezvous Point (RP).

PIM Join—A type of PIM message that a router sends in an upstream direction. One type of PIM Join is sent toward a multicast source and the other is sent to an RP when a PIM-ASM client wants to join a multicast tree. When a router is part of a multicast tree, it receives the multicast group if there is active traffic.

PIM-SSM—PIM Source-Specific Multicast. A newer type of multicast that gives more control over what sources can send data to the network. PIM-SSM requires inserting the source unicast address into the Join packet rather than using an RP to link the source and the receivers.

PNNI—Private Network-to-Network Interface. A powerful routing protocol, usually used to distribute ATM PVC and SVC routing information throughout a provider backbone. It uses the same SPF algorithm as OSPF and IS-IS.

point-to-multipoint LSP—A way to set up an MPLS LSP in a point-to-multipoint fashion, similar to a point-to-multipoint ATM PVC. It enables efficient IP and IPv6 multicast replication on top of an MPLS network.

policing—Also known as rate-limiting. A mechanism to limit the throughput of a given type of traffic. A common use is on the ingress of a customer interface on a BNG to restrict the rate at which a customer can send data to the network.

PON—Passive Optical Network. A method to run multiple data channels over a fiber cable that runs from the service provider to the premises (could be premises, curb, or home) using unpowered (that is, passive) equipment for any optical splitting requirements.

POTS—Plain Old Telephone Service. The telephone service that has been around for many decades. Provides a voice telephony service from a central exchange to the customer premises.

PPP—Point-to-Point Protocol. An encapsulation protocol standardized by the IETF that provides a point-to-point link-management protocol. PPP provides features including authentication, loop detection, encapsulation, and link continuity detection.

PPPoA—PPP over ATM. An IETF standard describing how to encapsulate PPP frames to be sent over an ATM network. This protocol is natively encapsulated on the ATM layer. In contrast, PPPoE uses Ethernet as its transport protocol.

PPPoE—PPP over Ethernet. A way to create a PPP link over a multi-point Ethernet network. To compensate for the extra PPPoE overhead, the link's IPMTU has traditionally been limited to 1492 bytes.

PPPoE discovery phase—The first of the two PPPoE phases. The discovery phase is intended for a CPE to discover the PPPoE access concentrators (or servers) and set up a PPPoE session.

PPPoE intermediate agent—An agent sitting between the PPPoE client and PPPoE server that can add informational data to the PPPoE header. This information could include the physical port designation on the DSLAM. This works in a similar fashion to DHCP option 82.

PPPoE session phase—The second of the two PPPoE phases. The session phase is where the client and server are in a steady session state.

P router—Provider router. A term coined in RFC 2547 to identify a router inside the provider's core that performs MPLS switching. This reduces the complexity required in the router, because it is optimized for MPLS switching. A PE needs more capability to manage edge services.

PSD—Power Spectral Density. The power in use across given spectra. This is commonly used in an ADSL environment where some parts of the spectrum need to be unused by the ADSL transmitter/receiver, such as the POTS frequencies.

pseudowire—A way to emulate a physical or Layer 2 path through an MPLS network. It is also known as a pseudowire edge-to-edge (PWE3). The service is also called a Virtual Private Wire Service (VPWS).

PSN—Packet-Switched Network, such as IP.

PSTN—Public Switched Telephone Network. The system that provides a plain old telephone service.

PVC—Permanent Virtual Circuit. A logical circuit that runs between two endpoints in an ATM or Frame Relay network.

PVP—Permanent Virtual Path. A path through an ATM network that can contain one or more PVCs. Its strong advantage is when grooming ATM PVCs in an ATM network. Rather than dealing with many individual PVCs, they can be managed on an aggregate level using a PVP. These can also be thought of as a tunnel for PVCs through an ATM network.

PWE3—See *pseudowire*.

QAM—Quadrature Amplitude Modulation. A modulation scheme that uses two sinusoidal carrier waves that are out of phase with each other by 90 degrees. The waves' amplitude is modified to affect the modulation changes.

Q-in-Q—See *stacked VLAN*.

QoS—Quality of Service. Can refer to many aspects of the quality of service delivery—availability, packet reordering, timing accuracy, time-to-repair, time-to-provision, and accuracy of billing. A subset of QoS capability also refers to more CoS-related aspects, such as traffic differentiation and treatment using techniques such as scheduling, marking, shaping, and rate-limiting.

RADIUS—Remote Authentication Dial-In User Service. A protocol that runs between network elements and authentication servers. Authenticates and authorizes users into the network and provides accounting services.

RAM—ANCP Rate-Adaptive Mode. A method for the AN to communicate any changes in the DSL line synchronization in real time to the BNG over an ANCP session.

RAS—Remote Access Server. Usually synonymous with a narrowband RAS, although it can sometimes refer to a BRAS.

rate-limiting—See *policing*.

RED—Random Early Discard. An active queue management algorithm that routers implement as part of their buffer-management mechanisms. A RED system has two important variables. The first is the average queue length, which is how full the queue is of packets over a given time (the time being on the order of microseconds). Usually this is simplified to the instantaneous queue length. The second is the discard ratio, which indicates how aggressively or how probable it is that packets below a certain threshold will be discarded.

RF—Radio Frequency.

RFC—Request for Comments. A system developed to produce advisory standards. First a protocol, feature, or algorithm goes through an Internet draft process. After "rough consensus" is reached, the Internet draft becomes an RFC.

RG—In a corporate or commercial context, RG means routing gateway. In a residential environment, it stands for residential gateway. In both instances, it is another term for CPE.

RIP—Routing Information Protocol. A distance-vector routing protocol that announces its routing table every 30 seconds and uses a simple hop metric to determine route cost.

route leaking—In Layer 3 VPN networks, routes are isolated to a single routing domain with the use of VRFs and community tags. Route leaking allows some routes to be distributed from one VPN to another.

route reflector—Internal BGP networks require a full mesh of BGP speakers to ensure that all routers are properly synchronized. One exception to this rule is route reflectors. BGP speakers peer with a route reflector, which acts as an IBGP route distribution router.

route target—When MPLS VPN routes are announced to other BGP peers, a route target, which can be thought of as a tag, is added to each route. It is used as a unique identifier that can be used to collate routes under a common domain. For example, all routes in a standard Layer 3 VPN would share the same route target.

routed mode—Used in this book to denote the forwarding mode of a CPE or RG. Routed mode means that the CPE/RE routes Ethernet frames between the WAN and LAN ports based on destination IP address. If there are multiple PVCs or VLANs on the WAN port, static or dynamic routing protocols manage the traffic forwarding between the logical paths. Traffic filtering at the IP level is also possible when the CPE runs in routed mode.

RP—Rendezvous point. Used in a PIM-ASM network. Identifies multicast senders and distributes groups to interested receivers.

RPF—Reverse Path Forwarding. There are several types of RPF. One simple way is a technique to verify that the source address of traffic entering an interface matches the source route back to the destination. This prevents IP address spoofing. A less aggressive version can just match the existence of the route in the routing table.

RPT—Rendezvous Point Tree. In a multicast topology, an RPT is a topology between the interested receiver and the rendezvous point.

RR—See *route reflector*.

RSVP—See *RSVP-TE*.

RSVP path—Resource Reservation Protocol path. A type of RSVP message that is sent from the network's ingress point in a hop-by-hop fashion to set up an LSP.

RSVP-TE—Resource Reservation Protocol with Traffic Engineering. The current, most popular use is an enhancement to the original RSVP specification to enable MPLS signaling with traffic engineering capability over an MPLS network. RSVP-TE can constrain LSP routing through a network using features such as link color, setup priority, and loose and strict hops.

RTP—Real-time Transport Protocol. A standardized packet format for delivering video and audio over a packet network.

RTSP—Real-time Transport Streaming Protocol. A control protocol to enable a device to issue commands to a streaming server to control the media stream.

RTT—Round-Trip Time. The two-way latency between two devices on a network.

SBC—Session Border Controller. A device that arbitrates connections on a network. This is commonly used in VoIP networks to separate the SIP servers from the UA.

SCCRP—Start-Control-Connection-Reply. A reply sent from the LNS to the LAC when setting up an L2TP tunnel.

SCCRQ—Start-Control-Connection-Request. A request sent from the LAC to the LNS when setting up an L2TP tunnel.

SDH—Synchronous Digital Hierarchy. A successor to PDH that uses a synchronized network clock, which enables much higher data rates than PDH.

SD-TV—Standard-Definition Television. The most common set of digital television resolutions used in IPTV networks today. As CPE HD-TV decoding engines proliferate and are commoditized, and provider bandwidth increases, HD-TV will overtake SD-TV in popularity.

serialization delay—The latency required to transmit a number of bytes onto the wire based on the transmission speed. This is more noticeable on slower-speed links.

service VLAN—In DSL access terminology, refers to a VLAN that is dedicated to a service. A 1:1 VLAN is a multiservice VLAN that is dedicated to a customer.

session phase—See *PPPoE session phase*.

shaping rate—Specifies a peak rate at which traffic can be sent from a QoS object. Any traffic exceeding the peak rate is queued if queue space is available. Smoothes traffic bursts.

SHDSL—A high-speed DSL service usually operating in symmetric mode. Multiple copper pairs can be inversely multiplexed to achieve higher bit rates.

SIP—Session Initiation Protocol. A protocol for creating and managing sessions with other peers. It uses a SIP server and a user agent (UA), which is the client handset or device.

SMPF—Shared Metallic Path Facility. An unbundled cable that has the voice and DSL components split into separate components by the wholesaler.

SNMP—Simple Network Management Protocol. A simple UDP-based protocol that retrieves statistics from network elements. SNMP also lets you configure a device with the use of SET commands.

SNR—Signal-to-noise Ratio.

SOAP—Simple Object Access Protocol. A way to transfer XML-based messages over a network.

SONET—A digital communications method that replaced PDH. Is very similar to SDH, except for some framing differences.

SPF—Shortest Path First. Another name for the Dijkstra algorithm, which is named after its Dutch inventor. SPF is a key feature of several routing protocols that find the closest path to a destination. Such protocols include OSPF, IS-IS, and PNNI.

splitter—A device that works much like a DSL filter, except that the DSL modem connects directly to the local loop. The POTS signals are filtered out by a high-pass filter on the DSL modem. All POTS devices connect to the splitter, rather than attaching a low-pass filter to each POTS line. The splitter contains a low-pass filter for the POTS circuit to ensure that DSL signals do not interfere with the telephone service.

SPT—Shortest-Path Tree. In multicast, the SPF is the shortest path back to the source of a multicast stream. It is used at all times in a PIM-SSM domain. It is also used in PIM-ASM networks when a DR switches from the RPT to the SPT.

SSL—Secure Sockets Layer is a cryptographic protocol that creates a secure communications channel between two devices on a network. It is commonly used on many websites where the contents of the data need to remain secure as they are sent over the network.

stacked VLAN—A term coined by the DSL Forum. Refers to an Ethernet frame that has a second 802.1Q tag. Usually a stacked VLAN (S-VLAN) refers to the second VLAN header that is added to identify the AN or switch to which the subscriber is connected.

STB—Set-top Box. A device located at the home that decodes and at times decrypts IPTV, video on demand, radio over IP, or any other multimedia services that are received from the network. The STB then outputs the content to a TV screen via a SCART, RGB, HDMI, or other type of interface. The STB also renders the SUI on the screen.

STP—Spanning Tree Protocol. A protocol used in Ethernet networks to monitor the network for redundant and potentially loop-causing paths. Blocks any potentially harmful switch ports that might cause a loop as soon as the port is enlivened.

Strict Priority Scheduling—A term used by Juniper Networks to denote traffic that must be sent without delay and with minimal jitter. Normally used for VoIP traffic.

sub-carrier—A DMT frequency block in a DSL system. Also called a bin.

SUI—Set-top box User Interface. An interface rendered by the STB and displayed on the television.

SVC—Switched Virtual Circuit. A circuit that can be created on-demand through an ATM network. This type of circuit is not too widespread.

S-VLAN—See *stacked VLAN*.

symbol—A collection of binary digits that are modulated onto a wire using a scheme such as PAM. Transmitting data by converting symbols to a wave pattern rather than modulating individual bits is much more efficient.

TCM—See *Trellis Code Modulation*.

TCP—Transmission Control Protocol. A transport protocol residing at Layer 4 of the OSI stack. TCP is commonly called TCP/IP, which refers to TCP communications over an IP network. TCP ensures the reliable transmission of data from one endpoint to another over a connectionless protocol such as IP. TCP is the most common transport protocol on the Internet.

TDM—Time Division Multiplexing. Splitting a channel into multiple timeslots, with a portion of the data being transmitted in each timeslot. Data multiplexing is achieved by different channels occupying different timeslots. Examples of TDM networks are the GSM mobile network and digital PSTN voice trunks.

TFTP—Trivial File Transfer Protocol. A lightweight file transfer protocol that operates over UDP.

token bucket rate-limiter—A policer that uses the concept of a bucket of tokens or credits. A router or switch works with the bucket to determine whether packets can be sent or dropped if they exceed a given rate.

ToS—Type of Service. An 8-bit field in the IP header, of which 6 bits have been defined for use so far. These 6 bits are used by the DiffServ architecture.

traffic class—A grouping of traffic that shares common QoS characteristics.

traffic flow—A data flow related to an application session. For example, an HTTP session between a user and a server is a single session. Identifying characteristics of the session can be just addressing information or the complete 5-tuple.

transmit rate—A term used in Juniper JUNOS software that specifies the desired minimum rate of throughput that a QoS object shall receive in the event of congestion.

Trellis Code Modulation—A more effective way to encode and modulate data for transmission by a radio system. It improves a channel's power efficiency and better decoding data from the wire at given signal-to-noise ratios.

TTL—Time To Live. A field commonly found in the packet header of packet-based networking systems. IP and MPLS are two protocol examples that have a TTL field, which is decremented by 1 at each router hop. The TTL field is intended to detect routing loops and discard a packet if its TTL is 0.

UA or user agent—See *SIP.*

UDP—User Datagram Protocol. A connectionless transport protocol that resides at Layer 4 of the OSI seven-layer stack.

unicast—A method of sending IP or IPv6 packets from a single host to a single destination.

VCI—Virtual Circuit Identifier. A value in an ATM cell header that indicates to which PVC a cell belongs.

VDSL—Very high-speed Digital Subscriber Line. A specification released by the ITU that increases the data rate on DSL connections. It allows simultaneous operation of POTS and DSL services.

VLAN—Virtual Local-Area Network. A technique standardized by the IEEE to isolate LAN traffic into its own broadcast domain, usually using an 802.1Q VLAN tag.

VoD—Video on Demand. Allowing a user to request multimedia content on-demand, usually using a remote to browse and buy or view content.

VoIP—Voice over IP. A way to transfer a voice call over an IP network. VoIP is one of the services in a triple-play or multi-play bundle.

VPI—Virtual Path Identifier. A value in an ATM cell header that indicates to which PVP a cell belongs.

VPLS—Virtual Private LAN Service. A way of emulating a point-to-multipoint LAN service over an MPLS network of LSPs.

VPN—Virtual Private Network. A collection of Layer 2 or Layer 3 endpoints in a private switching or routing domain.

VPWS—See *pseudowire.*

VRRP—Virtual Router Redundancy Protocol. A protocol that runs between two or more routers to ensure that a default gateway on a LAN always can be reached by hosts. If one VRRP router fails, another router detects this and takes over the duties of the default gateway.

VSA—Vendor-Specific Attribute. Used most commonly in RADIUS to indicate that an attribute-value pair (AVP) has been created by a vendor, rather than being part of a standard. Also found in the PPPoE header.

VTU-O—VDSL Transceiver Unit at the Optical Network Unit.

VTU-R—VDSL Transceiver Unit at the Remote End.

wave division multiplexing—A way to multiplex multiple frequencies of laser-generated light onto a single fiber strand. Coarse Wave Division Multiplexing (CWDM) multiplexes a handful of laser-generated light onto a single fiber strand. Dense Wave Division Multiplexing (DWDM) is a system that can support many more wavelengths.

WEP—Wired Equivalent Privacy. A protocol that is part of the initial WiFi 802.11 standard. It attempts to secure the radio channel from eavesdropping. However, the protocol is not considered very secure. A successor, WPA, is considered a better alternative.

wire gauge—A general term for the width of a piece of wire. In telecommunications, its most popular application is to identify the width of the cable that connects the customer to the exchange.

WRED—Weighted Random Early Discard. A queue management algorithm that randomly discards packets in a queue. Is aware of packet coloration to modify discard aggression.

GLOSSARY OF PACKET DIAGRAMS

IPv4 (RFC 791)

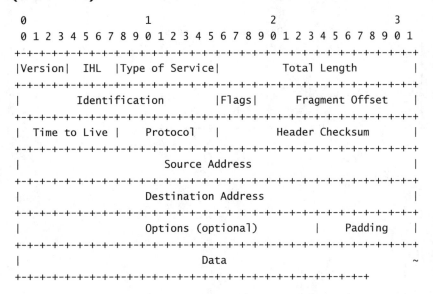

```
 0                   1                   2                   3
 0 1 2 3 4 5 6 7 8 9 0 1 2 3 4 5 6 7 8 9 0 1 2 3 4 5 6 7 8 9 0 1
+-+-+-+-+-+-+-+-+-+-+-+-+-+-+-+-+-+-+-+-+-+-+-+-+-+-+-+-+-+-+-+-+
|Version|  IHL  |Type of Service|          Total Length         |
+-+-+-+-+-+-+-+-+-+-+-+-+-+-+-+-+-+-+-+-+-+-+-+-+-+-+-+-+-+-+-+-+
|         Identification        |Flags|      Fragment Offset    |
+-+-+-+-+-+-+-+-+-+-+-+-+-+-+-+-+-+-+-+-+-+-+-+-+-+-+-+-+-+-+-+-+
|  Time to Live |    Protocol   |         Header Checksum        |
+-+-+-+-+-+-+-+-+-+-+-+-+-+-+-+-+-+-+-+-+-+-+-+-+-+-+-+-+-+-+-+-+
|                        Source Address                         |
+-+-+-+-+-+-+-+-+-+-+-+-+-+-+-+-+-+-+-+-+-+-+-+-+-+-+-+-+-+-+-+-+
|                      Destination Address                      |
+-+-+-+-+-+-+-+-+-+-+-+-+-+-+-+-+-+-+-+-+-+-+-+-+-+-+-+-+-+-+-+-+
|                    Options (optional)         |    Padding     |
+-+-+-+-+-+-+-+-+-+-+-+-+-+-+-+-+-+-+-+-+-+-+-+-+-+-+-+-+-+-+-+-+
|                             Data                              ~
+-+-+-+-+-+-+-+-+-+-+-+-+-+-+-+-+-+-+-+-+-+-+-+-+-+-+-+-+-+
```

IPv6 (RFC 2460)

```
 0                   1                   2                   3
 0 1 2 3 4 5 6 7 8 9 0 1 2 3 4 5 6 7 8 9 0 1 2 3 4 5 6 7 8 9 0 1
+-+-+-+-+-+-+-+-+-+-+-+-+-+-+-+-+-+-+-+-+-+-+-+-+-+-+-+-+-+-+-+-+
|Version| Traffic Class |           Flow Label                  |
+-+-+-+-+-+-+-+-+-+-+-+-+-+-+-+-+-+-+-+-+-+-+-+-+-+-+-+-+-+-+-+-+
|         Payload Length        |  Next Header  |   Hop Limit   |
+-+-+-+-+-+-+-+-+-+-+-+-+-+-+-+-+-+-+-+-+-+-+-+-+-+-+-+-+-+-+-+-+
|                                                               |
+                                                               +
|                                                               |
+                     Source Address                            +
|                                                               |
+                                                               +
|                                                               |
+-+-+-+-+-+-+-+-+-+-+-+-+-+-+-+-+-+-+-+-+-+-+-+-+-+-+-+-+-+-+-+-+
|                                                               |
+                                                               +
|                                                               |
+                  Destination Address                          +
|                                                               |
+                                                               +
|                                                               |
+-+-+-+-+-+-+-+-+-+-+-+-+-+-+-+-+-+-+-+-+-+-+-+-+-+-+-+-+-+-+-+-+
|                         Data                              ~
+-+-+-+-+-+-+-+-+-+-+-+-+-+-+-+-+-+-+-+-+-+-+-+-+-+-+-+-+
```

TCP (RFC 793)

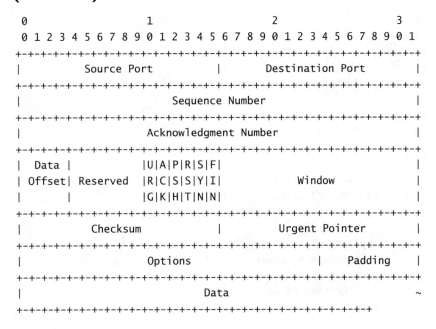

```
 0                   1                   2                   3
 0 1 2 3 4 5 6 7 8 9 0 1 2 3 4 5 6 7 8 9 0 1 2 3 4 5 6 7 8 9 0 1
+-+-+-+-+-+-+-+-+-+-+-+-+-+-+-+-+-+-+-+-+-+-+-+-+-+-+-+-+-+-+-+-+
|          Source Port          |       Destination Port        |
+-+-+-+-+-+-+-+-+-+-+-+-+-+-+-+-+-+-+-+-+-+-+-+-+-+-+-+-+-+-+-+-+
|                        Sequence Number                        |
+-+-+-+-+-+-+-+-+-+-+-+-+-+-+-+-+-+-+-+-+-+-+-+-+-+-+-+-+-+-+-+-+
|                    Acknowledgment Number                      |
+-+-+-+-+-+-+-+-+-+-+-+-+-+-+-+-+-+-+-+-+-+-+-+-+-+-+-+-+-+-+-+-+
| Data  |           |U|A|P|R|S|F|                               |
| Offset| Reserved  |R|C|S|S|Y|I|            Window             |
|       |           |G|K|H|T|N|N|                               |
+-+-+-+-+-+-+-+-+-+-+-+-+-+-+-+-+-+-+-+-+-+-+-+-+-+-+-+-+-+-+-+-+
|           Checksum            |         Urgent Pointer        |
+-+-+-+-+-+-+-+-+-+-+-+-+-+-+-+-+-+-+-+-+-+-+-+-+-+-+-+-+-+-+-+-+
|                    Options                    |    Padding     |
+-+-+-+-+-+-+-+-+-+-+-+-+-+-+-+-+-+-+-+-+-+-+-+-+-+-+-+-+-+-+-+-+
|                             Data                              ~
+-+-+-+-+-+-+-+-+-+-+-+-+-+-+-+-+-+-+-+-+-+-+-+-+-+
```

UDP (RFC 768)

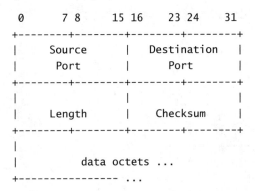

```
 0      7 8     15 16    23 24    31
+--------+--------+--------+--------+
|     Source      |   Destination   |
|     Port        |      Port       |
+--------+--------+--------+--------+
|                 |                 |
|     Length      |    Checksum     |
+--------+--------+--------+--------+
|
|         data octets ...
+--------------- ...
```

ETHERNET II

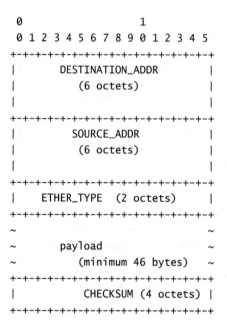

```
0                     1
0 1 2 3 4 5 6 7 8 9 0 1 2 3 4 5
+-+-+-+-+-+-+-+-+-+-+-+-+-+-+-+-+
|          DESTINATION_ADDR      |
|             (6 octets)         |
|                                |
+-+-+-+-+-+-+-+-+-+-+-+-+-+-+-+-+
|            SOURCE_ADDR         |
|             (6 octets)         |
|                                |
+-+-+-+-+-+-+-+-+-+-+-+-+-+-+-+-+
|      ETHER_TYPE   (2 octets)   |
+-+-+-+-+-+-+-+-+-+-+-+-+-+-+-+-+
~                                ~
~        payload                 ~
~        (minimum 46 bytes)      ~
+-+-+-+-+-+-+-+-+-+-+-+-+-+-+-+-+
|           CHECKSUM (4 octets)  |
+-+-+-+-+-+-+-+-+-+-+-+-+-+-+-+-+
```

ATM AAL5 PDU

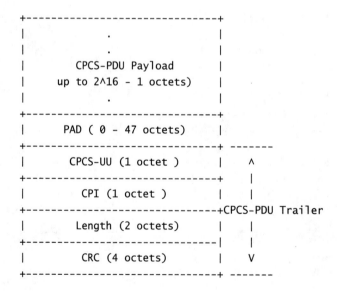

```
+------------------------------+
|              .               |
|              .               |
|        CPCS-PDU Payload       |
|     up to 2^16 - 1 octets)    |
|              .               |
+------------------------------+
|     PAD ( 0 - 47 octets)     |
+------------------------------+ -------
|     CPCS-UU (1 octet )       |   ^
+------------------------------+   |
|        CPI (1 octet )        |   |
+------------------------------+CPCS-PDU Trailer
|      Length (2 octets)       |   |
+------------------------------|   |
|        CRC (4 octets)        |   V
+------------------------------+ -------
```

LLC Encapsulated PPP over AAL5 (RFC 2364)

```
+-----------------------+ --------
|  Destination SAP (0xFE) |      ^
+-----------------------+      |
|  Source SAP (0xFE)    | LLC header
+-----------------------+      |
|  Frame Type = UI (0x03) |    V
+-----------------------+ --------
|  NLPID = PPP (0xCF)   |
+-----------------------+ --------
|   Protocol Identifier |      ^
|     (8 or 16 bits)    |      |
+-----------------------+ PPP payload
|          .            |      |
|          .            |      |
|  PPP information field |      |
|          .            |      |
|          .            |      |
+-----------------------+      |
|        padding        |      V
+-----------------------+ --------
|  PAD ( 0 - 47 octets) |
+-----------------------+ --------
|  CPCS-UU (1 octet )   |      ^
+-----------------------+      |
|   CPI (1 octet )      |      |
+-----------------------+CPCS-PDU Trailer
|  Length (2 octets)    |      |
+-----------------------|      |
|   CRC (4 octets)      |      V
+-----------------------+ --------
```

PPPoE Ethernet Payload (RFC 2516)

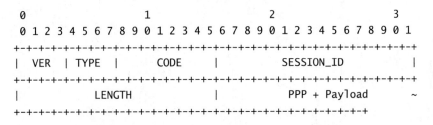

```
 0                   1                   2                   3
 0 1 2 3 4 5 6 7 8 9 0 1 2 3 4 5 6 7 8 9 0 1 2 3 4 5 6 7 8 9 0 1
+-+-+-+-+-+-+-+-+-+-+-+-+-+-+-+-+-+-+-+-+-+-+-+-+-+-+-+-+-+-+-+-+
| VER | TYPE |    CODE    |           SESSION_ID              |
+-+-+-+-+-+-+-+-+-+-+-+-+-+-+-+-+-+-+-+-+-+-+-+-+-+-+-+-+-+-+-+-+
|            LENGTH       |          PPP + Payload            ~
+-+-+-+-+-+-+-+-+-+-+-+-+-+-+-+-+-+-+-+-+-+-+-+-+-+-+-+-+-+-+-+
```

PPPoE TAG TLV (RFC 2516)

```
 0                   1                   2                   3
 0 1 2 3 4 5 6 7 8 9 0 1 2 3 4 5 6 7 8 9 0 1 2 3 4 5 6 7 8 9 0 1
+-+-+-+-+-+-+-+-+-+-+-+-+-+-+-+-+-+-+-+-+-+-+-+-+-+-+-+-+-+-+-+-+
|            TAG_TYPE           |          TAG_LENGTH           |
+-+-+-+-+-+-+-+-+-+-+-+-+-+-+-+-+-+-+-+-+-+-+-+-+-+-+-+-+-+-+-+-+
|          TAG_VALUE ...                                        ~
+-+-+-+-+-+-+-+-+-+-+-+-+-+-+-+-+-+-+-+-+-+-+-+-+-+-+-+-+-+
```

PPPoE PADI (RFC 2516)

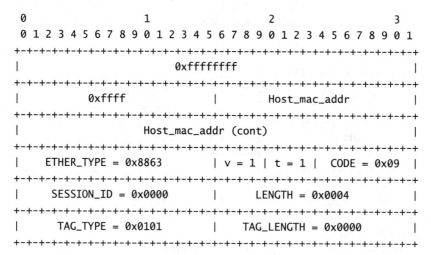

```
 0                   1                   2                   3
 0 1 2 3 4 5 6 7 8 9 0 1 2 3 4 5 6 7 8 9 0 1 2 3 4 5 6 7 8 9 0 1
+-+-+-+-+-+-+-+-+-+-+-+-+-+-+-+-+-+-+-+-+-+-+-+-+-+-+-+-+-+-+-+-+
|                          0xffffffff                           |
+-+-+-+-+-+-+-+-+-+-+-+-+-+-+-+-+-+-+-+-+-+-+-+-+-+-+-+-+-+-+-+-+
|            0xffff             |         Host_mac_addr         |
+-+-+-+-+-+-+-+-+-+-+-+-+-+-+-+-+-+-+-+-+-+-+-+-+-+-+-+-+-+-+-+-+
|                      Host_mac_addr (cont)                     |
+-+-+-+-+-+-+-+-+-+-+-+-+-+-+-+-+-+-+-+-+-+-+-+-+-+-+-+-+-+-+-+-+
|      ETHER_TYPE = 0x8863      | v = 1 | t = 1 |  CODE = 0x09  |
+-+-+-+-+-+-+-+-+-+-+-+-+-+-+-+-+-+-+-+-+-+-+-+-+-+-+-+-+-+-+-+-+
|       SESSION_ID = 0x0000     |        LENGTH = 0x0004         |
+-+-+-+-+-+-+-+-+-+-+-+-+-+-+-+-+-+-+-+-+-+-+-+-+-+-+-+-+-+-+-+-+
|       TAG_TYPE = 0x0101       |      TAG_LENGTH = 0x0000       |
+-+-+-+-+-+-+-+-+-+-+-+-+-+-+-+-+-+-+-+-+-+-+-+-+-+-+-+-+-+-+-+-+
```

PPPoE PADO (RFC 2516)

```
 0                   1                   2                   3
 0 1 2 3 4 5 6 7 8 9 0 1 2 3 4 5 6 7 8 9 0 1 2 3 4 5 6 7 8 9 0 1
+-+-+-+-+-+-+-+-+-+-+-+-+-+-+-+-+-+-+-+-+-+-+-+-+-+-+-+-+-+-+-+-+
|                        Host_mac_addr                          |
+-+-+-+-+-+-+-+-+-+-+-+-+-+-+-+-+-+-+-+-+-+-+-+-+-+-+-+-+-+-+-+-+
|      Host_mac_addr (cont)     | Access_Concentrator_mac_addr  |
+-+-+-+-+-+-+-+-+-+-+-+-+-+-+-+-+-+-+-+-+-+-+-+-+-+-+-+-+-+-+-+-+
|            Access_Concentrator_mac_addr (cont)                |
+-+-+-+-+-+-+-+-+-+-+-+-+-+-+-+-+-+-+-+-+-+-+-+-+-+-+-+-+-+-+-+-+
|     ETHER_TYPE = 0x8863       | v = 1 | t = 1 |  CODE = 0x07   |
+-+-+-+-+-+-+-+-+-+-+-+-+-+-+-+-+-+-+-+-+-+-+-+-+-+-+-+-+-+-+-+-+
|    SESSION_ID = 0x0000        |      LENGTH = 0x0020           |
+-+-+-+-+-+-+-+-+-+-+-+-+-+-+-+-+-+-+-+-+-+-+-+-+-+-+-+-+-+-+-+-+
|      TAG_TYPE = 0x0101        |    TAG_LENGTH = 0x0000         |
+-+-+-+-+-+-+-+-+-+-+-+-+-+-+-+-+-+-+-+-+-+-+-+-+-+-+-+-+-+-+-+-+
|      TAG_TYPE = 0x0102        |    TAG_LENGTH = 0x0018         |
+-+-+-+-+-+-+-+-+-+-+-+-+-+-+-+-+-+-+-+-+-+-+-+-+-+-+-+-+-+-+-+-+
|     0x47      |     0x6f      |     0x20      |     0x52       |
+-+-+-+-+-+-+-+-+-+-+-+-+-+-+-+-+-+-+-+-+-+-+-+-+-+-+-+-+-+-+-+-+
|     0x65      |     0x64      |     0x42      |     0x61       |
+-+-+-+-+-+-+-+-+-+-+-+-+-+-+-+-+-+-+-+-+-+-+-+-+-+-+-+-+-+-+-+-+
|     0x63      |     0x6b      |     0x20      |     0x2d       |
+-+-+-+-+-+-+-+-+-+-+-+-+-+-+-+-+-+-+-+-+-+-+-+-+-+-+-+-+-+-+-+-+
|     0x20      |     0x65      |     0x73      |     0x68       |
+-+-+-+-+-+-+-+-+-+-+-+-+-+-+-+-+-+-+-+-+-+-+-+-+-+-+-+-+-+-+-+-+
|     0x73      |     0x68      |     0x65      |     0x73       |
+-+-+-+-+-+-+-+-+-+-+-+-+-+-+-+-+-+-+-+-+-+-+-+-+-+-+-+-+-+-+-+-+
|     0x68      |     0x6f      |     0x6f      |     0x74       |
+-+-+-+-+-+-+-+-+-+-+-+-+-+-+-+-+-+-+-+-+-+-+-+-+-+-+-+-+-+-+-+-+
```

PPP LCP (RFC 2516)

```
0                   1                   2                   3
0 1 2 3 4 5 6 7 8 9 0 1 2 3 4 5 6 7 8 9 0 1 2 3 4 5 6 7 8 9 0 1
+-+-+-+-+-+-+-+-+-+-+-+-+-+-+-+-+-+-+-+-+-+-+-+-+-+-+-+-+-+-+-+-+
|                 Access_Concentrator_mac_addr                  |
+-+-+-+-+-+-+-+-+-+-+-+-+-+-+-+-+-+-+-+-+-+-+-+-+-+-+-+-+-+-+-+-+
|Access_Concentrator_mac_addr(c)|        Host_mac_addr          |
+-+-+-+-+-+-+-+-+-+-+-+-+-+-+-+-+-+-+-+-+-+-+-+-+-+-+-+-+-+-+-+-+
|                     Host_mac_addr (cont)                      |
+-+-+-+-+-+-+-+-+-+-+-+-+-+-+-+-+-+-+-+-+-+-+-+-+-+-+-+-+-+-+-+-+
|     ETHER_TYPE = 0x8864       | v = 1 | t = 1 |  CODE = 0x00  |
+-+-+-+-+-+-+-+-+-+-+-+-+-+-+-+-+-+-+-+-+-+-+-+-+-+-+-+-+-+-+-+-+
|     SESSION_ID = 0x1234       |       LENGTH = 0x????          |
+-+-+-+-+-+-+-+-+-+-+-+-+-+-+-+-+-+-+-+-+-+-+-+-+-+-+-+-+-+-+-+-+
|    PPP PROTOCOL = 0xc021      |        PPP Payload            ~
+-+-+-+-+-+-+-+-+-+-+-+-+-+-+-+-+-+-+-+-+-+-+-+-+-+-+-+
```

L2TPv2 Stack Overview (RFC 2661)

```
+-------------------+
|Subscriber         |
|Packet Payload     |
+-------------------+
| Subscriber        |
| IP header (if IP) |
+-------------------+
| PPP Frames        |
+-------------------+     +-----------------------+
| L2TP Data Messages|     | L2TP Control Messages |
+-------------------+     +-----------------------+
| L2TP Data Channel |     | L2TP Control Channel  |
| (Unreliable)      |     | (Reliable)            |
+---------------------------------------------------+
|                      UDP                          |
+---------------------------------------------------+
|                      IP                           |
+---------------------------------------------------+
|     Packet Transport (UDP, FR, ATM, Eth.)         |
+---------------------------------------------------+
```

L2TP Header (RFC 2661)

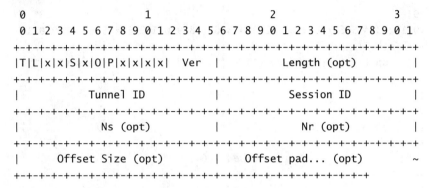

```
 0                   1                   2                   3
 0 1 2 3 4 5 6 7 8 9 0 1 2 3 4 5 6 7 8 9 0 1 2 3 4 5 6 7 8 9 0 1
+-+-+-+-+-+-+-+-+-+-+-+-+-+-+-+-+-+-+-+-+-+-+-+-+-+-+-+-+-+-+-+-+
|T|L|x|x|S|x|O|P|x|x|x|x|  Ver  |          Length (opt)         |
+-+-+-+-+-+-+-+-+-+-+-+-+-+-+-+-+-+-+-+-+-+-+-+-+-+-+-+-+-+-+-+-+
|           Tunnel ID           |          Session ID           |
+-+-+-+-+-+-+-+-+-+-+-+-+-+-+-+-+-+-+-+-+-+-+-+-+-+-+-+-+-+-+-+-+
|             Ns (opt)          |            Nr (opt)           |
+-+-+-+-+-+-+-+-+-+-+-+-+-+-+-+-+-+-+-+-+-+-+-+-+-+-+-+-+-+-+-+-+
|          Offset Size (opt)    |      Offset pad... (opt)      ~
+-+-+-+-+-+-+-+-+-+-+-+-+-+-+-+-+-+-+-+-+-+-+-+-+-+-+-+-+-+-+-+
```

L2TP AVP (RFC 2661)

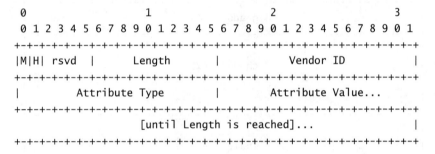

```
 0                   1                   2                   3
 0 1 2 3 4 5 6 7 8 9 0 1 2 3 4 5 6 7 8 9 0 1 2 3 4 5 6 7 8 9 0 1
+-+-+-+-+-+-+-+-+-+-+-+-+-+-+-+-+-+-+-+-+-+-+-+-+-+-+-+-+-+-+-+-+
|M|H| rsvd  |       Length      |           Vendor ID           |
+-+-+-+-+-+-+-+-+-+-+-+-+-+-+-+-+-+-+-+-+-+-+-+-+-+-+-+-+-+-+-+-+
|         Attribute Type        |        Attribute Value...
+-+-+-+-+-+-+-+-+-+-+-+-+-+-+-+-+-+-+-+-+-+-+-+-+-+-+-+-+-+-+-+-+
|                  [until Length is reached]...                 |
+-+-+-+-+-+-+-+-+-+-+-+-+-+-+-+-+-+-+-+-+-+-+-+-+-+-+-+-+-+-+-+-+
```

DHCP (RFC 2131)

```
 0                   1                   2                   3
 0 1 2 3 4 5 6 7 8 9 0 1 2 3 4 5 6 7 8 9 0 1 2 3 4 5 6 7 8 9 0 1
+-+-+-+-+-+-+-+-+-+-+-+-+-+-+-+-+-+-+-+-+-+-+-+-+-+-+-+-+-+-+-+-+
|     op (1)    |   htype (1)   |    hlen (1)   |    hops (1)   |
+---------------+---------------+---------------+---------------+
|                            xid (4)                           |
+-------------------------------+------------------------------+
|           secs (2)            |           flags (2)          |
+-------------------------------+------------------------------+
|                          ciaddr  (4)                         |
+--------------------------------------------------------------+
|                          yiaddr  (4)                         |
+--------------------------------------------------------------+
|                          siaddr  (4)                         |
+--------------------------------------------------------------+
|                          giaddr  (4)                         |
+--------------------------------------------------------------+
|                                                              |
|                          chaddr  (16)                        |
|                                                              |
|                                                              |
+--------------------------------------------------------------+
|                                                              |
|                          sname   (64)                        |
+--------------------------------------------------------------+
|                                                              |
|                          file    (128)                       |
+--------------------------------------------------------------+
|                                                              |
|                          options (variable)                  |
+--------------------------------------------------------------+
```

DHCPv6 Client/Server (RFC 3315)

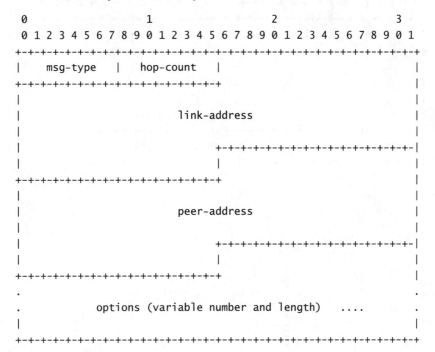

```
 0                   1                   2                   3
 0 1 2 3 4 5 6 7 8 9 0 1 2 3 4 5 6 7 8 9 0 1 2 3 4 5 6 7 8 9 0 1
+-+-+-+-+-+-+-+-+-+-+-+-+-+-+-+-+-+-+-+-+-+-+-+-+-+-+-+-+-+-+-+-+
|    msg-type   |               transaction-id                  |
+-+-+-+-+-+-+-+-+-+-+-+-+-+-+-+-+-+-+-+-+-+-+-+-+-+-+-+-+-+-+-+-+
|                                                               |
.                            options                            .
.                           (variable)                          .
|                                                               |
+-+-+-+-+-+-+-+-+-+-+-+-+-+-+-+-+-+-+-+-+-+-+-+-+-+-+-+-+-+-+-+-+
```

DHCPv6 Relay (RFC 3315)

```
 0                   1                   2                   3
 0 1 2 3 4 5 6 7 8 9 0 1 2 3 4 5 6 7 8 9 0 1 2 3 4 5 6 7 8 9 0 1
+-+-+-+-+-+-+-+-+-+-+-+-+-+-+-+-+-+-+-+-+-+-+-+-+-+-+-+-+-+-+-+-+
|    msg-type   |   hop-count   |                               |
+-+-+-+-+-+-+-+-+-+-+-+-+-+-+-+-+-+                               |
|                                                               |
|                          link-address                         |
|                                                               |
|                               +-+-+-+-+-+-+-+-+-+-+-+-+-+-+-+-+|
|                               |                               |
+-+-+-+-+-+-+-+-+-+-+-+-+-+-+-+-+                               |
|                                                               |
|                          peer-address                         |
|                                                               |
|                               +-+-+-+-+-+-+-+-+-+-+-+-+-+-+-+-+|
|                               |                               |
+-+-+-+-+-+-+-+-+-+-+-+-+-+-+-+-+                               |
.                                                               .
.            options (variable number and length)   ....        .
|                                                               |
+-+-+-+-+-+-+-+-+-+-+-+-+-+-+-+-+-+-+-+-+-+-+-+-+-+-+-+-+-+-+-+-+
```

DHCPv6 OPTION TLV (RFC 3315)

```
 0                   1                   2                   3
 0 1 2 3 4 5 6 7 8 9 0 1 2 3 4 5 6 7 8 9 0 1 2 3 4 5 6 7 8 9 0 1
+-+-+-+-+-+-+-+-+-+-+-+-+-+-+-+-+-+-+-+-+-+-+-+-+-+-+-+-+-+-+-+-+
|          option-code          |           option-len          |
+-+-+-+-+-+-+-+-+-+-+-+-+-+-+-+-+-+-+-+-+-+-+-+-+-+-+-+-+-+-+-+-+
|                          option-data                          |
|                      (option-len octets)                      |
+-+-+-+-+-+-+-+-+-+-+-+-+-+-+-+-+-+-+-+-+-+-+-+-+-+-+-+-+-+-+-+-+
```

RADIUS (RFC 2865)

```
 0                   1                   2                   3
 0 1 2 3 4 5 6 7 8 9 0 1 2 3 4 5 6 7 8 9 0 1 2 3 4 5 6 7 8 9 0 1
+-+-+-+-+-+-+-+-+-+-+-+-+-+-+-+-+-+-+-+-+-+-+-+-+-+-+-+-+-+-+-+-+
|     Code      |  Identifier   |            Length             |
+-+-+-+-+-+-+-+-+-+-+-+-+-+-+-+-+-+-+-+-+-+-+-+-+-+-+-+-+-+-+-+-+
|                                                               |
|                         Authenticator                         |
|                                                               |
|                                                               |
+-+-+-+-+-+-+-+-+-+-+-+-+-+-+-+-+-+-+-+-+-+-+-+-+-+-+-+-+-+-+-+-+
|  Attributes ...
+-+-+-+-+-+-+-+-+-+-
```

INDEX

THIS BOOK IS SAFARI ENABLED

INCLUDES FREE 45-DAY ACCESS TO THE ONLINE EDITION

The Safari® Enabled icon on the cover of your favorite technology book means the book is available through Safari Bookshelf. When you buy this book, you get free access to the online edition for 45 days.

Safari Bookshelf is an electronic reference library that lets you easily search thousands of technical books, find code samples, download chapters, and access technical information whenever and wherever you need it.

TO GAIN 45-DAY SAFARI ENABLED ACCESS TO THIS BOOK:

- Go to **http://www.prenhallprofessional.com/safarienabled**

- Complete the brief registration form

- Enter the coupon code found in the front of this book on the "Copyright" page

If you have difficulty registering on Safari Bookshelf or accessing the online edition, please e-mail customer-service@safaribooksonline.com.

PRENTICE
HALL